············ **mental_floss** *presents:* ············

CONDENSED KNOWLEDGE
and FORBIDDEN
KNOWLEDGE

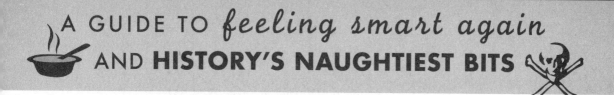

A GUIDE TO *feeling smart again*
AND **HISTORY'S NAUGHTIEST BITS**

ISBN 978-0-06-234824-1

14 15 16 17 18   RRD   10 9 8 7 6 5 4 3 2 1

·········· mental_floss *presents:* ··········
CONDENSED KNOWLEDGE
and FORBIDDEN KNOWLEDGE

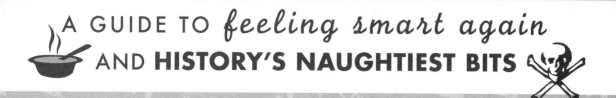

A GUIDE TO *feeling smart again*
AND **HISTORY'S NAUGHTIEST BITS**

Edited by WILL PEARSON, MANGESH HATTIKUDUR,
and ELIZABETH HUNT

HARPER

NEW YORK · LONDON · TORONTO · SYDNEY

Also available from **mental**_floss:

The mental_floss *History of the United States*

The mental_floss *History of the World*

mental_floss *presents: Be Amazing*

mental_floss *presents: Condensed Knowledge*

mental_floss *presents: Forbidden Knowledge*

mental_floss *presents: In the Beginning*

mental_floss: *Cocktail Party Cheat Sheets*

mental_floss: *The Genius Instruction Manual*

mental_floss: *Scatterbrained*

mental_floss: *What's the Difference?*

mental_floss presents:

Condensed Knowledge

mental_floss *presents:*

Condensed
Knowledge

Edited by
Will Pearson, Mangesh Hattikudur, *and* **Elizabeth Hunt**

HARPER

NEW YORK • LONDON • TORONTO • SYDNEY

To Jane Cee, Henley, Umesh-uncle and Chitra-auntie, and Barbara Roewe.

Acknowledgments

The editors would like to thank Abigail Myers, John Chernoff, Carol Hunt, Clif Hunt, Carla Kingery, Betsy Marsey, Patsy Jones, Terry Finley, Ellen Sullivan, Tom Gallagher, Jerry Footlick, Ceil Cleveland, and Jackie Leo.

Condensed_Knowledge

Try all 15 delicious varieties!

Introduction

mental_floss magazine was just one of a hundred semiamusing ideas that came out of our floor's late-night dorm room conversations at Duke University. There was, of course, the heated driveway company, that hoped to melt away morning frost and make snow shoveling a thing of the past. And the pet lobster farm, which not only intended to breed pedigree lobsters as domestic companions, but also carry fine lobster accessories . . . such as tiny leashes, sweaters, and mittens. And who could forget the Great American Pudding Truck? The idea was to get a cement mixing truck, fill it with pudding, and roam the country squirting gelatinous goodies into the pudgy hands of kids on every block. Brilliant, right? Well, if one thing was made abundantly clear to us in college, it was that there was a whole world of opportunities just waiting to be tapped by dreamers like ourselves. So, why then did we pursue *mental_floss*? Maybe because of all the ideas on the table, it's the one that made us grin the widest.

Statistically speaking, *mental_floss* never should have launched. Consider the facts: two 21-year-old kids with no industry experience, no journalism background, and no real money to throw around decide to start a national publication. Add to that the fact that the year we decided to launch was considered the worst economy for magazines since World War II. Ad money was down dramatically, and high profile publications like *Talk, George,* and *Mademoiselle* were all forced to close shop.

Not exactly the best timing. But when you're as quietly mischievous as we are, stats don't faze you. *mental_floss* was exactly the sort of magazine we wanted to find in our mailbox every month—something that was hip and quick and quirky and fun, but really left you feeling smarter. You know? A sort of bible for trivia addicts. A quick fix for knowledge junkies. Something that truly blurred the lines between education and entertainment. So we hunted for it. We scoured bookstores. We rummaged newsstands. And when we couldn't find the magazine we were looking for, we decided to go out and create it.

Fast forward a few years later, and *mental_*

floss still has us smiling. After all, we've managed to get away with a "Swimsuit" issue (featuring 15 geniuses, from Einstein to Eleanor Roosevelt stripped down to their skivvies), a "Saints and Sinners" issue (that had Mother Theresa, Gandhi, Nelson Mandela, and Madonna all fighting for cover space), and even a "Lies Your Mother Told You" issue featuring all the so-called facts people have been trying to slip past you for years. But now that we're growing older, wiser, maybe even a little more mature (emphasis on little), we're starting to branch out. *Condensed Knowledge* is *mental_floss's* first adventure in the book world, and well, we're pretty darn excited about it. We've gathered seventeen experts, thousands of facts, and slapped the work silly in typical *mental_floss* style. So go ahead: skim a few pages, ease into the paragraph of your choice. And if you're not hopelessly addicted in a matter of minutes, we'll do our best to understand. After all, we still have the pudding truck business to fall back on.

Happy flossing,
Will and Mangesh

A Feast for Hungry Minds

People love to feel smart, but would prefer not to have to work for the knowledge. There's a good reason we like the Dummies books, Cliff's Notes, and bulleted summaries; we're active people without a lot of time on our hands. It's the same reason fast food, insta-photos, and dry cleaning are so popular. We want it all, we want it quickly, and—if possible—we'd like it supersized (no mayo).

You think you have the time or energy to delve into ancient religious tomes to uncover the basic tenets of Islam by yourself? We think not. Learning Arabic, even on tape, is a four-month process in and of itself. Besides, you've got better things to do.

Sadly, when it comes down to it, we're just not all that book-smart. We're fuzzy on the facts. We have trouble telling the Bill of Rights from a bill of lading, astronomy from astrology, or Madonna from, well, Madonna. Most people think Hercules is a pro wrestler, and Descartes a snail or dessert wine.

It's not our teachers' faults: our hormones were raging, we were bored out of our minds, hungry, afraid of the class bully, and looking to hitch a ride with the first trucker who'd take us far from our wretched neighborhood. And that was just elementary school.

We're not stupid, either; we used to know all kinds of stuff—we've just forgotten. Given our study habits, you can hardly blame us for our academic amnesia. Procrastination was the name of the scholastic game: we waited until ten minutes before class to attempt memorizing the names of every U.S. president, the 206 bones in the human body, that frickin' chemistry chart, or some Shakespearean sonnet—only to pass by the skin of our braced teeth. We crammed, we jammed, we purged.

The idea of *Condensed Knowledge* is for readers to stroll up to the buffet line of basics and take a heaping plateful of smart(aleck). And one helping surely won't be enough to fill that big noggin of yours, so like Pavlov's puppies, you'll ring the bell again and again. In this process, you will begin to make connections you never thought possible: like how the Industrial Revolution was critical to the invention of the snowboard, that without space travel there'd be no Twinkie, and that there are simple dance steps that can bring you closer to God.

Most of us are more interested in the big picture than in the microscopic minutiae of molecules, Sanskrit, or caloric intake; we leave that to folks like Einstein, Bill Gates, and Oprah. And now, thanks to the insanely bright crew of expert authors assembled here, critical events and ideas in fifteen fields of study have been distilled into easy Mc-Nugget-size chunks. Then it's up to you to connect the dots.

Confucius said, "To know that we know what we know, and that we do not know what we do not know, that is true knowledge." All we know is, that makes our heads hurt, and that Sir Francis Bacon (no relation to Kevin Bacon) said it better: "Knowledge is power."

You'll become top dog at the water cooler, a whiz at home Jeopardy!, an arbitrator of stupid bets your friends make. Kids will gather at your feet to hear your tales of wisdom, your lovers will finally be impressed, politicos will beg you to run for president. What you *do* with this newfound power is up to you. We hope you use it wisely.

Michael A. Stusser, a regular contributor, still remembers meeting the first issue of *mental_floss* magazine. The pair have worked happily ever after ever since, spending their waking hours making sweet, sweet, articles together.

mental_floss *presents:*

Condensed
Knowledge

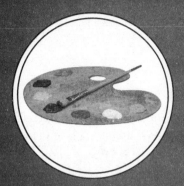

by
Robert Cumming

Condensed ART HISTORY

Contains

5 Scandals That Rocked Art ✳ 7 Styles to Keep at Your Fingertips ✳ 6 Masters of the Modern ✳ 9 Champions of the Old School ✳ Wheeling and Dealing: 6 Dealers and Auctioneers the World Reveres ✳ 5 Greatest Sculptors of All Time ✳ 5 Bank-Breaking Works of Staggering Genius: The Priciest Artists in the World ✳ 4 Nudes You Ought to Know by Name (and Have as Fridge Magnets) ✳ 4 Artists (and 1 Exhibition) Bent On Shocking the Masses ✳ This Bold House: 5 Architects Who Defy Convention

5 Scandals That Rocked Art

Forgeries, thefts, and outright vandalism? That's right. Art history's about to get a whole lot more interesting.

_01:: The Vermeer Forgeries

Every age sees art through its own eyes, and the cleverest forgers play up to this. One of the most notorious forgeries ever occurred in the 1930s. A Dutchman named Han van Meegeren (1889–1947) produced forgeries of early works by the Dutch 17th-century master Jan Vermeer. They were technically brilliant and faultless, using old canvas and the correct 17th-century pigments. Cunningly, van Meegeren chose religious imagery that some experts believed Vermeer had painted, but very few examples of which existed. Most (though not all) of the greatest experts were completely taken in, but when you see the paintings now, you'll wonder why. All the faces look like the great film stars of the 1930s, such as Marlene Dietrich and Douglas Fairbanks.

_02:: The *Mona Lisa* Theft

It's sometimes suggested that rich criminals arrange for famous works of art to be stolen so that they can have them exclusively to themselves in private. Such theories have never been proven, and the truth is usually just a bit simpler. One of the most bizarre thefts was of the *Mona Lisa* from the Louvre in 1911. An Italian workman, Vincenzo Perugia, walked into the gallery, took the painting off the wall, and carried it out. Security was nonexistent.

About two years later it was discovered in a trunk in his cheap lodging rooms in Florence. So, why did he take it? It was nothing to do with money. He said that as the painting was by an Italian, Leonardo da Vinci, it was part of Italy's national cultural heritage, and he was simply taking it back to where it belonged: Florence. (The painting was returned to the Louvre.)

_03:: The Auction Houses Scandal

The major commercial scandal of recent years has been the alleged collusion between the two big international auction houses Christie's and Sotheby's. As the supply of expensive masterpieces began to run out, competition between the two firms became increasingly fierce and each of them found it difficult to make a profit. They got together secretly to fix not the price of works of art themselves but the commission that they would each charge to sellers. In certain parts of the world, such an arrangement is quite legal but not in the United States. Eventually the practice came to light. The federal authorities imposed fines running into hundreds of millions of dollars, and prison sentences were also handed out.

_04:: The Portland Vase

Wanton acts of destruction in the art world are fortunately rare. One of the strangest occurred in 1845 in the British Museum, London, and is worthy of a Sherlock Holmes story. The Portland Vase, the most famous example of ancient Roman glass, decorated in dark-blue-and-white cameo technique, was brought from Italy in 1783 and purchased by the Duchess of Portland. A drunken young man entered the museum and without explanation smashed the vase and its glass display case. He was imprisoned for breaking the case but not the vase, as British law didn't impose penalties for destroying works of art of high value. The vase has since been repaired; however, you can still see the bruises.

_05:: Cellini's *Saltcellar*

A recent art world disaster/scandal occurred on May 13, 2003 (and it wasn't even a Friday!). Thieves climbed scaffolding and smashed windows to enter Vienna's Art History Museum and stole the *"Mona Lisa* of sculptures"—Cellini's *Saltcellar*. This intricate 16-centimeter-high sculpture was commissioned by François I, king of France, from Benvenuto Cellini (1500–1571), the Renaissance's most ingenious and gifted goldsmith. Crafted with amazingly rich detail and skill, its principal figures are a naked sea god and a woman who sit opposite each other, with legs entwined—a symbolic representation of the planet earth. The thieves set off the alarms,

What's the Difference?
FAKES VS. FORGERIES

While the two words are seemingly interchangeable, there's a real distinction here. A fake is a work of art that is deliberately made or altered so as to appear better, older, or other than what it is. When you go browsing round the stalls of the local flea markets and think you have found a bargain, be cautious because you may well be looking at a fake. A forgery, on the other hand, is something made in fraudulent imitation of another thing that already exists. Throughout history, people have come forward with what they claim are lost masterpieces by Leonardo or Vermeer, for example, which they themselves have created with great skill in their studios. Such works are not fakes but forgeries.

but these were ignored as false, and the theft remained undiscovered until 8:20 a.m. The reasons for the theft are as yet unknown. The fear is that these thieves will destroy the sculpture or melt it down, an act of vandalism that would be the equivalent of burning the *Mona Lisa.*

Styles to Keep at Your Fingertips

If you're looking to impress, you'll need to know more than just a handful of painters and their masterpieces—you're going to have to know some styles too. That's why we're giving you the lowdown—a revealing guide to the key movements and the reasons they matter.

_01:: Giving Birth to the Renaissance

Literally meaning "rebirth," the Renaissance ushered in the flowering of new ideas in Italian art between the 14th and 16th centuries, and the impact has been felt in the Western art world ever since. Like no style before it, the Renaissance brought three new ideas to the table and explored them with increasing sophistication. In this period you find art as a window on the world, with light and "real" space being continually explored; you find man as the measure of all things, from human scale and proportion to human emotions and ideals; and you find a strong reverence for Christianity, the Bible, and classical antiquity, with Christian messages from the Old and New Testaments along with the adaptation of classical Greek and Roman ideas incorporated into the style. If you want to see all of this together in one place and at its most magnificent, take a closer look at Michelangelo's ceiling in the Sistine Chapel, Rome.

_02:: Going for Baroque

The dominant style of the 17th century, the baroque period was filled with elaborate and ornate art, the theatrical world of illusion, endless drama, a love of rich color and materials, and, most important, heaviness, seriousness, and pomposity. The Catholic Church used the baroque style to illustrate Christian religious subjects and to proclaim the power of the established church as it fought back against austere Protestant ideals during the Reformation. Hence, the best examples of baroque style are found where the Catholic faith prevailed—Italy (especially Rome), Austria, southern Germany, central Europe, Spain, and France. Similarly, absolute monarchs used the baroque style for secular subjects to proclaim their worldly power, and to celebrate the richness of their possessions and lifestyles. Baroque's best work can be found in Bernini's churches and fountains in Rome and in the work of the Catholic monarchs' favorite artist, Rubens.

_03:: Cuckoo for Rococo

As the baroque began to fade, rococo art emerged as an 18th-century reaction to the heavy, ornate work that had characterized the previous century. Look for paintings, buildings, porcelains, sculpture, and furniture that are full of curves. You'll find an art style that is filled with pretty colors, playfulness, youthful exuberance, elegance, fine craftsmanship, extravagance, carefree attitudes, and references to real and fanciful nature (flowers, leaves, rocks, birds, monkeys, or dragons). Rococo reached its fullest expression in 18th-century France (it is the Louis XV style) and central Europe (Bohemia). In fact, it was Louis

XV's mistress, Madame de Pompadour, who encouraged the creation of rococo's most sumptuous and decorative masterpieces, such as the paintings of François Boucher and Sèvres porcelain.

_04:: **Neoclassicism and Napoleon?**

The fashionable art style from about 1770 to 1830, neoclassicism emphasized the spirit and appearance of classical Greece and Rome. While the style tends to be severe, authoritative, didactic, well made, and architectural (preferring straight lines), it originally trumpeted a more decorative and cerebral note. After the French Revolution and Napoleon, however, neoclassicism became heavy-handed, with an emphasis on magnificence and grandiosity. The style succeeds best in architecture, furniture, and sculpture, and can be seen at its finest in England (where it starts as the Adam style and ends up as Regency) and France (where it starts as the Louis XVI style and ends up as the Empire style). The key painter of the movement was Jacques-Louis David.

_05:: **Isn't It Romantic?**

The key movement in art, music, and literature in the late 18th and early 19th centuries, Romanticism produced some of the greatest and best-loved works of all time. The Romantics believed in new experiences, individuality, innovation, risk taking, heroism, freedom of imagination, love, and living life to the fullest. In painting and sculpture they introduced new and dramatic subjects, innovative styles and techniques, rich and vigorous colors and brushwork, and a tendency to see and experience everything as larger than life. Romanticism appealed particularly to the

northern European temperament and flourished at its fullest in Germany, Britain, and France. Delacroix, one of the greatest painters of the Romantic movement, summed it all up in his well-known painting *Liberty Leading the People*, a key image celebrating the popular democratic uprising in Paris in 1830, whose spirit is celebrated in the hit musical *Les Misérables*.

_06:: **Works That Leave an Impression**

Impressionism was the famous progressive movement that started the dethronement of academic art and the traditions that had stemmed from the Renaissance. The impressionists ignored artistic "style" and went back to nature with the intention of painting only what the eye could see. They created small-scale works of contemporary scenes, notably landscapes, that were freely and directly painted *en plein air* ("out of doors"), portraits, and still lifes. The impressionists' trademark technique was short brush strokes and a rainbow palette. Talk about an explosive launch, though; the first impressionist exhibition took place in 1874 and featured the works of such heavyweights as Cézanne, Degas, Monet, Morisot, Pissarro, Renoir, and Sisley.

_07:: **Modernism in a Modern Age**

The great flowering of modern art occurred between 1880 and 1960, and it embraces all the avant-garde works produced at that time. Beginning with Manet and the impressionists, modernism continued on until Jackson Pollock and the New York school hit the scene. No doubt, modernism's greatest innovator and exponent was Picasso, whose style itself broached a variety of looks and feels. As modernism unfolded, three major characteristics

Fake Your Way through a Conversation
(AT AN ART OPENING!)

The art world loves jargon, and the more art buzz words you can cram in, the more impressed people will be. The next time you meet a work of art that has you stumped, and you're being pressed for a response, just play with the following:

Quote some Latin! Who says dead languages aren't useful? When confronted, try sprinkling a bit of the old language into your response, like: "What you say is all very well, but always remember that *ars longa, vita brevis*" ("art is long-lasting but life is short"). Another good one is *ars est celare artem* ("the purpose of art is to conceal art's artfulness"). And if all else fails, say, "*de gustibus non est disputandum*" ("there's no accounting for taste").

Use entropy! Entropy is a scientific term that's been hijacked by the art world. And while it means that the amount of disorder in the universe is bound to increase (this is the second law of thermodynamics: heat is disordered energy), it's pretty useful at openings. If the thing you're looking at appears to be irredeemably chaotic and incomprehensible, try saying, "The artist appears to be a supreme master of entropy." You will sound deeply knowledgeable while seeming to praise the work (when, in fact, you're cleverly condemning it!).

Isn't it ironic? Simply claim that "Fundamentally, this work is an extremely skillful use of irony." By definition, irony means to convey a meaning by expressing the opposite. If you have no idea what the artist is trying to say and suspect that the artist doesn't have an idea either, this is a crafty way of implying that you've penetrated to the heart of the work's nonexistent meaning. If you're asked what or where the irony is, look inscrutable, nod wisely, and walk away.

The final nod: If you find a work of art meaningless or someone's point of view incomprehensible, unacceptable, or futile, you can always shake your head and declare the whole issue to be "problematic." Just whatever you do, don't admit defeat or tell the truth.

---

emerged: (1) a strong desire to break with the past, unlike previous art movements that emphasized their inheritance from, or rejuvenation of, the art of the past; (2) a defiance of all art institutions and the creation of works of art that were intentionally "homeless," in the sense that they belonged in no official art institution; and (3) the incorporation of a plethora of styles and ideas. In essence, modern artists were at their most active in those places where freedom of speech and thought were newfound liberties, or in those places where those liberties were most actively fought for, such as late 19th- to early-20th-century France, post-Revolutionary Russia, interwar Germany, or post–World War II

United States. Modernism's two major homes, however, lay in France and the United States. Paris remained its center of gravity between 1880 and 1939, while New York was its home from 1945 to the 1960s.

6 Masters of the Modern

It's almost impossible to talk about modern art without tipping your hat to these greats. Here are the masters who gave birth to the modern.

_01:: Pablo Picasso (1881–1973)

Picasso is the undisputed master of the modern movement. You have to go back to Michelangelo to find anyone of equal genius or stature. Convivial and energetic, he had a voracious appetite for the female sex, although his relationships with women were not always happy. Creator of a vast output of work, he was equally inventive as a painter, sculptor, printmaker, ceramicist, and theater designer. His work displays a bewildering change of technical and stylistic originality with a wide-ranging Freudian response to the human condition, including many intimate references to sex and death, sometimes blissful, sometimes anguished. Always highly autobiographical, Picasso had the rare ability to turn self-comment into universal truths about mankind.

_02:: Henri Matisse (1869–1954)

Matisse was the king of color and celebrated the joy of living through the exploration of his palette. One of the founders of the modern movement, Matisse achieved a joyous combination of subject matter (notably the open window, the still life, and the female nude) and a glorious exploitation of color, and proclaimed a new freedom to do his own thing without necessarily imitating nature. Matisse explored color independently from subject matter and turned color into something you wanted to touch and feel. While he was at his best with paint and paper cutouts, he was also a brilliant and innovative printmaker and a gifted sculptor. As a personality, however, he was professorial, social, but a bit of a loner.

_03:: Wassily Kandinsky (1866–1944)

Kandinsky was one of the key pioneers of the modern movement and reputedly the creator of the first abstract picture. Russian born, he initially trained as a lawyer, which made him at ease with abstract modes of thought. Possessor of a complex, multifaceted personality, Kandinsky cultivated an intellectual rather than an instinctive approach to art, backed up by much theoretical writing. Starting as a figurative artist, he worked his way via freely painted abstracts to a complex geometrical form of abstraction. The common thread in all his work is color. He intellectualized his ideas and his art, but at the same time he had such a strong physical sensitivity to color that he could literally hear colors as well as see them (a phenomenon known as synesthesia; see page 289 in Psychology).

_04:: Piet Mondrian (1872–1944)

Mondrian was one of the pioneers of a pure abstract art. His most recognizable works have the simplest elements: black horizontal and vertical lines, a white background, and only the primary colors. His aim was to find and express a universal spiritual perfection, but his imagery had a profound influence on 20th-century commercial and architectural design and has been endlessly recycled with little or no understanding of its underlying purpose. As a personality he was austere and reclusive; he hated the green untidiness of nature but was addicted to jazz and dancing. Sadly, in his own lifetime he had no commercial success, but Mondrian was highly revered and tremendously influential on the movers and shakers of modern art and design.

_05:: Jackson Pollock (1912–1956)

"Jack the Dripper" was the leading artist of the pioneer New York school. He was a tortured, monosyllabic, alcohol-dependent soul, swinging between sensitivity and machismo, elation and despair. At his best he produced magnificent work that needs to be seen on a large scale to fully appreciate the passionate, heroic, and monumental nature of his achievement. When he rolled his canvases out on the floor and stood in the middle of them with a large can of house paint, he was literally and physically part of his work, thereby achieving an integration of the artist's personality and the activity of artistic creation that had never before been realized with such expressive freedom.

_06:: Andy Warhol (1928–1987)

Sure, Andy Warhol may have been a neurotic surrounded by drug addicts, but that doesn't mean he wasn't a key artistic figure. Warhol's work represents one of art's turning points because he changed the role model of the artist into one that all aspiring young contemporary artists now follow—no longer the solitary genius expressing intense and personal emotion (like Pollock) but the artist as businessman. He placed artists on a par with Hollywood film stars and Madison Avenue advertising executives. Understandably, he loved and exploited iconic images drawn from the world of glamour, mass media, and advertising, and you can still find his Campbell soup cans and Marilyn Monroe–themed prints everywhere. The son of Czech immigrants, Warhol acted out an oft-repeated American dream cycle—pursuing a driving need to be famous and rich (like his subjects) but destroying himself in the process.

9 Champions of the Old School

If you're waxing nostalgic for the good stuff, you can't go wrong with the classics. Here are some of the greatest men ever to wield a paintbrush, sorted by nationality.

_01:: Italy's Raphael (1483–1520)

So, why Raphael? Consider that Michelangelo was principally a sculptor, and Leonardo produced very few paintings. And while Giotto (ca. 1267–1337) first established a new level of realism in art, and Masaccio (1401–1428) pioneered deeply moving works with simple and profound human gestures and emotions, first place undoubtedly has to go to Raphael. A child prodigy, Raphael actually died young, but he had a complete mastery of all Renaissance techniques. In fact, he explored subjects and ideas and developed them with apparent ease, yet he managed to endow them with the deepest emotional and intellectual expression. Raphael projected an ideal at almost every level, which is why he was held up as the model for all ambitious artists to follow—until the overthrow of the Renaissance and academic traditions by the modern movement.

_02:: Spain's Diego Velásquez (1599–1660)

It's a close call between Velásquez and Goya, but we had to go with Velásquez, even though he wasn't prolific and his style changed considerably. Velásquez's early work is notable for its pinpoint-sharp realism, whereas his later works are loose and softly focused. By far, Velásquez's greatest achievements are his portraits, where he manages to balance grandeur, realism, and intimacy as no one has ever done before or since. And his sensitivity to light and sensational color harmonies were hugely influential on avant-garde painters (such as Manet) of the late 19th century. Goya (1746–1828), on the other hand, had a profound understanding of human character— youth and old age, hope and despair, sweet innocence and brutal savagery—yet he was never judgmental, simply showing human nature as it was (and still is). Nevertheless, the quality of Goya's work is variable, whereas Velásquez never seemed to put a foot wrong, which is why, by a hairbreadth, Velásquez takes the prize.

_03:: France's Nicolas Poussin (1594–1665)

Three names are in the frame here: Poussin, David, and Cézanne. Cézanne (1839–1906) is here because, although a solitary, pioneering, difficult workaholic who considered his life and work failures, he was nonetheless the mother and father of modern art. David (1748–1825) was the passionate, volatile founder of French neoclassical painting. Like his hero Napoleon, he was dictatorial, austere, and inflexible, and his art in the service of the state radiates a powerful ideological, political, and artistic commitment. Poussin was the founder of French classical painting, who lived and worked in Rome, creating complex allegorical subjects on moral themes that were severe, intense, highly intellectual, and composed with an underlying geometry of verticals, horizontals, and diagonals. So, why's he the greatest? For the simple reason that both Cézanne and David, both of whom knew what they were talking about, said he is.

The Low Countries'
_04:: Rubens (1577–1640) and
_05:: Rembrandt (1606–1669)

There needs to be a joint prize here because of national politics. In the 17th century the Low Countries split politically into the New Republic of Holland and Flanders (effectively modern Belgium). The greatest Flemish painter is Sir Peter Paul Rubens, the widely traveled man of many talents who was a painter, diplomat, businessman, and scholar. His studio had a huge output of large-scale altarpieces, ceiling decorations, and portraits, which were staunch favorites with the Catholic Church and monarchs wishing to proclaim the divine right of kings. The greatest Dutch master, on the other hand, is Rembrandt. His elusive work is completely different—out of the mainstream, gritty, and deeply personal. Fascinated by emotional crisis and moral dilemmas, Rembrandt's work makes you sense that he has genuinely experienced the intensity of the emotions he portrays.

_06:: Germany's Albrecht Dürer
(1471–1528)

The prize goes to Albrecht Dürer, the greatest Northern artist of the Renaissance (he was the same age as Michelangelo). Prolific, tenacious, and immensely ambitious, Dürer uniquely

and subtly synthesized the old Northern medieval traditions and the new Italian humanist discoveries. His subjects include the New Testament, nudes, landscapes, and classical mythology, and he was equally fascinated by plants and animals. And though his oil paintings are skillful, they are clearly self-conscious. Dürer was more at ease with drawings and watercolors, and he excelled at printmaking, where his technical mastery of woodcut and engraving has never been equaled.

_07:: Britain's J. M. W. Turner (1775–1851)

There are only two contenders here: Turner and Constable (1776–1837). The British are probably more at ease with nature than they are with people, so not surprisingly they produced two of the world's pioneering landscape painters. Constable's peaceful, silvery green, dewy-fresh scenes of the English countryside were tremendously influential on the French, but he was a stay-at-home artist and didn't have the scope and originality of Turner in terms of subject matter and technique. Turner's travels took him all over Europe, where he saw the works of classical antiquity, and the Industrial Revolution fired his imagination. All of nature's moods and all her seasons are included in his work, and he was so innovative in his techniques with oils and watercolors that contemporary critics thought he must have gone mad.

_08:: U.S.A.'s Winslow Homer (1836–1910)

The two contenders for the American award are Winslow Homer and Thomas Eakins (1844–1916). Eakins was from Philadelphia and studied in Paris and Spain. Pragmatic but with an unyielding personality, he was little honored in his lifetime. He produced frank and candid portraits of matter-of-fact successful professionals (notably doctors and scientists). However, he lacks the masterly confidence of Winslow Homer who, although self-taught, produced satisfying, virile images that convincingly reflect the American pioneering spirit. Homer's work has a strong narrative content (he started as a magazine illustrator), and he's at his best with children and images of practical people coping with adversity. Homer lifted his art beyond the ordinary by infusing it with a sincerely felt underlying moral message.

_09:: Europe's Titian (ca. 1488–1576)

It may seem special pleading to classify Titian, who was Venetian born, as a European, but (with the exception of Raphael) he significantly influenced all the other artists selected here. Even in his own lifetime his influence and following were truly pan-European. He's also the only great master whose style and reputation over time have never been seriously questioned or suffered an eclipse. He is to painting what Shakespeare is to literature.

Alphabet Soup
(WITH ART-OFFICIAL FLAVORING!)

aesthete: [ES-theet] *n* Someone who claims to be particularly sensitive to beauty and who thinks as a result that he or she is superior to others (for example, Oscar Wilde).

vernissage: [ver-nih-SAZH] *n* French word for "varnishing," aka the day before an exhibition opened, when artists added the finishing touches to their work already hanging on the wall. Nowadays it's simply the chic word for a private viewing.

Both were masters of their craft, constantly innovative, producing thrilling new subjects or brilliant reinterpretations of classical themes, with a profoundly sympathetic response to the human condition.

Wheeling and Dealing:
Dealers and Auctioneers the World Reveres

6

What good's a great work of art if no one will buy the thing? Here are a few of history's slickest salesmen and their "off the wall" antics.

_01:: Jacopo Strada (1515–1588)

One of the cleverest and most successful dealers of the Renaissance, Jacopo dealt in statues, coins, drawings, and pictures. By luck or cleverness he had his portrait painted by Titian, the greatest master of portraiture, and so is remembered forever. Since Titian was brilliant at showing people's inner character, he shows Strada as a sly and cunning man with grasping hands. What's clear is that Titian did not like the guy, but he definitely needed his help to sell some pictures. The paintings in question had been done by studio assistants, but the crafty Titian wanted to pass them off as his own. Strada obliged, and Titian painted his portrait in return. Such deals have been done throughout the history of art, though usually not with such memorable artistic consequences.

_02:: James Christie (1730–1803)

Eighteenth-century London was thick with auctioneers, but James Christie soon established himself as the leading fine art auctioneer. In fact, he's the only one whose business has continued to the present day. (Sotheby's started as book auctioneers and did not deal in fine art until the 20th century.) Christie came from Ireland and had charming manners and a fluent tongue (he was known as the "specious orator"). A great favorite with the ladies, he would extemporize florid descriptions of the objects as he sold them from the auctioneer's box, literally talking the prices up as he took the bids. Such practices would now break every rule in the book. Since Christie's heyday, the art world has become more regulated and a little less colorful as a result.

_03:: Joseph Duveen (1869–1939)

Duveen was king of the commercial art world in the 1920s and 1930s, when dealers were the dominant force. He was the most successful art dealer ever and was the trusted agent of both the British aristocracy, who were forced sellers of their great treasures, and the new American industrial millionaires, who were enthusiastic buyers. One of Duveen's tricks was to refuse to sell to his American clients the thing they most wanted (e.g., a Rembrandt), telling them that they were not yet ready for such a fabulous masterpiece because they were not yet capable of appreciating it. He would then sell them lesser works, and when he finally announced that they were ready for the Rembrandt, they felt so honored by his judgment that they would pay almost any price for it.

_04:: Ambroise Vollard (1867–1939)

The best-known route to success as an art dealer is to think big, buy cheap, and sell expensive. The big money has always been in the big established names, but there are exceptions. Vollard supported the impressionists and the young modern avant-garde in their early penniless days, (e.g., Gauguin, Cézanne, Bonnard, Picasso). In retrospect, he was in the right place at the right time. He gave many of them their first shows when their work was basically impossible to sell, and he gave them contracts that paid them regular monthly allowances in anticipation of works to come. First and foremost Vollard believed in their art, and when his judgment was finally vindicated the financial rewards were considerable.

_05:: Peggy Guggenheim (1898–1979)

She was the grande dame of all 20th-century art dealers. Born into a wealthy dynasty with a famous name—Guggenheim's grandfather had made a fortune in mining, and her playboy father went down with the *Titanic*—Peggy opened her first gallery in London in 1938, but she made her reputation in New York with the Art of This Century Gallery, where she showed surrealist and abstract art. In fact, Jackson Pollock was one of her biggest discoveries. In 1947 she went to live permanently in Venice. And though her galleries thrived, Peggy's passions weren't restricted just to art. Once asked how many husbands she had had, Peggy replied, "Mine, or other people's?"

_06:: Peter Wilson (1913–1984)

Wilson was the suave aristocratic chairman of Sotheby's who, in the post–World War II era, turned fine art auctioneering into a multimillion-pound international phenomenon. Blessed with a true connoisseur's eye and a love of deals and risk taking, he was nevertheless better at recognizing a lost masterpiece than making money. His breakthrough came in 1958, when he held the first glamorous black-tie evening sale of just seven impressionist masterpieces from the Goldschmidt collection. Many of his partners were bitterly opposed to the project, fearing a disaster, but Wilson conducted a triumphantly successful sale, and the event launched a new and glamorous chapter in the history of auctioneering. He sold all the pictures in a mere 21 minutes.

5 Greatest Sculptors of All Time

Playing in two dimensions is easy enough, but what truly separates the men from the boys? Maybe it's when you give up your easel for a tool belt and get to work with a hammer and chisel. These amazing sculptors took their talents 3-D.

_01:: Donatello (1386?–1466)

Unquestionably the greatest sculptor of the early Renaissance, Donatello was born in Florence, though he traveled widely and was famous throughout Italy. Donatello had complete mastery of bronze, stone, wood, and terracotta, and nothing escaped his extraordinary capabilities: relief sculpture, nudes, equestrian statues, groups of figures, and single figures seated or standing. In fact, he reinvented the art of sculpture just as other contemporaries were reinventing the art of painting, and his innovations and discoveries were profoundly influential. Above all, Donatello seemed to be able to bring sculpture to life by his ability to tell a story, combine realism and powerful emotion, and create the impression that his figures were more than mere objects of beauty for passive contemplation, but creations filled with energy and thought, ready to spring into action.

_02:: Michelangelo (1475–1564)

Clearly an outstanding genius, Michelangelo's influence dominated European art until Picasso changed the rules. A sculptor first, painter and architect second, Michelangelo was a workaholic—a melancholic, temperamental, and lonely figure. He had a profound belief in the human form (especially the male nude) as the ultimate expression of human spirituality, sensibility, and beauty. In fact, Michelangelo's early work shows the human being as the measure of all things: idealized, muscular, confident, and quasi-divine. Gradually that image becomes more expressive, more human, less perfect, fallible, and flawed. He loved turning and twisting poses full of latent energy, and faces that expressed the full range of human emotion. Endlessly inventive, he never repeated a pose, although being a true Renaissance man, he was proud to borrow from Greek and Roman precedents.

_03:: Gian Lorenzo Bernini (1598–1680)

Bernini set sculpture free from its previous occupation with earthly gravity and intellectual emotion, allowing it to discover a new freedom that permitted it to move, soar, and have a visionary and theatrical quality. A child prodigy, Bernini had a sparkling personality and brilliant wit (he wrote comedies)—qualities that shine through his sculptures. He was also a true virtuoso technically, able to carve marble so as to make it seem to move or have the delicacy of the finest lace. At his best he blends sculpture, architecture, and painting into an extravagant theatrical ensemble, especially in his fountains, where the play of water and light over his larger-than-life human figures and animals creates a vision that is literally out of this world.

_04:: Auguste Rodin (1840–1917)

Rodin is the glorious, triumphant finale to the sculptural tradition that starts with Donatello. He is rightly spoken of in the same breath as Michelangelo, although they're very different: Michelangelo carved into marble whereas Rodin molded with clay. A shy workaholic, untidy, and physically enormous, Rodin emerged from impoverished beginnings. He became an international celebrity and was deeply attractive to smart women. Rodin was also well known for loving the fluidity of clay and plaster, and was able to retain this quality even when his work was cast in bronze, thereby magically releasing in his figures an extraordinary range of human feelings and a sense of the unknown forces of nature.

_05:: Constantin Brancusi (1876–1957)

Brancusi is one of the seminal figures of 20th-century art with a profound influence on sculpture and design. Born into a Romanian peasant family, he settled in Paris in 1904, becoming a student of Rodin. Amazingly, Brancusi remained indifferent to honor and fame. At the heart of his work is a tireless refinement and search for purity. Never abstract, his work always references something recognizable in nature. Brancusi believed in the maxim "Truth to materials," and he always brought out the inherent quality of each material that he used. The purity and simplicity of his

What's the Difference?

CONSERVATISM VS. RESTORATION

And you thought they were the same! As you well know, works of art are fragile and often made from organic materials, so even the most humble works need careful looking after. Conservation is the creation of the environment in which a work of art is properly looked after, without undue interference and without the need to restore and repair. A good example would be not hanging paintings on the wall above a radiator. Restoration, on the other hand, is the repairing of a work that has become damaged through accident, decay, or neglect. The science and technology of restoration are intricate, and the ethics are as complicated as medical ethics. How much transplanting, patching up, and cleaning can be done before the object dies aesthetically or becomes unrecognizable? The best motto is "If in doubt, leave well alone," because once a work is dead or ruined, there's nothing you can do. A terrifying number of paintings have been ruined by over-restoration in the last 50 years, and as yet no one has properly faced up to the fact. Case in point, *Mona Lisa* once had eyebrows—until an unwise restorer accidentally removed them.

forms touch something very basic in the human psyche, just as does, for example, the sound of the waves of the sea.

5

Bank-Breaking Works of Staggering Genius: The Priciest Artists in the World

If you take the 10 most expensive paintings ever sold at public auction, you'll find 5 names dominate the list.

_01:: Van Gogh

Van Gogh has three paintings on the list and holds the "honor" for the most expensive painting ever—the famous portrait of Doctor Gachet (1890). Van Gogh's doctor and an expert on melancholia, he asked Van Gogh to paint the picture, and it's one of the artist's last works (within eight weeks of completing it Van Gogh took his own life). In fact, he painted two versions, and the subsequent history of this one is extraordinary. Unsold at Van Gogh's death, it subsequently was owned by several different collectors, and in 1938 it belonged, astonishingly, to the Nazi supremo Hermann Göring. The Kramarsky family then acquired it, and they sold it at Christie's in 1990 for $82.5 million. The buyer was Japanese businessman Ryoei Saito, but he didn't get to enjoy his masterpiece for long. Shortly after his purchase the Japanese economy took a tumble, and Siato's businesses went down the plug, allowing the banks to take possession of his works of art. Van Gogh also pulls rank at number four with a self-portrait ($65 million) and at number eight with *Irises* ($49 million).

_02:: Renoir

Renoir weighs in at number two with *Au Moulin de la Galette*, selling for a cool $78.1 million. The piece is one of the most famous of all impressionist works, a busy open-air scene of an outdoor café, with Renoir's characteristic softly dappled sunlight. The café was an unpretentious meeting place with a happy holiday atmosphere attended by ordinary working-class people who liked to have a drink and a dance and eat the excellent little cake known as a galette. It was exactly the type of easy-on-the-eye picture that most appealed to speculative collectors at the height of the frenzied art market boom in the 1990s. The painting was sold by Sotheby's New York two days after Christie's sold Van Gogh's portrait of Doctor Gachet. Guess who the buyer was? None other than the same Mr. Ryoei Saito.

_03:: Rubens

The Flemish master Sir Peter Paul Rubens pulls in at number three with his *Massacre of the Innocents*. Painted between 1609 and 1611, the work is a huge and dynamic composition with plenty of naked flesh (a nudie pic!) illustrating the moment when Herod ordered the killing of innocent young babies because he'd been told that one of them would become king of the Jews. Part of the excitement was because the painting had sat unrecognized for over 100 years in the collection of a German family until a Sotheby's expert (in 2002) recognized it for what it was. The auction house predicted a price of $6–8 million and were as astonished as the owner when it eventually sold for a staggering $68.4 million.

_04:: Cézanne

Cézanne is at number four with a still life called *Curtain, Pitcher, and Bowl*. It's as different from the Rubens piece as can be imagined. A simple wooden table, a white tablecloth, an earthenware pitcher, a plate, a blue curtain in the background, and 20 or so apples and pears. But it came to the market at the right moment and was the star exhibit in a 1999 lot sale of 50 impressionist and modern art pieces in New York. The auction was held by the estate of a late New York socialite and philanthropist, Betsey Cushing Roosevelt Whitney, wife of the former American ambassador to London, John Hay Whitney. The sale was a huge success, and the painting fetched $55 million.

_05:: Picasso

Picasso can claim 4 out of the top 10. His most expensive is a Blue Period work (1905) called *The Marriage of Pierette*, painted when Picasso was living in poverty. The work was sold in Paris at the height of the 1989–1990 boom to, yes, another Japanese businessman, and the work is currently on the market waiting to be resold. The auctioneer who sold it for $51.72 million was a colorful character rumored to have owned the picture. In May 2000, however, he was arrested on charges of having forged auction sales documents in 1995. The other Picassos are a 1901–02 *Woman with Folded Arms* ($50 million in 2000), a 1938 portrait of his prewar mistress Dora Maar ($45 million in 1999), and an erotic 1932 portrait of his previous mistress, Marie-Thérèse Walter, asleep in a red armchair ($44 million in 1997).

Nudes You Ought to Know by Name (and Have as Fridge Magnets)

You've probably seen them out about town, and you've definitely witnessed them in all their glory. So, isn't it time you learned their names?

_01:: Michelangelo's *David*

This is the one you probably do have as a fridge magnet. In real life he's huge, 17 feet high, carved out of a single block of marble. Created by Michelangelo in 1501–1504, *David* stood outdoors in public view in the middle of Florence. The biblical hero is the little guy with a sling who killed the Philistine giant Goliath with a single shot. The Florentines revered him—he was the symbol of their small city-state, constantly under threat from bigger political powers. Artistically, however,

David is a mishmash, heroically ideal in the classical tradition, but in parts realistic (big veined hands, no fig leaf), imperfect (the head is too big), and also sexy (which is why your fridge magnet allows you to dress and undress him).

_02:: Venus de Milo

Once considered the perfect example of female beauty, Venus de Milo stands carved in white marble, naked from the waist up (her lower half is covered by a garment). She turns and seems to grow out of the cloth like an opening flower. Memorably, she has no arms because they were broken at some time, so you could have fun adding on your own to your fridge door. The statue is one of the most famous treasures in the Louvre, in Paris. Created during the Hellenistic period (fourth to first centuries BCE), the high point of ancient Greek art, she came to the Louvre in 1820, after she had been dug up on the island of Mílos by a Greek peasant.

_03:: Apollo Belvedere

Two hundred years ago the Apollo Belvedere was the most famous work of art in the world. Copies and replicas of the athletic young god were everywhere. Pulses raced at the sight of him stepping forward, left arm outstretched, with a cloak slung loosely over his shoulders and left arm. He wears a fig leaf, and both arms are broken, so a fridge magnet would give you scope to add and take away. Apollo, the son of Zeus and twin brother of Diana, was the god of prophecy and the ideal example of masculine beauty and rational civilized behavior. He is still one of the glories of the papal collections in the Vatican, but few visitors swoon before him now.

Strange but True

BRUSHES WITH CONTROVERSY

One of America's best-known artists, John James Audubon (1785–1851) (famous for his *Birds of America*, which illustrates in stunning detail and artistry 435 species), was the bastard son of a Haiti slave trader. To paint the birds, he first shot them and then wired their dead bodies into lifelike poses.

The painter and sculptor Daniele da Volterra (ca. 1509–1566) was nicknamed "braghettone" (i.e., "putter on of pants") because the Counter-Reformation pope Paul IV (1555–1559) employed him to cover up the most critical parts of the sacred nudes with decorous draperies, including Michelangelo's nudes on the Sistine Chapel ceiling.

The most faked and forged artist is probably Camille Corot (1796–1875). Over 10,000 fakes and forgeries have been recorded, and to complicate matters, Corot himself often added his signature to copies made by his pupils. When Corot died, the demand for his works was quite extraordinary, and there was a big market for unscrupulous dealers, who sold dozens of forgeries to foreign buyers, notably Americans.

The cherub-faced aristocrat and Italian artist Piero Manzoni (1933–1963), who died at the age of 29, created as a work of art a series of 30-gram tins containing "artist's shit." They were labeled with the same name and "naturally preserved," arranged in piles or randomly on a surface. Ninety versions were made, each designed to be sold for its weight in gold.

_04:: *Olympia*

Olympia became famous overnight in 1865. Exhibited at the Paris Salon, she was instantly condemned as indecent and disgusting. What was the problem? Pictures of naked women lying full length on a bed had been done by the greatest artists for centuries. Called Venus, goddess of love, they earned the highest praise. This picture was different, however. Although the subject was posed like a Venus, it was clear that this was no goddess.

With her fashionable shoe dangling on her foot, a come-hither look, a black ribbon round her neck, earrings, a black cat, and in a setting that is clearly a bedroom, Olympia is unmistakably a high-class prostitute. With one unforgettable picture, Manet destroyed all the old fictions and conventions, saying that art should show things (and people) to be as they are rather than dress them up to be what they are not. (Which is why you should have her on your fridge.)

Artists (and 1 Exhibition) Bent On Shocking the Masses

While refusing to decorate a saint's head with a halo or putting a toilet on display at a museum might seem tame by today's standards, these are the artists and events that pushed art forward. Take a closer look at the masters who sent the art world spinning.

_01:: Caravaggio (1571–1610) and Jesus

In spite of their reputations for unconventional behavior, most artists live peaceful and relatively uneventful lives. The only major artist with a serious criminal record is Caravaggio. He was regularly in trouble for hooliganism and was even charged with murder. Brilliantly talented as a painter, Caravaggio displayed a complete disregard for all the accepted proprieties and rules, and seems to have lived in a state of constant hyperexcitement. He loved sensational subjects, including severed heads, martyrdom, and corrupt-looking young men (although his tastes leaned to the heterosexual). He also caused deep offense by using peasant models for his images of Jesus Christ and the saints. This vexed plenty of people who thought that true art required idealization and that Christ and the saints needed to be depicted as superhuman angels instead of ordinary human beings.

_02:: Gustave Courbet (1819–1877) and the Working Masses

Courbet was a larger-than-life character, physically and mentally, who regularly shocked the bourgeoisie of the French Second Empire (1848–1870). Coming from a peasant background, Courbet established himself in Paris as a champion of realism. Courbet painted enormous pictures of working-class people doing humdrum, everyday things. To those who believed that art should be about pure beauty and that the working classes should be kept firmly in their place, this amounted to dangerous socialism and political revolution. In the end Courbet was put in jail for a brief period, but he won the argument for his art, and he became a model for the next generation of pioneers such as Degas, Toulouse-Lautrec, and Picasso.

_03:: Marcel Duchamp (1887–1968) and a Well-Lighted Urinal

Duchamp created very few works of art, and few of those are very interesting to look at. Today he's applauded as one of the great gurus and fathers of conceptual art. He was the first 20th-century artist to propose that the interest and stimulus of a work of art can lie solely in its intellectual content. The most famous example of this is his *Fountain Urinal* (1917). He took a used men's urinal, signed "R Mutt," and put it on display, saying, "Anything is a work of art if I, the artist, say it is." In 1917 this was a genuinely shocking idea, although now it's been repeated to the point of boredom.

_04:: America and the Scandalous Armory Show

The press loves scandal because it sells newspapers, and exhibition organizers enjoy it when it brings in the crowds. Both parties were satisfied at the famous Armory Show held in New York in 1913—so-called because it took place in the building of the 69th Regiment Armory, where half a million visitors turned up to gasp at and be shocked by the horrors of modern art. Cézanne, Picasso, Rodin, Brancusi, as well as the major impressionists were included in this show. It was, however, a turning point for art in America. The Metropolitan Museum bought its first Cézanne, and American artists realized that they had a long way to go to catch up with the latest developments in Europe. Half a century later, abstract expressionism and pop emerged, indicating that the Americans had not only caught up but actually overtaken the Europeans.

_05:: Picasso's *Guernica*

When Picasso painted *Guernica* he wanted to shock people—not to cause them offense but to wake them up to man's inhumanity. *Guernica* was first exhibited in the Spanish Pavilion at the International Exhibition in Paris in 1937. Its stark, terrifying, black-and-white imagery referred to the recent destruction of the Basque capital of Guernica in broad daylight in April 1937, when over 1,500 innocent civilians were killed. Nazi planes with German pilots under the command of General Franco carpet bombed the town so as to cause maximum death and devastation. Picasso kept the painting in his studio in Paris. In 1942 he was visited by some Nazi military officers who looked at the painting and asked Picasso, "Did you do this?" "No," replied Picasso, "you did it."

This Bold House:
Architects Who Defy Convention

If you're looking to renovate, forget the do-it-yourself approach. Instead, why not just contract out the job to one of the best? Here's a helpful guide for determining which architectural great deserves to design your dream home.

_01:: Frank Lloyd Wright (1867–1959)

A key figure in American architecture, Frank Lloyd Wright will build you a beautiful, harmonious house. It might have only a few rooms, but everything will be carefully integrated. The colors will be warm, and the materials natural and truthful. Daylight, of course, will be important, and it's a safe bet that the building will sit comfortably and easily in its natural setting. In fact, the house just might provoke gasps of admiration . . . but will you enjoy living in it? A stickler for his own views, Frank Lloyd Wright was obsessed with controlling everything, from the furniture to the ornaments to even the appliances—so much so that you may find you have a house in which Frank Lloyd Wright's personality is so dominant that you feel like a guest in your own home.

_02:: Andrea Palladio (1508–1580)

With Palladio, you've chosen not just the finest Renaissance domestic architect but one of the most skillful and intelligent architects of all time. The proportions will be so perfect and human that you will feel physically bigger and morally better the moment you step inside the front door. The classical details will be handled with the greatest understanding, but you will have a genuinely innovative house, not a pastiche of ancient architecture. Best of all, Palladio will have taken into account the full potential of your site, overcome any difficulties it presents, and created a design that fits your budget (well, he will be less tempted than most architects to spend your money as if it were in unlimited supply).

_03:: Le Corbusier (Charles-Edouard Jeanneret) (1887–1965)

Le Corbusier, one of the key pioneer architects of the modern movement, coined the phrase "a machine for living in," and that's exactly what his house will be. Simple in design, it will have minimal ornamentation, open plan spaces, white walls, and windows that run the full length of those walls like ribbons. But to appreciate your house to the fullest you'll need to have an understanding of his architectural and social theories, and be thrilled by the way they've been applied. You'll also need to dispense with clutter and have very few visible possessions; otherwise you'll be accused of desecrating the purity of his architectural principles.

_04:: Robert Adam (1728–1792)

Robert Adam was a canny Scotsman who became the architect of choice for the British nobility and gentry at the height of their powers. If your taste is for living in the grand manner with impressively proportioned rooms in the classical style (for receiving and impressing your guests, of course), then this guy's the architect for you. Especially good at converting existing houses, Adams pays breathtaking attention to detail and he would expect to design the furniture to go with your impressive rooms. He will also dictate the colors and the moldings, which are part of the overall scheme. Above all you'll require a taste for huge houses, an army of servants, deep pockets to keep the establishment going, and an overwhelming desire to entertain your guests in the style your house will lead them to expect.

_05:: Antonio Gaudí (1852–1926)

If your taste runs to the unusual and exotic, then Gaudí, the quirky Spanish interpreter of the art nouveau style, is probably the architect for you. You will see hardly a straight line on the outside, and your friends may think seeing too many old Disney movies has influenced your taste. Your house will look as though it's been molded rather than constructed, and don't be alarmed if you see the workers actually building it from rubble (one of Gaudí's favorite materials). The rubble will soon be covered in patterns made from brightly colored ceramic and glass. But be forewarned: you had better enjoy living on a building site, for it's highly probable that your house will never get finished.

by
Karen Bernd

Condensed
BIOLOGY

Contains

6 Critical Moments in the Fight against Diseases ✳ Slaphappy Science: 5 Great Reasons to Swat Mosquitoes ✳ 4 Ways Doctors Scope You Out ✳ Better Off Dead: 3 Parts of Your Body That Are Not Alive ✳ Biology That's Skin Deep: 3 Secrets to Unnatural Beauty ✳ 4 Things Your Boss Has in Common with Slime Mold ✳ Alien Invaders: 5 Guests That Overstayed Their Welcome ✳ 5 Extreme Mammals ✳ 7 Things Smarty-Plants Can Do ✳ 4 Excuses to Get a Prescription for Chocolate ✳ Behind the Equations: The Juicy Backstories on 5 Famous Biologists ✳

6 Critical Moments in the Fight against Diseases

In the Middle Ages a man considered himself lucky if he made it to the ripe old age of 35. Now, thanks to a few key health discoveries, the 30s are just a pit stop on the geriatric highway.

_01:: Bridging over Troubled Waters

The power of good plumbing is incredible. While good sanitation can't rid the world of all diseases, it has made a huge dent in epidemics caused by water-borne infectious diseases. Around 1700 BCE indoor plumbing came to royalty on the island of Crete. A millennium later Hippocrates (ca. 460–ca. 377 BCE) saw the importance of clean water and recommended that ancient Romans boil water to remove pollutants. The Romans hadn't a clue about bacteria and viruses, but we do. An easy way to pass bacterial diseases like cholera and intestinal infections is to come in contact with things that "pass through" people and animals. The moral: Don't wipe with the hand that feeds you.

_02:: Cider House Rules

Milk and cider are routinely pasteurized by a process developed by Louis Pasteur (1822–1895) in the 1860s. Sure, the name looks egomaniacal, but in fact, Pasteur's work deserves a namesake or two. Realizing that heat treatment of foods like milk could render "germs" harmless without altering the foods' taste was a big breakthrough. In addition to giving us fresh milk, Pasteur was the one who showed that spontaneous generation couldn't occur. Up until that point people believed that things appeared like magic—frogs in wet mud, maggots in meat. Showing that magic wasn't to blame, and that you could indeed keep maggots out of meat, was a major leap in preventing communicable diseases.

_03:: Pea-Brained Schemes

The saying that nothing in life is more important than good breeding holds true when it comes to diseases. Some diseases aren't caught; they're based on genes you got from your parents. Gregor Mendel (1822–1884) first noted the idea that living things had a genetic basis in 1865. At a time when people believed that babies grew from preformed beings, Mendel grew pea plants and studied the inheritance patterns of certain traits like height and seed shape. From simple, detailed observations he developed laws of inheritance showing a contribution from male and female plants. Knowing this made it possible to better understand appearance patterns for diseases like sickle cell disease, cancer, and Huntington's disease.

_04:: An Antibiotic Arsenal

Antibiotics kill bacteria. So, why can you ingest these things? Why don't they kill *you*? Many antibiotics are safe for humans because we aren't built like bacteria. Bacteria have cell walls protecting them from the environment (your gut). Antibiotics mess up cell wall synthesis or function. And while the drugs do little to our cells, they cause bacteria to lose their armor and die. And since bacteria are at the root of diseases ranging from colds to tetanus, syphilis, and leprosy, having the ability to zero in on their unique characteristics added a big gun to the antidisease arsenal. Note: antibiotics do not kill, maim, or even weaken viral infections, so don't bother asking for them if you've got the flu!

_05:: The Vaccination Emancipation

Prior to 1725 smallpox killed more than 100 million people. Today the virus lives only in laboratories. How did we get so lucky? It occurred to scientists to inject the virus that causes cowpox to fight smallpox. Makes a whole lot of sense, right? Turns out that the human immune system can remember being exposed to an invader and mount a better defense next time. Cowpox virus is very similar to smallpox virus, so a person who had a harmless case of cowpox would be immune to the much more harmful smallpox virus. Today vaccines are developed using mimic viruses (like cowpox for smallpox), heat-killed viruses, and even just bits of virus proteins. The vaccination causes your body to be ready so that the bad virus can't ambush it later in life.

_06:: DNA Cut-and-Paste

Mendel laid out the rules of genetic inheritance, and in 1952 Alfred Hershey and Martha Chase determined that you inherit DNA. James Watson and Francis Crick published the structure of DNA in 1953, and well, scientists have been studying it ever since. Recombinant DNA, however, is not the stuff of bad sci-fi movies. It involves making new combinations of DNA in a test tube, much like using the cut-and-paste feature on your computer. So, why is this an advance in the fight against disease? Being able to manipulate virus genes has led to new vaccines that have no possibility of causing infections. Studying inherited diseases at the DNA level has led to better, more focused treatments and could possibly lead to cures.

Fake Your Way through a Conversation

(ABOUT GENES AND GENE EXPRESSION)

To use a construction analogy, genes are like blueprints for cellular parts. If you want to build a house (a protein) you go to an architect's office (the nucleus), which holds a collection of blueprints (the genome made of DNA). A copy of one blueprint is made (transcription of gene into mRNA, or messenger RNA) and given to a contractor (the ribosome). The contractor uses the paper plans to build your three-dimensional house out of brick (translation of mRNA into protein). The contractor may also make many other copies of that house (a subdivision) until the blueprint wears out. Every cell in your body contains the same genome, but not every cell has the same proteins. Just as branch offices of architectural firms can build subdivisions that look different, cells choose a subset of genes to express. The blueprints they pick determine what the cell contains and does.

Slaphappy Science:
5 Great Reasons to Swat Mosquitoes

Poor little mosquitoes. One minute they're just minding their own business, stopping to quench their thirst, and then whap! Suddenly their lives come to a screeching halt. Well, don't feel too sorry for the suckers. Here are five reasons to keep on swatting.

_01:: Malaria

Malaria occurs in more than 100 countries and territories and causes more than 1 million deaths each year. This disease comes from four species of *Plasmodium* parasites and is transmitted through, you guessed it, mosquito bites. In each case the mosquito picks up the invader when it bites an infected individual. The parasite then uses the mosquito as a reproduction center and food source (eww). After about a week, enough plasmodium to do some damage accumulates, and a little bit is passed along with the mosquito's saliva when it bites someone new. After multiplying in that person's liver, the parasite causes red blood cells to burst and releases toxins into the blood, making the person feel lousy. Hurray for citronella candles!

_02:: Dengue Fever and Dengue Hemorrhagic Fever

These sister diseases are caused by four related flaviviruses that use the *Aedes aegypti* mosquito as a flying hypodermic needle. Although the name *flavivirus* may sound yummy, a disease that causes you to hemorrhage probably isn't good dinner conversation. While infection sometimes results in only flulike symptoms, there are 50–100 million cases and more than 15,000 deaths from the diseases each year. The first reported epidemics occurred in Asia, Africa, and North America from 1779 to 1780; however, a current pandemic in Southeast Asia has brought the disease back to the forefront. The good news is that not all people hemorrhage and many immune systems can fight off the disease. The bad news is that the *aegypti* mosquito is currently in Texas and the southeastern United States, air travel makes disease movement easier, and there is no vaccine.

_03:: West Nile Virus

West Nile virus used to be found only in Africa, Eastern Europe, West Asia, and the Middle East. However, in 1999 cases were documented in the northeastern United States. That means that our generation is witnessing this disease's territory expand. Culex mosquitoes transmit the virus, and birds act as virus reservoirs, where the virus can multiply so more mosquitoes can pick it up. People are known as dead-end hosts because while we do get sick, we don't pass on the germs. Short-term symptoms of West Nile fever resemble the flu, and this form of the disease is more common because a healthy immune system can usually fight off the virus. And while West Nile encephalitis affects less than 1% of infected people, it is much more serious. In this form the membranes around the brain become inflamed, which can result in neurological damage or death.

_04:: St. Louis Encephalitis

If encephalitis is an inflammation of the brain, then St. Louis encephalitis refers to big-headed people from the Midwest, right? Actually, the disease is caused by another arbovirus—a virus transmitted by mosquitoes. The St. Louis part came, presumably, because of cases identified in that city. Symptoms range from fever and headaches to more severe infections resulting in stiffness, stupor, and spastic paralysis. There was a major epidemic of the disease during 1974–1977, but since then outbreaks have been sporadic and small. Like West Nile virus, the virus causing St. Louis encephalitis is a flavivirus passed through birds, which act as growth chambers, and transmitted by the *Culex* species of mosquitoes. Even though there are only about 128 cases per year, it still sounds like a good excuse for mosquito netting.

_05:: Yellow Fever

Yellow fever is perhaps the strongest advertisement for insect repellent—those infected can go from healthy to dead in three days. The symptoms include a progression from fever to extremity pain to "black vomit" (vomiting blood clots) to jaundice (making the skin yellow) to death. While not everyone dies, who wants to take the chance? Before we knew that only mosquitoes transmitted the virus (not human contact), yellow fever caused en-

forcement of strict quarantines. In 1793 yellow fever practically emptied Philadelphia. During the epidemic 5,000 Philadelphians died in three months, and many people—including notables like George Washington—fled the city in terror. The development of a vaccine against the disease has reduced the number of cases, but it still occurs widely in Africa and South America.

What's the Difference?

SEWAGE PLANTS VS. SEPTIC TANKS

While you probably don't want to be downwind of either a sewage treatment plant or a septic tank, you probably do want to know the difference. Though both have bacteria that eat waste, the two differ in the kinds of bacteria at work. Sewage treatment plants use large, open vats with moving multivalve spigots and rely on oxygen-loving (aerobic) bacteria. Constant stirring of the waste provides the aeration needed for aerobic bacteria to eat quickly and reduce the waste to filterable forms. Septic tanks, however, are built closed off and underground, an environment that spells death for aerobic bacteria. Septic tanks use oxygen-hating (anaerobic) bacteria, which are actually killed by oxygen. The anaerobic bacteria break down waste but are slower eaters than their aerobic cousins. Their slow-working nature and aversion to oxygen explain why septic tanks can fill up and why a hole in the tank can cause an awful stench. If the contents get out, the processing bacteria are killed and, well, yuck.

Ways Doctors Scope You Out

Doctor visits were always fun: paper gown with peek-a-boo flaps, cold stethoscopes up the back, annual weigh-ins. Just in case you're not feeling exposed enough, though, modern science has given us the scopes.

_01:: Endoscope: Glancing Where the Sun Don't Shine

Endoscopy refers to diagnostic devices that look into natural body orifices, like the ear, nose, and rectum, or cuts made by a surgeon's blade. The first designs, by Philip Bozini in 1805, consisted of a rigid shaft, a candle, and a concave mirror. Yoww! No flexibility and a lot of heat made insertion of this device unpleasurable, to say the least. Luckily, low light and poor visibility made it of minimal use to the physician, so the device fell out of favor. But not to worry. Two German physicians developed the semiflexible Wolf-Schindler gastroscope in 1933 and brought it to America. Modern forms use flexible shafts that contain video equipment within their mere 2.8-millimeter diameter—a big improvement for those on either end of the device.

_02:: Laparoscope: Tinier Scars in the OR

This device is the reason you can have your appendix removed without a scar above the bikini line. Laparoscopy is the younger cousin of endoscopy and refers to looking inside the abdomen. Although it was first performed in 1901, this procedure came into its own with the development of very small charge-coupled device (CCD) cameras and disposable laparoscopic instruments in the 1980s and 1990s. Currently, procedures ranging from gynecological to gall bladder surgeries can combine the visualization properties of endoscopy with high-tech laser surgery so that surgeons can remove a 6-inch-long organ through a 1-inch space.

_03:: Ophthalmoscope: For When the Eyes Have It

Looking into someone's pupils provides ways to monitor eye health. However, there is a basic problem—light enters and is reflected from the eye along the same path. If you want to look into someone's eye (at the retina), you have to put your eyes or a camera in front of the subject's. This gets complicated since the observer's head must necessarily block the light coming into the subject's eyes, leaving nothing to bounce back. Enter Hermann von Helmholtz. In 1851 Hermann developed an ophthalmoscope made of reflective plates and concave lenses, which provided indirect light while allowing a clear image of the retina. Besides exposing eye problems, the ophthalmoscope also helps in diagnosing a range of neurological, kidney, and heart disorders.

_04:: Microscope: For Looking Deep Within

To look beyond the organs and into the cells, a microscope is the way to go. Light microscopes in modern labs can make cells appear 1,000 times larger than they are. And though the microscope's inventor isn't known, its earliest descriptions date back to 1621. Original versions used a single glass lens and were plagued by problems with glass quality. How does the microscope work? The sample sits on a stage below a tube containing the lenses, and light shines up through the sample and into the tube to the user's eye. Modern light microscopes use glass of the highest specifications and exact curvatures. Compound microscopes can use up to three separate lenses and provide images with amazing details. Skin cells versus kidney cells, normal cells versus cancerous ones—a microscope can help you tell the difference.

Better Off Dead:

3 Parts of Your Body That Are Not Alive

If you think your hair is the only part of your body that isn't alive, maybe it's time you got a second opinion?

_01:: Cartilage

If you've had a nose job (don't worry, we won't tell), your plastic surgeon worked at least somewhat with a plasticlike tissue called cartilage. Chondrocyte cells make cartilage and then live in small pockets within the structure. The chondrocytes' secretions include a network of collagen and chondroitin sulfate that is strong enough to be the skeleton of humans during early development. Eventually, you develop a bone skeleton, but you still have cartilage in the flexible structures of the ear, nose, and windpipe.

_02:: Bone

The hard part of bone is a nonliving matrix of collagen and calcium phosphate. The catch is that the solid part of bones is nonliving, but it isn't unchanging. Just as you live in a house that you can renovate, osteoblasts and osteoclasts live in and remodel bone. When the diet is good and the bone is bearing weight, the osteoclasts are in charge of building, and new bone is laid down. It's why athletes have thicker bones than couch potatoes. On the other hand, cells use a lot of calcium and bones are the calcium store. If the body doesn't have enough dietary calcium or the bone is not bearing weight routinely, osteoclasts come in, tear down the matrix, and recycle the calcium to other parts of the body.

_03:: Tendons

Imagine a tow truck arrives to pull your car out of a ditch. If the driver uses a winch and a heavy rope, you'll be good to go. If he uses a

Myths and Misconceptions

CLONING FROM THE COMFORT OF YOUR OWN HOME!

Public perception suggests that it's easy to clone animals and make perfect copies of the parent. But public perception is wrong. First, to create, say, a cow clone, you need two cells: the nucleus (containing the DNA) of a cell from cow 1 and an unfertilized egg from cow 2 that has had its own nucleus removed. The cow 1 nucleus is placed in the enucleated cow 2 egg and implanted into a third cow's uterus to develop—a highly inefficient process. Gathering eggs, removing nuclei, inserting "new" nuclei, and getting the egg to implant are each very difficult steps, and having them all work at the same time is rare. Then, even when the procedure works, the calf is not a truly complete genetic clone. While nuclei contain a majority of a cell's genetic material (DNA), mitochondria have small amounts. Because the cell contains many mitochondria, true genetic cloning requires that the nucleus and egg come from the same individual (which means the cloned animal can't be dead and can't be male—no egg).

winch and a rubber band, you're stuck. Tendons are the body's equivalent of that heavy rope. They connect muscles (the winch) to bones (your car) and are used to generate movement during muscle contractions. Each tendon is made of millions of tropocollagen strands, and each tropocollagen strand is made of collagen fibers. This is a different form of the same collagen used in collagen injections. Alone, each collagen molecule is short and somewhat weak. However, a collagen "rope" with a mere 1-millimeter diameter can support at least 10 kilograms (4.5 pounds) before breaking.

Biology That's Skin Deep:
Secrets to Unnatural Beauty

3

Helen of Troy may have awoken to her ship-launching beauty every day, but many of the rest of us turn to chemicals, rubs, and treatments for that "all-natural" look. Here's the dirt on why they work.

_01:: Exfoliants

Your skin has layers of dead cells making you look older (sorry), but exfoliants can come to the rescue. Exfoliants contain small abrasive particles, like bits of nutshells, rocks, or other exotic debris. When you rub the abrasives on the skin (in a circular motion, of course), they remove cells much the same way that sandpaper removes the top layer of a piece of wood. When used properly, the particles rub off only dead skin and result in the advertised healthy glow. Younger skin is revealed because skin cells are examples of epithelia—the same cells that line and cover every organ in your body and act as barriers and protectors. In every case the body knows that normal wear and tear damages this line of defense, and so new skin cells are always being made. The cells mature and end up on the surface when old cells on top of them die and fall off; it happens all the time. Rough exfoliation can cause their death, but correct use just speeds the cleanup process.

_02:: Perms

The grass is always greener on someone else's head. Those with curly hair spent hours smoothing it straight, while the straight-haired lot yearned wistfully for curls that wouldn't flop by happy hour. Then along came the invention of permanent waves and hair relaxers to address these serious issues. Both processes rely on the chemical structure of hair. Each hair is actually a bundle of proteins called keratins that are secreted from the hair follicle cell. The amount of bounce in your locks is a result of the pattern of cross-linking between keratins in a hair and protein components that contain sulfur. To make more lasting change in your hairdo, hairdressers use solutions that break the natural sulfide cross-links and reform them in a new way. When you get a whiff of the sulfur, you can be sure you're smelling biochemistry.

_03:: Botox Injections

Think of beauty and you probably don't conjure up images of food poisoning, but trends in cosmetics are sometimes unpredictable. Botox treatments are a case in point. Botox (botulinum toxin) is secreted by the *Clostridium botulinum* bacterium. If eaten, the bacterium lives in the gut, releases its toxin, and causes potentially fatal food poisoning. However, when injected (in small doses), it eliminates crow's-feet and worry lines. How? It causes paralysis. Botox inhibits neurons that normally tell muscles to relax. When the neurons can't signal, the muscle remains paralyzed in its contracted form. So it follows that injecting a small amount locally reduces wrinkles. However, injecting large amounts paralyzes vital organs and results in death—truly a case where dosage counts.

Things Your Boss Has in Common with Slime Mold

There have been times when you were sure your boss was a lower life form. Finally! Here's the biological proof you've always wanted.

_01:: They Both Respond to External Stimuli

Slime mold can, and does, move (a fact responsible for notorious B movie *The Blob*). The movement is known as chemotaxis because the slime mold senses a chemical (chemo) and moves (taxis). To understand the directional nature of the movement, think of freshly baked chocolate chip cookies and a skunk's smell. Anything the slime moves toward is a chemoattractant. If the mold moves away, the substance is a chemorepellant. Just as you follow the cookies' aroma to the kitchen or flee desperately from the skunk's spray, slime molds detect chemical gradients to determine the direction of their motion. Either the mold goes toward the higher concentration of an attractant chemical, or it slithers toward lower concentrations if the chemical is a repellant.

_02:: They're Both Eukaryotic

There are two basic cell types. Prokaryotic cells have an external membrane, and all their other parts float in the cytoplasm within it. Eukaryotic cells have an external membrane as well, but they also have smaller membrane sacks inside. The sacks are called organelles, and each kind of organelle is specialized for a different function. Slime mold (*Dictyostelium discoideum*) and your boss share this quality. Not only do they both have organelle-containing cells, but they also have the same kinds and similar numbers of each type of organelle.

_03:: They're Both Multicellular

Your boss started out as a single cell that divided to become the millions of different cells in the body. And while slime mold may look simple, it too has a multicellular stage in its life cycle. During times of plenty (food and moisture), each slime mold cell is an independent unit that lives as part of a swarm. However, when resources are scarce, these swarmer cells will clump and work together in a slug to produce reproductive structures called fruiting bodies. Just make sure to note two things: first, this slug is not the kind in your garden;

and second, unlike your boss, the slime mold "chooses" between single cell and multicellular existence, wherein all of the cells must work together for survival.

_04:: They Both Reproduce Sexually

This is true for humans certainly, since a sperm and egg must fuse to get things started. That fertilized egg, or zygote, will go on to divide thousands of times for the human body to develop. For humans, there's the hope of happily ever after, but not for slime molds. Once two swarmer slime mold cells fuse, the new cell goes on to divide two, and only two, times to produce four daughter cells. Each of these cells is a swarmer that can either remain solitary or clump with hundreds of others to form a slug. This mold can even do something your boss can't: it can reproduce asexually by having one swarmer cell divide in half to make two identical clones. Let's hope the boss never develops that ability!

Alien Invaders:
5 Guests That Overstayed Their Welcome

When these poor countries couldn't solve their own environmental dilemmas, they enlisted aid from overseas creatures. Here are a few foreign "friends" that didn't bother to help out, making the quick transition from guest to pest.

_01:: Cane Toads

Cane toads (*Bufo marinus*) aren't native to Australia, but they are becoming a large ecological problem there. The toads were introduced as a natural means of controlling the grayback beetle population that plagues the country's sugarcane fields. There are three slight problems. First, the toads reproduce very rapidly. Second, the cane toad has no natural predators to keep its population in check. And third, even though the toads have voracious appetites, they don't eat many of the beetles, because the grayback beetle lives inside the sugar cane and the toad can't get to it. Now instead of just an insect problem, Australia has beetles in the cane and toads underfoot.

_02:: European Starlings

Introducing a new animal to control an old pest seems to be a recurring theme. The European starling (*Sturnus vulgaris*) was brought to the United States as a means of controlling insects such as locusts. In 1890 a flock of 100 of the small black birds was released in New York City's Central Park. This small flock aggressively competed with native species for nesting cavities and food, and the birds are now found throughout the United States and Canada. This competition has resulted in declining numbers of native species, like the Eastern bluebird. As if that wasn't enough, starlings are responsible for damaging fruit crops as well. The upside is, at least they do eat locusts.

_03:: Zebra Mussels

Originally found in Europe, this freshwater mussel probably invaded the United States by stowing away in the ballast water of transatlantic ships. First seen in the Great Lakes, their range nearly doubled between 1986 and 1988. Since their larvae swim and the adults love boat hulls, they'll probably be found in more lakes soon. Zebra mussels are particularly unpopular with native clam lovers because the mussels compete with the clams for resources and space. Water intake structures don't fare well either: the cost of the damage from the adults' presence goes well into millions of dollars. On the other hand, the presence of millions of hungry filter feeders has led to a decrease in algae, allowing sunlight to penetrate into deeper water and helping some invertebrates and aquatic plants—a lot of power for a little mollusk.

_04:: House Sparrow

What is it about New Yorkers and birds? Like the European starling, the house sparrow (*Passer domesticus*) was released in New York City's Central Park in the 1800s. As settlers moved west across the United States, the house sparrows moved with them, and their range currently extends from sea to shining sea. This small brown, black, and white bird is a common sight at backyard birdfeeders since its diet consists of seeds. Its eating habits, however, have made it less than welcome on farms, where it can eat enough seed to reduce crop yields. Like many introduced species, house sparrows did muscle in on someone else's territory, so they too have been blamed for the population decline of some native bird species.

_05:: Kudzu

As interstate highways began crisscrossing the southern United States, a need developed for low-maintenance ways to control roadside erosion and beautify the landscape. Enter the kudzu (*Pueraria lobata*), a low-growing vine that requires basically no maintenance, can withstand hot southern summers, and has pretty green leaves and flowers in July. Problem is, kudzu is highly invasive and grows very quickly. A short visit to a southeastern state will introduce you to kudzu next to roads, in fields, and covering old barns. It may be picturesque and it does fight erosion, but it also outcompetes and kills all plant life in its path. There are even cases of livestock and pets wandering into kudzu fields, becoming entangled, and dying. On the other hand, kudzu is said to be quite tasty in salads.

5 Extreme Mammals

Mammals are warm-blooded, covered with hair, bear live young, and produce milk to feed them, and we like to think of ourselves as the best mammal around. However, in many categories other animals have us beat, paws down.

_01:: The Biggest

Some people argue that a vegetarian diet can't support a large life-form. They obviously haven't met the blue whale (*Balaenoptera musculus*), a massive creature that survives on plankton. Weighing in at 150 tons, the blue whale isn't only the largest mammal but, in fact, the largest animal known. Its ability to maintain life on such a grand scale is aided by its oceanic lifestyle. In comparison, the bull African elephant (*Loxodonta africana*) is the largest land animal, and it weighs a mere 12 tons.

_02:: The Smallest

The title "smallest mammal" is only slightly smaller than the animal it describes. A native of Thailand, measuring 1.14–1.3 inches and weighing 0.06–0.07 ounces, Kitti's hog-nosed bat (*Craseonycteris thonglongyai*), or bumblebee bat, truly earns its title. The smallest land mammal, the pygmy shrew (*Suncus etruscus*), is only slightly larger, tilting the scales at a hefty 0.05–0.09 ounces. These pipsqueaks are so small that they're outweighed by two standard paper clips. Even though their diminutive stature places them eye to eye with many snails and insects, these two animals are true warm-blooded vertebrates: they are covered with hair, and their females produce milk—mammals to the core.

_03:: The Fastest

As might be expected, the winner in this category depends on the terrain. Mammals are found in the air, water, and land, and each domain requires different types of locomotion skills. The fastest air mammal is the big brown bat (*Eptesicus fuscus*), which can flap its way up to 15.5 miles per hour. The fastest water mammal reaches a significantly higher 34 miles per hour—and at this speed the killer whale (*Orcinus orca*) can definitely have its choice of the catch of the day. However, clocking in at 70 miles per hour, the overall fastest mammal is a land creature, the cheetah (*Acinonyx jubatus*). Due to the amazing amount of energy required, this cat can pour on the power only for short periods of time, but that's of little comfort to the gazelles it sets its sights on.

_04:: The Slowest

In a competition over slowness, three animals come to mind: the tortoise, the sloth, and the snail. Of these contestants the snail is definitely the winner hands down. The garden snail clocks in at a molasses-like 0.03 miles per hour. Moving at a steady pace, it would take the snail 12.5 hours to go around a standard city block. However, the category is the slowest mammal, and snails (and tortoises) aren't mammals. On that technicality the three-toed sloth (*Bradypus variegates*) pulls into the winner's circle. Three-toed sloths, believe it or not, have three toes and spend the vast majority of their lives in the rain forests of Central and South America. These speedsters register 0.15 miles per hour, making them 5 times faster than the garden snail but 467 times slower than the cheetah.

_05:: The Thickest

No, this award doesn't refer to mental capacity; that could be a much tougher call. The rhinoceros (*Diceros bicornis michgeli*) is the land mammal with the thickest skin. In fact, for its size, the rhino has the thickest skin of any animal. Rough boss, critical spouse—with 1-inch-thick skin, these tough guys can handle it all. Well, maybe not the boss.

Strange but True
X-TREME MATING

The male platypus is one of only two known venomous mammals. The venom, however, is delivered not by fangs but by retractable spurs on the male platypus's hind legs. Even more strange, these spurs aren't really used on predators and prey. Instead, platypus venom is reserved for battles with rival males during what must be an extreme mating season. In the very few documented cases where humans have been envenomed, the results were intense. The unfortunate victims reported tremendous pain that did not respond to morphine and lingered for months.

7 Things Smarty-Plants Can Do

Not to get you down, but plants can do everything you can do and then some.

_01:: Reproduce

Whoever argued that sex doesn't require a lot of brainpower was right. This applies not just for humans but for all plants as well—they reproduce without even having a brain. The way it works with plants is the same way it works with humans, with a few G-rated substitutions. The plant equivalent to sperm is pollen (think about that as you wash your car this spring), and the plant equivalent of an egg is an ovum. Pollination is the process of getting the pollen near the ovum. The pollen catches a ride on the wind or on a variety of insects like bees or moths. Once the pollen reaches its destination, it grows a tiny tube toward the ovum. When the tube penetrates the ovum, fertilization occurs, and a short time later the seeds are ready.

_02:: Reproduce All Alone

Most plants mate in pairs, but a few plants are monoecious (from the Greek "one house"), meaning that both sexes are present in the same plant. For example, one corn stalk can fertilize itself. This contrasts with the way animals and some plants, like oak trees, arrange things. Oak trees and people are dioecious (from the Greek "two houses"), meaning that different organisms produce the two types of sex cells. Being monoecious has some interesting consequences: it greatly promotes pollination by wind or even gravity, and it also favors inbreeding (believe it or not, intelligence is not a factor in that either).

_03:: Respond to Stress

What could a plant have to be stressed about? A lot. Once a seed begins to grow, the plant is quite literally rooted to the spot, unable to get up and move if the weather is lousy. Because of this, plants have developed ways of surviving abiotic stresses like drought, high salinity, heat, and chill. The defenses aren't always successful, though, and long-term stresses kill most plants. As an example, to combat drought, plants quite literally close up shop. Water pressure within plant cells provides much of their rigidity (called turgor), and without water the plant wilts. To combat wilting, cells harden their cell walls and leaves and shut their ventlike stomata to reduce water loss. Some plants have evolved amazing water conservation mechanisms, as errant houseplant owners know. However, most plants (both indoor and outdoor) will die during long droughts.

_04:: Produce Their Own Food

Forget TV dinners; plants know how to take in light and convert it to food. Translated into biology lingo, plants use photosynthesis to convert solar energy into usable chemical energy forms. Without thinking, the pigments in the chloroplasts of a leaf cell capture photons of light. The energy from those photons is passed through more than 10 protein complexes to produce glucose and other cellular building blocks. This process is a definite reason to go hug a tree. We humans need not only the end products but also what the plant considers waste—a gas called oxygen. Without plant life, we don't eat or breathe. Contrary to popular belief, without us they get along just fine (if not better).

_05:: Kill You

There's no reason to be paranoid. Plants aren't out to get you, personally, but many are killers. Some plant poisons are just plant waste products (think of the waste you produce). Others have developed because plants cannot run away from their predators. Toxins like ricin in castor beans or alkaloids from delphiniums make the animals that eat them sick or dead. Either way the animal is unlikely to eat leaves from that plant again. In a bizarre twist, humans are learning how to harness some of these poisons for medicinal purposes. Foxglove produces a toxic glycoside that in low doses is the heart medication digitalis. The power of opium poppies, a deadly alkaloid, has been used medicinally for centuries in the forms of morphine and codeine.

_06:: Coordinate Functions in an Organism More Than 100 Feet Tall

Sequoia trees tower overhead. Easily made up of many billions of cells, these giants, as well as all other plants, employ coordinated actions. Resources gathered through the roots or via photosynthetic leaves are shared throughout the plant. The organism bends toward the light and seems to know just when to do things like dropping leaves. And all this occurs without a brain, in part due to the plants' vascular system made of xylem and phloem. These tissues could be compared to the blood and lymph systems in the human body. Xylem is plant tissue that transports water and minerals up from the roots and provides support. Phloem moves the products of photosynthesis (food) from leaves to other sites for use or storage.

_07:: Fight Off Invaders

It may be surprising, but plants can actually detect invasion and mount counterattacks in a manner similar to humans' immune systems. When a fungus or bacteria attacks, the plant detects that something is amiss and does two things. First, cells around the infected cell die, forming a barrier that the original invader can't cross. Second, signals travel throughout the plant system warning other cells. The other cells change their content and functions so that they can resist invasion. The systemic nature of this signal is important because invaders usually don't come alone and plants can't run away. It is interesting to note that one of the chemicals in the resistance response is salicylic acid, the natural precursor of our painkiller aspirin.

Excuses to Get a Prescription for Chocolate

It's true: chocolate is good for you, so why not stock up? (Unfortunately, there's nothing we can do about french fries.)

_01:: Love at First Chemical Reaction

Chocolate contains compounds like phenylethylamine (PEA), tryamine, and theobromine, all of which can make you feel swell. These compounds have mildly stimulatory and pleasure-causing effects because their shapes are similar to neurotransmitters, the brain chemicals that travel between nerve cells to help you interpret and react to your environment. Neurotransmitters like the catecholamines are responsible for feelings of well-being and contentment. Guess what? The chocolate compounds look a lot like these feel-good neurotransmitters. When PEA bumps into a nerve cell, a regular love-fest ensues, and all feels right with the world. Since the "love compounds" are present in only small amounts, you need to eat more, right?

_02:: Help Your Heart

A bar of dark chocolate contains 10 times as many phenols as an orange and 4 times as much as beets. Why calculate phenol content? Phenols have been shown to inhibit blood clots by thinning the blood. Thinner blood is easier for the heart to pump, and the decrease in clots means fewer heart attacks. And science is finally supporting what lovers have in-

---

Strange but True

EXERCISING'S "BURN" EXPOSED

While "Feel the burn" is the rallying cry of the exercise conscious, there are actually two burns. One signifies damage due to a muscle tear. The other indicates you're in oxygen debt and shouldn't overdo it. Muscles use oxygen as part of aerobic respiration, which consumes carbohydrates and produces cellular power. In times of exertion, even though your heart is pounding, power needs exceed the amount of oxygen your blood can deliver. When this happens, muscle cells use anaerobic respiration, an alternate power pathway that doesn't use oxygen but isn't as efficient. The burn then comes from the pathway's byproduct—lactic acid. Lactic acid is a weak acid, but it is an acid. If the blood doesn't remove enough and it accumulates in the muscle, it hurts. Too bad we don't use the anaerobic respiration pathway that yeast does—its byproduct isn't lactic acid but alcohol.

tuited for centuries—the gift of chocolate isn't only *from* the heart, it's also good *for* the heart. That being said, remember: moderation is the key. Some doctors now recommend a glass or two of red wine to add phenols to the diet, and eating only 1.5 ounces of dark chocolate will equal that phenol intake. Quadrupling that dosage is fun, but don't expect your doctor to recommend it.

_03:: Ward Off Magnesium Deficiency

Many of the enzymes (protein machines) in your cells require metals like magnesium to work. A magnesium deficiency can be a factor in anything from asthma to diabetes, migraines, stuttering, or even premenstrual syndrome. Food cravings can be the body's way of telling you about diet deficiencies, so to satisfy your craving, why not grab a chocolate bar and enjoy? It's a good source of magnesium. (For the record, so is broccoli, but broccoli cravings are less common for some reason.)

_04:: Put a Little Zip in Your Step

A "little" zip is the key part of this chocolate fact—chocolate contains caffeine. In a normal serving size of milk chocolate (about 6 ounces if you're feeling virtuous) there are 36 milligrams of the stimulant. You'd have to have almost three servings to compare with the jolt you'd get from a cup of coffee. Either way, candy bar or morning coffee, caffeine is the stimulant of choice, as it works to block the Off button for a stimulatory pathway found in all cells. When caffeine is around there's no signal to stop, so the pathway keeps on going and going and going—and so do you.

Behind the Equations: The Juicy Backstories on Famous Biologists

5

In most textbooks it seems like scientists just waltz into their labs, fiddle around for a bit, then wait for the Nobel Committee to call. Sadly, the road to discovery is rarely that simple, and speed bumps pop up constantly. Call it historical context or call it dirt; there's always more to the story.

_01:: Give Peas a Chance

Who would have guessed that Gregor Mendel (1822–1884), the "father of modern genetics," began his work in remedial training? In 1843 Mendel was an ordained priest attempting to get a job teaching natural science at a local school in Brno, Moravia. Problem was, he failed the teaching certificate exam. No social promotions allowed here; to fix him up, his abbot had Mendel attend the University of Vienna to study physical and biological sciences. Sticking with it seems to have worked.

At Vienna, Mendel began his legendary work with pea plants, which demonstrated that patterns of inheritance hold from peas to humans. Oh, and even though his work in genetics remained unrecognized by scientists until the 1900s, Mendel did achieve his goals. He finally received his teaching certificate, taught high school, and became the abbot of his monastery.

_02:: Naturally Selected

Charles Darwin (1809–1882), a young graduate from the University of Cambridge, almost didn't get to go on the 1831 voyage of the HMS *Beagle,* the five-year voyage that provided the basis for Darwin's historic *Origin of Species.* Initially, the ship's captain wanted to reject him based on the shape of his nose. It seems Captain Fitz-Roy judged a man's character by his profile, and Darwin's nose just didn't indicate "sufficient energy and determination." Also, Darwin's father thought the trip was a frivolous attempt to avoid getting a real job (like joining the clergy). What to do? A three-day test voyage with the captain and a well-worded letter from Darwin's uncle soon removed the barriers, and Darwin was on his way.

_03:: Rest in Peace Prize

Many people have heard about Watson and Crick, the dynamic duo of DNA. Fewer have heard of Rosalind Franklin, unless they've heard about the Nobel controversy. Franklin (1920–1958) took the X-ray photographs that are credited with making DNA structure clear to Watson and Crick and leading to the Nobel Prize the men shared with Maurice Wilkins. So, why didn't she just look at the picture and see it herself? Well, for one thing, an X-ray diffraction picture looks a lot like children's spin-art. Taking such pictures is difficult and interpreting them, an art. Also, many times breakthroughs require the perspectives of people from different areas. But was Rosalind Franklin denied a Nobel Prize due to sexism? Absolutely not. The proof: Watson, Crick, and Wilkins were awarded the Nobel Prize in 1962. Franklin died of ovarian cancer four years earlier, and Nobels are not awarded posthumously.

_04:: Albert in Wonderland

One safety rule for scientists is "Don't eat in lab." Albert Hofmann's (1908–) choice to ignore that rule took him not just down a different path but on a whole new kind of trip. In 1938, while trying to develop treatments for migraine headaches, Hofmann made a new chemical, but then had to leave work early due to feelings of "not unpleasant delirium." The next day he thought that there might be a connection between the chemical he inhaled accidentally and his altered mood, so he did the next logical (albeit crazy) thing. He ate some. The chemical was lysergic acid diethylamide, or LSD, and that day Hofmann became the first person ever to "drop acid." LSD has some therapeutic potential, but LSD abuse led Sandoz to stop producing it in 1966.

_05:: Cell Block

As a little guy, what do you do when your results fly in the face of current dogma? This was Leonard Hayflick's dilemma. In the 1960s scientists knew that if they put cells in a petri dish with the right nutrients and enough room, the cell culture would stay alive and keep dividing indefinitely. However, Leonard

Hayflick and Paul Moorhead had evidence that fibroblast cells in culture would divide only a certain number of times (about 50), and then they would die. To confirm their findings and convince skeptics, these young guns had colleagues working in leading labs, repeating their experiments. Good try, but it didn't work. Hayflick's first paper describing the work was rejected because it was contrary to the current line of thinking. Fortunately, the pair persevered and the paper was published in a different scientific journal. The evidence was so compelling that other researchers listened and the entire field of biogerontology, the study of how cells age, was born.

by
Joe Schwarcz

Condensed
CHEMISTRY

Contains

Elemental Floss: 4 Chemists Who Lived for the Lab ✳ 3 Sexy Insects ✳ Gills with Frills: 2 Fishy Health Benefits ✳ 3 Drugs That Save Lives ✳ 1 Backyard Narcotic ✳ 2 Religious Mysteries Solved by Chemistry ✳ 3 Fantastic Side Effects of Neutering ✳ Urine Trouble: 4 True Tales of Tee-Tee ✳ 3 Facts with Silver Linings ✳ 4 Metals That Meddle with Your Body ✳ Lady Killers: 3 Deadly Cosmetics ✳ 3 Tips for Brisk Business ✳ 4 Simple Cures Straight from Momma's Cupboard ✳ All Fired Up: 3 Smokey the Bear Nightmares ✳ Last Calls for Alcohol: 3 Tips for Imbibing ✳ 5 Facts in Poor Taste ✳

Elemental Floss:
Chemists Who Lived for the Lab

The life of a chemist isn't always easy . . . or safe for that matter. Hats off to these cats for braving the elements in the name of pushing science forward.

_01:: Antoine-Laurent Lavoisier
(1743–1794)

While Lavoisier was the father of modern chemistry, he certainly wasn't the father of *modest* chemistry. A brash Antoine once said, "I am young and avid for glory." He may have been somewhat full of himself, but he did deliver the goods. His contributions range from helping to light the streets of Paris to establishing the law of conservation of mass. And though he often took too much credit for the ideas of others, his own contributions have lasted as well. (He named oxygen and hydrogen—beat that!) Like all scientists, Lavoisier ran into some funding problems, so against the advice of his friends, he took a job as farmer-general (tax collector). That was his first mistake. His second was blackballing Jean-Paul Marat from the Academy of Science. During the French Revolution, the combination of Lavoisier's status as a tax collector for the government and Marat's influence landed Lavoisier at the guillotine. He supposedly begged for a few weeks to finish his experiments. Motion denied. Lavoisier was beheaded immediately. A fellow scientist who observed the tragic event commented that "it required only a moment to sever his head, and probably one hundred years will not suffice to produce another like it."

_02:: Henry Cavendish (1731–1810)

Cavendish was a notoriously shy, absent-minded English chemist and physicist with a pronounced fear of women (he had female servants but could communicate with them only through notes). Despite tons of experiments, he published only 20 articles, and many of his contributions weren't realized until they were rediscovered. Lavoisier (see above) repeated Cavendish's study of the collection of gases above water and renamed inflammable air—hydrogen. Similarly, James Maxwell repeated Cavendish's experiments on electricity, although he didn't go to quite the same lengths in the name of science. During his studies of capacitance (a measure of the ability to hold an electric charge), Cavendish shocked himself repeatedly and estimated the strength of a current by measuring the amount of pain he felt as it flowed through his body. Where would modern science be if a few crazy men hadn't been willing to shock themselves silly? The world may never know.

_03:: Marie Curie (1867–1934)

The Polish-born French chemist Marie Curie was the first person ever to win two Nobel Prizes: she shared the 1903 prize in physics with her husband, Pierre, and Henri Becquerel (for the discovery of radioactivity), and she later won the 1911 prize in chemistry (for the isolation of radium). But radiation turned out to be a poor friend to the Curies. In 1906 Pierre, sickened by his prolonged exposure to radiation, died when a horse-drawn wagon ran him over. Amid some controversy, Marie Curie accepted his physics chair at the Sorbonne and became the institute's first female professor. A classroom full of celebrities and politicians greeted her with a standing ovation, but of course, Marie skipped the niceties and began teaching her husband's lecture exactly where he left off. After a career of many more firsts, in 1934 Marie died of leukemia, likely brought on by exposure to high radiation levels during her research. The Radium Institute was renamed the Curie Institute in her honor.

_04:: Christian Friedrich Schönbein (1799–1868)

Note to spouses of chemists: hire your sweetie a babysitter. German chemist Christian Schönbein, who discovered ozone in 1840, didn't always listen to his wife's number-one rule: no experiments in the house. On an otherwise uneventful day in 1845, Schönbein accidentally spilled a mixture of nitric and sulfuric acids. He didn't want his wife to find out, so he quickly grabbed her apron to sop up the liquid. There was just enough time for the apron to dry out (over the stove) before his wife came home. All would have gone smoothly, except that the apron burst into flames and disappeared without producing any smoke. Fortunately, his wife wasn't wearing it at the time. On the bright side, Schönbein had discovered nitrocellulose (or guncotton), which effectively took the place of gunpowder on the battlefield.

3 Sexy Insects

If your cheesy pickup lines and B-grade courting tactics just aren't up to par, maybe it's time you took some tips from the Don Juans of the insect world.

_01:: Spanish Fly

Mention Spanish fly, and people's thoughts turn to carnal activities. Actually, Spanish fly isn't a fly at all, but a beetle that produces a compound called cantharidin, an irritant of the urogenital tract. While it isn't an aphrodisiac, Spanish fly can produce an erection. It can also pose a serious threat to human health. Luckily, it poses no threat to the male pyrochroid beetles, which rely on the stuff for mating purposes. During the mating ritual, the male secretes a gooey substance, which the female tastes. Only if she tastes cantharidin does mating become a possibility—a good example of chemical warfare and species survival. The female passes the cantharidin on to her eggs, which are then less appetizing to predators such as ladybugs.

_02:: Moths That Use Protection

Talk about clever dating tactics, the red male moth of the *Cosmosoma myrodora* species dines on the fluid from the leaves of the dog fennel plant and stores some of its chemical contents in a pair of pouches under his abdomen. Then, when the little guy goes a-courting, he discharges the pouch contents all over the female, sort of like nuptial confetti. The fluid contains a variety of alkaloids from the plant that repel predators, such as spiders. Indeed, virgin female moths coated with the stuff and placed into spiders' webs are quickly cut loose by the spider. This chemical protection seems vital since the moths spend up to nine hours copulating! The male wants to ensure that his mate doesn't become a meal while he attempts to impregnate her.

_03:: Meat and Greet

Plants use some fascinating techniques to spread their pollen. The voodoo lily, for example, depends on carrion beetles for pollination. Because these beetles normally feast on decaying flesh, the lily has evolved an ideal mechanism. Its fragrance is composed of two

---

Strange but True

OZONE AND CONDOMS

We think of ozone as a useful gas. And indeed it is, as long as it's up there in the stratosphere where it belongs. Ozone forms when oxygen is exposed to ultraviolet light, and it's a good thing because ozone's a great absorber of ultraviolet radiation, thus protecting us from skin cancer. At ground level, however, ozone is a pollutant, forming as a result of internal combustion in our car engines. It's also the characteristic smell you sniff around photocopiers or other electrical devices. While ozone irritates our lungs, it can also affect our sex lives. The most widely used condoms are made of natural rubber, a substance that degrades when exposed to ozone. In laymen's terms, this means that your protection needs protection if you're storing it around a photocopier.

---

delightful chemicals, putrescine and cadaverine, which smell just like rotten meat. And while they smell awful to humans, they're pretty appealing to carrion beetles. When the bugs come a-crawling in search of the odor, they are undoubtedly disappointed—no rotting meat in sight, only some weird flower. But as the beetles explore the plant they pick up pollen, which they then unwittingly spread around.

Gills with Frills:
Fishy Health Benefits

Stop heaping those ribs on your plate, put down that pork chop, and lay off the steak for just a sec! We've got the chemically justified reasons why you need to "go fish."

_01:: Fish for the Brain

Here's something to think about. Docosahexaenoic acid, or DHA for short, is a fatty acid. In fact, DHA is a major component of the brain, nerve, and eye tissue, and may just be the right substance for pregnant mothers to dose up on if they want brainy children. A British study showed that children born to mothers who ate oily fish such as sardines or mackerel at least once every two weeks showed superior brain development. In fact, the potential benefits of DHA are so great that there's talk of adding it to baby formula. Another encouraging finding is the reduction in the risk of dementia in people who eat fish at least once a week. It seems polyunsaturated fatty acids, such as DHA, reduce inflammation in the brain and aid in nerve cell regeneration. Holy mackerel!

_02:: And Fish for the Teeth?

Fish is so good for you that even its condiments have nutritional value. Along with your raw fish (sushi), try a little of the pungent, green horseradish known as wasabi. This spicy side might actually do more than just improve the taste: it could keep you smiling longer. Chemicals called isothiocyanates, found in a good dose in wasabi, have been shown effective at killing the bacteria that cause tooth decay and likely fight other germs as well. Perhaps that's why wasabi evolved in the first place as a traditional accompaniment to raw fish! And if that wasn't enough, here's another sushi surprise: isothiocyanates also have anticancer properties, which should have you grinning even wider.

What's the Difference?
REAL OJ VS. FAKE OJ

The orange juice market is huge. Unfortunately, some processors try to cut corners by extending the juice with sugar, pulp wash, and water. But a true orange juice purist can detect the ruse with some clever science. Oxygen in nature occurs as two possible isotopes, O-16 and O-18, which differ slightly in mass. That's right: all water is not created equal. A juice diluted with water from nonbiological sources will have a different isotope distribution, and this can be detected by an instrument called a mass spectrometer. In fact, the authorities have already used this method to put the squeeze on some OJ fraud artists. They may fool the taste buds, but not the mass spectrometer.

3 Drugs That Save Lives

Sometimes the solutions to life's biggest problems (like tuberculosis) are found in the most unexpected places . . . like in the fungus at the back of a chicken's throat. Here's to unusual drugs from unusual sources that continue to save lives.

_01:: Aspirin and the Willow

It's a common belief that aspirin is found in the bark of willow trees. It's not! A related compound called salicin does indeed occur in willow bark, thereby explaining the traditional use of the bark as a medication. But salicin is irritating to the stomach, a problem that prompted the Bayer company to look for an alternative. When one of their chemists synthesized acetyl salicylic acid in 1898, he found it to be a great improvement over other salicylates—a triumph of chemistry over nature! Aspirin has since been found to do much more than alleviate pain. It's an excellent anti-inflammatory substance, as many arthritis patients will vouch. ASA, as it is commonly known, also has an anticoagulant, or blood-thinning, effect, which can reduce the risk of heart attacks. In fact, today more aspirin is consumed as a heart-attack preventer (generally in doses of about 80 mg a day) than as a painkiller!

_02:: Streptomycin and a Sick Chicken

In the 1930s Selman Waksman, working at Rutgers University, became interested in isolating antibiotics from fungi, hoping to find another penicillin. To aid his quest, he asked his colleagues to send him samples of any unusual species they encountered. One day a farmer came to see a Rutgers veterinarian with a sick chicken in tow. All of his chickens, the farmer said, were suffering from the same kind of disease as the sample. The vet found that the bird had a fungal throat infection, but remembering Waksman's request, he sent him a throat swab. From a culture of this fungus, Waksman eventually isolated streptomycin, an antibiotic that revolutionized the treatment of infections, particularly tuberculosis.

_03:: Sister Morphine

When you're in pain, nothing else matters. Jobs, the vagaries of the stock market, and politics all take a backseat to dealing with the affliction. Unfortunately, about 10 million North Americans are permanently disabled by back pain, and nearly 75% of cancer patients experience severe pain. For these people, pain-killing medication can make life worth living. Oxycodone (OxyContin) is a semisynthetic analogue of morphine and is available in a time-release form for effective pain relief. But instructions must be carefully followed. Cutting a pill in half destroys the time-release effect, and all of the active ingredient is released at once, potentially causing a fatal overdose. Unfortunately, oxycodone has become a very popular drug for people who want to achieve a chemical high. They cut open tablets and chew, snort, or mainline the contents. Sadly, many have paid with their lives.

1 Backyard Narcotic

Not to get all Nancy Reagan on you, but it's probably best not to go around licking toads just to get a high. In fact, trial and error might not be the best policy when it comes to backyard narcotics. Here's a case that ended up in error.

_01:: Cane Toads Take a Licking

In the 1930s "sugarcane" toads were introduced into Australia from Hawaii with the idea that they would control the grayback beetle, a sugarcane pest (see Alien Invaders: 5 Guests That Overstayed Their Welcome, p. 33). Bizarrely enough, cane toads can secrete a toxic compound known as bufotenin from a couple of glands behind their eyes (when attacked by predators, of course). But the toxic goo is also a hallucinogen, albeit a dangerous one. In their endless quest to get high, Australian teenagers have taken to drinking the slime produced when toads are boiled. Clearly, emulating this behavior isn't the brightest idea, as two Canadian kids learned. They purchased a couple of toads from an exotic pet store and licked them, hoping for euphoria. They got hospital beds instead.

2 Religious Mysteries Solved by Chemistry

There are some mysteries that we just can't explain. Then again, there are plenty of others that make a lot more sense if you know a little chemistry.

_01:: Where the Hell Is It?

Does hell exist? The ancient Greeks thought so. They even knew where the entrance to the underworld could be found: right beside the temple of Apollo in Pamukkale, in what is now Turkey. The gateway looked like the entrance to a cavern, but this was no ordinary cavern. No animal or man who wandered into the misty cave ever returned. Today we have a good idea why—the area around the cave is permeated with subterranean hot streams. As the hot water flows over deposits of limestone, namely calcium carbonate, it liberates carbon dioxide into the water (sort of a natural carbonation process). Then as the carbonated water reaches the cave, the pressure is released and the gas escapes—kind of like opening a bottle of soda pop. Since carbon dioxide is heavier than air, it pushes the air out of the cave. So anyone entering is quickly overcome by a lack of oxygen . . . a hell of an explanation!

_02:: Popcorn's Devilish Origins

English colonists were introduced to popcorn at the first Thanksgiving in Plymouth by Quadequina, a Native American chief. They were told that popcorn pops because a demon living inside each kernel gets angry and has to escape when placed near heat. If you're looking for a better explanation, look to the steam. Each kernel of corn has a small amount of moisture inside that changes to steam when heated. Gases expand as the temperature increases so that pressure builds up inside the kernel until it can take it no more. Then there's a sudden explosion, and the kernel is

Alphabet Soup

FRESH OUT OF THE COVEN

belladonna: [bel-uh-DON-uh] *n* Derived from the Italian for "beautiful woman," belladonna was a favorite among witches, the forerunners of our modern chemists and physicians. In their attempts to make various poisons and potions, they discovered the physiological properties of many plants and herbs. An extract placed in the eye dilates the pupil and supposedly increases sex appeal. Similar compounds are used today by ophthalmologists when they examine the eyes. When belladonna is rubbed on the skin, its active ingredient, atropine, is absorbed and can give rise to hallucinations. That's why belladonna was incorporated into "witches' ointment," which was applied to the skin during coven meetings. Knowing that, it isn't hard to believe that witches really did fly (at least in a chemical fashion!).

literally blown inside out. If a small hole is bored into an unpopped kernel, it won't pop because the steam has a means of escaping.

Fantastic Side Effects of Neutering

3

There's always a silver lining, right?

_01:: Keep Your Hair

It may seem hard to believe, but as late as 1942 male patients in some mental hospitals were castrated to quiet them. And you thought what they did in *One Flew over the Cuckoo's Nest* was bad. As a result, Winfield State Hospital, a mental institution in Kansas, became an ideal place for Yale anatomist James Hamilton to conduct a study of castrated men. One day one of the patients who had been stripped of his manhood received a visitor, his identical twin. Dr. Hamilton was struck by the fact that the visitor was completely bald, while the inmate had a full head of hair. Could testosterone have something to do with baldness, the researcher wondered? To investigate this possibility, Hamilton got permission to inject the castrated man with testosterone. Within six months the mental patient became as bald as his brother, who had been progressively going bald over a 20-year period. The baldness was unfortunately irreversible, but Dr. Hamilton had demonstrated clearly that testosterone levels could be linked to hair growth.

_02:: Avoid Breast Cancer

The first scientific observation related to breast cancer was made in 1896, when it was noted that the disease sometimes regressed if the ovaries were removed. Eventually this connection was understood in terms of estrogen, the female hormone produced by the ovaries. Some types of breast cancer cells are stimulated to divide by estrogen, and so blocking this effect constitutes a form of treatment. In fact, many antiestrogen drugs have been tried

---

Inventions and Innovations

ICE CREAM DIPPED IN CELLULOSE

Just about everyone enjoys licking sweet frozen colloidal foam, known to simple folk as ice cream. Bizarre, eh? If you examined ice cream under a microscope, you would see a mix of ice crystals, air pockets, and fat globules embedded in a sugary syrup. Fresh ice cream, of course, tastes great. But as it ages it develops a crunchier texture. That's because every time you take it out of the freezer, a little bit melts and refreezes into larger crystals. The solution? Stabilizers like microcrystalline cellulose or guar gum have a remarkable ability to absorb moisture so that the water that forms as ice cream melts becomes unavailable for refreezing. The additives help you enjoy the product longer without worrying about the dreaded "heat shock."

with various degrees of effectiveness, and some plant products also contain compounds that can block the action of the body's estrogen. That's why soy beans and their derivatives, such as tofu, are being promoted as anticancer foods. Flaxseeds also contain anti-estrogens, and a study at the University of Toronto showed that about 25 grams of flaxseed in a daily muffin improved the outcome for estrogen-sensitive breast cancers.

_03:: Prevent Prostate Cancer

We've known for a long time that eunuchs don't develop prostate cancer. Removing the testes lowers the level of male hormones in the blood—the same hormones that stimulate prostate cancer. Indeed, prostate cancer is sometimes treated by surgical removal of the testes, but it ain't the only way. Today there are also drugs, known as antiandrogens, that can block the action of male hormones. Of course diet can also play a role. Reducing the animal fat in your diet and increasing consumption of foods that contain the red pigment lycopene can offer protection against the disease. On that note, tomato products are the best source of lycopene, and the compound is made more available by cooking—a point well worth remembering for men who'd like to hang on to some important parts of their anatomy.

Urine Trouble:
True Tales of Tee-Tee

Who says there's no place in chemistry for bathroom humor? Here are four tales that should have you laughing all the way to the loo.

_01:: Peeing for Napoleon

When Napoleon ran short of gunpowder, he issued an ordinance for people to urinate on niter beds—or compost heaps, as we would now call them. Potassium nitrate, or saltpeter, is an essential component of gunpowder and forms as organic waste decomposes. The other main components of gunpowder, sulfur and charcoal, were abundantly available, so Napoleon had no worries there. Oddly enough, patriotic Frenchmen who increased their fluid intake to help the emperor's war effort may have reaped some unexpected benefits. A recent study has shown that men who pee more often have a reduced risk of bladder cancer. In fact, Israeli researchers have shown that rural men urinated more often and drank more fluids, while urban urine was more concentrated and stayed in the bladder longer, possibly promoting greater contact of carcinogens with the bladder.

_02:: Copper and Squatting Cowboys

A few cowboys were squatting around a campfire when one suddenly let out a painful yelp and grabbed his crotch. An excellent conductor of heat, the copper rivet in his jeans had apparently warmed up and burned the poor chap in a rather sensitive part of his anatomy. Levi Strauss, who had patented the riveted work pants made of denim in 1873, heard about the problem and issued an immediate order that copper rivets should be used only on pockets and not in the crotch. Thankfully, today's rivets are made of nickel coated with copper. The fact that copper is an excellent conductor of heat also explains why the most noted chefs use copper utensils. There are no hot spots on the bottoms of copper sauce pans, and the rate of heating the contents can be readily controlled.

_03:: Ben Franklin and Asparagus

Benjamin Franklin made many contributions to science, including bifocals, the Franklin stove, and lightning rods. But he was also the first to record that some people produced urine with a disagreeable odor after eating asparagus. You'll be grateful to know that the smell has now been identified and is due to sulfur-containing compounds produced when asparagus is metabolized. It seems, however, that not everyone can generate these compounds. A study examined the urine of 115 people who dined on the green vegetable, and only 46 produced the smell. Strangely, not everyone can smell it either.

_04:: Beets and Urine

You probably haven't given much thought to beets unless you've had an alarming bathroom experience after eating them. The naturally occurring pigment in beets, called betacyanin, is a deep red color, and it can give you quite a start if it shows up in your urine! Like asparagus, however, it doesn't affect everyone, only the folks who can't metabolize betacyanin. While this is a genetic trait, it has no health consequence other than to explain why some people will see red after eating beets and going to the restroom.

Facts with Silver Linings

We all know second place is the first loser. But if you're itching to justify all those second-place trophies on your shelf with stories of why silver's actually the best, look no further. Here are some reasons to get up with silver.

_01:: Scents and Sensibility

According to the legend, Sir Lancelot, who wooed Guinevere away from King Arthur, wore silver armor, while the king wore gold. Surely it was hot inside those suits, and conditions were conducive to bacterial growth. Amazingly, though, silver has an antibacterial effect, so Lancelot may not have smelled quite as ripe as Arthur. Today some water filters are impregnated with silver to kill bacteria. Silver-treated socks are also available for the control of foot odor, and experiments are even under way to determine if underarm aroma can be solved with a silver lining. In addition, some people claim that ingesting silver as a "colloidal" preparation destroys undesirable microbes in the body. While there's no scientific evidence that this is true, the practice may turn a person's skin color permanently gray.

_02:: Liquid Silver

The Romans named this element after Mercury, the messenger of the gods in mythology. Its symbol, Hg, is derived from the Latin *hydrargium*, meaning "liquid silver." Both of these refer to mercury's mobility, and indeed it's a mobile element in more ways than one. Liquid mercury scatters in an impressive way when hit, but mercury and mercury com-

pounds can also spread through the environment. Coal contains small amounts of mercury

Myths and Misconceptions
THE HUSBAND ALLERGY

Doctors used to laugh when ladies came in complaining that they must be allergic to their husbands, but now we know that you can develop an allergy to anything—including husbands! One lady became allergic to her hubby after 25 years of happy marriage. As soon as he came into the house she became uncomfortable with various aches and pains for which her physicians could find no solution. The couple was actually forced to live apart for months before the source of the problem was discovered: the husband was a dentist and had switched to a new type of anesthetic for his patients, and his unfortunate wife was reacting to the residues of these substances. So, how'd they solve their problems? Thorough washing by the dentist and a quick change of clothing before coming home restored their conjugal bliss.

compounds, which are released into the air when burned. They are then returned to lakes and oceans by rain, eventually concentrating in fish. Shark, swordfish, and mackerel can contain enough mercury to present a risk to pregnant women, nursing mothers, and young children. In fact, experts warn that even tuna shouldn't be eaten more than a couple of times a week, for fear of mercury's effect.

_03:: Hi Ho, Silver!

Everyone knows that the Lone Ranger fired silver bullets from his gun. Was this of any consequence? Maybe. If we compare a lead bullet and a silver bullet fired with the same amount of explosive charge, the silver bullet will get to its target faster. That's because silver is lighter than lead, so it's more readily accelerated by the exploding charge. While the silver bullet may get to its target a couple of milliseconds faster, it will likely do less damage than the softer lead, which spreads on impact. Since the Lone Ranger never actually shot anyone (and only knocked the gun out of the criminal's hand), the faster, harder, silver bullet was preferable.

4 Metals That Meddle with Your Body

Sure, they seem friendly enough when they're given cute Latin names and boxed neatly away on that periodic table you've got. But if you truly want to see these elements at their worst, here's a little metal floss to put things in perspective.

_01:: Putting the Mad in Mad Hatter

Danbury, Connecticut, used to be the center of the American hat industry. It was also known for the Danbury shakes, a condition that encompassed tremors, incoherent speech, difficulty in walking, and eventual feeble-mindedness. But why were the people of Danbury so prone to the disease? It seems the main victims of the shakes were hatters, or hat makers, who used mercury compounds in the processing of their felt. Oddly enough, this condition was also known in Europe, as evidenced by Lewis Carroll's Mad Hatter character in the famous *Alice in Wonderland* stories.

_02:: Mercury, Take II

The lighthouses along Canada's coasts are great tourist attractions. But some have recently been closed to the public because, of all things, mercury pollution. Virtually all lighthouses built in the 19th and early 20th centuries featured rotating lens assemblies that floated on a pool of mercury to reduce friction. At the time, the toxicity of mercury vapor wasn't recognized, and many a lighthouse keeper suffered ill effects such as tremors, delusions, and depression. In fact, the lighthouse on Rottnest Island in Australia is famous not only for being the first rotating beam lighthouse on that continent but also because its first three keepers all committed suicide! Today most exposure to mercury vapor comes from broken mercury thermometers.

_03:: Biting Humor

Anyone who's ever chomped on a piece of aluminum foil may have learned the hard way that dissimilar metals that come in contact can generate electric current. Since dental fillings contain metals, contact with aluminum can cause an intense jolt of pain. Imagine having such pain constantly! That's what happened to a lady who had a tooth filled next to a gold crown. Whenever she ate acidic foods, which provided the electrolyte needed to conduct current, she experienced intense facial pain, which at first was misdiagnosed as trigeminal neuralgia, a horrific neurological disease. When the filling was replaced with porcelain, the pain disappeared. This also provides a lesson for keeping cutlery made of dissimilar metals separate in the dishwasher. We're not worried about causing the cutlery pain, but the electric current will cause corrosion.

_04:: Around-the-Clock Dangers

In the 1920s the Radium Dial Company opened a new watch factory in the small town of Ottawa, Illinois. Many young women were hired to paint the numbers on the watch faces with glow-in-the-dark, radium-laced paint. They were told the paint was harmless even as they licked their paintbrushes into fine points. The paint *wasn't* harmless—radium is a radioactive element, which after prolonged exposure can accumulate in bones. It decays

---

Myths and Misconceptions
THE LEAD IN LEAD PENCILS

This may come as a shock to some people, but lead pencils do not, we repeat DO NOT, contain any lead. Never did. The so-called lead is actually a mixture of graphite and clay. The more graphite, the softer and darker the point. The mistake in terminology can be traced back to the ancient Romans, who actually used pieces of lead to draw lines on papyrus scrolls to guide them in writing with a tiny brush called a *pencillus*. Lead is a very soft metal and pieces readily rub off. The Romans never realized, however, that lead was potentially toxic. Of course, today we know that even tiny amounts ingested can result in poisoning. On the brighter side, though, it looks like you're not going to die of lead poisoning for chewing on your pencils way back in grade school.

---

by releasing alpha particles, which can destroy cells in the bone marrow, and it can often lead to bone cancer. Many factory workers developed health complications despite the team of doctors who routinely checked the women's radium levels. While few of the workers ever came forward with their complaints, the Radium Dial Company dealt with those that did—quickly and quietly. In a bizarre twist, as late as the 1940s radium was used by some physicians to treat arthritis. Not only was this treatment dangerous but it was also useless.

Lady Killers:
Deadly Cosmetics

Yeah, we all know beauty's in the eye of the beholder. And while a dab of makeup here and there generally helps the cause (Tammy Faye aside), the following are three cases where the price of beauty became excruciatingly high.

_01:: Dynamic Weight Loss

During World War I, French munitions workers manufacturing trinitrotoluene (TNT) commonly developed unusual sweating, fever, and weight loss. Apparently, inhaled TNT vapors increased their metabolic rate. And though TNT was too dangerous to use as a medication, in 1931 dinitrophenol, a chemical relative, was introduced in the United States to step up metabolic rate. It seemed so safe in small doses for weight loss that it was actually available without a prescription. But by 1935 toxic reactions involving the bone marrow and skin were noted, and eventually a few deaths were associated with the product. Dinitrophenol also caused cataracts, and about 100 users lost their sight. The drug is no longer legal in Canada or the United States but is still sometimes illegally obtained from Mexico.

_02:: Nail Files: Acetone vs. Acetonitrile

Acetone is the active ingredient in many nail polish removers, while acetonitrile is the active ingredient in the solution used to take off artificial nails. These two compounds are very different in their levels of toxicity. In an unfortunate case, a 16-month-old child ingested about 15–30 milliliters of the latter, and her panic-stricken mother immediately called a poison control center. The mother didn't transmit the information properly, and the doctor thought she was talking about nail polish remover. He informed her that there was no great risk. Had he realized that acetonitrile had been swallowed, he would have declared an emergency immediately because the compound releases cyanide once metabolized in the liver. Sadly, the child was found dead in the morning.

_03:: Perfume and Regurgitating Whales

Whales can finally relax! Today's chemists have learned how to mimic ambergris in the laboratory, causing high-pitched sighs of relief in oceans across the world. Ambergris, the waxy liquid coating the stomachs of sperm whales, protects them from the sharp bones of the cuttlefish they eat. When fresh, ambergris is soft and black and smells awful. When exposed to sun and water, it hardens, becomes lighter colored, and develops a pleasant smell. Bizarrely, ambergris is an excellent fixative that keeps perfume's scent from evaporating too quickly, and for this reason was once prize booty for whalers. A piece of ambergris weighing 922 pounds was once found floating in the ocean, making its discoverer instantly wealthy. But synthetic analogues have now eliminated the need to kill whales for perfume manufacturing. And ladies no longer have to cope with the notion of anointing themselves with whale regurgitation.

3 Tips for Brisk Business

While Kermit is no doubt right in singing that "it ain't easy being green," having green is another story. Here are a few tales of chemistry, business, and the pleasant effect they have when you mix 'em up just right.

_01:: The Brewing of Bluing

The real Mrs. Stewart did not want her face on the bottle of bluing. Too bad, because she missed out on immortality. Her husband, Al, a traveling salesman in the late 1800s, sold bottles of liquid bluing and thought that a kindly face on the label would increase sales. When his wife refused, he used a picture of his mother-in-law! As white fabrics age, they take on a yellow tinge. That's because they begin to absorb the blue wavelengths of light instead of reflecting them. The answer, as Mr. Stewart discovered, was to add a touch of ferric hexacyanoferrate, or Prussian blue, to the wash. Mrs. Stewart's bluing is still making clothes "whiter than white" today. And don't worry about the cyanide; it is tightly bound to iron and is harmless.

_02:: Tint of Brilliance

Proving that teachers really should watch what they say to impressionable youngsters, in 1856 an English schoolboy named William Henry Perkin (1838–1907) started experi-menting in his home laboratory. His teacher had offhandedly remarked that a fortune could be made in synthetic quinine, so young Perkin went to work. Like most chemistry students, he ended up with little more than a failed experiment and a purple-tinted mess. Unlike most chemistry students, Perkin saw gold: he immediately left school and became a millionaire by opening a factory that produced the first synthetic dye.

_03:: About Face: Skin Peels and the Economy

Can the sales of trichloroacetic acid actually predict the state of the economy? Maybe. The chemical, used by dermatologists and plastic surgeons to carry out facial peels, is painted on to the skin. The skin immediately responds by trying to slough off the irritant. What results is a rapid turnover of cells whereby wrinkles are reduced, precancerous lesions are removed, and your skin is rejuvenated with a youthful glow. So what's this got to do with the economy? Skin peels aren't covered by medical insurance, and according to some doctors the number of patients desiring the procedure dropped dramatically before the recession in the early 1990s. So did the number of patients looking to have their breasts enlarged with implants. The same trend was repeated in the first couple of years of the 21st century.

Simple Cures Straight from Momma's Cupboard

No need to bother the doctor or visit the pharmacist; these are cures you'll find in the comfort of your own kitchen.

_01:: Dealing with Motion Sickness Gingerly

Motion sickness can be really unnerving. But would you believe that the solution might be as simple as ginger? A study at the University of Michigan Medical Center showed that subjects given about 1,000 mg of ground ginger fared much better than those on a placebo when placed on an amusement park–style ride famous for inducing motion sickness. And ginger may even help with the pain of arthritis. In India it's one of the most common remedies for the condition. How does it work? Ginger triggers the release of prostaglandins in the body, chemicals with anti-inflammatory properties. A word of caution though: People taking blood thinners have to be careful with ginger because it also has an anticoagulant (blood-thinning) effect. No need to worry about ginger ale, though, as there isn't much ginger in it.

_02:: Hyperventilation and the Paper Bag Trick

When we hyperventilate, we exhale abnormal amounts of carbon dioxide. And since carbon dioxide forms from carbonic acid in the blood, hyperventilation can affect our acid-base ratio and cause symptoms such as fainting. The ready remedy is to breathe into a bag so the exhaled carbon dioxide can be recycled. Of course, humans aren't the only ones left gasping for air—chickens can also hyperventilate, particularly in hot weather because they have no sweat glands. When they lose carbon dioxide, they start laying eggs with thinner shells. That's because eggshells are made of calcium carbonate. Less carbon dioxide in the blood means less carbonate available for eggs. The solution? Give the chickens carbonated water to drink. No need to pamper them with Perrier; cheap seltzer will do the trick.

_03:: Hate Hangovers? Drink Vodka!

Ever wonder what causes a hangover? It isn't the alcohol in the beverage—not the alcohol that most people think of, anyway. The alcohol that intoxicates is ethanol, but the stuff responsible for the hangover is a byproduct of fermentation known as methanol. Dark wines, cognac, fruit brandies, and whiskies contain the most methanol, while vodka has almost none. Enzymes in the body convert methanol to formaldehyde, which causes the symptoms. These enzymes actually prefer ethanol as their meal—hence the hair-of-the-dog treatment for hangovers. Taking another drink provides the enzymes with ethanol, and while they gorge on this, the methanol is excreted. In the doses found in beverages, methanol may be annoying but not dangerous. In high doses methanol can intoxicate and is sometimes passed off as regular alcohol by bootleggers, and in such amounts it can be lethal.

_04:: Cloves for the Breath

In the third century BCE officers of the court in China were required to carry cloves in their mouth when addressing the emperor. This was to prevent him from being exposed to bad breath. It was probably in this fashion that people discovered that cloves had local anesthetic properties. Eugenol, found in oil of cloves, is still used by dentists to anesthetize the gums before giving a needle, and in an emergency clove oil can be rubbed around an aching tooth for relief. Some interesting mythology surrounds cloves as well. Folklore suggests they have aphrodisiac properties because they resemble a certain part of the male anatomy. Not so. Cloves may improve your breath, but they won't leave you breathless.

All Fired Up:
Smokey the Bear Nightmares

Between the evolution of matches, mischievous children, and fiery fowl, there's plenty here to keep Smokey up all night.

_01:: The Stormy Petrel: A PETA Nightmare Too

The Shetland Islands are famous for sheep and wool. But did you know that they're also home to the stormy petrel? This unusual bird, so named because it was thought to appear before a storm, has a very high fat content. Fat, of course, is an excellent fuel and burns readily to produce carbon dioxide, water, heat, and light. Islanders used to catch the creatures, dry them, fix their feet in clay, and thread a wick through their beaks. Then they would light the wick and burn the dried bird for illumination. The Danes did the same with the great auk, a bird that has since become extinct. They inserted a wick into the dead bird's belly and burned it. The slightly less macabre were satisfied with burning whale oil.

_02:: Early Matches

We take many things in life for granted, like matches. Until the late 1700s if you wanted a flame, you had to be good with a flint and tinder. But then French chemist Claude Bertholet came along and discovered that a mixture of sugar and potassium chlorate could be ignited with a small drop of sulfuric acid. The first self-igniting matches had heads made of potassium chlorate, sugar, and gum, and were ignited by being dipped into a vial of sulfuric acid. The problem of carrying around open bottles of sulfuric acid was solved by sealing the acid in a glass tube that was wrapped in a paper saturated with the combustible chemicals. Small pliers were used to crush the tube and release the acid—which ignited the paper.

_03:: Mischievous Children and Methane

Children in Leeds, England, used to amuse themselves by throwing matches into the canal that was the receptacle for sewage output. However, the desired effect—a burst of flames—was seen only on very cold mornings. The decomposition of sewage due to the action of bacteria can generate lots of methane gas, and methane is highly flammable. While the spectacular display of flames angered bargemen on the canal and delighted wily children, it never lasted long. The gas is usually lighter than air, so it dissipates quickly. Only on very cold days did there seem to be enough lingering methane just above the surface of the water to cause the flaming effect.

3 Last Calls for Alcohol: Tips for Imbibing

Alcohol comes with enough of its own problems, so it seems unfair that people also have to worry about how they drink. Alas, here are some tips on getting tipsy.

_01:: Strong and Smooth with a Hint of Tungsten

There used to be a strange initiation rite for men drafted into an artillery regiment in France. Recruits had to drink a glass of white wine that had flowed through the barrel of a 155-millimeter gun after several shots had been fired. Then one day a 19-year-old soldier developed seizures and was taken to the hospital unconscious and unresponsive to stimuli. He had extremely high levels of tungsten in his blood, and doctors traced the source to the wine. It seems the composition of gun barrels had recently changed with the inclusion of tungsten for hardness, tungsten steel being especially hard. Other recruits were spared because they had vomited immediately after drinking the wine. Since then the French army has banned the hazing ritual.

_02:: Fill 'Er Up with Unleaded

An English couple moved to Spain and discovered the delights of sangria. To have some on hand all the time, they purchased a jug from a local potter that fit neatly into their fridge. Not a good move, as it turned out. Over a period of a few months the husband lost 25 kilograms (about 55 pounds) and began

Inventions and Innovations

SPRAY THAT UNFAITHFUL HUSBAND (S-CHECK)

For years people cheated on their spouses in the name of chemistry. Finally, chemistry is fighting back. Takeshi Makino, president of the Safety Detective Agency in Osaka, Japan, won the 1999 chemistry Ig Nobel Prize (for achievements that "cannot or should not be reproduced") for his unusual invention. His agency sells a pair of chemical sprays, called S-Check, that a wife can spray on her husband's underwear to see if he's been unfaithful. The sprays turn traces of semen bright green. And only showering will help. Unfortunately, the same company has also come up with a new idea for infidelity detection creams: the shower detector. Rub it into your mate's back, and a scab will form when he (or she) attempts to shower. Put it on socks or underwear, and they'll change color (from the change in temperature) if removed for longer than 15 minutes. When did cheating get so complicated?

to suffer from terrible abdominal cramps. Luckily, he called his brother, a British physician, who recognized the severity of the symptoms and urged him to get an immediate blood test. It showed toxic levels of lead! The jug had been improperly glazed, and the sangria leached lead from the decorative pigment. Immediate medical treatment to remove the lead from his system saved the man's life.

_03:: Meat, Fish, and the Color of Wine

Why does red wine go with meat and white with fish? The simplest explanation is that red wine has a more robust flavor and would overwhelm the delicate taste of fish. But if you're looking for more of a chemical explanation, here it is. Red grape skins contain plenty of tannic acid that ends up in the wine. Much of the flavor of red meat is due to compounds found in the fat, but unfortunately fat coats the taste buds so that subsequent bites don't taste as good as the first. This is where the tannic acid comes in. It has detergent properties, meaning that it can remove fat. So sipping red wine between bites cleans the palate. Fish has less fat, and tannic acid can also overpower the more subtle flavor. But contrary to what some may think, it isn't illegal to drink white wine with meat.

5 Facts in Poor Taste

Ever notice how some foods agree with you and some don't? Here are a few foods that aren't just out for an argument; they're looking to get the final word.

_01:: Bitter Cassava

Cassava roots have a bitter taste that prevents insects as well as hungry monkeys from eating them. This is great for African farmers, who grow a lot of cassava because it produces high yields in poor soil as well as in drought conditions. The bitter taste comes from a compound called linamarin, which the cassava root produces to protect itself from predators. How? By releasing cyanide of course! Amazingly, the cassava can cause human poisoning if the root is improperly prepared, so it has to be grated and soaked for days before being eaten. In fact, the resulting condition from eating raw cassava is known as konzo and is characterized by paralysis. Surprisingly, tapioca is actually made from cassava, but it contains no residual cyanide, so no need to worry about that pudding.

_02:: Bad Milk

One of the unfortunate victims of bad milk was Abraham Lincoln's mother, Nancy Hanks Lincoln, who died of milk sickness in 1818.

The sickness, which actually wiped out many pioneers, had nothing to do with bacteria and everything to do with a cow's diet. When the animals grazed on a plant called snakeroot, people who drank their milk got sick and often died. A naturally occurring substance in the milk called tremetone was converted by human body enzymes into a highly toxic substance. When chemists linked milk sickness to snakeroot early in the 20th century, farmers were counseled to rid their fields of the plant, and thus milk sickness was eliminated.

_03:: Hungry for Change

According to the *British Medical Journal*, coins are the most common items found after cremation of the human body. It seems some people ingest coins for good luck. Others think that they can correct dietary deficiencies in zinc or copper. Surgeons once removed $22.50 from a 31-year-old man who had been ingesting coins for 12 years and finally came down with zinc poisoning. Zinc reacts with hydrochloric acid in the stomach to form hydrogen gas and zinc chloride, which is very corrosive and can lead to ulcers. The world record for coin ingestion is 424, a feat outmatched only by the heartiest of piggy banks.

_04:: Beans, Beans, Good for the Heart . . .

Beans have been called the musical food because of their propensity to produce gas. That's because humans lack an enzyme needed to digest some of the carbohydrates in beans. Raffinose and stachyose are particularly problematic. Although we can't digest these compounds, microbes in our intestines can. Unfortunately, when the bugs eat the beans, they produce gas that eventually has to make a more or less dramatic exit. Now scientists have successfully isolated the required enzyme, alpha-galactosidase, which can be added to the first mouthful of beans (or broccoli or cabbage or stir-fry) to reduce the problem. And it's a good thing because beans are great. They're a wonderful source of fibers and also flavonoids, which can protect against cancer and heart disease.

_05:: A Mighty Wind

Restaurants often offer mints to their patrons after a meal. This is an old tradition because mint reduces the chance of untoward gaseous emissions (otherwise known as farting). You can get gas in your intestine in all sorts of ways. You can swallow air. Or carbon dioxide can be produced when the acid contents of your stomach mix with naturally occurring bicarbonate in the small bowel. However you get gas, the bottom line is the same: if there's a buildup of gas, it has to come out one way or another. And this is where mint works its charm. Peppermint contains natural oils that act as a carminative, meaning that they allow sphincter muscles to relax so that gases can be expelled steadily rather than in powerful explosive bursts. Long live the after-dinner mint!

by
Kenneth Silber &
Alexei Bayer

Condensed
ECONOMICS

Contains

Economists Everyone Should Know

Sure, the next time you're laid off, salaried down, underbudgeted, or wearing hand-me-downs, you *could* blame the economy. But why pick on the economy when you can pick on the economist instead?

_01:: Adam Smith (1723–1790)

Ever felt a push from behind on your way to work, but when you turned around no one was there? It was probably Smith's "invisible hand," the force that leads individuals pursuing self-interest to provide useful goods and services for others. Champion of the free market, Smith pretty much founded economics as a systematic discipline, and his ideas echo through the profession to the present day. If you don't believe in economic forecasting, read Smith's masterwork, *The Wealth of Nations* (1776). Smith, a native Scot, argued that Great Britain couldn't afford to hold its rebellious American colonies—an impressive conjecture considering Britain's world domination at the time.

_02:: David Ricardo (1772–1823)

Ricardo became the poster boy for middle achievers everywhere when he came up with the idea of comparative advantage. He showed how free trade allows countries to specialize in what they do best—even if they're not very good at anything. The same principle explains why Michael Jordan doesn't fix roofs, even though he might be better at it than many roofers; it's more efficient for him to focus on basketball. Disinherited for marrying outside his family's Jewish faith, Ricardo was originally a successful banker in London, then a member of Parliament, before he became an economist. In his "Essay on the Influence of a Low Price of Corn on the Profits of Stock," Ricardo presented the law of diminishing returns, which explains how adding more labor and machinery to a piece of land (or other fixed asset) after a certain point is just unproductive.

_03:: John Maynard Keynes (1883–1946)

Before Keynes, economics was in its classical phase. After him, it was in its Keynesian phase (just as there was Newtonian physics before Albert Einstein came along). The Great Depression convinced Keynes that the government had to engage in deficit spending to combat unemployment, a major break from the economic thinking of the time. He first became well known after World War I when he quit his British Treasury job, complaining that the Treaty of Versailles would wreak economic havoc. (He was right.) He also helped set up the system of fixed exchange rates used for decades after World War II. Unlike the majority of economists, Keynes led the life of a celebrity: he married a Russian ballerina, drank Champagne with literary figures, and made a fortune in the stock market. Keynes once said, "I would rather be vaguely right than precisely wrong," which may account for continued arguments between "new Keynesian" and "new classical" economists.

_04:: Joseph Schumpeter (1883–1950)

Schumpeter, born in Austria, reportedly vowed to become the best economist, horseman, and lover in Vienna—and later regretted not meeting the horseman goal. He argued that economists' traditional idea of competition (similar companies competing on price) was much less important than "creative destruction," whereby entrepreneurs create new products and industries. He predicted that capitalism would be undermined by its own success. But unlike Karl Marx, Schumpeter didn't look forward to the system's demise. He wrote, "If a doctor predicts that his patient will die presently, this does not mean that he desires it."

_05:: John Kenneth Galbraith (1908–)

Galbraith once said, "The only function of economic forecasting is to make astrology look respectable." A prolific author and adept debater, Galbraith stands among the economists best known outside the economics profession. The Canadian-born Galbraith moved to the United States in the 1930s and worked as a price controller in World War II, a Harvard professor, an advisor to President John F. Kennedy, and eventually a U.S. ambassador to India. A persistent concern of his long career has been with corporate power. In such books as *The Affluent Society* (1958) and *The New Industrial State* (1967), he argued that big companies have little to fear from competitors and exercise lots of influence over consumers. Not everyone likes the thesis, of course; critics have pointed out that big companies sometimes lose market share and go out of business.

_06:: Milton Friedman (1912–)

Friedman advocated free-floating exchange rates, school vouchers, the shift from the draft to a volunteer military, and for doctors to be allowed to practice medicine without a license. A proponent of free markets and limited government, Friedman challenged the Keynesian ideas that dominated economics in the decades after World War II and instead supported monetarism, an emphasis on the

---

Strange but True

THE STONE MONEY OF YAP

If you're frustrated by the market and you're looking for a currency that can stand the test of time, look no further. In the Caroline Islands in the South Pacific, there's an island named Yap (or Uap). In 1903 an American anthropologist named Henry Furness III visited the islanders and found they had an unusual system of currency. It consisted of carved stone wheels called *fei*, ranging in diameter from a foot to 12 feet. Because the stones were heavy, the islanders didn't normally carry their money around with them. After a transaction the *fei* might remain on a previous owner's premises, but it was understood who owned what. One family's *fei*, Furness was told, had been lost at sea many years earlier while being transported from a nearby island during a storm. But that stone was still used as currency, even though it was unseen and irretrievable beneath hundreds of feet of water.

role of money in the economy. Born to immigrants in New York City, Friedman spent much of his career at the University of Chicago. In 1976 he won the Nobel Prize for economics for, among other things, "his demonstration of the complexity of stabilization policy"—meaning, why government has so much trouble keeping the economy on an even keel. His fame, however, only grew. In 1979 Friedman's book *Free to Choose* (coauthored by his wife and accompanied by a public-television series) reached a worldwide audience.

Famous Bubbles That Popped

Everyone loves bubbles, right? Bubble gum, bubble tea, bubble baths. Fun, fun, fun! That is, until your lousy stockbroker calls up from Boca Raton to tell you that the surefire stock tip he gave you just bottomed out, and now he's going back to school to pursue his law degree. That's when bubbles are less fun—when they're of the economic nature and leave you cursing in the poorhouse. Here's a tribute to eight of the worst bubbles ever to pop.

_01:: The Ponzi Scheme

Being a scam artist is bad enough; having a type of scam named after you is a perverse sort of immortality. Consider the case of Charles Ponzi, who showed great chutzpah even by 1920s standards. Promising investors a return rate of 100% in just 90 days, Ponzi lured trusting thousands into his Security and Exchange Company (no relation to the Securities and Exchange Commission, which regulates U.S. financial markets). But the supposed whiz kid merely used the new funds to pay off existing investors, a practice now known as a Ponzi scheme. The arrangement collapsed when the authorities began investigating, and after doing a stint in the slammer, "the Ponz" finally got a real job—working for Alitalia, the Italian national airline.

_02:: The South Sea and
_03:: Mississippi Bubble

Don't you just love globalization? In the early 18th century this double bubble grew on both sides of the English Channel at the same time, probably the first example of globalization in financial markets. In England, investors snatched up shares of the South Sea Company, a firm that was supposed to monopolize trade with the Americas, while in France money flowed into a company set up by Englishman John Law to operate in the Mississippi Valley and other French colonial areas. Share prices of the companies rose so much that it became necessary to invent a new word for those who grew rich in the bubble: millionaires. Somehow the South Sea Company never made a profit; claims that Louisiana had mountains of gold turned out to be a little less than accurate. After share prices collapsed in 1720, France had a government crisis, and England passed the Bubble Law, forbidding companies to issue stock.

_04:: Florida's Real Estate Boom

President Andrew Jackson—whose face graces the $20 bill—won Florida for the United States in 1821, but for 100 years Americans couldn't quite figure out what to do with it (aside from removing the Native American population). But in the early 1920s developers descended en masse on the Sunshine State, realizing its potential as a giant vacationland for winter-weary northerners. A huge boom ensued, with prices rocketing to $1,000 per acre, a hefty sum of money in those days. At one point, an amazing one-third of Miami's population had become real estate agents. Right idea but bad timing—Florida weather helped burst the bubble with severe hurricanes in 1926 and 1928.

_05:: The Roaring '20s Stock Market

In the 1920s stocks could be purchased like real estate, by putting 10% down and taking out a 90% loan from the broker, secured by the value of the shares. This huge margin provided fantastic leverage—when stocks appreciated. And appreciate they did. The Dow Jones industrial average rocketed 344% between 1923 and 1929, and more and more Americans got caught up in the stock market frenzy. It was not all speculation or a pyramid scheme: there were legitimate reasons for investors to be optimistic. The '20s were a period of rapid economic growth and development of new technologies: radio, electricity, automobiles, and airplanes. Nevertheless, the bubble

burst in October 1929, and the Dow lost nearly 25% in just two days. The crash was promptly followed by the Great Depression, and the market bottomed a few years later, at just 11% of its 1929 peak.

_06:: Japan's Stock Bubble

In the 1980s Japanese companies could do no wrong, as far as investors were concerned. The Nikkei 225 index of the Tokyo stock market rose dramatically throughout the decade—dipping briefly only during the 1987 Black Monday crash—to hit almost 40,000 in 1989. Its market capitalization peaked at 611 trillion yen—larger than the New York Stock Exchange's. So convinced was everybody that stock prices had nowhere to go but up, Japanese stockbrokers offered their big clients guaranteed returns on their stock portfolios. It all came to an end when growth in Japanese exports failed to keep pace with investors' expectations, and for over 10 years the Nikkei slumped—ultimately giving up all the gains of the late 1980s and returning to the pre-bubble level of around 7,800 in early 2003.

_07:: Russia's Notorious MMM

When the Soviet Union collapsed in 1991, Russians were naive about financial markets. So, when in 1994 an obscure company called MMM (not to be confused with the 3M Company, the American blue chip) opened offices in Moscow and other Russian cities and began offering fantastic returns on its shares, Russians pulled their hard-earned rubles out of their mattresses. They didn't ask how MMM was going to earn such returns; after years of Communist propaganda, they had an unshakable faith in the capitalist system. Sergey

Mavrodi, MMM's founder, even got elected to the Russian parliament. The damage from the pyramid was relatively small; when the scheme collapsed in 1995, MMM had stolen an estimated $100 million, a mere pittance by the standards of Enron. But the number of Russians taken in was enormous; since record keeping was spotty, estimates ran as high as 50 million—which would make it the largest fraud of its kind in history.

_08:: The Internet Bubble

American investors have none of the excuses the Russian investors had. They're supposed to be the hard-nosed capitalists and the most sophisticated investors in the world. But in the second half of the 1990s they got caught in the Internet bubble on NASDAQ. This wasn't all that different from a pyramid scheme, even though it was touted by hotshot analysts working for the world's most re-spected investment banks. Internet companies that never made a profit were valued by the market at hundreds of times their annual revenues. The NASDAQ composite index, which traded at 1,500 in 1998, rocketed to over 5,000

Just the Facts

THE NATIONAL DEBT

U.S. federal debt—Jan. 1, 1791	$75,463,476.52
U.S. federal debt—Dec. 31, 2002	$6,405,707,456,847.53
U.S. federal debt owed to public—Dec. 31, 2002	$3,647,939,770,383.73
The rest, just between government agencies	$2,757,767,686,463.80
Debt owed to public as % of annual economy—1946	114
Debt owed to public as % of annual economy—2001	33

by March 2000, and serious analysts began measuring the number of mouse clicks visitors made at different Web sites. As in other bubbles, though, the fall was precipitous, and the shares of those few Internet start-ups that survived fell to a tiny fraction of their peak values.

5 Central Banks with Clout

William McChesney Martin, former chairman of the U.S. Federal Reserve, once claimed that central banks are like bad party hosts: they "take away the punch bowl just when the party gets going." The following are five of the worst party hosts around.

_01:: The Fed (the Leader)

U.S. dollars make up about 70% of central bank reserves around the world so, big surprise, the U.S. Federal Reserve holds the rank of world's leading central bank. The Fed sets American interest rates, controls the U.S. money supply, and regulates the country's commercial banks. If a commercial bank can't get money anywhere else, the Fed serves as the lender of last resort. Working for the Fed may not seem like the most glamorous job, but Fed chairman Alan Greenspan has certainly gotten his share of the limelight since taking office in 1987 (he's lasted through four presidents). Although Greenspan gets just one vote on the 12-member Federal Open Market Committee, the chairman's views usually carry a lot of weight, as was true of those of Greenspan's cigar-chomping predecessor, Paul Volcker.

_02:: The European Central Bank (the New Kid)

Don't discount the European Central Bank (ECB) just because it's the new kid on the chopping block. Since it was founded in 1998, the ECB has conducted monetary policy for the 12 countries that have adopted the euro, the single European currency. The ECB sets interest rates for the entire euro zone, but—-wouldn't you know it—in highly bureaucra-tized Europe, all countries still have their own national central banks. All of them, plus the ECB, are part of another organization called the European System of Central Banks. Setting a single interest rate for an entire continent is a pretty thankless task since not all countries are likely to be satisfied, so the ECB gets pulled different ways by political pressures. Even the location of ECB headquarters—Frankfurt, Germany's financial center, rather than Paris—was a matter of political horse trading.

_03:: The Bank of England (the Old Guard)

Nicknamed the Old Lady of Threadneedle Street, after its headquarters in London's financial district, the Bank of England stands as one of the world's oldest central banks—only the Swedish central bank is older. Founded way back in 1694 and nationalized in 1946, the Bank of England gained its operational independence only in 1997. In an ironic twist, it was the Labor government—the putative socialists—that finally decided not to meddle in the interest-rate-setting process. Although the pound is no longer the currency of an empire over which the sun never sets, London still acts as Europe's largest financial hub. As a member of the European Union, Britain is eligible to join the euro zone but has so far followed the conservative path of holding on to the pound—thus the Bank of England remains a force to be reckoned with.

_04:: The Swiss National Bank (the Safety Zone)

You know you're watching a good movie when the crook/tyrant/heiress utters the phrase "numbered Swiss bank account." The Swiss franc acts as the quintessential safe-haven currency—a reassuringly stable thing to invest in during times of crisis and turmoil. The Swiss National Bank maintains that sense of security, and the franc's safe-haven role has acquired even greater appeal for many investors since September 11, 2001. However, before hiding your money and heading for the border, you should know that Swiss bank secrecy laws have weakened in recent years.

_05:: The Bank for International Settlements (the Go-Between)

Sometimes you just need a go-between, and that's where the BIS comes in. A central bankers' bank, the BIS serves as a counterparty, or trading partner, for financial transactions between banks. The ultimate purpose of the BIS is to foster cooperation among central banks to ensure stability in the world's financial and banking systems. Located in Basel, Switzerland, the BIS was originally formed in 1930 to deal with the issue of German reparations after World War I, and it's been a fixture of global finance ever since. In contrast to the World Bank and the International Monetary Fund, however, you rarely hear about the BIS being targeted by antiglobalization protesters. Sometimes keeping a low profile keeps you out of trouble.

And **Without**

2

_01:: The Bank of Japan (the Has-Been)

For a while in the 1980s, the Japanese central bank trampled close on the heels of the U.S. Fed. The Japanese economy, the world's second largest, gained on its rival, and the yen won acceptance as a reserve currency, especially in Southeast Asia. But it all came a-cropper in the 1990s, when the speculative bubble in Japanese stocks and real estate burst. The Japanese economy entered a long period of stagnation, and Japanese banks, once the world's largest, became a weak link in the world financial system. The Bank of Japan has been powerless in reviving the economy—even though it has pushed interest rates down to zero.

_02:: The People's Bank of China (the Lame Duck)

The People's Bank of China is China's central bank (whereas the Central Bank of China is the central bank of Taiwan). Whether or not the institution really belongs to the people, the People's Bank has responsibility for the financial system of a nation with more than 1.2 billion people. The Chinese economy grows by 7–8% each year and will probably become the world's biggest sometime in the 21st century. But unlike other major central banks, the People's Bank doesn't really make key decisions about monetary policy. Interest rates in increasingly capitalist China are still set by bureaucrats in the Communist Party.

Gangs of New York:
Schools of Thought That Are Always at War

Winston Churchill once said, "If you put two economists in a room, you get two opinions, unless one of them is Lord Keynes, in which case you get three." Clearly, the legacy of Keynes lives on.

_01:: Keynesianism

In the world of economics, you're cool only as long as you're right. Based on the ideas of British economist John Maynard Keynes, Keynesianism dominated economics for several decades after his death in 1946. Keynesians focus on aggregate demand, or total spending in the economy by consumers, industry, and government. When there's a recession, in their view, consumers and industry aren't spending enough, so government should spend more to take up the slack. By the 1960s Keynesians had grown confident that government could fine-tune the economy, nicely smoothing out the business cycle. But 1970s stagflation (economic stagnation combined with high inflation) was a major blow to this confidence. You still see Keynesian prescriptions at work, though, whenever governments ramp up public-works projects to push the economy out of recession.

_02:: Monetarism (or How to Stand Up to Keynes 101)

If your date tells you that "money matters," simply tell her you don't associate with monetarists. It might sound like a dirty word, but in fact monetarists just believe that economies are profoundly affected by how much currency is in circulation. Led by economist Milton Friedman, the monetarists shredded Keynesian theory and argued that the Keynesian tolerance of inflation as a way of keeping unemployment low would result in escalating inflation—and lousy unemployment figures too. The experience of the 1970s gave monetarists considerable intellectual cachet, and in the early 1980s economic policy in the United States and Britain had a strong monetarist tinge. But monetarism ran into some trouble when it became clear just how hard it is to measure the money supply. (Do you count just cash? Also checking accounts? What about other financial instruments?) Moreover, central bankers were never entirely enthused about the idea of limiting their own decision-making power by adopting clear, stable rules for managing the money supply.

_03:: Supply-Side Economics (If You Trust the Man with the Napkin)

Nothing's better for a new school of economic thought than a bad economy. Similar to the monetarists, the supply-siders spent the late 1970s arguing that the Keynesians had made a mess of the economy. Of course, they thought that monetarist ideas were at best a partial solution. The supply-siders put their emphasis on tax cuts, and especially on reducing marginal tax rates (the high rates at which income above a certain level is taxed). Using a curve initially drawn on a napkin by economist Arthur Laffer (yes, the Laffer curve), the supply-siders argued that tax revenues could increase if rates were reduced, since people would work and invest more. The supply-siders hit a peak of influence in the 1980s, inspiring tax cuts in the United States and other countries. The results were controversial, with the supply-siders claiming to have boosted economic growth, while critics complained they had boosted government budget deficits.

_04:: Post-Keynesianism (When in Doubt, Recycle)

Garnish your Keynes with a hint of Marx, and you'll find you get a post-Keynesian. The post-Keynesians emphasize the uncertainty, instability, and problems of capitalist economies, drawing on Karl Marx's ideas about class struggle. They think that Keynes was on to something in seeing how markets can fail, but that regular Keynesianism doesn't sufficiently explore those insights. And although they may all look alike, post-Keynesians are a pretty diverse group. They're generally on the political left, but they don't rally around a specific set of policy proposals. Nor are there well-defined theoretical tenets that they all share. They don't even really agree on where they stand in relation to Keynes. Some post-Keynesians see themselves as building on the man's work.

Pure Genius

FRIEDRICH HAYEK

Friedrich August Hayek (1899–1992) knew a lot. He was a Nobel Prize–winning economist who also contributed to political science and psychology. But a key part of his work was pointing out that no one knows all that much because knowledge and data are scattered among numerous individuals and institutions. That, Hayek explained, is why socialist central planners can't run a halfway decent economy—they don't have the info. During the Great Depression, Hayek argued with British economist John Maynard Keynes about what makes economies go boom and bust. Many economists agreed with Keynes, but decades later Hayek's insights got new respect. By the 1940s Hayek was deep in the debate over socialism. In his book *The Road to Serfdom*, he argued that government control of the economy erodes political liberties. And although he was a hero to many conservatives, one of his most famous writings is an essay entitled "Why I Am Not a Conservative."

Spending over a decade at the University of Chicago, then later moving to Germany and finally back to Austria, Hayek shared the 1974 Nobel Prize and was still publishing at age 89.

Others think of themselves as truly *post-Keynesian*, moving beyond Keynes's ideas.

4 Kinds of Money: Old, New, and Funny

Sure, we believe all people are created equal. It's just that some of their currencies are created more equal than others.

_01:: Ecuador's Vanished Sucre

Nations like having their own currencies. First of all, they can print the portraits of great political leaders, or at least honor their famous writers and painters—or sexpots, if they're living in France. If they can't pay their bills, governments can also run the printing press and produce as much money as they need. But Ecuador is an exception to this rule. Until 2000 it had its own currency, the sucre, which existed for 116 years. But runaway inflation, the flight of capital, and entrenched economic crisis convinced the government that it would do better to adopt the U.S. dollar as its national currency. Inflation promptly fell and the economy began to grow. Panama is the only other sovereign state that uses the greenback in its domestic economy—although it never bothered to remove the balboa, its own currency, from circulation.

_02:: The Euro

After nearly a decade of preparation, the euro began circulating January 1, 2002. The euro replaced the national currencies of 12 nations of the European Union. Such venerable currencies as the German mark, the French franc, and the Greek drachma are gone. But three nations eligible to join the euro zone—Britain, Sweden, and Denmark—have so far opted not to do so. While euro banknotes are identical across euro-land, every nation mints its own coins, with its own national symbols on the

---

What's the Difference?

DISINFLATION VS. DEFLATION

Disinflation means the rate of inflation is going down. In other words, when there's disinflation, prices continue to rise but at a slowing pace. The United States has seen a good deal of disinflation since the late 1970s, which is usually regarded as a good thing.

Deflation, on the other hand, means that prices are going down. It's not just lower inflation but actually negative inflation. Deflation isn't considered a good thing at all. Like inflation, it creates uncertainty, distorts decision making, and transfers wealth in arbitrary ways. Deflation erodes the value of collateral, while the real value of loans goes up—which gives borrowers a good reason not to pay the money back. Take for example Japan, which has experienced deflation in recent years, exacerbating the country's economic woes. Not surprisingly, Japanese banks have ended up with a lot of dud loans on their hands.

flip side. There's even a Vatican euro, with a depiction of Pope John Paul II. Currency unions are nothing new in Europe, but the current European Monetary Union is the first attempt to introduce a single currency for some 300 million people at once.

_03:: Brazilian Money

In the 1970s and 1980s Latin America went through a nasty bout of hyperinflation. With prices rocketing by up to 3,000% per year in Brazil, its currency, the cruzeiro, disintegrated. In 1986 the government came up with the cruzado, which fared little better. In 1989 this had to be replaced with the new cruzado, then back to the cruzeiro, and then to the cruzeiro real. Since 1994 Brazilians have had yet another currency—the real—which so far

has been a bit more real. Because of inflation, the real, when it was introduced, was worth 2.75 billion 1986 cruzados. By the way, *real* is pronounced "ray-owl" by people who want to sound Brazilian, though true Brazilians call it something closer to "he-ow."

_04:: The Turkish Lira

The Turkish lira has the unfortunate distinction of having the highest exchange rate per dollar. The greenback was worth about 1,400,000 liras in 2003. Since Turkey's per capita gross domestic product is approximately $2,800, it means that each and every Turk—man, woman, and child—is on average a lira billionaire. It wasn't always that way. In 1980 the lira exchange rate was a modest 70 liras per dollar.

Stats That Drive the Market Wild

British prime minister Benjamin Disraeli once claimed, "There are three kinds of lies: lies, damned lies, and statistics." And, well, statistically speaking, economic data is rarely perfect. Here are just a few of the figures that make the markets move.

_01:: The Unemployment Rate

Here's how to tell if you're part of the unemployment rate: if you're out of work and looking, the U.S. Department of Labor counts you as unemployed; if you're out of work but just sitting around on the couch all day, it does not. (No one keeps statistics on laziness as of yet.) Every month the U.S. Department of Labor uses surveys and statistical methods to measure how many civilians are out of work, and

that percentage is known as the unemployment rate. When the unemployment rate goes up, investors tend to get nervous. It doesn't help that the rate is considered a "lagging indicator," meaning that it can stay high (bad) even after the economy starts to get better.

_02:: Gross Domestic Product

Financial traders across the world dash for their desks at 8:30 a.m. eastern time the last day of each quarter. No, no one's passing out discount stock coupons. Rather, it's the time of year when the U.S. Department of Labor releases the GDP figures. The GDP is the total output of goods and services within the United States, which includes spending by consumers, companies, and government, plus the trade balance (exports minus imports). So it's a big-picture look at how the economy is doing. The figure includes all goods and services produced inside the borders of the United States, regardless of the nationality of the producer. And while economists used to focus on Gross *National* Product, or GNP, which includes products made by U.S. companies abroad (and excludes stuff made by foreign-owned producers in the United States), in these days of globalization, the GDP is seen as the more meaningful figure.

_03:: Housing Starts

If you want to know which sectors of the economy are likely to thrive, check out the housing starts figures. Compiled by the U.S. Census Bureau, these figures show the number of residential units that start construction each month. When homes are built, it means work for construction workers, demand for lumber, and even potential refrigerator purchases. During troubled economic times in the first few years of the 21st century, the relatively strong housing sector helped keep the economy from sinking into a deeper downturn.

_04:: Consumer Confidence

Consumer confidence can be a tricky thing to measure; just ask the Conference Board, an organization that puts out a monthly index of consumer attitudes based on surveys of 5,000 households. The numbers reflect how consumers feel about their present economic situation, as well as their expectations for the next six months. Consumer spending accounts for two-thirds of the economy, so high consumer confidence is an indication that corporate profits and stock prices are likely to be healthy. Then again, bond traders sometimes start selling if it looks as if consumer confidence is getting too high—because that could mean that inflation will soon show up and erode the value of fixed-income bonds.

Stump the Expert

HOW HIGH IS NAIRU?

Economists believe in something called the NAIRU, or Non-Accelerating Inflation Rate of Unemployment. It's a level of unemployment at which inflation is stable. That means if the unemployment rate falls below the NAIRU, inflation will increase (the economy is booming, so companies hike prices and workers demand raises).

It would be nice to have an exact number for NAIRU, since this would allow for better economic forecasting and help policy makers steer the economy. But economists can only make estimates based on actual unemployment and inflation. Also, NAIRU changes over time, due to shifts in demography, productivity, and other factors. Some economists think the current U.S. NAIRU is around 5 percent, but no one knows for sure. And though the NAIRU has also been called the natural rate of unemployment, economists now tend to avoid implying that unemployment is a natural, or good, thing.

Things Karl Marx Believed

If you're sick and tired of free markets and Adam Smith's invisible hand waving at you with one finger, maybe you should consider joining the throngs of Marxists who think capitalism's beat. Here are three theories that should have you seeing red in no time.

_01:: A Working Theory

Karl Marx (1818–1883) wasn't all that radical for his day; earlier 19th-century economists, notably David Ricardo, held similar views on some subjects, but Marx took the ideas one step further. According to his labor theory of value, the value of a commodity is determined by how many hours of labor went into producing it. So, if it takes twice as long to make a combat boot as a stiletto-heeled shoe, then the boots will cost twice as much as the shoes, at least in the long run. Marx argued that la-

Fake Your Way through a Conversation
(ON RATIONAL EXPECTATIONS)

Mentioning "rational expectations" is an excellent way to demonstrate that you have some familiarity with economic theory. The idea of rational expectations, put forward by some economists, is that people are pretty smart when it comes to predicting economic phenomena (such as inflation or stock prices or their own incomes). That doesn't mean the predictions will be accurate, but it means they won't be off target in any regular or predictable way.

If your conversation partner asks, "So what?" point out that the rational-expectations theory sets limits on what government is able to do. For instance, in a recession, the government might cut taxes to get people to spend more. But if taxpayers have rational expectations, they'll realize the tax cut is temporary, and they'll keep their spending low in anticipation of the budget deficits and higher taxes coming next year.

At this point your conversation partner may express skepticism, questioning whether people in a shopping mall are really performing complex calculations about government policy. Don't worry, we've got an effective counter! Just note that some economists share these doubts, and then mention the alternative view of adaptive expectations, which says people form expectations based on the past. So, if inflation was high last year, shoppers will expect it to be high next year, even if the Fed is now gung-ho about stopping inflation.

bor, too, is a commodity, its value determined by how many labor hours society puts into getting a worker ready for work. This raises a question: how do capitalists make profits? Marx's answer: they do it by exploiting workers, squeezing "surplus value" out of them. His political ideas took a big hit when the Soviet Union collapsed in 1991, causing economists to reject his economic critique of capitalist society; however, he remains influential in sociology and political science and among lefty intellectuals everywhere.

_02:: A Falling Rate of Profit

As capitalists exploit their workers and compete against one another, profits generally tend to decline, according to Marx. This idea follows logically once you've accepted everything in Marx's labor theory of value. The capitalists take the surplus value they get from the workers and reinvest it in factories and machinery. But this means that exploiting the workers gets them less value than it used

to, in comparison to the overall size of their operations. So what do you do if you're a capitalist? Exploit the workers even harder, of course!

_03:: A Concentration of Wealth

Try as they might, many capitalists can't prop up that falling rate of profit for very long. Instead, they are beaten by their competitors and end up falling into the working class. The capitalists who remain on top, however, are increasingly wealthy. They form monopolies that dominate their markets. The trouble is, there are fewer and fewer successful capitalists, while the numbers of workers are growing—as is their misery. Therefore, Marx thought, history was moving inevitably toward revolution. Workers would rise up and displace the capitalist class, creating socialist societies instead. But he expected this to happen first in the most advanced economies, such as his native Germany, not in relatively backward places like Russia.

Nightmare on Wall Street:
6 Crises That Keep Economists Up at Night

Thomas Carlyle once called economics "a dismal science." Indeed, economists tend to be cautious and pedestrian, but can you blame them? After all, who could sleep easy after hearing these scary stories?

_01:: The Irish Potato Famine

When you think of economics, think of food. Until the late 1800s economic crisis usually meant agricultural crisis, with famine a not-

so-infrequent consequence. Before the advent of industrial agricultural methods, weather conditions and infestations of various kinds had the power to hold the economy hostage.

In 1845 a new fungus, *Phytophthora infestans*, struck the potato—the mainstay of Ireland's food supply. Although the blight lasted only a few years, its effects were far reaching. As many as 1.5 million died as a direct result of the famine, and many more emigrated in the second half of the 19th century. Even today, only half as many people live in Ireland as did before the famine.

_02:: German Hyperinflation

By November 1923 in Germany, $1 in the United States equaled 4.2 billion German marks, and even daily staples had to be purchased with wheelbarrows of cash. How did this happen? In 1918 Germany lost World War I, suffered a revolution, and became a republic when Emperor Wilhelm II was forced to abdicate. The Treaty of Versailles, signed a year later, saddled Germany with 6.6 billion British pounds' worth of reparations. With the German treasury empty, the government could pay—and conduct its ongoing business—only by printing lots of money: the quickest recipe for inflation. At the height of inflation in 1923, prices rose 40% *per day*. People rushed to the stores as soon as they were paid, before their money became worthless. The frightful experience of the early 1920s scarred the German national psyche and undermined faith in the Weimar Republic, which helped pave the way for Adolf Hitler and the Nazi Party. In fact, Hitler's early grab for power—the Beer Hall Putsch in Munich—came on November 8, 1923.

_03:: The Great Depression

During the Roaring '20s in the United States, the wealthy spent a lot of money they had, and the not-so-wealthy spent a lot of money they didn't have. The Great Depression began soon after the stock market crashed in October 1929, but economists still argue whether the bursting of the 1920s financial bubble caused the Depression or merely foretold the coming economic slump. Either way, by 1932 the economy contracted by 31%, and some 13 million were left jobless—a quarter of the workforce. When President Franklin Delano Roosevelt took office in 1932, he started the New Deal, a set of policies to boost federal spending and create government-financed jobs. Although the economy began growing again in the mid-1930s, the effects of the Depression lingered on until Pearl Harbor. The number of unemployed fell to 7.6 million in 1936 but rose again to 10 million in 1938—the same number of men drafted into the armed forces during World War II.

_04:: The '70s Oil Crisis

The price of oil tends to be slippery—something the economists forgot in the early 1970s when they confidently predicted that crude prices could fall as low as the cost of pumping oil out of the Saudi desert (estimated at less than $1 per barrel). Instead, following the Yom Kippur War between Israel and its Arab neighbors in October 1973, Arab oil producers declared an embargo. Oil prices tripled to more than $10 per barrel, and gasoline shortages ensued. By December President Nixon had to announce that because of the energy crisis, the White House Christmas tree would not be lighted. The 1979 Iranian revolution brought a second oil shock, and oil prices eventually peaked at around $35 per barrel. The oil crisis helped bring on a period of stagflation—meaning that even though the U.S. economy barely dragged along, inflation continued to rise.

_05:: The Asian Flu

The domino-like collapse of several Asian economies in the late 1990s seemed to come out of nowhere. The "tiger" economies of Southeast Asia had been booming for years, and the region widely expected to stay an economic powerhouse straight into the upcoming millennium. Yet in July 1997 things went spectacularly wrong. Thailand became the catalyst for the crisis, when severe pressure from speculators brought down its currency, the baht. The Philippine peso and the Malaysian ringgit fell next. Then the Indonesian rupiah was devalued in August, ushering in political and social turmoil. Finally, even South Korea, one of the strongest economies in east Asia, nearly went bankrupt and had to be bailed out. Economists were at a loss to fully explain the crisis. But as country after country succumbed to the financial bug, one lesson seemed clear: an interconnected global economy can transmit panic just as well as it can goods and services.

_06:: Argentina's Peso Crisis

During the 1990s Argentina was the star pupil of the International Monetary Fund. After two decades of runaway inflation and collapsing currencies, the Argentine government finally turned over a new economic leaf in 1992. Economy minister Domingo Cavallo helped set up a new currency, the peso, and firmly linked it to the U.S. dollar. The government decreed that one peso could always be exchanged for one dollar and that it would print only as many pesos as were backed by dollar reserves. The system functioned extremely well for a few years, but by late 1997 the overvalued peso and restrictive monetary policies helped bring on a prolonged recession, accompanied by turmoil in financial markets. Successive economy ministers and presidents could find no solution. In December 2001 the Argentine peso was devalued, and the government defaulted on some $140 billion in debt, the biggest default on record.

Go Directly to Jail:
3 Monopolies That Won't Be Building Hotels

We all played the board game. But real-life monopoly is a serious matter, at least as far as the government is concerned. Here are three giants that got some unwanted face time with Uncle Sam.

_01:: Standard Oil

Around the turn of the 20th century, Standard Oil was practically synonymous with ruthless corporate power. John D. Rockefeller's company cut secret deals with railroads, undermined its competitors, and gained control of some 90% of U.S. oil-refining capacity. In 1906 the federal government filed a lawsuit against Standard Oil under the Sherman Antitrust Act—a law designed to combat monopoly power and unfair business practices. The Supreme Court ruled in the government's favor in 1911, ordering the giant company to be broken up into relatively minuscule pieces such as Esso (later known as Exxon) and Socal (later known as Chevron). Oddly, though, the company's assets turned out to be worth more after the dissolution, so Rockefeller became even richer than before.

_02:: AT&T

Remember the days when there were no long-distance telephone commercials? For decades, if you wanted to make a phone call, you had little choice but to go to American Telephone & Telegraph, which handled the overwhelming majority of long-distance and local calls and also built most of the phones and telecom equipment. The Justice Department wrestled with Ma Bell in court in the early 1950s but achieved only minor limits on the company's monopolistic practices. The feds filed suit again in 1974, and eight years later AT&T was ordered to divest itself of its local phone operations; the reorganization took effect in 1984, and the regional "Baby Bells" were born.

_03:: Microsoft

For a while, it looked as though the software company founded by Bill Gates might be broken into "Baby Bills," but this never happened. An antitrust case filed by the Justice Department and state governments in 1998 accused Microsoft of abusing its dominance of operating systems (software that lets computers operate) so as to stifle competitors and take advantage of consumers. In November 2000 Judge Thomas Penfield Jackson ruled against

Timeline

FOLLOW THE BOUNCING INCOME TAX RATE

1913 The federal income tax begins. It's progressive, meaning that income at higher levels is taxed at higher rates. The top marginal rate (or highest tax bracket) is set at 7%.

1918 The United States needs money to fight World War I. Top rate jumps to 77%.

1929 Tax rates lowered throughout the Roaring '20s. Top rate bottoms out at 24%.

1933 Great Depression. Top rate goes to 63%, but you're lucky if you have any income.

1944 World War II is going on. Highest U.S. top rate ever: 94%.

1963 The war is long over. Why is the top rate 91%?

1965 Tax cuts initiated by President John F. Kennedy take effect. Top rate: 70%.

1982 "Reaganomics" means tax cuts. Top rate: 50%.

1986 Tax reform. Close the loopholes and lower the rates. Top rate drops to 28%.

1991 President George H.W. Bush breaks his "no new taxes" pledge. Top rate: 31%.

1993 "Clintonomics" means tax hikes. Top rate: 39.6%.

2003 President George W. Bush's tax plan would cut top rate to 35%.

Microsoft, but his decision was overturned on appeal. A settlement reached in November 2001 and modified the following year set some restrictions on Microsoft's practices but left the company fully intact. It's no surprise then that a number of state governments, not to mention Microsoft's corporate rivals, complained that the software goliath had gotten off with a slap on the wrist.

Money Makes the World Go Wrong:
Political Careers Wrecked by Economics

It's often said that people vote with their pocketbooks. Well, it's no doubt that thinning wallets and receding purse lines definitely played a big role in shoving these cats out of office.

_01:: Herbert Hoover

Considered a wonder boy of American politics, Hoover (1874–1964) organized relief efforts that fed millions around the world after World War I. In fact, he was a well-regarded secretary of commerce in the 1920s and was elected president in 1928 with a mandate to manage the nicely humming American economy. The next year, however, saw the stock market crash and the start of Great Depression. And Hoover's policies—such as keeping the budget in balance and imposing high tariffs on imported goods—seemed only to deepen the crisis. It didn't help that he had a gloomy demeanor, which led one historian to call him the Great Depressive. Hoover was trounced in the 1932 election by the upbeat Franklin D. Roosevelt, who adopted the more activist policies of the New Deal. And while Hoover got the Hoover Dam named after him, as well as the Hoover Institution, the famous vacuum cleaner brand bears no relation.

_02:: Jimmy Carter

In the years after the Watergate scandal, Americans were pretty sour about their political leaders. That's why former Georgia governor (and nuclear engineer turned peanut farmer) Jimmy Carter's reputation for honesty swept him into the White House in 1976. "I'll never lie to you," he told the public—and apparently he never did. When the economy tanked during his presidency, Carter was up-front about it, saying the country was in crisis in what came to be known as "the malaise speech." (Actually, Carter never used that word, but it was in a memo he'd gotten from a political consultant.) But things kept getting worse, and Carter didn't seem to have an answer. Inflation rose each year of his presidency, hitting 13.5% in 1980. And the "misery index" (which you get by adding inflation and unemployment) went to 20%. Carter lost the 1980 presidential race but won the 2002 Nobel Peace Prize for his international good works.

_03:: George H. W. Bush

The 41st U.S. president learned the hard way that success overseas isn't enough to get you reelected when the economy goes south. After a victory in the first Persian Gulf War in early 1991, Mr. Bush's approval ratings soared as high as 91%. Only 1 American in 10 didn't love him, and leading Democrats chose to sit out the 1992 presidential election for fear of being mauled by a popular incumbent. But the economy perversely went into recession—in part because of high oil prices before the war. Unemployment, which stood at 5.3% in 1989, rocketed to 7.5% by 1992. The president compounded his problems by appearing insensitive—fielding questions about the economy at the golf course. Defeated 18 months later by a cheeky unknown named Bill Clinton, Bush changed from the glorious war victor into another one-term wonder.

_04:: John Major

Becoming British prime minister in November 1990, after 11 years of often controversial rule by iron lady Margaret Thatcher, Major promised conservatism with a human face. His youthful enthusiasm appealed to British voters, and he led the Conservative Party (also known as the Tories) to an unprecedented third straight election victory in 1992. But then, in September of that year, selling of the pound by financial speculators forced the gov-ernment to ignominiously devalue the currency and abandon its link to continental European currencies. Inflation soared and unemployment peaked at 10.5% two months later. Major endured as a lame duck for another four and a half years—simply because the British parliamentary system didn't require him to hold elections. When the voters finally got a chance to vent their anger at the Tories, Major was defeated in a landslide by the bright new light of the Labor Party, Tony Blair.

_05:: Marie Antoinette

By the time Marie Antoinette became queen of France in 1774, at the ripe age of 19, she had already been married for five years. She was never popular because of her Austrian origins, but her extravagant ways and lavish lifestyle earned her the nickname Madam Deficit from her subjects. In fact, she was squarely blamed for the country's financial crisis, though the true cause was heavy debt from the Seven Years War (1756–1763) and French support for the American Revolution. More than half of the government budget went to service that debt, and inflation was massive. By the time the French Revolution broke out in 1789, over 80% of the average peasant's income was spent on bread. When told that her subjects had no bread to eat, Marie Antoinette reportedly replied, "Let them eat cake." (Historians doubt she ever said this, but the point is the peasants thought she had.) The monarchy was abolished in 1792, and in January 1793 King Louis XVI was guillotined. Madam Deficit followed her husband to the scaffold in October of that year.

by
Curry Guinn

Condensed
GENERAL
SCIENCE

Contains

The Naked Truth: 4 Bizarre Revelations about Sex ✳ Fun for the Feeble-Minded: 6 Useless Studies ✳ 4 Mind-Boggling Facts You'd Never Have Guessed ✳ 6 Little-Known Scientists (Who've Contributed as Much as Einstein) ✳ Accidents Waiting to Happen: 5 Mistakes That Became Medical Miracles ✳ And 6 That Became Marketable Merchandise ✳ 7 Technologies That Will Change the World (as Soon as We Invent Them) ✳ They Blinded Me with Science: 10 Frauds and Hoaxes That Duped the Masses ✳

The Naked Truth:
Bizarre Revelations about Sex

Don't look so smug, Casanova. Just when you thought you had the birds and the bees all figured out, it turns out Ma and Pa shorted you on the details. Here are four little-known sex facts every cad needs to add to his or her repertoire.

_01:: Even Cockroaches Have Standards

British scientists at the University of Manchester have determined that female cockroaches will lower their standards for a mate as their biological breeding clock begins to tick. By looking at the amount of cockroach wooing required by a male (similar to what's observed on college campuses worldwide), the researchers documented that females became less selective as their reproductive potential decreased. Males, however, seemed to show no difference in mating practices regardless of the female cockroach's age.

_02:: Are You My Lover? (Confused Birds without Bees)

Charles Paxton of St. Andrews University gave this sage advice: "You would not want to go into a pen with an amorous ostrich." And right he is! When Paxton set out to determine why ostriches on British farms weren't laying eggs despite their obvious mating displays, he quickly realized that the poor birds were "sexually confused." It turns out the species-curious ostriches were pointing their "affections" in the wrong direction, mistakenly directing their courtship behaviors toward the human farmers. In perhaps a sign of truly unconditional love, the ostriches seemed to be able to work up their mojo irrespective of the farmer's sex.

_03:: 7 Degrees of Separation

Forget Kevin Bacon; using DNA analysis, Professor Bryan Sykes of Oxford University has traced 95% of the people living in Europe back to one of seven women who lived approximately 11,000 to 45,000 years ago. Amazingly, he's bringing people one giant step closer to answering that eternal question,

---

Strange but True

SEXY ANIMAL FACTS

The strongest muscle in your body is the tongue.

A female ferret will die if it goes into heat and cannot find a mate.

After sleeping for 17 years, a cicada will awake, mate, and then die within two weeks.

Dragonflies live for only 24 hours.

Humans and dolphins are the only species that have sex for pleasure.

"Where do we come from?" By examining mitochondrial DNA—a genetic material that is passed on only by mothers—Sykes has been able to establish direct maternal links back to these "seven daughters of Eve." Though his research has focused on Europe and these seven clans in particular, Sykes estimates that there are 36 different clans around the world.

_04:: You Know What They Say . . .

It's time to squash those rumors! Despite what you may have heard, two Canadian scientists, Jerald Bain and Kerry Siminoski, studied the relationship between height, foot size, and penile length and found no significant correlation, seemingly disproving the myth. In addition, Chris McManus of University College London set out to determine once and for all the question of testicle asymmetry in reality versus ancient art. His "nutcase" study was based on the observation of 107 ancient nude statues. Despite previous research claiming that male testicles tend to be symmetrical, McManus observed that on real men, the right side of the scrotal sac is higher, but not lighter (as it is incorrectly portrayed in ancient Greek statues). Both studies won the Ig Nobel Prize (1 of 10 annual awards for research "that cannot, or should not, be repeated").

Fun for the Feeble-Minded:
6 Useless Studies

Do you ever get mad when you hear stories of scientists who were paid thousands of dollars to research, say, how many people can walk and chew gum at the same time? Well, we do! After all, we had to sit through 12 years of Career Days, and no one ever said science was this easy.

_01:: Sudden-Death Can Lead to Sudden Death

Scientists at Utrecht University in the Netherlands analyzed the incidence of death on the five days prior to, the day of, and the five days after the 1996 semifinals between the Netherlands and France in soccer. The game was particularly exciting, going to overtime before being decided by penalty kicks. (France ultimately won.) The average number of male deaths in the Netherlands by heart attack or stroke on the days surrounding the match: 150; on the day of the match: 173. It isn't known what the French death rate was during and after the match. Guess that means they'll have to do more research.

_02:: The Wave Factor

Did you know that the stadium wave, where eager fans jump out of their seats, throw their arms in the air, and then quickly sit back down, travels on average 40 feet per second?

Or that the average width of a stadium wave is 15 seats? Or how about that on average it takes roughly 30 fans to set a wave in motion? Well, thanks to Hungarian scientist Tamas Vicsek and his team of researchers, these numbers are now quantifiable science. In a study done in 2002, Vicsek and his team watched videotape of Mexican soccer matches (sounds exhausting) to create a mathematical model. Just use-less science? Not according to Vicsek. The research might actually be used to help predict how and when soccer fans will riot.

_03:: The Trouble with Stubble

Are you (or if you are female, your husband) having trouble relating to your cat? Perhaps you should think about shaving. A study led by Fairfield University indicates that cats re-

---

Alphabet Soup

(WITH JUST A PINCH OF TECHNOLOGY)

ambimousterous [AM-bee-MOUS-ter-ihs]: *adj* Proficient using a mouse with both the left and right hand.

Aunt Tillie [ANT TIL-lee]: *n* The quintessential naive user that must be taken into account when designing software. To pass the Aunt Tillie test means the software is idiotproof.

Batman factor [BAT-man FAK-tur]: *n* A measure of electronic geekness that looks at the size and number of items attached to one's belt. For instance, having a Palm Pilot, a cell phone, and a walkie-talkie would grant you a very high Batman factor.

bogosity [bo-GOS-ih-tee]: *n* The degree to which something is bogus.

chickenboner [CHIK-en BO-nur]: *n* A spammer generally thought to be a redneck in a darkened trailer with a litter of KFC chicken bones surrounding the workstation.

dancing frog [DAN-sing FROG]: *n* A computer bug that will not manifest itself when someone else is watching over your shoulder. (Remember the Warner Brothers frog that sang and danced for only one person?)

geekasm [GEE-KAS-em]: *n* Best understood by reading this quote by MIT professor Alex Slocum: "When they build a machine, if they do the calculations right, the machine works and you get this intense . . . uhh . . . just like a geekasm, from knowing that what you created in your mind and on the computer is actually doing what you told it to do."

kilogoogle [KIH-lo-GOO-gul]: *n* Unit of measurement to indicate the number of hits made on a term by a Google search. "mental floss" has 7.5 kilogoogles.

teledildonics [TEL-uh-dil-DON-iks]: *n* Virtual-reality sex.

zipperhead [ZIP-ur-HED]: *n* Someone with a closed mind.

act negatively to men with long, dark beards. They seem rather indifferent to short beards or unshaven men. In another study, Robert Bork's distinctive partial beard caused disorientation and paralysis in some cats. Of course, now all we need is a study to figure out *why* cats don't like facial hair. It will probably require a hefty chunk of grant money, but we're sure it would be worth it.

_04:: That Whole Shakespeare-Monkey Thing

If a million monkeys typed on a million typewriters for a million years, would they produce a work of Shakespeare by chance? This notion has been used to indicate how, over the vastness of time, complex creations could arise from chance. Well, researchers at Plymouth University in England have carried out a small-scale experiment by placing a computer in an enclosure with six macaques (short-tailed monkeys). After pounding on it with a rock, defecating on it, and urinating on it, some of the monkeys did hit a few keystrokes, producing mostly a lot of *S*s. Theoretically, the hypothesis defies statistics. The odds of striking the correct sequence is so small that you'd have to have a million monkeys typing at a rate of 31,000,000 strokes a year (one per second) each for a million years, and then multiply that amount by itself almost 200 times.

_05:: Toast Really Does Fall Butter-Side Down

Led by physicist Robert Matthews of Aston University, British schoolchildren dropped thousands of buttered and unbuttered pieces of toast from their tables. The results are in: the butter side will hit the ground first more often. In fact, the side of the toast facing up on the plate would hit the floor first more often than not, even if it has no butter. Simply put, when the bread falls, it begins to flip. It generally only has time to flip over before it hits the floor, given average kitchen table height. In a related experiment, when the toast is dropped from a significantly higher height, the unbuttered side would, on average, hit first.

_06:: Navel Academy

A study by Karl Kruszelnicki of the University of Sydney seems to raise more questions than it answers. In a survey of 4,799 people, Kruszelnicki determined that two-thirds of those surveyed detected the presence of belly button lint (BBL). A much higher percentage of men (72%) reported BBL as opposed to women (27%). But curiously, the color of the belly button lint didn't always seem to correspond to the clothes that people wore. The main question this study raises is, why?

Mind-Boggling Facts You'd Never Have Guessed

Some things are just too strange to be coincidence. Maybe the universe is more interconnected than we think?

_01:: There Are as Many Chess Games as Particles in the Universe

Want to know why the best human chess players can still beat the best computers? The secret, brought to you in math-speak, is that the primary game-tree search algorithm in chess faces a massive combinatorial problem. More simply, on average there are 40 moves for each chess turn. And chess games can last up to 70 turns (although most good players will resign well before if they see their position is lost). So the resulting tree describing all chess games is 10^{73}. Estimates for the number of particles in the universe range from 10^{70} to 10^{80}, which means the two are actually pretty close!

_02:: Happy as a Clam

Believe it or not, Gettysburg College researcher Peter Fong decided to dope up his subjects, fingernail clams, by putting them on antidepressants. And while the phrase "happy as a clam" didn't exactly originate with Fong's research, his unique Prozac prescription has kick-started their social lives. Prozac decreases the uptake of serotonin, making more of the neurosecretion available to the nervous system. In the bivalves' case, this led to an overwhelming urge for synchronous spawning, a boon both for clam farmers and gawky teenage clams alike.

_03:: You're Bananas!

If you took bio in high school, you learned that humans are primates. Fine. We accept that we have things in common with other animals—but not the produce aisle! DNA, the building block of life, is a common strand in all living organisms on earth. If the DNA in your body were stretched out it would be 500 million miles long, its average thickness 10 atoms. Here's the strange part, though: humans and bananas share approximately 60% of the same DNA structure. Of course, there are closer comparisons. Humans and mice share about 97% of the same structure, while humans and chimps, perhaps our closest relatives, share about 98%.

_04:: Spooky Particles

Albert Einstein called it "spooky action at a distance." The quantum process known as entanglement (also known as the Einstein/Podolsky/Rosen [EPR] effect, though it should be the ESP effect) allows one particle to "know" the change of state of another particle instantaneously. What's that mean? When paired quantum particles are sent off in different directions, and then one of the particles changes its spin, its pair immediately senses the change and alters its own spin. Eerily enough, experiments have confirmed that this "communication" across distance occurs faster than the speed of light.

Little-Known Scientists (Who've Contributed as Much as Einstein)

Sure, Albert Einstein and Marie Curie might have hogged the limelight back in the classroom (showoffs!), but they certainly weren't the only scientists on the scene. Here are six geniuses who deserve equal attention.

_01:: The Guy Who First Realized We've Been Drifting Apart

In geology, Alfred Wegener (1880–1930) is recognized as the father of continental drift. His theory, introduced in 1915, then ridiculed for years, was a paradigm-shifting idea that led to all of modern-day geology. In fact, you've probably seen simulations of what the world looked like back when all of the continents were joined together. Wegener's understanding of continental drift and plate tectonics has helped to explain phenomena such as earthquakes, volcanoes, and other action within the earth's crust. Further, his ideas have shed considerable light on how plants and animals have evolved and spread across the globe.

_02:: The Guy You Should Thank for Must-See TV

Philo T. Farnsworth (1906–1971) single-handedly dreamed up the cathode ray tube, which led to the invention of the television. By scanning and transmitting images in horizontal lines, the young eccentric pioneered an entirely new medium. Sadly, his claim to fame was quietly usurped. At just 21, Farnsworth presented his research to RCA executive David Sarnoff and Russian scientist Vladimir Zworykin. Zworykin and Sarnoff then replicated the technology and revised it. Using their resources at RCA, the two then began to dominate the marketing of this new technology. Farnsworth sued and seemingly won in court, but the power of the corporation proved mightier, and Farnsworth was never able to profit from the industry he helped launch.

_03:: The Guy Responsible for Your Speedy PC

William Shockley (1910–1989) and other scientists at Bell Labs were the first to use semiconductors to replace vacuum tubes in 1951. In fact, the use of transistors completely revolutionized modern computers. Shockley's use of the technology both as a transmitter of information, converting sound waves to electronic information, and as a resistor, to control the electronic current (spelling it out—TRANSmit + resISTOR), was unique. Transistors could perform the same function as vacuum tubes at one-millionth the energy required. The technology quickly became ubiquitous in electronic equipment, leading to revolutions in size, speed, and capabilities. Sadly, however, the genius tarnished his reputation in later years by espousing some shockingly racist theories.

_04:: The Guy You Should Thank for the World Wide Web (and We're Not Talking Al Gore!)

Tim Berners-Lee (1955–) helped launch an information revolution that has forever altered society. While the Internet is the product of many people's creative genius, the World Wide Web (WWW) itself has a unique parent. In 1980 Berners-Lee struck on the idea of having hyperlinked text available to him on his computer so he could easily follow his thoughts while working. But he didn't want to access data and information on just his own computer; he wanted information available from other computers on the network. And ultimately, that means the entire network of computers out there. Berners-Lee created the first language for Web pages, HTML, which is still the primary language of the WWW. In 1991 the WWW was introduced, and the whole world's gone dot-mad every since.

_05:: Just One Word—Plastic

Is there any substance that is more ubiquitous and more representative of the past 40 years than plastic? It's inexpensive, moldable, and incredibly functional, and we've got a genius named Leo Baekeland (1863–1944) to thank for it. In fact, Leo saw the immense potential for the fully synthetic material when he first invented it, way back in 1907. Dubbing his creation Bakelite, the inventor spent his life dominating the world of synthetic plastics, even subduing rival Thomas Edison. Bakelite itself became a predecessor to more advanced and malleable plastics (you can still find Bakelite products and collectors on eBay!), and his legacy clearly lives on: during this year alone, over 50 million tons of plastics will be produced.

_06:: The Guy Who Chose to Breed Flies instead of Swatting Them

Theodosius Dobzhansky (1900–1975) isn't a name that rolls off the tongue (or that immediately springs to mind when we think of the world's greatest scientists), but his contribution to the field of genetics is immense. Dobzhansky took Darwinian concepts of evolution and began studying them in terms of genes and gene pools. His research focused on the humble fruit fly, but his results weren't humble at all. He's credited with having first demonstrated evolution in action by showing how the genetic makeup of fruit flies changed to adapt to different environments. For the first time evolutionary theorists could point to the hard science of genetics to bolster their claims. No small feat, Dobzhansky laid the groundwork for all future science in evolution and genetics.

Strange but True

EINSTEIN'S PICKLED BRAIN

While Albert Einstein's cranium is now safely stored at Princeton Hospital, the genius's cranium was actually kept in a mason jar in a Wichita, Kansas, laboratory for many years. The brain, which has been subject to plenty of postmortem study, measures surprisingly smaller than average brains. It is, however, markedly denser in some of the regions associated with mathematical ability, and neuroscientists disagree over whether these differences are significant.

Accidents Waiting to Happen:
Mistakes That Became Medical Miracles

Mama always said you should learn from your mistakes. But did she really mean that you should take your daily gaffes and turn them into groundbreaking, earthshaking revelations in science? Here are a couple of cats who did just that.

_01:: That Stuff in the Back of Your Fridge

In 1928 Alexander Fleming famously left a culture of *Staphylococcus aureus* bacteria out under a microscope for too long. By chance, some mold spores landed on the culture and began to grow. Preparing to throw the culture out, Fleming noted something truly peculiar: the bizarre mold had killed all of the bacteria. Fleming capitalized on his mistake when he realized that the mold was nontoxic to animals, going on to develop the first truly effective antibiotic. The medicine, which you now know as penicillin, has saved millions of lives over the years.

_02:: The Original X-Man

Wilhelm Roentgen was setting up a primitive cathode ray generator projected through a glass vacuum tube when he noticed a faint green light on the wall across the room. The light was shining directly on a barium-platinocyanide-coated screen (isn't that always the case?). What was more astonishing, the light from the cathode ray generator seemed to travel through a variety of materials such as wood and paper. As Roentgen began putting various objects in front of the generator, he noticed the outline of the bones of his hand on the wall. For the next few weeks, Roentgen stayed in seclusion studying his accidental phenomenon, which he later dubbed X (for unknown)-rays.

_03:: The Reason You Don't Have a Larger Family

In 1951 Carl Djerassi was attempting to synthesize estradiol, a steroid primarily used to treat inflammatory disease. In the process, however, he accidentally produced a chemical that was similar to progesterone, only more active. Playing with his new product, Djerassi modified the chemical so that it could be taken orally. What resulted wasn't just any ordinary pill; it was the Pill. Still in wide use across the globe, the birth control drug Djerassi created had one of the most sweeping social impacts on the world in the 20th century. Djerassi went on to become a crusader for birth control, publishing and lecturing widely on the subject.

_04:: A Poodle's Piddle

Who could have known that a puddle of dog urine would spur a cure for diabetes? That's right! In studying the function of the pancreas (which wasn't well understood in 1889), two professors from the University of Strasbourg decided to remove the pancreas from a living dog. Later, flies were seen swarming around the canine's urine. Curious as to the cause, the professors analyzed the sample and found that it contained a higher than normal amount of sugar. The doggone discovery led the scientists to determine a relationship between the pancreas and its control of insulin. In turn, this led to the first effective treatment of diabetes through insulin injections.

_05:: Something to Stop the Burning!

German scientist Paul Ehrlich was looking for a treatment for sleeping sickness, an infection that can eventually lead to coma. Looking for an arsenic compound that would kill the disease without harming the patient, Ehrlich stumbled across a compound known as 606. The drug did little for sleeping sickness, but it did work wonders on syphilis. At the time (1999), syphilis was a hugely disabling and extraordinarily prevalent—though little talked about—disease. Ehrlich and his colleagues tested 606 on syphilitic mice, guinea pigs, and rabbits. Surprisingly, within just three weeks, the animals emerged cured. The resulting drug, Salvarsan (606), sold brilliantly across the globe and put Germany at the top of chemical and drug production.

Just the Facts

BODY-BASED STATISTICS

Amount of time it takes blood to make a complete circuit through your body: 60 seconds

Amount of saliva produced per day: 2 quarts

Length human hair grows on top of head in a month: 1 inch

Average number of blinks per minute: 25

Average number of blinks per year: 13,140,000

Number of bones a human is born with: 300

Number of bones an adult human has: 206

Increase in life expectancy if cardiovascular disease were eliminated: 9.78 years

And

6 That Became Marketable Merchandise

Forget the hard work and hours of research. If you want to make a lot of money as a scientist, maybe your best bet is a lucky lab find.

_01:: This Is What Happens When You Don't Wash Your Dishes!

In an act repeated thousands of times in thousands of science labs across the world, in 1903 Edouard Benedictus knocked a flask off a shelf and onto the floor. The glass shattered, but oddly, the container retained its shape. Upon questioning his lab assistant, Fast Eddy learned that the flask had contained cellulose nitrate. And while it had appeared empty (his assistant had done a shoddy cleanup job), the residue from this liquid plastic clung to the inside of the vial. Quick on the uptake, Benedictus realized that he could insert a layer of the celluloid between two sheets of glass, such that the composite would fracture yet retain its shape. The discovery led to safety glass being used in car windshields as well as thousands of other applications.

_02:: Bring the Heat

Corning scientist Dr. Eugene Stookey was experimenting with photosensitive glass. Unbeknownst to him, though, the oven he was working with malfunctioned and heated the glass to a much higher temperature than intended. Instead of finding a puddle of melted glass, though, Stookey opened the oven door to a hard milky white substance. As he pulled the overheated glass out, he accidentally dropped the material—but it didn't break! So, what's become of his discovery? Stookey and company used the process to create a little line of plates and pans you probably know as Corning Ware.

_03:: Is That a Candy Bar in Your Pocket or . . . ?

Radar and microwave technologies developed during World War II were credited with helping to turn the tide in the battle in Europe. But after the war, scientists like Percy Spencer stumbled across all sorts of new applications for the technologies. Percy, who was working for Raytheon at the time, happened to be in the path of powerful radiation emitted from a magnetron (ouch) when he noticed that the candy bar in his pocket had melted. He then, believe it or not, put popcorn kernels in front of the device and watched in fascination as the popcorn popped. He also demonstrated cooking an egg from inside out. (Don't do this at home, they tend to explode!) Of course, using low-density microwave energy to cook is now commonplace, and Spencer's use of popcorn as an early experimental substance was prescient—today the United States produces 500,000 tons of popcorn, most of which is cooked in microwave ovens.

_04:: A Weak Solution

Spencer Silver of 3M was experimenting with superstrong adhesives in 1970. One combination disappointingly led to something only mildly adhesive. In fact, the adhesive was so weak that it couldn't even be used to hold two pieces of paper firmly together! Finding no good use for it, Silver tossed the pitiful glue aside and continued to work. A few years later another 3M employee, Arthur Fry, was frus-

---

Timeline

ROBOTICS UP TO *BLADE RUNNER*

1206 Arab mechanical engineer al-Jazari writes a book on automatons, *The Book of Knowledge of Ingenious Mechanical Devices.*

1350 An automated rooster erected on top of the cathedral in Strasbourg in 1350 is designed to flap its wings and crow every day at noon.

1495 Leonardo da Vinci draws plans for a mechanical man.

1497 Two bell-striking giants are built on top of the great clock tower in Piazza San Marco, Venice.

1769 The Turk, a chess-playing automaton, is unveiled by Baron Wolfgang von Kempelen. Despite many years of playing, it is never fully revealed to be the fake it is during Kempelen's lifetime.

1818 Mary Shelley publishes *Frankenstein.*

1834 Charles Babbage begins designing the Analytical Engine, a steam-powered computer capable of manipulating and storing numbers.

1898 Nikola Tesla invents a remote-control boat.

1939 Elektro and Sparko cause a sensation at the New York World's Fair as Elektro dances, counts to ten, and smokes while his dog, Sparko, walks and barks.

1946 The first computer, the Eniac, is built by Eckert and Mauchly at the University of Pennsylvania.

1962 General Motors installs the first industrial robot on a production line in a car factory in Trenton, New Jersey.

1968 HAL, the computer, runs amok in Kubrik's *2001: A Space Odyssey.*

1976 The Viking Mars probes use a robotic arm to collect rock and soil samples.

1982 Ridley Scott's *Blade Runner* is released, an exploration of what it means to be human, based loosely on Philip K. Dick's 1968 novel, *Do Androids Dream of Electric Sheep?*

trated that his little paper markers wouldn't stay in place in his choir hymnal. Borrowing some of Silver's adhesive, Fry found that his markers would stay in place, and he could lift them off without damaging his book at all. Post-it notes were first marketed in 1980, spurring a whole revolution for office organizers and to-do list makers the world over.

_05:: Fishing for Answers

Roy Plunkett discovered Teflon (tetrafluoroethylene) in a Du Pont lab in 1938 during the search for a new refrigerating coolant. However, much like Spencer Silver's 3M solution (see above), it was tossed aside for lack of application. In fact, it wasn't even considered for commercial production until a Frenchman named Marc Gregoire went fishing. Gregoire found that the substance worked great on his tackle to reduce tangling. Of course, now Teflon is used in everything from car brakes to space suits to replacement arteries for the human heart. It's also used on microchips and

rockets, and surprisingly, it's even rubbed liberally on the Statue of Liberty's arthritic joints (Teflon apparently slows down the aging process in statues).

_06:: Delicious and Refreshing (Not to Mention Good for Your Teeth?)

Did you know that Coca-Cola started out as a medicinal syrup? It's absolutely true. In the late 1800s pharmacists frequently mixed up and sold cure-all potions. One such pharmacist, a guy named John Pemberton, stirred up a batch of what he thought was an excellent tonic for tiredness, nervousness, and sore teeth. He and his assistant then mixed the solution with ice water, tried it, and decided they wanted more than just a spoonful. In their next batch, though, Pemberton's assistant accidentally used carbonated water, and wow, a soft-drink giant was born! So, just how popular is Coke? According to the Coca-Cola company, the only word more commonly used than *Coca-Cola* in the *world* is *OK*.

Technologies That Will Change the World (as Soon as We Invent Them)

We know Louis Armstrong likes to sing about "What a Wonderful World" we've got, but seriously! Just think of how much better things will be when we finally get these objectives crossed off our list.

_01:: No More Flu!

Penicillin changed the state of health care for the entire world by helping to control bacterial infections. Viral infections, on the other hand, are still mostly untreatable. There's a

good deal of evidence to suggest that this will change in this century, though. Today's scientists have had some success in controlling viral fusion by inserting genetic material into healthy host cells in a class of envelope viruses (a class that includes HIV, influenza, rhinoviruses, and Ebola). The research definitely looks promising. And given these advances, it's not hard to see a future where many of the most common viral ailments are as treatable as common infections.

_02:: No More Fat!

While genetic engineering is becoming commonplace in agriculture (producing things like tear-free onions and nutritionally enhanced rice), this technology is only just starting in the treatment of humans. The real revolution in genetic engineering will occur when genes are routinely manipulated to eliminate the onset of heart disease, obesity, and cancer. Scientists have identified approximately 2,000 single-gene diseases that will one day be stopped through gene therapy. So, why isn't the technology commonplace yet? The problem is that often the manipulated gene fails to show up when inserted in the host. As we better understand the human genome sequence, though, it will become far easier to insert as well as delete genes without endangering the function of other chromosomes.

_03:: No More Memory Loss!

Think Keanu Reeves in *The Matrix* or *Johnny Mnemonic*. In both films he had a socket in the back of his head where information could be downloaded or uploaded. Believe it or not, this sort of technology will no longer be science fiction in the 21st century. Currently about 6,000 people have cochlear implants, electrodes that stimulate the auditory fibers in the brain. Amazingly, this technology gives the profoundly deaf the ability to actually

hear sounds. But that's just the start. At Emory University patients with an implanted computer chip connected to the cortical node can use the chip to move an object on a computer screen. Of course, this technology brings up huge debates about the line between man and machine, but the sheer scope of its application is staggering.

_04:: No More Automobile Accidents!

With trains in Japan and Europe routinely having no human operators, it seems only a matter of time before our highway systems will no longer be under the control of the 100 million drivers who take to the road every day. And considering the statistics, it seems like a logical step forward. Every year 50,000 road deaths occur, but does that mean people will be ready to turn the wheel over to their PC? If computer drivers had the same fatality rate as humans, would you get in the automated car? Probably not. How about if automated cars had a fatality rate of 20,000 lives? What about 10,000 lives? Or even 300 lives? Most people's gut reaction is that the fatality rate must be very, very low to give up that control. Of course, we're willing to take far greater risks and are far more accepting when it comes to human gaffes than when technology's to blame.

_05:: No More Blackouts!

Promises of pollution-free, unlimited power have been looming for a while. The idea is that we should be able to obtain energy by extracting hydrogen from water. And it sounds ideal. The reality is that if fusion can be harnessed in a safe way, our dependence on fossil fuels will be a thing of the past. Unfortunately, the power it takes to create nuclear fusion (1) either is higher than the power it creates or (2) necessitates a fission nuclear reaction. Plasma technologies, magnetic confinement, and laser-induced fusion are the most likely candidates for efficiently producing a fusion reaction that can be converted to useful power. But don't rule out hope, yet! The next leap forward will come soon, as the European Union continues the development of the Toka-mak fusion reactor, which will create a self-sustaining fusion reaction.

_06:: No More Age Spots!

In the 21st century the ability to replace worn-out organs will become commonplace by cloning new organs and cells from the host body. But more than just performing transplants, scientists will also be able to slow or halt the aging process in many cells. Current theories on aging indicate that the interaction of free radicals (reactive oxygen species) causes cells to degenerate over time. By neutralizing these free radicals, significant delays can occur in the aging of cells. So, what's that mean exactly? The natural lifespan might be increased to well over 100 years, and those later years might still be as productive (perhaps even reproductive) as earlier years. Such a change would revolutionize the way we structure society.

_07:: No More (Exorbitant) Power Bills!

Superconductors allow the transmission of electricity without any loss of energy, so scientists continue to strive toward making room temperature semiconductors. And why are room temperature semiconductors important to your well being? The end result of such

Fake Your Way Through a Conversation

NANOTECHNOLOGY'S GONNA CHANGE EVERYTHING!

It's confirmed—nanotechnology is one of the hottest buzzwords since . . . well, the buzzword *buzzword*. And the good part is that faking your way through a discussion of it is easy once you understand only a few things. First off, nanotechnology implies building things with atoms and molecules. The scale is obviously very, very small, a nanometer being a billionth of a meter. By comparison, a human hair is about 50,000 nanometers wide. But what exactly's the payoff? If you're arguing for the technology, just keep these things in mind: by applying it to medicine, nanomachines will actually be able to enter the body to destroy viruses, remove arterial plaque, and excise cancer cells. Even more amazingly, nanomachines will have the ability to build other nanomachines in a completely pollution-free production process, and the potential for these tiny machines is enormous. Of course, if you're lobbying against the technology, the potential for overreplication is a real threat. So, if you want to kill the conversation ASAP, just bring up the Terminator scenario: nanotech weapons have the potential to self-replicate as targeted killing machines to kill any sort of host system available (from computers to crops to livestock to humans). It should help you switch topics quickly.

technology will be an enormous increase in our ability to miniaturize devices. Computers, power transmission, and communication technology would become smaller and, as a result, faster. Further, billions of dollars will be saved as energy is conserved rather than lost in heat.

(See 4 Reasons to Have Your Physics Super-Sized on page 240 for more on superconductors.)

They Blinded Me with Science:
10 Frauds and Hoaxes That Duped the Masses

Sometimes scientists are brazen, sometimes they're power hungry, and sometimes they're just plain wrong. Hey, if you can't believe a scientist, who can you trust?

_01:: The Cold Fusion Incident

Fusion power has been heralded as the solution to our future power needs. After all, it promises to provide a nearly limitless supply of energy with minimal environmental impact. The current problem, though, is that it takes a tremendous amount of energy to fuse together nuclei. So, when Stanley Pons and Martin Fleischmann announced to a hungry scientific world that they'd discovered cold fusion in 1989 (a process that supposedly used much less energy), the duo were welcomed with splashy headlines. Other scientists were dubious, and when Pons and Fleischmann withdrew their paper from *Nature* magazine and refused to answer questions, charges of fraud were made. Pons and Fleischmann never gave enough details of the experiment to allow others to replicate it, and more than 10 years later no one has been able to replicate their results. There are still scientists who believe Pons and Fleischmann were on to something, but the premature claims of cold fusion cast such doubt on these two researchers that they were doomed to ignominy.

_02:: Scientist in on God's Prank

In the early 18th century Dr. Johann Beringer of the University of Würzburg devoted his research to the discovery of fossils that seemed to indicate prehistoric life. Beringer, however, believed that these fossils were "capricious fabrications of God," used to test man's faith. His beliefs seemed confirmed when at one site he discovered fossils of birds, beetles, moons, and stars. Little did he know that two mean-spirited colleagues had planted the fake fossils. Perhaps trying to get caught, they even planted tablets inscribed with the Hebrew and Arabic words for God. Beringer published a book, *Lithographia Wirceburgensis*, in 1726 describing his findings and his theory. But then he made another discovery: a similar buried tablet inscribed with his own name. He immediately began trying to buy back all the available copies of his book, but it was too late. Because of the hoax, his book became a bestseller.

_03:: George and the Cardiff Giant

George Hull had no patience with fools, but he exhibited great patience for making a fool of others. After arguing with a clergyman who claimed that giants had walked the earth because the Bible said so, Hull proceeded to carve a 10-foot gypsum statue of a man. He then buried his creation on a neighboring New York farm. In 1869, a full year later, Hull hired some well diggers, who discovered his stone man on the job. Of course people gathered to see this oddity, and rumors began to spread that it was a fossilized human of gigantic proportions. Many saw it for the hoax it was, but when two Yale professors declared it genuine, the proof of giants on earth became set in stone. Eventually Hull had to admit it was a fake after he sued P. T. Barnum for exhibiting a copy of it. Barnum claimed his statue was just a hoax of a hoax and was found not guilty.

_04:: The Most Unnatural of Selections

In the mid-1800s pollution from factories in Britain was darkening trees by killing the lichen, and scientists also noted a decline in the ratio between lighter-colored peppered moths and darker varieties. It was hypothesized that the lighter moths were easier to spot and thus were eaten more by birds. Here was evolution in action. Bernard Kettlewell sat in the woods and watched to see whether birds preferred the lighter version to darker, and he reported that indeed they were twice as likely to eat the lighter moths. Three problems, though: (1) Kettlewell was responsible

for nailing dead moths to the trees for the birds to feed on, (2) peppered moths rarely alight on tree trunks, and (3) birds don't normally feed on moths that are on the side of trees. Even after scientists were informed of these inconsistencies, many still clung to the validity of the experiment, perhaps because they wanted to believe it as the canonical example of observed natural selection.

_05:: Sex and the Seedy

Alfred Kinsey's landmark studies of the 1950s, known as the Kinsey Reports, were the major emphasis on late-20th-century views of human sexuality. The incidence of homosexuality, bisexuality, adultery, and childhood sexual behavior were higher than previously thought, which helped lead to different views of adult and childhood sexual behavior. According to Judith Reisman, however, Kinsey's research was fraught with very bad scientific method and possibly fraud. He obtained much of his data by interviewing prisoners, his interviewing technique was biased, and he used reports from pedophiles to hypothesize about childhood sexual behavior. Kinsey's estimates on the extent of homosexual behavior (38.7% in males ages 36–40) have not been validated in subsequent studies. In contrast, a Batelle report found that 2.3% of men reported having sex with another man. Nonetheless, Kinsey's landmark study still remains one of the primary sources for current sexuality discussions.

_06:: Anything for Albert

Arthur Eddington was so convinced of the theory of general relativity that he altered his data to support it. Eddington set out to put

Einstein to the test by carefully measuring how light was bent during a solar eclipse. But apparently the examiner went soft. When the results were in, Eddington threw out 16 photographic plates that didn't support Einstein's theory. Even worse, he then published his research without those 16 plates and showed how Einstein's theory accurately predicted the resulting data. It was this experiment that helped launch the public acceptability of relativity. Strangely enough, the hoax still has legs. You can still find the experiment listed in current textbooks as "proof" of Einstein's theory.

_07:: Errors of a Graphic Nature

A more recent incident of fraudulent science concerns Jan Hendrik Schön, a physicist at Bell Laboratories. Considered brilliant, Schön was on the fast track in the field of nanoelectronics. His name was even mentioned for a possible Nobel Prize. But his rate of publication (40 a year) and his amazing results began to make some colleagues curious. Eventually Schön was caught falsifying data when he presented identical graphs in two different papers—and the graphs were supposed to be on different topics. Bell Labs themselves initiated an investigation and were rightfully horrified to find gross misconduct.

_08:: The Great Tasaday Hoax

One of the most startling anthropological discoveries of the 20th century was the discovery of a primitive, cave-dwelling society in the Philippines in 1971. The Tasadays, as they were called, were a find of enormous proportions because they lived a life undisturbed by hundreds of years of society. And to many an academic's delight, anthropologists could now directly observe how people lived in such societies. The Tasadays even used stone tools. If you're thinking it's impossible that such an isolated group could exist in the Philippines as late at the 1970s, you're right. It turns out that their "discoverer," PANAMIN (Private Association National Minorities) secretary Manuel Elizalde Jr., paid local farmers to live in the caves, take off their clothes, and appear Stone Age. In return he gave them money and security from counterinsurgency and tribal fighting. The fact that the Tasadays were a hoax was not confirmed until the fall of Marcos in 1983, invalidating, no doubt, many PhD dissertations that had been written in the interim.

_09:: Don't Worry about the EMF, but Please Don't Talk and Drive

Concerns about the dangers of living close to high-tension wires or of frequent use of cell phones have been hot topics for the past decade. Unfortunately, one of the studies that warned about the dangers of electromagnetic field (EMF) damage was a case of fraudulent science. Robert P. Liburdy, a cell biologist at the Lawrence Berkeley National Laboratory, was a leading researcher looking into the dangers of EMF. No study up to that point had shown any increase in risk due to electromagnetic fields. Liburdy set out to change that, however, as his papers claimed that the fields could cause a disruption in calcium, which is important to cell function. According to external reviewers, however, Liburdy left out, manipulated, and otherwise misrepresented the data to support the conclusions he was looking for. While the intense debate about the possible dangers of EMF will continue, it will do so without Liburdy's findings.

_10:: Further Proof That Scientific Education Is Essential

The Quadro Corporation of Harleyville, South Carolina, had an impressive client list: public schools, police agencies, the U.S. Customs office, and Inspector General's offices to name a few. The product they sold, the top of the line Quadro QRS 250G (also known as the Quadro Tracker, available for $1,000), boasted the ability to find drugs, weapons, or virtually anything worth looking for. The small plastic box supposedly contained frequency chips of an advanced sort not known to regular science. Driven by static electricity, the Quadro would resonate at exactly the same frequency as the searched-for item. When the FBI opened the box, however, they found nothing inside. Quadro threatened to sue Sandia Laboratories when Sandia suggested that the device was fraudulent, but eventually Quadro became the bigger company, and just closed shop.

by
Martin W. Lewis

Condensed
GEOGRAPHY and
CULTURE

Contains

Major Mistakes on Your World Map: 3 Countries That Make Atlas Shrug ✷ 5 Tiny Nations That Get No Respect ✷ Home Alone: 4 Places That'll Make Any Misanthrope Smile ✷ 3 Swarming Megacities Where People Just Won't Leave! ✷ 3 Countries That Don't Take American Express (Don't Even Get Them Started on Travelers Cheques) ✷ 4 Places That Will Never See a Club Med ✷ Dysfunction Junction: 5 Crime and Kidnapping Capitals ✷ Sex and the Cities: 3 International Hubs of Prostitution ✷ English as a 102nd Language: 4 Places Where Subtitles Would Definitely Help ✷ 6 Lands Where Gods Collide ✷ 5 Assumptions That'll Help You Lose Friends ✷ 6 Places to Meet New People and Chew Their Saliva ✷

Major Mistakes on Your World Map:
Countries That Make Atlas Shrug

Forget about trying to find Waldo; what about Somalia? That's right! While your world map no doubt looks authoritative—with all those fancy colors and heavy lines—there seems to be a real problem locating some of these so-called countries on the ground.

_01:: Somalia

Somalia isn't really a country, but you can still find it on most world political maps. You can read all about in the reference books too: they'll tell you that almost all of the people of Somalia share the same ethnicity, speak Somali, and follow the Sunni Islam religion. Of course, the books usually forget to mention that Somalia hasn't been a unified state for years. After bouncing around as a pawn in Cold War geopolitics (first as a Soviet ally and then an American one), Somalia collapsed catastrophically in 1991. Now its "central government" doesn't even control all of its capital city, Mogadishu. As for the rest of Somalia, it's basically divided into squabbling clan territories.

_02:: Republic of Somaliland

The new, stronger government in northern Somalia transcends the squabbling clans to rule the Republic of Somaliland. So, what's the catch? The Republic of Somaliland is a phantom country—it hasn't received any international recognition, so it's almost impossible to locate in the reference works. Oddly enough, you can find Somaliland on the world map if you have a map made during the first half of the 20th century. At that time, northern Somalia was a British colony—called British Somaliland—and Italy ruled the rest of Somalia. It's surprising that arbitrary European-imposed boundaries have shown such staying power.

_03:: Democratic Republic of the Congo

The Democratic Republic of the Congo is another challenge to the geographically literate because (1) it's not democratic; (2) it's not a functioning republic; (3) it's not the same place as its neighbor, Congo; and (4) it goes through lots of name changes (Belgian Congo, Congo Leopoldville, Congo Kinshasa, Zaire). So, good luck with the atlas. Unfortunately, by the time we figure it all out, the Democratic Republic might not exist anymore. Its economy and infrastructure have been decaying for decades, and the government just doesn't control much of the territory. During the Cold War, Belgium, France, and the United States propped up the brutal and corrupt regime of Mobutu Sese-Seko, but subsequent coups and foreign invasions have turned the country into an empty shell.

5 Tiny Nations That Get No Respect

Every sovereign state deserves its own seat in the community of nations, right? But what happens when you make size a factor? These countries help put an end to the debate over whether size really does matter.

_01:: Luxembourg

With 448,000 people inhabiting 2,500 square kilometers, Luxembourg is a small place indeed. Luxembourg could easily fit into Russia 6,600 times, and the population of Luxembourg would have to be multiplied by more than 2,000 to equal China's. But Luxembourg counts as a significant member of the European Union and other international organizations—and it ranks as the world's richest country on a per capita basis (at US$43,000). Luxembourg also stands as something of a giant when contrasted with the world's true microstates. These are the internationally recognized sovereign entities that you might not find on a world map for the simple reason that they're too small (for example, the feudal remnants of Europe and a few of the islands of the Caribbean and Pacific).

_02:: Principality of Monaco

Everyone knows that American movie star Grace Kelly became Princess of Monaco, but what exactly is Monaco? The quintessential European microstate, Monaco could fit into tiny Luxembourg about 1,400 times. Covering less than two square kilometers, Monaco boasts a total population of 32,000 (fewer people than you could find at a large U.S. university). Of that small number, only 16% are actually classified as Monegasque; the rest are mostly French and Italian. So, what's so special about Monaco? For one thing, it has Monte Carlo, a well-known gambling haven for Europe's dissolute elite.

_03:: Nauru

Composed of 10,000 people on an island less than one-eighth the size of the District of Columbia, the nation of Nauru is both interesting and sad. In the 1970s Nauru was one of the most prosperous countries in the world, and the large profits from its phosphate industry were spread widely among its small number of citizens. The problem? The phosphate deposits are mostly gone, and with them went most of the country. What remains is largely a desolate, stripped-out wasteland. The people of Nauru now face an uncertain future, surviving on mismanaged trusts left over from the days of the phosphate boom. The government of Nauru, however, hopes to reinvent the island as an off-shore banking center.

_04:: Pacific Atoll Countries

Although the islands of Tuvalu and Kiribati are tiny specks, both states control vast expanses of the Pacific Ocean, with substantial fisheries and potentially significant mineral resources. Kiribati is only about four times the

rather large challenge. And looming over Kiribati and Tuvalu—as well as the Marshall Islands and the Maldives—is the threat of global warming. If sea levels rise as some models predict, the low coralline atolls of these countries will simply vanish beneath the waves.

_05:: Vatican City: The Holy See

Even such minuscule countries as Nauru and Monaco are substantial when contrasted with the world's smallest sovereign state: Vatican City. The Vatican (or the Holy See, as it is more properly called) is little more than a cluster of buildings in Rome, covering less than half a square kilometer. This speck of land, roughly three quarters the size of Washington's Mall, is all that remains of the Roman Catholic Church's once substantial territorial holdings. Here one can find a true, if tiny, theocracy: the pope enjoys full executive, judicial, and legislative powers, and the legal system is based on canon law. But despite its limited size, the Holy See is a highly international place, receiving pilgrims and financial contributions from Catholic churches all over the world.

size of the District of Columbia, but it extends across more than 3,000 miles of sea space—a substantial "territory" for its 78,600 inhabitants. Patrolling this expanse, however, is a

Home Alone:

Places That'll Make Any Misanthrope Smile

The most remote destination on earth is undoubtedly the center of Antarctica. Guarded by thousands of miles of rugged glacial terrain, not to mention the roughest seas on the planet, you're pretty likely to find all the alone time you need there. But if you're simply looking for a hiding spot, here are a couple other places no one will think to seek.

_01:: Tristan de Cunha

If you'd like to see another person or two, your best bet is probably Tristan de Cunha, in the south Atlantic. Tristan de Cunha, population 300 or so, is a rugged volcanic island largely ringed by sea cliffs up to 600 meters high. The best way to get to the island is by taking a fishing boat out of Cape Town, South Africa. Tristan is a dependency of the almost equally isolated St. Helena (population 7,300), famous as Napoleon's final place of exile. But St. Helena, itself one of Britain's last remaining colonies, lies over 1,500 miles away. The people of Tristan make a decent living by fishing and growing a few crops (mostly potatoes); the island's main exports are saltwater crayfish and postage stamps.

_02:: Pitcairn

The Pacific also contains a number of remote islands. One of the most famous is Pitcairn, another British territory. As oceanic islands go, Pitcairn is not that isolated, being only a few hundred miles from the Isles Gambier in French Polynesia, but it is rugged and lacks an anchorage site. In fact, it was selected as a refuge by Fletcher Christian and the other mutineers from the *Bounty*—along with their Polynesian wives—precisely for this reason. The subsequent history of Pitcairn was grim and bloody, resulting in a highly limited gene pool. Its population, moreover, is in serious decline; from a height of 233 in 1937, it now stands at only 47. Pitcairn's main export is (again!) postage stamps, and it's probably the only place in the world where everyone is a Seventh-Day Adventist.

_03:: Kyrgyzstan

Outside of the polar reaches, the world's most remote lands lie in Central Asia. Here one can find a number of landlocked countries far removed from the cosmopolitan cities and sea-lanes of global commerce. One could do little better that Kyrgyzstan, a former Soviet republic dominated by rugged mountains and deep canyons. It also boasts one of the most scenic lakes in the world, the 115-mile-long Issyk Kul. Kyrgyzstan joins four other landlocked states (Kazakhstan, Turkmenistan, Tajikistan, and Afghanistan) in surrounding Uzbekistan, making it the world's only double-landlocked country. Surprisingly, traveling to Kyrgyzstan is remarkably easy. The government is now encouraging tourism, and one can fly to Kyrgyzstan's capital, Bishkek, from a number of major airports. Flights on British Airways leave London several times a week, but if you're feeling more adventurous, try Kyrgyzstan Airlines flying out of Stuttgart, Germany.

_04:: Tuva

Even more isolated than Kyrgyzstan, however, is Tuva, an internal Russian republic nestled behind mountain barriers along the Mongolian border. Lying at the very heart of the Eurasian continent, Tuva is an odd geographical and cultural mélange. The Tuvinians speak a language related to Turkish, practice Tibetan Buddhism, and are famous (to ethnomusicologists, at least) for their throat singing. But access to Tuva is tough. Be prepared to pay top dollar if you want to book a flight to their capital, Kyzyl. (No shortage of the letters *k*, *y*, and *z* in Central Asia!)

Swarming Megacities Where People Just Won't Leave!

Some people seek solace in the world's empty lands, but making yourself another face in the crowd can be just as effective. Take your pick from hiding spots among urban populations exploding across most of the Third World.

_01:: São Paulo, Brazil

Most reference works inform us that greater Tokyo, with some 26 million inhabitants, is the largest urban cluster on the planet. Such a figure is somewhat misleading, however, because it fails to capture the greater density of settlement and rates of growth typically found in Third World megacities. Latin America already has some of the world's largest urban clusters, with both greater Mexico City and São Paulo containing roughly 18 million residents. São Paulo, the commercial, financial, and industrial center of Brazil, has seen particularly explosive growth. From a "mere" 8 million inhabitants in 1970, São Paulo is predicted to soon surpass 25 million. Its industrial suburbs were widely reputed to be the most polluted places in the world in the 1980s, but recent measures have resulted in some improvement.

_02:: Lagos, Nigeria

Megacities in other parts of the Third World are catching up with those of Latin America. Lagos, Nigeria, for example, was a small and manageable city of roughly 1 million inhabitants in 1960, but it had reached 12 million by 2000 and is predicted to top 23 million by 2015. As early as the 1970s, however, the city was becoming unmanageable, and at present conditions are often nightmarish: commute times of three to four hours are common, crime is surging, and the basic infrastructure isn't even close to keeping pace with the burgeoning population. Owing partly to the chaos of Lagos, the Nigerian government decided in 1976 to build a new capital at Abuja, in the center of the country. Although it has done little to halt the expansion of Lagos, Abuja's growth has also been impressive, if not frightening. From some 400,000 in 1991, when it officially became Nigeria's capital, Abuja had reached a population of nearly 4 million by 2003.

_03:: Calcutta

Third World urbanism in its starkest form—with the largest and most impoverished crowds—can be found in Calcutta (Kalikata). Greater Calcutta's 15 million inhabitants squeeze into a relatively small area, giving an average population density of 85,000 people per square mile. Millions live in crude plywood and plastic shacks—luxury homes compared to such housing units as small stretches of concrete piping or simply the sidewalks. Most of the city has a strong stench, and after the monsoon rains hit, much of the city floods, compounding the sanitation problem. But the common image of Calcutta—Mother Teresa caring for a leprous child—conveys only a half-truth. Despite its squalor and misery, Calcutta is culturally sophisticated. Not all of its people are impoverished, and even quite a few of its poor are well educated. Some reports claim that Calcutta has the highest level of cultural output—measured by such features as the amount of poetry published annually—in the world.

3 Countries That Don't Take American Express (Don't Even Get Them Started on Travelers Cheques)

If you're sick of traveling halfway around the globe just to see a McDonald's, a Starbucks, and an ad for American Express, here are a couple of spots to add to your itinerary. But be wary: leaving globalization behind may cost you.

_01:: Burma (Myanmar)

If you're looking for an entire country that until quite recently opted out of the global economic system, try Burma. But remember that opposition to globalization also means skepticism about international tourism, so don't expect an easy time. And don't necessarily expect a nice place; isolation is maintained in countries such as Burma (which now calls itself Myanmar) and North Korea by stringent repression. Up until the 1980s the Burmese government strictly limited tourism, but it's now encouraging it. Expect friendly people; a leisurely pace of life; a relatively unsullied natural environment; some of the world's most impressive temples, monuments, and ruins—and a nasty police state that still wants to limit your contact with its citizens.

Strange but True

POOR PLACES
THAT AIN'T SO POOR

Throughout most of the world there's a close correlation between levels of economic and social development. Wealthy places, in other words, generally have healthy and well-educated populations, whereas poor places don't. But there are some striking exceptions to the rule. Sri Lanka, for example, has a per capita gross domestic product of $820, which is a fraction of that of Mexico ($5,840), let alone that of the United States ($34,900). Yet Sri Lanka, despite its almost interminable civil war, boasts almost universal literacy as well as an enviable average longevity of 72 years. Even more remarkable is India's southwestern state of Kerala, an extremely crowded place with an average income even lower than that of Sri Lanka. Yet Kerala, with an average life expectancy of more than 70 years, has conquered malaria, boasts universal education, is virtually free of beggars and serious malnutrition, and is approaching population stabilization.

_02:: Bhutan

A more enticing option is Bhutan. Nestled along the southern slopes of the Himalayas adjacent to northeastern India, Bhutan is a lightly populated, environmentally pristine country noted for its stupendous mountains, Buddhist temples and monasteries, and determination to keep the modern world at bay. The Bhutanese government, however, recognizes that some forms of development are desirable, and it now looks to tourists as a potential source of revenue. But it has no desire to see mass tourism, which it views as culturally destabilizing, much less to welcome the throngs of hippie backpackers that once swarmed through nearby Nepal. Bhutan, therefore, invites well-heeled and short-term guests. Tourists in groups of three or more are required to spend at least $165 a day, and single tourists are levied an additional fee of $40 a day.

_03:: North Korea

If you really want to escape globalization, you might try sneaking into North Korea. Of course, you'll probably be arrested and executed, and you may even be captured and eaten by villagers. (Between one and three million North Koreans have starved to death over the past decade, and reports of cannibalism are growing.) But if you do survive the ordeal, you can bear witness to the most extravagant personality cult in history, one that makes the efforts of Hitler, Stalin, and Saddam Hussein look rather modest in comparison. Kim-Il Sung, the country's founding dictator, is still its official president—even though he died in 1994. (Why be president for life when you can have the position for all eternity?) His son, Kim Jong-Ill, now the country's "dear leader," is evidently doing his best to follow in his father's footsteps.

Places That Will Never See a Club Med

What exactly is the worst climate in the world? Whether a given climate is good or bad is subjective; to a native of northern Alaska, for instance, 75°F can seem miserably hot. But, in general, what makes for the worst climate depends on what you dread the most: fire or ice.

_01:: Jacobabad, Pakistan

Those averse to fire should avoid spending a summer in Death Valley, California, where the average July temperature is 101°F, or Marble Bar, Australia, which once recorded 161 days in a row when the mercury topped 100°F. Even hotter—or at least more sticky—times can be had in Jacobabad, Pakistan. Here the average June high temperature is 114°F, with relative humidity averaging nearly 60% in the morning hours. Dust storms are also frequent at this time of the year. Add to that the prevalence of Islamic extremism and clan feuds in the area, and Jacobabad might not be the ideal place for resort development.

_02:: Djibouti, Africa

At least Jacobabad, like Death Valley and Marble Bar, has relatively pleasant winters. For year-round heat and general unpleasantness, the best selection is probably Djibouti, in northeastern Africa, where it's always hot, always humid, and hardly ever rains. Djibouti's winters are marginally bearable, with average high temperatures in the mid-80s Fahrenheit and relative humidity at midday hovering at 70%, but the rest of the year is something else. By July expect a temperature range from 87°F at night to 106°F in the afternoon, with early morning relative humidity around 60%. The people of

---

Inventions and Innovation

THE CHRONOMETER

Early mapmakers and navigators had no problem determining latitude, which is fairly easily calculated on the basis of the height of the midday sun. Longitude, however, was mostly a matter of guesswork, resulting in distorted maps and innumerable shipwrecks. Geographers had long realized that the problem could be solved by a highly accurate clock; if it were noon onboard ship (determined by simple observation) and midnight at Greenwich, England (as revealed by the chronometer), then you had to be halfway around the world from Britain's Royal Observatory. But no one could build a clock that would remain accurate enough through rolling waves and temperature and humidity extremes, despite the lure of a £20,000 award promised by the British government. No one, that is, until the task was taken up by an ill-educated British craftsman named John Harrison (1693–1776). In 1773 Harrison was belatedly awarded the full prize much to the chagrin of a few gentleman scientists who continued to look down on Harrison with pure class contempt.

Djibouti are especially inclined to seek shelter during the summer months when the khamsin wind blows in from the desert, compounding the heat with ample quantities of dust and grit.

_03:: Sakha, Siberia

Ice haters should avoid the polar areas, but that's easy enough, since no humans live there. Roughly 1 million people, on the other hand, live in Sakha (or Yakutia) in east-central Siberia. In its capital city of Yakutsk, the average January temperature is −45.4°F. Further north, Verkhoyansk enjoys an average January high temperature of −54°F. Cultural practices exacerbate the nastiness: in the winter, the local people traditionally live with their horses and cattle, subsisting on milk tar—an intriguing blend of fish, berries, bones, and the inner bark of pine trees conveniently dissolved in sour milk. Not surprisingly, Russia's Czarist and Communist authorities used to enjoy exiling troublesome intellectuals to this region. But partially as a result, the people of Sakha are now noted for their intellectual and political sophistication.

_04:: Kerguelen

Despite its winter frigidity, Sakha's brief summers are sweet. For incessant unpleasantness, look to maritime locations between 50° and 60° latitude, where raw temperatures; brisk winds; and rain, sleet, and snow predominate year-round. Alaska's Aleutian Islands certainly fit the bill, but the best example is probably Kerguelen, a sizable French-owned archipelago in the southern Indian Ocean. Kerguelen experiences precipitation on more than 300 days a year, and its average temperatures range from 35.6°F in July to 45.5°F in January. Kerguelen has no flying insects—not too surprising considering its average wind speed of 35 kph, which would quickly send the hapless butterfly far out to sea. Thus even the ubiquitous Kerguelen cabbage, a former godsend for scurvy-racked whalers, has adapted to being pollinated by wind rather than insects.

Dysfunction Junction:
Crime and Kidnapping Capitals

5

If pickpockets, purse snatchers, and petty thieves just don't get your heart racing the way they used to, maybe you should take a trip to these five exciting locales. Of course, there's no guarantee that you'll ever return.

_01:: Yemen

In Yemen, kidnapping is culturally institutionalized. Yemen's tribal groups, which tend to be militantly independent, have long used hostages as a tool for negotiating with the central government. Outsiders are simply grabbed and held until the authorities make promises or deliver the goods. Traditionally, the victims are treated with courtesy, and a few have reported that they rather enjoyed the ordeal. But don't expect such treatment anymore, especially if you hold a U.S. passport. Yemen is the ancestral home of Osama bin Laden, and sympathy for Al Qaeda runs rather high throughout the country.

_02:: Colombia

Although kidnapping in Colombia doesn't have such deep cultural roots, it's widely prevalent and extremely dangerous. Ransom figures are often exorbitant, and murder is a relatively common outcome. Beset with several competing leftist revolutionary and rightist paramilitary organizations—all of which now seem more interested in the narcotics trade than in political action—Colombia has a well-deserved reputation for being the most violent, crime-ridden country in the world. But while the drug trade has greatly exacerbated the problem, violence, especially political violence, is nothing new. The period between 1948 and 1962, when some 200,000 Colombians perished, is commonly referred to in history texts simply as *la violencia*.

_03:: Sierra Leone

Maybe it's unfair to highlight Colombia's crime rate, as a number of places are actually far more dangerous. Colombia does have, after all, a competent government, police force, and judicial system—which is more than a lot of countries. In contrast, the western African states of Liberia and Sierra Leone have been torn apart by brutal rebel armies over the past decade. Rival warlords have sought control of lucrative diamond fields, and they've been joined in the gem and arms businesses by several questionable international organizations—

including Al Qaeda. Visitors to Sierra Leone will likely see many handless people, as hand-chopping has been a favorite technique of rebel leaders for instilling fear in, and ensuring cooperation from, wary villagers.

_04:: Liberia

In neighboring Liberia, on the other hand, the violence continues. Charles Taylor, a one-time guerrilla leader who was "elected" president in 1997, terrorized his own people while supporting brutal rebel movements in neighboring countries. Taylor, in turn, was challenged by the delightfully named LURD: Liberians United for Reconciliation and Democracy. Some observers believe that LURD is serious about democracy and reconciliation; others are skeptical, leery of a militia in which commanders sport such names as Dragon Master and Nasty Duke and favor American "gangster chic."

_05:: Ituri, Democratic Republic of the Congo

The Democratic Republic of the Congo, as noted on p. 108, is a textbook case of a failed state. It's important to note, however, that parts of this country have failed rather more spectacularly than others. In fact, nowhere is the violence and general mayhem more extreme than in the northeastern province of Ituri. After Uganda withdrew its pillaging troops in early 2003, the region's two main ethnic groups, the Hemas and the Lendus, set upon each other with ferocity. Numerous reports of cannibalism, conducted more for reasons of magic than of hunger, soon reached the global media. (When corpses are missing their hearts, livers, and brains, you can assume that *something* fishy is going on.) According to some reports, many Pygmies—innocent bystanders to the region's ethnic carnage—had been hunted down and partially

eaten. Colombia and Yemen are looking better all the time, no?

Sex and the Cities:
International Hubs of Prostitution

3

Like it or not, the world's oldest profession shows no sign of slowing down. And while your Lonely Planet guide probably won't clue you in to just how lonely some of this planet gets, the truth is sexual tourism remains a booming global business.

_01:: Bangkok, Thailand

Thailand supposedly has the largest number of prostitutes per capita in the world. While most Thai prostitutes cater to a domestic clientele, many in Bangkok are oriented to the international sex tourists coming from such countries as Germany, Japan, and the United States. Technically speaking, prostitution is illegal in Thailand—but that just makes it a highly lucrative source of income for corrupt policemen and army officers. This situation is nothing new, though. The Thai government evidently began to draw significant funding from prostitution in the 1680s after the king awarded a monopoly in the field to a state official, who in turn employed over 600 enslaved women for the purpose.

_02:: Angeles City, Philippines

While Manila has its share of prostitution, far more insidious is Angeles City, former site of a major U.S. Air Force base. After the United States pulled out and volcanic Mt. Pinatubo

catastrophically exploded, many experts predicted disaster for Angeles City. But instead of withering away, the city turned to one of the special "industries" that had arisen to serve the "needs" of American military personnel. Web sites advertise ever more lavish clubs, indicating that Angeles City may be seeking to emulate Las Vegas as an international adult playground, albeit one focusing on sex rather than gambling.

_03:: Havana, Cuba

In the 1950s the world's premier sin city, offering both gambling and sex, was probably Havana. When Castro came to power, however, all such aspects of "bourgeois decadence" were supposedly swept away, and Cuba was soon pronounced free of prostitution. But after the Soviet Union collapsed, bringing down the Cuban economy with it, the old ways returned with alacrity. As the government turned to foreign tourism as an income source, it soon became clear that the

Just the Facts

WHERE'S THE BEST PLACE TO BE A WOMAN?

Most female populations (# men per 100 women)*: Latvia, 83; Ukraine, 87; Russia, 88

Highest female life expectancy at birth**: Japan, 84.4; France, 82.4; Sweden, 82.2

Largest gender discrepancies in longevity (number of years women outlive men)**: Russia, 13; Belarus, 12; Ukraine, 11

Female unemployment rate as % of male unemployment rate***: South Korea, 71; UK, 79; Sweden, 87

Female professional and technical workers as % of total***: Lithuania, 70; Latvia, 67; Estonia, 67; Moldova, 67

Ratio of estimated female to male earned income***: Latvia, 0.72; Denmark, 0.70; Finland, 0.70

Women in Parliament, % of Total***: Sweden, 42.7; Denmark, 38; Finland, 36.5

Women in government at ministerial level, % of total***: Sweden, 55; Colombia, 47; Denmark, 45

Female students as % of male students in secondary education***: Lesotho, 194; Namibia, 148; Uruguay, 136

Composite gender empowerment index (women in important decision-making capacity), top three countries***: Norway, Iceland, Sweden

(Sources: *_The Economist_, Pocket World in Figures, 2001; **L. Rowntree et al., *Diversity Amid Globalization*, Prentice Hall, 2003; ***UN Human Development Reports: http://hdr.undp.org/reports/global/2002/en/indicator/indicator.cfm?File=index_indicators.html)

---

one commodity that would bring in substantial sums of hard currency was sex. *Jinateras*, as Cuban streetwalkers are commonly called, soon became a ubiquitous sight. Subsequently, the embarrassed Cuban regime began to crack down, but the underlying dynamics remain. Once again prostitution is shoring up the Cuban state.

English as a 102nd Language:
Places Where Subtitles Would Definitely Help

4

Sure, languages of business, like English, Spanish, and Chinese, are taking the world by storm. But don't throw out your pocket translators just yet! Since 3,000–4,000 distinct languages are still in existence, you might want to get, say, 30 or 40 more languages under your belt before you visit these places.

_01:: Papua New Guinea

No country has more linguistic diversity than Papua New Guinea (PNG). Over 800 languages are currently spoken in the country, and no one linguistic group contains more than a small percentage of the population. Many languages of the interior are poorly known, although missionary linguists are working hard to record them in preparation for bible translation. How does Papua New Guinea function as a country, considering this welter of tongues? Some form of common speech is necessary, and PNG has one in English. Well, not exactly English as we know it, but Melanesian Pidgin English, based on a simplified vocabulary and local grammatical and sound structures. Thus a foreign tourist would generally be labeled a *man bilong longwe ples* (or "man belong long-way place").

_02:: Caucasus Mountains

Even greater linguistic complexity is found in the Caucasus Mountains, stretching between the Black and Caspian seas. Some of its languages belong to large, widespread families that extend far beyond the area, such as Armenian and Ossetian (which belong, like English, to the Indo-European family). Most, however, fit into three totally distinct linguistic families that exist nowhere else in the world. A few Caucasian languages are nationally significant. Georgian, for example, is the official language of an independent country. Spoken by some 5 million people, it has an ancient and rich literary tradition. Most others, however, are never written, and many are limited to a single isolated valley. Complexity reaches its apogee in the small Russian internal republic of Dagestan in the northeast, where more than 50 distinct languages are still spoken.

_03:: Yunnan, China

Another linguistically intriguing area is the province of Yunnan in south-central China. Here the fertile valleys and plateaus are populated by people speaking Mandarin Chinese, but on the steep slopes and rugged hills one can find more than 20 separate languages belonging to three linguistic families. A similar situation exists across the border to the south, where the lowlanders speak the national languages of Vietnam, Burma, Laos, and Thailand but the hill tribes retain their own tongues. Laos alone has some 82 distinct languages. Such patterns are linked to a centuries-old process of Chinese expansion. Peoples who did not wish to be overwhelmed by the Chinese fled to the rugged slopes or moved southward along the ridgelines into Southeast Asia. Today this area—known as the Golden Triangle—is notoriously difficult to control, owing both to its rugged topography and to its ethnic complexity. Not surprisingly, it remains one of the world's main opium-growing zones.

_04:: Salt Lake City, Utah

Although the United States is one of the most monolingual parts of the world, certain parts of it—those attracting large numbers of immigrants—are truly polyglot: try standing on a corner in New York and counting the languages heard on the street. One of the most unexpectedly multilingual parts of the U.S., however, is Salt Lake City, which as a result now boasts a number of translation services. Linguistic diversity here derives not from ethnic complexity or from immigration, but rather from missionary activity. As the center of the globally expanding religion of Mormonism, Salt Lake City is home to tens of thousands of returned Mormon missionaries. And Mormon missionaries are famous not merely for walking around obscure Third World cities in their starched white shirts but also for assiduously learning the languages of their host societies. Since most young Mormon men go on missions, the resulting linguistic resources of Salt Lake City are impressive indeed.

6 Lands Where Gods Collide

Most world atlases divide the planet into large blocks of faith, showing a Muslim Middle East, a Hindu India, a Christian Europe, and so on. These maps are useful at the global scale, but they often prove misleading when you're looking at the smaller picture.

_01:: Kerala

In India's southwestern state of Kerala, roughly half the people follow Hinduism, and the rest are evenly divided between Islam and Christianity. Although Kerala is one of the few parts of India that was never under sustained Muslim rule, trade connections across the Arabian Sea brought Islam to the state centuries ago. Christianity came as early as the third century CE, and in the 1500s the Portuguese made another round of converts. The two Christian groups remained separate, however, and the older Syrian Christian community is still considered to have a much higher caste ranking than the Roman Catholics. (So much for caste being exclusive to Hinduism!) Kerala once had a thriving Jewish community as well, but all but a handful of its Jews have long since decamped for Israel. To make matters even more complicated, Kerala also has a substantial antireligious (or is it quasi-religious?) movement: that of Marxian communism. Hammer and sickle emblems are just as common as temples, mosques, and churches across the lush and densely populated landscapes of "Red Kerala."

_02:: Brazil

South America has surprising religious diversity. Even though Roman Catholicism still reigns in most areas, evangelical Protestantism has been spreading rapidly in recent years. Many Brazilians practice a variety of syncretic (or mixed) faiths that are more deeply rooted in traditional West African religious practices than in Christianity. The most widespread African faith in Brazil is probably Candomblé, which can be directly traced back to the Yoruba country of southwestern Nigeria. Candomblé, like other mixed faiths with African roots, involves the use of a wide variety of ritual plants, some of which are apparently intoxicating.

_03:: Suriname

South American religious diversity reaches its extreme in Suriname, a former Dutch colony north of Brazil. Both Roman Catholic and Protestant Christianity are well represented (at roughly 23% and 25% of the populace, respectively), but so are Islam and Hinduism (20% and 27%). (Under colonialism, many workers were imported from Indonesia and India to cut sugarcane, hence the Muslim and Hindu elements). In the interior, a sizable number of indigenous people practice traditional animism, worshiping nature spirits and their ancestors. The so-called bush blacks—people whose enslaved ancestors escaped to the interior rain forests—generally follow an African syncretic faith. To round things out, Suriname's small but commercially important

Chinese community tends, not surprisingly, toward Buddhism, Taoism, and Confucianism.

_04:: Lebanon

The Middle East is widely noted for its religious conflicts rather than its religious diversity. Lebanon, however, is fairly evenly divided between Sunni Muslims, Shiite Muslims, and Christians—and its Christians belong to roughly a dozen distinct sects. Throughout much of the Middle East, Christianity is both widespread and diverse; the re-

Myths and Misconceptions
EUROPE AS A CONTINENT

Textbook definitions tell us that Europe is a continent, bounded on the east by the unimpressive Ural Mountains and Ural River, which means that not only Russia and Turkey but also Kazakhstan lie partly in Europe but mostly in Asia. But reference works also tell us that continents are supposed to be mostly separated from each other by seas and oceans, disqualifying Europe from the category. Europe is thus perhaps best defined as a region, but regions are by their very nature slippery categories. Is Russia part of Europe? If so, Europe borders North Korea; if not, shouldn't Ukraine have to be excluded as well? (You can make such an argument, but it wouldn't make you very popular in Kiev.) Alternatively, one can redefine Europe as the collection of countries belonging to, or seeking to belong to, the European Union. No problem—provided that you are willing to exclude Switzerland and Norway.

ligion originated here, and certain forms survived that were stamped out as heretical in the West.

_05:: Turkey and Syria

Islam also exhibits marked diversity, especially in the region extending from southeastern Turkey through the mountains of coastal Syria and Lebanon. The Alevi of Turkey and the Alawites of Syria—who number in the millions—view the pillars of their faith metaphorically, and hence have no problem with such un-Islamic practices as drinking alcohol. The Druze take Islamic heterodoxy to an extreme, but it is hard to say what they really believe, since they purposely dissemble to outsiders while limiting knowledge of their innermost doctrine to a select few.

_06:: Iraq

Iraq is a religiously diverse country, with many Christians (an estimated 4% of the total population) as well as both Shiite and Sunni Muslims. More significantly, in northern Iraq and adjacent lands one can find some 150,000 Kurdish-speaking Yezidis, members of a profoundly antidualist faith who revere Satan, God's chief angel, in the form of a peacock. (The Yezidis cannot be considered Satanists, however, because in their version the rebellious devil later repented and was brought back into the fold by the benevolent deity.) Although the Yezidis have suffered periodic persecution, they have generally been allowed to worship in peace. Just imagine what their fate would have been had they lived in Europe during the Middle Ages or Renaissance!

5 Assumptions That'll Help You Lose Friends

Stereotyping is an indispensable part of geographical analysis, but it sure won't make you popular. The following misconceptions are five easy ways to lose footing on new grounds.

_01:: All Nicaraguans Speak Spanish

Surely Nicaragua is a typical Spanish-speaking, Latin American country, no? Visit the Caribbean shore of Nicaragua—the idyllically named Mosquito Coast—however, and you will find that English, Caribbean-style, is the dominant tongue, a legacy of the days of British imperialism. (Even Colombia has an English-speaking zone in the nearby islands of San Andrés and Providencia.) In the 1980s Nicaragua's leftist

Sandinista rulers discovered to their chagrin just how deeply entrenched their country's cultural divide was. When they tried to root out English as the language of imperialism, the Caribbean coast quickly rose up in rebellion.

_02:: All Europeans Are Traditionally Christian

Latin America isn't the only part of the world with zones of unexpected cultural juxtaposition. We do not tend to think of Tibetan Buddhism as a European religion, for example, but Europe includes within its supposed continental boundaries a community of some 150,000 Mongolian-speaking Tibetan Buddhists, the Kalmyks. The Kalmyks, whose internal Russian republic of Kalmykia lies to the northwest of the Caspian Sea, have formed a well-established European community for

several hundred years. Today the republic is noted for its charismatic, and perhaps criminal, leader, Kirsan Ilyumzhinov. A former chief of the World Chess Federation, Ilyumzhinov has engaged in such stunts as locking up drunks in iron cages along the streets of the capital for public humiliation.

_03:: There Aren't Any Jews in Ethiopia

Other such cultural oddities are much larger and much older. Most of the people of the central highlands of Ethiopia, numbering more than 25 million, speak Semitic languages that are more closely related to Hebrew than they are to the other languages of sub-Saharan (south of the Sahara) Africa. The central Ethiopians, moreover, began practicing Christianity roughly 1700 years ago, much earlier than did the people of northern Europe. Until recently Ethiopia also had a thriving Jewish community, that of the Falashas. The Falashas had long been isolated from other Jewish groups, and as a result they held only a small portion of the Jewish Holy Scriptures. A debate ensued over whether they should therefore be considered true Jews. Once the issue was decided in the affirmative, virtually the entire community migrated to Israel.

_04:: . . . Or in Zimbabwe for That Matter!

Jewish connections to sub-Saharan Africa do not end with the Falashas. More intriguing is the case of the Lemba, a tribal group from Zimbabwe. The Lemba have long been noted for a number of seemingly Jewish cultural practices, particularly those associated with diet and animal slaughter. Their own oral legends, moreover, point to a Middle Eastern origin. Recent analysis of genetic markers on the

---

Myths and Misconceptions

THE FLAT EARTH OF MEDIEVAL EUROPE

We all know that medieval Europeans believed the earth to be flat, a misconception conveniently put to rest by Christopher Columbus. Wrong! Not only did ancient Greek geographers know that the world was (roughly) spherical, but one of them (Eratosthenes) even worked out a fairly close approximation of its size. As heirs to the Greek intellectual tradition, medieval European scholars had good access to such information, and most fully accepted it. There were actually only a few eccentric thinkers who denied sphericity, most prominent among them being Cosmas Idicopleustes, author of *Christian Topography*. Columbus's major geographical departure was to argue for a small world, allowing easy access to Asia by sailing to the west. Here, of course, he was completely wrong. So why do most of us think that flat-earthers once prevailed? Simply put, during the battle over evolution in the late 1800s a few of Darwin's supporters got a bit carried away in denouncing the intellectual obstinacy of the Christian tradition.

Y chromosome indicates that many Lemba, particularly those of one clan, can indeed trace part of their ancestry back to ancient Jewish peoples. How they ended up in southern Africa, however, remains quite a mystery.

_05:: Islands That Were Never Colonized Follow Native Religions

The kingdom of Tonga was the only major archipelago in the South Pacific that was never colonized by a western power (although it was a British protectorate for many years), and it is still considered to be one of the most tra-ditional parts of Polynesia. But don't expect such tradition goes particularly deep when it comes to religion. Tonga is now one of the most devoutly Christian places in the world, resulting in a virtual shutdown of the country every Sunday. Four separate Methodist churches account for a majority of church attendance, but Mormonism is growing fast. By some accounts, up to one-third of Tongans are now Latter-Day Saints, making Tonga the most Mormon place—outside of Utah—in the world. Not surprisingly, Salt Lake City now has its own thriving Tongan community.

6 Places to Meet New People and Chew Their Saliva

If you're a firm believer in the "when in Rome, do as the Romans do" travel philosophy, be prepared to ingest some highly unusual substances when traveling to these places.

_01:: The South Pacific Saliva High

In much of the Pacific, kava is the traditional drug of choice. Kava supposedly reduces inhibitions and enhances conviviality, much like alcohol. However, it isn't the drug itself, so much as the traditional mode of preparation that often dismays outsiders. The active substance in kava is apparently released in interaction with chemicals contained in human saliva. Kava roots are thus thoroughly chewed, the masticated mass is wrung out in a twisted cloth, and the resulting liquid is then ready for drinking. Even though young people with good teeth and fresh breath are usually the designated chewers, kava drinking is still likely to put off the fastidious traveler.

_02:: Meet the Betels: A Southeast Asian Alternative

Kava drinking is, however, declining in parts of the western Pacific, where it is being gradually supplanted by betel chewing. Betel nut, actually the seed of a certain palm, chewed in combination with the leaf of a certain vine, is by some reports the third most popular recreational drug in the world (after alcohol and tobacco). From India through Southeast Asia and well into the Pacific, this mild intoxicant is often the drug of choice. Chewing it makes the saliva flow freely while coloring it deeply; if you see gloppy masses of red spittle all over the sidewalks, you know that you are in betel country. In many tribal societies of Southeast Asia, betel is a cornerstone of sociability; sharing one's stash is how friendships are cemented and courtships initiated. Whether it's good for the teeth, however, is a matter of some debate.

_03:: West African Cola

In much of West Africa, another area of habitual chewing, the drug of choice is cola. A mild stimulant, the main active ingredient of which is caffeine, cola has given its name—but not much more—to the common carbonated beverage of world renown. (Minute quantities of cola are, however, used in some colas.) Extremely bitter, cola itself has never found much favor outside of its place of origin. But West African history cannot be understood without reference to the nut. In earlier days, major caravans were organized to carry cola quickly from areas of production to areas of consumption, and major political struggles over the cola plantations were not unknown.

_04:: Leaves from the Andes

Coca-Cola itself derives its name, obviously, from coca as well as cola. Coca is the source of cocaine, but while the original recipe did indeed employ the real thing, the modern beverage uses only drug-free traces of coca extract. In the Andes Mountains, on the other hand, coca leaves are habitually chewed precisely for their stimulating effect. But a lot of patient chewing is required for even a fairly mild buzz, which prevents coca from causing

the kinds of psychological and social problems associated with cocaine. As a result, coca is fully legal in much of the Andes and is widely consumed. Intriguingly, in the days of the Incas coca chewing was tightly restricted, but when the Spanish came in its use was encouraged: the more the Indians chewed, the more silver they could mine.

Fake Your Way *through a Conversation*

THE ARMCHAIR GEOGRAPHER AS WORLD TRAVELER

There are few better ways to fake your way through cocktail party conversations than by learning geography. As people talk about their vacations to distant and exciting places, simply ask a few informed questions—and drop a few obscure place names—and they will tend to assume that you have been there yourself. If you really want to impress, you might focus on amusing place-names, especially if the conversation is focused on the British Isles. "When you visited Ireland," one might venture, "did you climb Macgillicuddy's Reeks or fish in the River Suck? It is especially noted for its pike, you know." "The Isle of Man is no doubt delightful, but the Calf of Man is really quite special." "My favorite Scottish islands are the threesome of Rhum, Eigg, and Muck, right off the Sound of Sleat." Or one can also compare Scotland's various firths, the best-named undoubtedly being the Firth of Forth. My own personal choice, however, has got to be the northernmost point of the Outer Hebrides: the Butt of Lewis.

_05:: Yemen's National Pastime

A somewhat similar drug of the Middle East is qat, the national obsession of Yemen. Every afternoon, much of Yemen simply shuts down as men gather together to chew great wads of qat and convivially discuss events. A few writers have gone so far as to blame Yemen's persistent poverty on the drug, largely because chewing it simply eats up so much time. A more reasonable concern is that qat cultivation is undermining Yemen's agriculture, as other crops are being abandoned in favor of the much more profitable drug. Yemen was once the world's major supplier of coffee, but those days are long gone. The Yemenis evidently think that they have found a better stimulant, even if most of the rest of the world begs to differ.

_06:: Siberian Mushrooms and More!

Qat, kava, cola, coca, and betel are all rather mild drugs that do little to truly alter one's consciousness. More powerful drugs, however, are central to a number of tribal societies across much of the world. The greatest diversity of psychoactive substances is found in the Amazonian rain forest, but the weirdest drug cult is probably that of fly agaric, a beautiful red-and-white mushroom. In Siberia and Lappland, shamans have traditionally used fly agaric to obtain sacred knowledge. In some Siberian societies, it is also popular with laypeople, but the mushrooms are rare and difficult to obtain. The poor thus sometimes take advantage of the fact that the active ingredient passes with almost full potency through the urinary tract (use your imagination!). The suggestion has even been made that the fly agaric cult infuses American popular culture in the person of a Lapp shaman nicely repackaged as Santa Claus. That would explain, after all, the flying reindeer.

by
Peter Haugen

Condensed
HISTORY

Contains

4 Civilizations Nobody Remembers ✳ 4 Regular Words with Epic Roots ✳ 3 Great Explorers You've Never Heard Of ✳ Bad Credit: 4 Bumbling Explorers History Still Adores ✳ A Row Is a Row Is a Row: 6 Misnamed Wars ✳ 4 Historical Commodities Brought to You by the Letter *S* ✳ 5 Women Who Proved to Be the Right Man for the Job ✳ 5 Women with Chops on the Battlefield ✳ You Say You Want a Revolutionary: 4 Reluctant Leaders ✳ 3 African Rulers Who Built Formidable (If Now Forgotten) Nations ✳ Rotten to the Corps: 8 Tyrants with Horrific Rap Sheets ✳ 7 World Leaders You Don't Know by Name ✳

Civilizations Nobody Remembers

Sure, you've got your Mesopotamians, your Egyptians, your classical Greeks, but the checklist of early civilizations—from military and trade powers to technological innovators—stretches quite a bit further. Here are four ancient cultures that rarely get their names dropped.

_01:: The Minoan Civilization

Around 3000 BCE a rich and resilient civilization arose on the Mediterranean island of Crete. The Minoans thrived there and on nearby isles for many centuries. While invaders, possibly sailing from Mycenae (an early Greek city-state) did prey on them, this civilization's death blow actually came from a massive volcanic explosion around 1500 BCE. It triggered tidal waves and released sky-choking clouds of ash. Some say the legend of Atlantis is based on this sea-swamped culture. Its ruins lay forgotten until 1900 CE, when British archaeologist Arthur Evans dug up Crete's fabulous palace of Knossos. Evans followed in the footsteps of Heinrich Schliemann, an inspired amateur who had earlier unearthed Troy, showing that the legendary city wasn't mere legend and that there really were lost civilizations.

_02:: The Hittites

By 1700 BCE these people, originally migrants from beyond the Black Sea, were thriving in Asia Minor (today's Turkey), where they built an empire that at its peak stretched east into Iraq and south to Syria. In the 1300s BCE Hittite power and wealth rivaled that of Egypt,

the Hittites' sometime enemy. About 100 years later, the Hittite civilization suffered a sudden, steep decline as Sea Peoples, who were raiding sailors, migrated into Hittite territories. Hittites kept historical records, but they stopped abruptly, so nobody today knows the details of their downfall. A few linguists even think that the Hittite language (they call it Indo-Hittite) was the root of all later Indo-European languages such as the various Germanic and Celtic tongues.

_03:: Sea Peoples

These marine raiders were like the Vikings, except much, much earlier (1200s and 1100s BCE instead of the 700s through 900s CE) and based in the Mediterranean. Sea Peoples terrorized far-flung ports for fun and profit and even waged wars against foes as formidable as Egypt. No one knows exactly who they were or why they were so aggressive, but these sailors most likely included Greeks and Sardinians—people from places with limited fertile land. This probably encouraged them to look elsewhere for economic advantage. In fact, one reason Hittites are little known is that invading Sea Peoples appear to have wiped out their empire.

_04:: The Nazca

From a plane flying over the Palpa Valley of southern Peru, you can make out figures of animals and geometric shapes made from massive lines etched in the earth atop surrounding mesas. A people called the Nazca dug them. Contemporary with the technologically advanced Moche people to their north (South American civilizations didn't begin with the Inca), the Nazca also made beautiful ceramics, paintings, and sophisticated fabrics woven of alpaca wool and cotton from about 1 to 900 CE. Their giant dirt sculptures, which can be recognized only from the air, have been cited as evidence of long-ago visits from other planets. More likely, they were laid out in accordance with astronomical observations and were meant to be viewed by sky gods.

Regular Words with Epic Roots

If you want to see your old professor swell with pride, try garnishing your sentences with some of this historically laced vocab.

_01:: Draconian

In the late 600s BCE the Greek city-state of Athens got a new set of laws, drawn up by an official called Draco. These weren't the first Athenian laws, or even the first to be written down, but they were systematic and codified as never before. They were also cruel. Even minor offenses were punishable by death. Draco himself died after guests at a reception in his honor showered him with their cloaks—a gesture of respect. He suffocated. Not long after, another lawgiver, Solon, struck down Draco's code in favor of a more compassionate system. Draco's laws may have been short-lived, but his name lives on as the adjective *draconian*, meaning unusually harsh. Solon's name is an English synonym for legislator.

_02:: Justice

Flavius Petrus Sabbatius (483–565 CE) was just a poor boy from Illyria (today's Albania) who became Byzantine emperor. Adopted by his uncle, the emperor Justin, young Flavius added *Justinianus* to his name and succeeded to the throne as Justinian I. Considered a great ruler, Justinian fought barbarians in Italy and corruption in Constantinople, but he is best remembered for collecting and organizing the best Roman statutes in the *Codex constitutionum* in 529 CE. (The Byzantine Empire was a latter-day, eastern extension of the Roman Empire.) Known as Justinian's Code, this system underlies many laws still used today. It's also a source of our modern concept of impartial judgment and fair punishment. Justinian's name, by way of Latin and French, became a word for that concept.

_03:: Guy

Guy Fawkes (1570–1606) almost succeeded in blowing up James I and the king's entire government in 1605. Although he was born in Yorkshire, Fawkes's pro-Catholic sentiments led him to a career in the Spanish army. When Catholic activists in England grew desperate over government persecution, they sent for Fawkes to attempt their assassination plan, the Gunpowder Plot. Caught in a Parliament cellar full of explosives, Fawkes was arrested, tortured, and executed. The English commemorate his arrest every November 5, Guy Fawkes Day, by burning him in effigy. Over the centuries, the word *guy* meant one of these effigies, then it evolved to mean any stuffed dummy, then a dull man, then a regular bloke. Now just about everybody is a guy.

_04:: Sandwich

Before it was food, Sandwich was a town in England. When Edward Montagu, an English admiral, was made an earl in 1660, he took the place name as part of his title. A century later his descendant John Montagu, fourth Earl of Sandwich (1718–1792), sat down to a game of cards and didn't leave the table for the next 24 hours. For this dedicated gambler, sleep was as nothing. Food, however, was another matter. To keep up his strength, he called for chunks of meat between two slices of bread. Voilà, a cuisine was born.

What's the Difference?
SPOTTING BC FROM BCE

On the one hand you've got the BC and AD camp, and on the other you've got BCE and CE supporters. So, what's the difference? As a young John Lennon once said about his flowing hair, "It's just fashion." If you grew up with BC and AD and now find yourself dealing with BCE and CE, remember that academic styles change. Late in the 20th century, some historians decided that BC and AD wouldn't do anymore. Those initials go back to Dionysius Exiguus (Denny the Little), who invented the modern calendar in 525 (AD or CE). As a Christian abbot, he keyed everything to Jesus's birth. AD, for *anno Domini* (year of Our Lord), counted forward from that date. BC, or Before Christ, counted backward. Recent scholars, however, felt the system was too centered on just one religion, so they changed AD to CE, for Common Era, and BC to BCE, for Before the Common Era. And wisely, they left the year numbers alone. So, doesn't that mean that the years still count from when Jesus was born? It would, except that Denny miscalculated. Most scholars now think that Jesus was born between 4 and 6 BCE.

Great Explorers You've Never Heard Of

Some guys have all the luck: Columbus got his own day, Lewis and Clark got their own university, and Marco Polo got his own water game. Sure, the following explorers were a little press-shy, but that doesn't mean you shouldn't know them.

_01:: Pytheas (ca. 300 BCE)

In the period just after Alexander the Great, a Greek sailor ventured through the Strait of Gibraltar, into the Atlantic, and up the coast of Europe. The Greeks were masterful navigators, who had planted their colonies all around the Mediterranean, but Pytheas (he lived in Marseilles) went far beyond their world. He reached Cornwall, explored the British Isles, and continued on, probably to the Baltic Sea and Norway, which he called Ultima Thule. Some historians think Pytheas might have landed on Iceland. Pytheas chronicled his travels in his book *On the Ocean*. While it hasn't survived, the historian Polybius wrote about Pytheas in the 100s BCE. That's how we know about his observations, including his accurate distance measurements, astronomical readings, and reports on fair-haired northern folk.

_02:: Abdullah Muhammad ibn Battuta
(1304–1368 or 1369)

In 1325 this well-born young man left his native Tangier, in North Africa, for a pilgrimage to Mecca. Going by way of Egypt, where he studied to be an Islamic judge, Ibn Battuta was bitten by wanderlust. Over succeeding decades he logged an estimated 75,000 miles—more than any other traveler before the steam age—visiting every part of the Muslim world and beyond, ranging as far as Sumatra and China to the east, Georgia to the north, Granada in Spain, and across the Sahara Desert to Sudan. Back home in 1353, Ibn Battuta hired a Moroccan poet to help him write his richly detailed travelogue, *Rihlih*. It vividly describes 60 rulers he met, including the treacherous sultan of Mogul India, Muhammad ibn Tughluq.

_03:: Cheng Ho (ca. 1371–ca. 1473)

In 1381 the Ming dynasty conquered the last Mongol stronghold in China. Ming soldiers captured Mongol boys, castrated them, and placed them in the emperor's service. Apparently holding no grudge, one of those boys grew up to command the emperor's great naval expeditions in the early 1400s—sailing to India, the Persian Gulf, and Africa. Cheng Ho (sometimes spelled Zheng He) made seven voyages, visiting capitals in Arabia, Egypt, and even Mozambique. Some modern theorists, notably British author Gavin Menzies and the Zheng He Association in London, argue that certain shipwrecks in the Caribbean, stone inscriptions in the Americas, and even a 1424 navigational chart prove that the Chinese traveled much farther, circumnavigating the earth a century before Magellan did.

Bad Credit:

Bumbling Explorers History Still Adores

So much for honesty being the best policy. These cats fell woefully short of their destinations but still nabbed the credit.

_01:: Christopher Columbus (1451–1506)

Columbus insisted throughout his life that he had found some fringe of Asia. He had no interest in discovering new continents in 1492. He wanted storied lands of old. China, India, and Indonesia were the prize destinations sought by European explorers of the late 1400s, not wild new places. Columbus took some comfort and derived a bit of wealth from the gold he found in the Caribbean, but through the troubled rest of his life, including two more voyages to the New World, he never gave up on the idea that Haiti must be Japan, Cuba was China itself, and South America could be a biblical earthly paradise. Imagining India nearby, he kept seeking a passage to it.

_02:: Ferdinand Magellan (ca. 1480–1521)

Everybody learns in school that Ferdinand Magellan was the first sailor to go around the world, proving that the world is, indeed, round. Few remember that he conceived the voyage and commanded the mission but never completed it. Magellan died in May 1521 when he unwisely got involved in a fight between two tribes of natives in the Philippines. Late the next year only one of his five ships, captained by Juan Sebastián de Elcano and manned by a tattered, starving skeleton crew, arrived back

in Spain. Still, it had been Magellan's determination that got them through the treacherous strait (named for him) at the southern end of

---

Fake Your Way through a Conversation

WHY WE'LL TAKE VASCO DA GAMA OVER COLUMBUS ANY DAY

Love him for "discovering" America or hate him for despoiling it, Christopher Columbus today ranks as main man among explorers of the late 1400s, while Vasco da Gama of Portugal gets honorable mention. Yet in their time it was Gama, not Columbus, who grabbed more glory. How? It's simple. Both Columbus in 1492 and Gama in 1497 went looking for a sea route from Europe to the rich trading ports of Asia. Columbus, sailing west, ran into a strange part of the globe that nobody cared about—not yet, anyway. Gama, on the other hand, hit pay dirt. Heading south around Africa and then north and east, he landed in Calicut, on the west coast of India. In other words, he accomplished what he set out to do. By that standard, Columbus failed miserably.

South America and across the Pacific, which he named, mistakenly, for its "calm" waters.

_03:: Juan Ponce de León (1460–1521)

After joining Columbus on his second voyage to the Americas in 1493, Ponce de León became Spanish governor of both Hispaniola (the island that today includes the Dominican Republic and Haiti) and then Puerto Rico. Puerto Rican natives told him a legend of a spring on the island of Bimini in the Bahamas that would make anyone who drank its water young again. Trying to find this island and its miraculous fountain of youth, Ponce de León landed instead on the east coast of Florida. Not knowing he had found the North American continent, he named the new "island" for the time of year and for its lush plant life (*Pascua Florida* is Spanish for "flowers Easter"). On his next visit to Florida, Ponce's quest for the fountain of youth was tragically cut short when he was hit by a Seminole arrow.

_04:: Sir John Franklin (1786–1847)

Franklin, late in his career as a British navy officer and explorer, set off in 1845 to find the Northwest Passage, a northern water route from the Atlantic to the Pacific. He died lost midway between the oceans. By 1850 every member of his expedition was starving or frozen. After ice trapped their two ships, sinking one, crew members set off on foot. Remains of a few were found years later near a waterway that connected with the Pacific. Franklin failed, but the many expeditions sent to find his missing party learned a great deal more about the geography of the far north. So, indirectly, his voyage proved the Northwest Passage really existed. Roald Amundsen of Norway finally sailed it successfully in 1905.

Timeline

COME AND KNOCK ON MY DOOR (WHEN ADVENTUROUS OUTSIDERS FIRST GOT THERE)

326 BCE Alexander the Great leads his army east across the Indus River and invades India.

300 BCE Greek navigator Pytheas sails west from Massalia, Gaul (Marseilles, France), past Gibraltar, heads north, and ends up in Norway.

55 BCE Julius Caesar invades Britain.

1000 CE Norse sailors from Greenland, led by Leif Eriksson, land in North America.

1265 Venetian brothers Niccolò and Maffeo Polo visit Mongol emperor Kublai Khan in Shangdu, Inner Mongolia. (Niccolò's son, Marco, will accompany the merchants on their next trek east.)

1413 Admiral Cheng Ho of China, having already visited Arabia and Egypt, sails to Malindi (in what is now Kenya).

1492 Columbus lands on his first New World island, probably San Salvador in the Bahamas.

1498 Vasco da Gama sails into the port of Calicut, in southwestern India.

1616 Dirk Hartog of Holland, a sea captain on his way to Indonesia, sets foot on the west coast of Australia. Seeing nothing of interest, he sails away.

1642 Dutch navigator Abel Janszoon Tasman lands on New Zealand. Islanders attack his landing party and kill several crewmen.

1980 Hollywood actor Harrison Ford moves to Jackson Hole, Wyoming.

A Row Is a Row Is a Row: Misnamed Wars

6

Sometimes not everybody agrees on what to call a war. Sometimes the name choices seem deliberately calculated to confuse you on a history test. The following wars came out with mixed-up monikers.

_01:: The Hundred Years War

Depending how you do the math, the war took more or less than a century. From 1337 to 1453, the English kept attacking France. But the foes didn't fight the whole time. The war started as a quarrel over English-held lands on the European continent. Also, England's Edward III thought he should rule France. Naturally, French king Philip VI disagreed. Phil tried to snatch Aquitaine, a French region ruled by Ed. This led to generations' worth of battles, but there were truces—some quite long. Peace broke out in 1360, for example, and lasted nine years. In 1396 England's Richard II married the daughter of France's Charles VI. That truce lasted 28 years. It finally took an internal conflict called the Wars of the Roses (see below) for England to give up the cause.

_02:: The Wars of the Roses

A battle over bouquets? Nope. The Wars (or War) of the Roses consisted of a fight between Yorks and Lancasters—two English families descended from Edward III (see above). They battled from 1455 to 1487. After Henry VI, a Lancaster, had a mental breakdown, his cousin Richard, Duke of York, took over as Protector of the Crown. Henry recovered. Richard, cit-

ing his own hereditary claim to the throne, refused to hand back the reins. Richard's son became Edward IV, whose rule was interrupted when Henry briefly regained power. So it went for decades, getting even more sordid in 1483. That's when Richard III (a York) came to power, but only after he had his little nephew Edward V (another York) declared illegitimate and then allegedly murdered the boy. Finally, Henry Tudor, a Lancaster on his mother's side, defeated Richard III in battle and became Henry VII. So, how did Hank restore the peace? He married a York. Oh, and those roses? They were family symbols—red for Lancaster, white for York.

_03:: The War of Jenkins's Ear

By some accounts, he was a slave trader, smuggler, and pub brawler. Others paint Robert Jenkins as a respectable English sea captain. As Jenkins told it, Spanish coast guards in 1731—trying to keep the British from trading in Spain's Caribbean colonies—boarded his ship, *Rebecca*; seized the captain; and cut off one of his ears. Doubters charged that he had lost the appendage in a drunken melee. Either way, Jenkins saved his ear in a jar of alcohol. The memento came in handy in 1738 when London politicians, arguing in favor of war with Spain, displayed both Jenkins and the severed ear before the House of Commons. It worked. Britain declared war. Fought in the West Indies from 1739 to 1741, this naval conflict blended into the more wide-ranging King George's War (see below).

_04:: French and Indian/Seven Years' War

Colonists in America named the 1754–1763 fight after the enemy (French troops and their Native American allies), but math-impaired Londoners named it for its duration. Actually, the F&I War was the final episode of a four-part struggle between France and England for control of North America. Marked by shifts in alliances and fought in Europe and Asia as well as in the New World, these wars would be confusing even if every one *didn't* have a different name on either side of the Atlantic. They also included:

1689–1697 King William's War (America)/
    the War of the Grand Alliance (Europe)
1701–1713 Queen Anne's War (America)/
    the War of the Spanish Succession
    (Europe)
1744–1748 King George's War (America)/
    the War of the Austrian Succession
    (Europe)

In the end, the British emerged victorious, gaining French Canada and other territories.

_05:: The Civil War/War Between the States/The War for Southern Independence

The brutal 1861–1865 conflict, in which the U.S. government fought to reign in a breakaway region, is best known as the Civil War. But many southerners prefer War between the States or, among the real Dixie diehards, the War for southern independence. If you're an American using the term *Civil War*, remember that other countries, England and Spain among them, have suffered their own internal uprisings. It could be a good idea to specify which civil war you mean.

_06:: World War I/The Great War

It wasn't called World War I until World War II came along. In the intervening decades this massive, Europe-centered fight was generally referred to as the Great War (*great* in the sense of *big*, not *extra good*). Lasting from 1914 to 1918, this war—fought largely from hand-dug defensive trenches—pitted the Central powers (Germany, Austro-Hungary, and the Ottoman Empire) against the Allied powers (Britain, France, Russia, Italy, and the United States, which finally waded into the brawl in 1917). Some old-timers continued to call the hostilities "the big one," even during and after the second big one. Another popular phrase, coined by U.S. President Woodrow Wilson, was "a war to end all wars." Obviously, that didn't work out.

Historical Commodities Brought to You by the Letter *S*

Just as the petroleum oil trade plays a major part in coloring today's international politics, it's tough to understand history without considering the crucial role these four *S*-words have played.

_01:: Silk

By 2500 BCE China already had a silk industry. By about 1000 BCE they were exporting silk to India, Turkistan, and Persia. More than any other commodity, silk was the basis of early trade along a 4,000-mile caravan track from China to the Mediterranean still known as the Silk Route (or Silk Road). Silk's value was such that you could buy livestock or pay taxes with it. The ability to make silk became such an economic advantage that in the 500s CE Byzantine emperor Justinian I sent two Persian monks on an undercover mission to smuggle silkworms out of China. During the Song dynasty (960–1279 CE), Chinese emperors doled out more than 500,000 bales of silk annually to bordering rulers, buying their goodwill.

_02:: Spices

Along with silk, spices such as cinnamon and ginger traveled overland from the Far East to the Middle East from early times. But even in the Renaissance, spices were rare and expensive farther west. Merchants of Venice, which ruled a small empire in the eastern Mediterranean, got very rich bringing spices to western Europe in the 1300s and 1400s. That's why Spain and Portugal wanted sea routes to India and why Columbus tried to sail to China. Magellan's round-the-world quest was such a success because the one ship that made it home in 1522 (out of five that set out in 1519) carried a fortune in cloves. Sailors on pepper ships later had their pockets sewn shut so they wouldn't steal the pricey cargo.

What's the Difference?

HOW TO TELL A QUEEN FROM A QUEEN MOTHER

In other words, when is a queen not *the* queen? Cross-dressers aside, the word *queen* refers to a female ruler, such as England's Queen Elizabeth I of the 1500s. The current Elizabeth's late mother was also considered a queen, but not *the* queen. As George VI's wife, she was queen consort, or spouse. When George died, his daughter Elizabeth succeeded him, so her mom (also named Elizabeth) then changed from queen consort to queen mother. While there's no such thing as a king consort, Elizabeth has given her husband, Philip, the title "prince of the United Kingdom."

_03:: Salt

An essential part of the human and animal diet and a crucial tool in preserving meat, fish, and dairy products, salt has been a lynchpin economic and strategic commodity throughout history. Soldiers of the Roman Empire even received an allowance of salt (the origin of the English word *salary*). In various eras people in Ethiopia and other parts of Africa have used cakes of salt to pay their debts. "Without salt they cannot make bacon and salt beef," said Union general William Tecumseh Sherman about his enemy in the U.S. Civil War. "Salt is eminently contraband, because [of] its use in curing meats, without which armies cannot be subsisted." In fact, Sherman even charged one of his captains with aiding the enemy for letting the rebels acquire the seasoning.

_04:: Slaves

What's most distressing about slavery is how widespread and common it was. Egyptians kept and dealt in slaves. So did classical Greeks, Romans, Arabs, and Vikings. Although rooted in warfare (prisoners of war were among the first slaves), economic advantage sustained slaving. In the 1500s and 1600s, colonists in the Americas looked to Africa for a forced labor base. Portuguese ships (followed by Spanish, English, and Dutch) obliged. A triangular trade developed in which molasses, rum, and tobacco went to Europe (or New England), where profits bought manufactured goods that were traded in West Africa for slaves to be shipped back to the Americas. It was usually more complicated than that (isn't it always), but to the traders, human beings were just another commodity.

5

Women Who Proved to Be the Right Man for the Job

Turns out, there isn't a correlation between testosterone and brain power after all. Who knew?

_01:: Elizabeth I of England (1533–1603)

Her daddy, Henry VIII, wanted a boy to succeed him (his life, not to mention England's history, was notoriously complicated by this desire), and young Bess didn't seem destined to rule. She was the third of Henry's children to wear the crown. Yet she proved the only one with a talent for government. Unlike her sickly half-brother, Edward, and unlike their spendthrift half-sister, Mary, known as Bloody Mary for her persecution of the Protestants, Bess knew how to manage people. Over a long reign, from 1558 to 1603, the Virgin Queen used sharp political instincts to solidify her power at home and internationally. Her firm rule gave foundation to a golden age, as English sea power, world exploration, trade, and arts (including the playwright Shakespeare) ascended.

_02:: Jinga Mbandi of Ndongo
(ca. 1580–1663)

She preferred the title "king," and she kept a harem of young men, whom she dressed in women's clothes. This monarch of west central Africa made her mark first in nervy negotiations with the encroaching Portuguese, but she was just as adept at the use of force. Over the course of a long, eventful reign, she personally led forces into battle both against neighboring tribes and against encroaching Europeans. Jinga came to power only after her brother, who preceded her as ruler, met a mysterious death. Legend says she killed both him and his young son to secure the throne. Far from delicate in her sensibilities, she reportedly devoured the slain prince's heart and drank human blood.

_03:: Nellie Bly (1867–1922)

Elizabeth Cochrane was a poor Pennsylvania teenager in 1885 when she wrote an angry letter to the *Pittsburgh Dispatch*, responding to an article saying women were meant for housework and child rearing. The *Dispatch* editor hired her and even sent her to Mexico to write about poverty. Soon, her byline—taken from a Stephen Foster song—caught the eye of Joseph Pulitzer. He hired "Nellie Bly" for his sensationalist *New York World*. Pulitzer made his star reporter the best-known American woman of a century ago. Most celebrated for a Pulitzer stunt—a 73-day trip around the world, beating author Jules Verne's fictional 80-day trip—Bly also wrote exposés of incompetence and corruption in mental asylums, jails, and sweatshops, and her stories prompted reform.

_04:: Golda Meir (1898–1978)

A wife and mother of two, Goldie Mabovitch Myerson dedicated her public life to the dream of a strong, independent Israel. Born in Russia, she grew up in Wisconsin, and after a stint as a Milwaukee schoolteacher, she moved with her husband to a kibbutz, or communal farm, in what was then British Palestine. She began rising through decades of labor union, political, and government positions—including legislator, envoy, and foreign minister. Golda Meir (as she renamed herself) became Israeli prime minister in 1968. Renowned for tough-mindedness, she nevertheless took the blame after a concerted attack by Arab nations caught Israel unprepared in the Yom Kippur War of 1973. At great cost, Israel won the war. Meir's party won that year's elections, but she soon resigned.

_05:: Indira Gandhi (1917–1984)

The daughter of independent India's first prime minister, Jawaharlal Nehru, Indira Gandhi served as his official state hostess. After the death of her politician husband, she won election to India's Parliament in 1964 and two years later became prime minister. She quickly won great popularity—especially after India defeated Pakistan in a 1971 border war. But she also made enemies and mistakes. Convicted of illegal campaigning, she defied a 1975 court order to resign. Instead she suspended civil rights, censored the media, and persecuted critics. Although voted out of office in 1977, she won the prime minister's post again three years later. Fighting a separatist movement, she ordered a military attack on a Sikh shrine in 1984. Two of her bodyguards, militant Sikhs, took revenge, assassinating her.

5 Women with Chops on the Battlefield

A few women leaders have taken a distinctly hands-on—not to mention violent—approach to conflict. Here's the dirt on women who were much happier playing the field than cheering from the sidelines.

_01:: Trung Trac and her sister,
_02:: Trung Nhi (birth dates unknown, died 43 CE)

In 39 CE two noblewomen led Vietnamese aristocrats in an armed march against their Chinese rulers. Trung Trac took up the cause after a Chinese officer killed her husband, a local lord, for plotting against China's Han dynasty. First, Trac and Nhi drove out the Chinese general in charge of Lien Lau. Within a year they conquered 65 other Chinese strongholds. They ruled as queens until 43 CE, when China attacked. With neither a professional army nor peasant support, Vietnam's nobles could not withstand the assault. The Trungs fought the invasion near present-day Hanoi, then retreated and regrouped for one last battle. Defeated, the sisters refused to surrender. Instead, they held hands, jumped into a river together, and drowned.

_03:: Boudicca (died 60 CE)

Romans in 60 CE Britain didn't know whom they were messing with. When tribal king Prasutagus (in what is now Norfolk) died leaving no male heir, the Romans grabbed his kingdom. They persecuted his family and the chiefs that had been under Prasutagus's protection. The king's angry widow, Boudicca, responded by rallying locals and charging through East Anglia, slaughtering thousands of Romans (and Britons who supported them) and burning towns from Camulodunum (Colchester) to the Roman outpost of Londinium (London). Boudicca's rebels sliced to pieces the Roman Ninth Legion. Finally the Roman governor, Suetonius Paulinus, who had been out of the country, came back with troops enough to beat her, although it was a tough fight. Boudicca died soon after, most probably after drinking poison.

_04:: Joan of Arc (ca. 1412–1431)

France's national heroine was an earnest teenager who heard saints telling her to fight for Charles, heir to the French throne. Pious and persistent at only 16, she convinced Charles (later Charles VII) to let her lead troops in the Hundred Years War. In 1429 she shrewdly took advantage of a military diversion to enter the besieged city of Orléans with much-needed supplies. Then she led successful attacks on surrounding English forts. This swung the war's momentum in Charles's favor. Later captured, Joan endured a torturous trial by French church officials aligned with the English. They convicted her of crimes that included heresy and wearing men's clothes. Burned as a heretic, she became a martyr. The Vatican later rescinded the heresy verdict and finally, almost five centuries after she died, consecrated her as a saint.

_05:: Lakshmi Bai (died 1858)

When the maharaja of Jhansi, a principality in northern India, died in 1853, the British governor general announced that since the ruler had left no heir, Britain would annex Jhansi. If the governor had studied his own country's history (see Boudicca, above) he might have seen what would happen next. The maharaja's widow (her title was maharani or rani for short) tried reason, pointing out that she and her late husband had an infant son. The governor said the boy didn't count because he was adopted. Angered, Rani Lakshmi Bai assembled an army to defend Jhansi. They fought valiantly but eventually fell to the overwhelming British onslaught. Instead of surrendering, the maharani slipped away on horseback and led a wide-scale Indian rebellion. She died in battle.

You Say You Want a Revolutionary: Reluctant Leaders

Some men are born revolutionaries, some men achieve revolutions, and some men have revolutions thrust upon them. The following can be lumped with the last.

_01:: Martin Luther (1483–1586)

A Catholic priest and university professor, Luther nailed his 95 Theses (arguments against the sale of indulgences, a Church method of raising money) on a church door in Wittenberg in 1517 as a call for debate. Instead, he triggered the Protestant Reformation, an upheaval not just of religious practice but also of Europe's entire power structure. At first Luther was appalled at the popular revolt, but when Holy Roman Emperor Charles V asked him to recant, Luther refused with a line that became famous: "Here I stand. I can do no other. God help me. Amen." He meant "nope." Expecting to be arrested and killed, Luther instead found himself kidnapped— not by the emperor, but by the sympathetic prince Frederick the Wise of Saxony. Fred snatched Luther for his own protection and kept him safely locked away in a cozy castle, where Luther wrote more arguments against Church excesses.

_02:: Benjamin Franklin (1706–1790)

For most of his prolific career as a printer, publisher, author, scientist, and inventor, Franklin remained a devoted British subject. He lived in London briefly as a young man and again for 17 years (1757–1775) just before the American Revolution. Although proud of his colonial origin, he referred to himself as "an Old England man" and artfully negotiated the post of British royal governor of New Jersey for his son, making Will Franklin the first American-born appointee to such an office. Ben Franklin tried to avert the split with Britain, but he was alarmed when some colonists tried to blame him for the hated British tax law called the Stamp Act. When Ben saw the inevitable, he sided with his fellow Americans.

_03:: Simón Bolívar (1783–1830)

Inspired by some of the same ideas that fired the American and French revolutions, Bolívar led South Americans in Venezuela, Ecuador, Colombia, Bolivia, and Peru as they threw off Spanish rule in the early 1800s. Yet "the Liberator" (as he was known) never quite embraced democracy. A wealthy aristocrat by birth and upbringing, Bolívar envisioned Hispanic-American republics in which hereditary power—as in the British House of Lords—restrained the popular will. And he argued that the office of president should be held for life. As president himself (in both Gran Colombia—later split into Venezuela, Ecuador, and Colombia—and Peru), he was more dictator than public servant. When he drafted a constitution for Bolivia (named for him), Bolívar restricted the right to vote to an elite class.

_04:: Robert E. Lee (1807–1870)

The Confederacy's greatest general started out as an opponent of Southern secession. As a U.S. Army officer and the son of a Revolutionary War hero ("Light-Horse Harry" Lee),

Strange but True

BEN FRANKLIN LIKED TO WORK IN THE BUFF!

It's true! Benjamin Franklin sat around naked, usually with the window open for the breeze. In a 1768 letter to a friend, Jacques Barbeu-Dubourg, Franklin described his "air bath" ritual in detail: "I rise early almost every morning, and sit in my chamber, without any clothes whatever, half an hour or an hour, according to the season, either reading or writing. This practice is not in the least painful, but on the contrary, agreeable; and if I return to bed afterwards, before I dress myself, as sometimes happens, I make a supplement to my night's rest, of one or two hours of the most pleasing sleep that can be imagined. I find no ill consequences whatever resulting from it."

Robert E. Lee felt strong allegiance to the United States. Yet he also felt that the nation should *not* go to war against its breakaway states. In 1861 Lee was offered command of a U.S. force being assembled to attack the Southern rebels. He turned it down. Later that year, after his beloved home state, Virginia, joined the Confederacy, Lee regretfully resigned his U.S. Army commission after 36 years of service and offered his allegiance to the South.

African Rulers Who Built Formidable (If Now Forgotten) Nations

In the 1800s the African map became a colonial patchwork of European flags, obscuring the memory of what had come before. But whites didn't just march in and take over; they had to deal with accomplished home-grown leaders.

_01:: Usman dan Fodio (1754–1817)

In the early 1800s Usman, an Islamic teacher and philosopher descended from the nomadic Fulani people, accused the king of Gobir (in what is now northern Nigeria) of failing to rule by Muslim law. Winning widespread support, Usman led a revolt that brought down the king and allied rulers of the region. He became caliph of a theocratic Fulani empire encompassing much of Nigeria and parts of Mali, Niger, Cameroon, and Chad. More interested in religious practice than administration, the pious Usman put his brother and son in charge of running the empire's emirates while he continued to teach. Decades of British pressure eventually wore away Fulani rule. The emirate of Sokoto, last bastion of Fulani power, finally fell to Britain in 1903.

_02:: Shaka (ca. 1787–1828)

Shaka's parents were of different tribes but the same clan, which broke a taboo in what is now South Africa. During his late-1700s boyhood, members of his mother's Langeni tribe persecuted Shaka for her sin, instilling in him a deep rage. In 1816 Shaka succeeded his father as chief of the small Zulu tribe. He quickly reorganized its army into a ruthless

---

Strange but True

ALEXANDER THE GREAT'S SWEETER SIDE

It can't be proved, but tradition says that after he died, Alexander the Great's body was preserved in honey. Why? As the most famous, most powerful person in the world, an elaborate funeral carriage was commissioned to escort his body from Babylon, where he died, to his birthplace in Macedon. This ornate hearse took two years to build—24 months in a hot climate, 24 centuries before refrigeration. And that's where the honey probably came in. The thick, sweet substance works as a natural preservative, admitting no oxygen, so the young conqueror's body maintained that dewy-fresh look (as opposed to mummification, which involves drying). As it turned out, though, the corpse never got home. Ptolemy Sotor, Alexander's appointed governor in Egypt, hijacked the funeral caravan to Memphis (not the one in Tennessee) and put his body on display before entombing it.

force that wiped out rivals and absorbed survivors of other tribes, including the Langeni. More bold and arrogant than shrewd, Shaka allowed Europeans to come ashore at Durban because he considered his own culture so far superior that the strangers presented no threat. Becoming murderously insane after his mother's 1827 death, Shaka angered his top officers, including his two half-brothers. They assassinated him. The Zulus finally fell to the British in 1879.

_03:: Samory Touré (ca. 1830–1900)

A West African reformer, religious leader, and military commander, Touré, a Muslim from a Mande village in what is today Guinea, proclaimed himself a chief in 1868 and by the 1880s had put together a big, rich, well-run kingdom. Trading gold and ivory for guns, he attacked and defeated neighboring chiefs, and also fought the French, whose growing African empire was threatening to nibble away at his borders. After his forces failed to turn back a French attack in 1883, he accepted French dominance, but only temporarily. He turned on the Europeans again in 1891. Eventually they pushed Touré out of his territory and then, when he tried to set up a new coastal kingdom, captured him in 1898. Exiled to Gabon, he died two years later.

Rotten to the Corps:
Tyrants with Horrific Rap Sheets

Hitler is squarely to blame for the six million Jews shot, gassed, or worked to death in his government's concentration camps, but should he also be charged with *all* the estimated 50 million deaths in World War II, a conflict he started? It's impossible to rank the world's deadliest leaders, but all these guys would make the list.

_01:: Adolf Hitler (1889–1945)

He wasn't crazy but calculatingly brutal. No surviving document shows that Hitler personally ordered the deaths of millions of Jews, Romany (Gypsies), homosexuals, the disabled, and other "defectives" in the Nazi camps, but it's clear that he did it. Hitler revealed his ambition for a Germany purged of Jews in many speeches and conversations, later collected in book form and in other writings, including his autobiography, *Mein Kampf*. In a way, he actually did create the New Germany he dreamed about. The Jewish population of Europe was drastically reduced, not only through mass murder but through emigration—before, during, and after the war. When Jewish survivors were finally liberated from the death camps, many had nobody left and nowhere to return. Their families were dead, their houses confiscated or destroyed.

The Nazis had wiped out entire villages. Of course, Hitler did not limit himself to picking on the powerless. He also took on rivals such as Ernst Röhm, commander of the Nazi storm troopers. In 1934, after they had helped bring him to power, Hitler ordered the murders of Röhm and dozens of other *Sturmtruppen* leaders.

_02:: Joseph Stalin (1879–1953)

As secretary-general of the Communist Party of the Soviet Union (1922–1953) and Soviet premier (1941–1953), "Uncle Joe" ruthlessly asserted his will. When his program to turn Russia's farms into collectives met resistance, he sent soldiers to shoot uncooperative peasants, killing perhaps 100,000 of them. When he sought to consolidate his power, he arranged for the murder of Sergei Kirov, his chief rival. Then, on the pretext of rooting out the assassins, he had his former party comrades sent to death camps, along with millions of other Russians perceived as threats to his absolute authority. The Soviet Union lost not just party bosses and farmers but military leaders, government officials, industry managers, diplomats, artists, and more. Nobody knows exactly how many Stalin killed. Estimates range from ten million to three times that.

_03:: Mao Ze-dong (1893–1976)

Unlike Stalin, he never ordered assassinations; unlike Hitler, he did not attempt genocide. The peasant-born Mao became a revolutionary as a young man, took over leadership of the Chinese Communist Party in 1931, served as chairman (head of state) of the newly declared People's Republic of China from 1949 to 1959, and remained party chair until his death. By pushing endless class warfare and ordering violent political and social reforms, Chairman Mao brought about horrible famines in which some starving peasant families resorted to cannibalism. He inspired repression, torture, and widespread humiliation that led to mass suicides. Victims of his Great Leap Forward—a failed attempt to build a rural industrial base in the 1950s—and his Cultural Revolution—a mass attack on intellectuals and the privileged in the 1960s and 1970s—probably number in the tens of millions.

_04:: Ismail Enver Pasa (1881–1922), _05:: Mehmed Talat Pasa (1871–1921), and _06:: Ahmed Cemal Pasa (1872–1922)

The Young Turk revolution of 1908 brought this triumvirate to power in the Ottoman Empire (Turkey) before World War I. ("Pasa" or "pasha" is a Turkish title of high rank and respect.) In 1915 and 1916 perhaps 600,000 (some estimates range as high as 2 million) members of the country's Armenian population died during a forced relocation. Armenian activists and the Turkish government still disagree over what caused the deaths—a deliberate genocidal drive carried out against a minority group or an unfortunate side effect of harsh wartime necessity. Some historians blame Talat; as minister of the interior, he directed the forced relocation. But there's plenty of responsibility to go around. All three fled Turkey in 1918, and all three were assassinated. Talat's killer was an Armenian seeking revenge.

_07:: Pol Pot (1925 or 1928–1998)

As prime minister of Cambodia's Khmer Rouge government between 1975 and 1979, Pol Pot enacted radical reforms that forced city dwellers into the countryside to work as farm slaves of the state. A million people died of starvation and disease. Pol Pot's government thugs tortured and executed many more, starting with anybody who resisted or dissented. After Vietnam invaded Cambodia in 1979, forcing him into hiding in the mountains, Pol Pot directed Khmer Rouge guerrillas against the new Hanoi-supported government. Although he officially lost his job as Khmer Rouge top boss in 1985, he continued to play a leadership role in a disintegrating Khmer Rouge until 1997, when his former comrades placed him under house arrest. He died without having been called to account for the people he killed.

_08:: Idi Amin (1924 or 1925–2003)

The head of Uganda's armed forces seized control of the country in 1971. At first Amin's strong leadership was welcomed by Ugandans, as well as by observing nations such as Britain, which had feared his predecessor Milton Obote's flirtation with socialism. But Amin's idea of statesmanship was to slaughter anyone who opposed him. Dependent on the support of his own Kakwa ethnic group, he ordered the persecution of other tribes. Amin's Uganda was notorious for torture chambers, cruel prisons, and executions numbering in the hundreds of thousands. He won popularity by deporting thousands of Asian Ugandans. But the Asians had run much of the economy, which then collapsed. After his 1978 invasion of Tanzania backfired (thousands of Ugandan exiles helped the Tanzanians), Amin fled to Libya and then to exile in Saudi Arabia.

7 World Leaders You Don't Know by Name

Be it an identity crisis, canny marketing, or simply a way to fool the authorities, many powerful people have gone by names their parents didn't give them. Here are seven leaders you know by their aliases.

_01:: Akhenaton aka Amenhotep IV (died 1336 BCE)

In the 1300s BCE a new king shook up Egypt by abandoning the centuries-old state religion. Forsaking other gods, he fixed on one only—the formerly obscure god of the sun disk, Aton. Polytheistic priests held enormous power in ancient Egypt, and Amenhotep may have been trying to slip their influence. He moved his capital from Thebes to a new site, far to the north, which he called Akhetaton, or "place of Aton's power," and renamed himself Akhenaton, or "useful to Aton." His radical changes ultimately failed as the military faltered and the empire withered. When son-in-law Tutankhaton became king, he changed his name to Tutankhamen (dropping the reference to Aton) and moved the capital back to Thebes. Tutankhamen died young but left a great-looking mummy.

_02:: Augustus Caesar aka Gaius Octavian (63 BCE–14 CE)

Only 18 when his great-uncle Julius Caesar was stabbed to death in 44 BCE, the boy learned that he was the Roman dictator's designated heir. Although Caesar's aide Mark Antony also wanted the job and had more experience and clout, the kid went for it. As Uncle Julius's adoptive son, Octavian changed his name to Gaius Julius Caesar Octavianus. After more than a decade of turbulent fighting among co-rulers and rivals, he emerged as unchallenged boss of the Roman Empire. His new government paid homage to old Roman republican institutions, but it rested entirely in Octavian's hands as emperor. In 27 BCE the Roman Senate, which he controlled, renamed him Augustus, connoting superhuman or even godlike stature.

_03:: James I of England aka James VI of Scotland (1566–1625)

When Elizabeth I of England died in 1603, she left no heir. The best claim came from James VI of Scotland. That's because James's great-grandmother was the sister of Elizabeth's father, Henry VIII. James also remained ruler of Scotland, but the scholarly king (he actually wrote a book) is better known as James I, England's first Stuart king. When he moved south he was not quite 37 but already long-accustomed to rule. He put on his own country's crown (figuratively, anyway) when he was a baby. That was after his mom, Mary Queen of Scots, had to skip the country. (The nobles didn't like it that she had married for a third time to a man suspected of killing her second husband, baby James's dad.) James the boy king began making state decisions as a teen. Once he got to England he called himself King of Great Britain (although legally, there wasn't any such nation yet), and he tended to argue with Parliament, who found him high-handed. Whatever the number after his name, James firmly believed in his own absolute power.

_04:: Vladimir Lenin aka Vladimir Ilich Ulyanov (1870–1924)

Raised in middle-class comfort, young Ulyanov and his four siblings all joined the revolutionary movement in Russia in the late 1800s. When Vladimir was only 17, his older brother, Aleksandr, a college student, was accused of conspiring to assassinate the czar and was hanged. Vladimir became a lawyer, but in 1895 he was arrested for trying to publish a revolutionary newspaper. After questioning him for more than a year, the government sent him into exile in Siberia. He kept up the radical journalism, however, publishing the book *The Development of Capitalism in Russia* in 1899 and founding the leftist newspaper *Iskra*. In 1901 he began writing under the by-line Lenin. At first the pen name was meant to cloak his identity, but the name stuck so well that the Soviet Union's founding leader will always be remembered by it.

_05:: Ho Chi Minh aka Nguyen Sinh Cung (1890–1969)

The Vietnamese leader used many aliases. Signing on as Ba, the former schoolmaster, also known as Nguyen That Thanh, he took a berth as cook on a French steamer in 1911 and sailed around the world. Settling in France in 1917 and becoming a socialist organizer, he went by the name Nguyen Ai Quoc, or "Nguyen the patriot." Around 1940 he called himself Ho Chi Minh ("he who enlightens"). As Ho, he declared Vietnam independent of France in 1945. He fought the French, who withdrew in 1954, leaving a partitioned Vietnam with pro-French nationals headquartered in the south. With U.S. support, South Vietnamese leaders scuttled a scheduled 1956 election that would have reunited Vietnam under the popular Ho. During the civil war that followed, the north sent weapons to its southern guerrilla allies, the Viet Cong, by way of a jungle path, the Ho Chi Minh Trail. After the north won the Vietnam War in 1975

Myths and Misconceptions
A LOPPING MISTAKE

Dr. Joseph-Ignace Guillotin (1738–1814) did *not* invent the guillotine, a French execution machine named for him. The doctor's name was Guillotin, with no final *e*, and he was deputy to the French Estates General in 1789. A supporter of capital punishment, he thought it should be done uniformly, with merciful efficiency, and proposed a head-chopping device. Of course, such machines had been around for centuries. After the Estates General became the revolutionary General Assembly, French Procureur General Pierre-Louis Roederer turned not to Guillotin but to another doctor, Antoine Louis, for a design. And in fact it was a German engineer who built the first working model. While it's not clear how the machine came to be named for Guillotin, we do know why it's spelled that way. The final *e* was added to make it easier to rhyme within revolutionary ballads.

(more than five years after Ho's death), the former southern capital, Saigon, became Ho Chi Minh City.

_06:: Marshal Tito aka Josip Broz
(1892–1980)

In 1928 Yugoslav police found bombs in Broz's apartment in Zagreb, Croatia. They accused the sometime mechanic of working for a Soviet-sponsored revolutionary group. (Broz had embraced Marxism while in a Russian prisoner-of-war camp during World War I.) Convicted of conspiracy against the Yugoslav monarchy, he served five years in jail. When he got out, he used aliases to avoid another arrest. Under one of those names, Tito, he was brought into the politburo, or controlling committee, of the Communist Party of Yugoslavia (CPY). When Germany and Italy occupied Yugoslavia in World War II, the royal government fled, leaving the CPY, now led by Tito, as the only effective Yugoslav resistance. This drove the exiled royals into an alliance with the Axis powers. When the Allies won the war, the CPY and Tito took control, creating the Federal People's Republic of Yugoslavia. As leader until his death, he held offices including party chair and president, but was best known by his preferred title, Marshal Tito.

_07:: Gerald Ford aka Leslie Lynch King
Jr. (1913–)

Born in Omaha, he was named for his dad, Les King. But when Leslie Jr. was very young, his parents divorced. Mom moved to Grand Rapids, Michigan, and married Gerald Rudolph Ford, who adopted the baby. They decided to rename the little guy Jerry Jr. Jerry won a seat in the House of Representatives in 1948, became House minority leader in 1965, and in 1973, President Richard Nixon appointed him vice president, replacing the disgraced Spiro T. Agnew. The next year Nixon himself, also disgraced, resigned from office, and Ford stepped up. That's how a Ford, not a King, came to occupy the White House from 1974 to 1977. Ford is the only U.S. chief executive never elected either president or vice president. Ex-pres Bill Clinton, born William Jefferson Blythe, also uses a stepfather's surname.

by
John Timpane

Condensed
LITERATURE

Contains

7 Literary Works That Changed Everything ✳ What a Famous Thing to Say: 6 Quotable Lines
and How to Use 'Em ✳ Girls Just Want to Have Fame: 5 Female Authors You Need to Know ✳
High Art: 5 Classics Written under the influence ✳ 6 Writers Who Didn't Need No Degree ✳
Arrest That Writer!: 6 Authors Too Dangerous to Let Loose ✳ 15 for All Time: The Ultimate
Desert Island Reading List ✳

Literary Works That Changed Everything

If you're looking for a cheat sheet of lit's movers and shakers, you've come to the right paragraph. Here are seven figures that shifted paradigms on the strength of their pens.

_01:: *Sonnets to Laura* by Francesco Petrarch (1304–1374)

A poet becomes obsessed with a young woman and makes her his ideal, his way to God through love. In many ways this tale is still the paradigm for the love story. Now, did Petrarch *invent* the love poem? A good question, and one that people still fight over. Some feel that the Roman poet Catullus was the first to write poems we would call love poems. Others say that love (and love poetry) as we know it arose among the troubadour poets of 11th- and 12th-century France. And some cast their vote solidly with Petrarch. In any case, he certainly did show centuries of poets how to write about very personal emotions, and his influence can be seen in almost every love song written ever since.

_02:: *The Canterbury Tales* by Geoffrey Chaucer (1343–1400)

We think he spells his first name the cool way too. It's no mean trick to write a long series of narrative poems that stay fresh and funny and full of life for 600 years. And, at first glance, you wouldn't think a pilgrimage to a saint's shrine would make such great reading. But the *Tales* did do something that was new and different: they portrayed people as people often are. Some call it realism; some simply call

it honesty. Chaucer had an eye for human foibles, and he presents them in comic detail, with an attitude that's both honest and sympathetic. As his characters pose, steal, lie, fornicate, and mess up, he looks on them all with a forgiving, amused detachment. The *Tales* aren't modern, but they sometimes feel like it. They really began the history of the English language (Chaucer wrote in what we now call Middle English) as a powerful literary device.

_03:: *Les Fleurs du Mal* ("Flowers of Evil") by Charles Baudelaire (1821–1867)

Baudelaire's book is important because it showed that a poet can create his own intense, suggestive world by weaving symbols into a new emotional language. This became a poetic movement called Symbolism, and it's still going strong. (This is different from the small-*s* symbolism—that's just the use of symbols. We all do that. Large-*S* Symbolism, which only poets and other writers do, is a whole way of creating a language and a landscape out of symbolic language. Sometimes the symbols will really refer to things, as most symbols do, and sometimes no one, not even the poet, will know the precise meaning of the symbols that emerge from the unconscious.) He fearlessly explored the underside of life, the perversities, the sensual overloads, the almost painful longings. Baudelaire is everywhere.

_04:: *Ulysses* by James Joyce
(1882–1941)

Joyce did not (we repeat, DID NOT!) invent the stream of consciousness technique. That honor goes to the novelist Dorothy Richardson, whom you should read. And in fact, other writers, such as Virginia Woolf and William Faulkner, may have done it better. (Your pick.) But Joyce certainly helped perfect it. We watch the world slide in front of the brain of Leopold and Molly Bloom and Stephen Dedalus. All the time, they're thinking to themselves of this and that. Outer and inner worlds intersect and combine. One of the beautiful things in this novel is how the forces of time and history make their appearance in the supposedly private thoughts of individuals. Also, getting behind people's eyes turns out to be a great way to see them at their frankest. Although difficult for the untrained reader, this book is a taste of life itself, a comic masterpiece if ever there was one.

_05:: Short Stories by Ernest Hemingway
(1899–1961)

If Hemingway didn't invent it, he certainly perfected a new way to tell tales, showing us action but refraining from interpreting it, letting us figure out the significance of things for ourselves—as we have to do much of the time in the nonliterary life. In his story "Hills Like White Elephants," a man and a woman have a conversation. But we're not told the topic. We figure it out by *listening*. Little by little, the painful ironies we're observing draw us in, involve us as if we were seeing this angry chat going on right in front of us. Hemingway's stories walk a tense tightrope strung between hopelessness and the ecstatic celebration of strength and courage. The standoff between the sexes has never been presented so uncompromisingly. And has there ever been a better appreciator of nature? Probably not. Ever since Ernest took hold of his number two pencil, fiction just hasn't been the same.

_06:: *Howl* by Allen Ginsberg
(1926–1997)

The madness of postwar America; sex and drugs; beatific, crazy exaltation. Ginsberg's poem was the opening of the Beat era, and also its high point. His poetry, his embrace of the forbidden, and his nutty, beatific energy have had a great deal of influence on music and the arts. In fact, many people cite *Howl* as the beginning of the counterculture years: the years of free thinking; sex, drugs, and rock and roll; and social ferment. Years when the civil rights movement swelled, antiwar protests built, and the general standoff between an older generation with their hands on the reins of power and a younger generation looking for a newer, wider world came to a head. Now, one poem can't be responsible for all that. But it *did* free many writers to think more expansively, with less fear, with more possibilities. And it still retains its haunting, mad power.

_07:: *One Hundred Years of Solitude*, by Gabriel García Márquez
(1928–)

In the 20th century the world of literature stopped being almost exclusively the province

Fake Your Way through a Conversation

(ON LITERATURE!)

Step one: Listen to what most of the people think about the book/poem/play you haven't read.

Step two: Agree with them.

Step three: Venture a brief opinion of your own, using the table below.

IF THEY LIKED IT, USE	IF THEY DIDN'T, USE
dense	*loose*
intense characterization	*stereotypes*
tight	*discursive*
suggestive, full of inference	*obvious*
questions accepted ideas	*naive*
original	*imitative*
clever	*intrusive*
compelling	*irritating*
tough	*self-indulgent, maudlin, sentimental*
bold	*pretentious*
down to earth	*stilted*
hilarious	*cartoonish*
unexpected resonances	*predictable*
experiment	*exercise*

Let's say they're speaking of *The Possum of Desire* by Alicia van Hollenbeck-Jiménez. If you see that folks like the book, you can say, "I found it full of unexpected resonances, intensely depicted characters that question established ideas. Her style is dense, suggestive. I liked the clever narration. The novel's theme is tough and bold, yet the prose is down to earth and hilarious. Very compelling." Use the words *yet* and *still* a lot.

If they hate it, you can say, "I found it predictable, full of imitative stereotypes. And the writing—it struck me as loose, discursive, maudlin. Didn't you think the author was being a little pretentious? Even when she was being funny, it just seemed a little cartoonish in the end. Naive. The whole thing was a rather irritating exercise."

That oughta do it.

of Europe and the United States, as new lit from across the globe elbowed its way to the table. *One Hundred Years of Solitude* by Colombian author Márquez was a worldwide smash, and its success helped bring the Central and South American voice into the world theater. What's different about that voice? Well, it's exotic: its view of history (and its environment—the steamy, mysterious, mythical rain forests and jungles of Central America) is wholly different from that of Europe. Of course, Europe's in there, but you also have the indigenous imagination, the postcolonial present, the beliefs of the past, and the disbe-lief of the present. Márquez's mind seems to be a fountain of stories. For many readers, his novel introduced magic realism, a world in which reality and our sense of the magical find new ways to interact.

What a Famous Thing to Say:
6   Quotable Lines and How to Use 'Em

The great thing is, when you drop these lines at your next cocktail party and people ask, "Where's that from?" you're actually going to know!

_01:: "Rule a large country as you'd cook a small fish."—Lao-tzu, *The Way of the Tao*

Very little is known about Lao-tzu. The very name actually means "old master," so it may simply be a name—like Homer, or the Preacher in the book of Ecclesiastes—ascribed to someone supposed to have written an ancient, famous work. There's even some doubt as to whether Lao-tzu, or any one person, wrote *The Way of the Tao*. Still, this work founded a religion/way of life followed by 20 million people today. The famous line, with its piquant terseness, even a trace of humor, appears to counsel political moderation and wisdom. The wise governor governs least, interferes least. Use this line whenever folks are discussing taxation, welfare, or other social programs. Heck, use it whenever an extremely big thing must be done with extreme care.

_02:: "Abandon all hope, you who enter here!"—Dante, *The Inferno*

This is the slogan written over the main entrance into Inferno. The message is clear. Hell is pretty definitively The End. If this is where you end up, ain't no bus out. You know how most of the time, if stuff gets you down, your friends will say, "Hey, come on, cheer up. It'll get better. Just you wait"? Well, not here. This is the ultimate Line to Use When Things Are Irretrievably Bad. Use it whenever you or your friends are about to go into some doubtful place, such as an Internal Revenue Service office, a bar, a dentist's office, or a draft office in wartime. And remember, it also comes in handy just before entering the dwellings of parents-in-law, loan officers, or difficult lovers.

_03:: "Now is the winter of our discontent."—William Shakespeare, first line of *Richard III*

Most people don't realize that Richard III, the guy who speaks this line, is a *villain*. The next line—"Made glorious summer by this sun of York"—is totally sarcastic, directed at the present resident of the throne, which Richard really really really wants. Richard III is a scheming, morally challenged evildoer who compounds outrage upon outrage in his quest for power. He seduces a woman by the casket of her husband (one that Richie killed), drowns his brother in a cask of wine, and performs other charming stunts along the way. So this line is the all-time expression of virulent impatience. Use it whenever you or someone you know has entered a stretch of misfortune, bad luck, or frustration. Makes a nice statement of empathy. Suppose your pal says, "Man, I haven't had a date in 20 years." Nod your head sympathetically and say, "Now is the winter of our discontent!"

_04:: "It was the best of times, it was the worst of times." —Charles Dickens, *A Tale of Two Cities*

This line hits maximum potential when you use it to describe your childhood, a party, your family, a class reunion, or any other event about which you are completely ambivalent. "How was the boss's Christmas party last night?" "Oh, it was the best of times, it was the worst of times." "Daddy, what was it like growing up in 1974?" "Oh, Junior, it was the best of times, it was the worst of times." So many memories and gatherings inspire ambivalence that folks will probably never stop

using this line. (Note: *A Tale of Two Cities* also has a pretty great ending, which contains the line "It is a far, far better thing I do, than I have ever done." You can say this aloud when you want to be praised for some selfless deed you're about to perform.)

_05:: "Things fall apart; the center cannot hold."—William Butler Yeats, "The Second Coming"

Throughout recorded history, human beings have looked around at the world and exclaimed, "Everything is falling apart!" And

---

Pure Genius

EMILY DICKINSON

Maybe she spent her whole life in her dad's house and seldom left her hometown of Amherst, Mass. And yeah, she might have fallen in love once or twice but never married. But whether you call her an eccentric, a spinster, or a recluse, Emily Dickinson (1830–1886) also almost single-handedly started modern American poetry (along with her contemporary Walt Whitman, whom she didn't know about). She invented a new way to write, in the form of the hymns she heard in church but full of mental and musical experiments. And dashes: she liked to punctuate her poems with dashes. Dickinson wrote fearlessly of nature, God, love, and the life of the emotions. Many of her individual lines—"I heard a fly buzz when I died"; "Much Madness is divinest Sense"; "Tell all the Truth but tell it slant"—are burned into the memory of the world.

they have always been wrong. The sun rose in the morning, and there was a world. Maybe not the greatest world, but *a* world. Still, that nagging human sense remains: things are getting bad, and they can only get worse. The 20th century was like that, personally and internationally. That may be why Yeats's line is possibly the most-quoted line of modern poetry. Use it vigorously whenever everything is just crumbling around you. (Boss: "We lost our biggest account!" You: "Things fall apart; the center cannot hold.") Also good when a very embarrassing situation happens, such as, for example, when someone's brassiere falls open, someone's pants fall down, or a plant comes crashing down from a mantelpiece.

_06:: "Never laugh at live dragons." —J. R. R. Tolkien, *The Hobbit*

This line is a version of Shakespeare's famous "Discretion is the better part of valor." It's not a good idea to dare forces that are stronger than you are—especially if those forces don't have anything holding them back. In other words, don't play chicken with a universe that doesn't have your best interests at heart. Don't dance in front of the onrushing train; you might get caught on the tracks. Use this wise and hilarious line when it's better to be quiet than confrontational. "Let's go tell the boss she's a pain in the butt." "Ah, never laugh at live dragons." "Let's go to the police station and tell them we aren't paying that drunk-driving ticket." "Ah, never laugh at live dragons."

Girls Just Want to Have Fame: 5 Female Authors You Need to Know

Sure, you might have overheard their names in classrooms or at cocktail parties, but isn't it time you were formally introduced? Don't be shy—these are ladies everyone needs to know.

_01:: Enheduanna: Hymns for Nanna

"Who?" you might ask. Well, we're both shocked *and* disappointed. Enheduanna was only the earliest poet ever recorded. The daughter of Sargon, a great ruler of Mesopotamia (2350–2330 BCE) and the guy who founded the kingdom of Akkad (as in the Akkadians), this princess spent her days penning dreamy poems. And while we don't know her given name, we do have her official name: pronounced En-head-WAN-na, which means "high priestess of Nanna." And basically, that was her job: to preside over ceremonies and write official hymns to Nanna, the moon goddess. Amazingly enough, several of these hymns have made their way down to us, and they're among the oldest poems known. The hymns show a powerful incantatory quality, possibly with a call-and-response thing going on.

_02:: Sappho: The Barry White of Her Day

If you're hunting for the roots of the poetry of love, look no further. One of the earliest Greek lyric poets, Sappho lived on the island of Lesbos around 600 BCE. And evidently she had quite a nice business running a school for women and writing wedding songs. Today most of her poetry survives in fragments; in one, the speaker undergoes the mania of love and describes herself as "paler than grass." In another, the speaker longs for her loved one and watches the Pleiades crawl across the sky. Because her love poems are directed to both men and women, she's become an eminent symbol of same-sex love, but really it's best to understand her as one of the first great love poets of all time, of all love.

_03:: Jane Austen's Powers (1775–1817)

After reading a Jane Austen novel, you realize two things: (1) It would have been humbling to know this woman, because she was sharp—she noticed *every* nuance about people. And (2) hers is about as female an art as you could wish for. Some people think her world is too restricted: middle-class women in the early 1800s trying to find themselves and find mates. Within that world, however, Austen unlocks our interior universes: what we pretend to be vs. what we really are. Prejudice is one of her great themes; in her three major novels (*Pride and Prejudice*, *Emma*, and *Persuasion*), a person has to unlearn those prejudices somehow. Oh, and did we mention that her stories make great movies?

_04:: Colette, the Original Vagabond (1873–1954)

Colette's life is almost as famous as her writings. But we shouldn't let the former overshadow the latter. Colette is the great chronicler of women in the world of love. Her worlds are full of humor and disappointment, revelation and bitterness. The Chéri novels portray the attempts of an older woman to hold on to a younger man, even after his marriage. *The Vagabond* may be Colette's best, as it follows a lonely single woman through the bruising turns of her theatrical career; it's pretty close to an autobiography. The Claudine novels, originally written as a kind of penny-porn under the brutal regime of her first husband, the infamous Willi, amount to an epic about a woman's sexual coming of age. Here we first see a theme running throughout Colette's work: loving men is so painful that it's no wonder women turn to other women. Melodramatic at times, perverse at others, Colette definitely created a world worth entering.

_05:: Virginia Woolf: Be Afraid! (1882–1941)

Her quiet, insistent, original voice has a way of staying on your mind. She is, let's face it, a modernist, meaning that for many readers her writing takes some getting used to. It seems difficult until you get the hang of it: that it's really being told from within people's minds, and that we're hearing the flow of their interior thoughts. We also encounter fascinating characters, such as the Ramsay family and Lily Briscoe of *To the Lighthouse*. If anyone wants a short segment that shows what great writing can do, how it can embrace time and passion and give us a new vision of our lives, you can't do better than the "Time Passes" passage of this novel. *Mrs. Dalloway* is just about as good. The high point of her technique and vision is *The Waves*, a series of internal mono-logues by a group of friends as they pass through time. And Woolf's last novel, *Between the Acts*, is her funniest and most frightening, a stroke of genius to end a singular career.

High Art:
5 Classics Written under the Influence

Many writers seek extreme experiences, including getting drunk/high/ecstatic/wasted/buzzed. And while we're not exactly advocating altered states here, it did seem to take the edge off their writer's block.

_01:: Collected Poetry, Li Po (701–762)

One of the best of the T'ang dynasty poets in seventh-century China, Li Po wrote many po-ems about drinking. In his poems and in many poems of the classic era of Chinese poetry, al-cohol has two functions. First of all, it brings friends together to sing, to reminisce, to have great little parties at which everybody gets tight and starts having poetry contests. Well, great! Second, it acts as a muse, a way to relax and release the poet into fantasies and media-tions that are good for the creation of poetry. See? Nothing new. Artists have been saying for centuries that if you take drugs, you make better art. They've often felt that the percep-tual expansion offered by drugs lets them have better, more surprising insights. Or at least *think* they do! Li Po and his pals obvi-ously felt that wine helped you be a better poet. Of course, being continuously sozzled comes with its own problems. Legend has it that Li died when, in a drunken state, he tried to embrace the reflection of the moon in a lake and fell in.

_02:: "Kubla Khan," Samuel Taylor Coleridge (1772–1834)

After smoking opium, Coleridge fell asleep, and when he awoke he was on fire with im-ages. He set to writing at a white-hot pace—until he was interrupted. When he returned to the poem an hour later, the vision was gone. He'd lost the moment. The result is one of the wildest, most puzzling poems of all time. A lot of people like the fact that it was written un-der the influence: it had a period of great pop-ularity in the 1960s. And back when it was published (1816), people took it as *the* quin-tessential Romantic poem: passionate, sponta-neous, beyond conscious control. They also liked how "he had it all there—and then lost it," which is a nice little fable about how fleet-ing inspiration is.

_03:: *The Sun Also Rises*, Ernest Hemingway (1899–1961)

Like many famous writers, Hemingway battled alcoholism all his life. In *The Sun Also Rises*, one of his best novels, almost every character drinks continually. They're trying to ignore the realities of life after World War I, trying to ignore their hangovers, and, often, just having a great party. War has torn apart the old ways, and the new ways—ways of nation building, ways of writing, ways of love, ways of being men and women—are full of pain and uncertainty. And these people, though they're adults, in many ways are incomplete, crippled. Jake Barnes, the protagonist, has suffered a war wound greatly compromising his sexual function (how's that for a delicate way to put it?), and the wound becomes a metaphor for the incompleteness that everyone's drinking to forget.

_04:: *Being and Nothingness*, Jean-Paul Sartre (1905–1980)

Sartre apparently was a big ingester of mescaline to get him, er, up to speed. He also took downers to let him sleep. These facts create a big question for the history of philosophy, don't they? Now, many readers have felt that despite his fame as the inventor of existentialism and despite his importance in many fields of literature, thought, and politics, he's completely unreadable. *Being and Nothingness* is supposed to be Sartre's great investigation of the experience of the absurdity and lack of intrinsic meaning in existence. When you discover nothingness, it's like a huge turning point, and there's no turning back. Sure wish the *book* was better. This thing is a twisty-turny, pompous, sloppy, contradictory mess, written in a celebratedly bad prose, whether

---

Strange but True

WRITERS IS THE CRAZIEST PEOPLE

While living in a hotel room in Brussels, Belgium, French poet Charles Baudelaire (1821–1867) captured a bat in a nearby graveyard, brought it back to his room, and kept it as a pet, feeding it bread and milk.

Russian playwright and fiction writer Anton Chekhov (1860–1904) didn't have long to live. His doctor bought a bottle of Champagne and poured Chekhov a glass. He drank it down with great appreciation and remarked: "It has been so long since I've had Champagne." Then he rolled over, and Chekhov checked out.

One of the strangest novels ever written may be *Gates of Paradise* by Polish writer Jerzy Andrzejewski (1909–1983). It is one-sentence long, unpunctuated, 40,000 words.

Speaking of strange, how about *Pugna Porcorum* ("Battle of the Pigs"), published by the Dominican monk Léon Plaisant (Placentius) in 1530? The poem extends to more than 250 verses, and *every word begins with the letter* P! Talk about pig Latin. Playful priest produces porky poetry!

French poet Gérard de Nerval (1808–1855) had a pet lobster that he took for walks, guiding it through the park of the Palais Royal on a pale blue ribbon.

Irish novelist James Joyce (1882–1941) wore five wristwatches on his arm, each set to a different time.

French or English. It may be a brilliant book, but it's not a good one. Maybe, applying the Li Po principle above, Sartre should have taken *more* drugs.

_05:: *Naked Lunch*, William Burroughs
(1914–1997)

Burroughs was a Beat writer and a heroin addict. His surrealistic novel influenced poets, musicians, and other addicts for the rest of the 20th century. This may be the ultimate in underground cult novels. You'll find its influence in everything from the art of Keith Haring to the poetry of Jack Kerouac to the lyrics of Steely Dan. One thing that's very impressive (besides the amount of drugs Burroughs reputedly took while compiling *Naked Lunch*) is how Burroughs uses addiction as a key metaphor for human existence. Everyone is a junkie for something—and everyone is also a narc, an agent of judgment and punishment. It's a brilliant insight, and it emerges from the jumble of this novel like a flash of drug-induced wisdom. Now, how many films have you seen that explore this theme? *Naked Lunch* is often called a novel, but it's really a collection of scenes and characters held together by the aforesaid metaphor. In fact, it doesn't hold together. Its existence is more important than its actual worth as literature. But its impact, which continues today in artists, writers, and filmmakers all over the world, is, well, psychedelic.

6 Writers Who Didn't Need No Degree

"Never let your schooling interfere with your education." And while Mark Twain might have said it, these cats definitely lived it. Here are six writers who skipped the degree and still did pretty OK for themselves.

_01:: Homer (ca. ninth century BCE)

"Well, OK," you say. "There were no colleges then, and Homer is just a name, not a person." True on the former; on the latter, scholars disagree. Many readers believe that the *Iliad* and the *Odyssey* are compilations of stories well-known around the Mediterranean world. The notion is that itinerant businessmen spread these stories around, along with the Greek language, and that after a while someone wrote them all down. But there's another idea: the name *Homer* may derive from an ancient word meaning "black," which leads some scholars to believe that Homer may have been a real person—an African businessman who spoke Greek, had a wide-open mind and a sharp ear, and wrote down tales that travelers around the Mediterranean told to while away those long nights between business deals. Who needs college when you have a road trip for a life?

_02:: William Shakespeare (1564–1616)

There's no evidence that this guy went to *any* school. Makes you sick, doesn't it? We don't know much about his youth in the provincial town of Stratford-upon-Avon, but one interesting guess is that he left town with a traveling acting troupe. With the troupe, Shakespeare may have worked his way to London and caught on with a band of actors there. Of course, living in London in the explosive last 20 years of the 16th century was bound to educate anyone. It was a world capital of trade, power—and theater. When Shakespeare became a playwright, he also became a literary bandit, cribbing tales and characters from wherever he could find them, from ancient Greek and Latin authors to contemporary (for him) tales from Italy, Spain, and France. Not a single book he owned has come down to us—so he must have been quite a borrower.

_03:: Leo Tolstoy (1828–1910)

Tolstoy has a reputation as an encyclopedic writer—a writer likely to allude to philosophy, history, industrial methods, military lore, social and educational theory, almost anything that's relevant to his story, and some that, well . . . isn't. So, how did he get such an encyclopedic mind? Not in college. He got a pretty good private education but dropped out of university. He hung out in Moscow and St. Petersburg, had a wild time, and developed venereal disease and a gambling habit. Then he joined the army, where among other things he commanded an artillery unit and witnessed the siege of Sebastopol. He traveled to Europe, started a school for kids, went back to Europe to learn about education, and read his head off. (He also married a woman who bore him 13 chil-

---

Alphabet Soup
WITH MULTISYLLABLE WORDS

Literary studies have some of the most jawbreaking technical language you can find. What's funny is how these hard words (*anacephalaeosis*) sometimes have simple meanings ("recap").

hendiadys: [hen-DIE-uh-diss] *n* You know how you say *good and mad* when you mean *very mad*, or *nice and soft* when you mean, er, *nicely soft?* You've expressed an idea in two words connected by *and* when you could've used just two words (a word and its modifier) to do it. So, what's a really crazed Greek word we could use for that? Oh, we know: hendiadys.

homoioteleuton: [ho-mee-oh-te-LOOT-on] *n* Again, a big, hard word for a pretty simple thing. This refers to the trick of using several adjacent words with the same ending: "He sneezed mightily, showered cheerfully, ate hungrily, dressed carelessly, and drove crazily."

Now for the one that everyone learns, the word that makes you *know* you've really learned something about literature:

onomatopoeia: [oh-no-mah-to-po-EE-ah] *n* The naming of something by imitating a sound associated with that thing, such as when we write *hiss* when we want to name a, er, a hiss. Or a sonic *boom*. People get apoplectic over another use, which many swear isn't really onomatopoeia, but who cares? That's the use of words that sound like the thing they stand for, such as *moan*, *dribble*, *bounce*, and so forth.

dren and was his secretary.) In the process, Tolstoy kept a huge personal diary and mined it for his earliest fiction. His experience in the army furnished some of the foundations for his masterwork, *War and Peace*, and a spiritual turning point later in life led to his later mystical writings. So, once again one of literature's most educated writers got that education almost anywhere but in school.

_04:: W. B. Yeats (1865–1939)

OK, he went to art school, but does that *really* count? Like many of the people on our list, Yeats was largely privately and self-taught. His interest in mythology and spiritualism led to intense reading in those directions and informed his poetry throughout his life. His interest in theater and politics helped lead to the founding of the Irish National Theatre, and he wrote most of his best-known plays (most of them based on Irish mythology) for performance there. His self-taughtness also led to a rejuvenation of his poetry in the early decades of the 20th century, when he found a new, harder, modern voice, partly through meeting Ezra Pound and other modern poets. Another engine for his muse was Ireland's struggle for independence. Writing powerful poetry of the highest order well into his seventies, Yeats was brilliant at continually reinventing his style and work.

_05:: Robert Frost (1874–1963)

This guy came pretty close to being a total failure. He dropped out of Dartmouth, taught school, was a newspaper man, worked in a factory, dropped out of Harvard, bought and ran a number of farms. Of course, none of these pursuits made him rich or famous. He published a poem here and there, but in one of the riskier life decisions you'll find in any poet's biography, Frost up and packed his family off to England. That's where he got his first two books of poetry published. And he was in his forties—so he was no spring chicken. England's where Frost met Ezra Pound and many other fine contemporary poets. They spread the word: this guy was the real thing. Upon returning to the United States, Frost became famous and then became a college professor (though not a college graduate).

_06:: Maya Angelou (1928–)

To continue our theme, who needs college when you have life? Angelou has been an actress, a nightclub singer, a civil rights activist, a screenwriter, a producer and director, a playwright and . . . a lot of other things. She's lived in Egypt, Ghana, Arkansas, and California. And the time she didn't have for college she's more than lavished on her writing, her poetry, and her memoirs. And that's a good thing. She was one of the first black cable car conductors in San Francisco; joined in the civil rights movement in the United States (she had already been involved in African civil rights) as a regional coordinator for the Southern Christian Leadership Conference; was associate editor of a newspaper in Cairo; and became an eminent poet, teacher, and writer. Once again, an incredible life. The gal ended up teaching college rather than attending it!

Arrest That Writer!:

6 Authors Too Dangerous to Let Loose

Writers agree that pens are mightier than swords. And apparently, tyrants and despots agree that jails are mightier than pens. The following are a few of the writers, poets, and playwrights who ended up behind bars just when their writing started to get interesting.

_01:: Ovid

In 8 BCE the Roman poet Publius Ovidius Naso, better known to us as Ovid, was banished from Rome by the emperor Augustus. Why? Tradition says the cause was the immorality of his verses. That might be, since Ovid was a very accomplished erotic poet—although his erotic poems are seldom if ever pornographic. But Augustus was a bit of a prude, and (alas for Ovid) the most powerful person in the world. He also had been a friend and supporter of Ovid's, in the days when Ovid was writing the *Metamorphoses* and other works based on myth and more "moral" stuff. So, this is the story not just of a political punishment but also of the breakdown of a friendship. In fact, we're not even sure why he was banished, but banished Ovid was—to the town of Tomi on the Black Sea. Ovid desperately tried to change his ways, tried to produce poetry that was less, er, racy, but in fact, he never saw Rome again.

_02:: John Milton (1608–1674)

It's hard to imagine that the author of *Paradise Lost* was ever anything but saintly and studious. But in fact, he had a tumultuous life. Milton was a convinced, aggressive Puritan.

And the Puritans weren't exactly fond of the Church of England or the king. With Milton as one of their main firebrands in print, they fomented a revolution that led to the beheading of Charles I in 1649. When the Puritans took power, Milton was appointed Latin secretary to the ruling Council of State. But the rule of the Puritans lasted a scant decade. When their government collapsed in 1659, so did Milton's fortunes. He was imprisoned between October and December 1660, and his works burned in public bonfires. After his release, he lived under modified house arrest for the rest of his life. What to do? He kept himself occupied by penning *Paradise Lost* (1667), *Paradise Regained* (1671), and *Samson Agonistes* (1671).

_03:: The Marquis de Sade (1740–1814)

How great would it be to have sadism named after you? Of course, you'd have to go to certain lengths, as this fellow did. His family married him off to a woman for the money, and he immediately began to busy himself (quite publicly) with prostitutes and with a sister-in-law. His mother-in-law didn't like that, and she had him imprisoned. So he spent 14 years in jail, including being condemned to death in the town of Aix for his sexual practices. Yet somehow he got out of that one. Then he was again imprisoned in 1777, and again for six years at the Bastille in Paris in 1784. Imprisonment gave him lots of time to keep churning out the vigorous pornography that made him famous. In fact, the marquis spent his last 12 years in the insane asylum at Charenton, where he wrote and directed plays starring the staff and inmates.

_04:: Václav Havel (1936–)

This brave poet and playwright was jailed repeatedly in the 1970s for works critical of the communist government in then-Czechoslovakia. With civil unrest rising, he was jailed in February 1989 but kept turning out influential plays, poems, and essays, and even winning literary awards. Set free in May, he helped stoke a peaceful resistance movement known as the Velvet Revolution. Havel became the focal point of a largely peaceful revolution, where large crowds of nonviolent demonstrators showed their disapproval of the ruling communists. Havel addressed crowds that sometimes numbered almost a million. By the end of the year, the communist government was out and Havel had been elected president. He served as president of Czechoslovakia—and later, when the country split in two, of the Czech Republic—for 13 years, retiring in 2003. The tally? Poetry 1, communism 0!

_05:: Salman Rushdie (1947–)

A lot of people think literature is just, well, a particularly brainy sort of fun, not dangerous at all. But woe to those who step out of line. In 1989 Indian novelist Salman Rushdie published a novel titled *The Satanic Verses*. On

---

Inventions and Innovations
KEEPING LIT LIT

It's about recording and reproduction, baby. The root word of *literature* means "letter." That figures: if you can't write a piece of literature down, it stays *talk*—which is fine if people have great memories, but less fine for stretches of longer than, say, 30 minutes. So all the inventions that have helped people set words down in locatable form—papyrus, the Gutenberg press, the Internet—they keep lit lit. And like any human endeavor, literature has been full of inventions. How about the novel? That's a good one. Scholars disagree about what and when the first novel was (Was it *The Golden Ass* by Lucius Apuleius, of around 150 CE? Was it *The Tale of Genji* by Murasaki Shikibu, of around 1000? Was it *Don Quixote* by Miguel de Cervantes, of around 1605?), but the progression is pretty clear. As of 1400 you really didn't have that many; as of 2003 you see tens of thousands of new ones every year. At one time poetry reigned supreme; now prose is king.

October 14, 1989, Ayatollah Khomeini, theocratic ruler of Iran, published a *hukm* against Rushdie for his novel because some parts were considered blasphemous against certain tenets of Islam. The text of the *hukm* was pretty serious: "I call on all zealous Muslims to execute [Rushdie and all those involved in publishing the book] quickly, wherever they may be found, so that no one else will dare to insult the Muslim sanctities." Rushdie was forced to go into hiding for several years, but he continued to publish. The bounty on his head was raised to more than $5 million. With the death of Khomeini and comparative relaxation of Iranian politics, however, Rushdie's begun to make public appearances again.

_06:: María Elena Cruz Varela (1953–)

A Cuban poet, Varela was self-taught, a true flower of the countryside. She won Cuba's National Award for Poetry in 1989. In May 1991, however, she and nine other writers wrote a letter to Fidel Castro, calling for greater openness in Cuba, direct elections, and the release of political prisoners. State-run newspapers attacked these writers as agents of the CIA. Then a state security brigade broke into her apartment, where she lived with her husband, daughter, and son. She was dragged by her hair into the street and made to eat some of her published work. Then she was thrown into jail, beaten, and starved. She was released in 1994 and went into exile in Puerto Rico.

15 for All Time: The Ultimate Desert Island Reading List

A miniature history of world literature fits into a good-sized trunk. Here are fifteen titles to keep you occupied while Skipper and the Professor try to fix the hole in that boat.

_01:: *The Iliad* and *The Odyssey* by Homer

These got Western Civ started; might as well keep it going! The two epics are very different. The *Iliad* portrays the nine-year battle of Troy as a series of individual battles. The sorrow and pity of war has never been as well portrayed. It's told in the most elevated of all voices—and yet, its concerns always stay close to the human heart. If ever there was a cast of characters that were epic, this one has it: Paris, Priam, Hektor, Odysseus, Menelaos, Agamemnon, Akhilles, Patroklos, Ajax, and old whatsername, Helen of Troy. The *Odyssey* follows Odysseus on a trip around the world, encountering (and surviving his encounters with) a range of gods and monsters. Meanwhile, his patient wife, Penelope, waits for him and fends off suitors who want her hand and her land. Both books are worth reading if only for the moment Odysseus's dog, Argos, recognizes his master when he finally returns, and then the faithful pet dies.

_02:: *The Tale of Genji* by Lady Murasaki Shikibu

A panoramic, passionate story of Japanese courtly life, *The Tale of Genji* is thought of by many as the first novel. Its central character is a man known as Genji. He is never the emperor, but he is the most admired, most desired, most accomplished man in the court. Yet he isn't exactly the most self-aware person in the world; he doesn't always know why he does things. Which may be why he makes love to so many different women and thus causes confusion and heartache of all sorts. One of this book's many delights is the delicate, reserved tone of the narrator. Another is the way lovers exchange tanka (short poems) to allude to their feelings; this practice makes *Genji* an anthology of poetry as well as a novel. Like many great works, this ancient book often strikes us as fresh and aware in a contemporary way.

_03:: *The Divine Comedy* by Dante Alighieri (1265–1321)

Hell, purgatory, and paradise—who could ask for anything more? Dante grew up in the city-state of Florence, and he strove to reach the top of the society that bore him. But in the political battles that tore Florence apart in the late 13th century, Dante was expelled from his home (1302) and forced to be a gypsy-exile-scholar for the rest of his life, during which he tried to make sense of this cataclysm. In the poems that came to be known as *The Divine Comedy*, Dante goes on a guided tour (his guide is the great Roman poet Virgil) of, well, those three places. The *Inferno* is best known: that's because, as the cliché goes, it's easier to imagine hell than heaven. Dante makes the poem sort of an autobiography, putting many of his enemies and rivals in the heated place and elevating Beatrice, the love of his life, to the apex of divine realization in the *Paradiso*. The story remains one of the most sustained examples of the sublime in any language.

_04:: *Don Quixote* by Miguel de Cervantes (1547–1616)

Self-delusion is one of the greatest themes a writer can wade into. It's at once what is very funny about people and very tragic about them. The good don, also known as the Knight of the Doleful Countenance, believes that the era of knights and damsels and dragons and such still exists, and that he can win glory and fame by defending the weak and attacking the evil. His sidekick, Sancho Panza, tries to talk him out of his deluded ways, but a combination of nearsightedness and a simple refusal to believe all available evidence makes Quixote impregnable to good sense. It's a huge collection of stories, many of them taken from Cervantes' own painful, eventful life, but it feels like a novel because it has a great, arching coherence to it. It gives us a great hero, a great sadness, and much laughter in the bargain.

_05:: Shakespeare's Collected Works

Without them, you might as well not have anything else. If you take this with you to your desert island, you will have the company of hundreds of characters trooping across the stage of life, matching wits, swords, passions, and words. You'll see Hamlet in the graveyard, Othello in the bedroom, Julius Caesar on the ground, Sir John Falstaff on the battlefield (hiding), Juliet up there and Romeo down there. You'll encounter hundreds of lines and phrases you didn't know you knew ("Oh, *that's* where that's from?"). And in the sonnets you will meet one of the most compelling and perplexing triangles ever created: the speaker, the beloved gentleman, and the Dark Lady. And running through it all like a rainbow river, the unconscious, superlative music of Shakespeare's poetry. We're not saying it's any good. But it may help you while away the time before getting rescued.

_06:: The King James Version of the Bible

Even the least religious reader can savor the words and tales; you know many of them already, as well as the great phrases reverberating throughout the English language. It is famously divided into the Old Testament, a collection of sacred scriptures of the Jewish people, dating from between about 1000 BCE and 200 BCE; and the New Testament, a collection of writings about the life of Jesus Christ and the works of his followers. So why not treat the Bible as it is: the greatest anthology of prose and poetry ever? Read the book of Job tonight, then 2 Corinthians tomorrow night. Read the book of Psalms for a couple of weeks, savoring it psalm by psalm; then read the book of Matthew. Go from the lovely, erotic Song of Songs to the book of John. From Ruth to Paul, from Isaiah to Luke, from Genesis to the book of Revelations. It'd be worth rowing to an island just to have the privilege.

_07:: *Tom Jones* by Henry Fielding (1707–1754)

What is life without laughter, and plenty of it? Several of our desert-island books have yuks in them, but none of them have more than *Tom Jones*. There's a wide-open good nature to the humor, an energetic affection for the characters, that comes through on every page. We meet Tom, an orphan who has a lot of life in him, meaning he gets into a lot of beds, a lot of trouble, and a lot of hearts. Mr. Allworthy is his kind benefactor. Tom is in love with the virtuous Sophie Western, but because of the sneaky Blifil, Tom is expelled from Mr. Allworthy's affections and hits the road. (See *The Odyssey*.) It's really a story about sin and forgiveness: Tom sins a whole lot, but deep down inside, he's a good person, as we (and Sophie) can see. Many people have said that the plot of this wonderful, racy book is one of the best ever concocted. The film *Tom Jones* is also a good intro to the book (if your island is somehow equipped with DVD), but it's certainly no replacement for it.

_08:: *Eugene Onegin* by Aleksandr Pushkin (1799–1837)

It's sometimes said that Russian literature begins and ends with Pushkin, especially with this exquisite novel in verse. As with Shakespeare in English and Ghalib in Urdu, lines and phrases of Pushkin's are on Russian lips every moment. Eugene Onegin is a young man with all the advantages. He's in the midst of society, the midst of luxury. And then it hits him—he loses his taste for life. Everything suddenly bores him. He can find no savor in existence. Natalya is a young girl who falls passionately, romantically in love with Eugene, and even though he is drawn to her, he is unable to come out of his boredom to respond to her. It's one of the most poignantly frustrating frustrated loves in all of literature. Considering the fate of their relationship, the fate of Eugene's friendship with the proud poet Lensky, and the fate of life itself—there's a profound perfection to this tale that has seldom been equaled.

Myths and Misconceptions

ANOTHER MAN BY SHAKESPEARE'S NAME?

At the turn of the 20th century, certain folks started whipping themselves into a lather over the notion that Shakespeare had not written his plays. They started reading between the lines, smelling a rat. The favorite theory was and is that a nobleman wrote the plays—the Earl of Oxford, maybe, or Francis Bacon—and didn't want people to know he'd indulged in this disgraceful pursuit. So he tapped Shakespeare as the front man. Some pretty famous people got into the act, including that all-time sleuther-behind-the-scenes, Sigmund Freud.

Here are a few of the reasons people think Shakespeare didn't write his plays:

1. There's no record that he ever went to any school.
2. Many of his plays were published without his name on them.
3. The plays are too smart to have been written by a middle-class guy with no university education.
4. There are clues in the plays that other people wrote them.
5. If Shakespeare wrote all this great stuff, why don't we know more about him?

Maybe they're right. Maybe we should tell the old joke: "Shakespeare didn't write his plays—it was another man by the same name." But there are pretty good replies to these notions:

1. Records were pretty bad back then, so that might be why there's no record of him in school.
2. True. So what? Later they were. And it's possible he didn't want them published (come pay to see *Hamlet*; don't buy the book), didn't care, or didn't want his name on them. And we have a fair number of contemporaries who say he did write many of these plays.
3. There really isn't much in the plays that a voracious reader couldn't have learned. We know a lot of the books and stories the "author of Shakespeare's plays" ransacked for plots and ideas. You didn't need to be an upper-class university student to read them.
4. Most of these "clues" are clues only if you want to see them that way.
5. Shakespeare isn't that mysterious a figure. We actually know a lot about the guy for a nonroyal person of 400-plus years ago.

_09:: *Little Dorrit* by Charles Dickens
(1812–1870)

Dickens wrote so many wonderful novels that this one might come as a surprise choice. And, hey, if you'd rather take *Oliver Twist, David Copperfield, The Pickwick Papers, Bleak House, A Tale of Two Cities,* or *Great Expectations,* well, fine. But to Dickens fans this choice will be no surprise. The novel has all the Dickens hallmarks: the sweeping sense of teeming human life in the midst of history; biting satire on unfeeling government institutions in the Circumlocution Office; stories of class snobbery and true love; wacky humor; a mystery to be solved; and a (fairly) happy ending tempered by the wisdom that life, even at its best, is pretty hard. *Little Dorrit*, like many Dickens novels, invites us not only to read it but also to live it.

_10:: *The Brothers Karamazov* by Fyodor Dostoevsky (1821–1881)

There are a few novels—and this is certainly one—that are so huge you can't pin a meaning on them. You can find lots and lots of meanings, but not a single strand. *The Brothers K* is the best of one of the very best writers ever. As many of the greatest literary works do, this book concerns the cataclysmic forces within a family: father Fyodor Karamazov and his sons Dmitri, Ivan, and Alyosha. This huge novel has that obsessive (and obsessing), dry-mouthed, feverish intensity for which Dostoevsky is famous. Again and again, we keep colliding with the profoundest themes in life: What are good and evil? Can human sin be redeemed? Is love possible? Where, if anywhere, is God? (In this regard, the high point of the novel is the segment titled *The Grand Inquisitor*, an interrogation of Christ come back to earth.) Reading this book feels like living an intense, maddening, poetic life.

_11:: *The Adventures of Huckleberry Finn* by Mark Twain (1835–1910)

This is one of the funniest books you'll read while on the island, yet it's no less profound for all that. It's got the Mississippi River—the ultimate symbol of freedom—life on the road,

the American dream. It's got the tension between young and old, slave and free, black and white. It has perhaps the most likable cast of characters to be encountered in any novel, including Huck, Tom Sawyer, the slave Jim, and the whole rogues' gallery of swindlers, killers, would-be's, has-been's, and never-will-be's all along the river. During the novel Huck realizes that living his kind of life is a way to hell in some people's eyes. All right, then, he says, I'll go to hell. It's an act of courage, and a shocking one at the time. But it's also the ultimate moral act, as this surprisingly subtle novel shows us. Warning: This novel is much different and much more perplexing than advertised. All aboard.

_12:: *Light in August* by William Faulkner (1897–1962)

Faulkner created dozens of novels and stories we could have recommended, most of them set in the mythical southern county of Yoknapatawpha. The central figure of *Light in August* is a fugitive named Joe Christmas. Uh-oh! Red lights, sirens, SWAT teams of the mind: Christ figure Christ figure Christ figure. Well, all right, but in Faulkner's hands, even this most overdone of symbols assumes new meanings in the early-20th-century South. Joe is an orphan and doesn't really know where he's from, but he believes he's part black. That means he never fits in anywhere and is doomed. We also meet the similarly symbolic and out-of-place Joanna Burden. Everyone has his or her own special burden in this novel: the burden of memory, identity, history, and race. Out of the wreckage emerges the human will to endure. Not a bad message for an island castaway.

_13:: *The Plague* by Albert Camus
(1913–1960)

OK, the existentialists were good at thinking, or at least in talking in cafés, but were they good writers? Answer: not always! Jean-Paul Sartre, for example, is wholly overrated. But one born writer who would have been a genius whether he'd been an existentialist or not is Albert Camus. *The Plague* is one of his widest-ranging myths. Bubonic plague grips a small Algerian town, and Dr. Rieux battles the disease even though he can't really stop it and can't really help people once they're infected. So, why carry on? There's an answer: We try to help one another bear the burden of a universe without answers. We battle against evil in protest against evil, in solidarity with one another. It's sad, it's grueling, but it's ultimately a beautiful exploration of how friendship can redeem the worst of experience.

_14:: *Catch-22* by Joseph Heller
(1923–1999)

This book is still hanging around. Why? For one thing, it is funny. Brilliantly funny. And it does gets serious about three-quarters of the way through, but then thinks better of it and ends on a genius high note. *Catch-22* is a war novel, and much of the humor is black humor. The main character is a guy by the name of Yossarian who is afraid to die and is trying to get out of flying dangerous bombing missions. But the true central character is the Catch-22 itself: that the only way you can't go on the bombing run is if you're crazy, and if you're crazy, you are normal, so off you go. Some catch. Along the way we get great satire: of the American Organization Man, of the McCarthy hearings, of organized and disorganized religion, and, above all, of the army.

_15:: *The Color Purple* by Alice Walker
(1944–)

Alice Walker's novel operates on many levels at once. It's a story about how whites oppress blacks and how men oppress women. It's also a story about how a woman who does not value herself learns to love herself. And it's also a story about what's valuable and singular about being an American of African descent, about the birthright of pain and joy waiting for the black person willing to acknowledge it. And on top, in between, and underneath all that, this is an intensely religious novel, at least in the sense of discovering what God is: the principle of beauty waiting for us to pay attention to it. God is, in a lot of ways, the color purple. But there's no seeing that until we've seen our way through history, self, family, sex, and culture. Enough joy here to make the whole island happy.

by
Bill Hauser &
Scott Speck

Condensed
MUSIC

Contains

6 Classical Scandals Straight from the Tabloids*   My 4 Dads: Men Who Sired Rock and Roll

3 Country Outlaws Who Became Folk Heroes   9 Composers Who Pull Our Strings*

3 Bandleaders Who Made Swing the Thing   5 Classical Tunes You Know from the Movies*

3 Rock Gods Who Died at 27   Miles Ahead: 4 Candidates for the Miles Davis Cosmic Jazz

Combo   2 Reasons Why Motown Saved America   The Great Divides: 4 Breaks in Classical

Music*   3 Skirts Who Shook the Music World   6 Political Moments in Rock and Roll

*Written by Scott Speck

6 Classical Scandals Straight from the Tabloids

Every generation thinks it invented sex and scandal, but that just isn't true. Musicians, even the classical ones, have always walked on the wilder side.

_01:: First Conductor Dies from Conducting!

Jean-Baptiste Lully (1632–1687) was the first documented conductor. Before him, most musical groups followed their first violinist or their keyboard player. Lully was the first musician ever to use a baton. However, his "baton" was a heavy staff six feet long, which he pounded on the ground in time to the music. Unfortunately, this staff proved to be his undoing. One day, while merrily beating time (in a concert to celebrate the king's return to health), he stuck the staff into his foot by mistake. He developed gangrene and died. Not a good role model for conductors worldwide.

_02:: Haydn Nearly Castrated!

Franz Joseph Haydn (1732–1809) was the father of the symphony as we know it. During more than 30 years of experimentation, he came up with the form that has influenced composers to this day. But as a little boy, Haydn was known for something else—his beautiful voice. He was the star soprano in his church choir. As he got older and his voice was about to change, his choirmaster came to him with a little proposition. If he would consent to a small operation, he could keep his beautiful soprano voice forever. Haydn read-ily agreed and was just about to undergo the surgery when his father found out and put a stop to the whole thing.

_03:: Paganini Allegedly Sells Soul to Devil! (Fetches Good Price)

The Italian violinist and composer Niccolò Paganini (1782–1840) was one of the most astounding virtuosos of all time. He had amazing technique and enormous passion. He also promoted himself shamelessly, doing tricks to astonish his audience. Often before a concert he would saw partway through three of the four strings on his violin. In performance, those three strings broke, forcing him to play an entire piece on one string. Rumors flew that Paganini had sold his soul to the devil in order to play so well. Sometimes Paganini would order the lights dimmed while he played particularly spooky music. Everybody fainted—when the candles were lit again, the room appeared to be full of dead bodies, sprawled everywhere. (It didn't take much to make an audience faint in those days.)

_04:: Cross-Dressing Berlioz Nearly Snuffs Out Rival!

The renowned French composer Hector Berlioz (1803–1869) was, among other things, wacky. While away in Rome studying on a scholarship, he heard that his beloved girlfriend, Camille, back in Paris, had started seeing another guy. Furious, he resolved to kill his rival. But he needed to disguise himself. So he bought a gun, put on a dress, and boarded a train for Paris. Halfway home, however, Berlioz chickened out and threw himself into the Mediterranean. Luckily for us, and for music, he was fished out (minus the gun).

_05:: Liszt's Lucky Fans Receive Canine Surprise!

There's a reason musicians give out only autographs these days. The Hungarian Franz Liszt (1811–1886), a virtuoso in the tradition of Paganini, played the piano and created a sensation all throughout Europe. Everywhere he played, women swooned—and he sometimes swooned himself. Liszt was one of the first rock stars, and the word *Lisztomania* was coined during his lifetime. He received so many requests for a lock of his hair that he finally bought a dog, snipping off patches of fur to send to his admirers—an unexpected use for your best friend.

_06:: Peter Tchaikovsky Nearly Loses Head!

The magnificent Russian composer Peter Tchaikovsky (1840–1893) was yet another in the line of geniuses who sometimes came unhinged. Tchaikovsky loved to compose, but he hated to conduct. Unfortunately, conducting opportunities came up way too often for him—including the gala opening concert of Carnegie Hall in 1891. Neurotic to the core, Tchaikovsky conducted with one hand firmly on top of his head, in the desperate belief that otherwise his head would fall off.

My 4 Dads: Men Who Sired Rock and Roll

When rhythm and blues went on the sly, it gave birth to rock and roll. in the paternity suit that followed, a few too many men claimed to be the father.

_01:: Chuck Berry

Roll over, Beethoven; Chuck Berry (1926–) straddled the racial chasm in music, blending blues, country, and teenage pop music, and tailoring performances to black or white crowds. Berry's witty lyrics, entertaining stage presence, and signature "duck walk" made him one of the most sought-after early rock performers of the 1950s. Berry didn't even have a demo tape when Muddy Waters sent him to meet Leonard Chess, co-owner of Chess Records, in 1955. But within a week he'd written four songs, including "Maybellene," his first Top 10 hit. Unfortunately, his celebrity made him a target, and after a racially charged trial in 1959 Berry spent two years in prison for "transporting a minor across state lines for immoral purposes." He went right back to recording afterward, though, and over the past 50 years Berry's songs have influenced countless rock musicians, from the Beatles to the Stones.

_02:: Little Richard

At a time of political and social conservatism, Little Richard's frantic piano pounding, falsetto singing, and no-holds-barred stage presence were enough to drive teenagers into a frenzy, and their parents into cardiac arrest. His appearance—mascara-coated eyelashes and pompadour hairdo—was, well, different and personified the sexuality and rebelliousness of the new music called rock and roll. During the 1950s he recorded classics like "Tutti-Frutti," "Lucille," and "Good Golly, Miss Molly." However, the performances, lyrics, and even his race helped to fire the 1950s backlash against rock and roll. The music didn't go away, but in 1957, at the height of his success, Little Richard did: he had a premonition of his own damnation and quit rock and roll to become a minister. Luckily for rock fans, he returned in 1964.

_03:: Bill Haley

Originally the lead country singer of the Saddlemen, Bill Haley tossed his cowboy hat in 1952 and renamed the group Bill Haley and His Comets. A year later Haley's "Crazy Man Crazy" became the first rock and roll record to make the *Billboard* pop chart. However, his

"Rock around the Clock" had only moderate sales until it was rereleased in 1955 as part of the soundtrack for *Blackboard Jungle* (a movie about juvenile delinquents). Rock and roll and the movies have been inseparable ever since. With hits like "Shake, Rattle, and Roll" and "See You Later Alligator," Haley was considered the most popular rock performer in the world in the mid-1950s. By the early

1960s Haley's star had sunk in the United States, but it grew even stronger in England, where he was viewed as a young rebel. By that time Haley was middle-aged and nearly bald.

_04:: Ike Turner

Despite notoriety as the ex-spouse of Anna Mae Bullock (Tina Turner), Ike Turner should be remembered for his early contributions to rock and roll. Considered one of the best session guitarists, talent scouts, and producers of the 1950s, Turner landed gigs on many early R&B and rock and roll recordings but often got stiffed on the credits. He recorded a song in 1951 called "Rocket 88" at Sam Phillips's Sun Records studio in Memphis, Tennessee, with saxophonist Jackie Brenston of the Delta Cats performing the lead vocals. The Delta Cats, not Turner, got the label credit, and "Rocket 88" became a number one R&B hit—considered by many the first rock and roll recording.

3 Country Outlaws Who Became Folk Heroes

"There's always that other 20% who just don't fit in. That's what happened to me, and it happened to Johnny Cash, and it happened to Willie Nelson. We just couldn't do it the way it was set up."—Waylon Jennings on the Nashville scene.

_01:: Johnny Cash

Think Ozzy Osbourne's "bad"? You must not have met the "Man in Black." When Johnny Cash first sang, "I shot a man in Reno/Just to watch him die," he wasn't serenading radio listeners; he was playing to a roaring crowd at Folsom State Prison. True to the outlaw mantra, Cash crooned on both sides of the bars: in 1965 he was nabbed at the Mexican border for trying to smuggle drugs into the States in his guitar case. Despite doing some time (or maybe because of it), Cash still had enough mainstream clout in 1969 to host his own prime-time variety show, showcasing the talents of artists like Bob Dylan. By the fall of '69 Cash's *Folsom Prison* and *San Quentin* albums had outsold even the Beatles.

_02:: Waylon Jennings

Waylon Jennings barely escaped "the day the music died"—February 3, 1959—by giving up his plane seat to the Big Bopper. The flight crashed, killing the Big Bopper, Buddy Holly, and Richie Valens, but Jennings survived to found the "outlaw" country music movement. In the 1970s he twisted out of Nashville's grasp and started singing a more rebellious style that mixed country, rock, and rockabilly. His recording of "The Eagle" in 1991 became the anthem for troops in Operation Desert

Storm, solidifying his hero status. But by 1988 hard living caught up with Jennings, and he had to undergo triple bypass surgery (partner in crime Johnny Cash had heart surgery across the hall at the same time). Jennings recuperated to perform nearly 100 shows a year.

_03:: Willie Nelson

The man in braids, Willie Nelson, grew up working the cotton fields of Texas and selling Bibles door to door. As an adult, he often played honky-tonk bars Saturday nights and taught Sunday school the next morning. But when told to choose between the two, Nelson couldn't resist the honky-tonks. He moved from Texas to Nashville, where his songwriting skills created hits for Patsy Cline, Faron Young, and Roy Orbison. By the 1970s Nelson's own singing career skyrocketed with a string of solo hits, duets with Waylon Jennings, and collaborations with the Highwaymen, all blending redneck country with rock. True to the outlaw spirit, Willie didn't get along with "the man," and in 1991 the IRS presented him with a past-due tax bill for $16.7 million.

9 Composers Who Pull Our Strings

Even if you're living in a soundproof box, you've probably heard of these guys. But can you list one thing about any of them that you didn't see in *Amadeus* or *Immortal Beloved*? Improve your repertoire.

_01:: Bach: Placing His Faith in Music

The granddaddy of all the great composers is Johann Sebastian Bach (1685–1750), who lived during the baroque period and influenced all composers after him. In his day Bach was revered not as a composer but as an organist—and his flying feet on the organ pedals attracted tourists and gawkers from all over. He was also incredibly prolific. (See sidebar Just the Facts, page 184.) In Bach's day, most music was written for a single occasion; nobody ever thought of performing it more than once. Many a Bach masterpiece was saved from certain oblivion immediately before being used for wrapping fish (or toilet paper). Bach was extremely religious, and he wrote much of his music to express his faith. Among his magnificent masterpieces are the *St. Matthew Passion*, the B-minor Mass, the six Brandenburg Concertos, and forty-eight preludes and fugues for keyboard. (In his day, these keyboard pieces were played on some form of organ or harpsichord—the piano hadn't been invented yet.)

_02:: Mozart: The Prodigy Son

Born in Austria, Wolfgang Amadeus Mozart (1756–1791) was a boy genius—so much so that his father took him out of school for weeks at a time, dragging him all around Europe to showcase his talents in the violin, piano, and composition. Mozart was the quintessential composer of the classic period in music. His works show perfect proportion and restraint. Mozart wrote 41 symphonies, 27 piano concertos, 5 violin concertos, numerous sonatas, and an awesome bunch of operas, including *The Marriage of Figaro*, *Don Giovanni*, and *The Magic Flute*. Although he couldn't remain a child prodigy forever, he never lost his amazing gifts. He could compose a piece of music in a few minutes, and often did. Music spoke to him from some higher place; all he had to do was write it down. But despite some popular successes, Mozart died a pauper at age 35 and was buried in an unmarked mass grave.

_03:: Beethoven: The Original Deaf Jam

Impetuous and hot-tempered, German composer Ludwig van Beethoven (1770–1827) wrote music that burned with an inner fire. He carried sketchbooks with him and polished his musical ideas until they shone with an unprecedented intensity. His Fifth Symphony is one of his most recognized works, with that famous (and violent) "duh duh duh DAAAAAAAH" rhythm, often described as "fate knocking on the door." The movie *Immortal Beloved*—while not completely accurate—gives us an enlightening look at Beethoven's personality and a brilliant sampling of his music. He holds a special place in the musical pantheon: many musicians consider him the ultimate composer. In Boston's legendary Symphony Hall, one word is emblazoned above the concert stage: "Beethoven."

_04:: Brahms: The Boy from the Brothel Makes Good

As a kid, Johannes Brahms (1833–1897) made his living playing the piano in houses of ill re-

pute. (How many composers can say that?) As he grew up, Brahms perfectly combined the restraint and structure of the classic style with the strong emotions of the Romantic. His pieces are put together as perfectly and intricately as a jigsaw puzzle, and yet they also have overwhelming emotional force. He became known as the successor to Beethoven—a reputation that saddled him with an incredible feeling of responsibility. Notoriously self-critical, he destroyed dozens and dozens of pieces before they ever saw the light of day. He didn't publish his first symphony until he was 43 years old. (By that age, Mozart had written 41 symphonies and been dead for 8 years.) Among his most beautiful pieces are all four of his symphonies, his intermezzi for piano (especially opus 118), his violin concerto, and his two piano concertos.

_05:: Dvořák: Bohemian Rhapsodies

If any composer represented the common people, it was Antonin Dvořák (1841–1904). Born in a small town in Bohemia (now part of the Czech Republic), Dvořák was surrounded by farmers and tradespeople as a child. He studied music with village schoolmasters and played in a local band. It was Johannes Brahms (see above) who "discovered" Dvořák and championed his music. Dvořák's gift for melody and musical inventiveness took him far—specifically, to America, where he became director of the National Conservatory in New York. While in the United States, he wrote one of his best-known works: the Symphony no. 9 (subtitled *From the New World*). But even at the height of his fame, Dvořák maintained a nostalgic love for his native Bohemia. A rustic, folksy quality can be found in almost every piece he ever wrote. Dvořák was one of the composers who started a *nationalist* trend—writing classical music based on the folk tunes of his homeland.

_06:: Verdi: Songs in the Key of Strife

Some musicians think that the Italian Giuseppe Verdi (1813–1901) was the greatest opera composer who ever lived. Verdi (whose full name means "Joe Green" in Italian) had an immense talent for creating some of the catchiest, most hummable melodies ever written for the human voice. Even today, Verdi's operas are favorites for that reason—and also because they tackle such primal human subjects as love, sex, jealousy, passion, murder, and more sex. Verdi was a master of dramatic pacing that still keeps his audiences on the edge of their seats. Among his 28 masterful operas are *La Traviata*, *Il Trovatore*, *Rigoletto*, *Otello*, and, most beloved of all, *Aïda*—that grand drama set in Egypt, complete with an elephant-laden triumphal march.

_07:: Tchaikovsky: The Great Communicator

If ever a composer deserved to be called Romantic, it was the Russian composer Peter Tchaikovsky (1840–1893). Emotionally, Tchaikovsky was a mess—neurotic, insecure, intense, overly sensitive, easily depressed, and easily elated. But luckily, he had the talent to express those feelings with glorious melodies. Tchaikovsky mastered the art of direct communication with his audience. When you hear his pieces, there's nothing between him and you; you feel as if you know the guy, and you like him. His music came to the attention of a wealthy widow, Nadezhda von Meck, who sent him a monthly allowance so that he could compose freely—on the condition that they never meet. When Tchaikovsky dedicated his Fourth Symphony "To My Best Friend," he was referring to her. Tragically, Tchaikovsky died at age 53 from cholera. (For years scholars have debated whether or not he purposely drank a glass of contaminated water in order to kill himself.) His credits include *Romeo and Juliet* and the ballets *Swan Lake*, *Sleeping Beauty*, and, most famous of all, *The Nutcracker*.

_08:: Debussy: Great First Impressions

The French composer Claude Debussy (1862–1918) brought about a new revolution in classical music. He tried to do with his music what the impressionist painters were doing with art—evoking the impressions of sights, sounds, fragrances, and even tastes. To do this, Debussy threw away traditional harmony and invented his own combinations of notes. Needless to say, he flunked out of the Paris Conservatory. He is celebrated for inventing the "whole tone scale"—that gauzy up-and-down scale you hear played by a harp whenever a character on TV has a flashback. Debussy's first important piece was *Prelude to the Afternoon of a Faun*, which caused a stir for its way-out harmonies. Years later a ballet set to the music caused as much of a stir for its racy choreography. His most evocative piece is the extraordinarily powerful three-movement work *La Mer* (The Sea), an incredible tour de force of imagery. When you hear the music, you can hear the howling of the wind, smell the salt air, feel the ocean spray on your face, and experience the first signs of motion sickness.

_09:: Copland: An American Original

American composer Aaron Copland (1900–1990) is beloved because he created, for the first time, a truly American sound. His music echoes the sounds of the great outdoors—the Wild West, the rolling hills of Appalachia, and even the bustle of New York City. By far Copland's best-known work (and the most recognized piece of American classical music) is *Appalachian Spring*. This music, originally written for ballet, tells the story of a young couple setting up a house and beginning their new life together. Copland also scored big with *Fanfare for the Common Man*, a short piece for brass and percussion that gets ripped off in nearly every Olympic theme you've ever heard.

3 Bandleaders Who Made Swing the Thing

It's true: swing existed even before there were Gap commercials. Way back in the 1930s, with the Depression raging and Prohibition ending, people started looking for a release—they found it in swing.

_01:: Benny Goodman

In 1934 jazz clarinetist Benny Goodman, the "king of swing," became a regular on a national radio show that featured the three popular dance themes of the time: traditional, Latin, and big band. Goodman used these broadcasts to feature a new jazz-oriented sound called swing, integrating African American jazz sounds into traditional dance band music. Goodman and his band always played last on the show, usually after midnight, when most people east of the Rocky Mountains were already in bed. When the band went on national tour, it played to small audiences—until reaching California, where radio fans lined up for blocks. Based on that solid fan base, Goodman's reputation and musical stylings quickly grew. Because Goodman was white, he was given more opportunities to use his media savvy—unusual among African American swing bands of the time—to help bring swing to the masses.

_02:: Count Basie

While working the vaudeville circuit in the 1920s, William "Count" Basie got stranded in Kansas City, Missouri, when his tour fell apart. The rough-and-tumble frontier town turned out to be a hotbed for jazz, though, and by 1929 Basie had joined Kansas City's leading jazz band. After moving the band to New York City in 1936, he renamed it Count Basie and His Orchestra. Freddie Green on guitar, Walter Page on bass, Jo Jones on drums, and Basie on piano made up the rhythm section at the heart of the band. The four took the prevailing bluesy jazz melodies and created fast-moving, polished versions, fusing blues and ragtime into a jazz style that evolved into swing. Basie continued to innovate his style to meet the times, but creating and popularizing swing stands as his greatest contribution to music.

_03:: Duke Ellington

Duke Ellington didn't invent swing, but he definitely made it "the thing." During his lifetime Ellington composed close to 2,000 works that ranged from big band swing music to opera. In the 1920s Ellington and his band began performing at the Cotton Club in Harlem. Their regular appearances on radio broadcasts from the Cotton Club quickly gained them a national audience and an international reputation. In 1932 Ellington composed "It Don't Mean a Thing (If It Ain't Got That Swing)," correctly anticipating that swing would quickly become a national obsession. Like

Goodman, Ellington could attract a large national radio fan base of both black and white

dance audiences looking for fun during the Depression-ridden, post-Prohibition 1930s.

5 Classical Tunes You Know from the Movies

Classical music is the perfect movie backdrop: lots of emotion, without those pesky lyrics that conflict with the plot. Here are five hummable tunes you'll recognize from the silver screen.

_01:: That Tune from *Die Hard*

Ludwig van Beethoven's Ninth Symphony is one of the most thrillingly triumphant pieces ever written, so naturally Hollywood exploits it whenever possible. The symphony begins in a somber and severe minor key; the composer seems to be struggling mightily against fate. But in the final section—for the first time ever in a symphony—a chorus and soloists join in, singing the "Ode to Joy" (*"Freude, schöner Götterfunken . . ."*). This theme brings the music from darkness to light, and the symphony ends in a titanic blaze of optimistic glory. Several film directors have made use of the extreme emotions of this piece in their films—from *A Clockwork Orange* to *Die Hard*. And Audi once released a hilarious commercial where a bevy of crash-test dummies comes to life, singing the "Ode to Joy" in tribute to a particularly safe car.

_02:: That Tune from *Moonraker*

Peter Tchaikovsky's wildly popular symphonic poem depicts in musical notes Shakespeare's beloved story of star-crossed lovers.

The piece, *Romeo and Juliet*, has long been a favorite on the concert stage, but nowhere has it enjoyed more success than in movies and on TV. The lush, soaring love theme from *Romeo and Juliet* seems to come up every time two characters fall in love. And in many cases the music swells onscreen when two unlikely characters fall in love (as in the James Bond movie *Moonraker*, when the evil steel-toothed character, Jaws, falls for a similarly scary-looking woman).

_03:: That Tune from *Apocalypse Now*

When German composer Richard Wagner (1813–1883) wrote his "Ride of the Valkyries" for his opera *Die Walküre*, he was depicting mythical, powerful god-women riding winged horses, swooping down over the battlefield, scooping up fallen soldiers, and carrying them up to Valhalla to defend the gods. But film director Francis Ford Coppola had an even better use for this music. This is the piece that Robert Duvall blares from the helicopters in *Apocalypse Now* as soldiers swoop down and attack a Vietnamese village. In this context, the music is more than awesome—it's absolutely horrifying. This is one of the most effective uses of preexisting classical music in all of moviedom—second only to the following example.

_04:: That Tune from *2001*

German composer Richard Strauss (1864–1949) wrote the opening of *Also sprach Zarathustra* ("Thus Spake Zarathustra") to depict the awe of a primal sunrise—which inspires the prophet and thinker Zarathustra to come down from his self-imposed exile in the mountains to begin enlightening the masses. You know this music: three long notes ascending in the trumpets, followed by an enormous "da-DAAAAH" for the whole orchestra, followed by pulsing in the kettledrums. Director Stanley Kubrick used Strauss's music three times in his movie *2001: A Space Odyssey*—also to accompany a moment of enlightenment. You hear it at the very beginning, "The Dawn of Man," where one ape realizes that he can use a bone as a weapon and elevates himself above all other apes; in the middle, when astronauts discover that Great Black Monolith on the moon; and at the end, when the Star Child is born. Don't ask us what it means—we don't know. But, man, is it primal.

_05:: That Tune from *10*

Bolero by French composer Maurice Ravel (1875–1937) is nothing but a single melody, repeated over and over, to a simple Spanish rhythm. The piece begins simply, with an innocent flute playing the melody quietly over a hushed snare drum. Over the next 15 minutes, the sound grows and grows (making a crescendo) and ends with an overwhelming, monstrous climax. Not surprisingly, the piece has long been associated with sex. Director Blake Edwards took advantage of this fact in his movie *10*. Everyone knows the scene where Bo Derek and Dudley Moore finally have their romantic moment, accompanied by this seductive number, with hilarious results.

3

Rock Gods Who Died at 27

Over the years many rockers chanted the "hope I die before I get old" mantra from the Who's "My Generation." But why have so many left us at age 27? (Jimi Hendrix also belongs on this list—check out his story on page 260.)

_01:: Jim Morrison (1943–1971): The Lizard King

Unlike the Beatles, Jim Morrison and the Doors explored the darker side of rock with lyrics focusing on violence and death. Between 1967 and 1970, the Doors poured out such hits as "Light My Fire," "Riders on the Storm," and "Hello, I Love You," but by 1969 Morrison's alcohol and drug problems provoked erratic concert performances often interrupted by drunken confusion, culminating in his arrest for indecent exposure and public drunkenness at a Miami concert. Physically and emotionally drained and facing legal problems, Morrison moved to Paris to recuperate. On July 3, 1971, he was found dead in his bathtub, a victim of a heart attack. Due to the secretive and confusing circumstances surrounding his death and burial, many fans refuse to believe that Jim Morrison is really dead and buried in a Paris cemetery.

_02:: Janis Joplin (1943–1970): Hard-Edged Soulstress

The gritty, R&B-infused vocals and legendary hard living of white soul singer Janis Joplin revived the role of the female blues singer in contemporary rock music. As the lead singer of Big Brother and the Holding Company, Joplin scored a number of hits in the mid-1960s such as "Piece of My Heart," "Ball & Chain," and "Summertime," and she mesmerized the crowd at the 1967 Monterey Pop Festival with her now legendary performance. But shortly after completing the recording of her classic rock album *Pearl*, Joplin was found dead of a heroin overdose in a Hollywood hotel October 4, 1970. While the drug overdose is listed as the official cause of death, many feel that the years of living life at light speed took its toll on Joplin.

_03:: Kurt Cobain (1967–1994): Rock's Reluctant Prince

The life of Kurt Cobain, the lead singer/songwriter for Nirvana and one of the founders of the Seattle grunge movement in the early 1990s, was one of contradictions. His anti-establishment message became the rallying cry for a new generation of youth, but as the band became more popular and successful, Cobain became increasingly depressed, saying that fans were missing his message. Between May 1993 and April 1994 Cobain overdosed at least three times and often threatened suicide. Police were called to Cobain's home in March 1994 when he locked himself in a room with a revolver, and Cobain then checked himself into a Los Angeles hospital for treat-

ment. He stayed only two days. A little over a
week later Cobain was found dead in a room
above his garage with a shotgun wound to the
head.

THE JAZZ TIMELINE

Jazz is an American original. Emerging from the postbellum south, the music has continued to evolve and change along with culture and the dramatic events of the last century. And although there have been numerous variations of the style, the history of jazz can be placed into six distinctive periods.

Dixieland   Colorful and brassy, Dixieland music emerged in and around New Orleans at the end of the 19th century. Dominated by marching bands performing an upbeat form of gospel and march music, the style is typified by songs like "When the Saints Go Marching In."

Swing   Appearing on the scene during the 1930s, just in time for the Depression and post-Prohibition times, swing caught on as the public was looking for a release from their problems. Swing allowed them to dance the night away. Featuring elaborate big band arrangements with layers of synchronized instrumentation, swing era jazz is exemplified by the big band music of Benny Goodman, Duke Ellington, and Glenn Miller.

Bebop   The 1940s witnessed a musical backlash against the big band swing sounds. Bebop is the antithesis of swing, with its followers avoiding melody altogether and emphasizing chordal improvisation. With big bands replacing smaller ensembles emphasizing solo performances, the bebop period is considered the most significant period in jazz. Among the leading contributors to this era are Dizzy Gillespie and Charlie Parker.

Cool jazz   By the late 1940s jazz was again changing its style from the hard bop sound to a softer, warmer, more textured harmonic style. Cool, or West Coast, jazz is a mixture of swing and bebop. Ensembles became the in thing again, and the work of Miles Davis (the album *Birth of the Cool*) ushered in the era.

Free jazz   In the late 1950s jazz was once again ready for a change. As in the past, this change was dramatic and the opposite of the existing style. Free jazz is all about experimentation and improvisation. Soloists shed ensembles and were totally free to experience the music, providing their own unique interpretations. The music of John Coltrane and Ornette Coleman is the music of free jazz.

Fusion   Bursting on the scene in the late 1960s, fusion blurred the popular electric sounds of rock and funk with jazz. Popularly embraced when Miles Davis began using electronic devices (e.g., wah-wah pedal) to give his trumpet a unique sound, the fusion movement was expanded by a legion of artists including Herbie Hancock and Chick Corea. This style of jazz continues to evolve today as jazz crosses paths with such contemporary sounds as hip-hop.

Miles Ahead:

4

Candidates for the Miles Davis Cosmic Jazz Combo

Pure jazz is the perfect syncopation of sound, and the following four artists are the soul of syncopation. With this cosmic combo in place, somewhere in the universe cats are grooving to jazz that's out of this world.

_01:: John Coltrane: Sax

John Coltrane almost single-handedly introduced the tenor saxophone to jazz. His groundbreaking style of playing long notes in a piercing, screaming manner coupled with his talent for improvisation has become the standard for jazz saxophonists today. After leaving the navy in 1947, Coltrane moved to Philadelphia, where he played in a number of bands, including Dizzy Gillespie's. In 1955 he joined Miles Davis's group and over the next six years gained an international reputation as the premier tenor jazz saxophonist. Always experimenting, Coltrane moved to the free jazz style in the 1960s, which allowed him to develop his unique sound even further and create music that was unquestionably pure Coltrane.

_02:: Thelonious Monk: Piano

Growing up in New York City, Monk began taking piano lessons at age 5 and by 13 was so accomplished that the Apollo Theater banned him from the weekly amateur contest because he'd won too many times. Along with Charlie Parker and Dizzy Gillespie, Monk created the jazz style called bebop in the early 1940s. By 1945 Monk's innovative form of bop stretched so ahead of its time that most other bebop players thought he was crazy; however, the style remained in vogue for the next 25 years. During his career, Monk played with many of the greats, including fellow cosmic combo members John Coltrane, Miles Davis, and Dizzy Gillespie. Classic pieces like "Round Midnight," "Straight No Chaser," and "Blue Monk" have been praised for their depth, complexity, and innovation.

_03:: Dizzy Gillespie: Trumpet

John "Dizzy" Gillespie was the heart and soul of bebop jazz. After moving to New York City in 1937, Gillespie jammed with the hottest jazz bands before he joined Cab Calloway's orchestra in 1939. During a session with Lionel Hampton, Gillespie became the first musician to record in the new bebop jazz style. Later, with Charlie Parker, he perfected the new jazz style, which took the place of swing and remained the primary force in jazz until Miles Davis's cool jazz movement replaced it in 1948. By the 1950s Gillespie transitioned from big bands to smaller combos, where he aided the development of upcoming players like John Coltrane. Gillespie's musical style and unique appearance—puffed cheeks, goatee, black horn-rimmed glasses, and beret—became the symbols of modern jazz and its rebellious nature.

_04:: Miles Davis: Bandleader

While best known for his trumpet work, Davis was an innovative bandleader and composer. Unlike the high-energy bebop style of Dizzy Gillespie, the West Coast cool jazz style that Davis created relied on phrasing and timing restraint. Davis's unique use of note placement and silence led to an intimate form of improvisation. Davis also had a knack for re-cruiting fantastic sidemen: he performed with Thelonious Monk in 1954 and formed a quintet with John Coltrane in 1955. In fact, almost every modern jazz great seemingly emerged from one of his bands, including Wayne Shorter, Herbie Hancock, Freddie Hubbard, and Chick Corea. Always pushing jazz forward, Davis formed an experimental quintet in the early 1960s that drifted from traditional jazz to avant-garde material to funky keyboard fusion. Even though this dismayed Davis's critics, the fans loved it.

2 Reasons Why Motown Saved America

The British are coming! The British are coming! Thank God for Hitsville, U.S.A.

_01:: The Sound Track for a New America

The growth of the black movement after the Civil Rights Act of 1964 happened just when rock and roll was ready for something new. Baby boomers hit young adulthood, bringing with them different attitudes, ideals, and disposable income. Building on the late 1950s doo-wop and girl group phenomena, Berry Gordy borrowed $800 from his family and founded Motown Records. Gordy intended to groom young black artists to be accepted by mainstream America. In this way, black rock and roll became more polished and acceptable to a wide spectrum of listeners. Not only did this appeal to the older adult audience, but it created the love songs for an entire generation. Most importantly, it became a subtle impetus for racial integration, with a young and powerful generation of black and white baby boomers sharing not only the same music but also the same attitudes and behaviors.

_02:: Motown Was America's Only Defense against the British Invasion

With the arrival of the Beatles in 1964, American rock and pop music became British. British music, dress, and style permeated all aspects of American culture, and British groups dominated Top 40 lists, radio play time, and record sales. Even most American bands sounded British. Only one rock genre survived and thrived during this onslaught: Motown. Between 1964 and 1967, Motown scored 14 number one singles and 46 Top 15 hits on the pop charts while also producing huge hits on the R&B charts. In 1967, at the pinnacle of Motown's success, 75% of its releases made

the charts. Motown music peacefully coexisted with British rock because both evolved from the same African American roots. Motown even became the "safe" music for parents and older adults who had decried black rock and roll as "jungle music" just a few years earlier.

The Great Divides:
Breaks in Classical Music

If you think all classical music sounds the same, it's time to get your ears checked . . . or you could study up on the differences.

_01:: Baroque: Ornamental Floss

The earliest classical music you are likely to hear in concert comes from the baroque era (from about 1600 to 1750). The artists, painters, architects, and composers of this period filled their works with fancy little swirls and curlicues. Although baroque music might sound tame to us now, back then it was seen as highly expressive—and its complex melodies, running up and down, were seen as extremes of emotional abandon. Some of the superb composers of the baroque period were Antonio Vivaldi, George Frederick Handel, and Johann Sebastian Bach. At one time or another all of the baroque composers worked either in a noble court, in a rich man's house, or in the Christian church.

_02:: Classic: A Return to Form

All of the music in the first half of this chapter is called classical music, but just to confuse you, one of the time periods within classical music is known as the classical period (from about 1750 to 1825). The classical period was an overreaction to the excesses of the baroque—a pendulum swing in the opposite direction. Whereas baroque music had been florid, extravagant, and emotional, the classical style was sparer, more reserved, and more controlled—a return to the clean, perfectly proportioned ideal of ancient Greece. (Think white marble temples, and you'll get the idea.) Great composers of the classical period include Franz Joseph Haydn, Wolfgang Amadeus Mozart, and, in his early years, Ludwig van Beethoven. All of them wrote music in certain forms: symphonies (which Haydn basically invented), sonatas for one or two instruments, and concertos for a solo instrument with orchestra.

_03:: Romantic: A Heartfelt Response

If the restraint of the classical period had been a reaction to baroque emotion, the Romantic period (from about 1825 to 1900) was a counterreaction. In Romantic music, what mattered most was personal expression. Not surprisingly, some of the most popular music in the world comes from this period. In Romantic music you often find huge orchestras, extremes of loud and soft, and enormous passionate outbursts. To express this emotion, Romantic music often makes use of different harmonies—stretching our sense of "what key we're in" almost to the breaking point. The music sometimes seems to be crying, as in the last movement of Peter Tchaikovsky's Sixth Symphony (*Pathétique*). Because the expression of individual feelings was so important, a lot of concertos for solo instruments with orchestra were written during this period. The most celebrated composers of the Romantic period include Robert Schumann, Frédéric Chopin, Johannes Brahms, Peter Tchaikovsky, Franz Liszt, Richard Wagner, Richard Strauss, Gustav Mahler, and Antonin Dvořák.

_04:: Twentieth Century . . . and Beyond

Around 1900 composers began to break all the rules. There was no longer one reigning style—the new rule was "anything goes." After stretching harmony almost to the breaking point, composers such as Arnold Schoenberg (1874–1951) decided to break it completely. Now nothing was in any key at all—the music

---

Alphabet Soup

4 SINGER TYPES FROM THE WORLD OF OPERA

castrato [kuh-STRAH-toe]: *n* A male singer, castrated in the early years of his life, in order to prevent his voice from changing. In centuries past a castrato's voice was prized for its combination of male strength and female beauty. The most famous castrato of all time was Farinelli, who became extremely rich off his rare talent. As you can read in 6 Classical Scandals Straight from the Tabloids on p. 174, the composer Franz Joseph Haydn narrowly escaped this particular career path.

heldentenor [HEL-den-teh-NOR]: *n* The tenor (high-voiced male singer) in a dramatic opera who has a *huge* voice—big enough to trumpet over a large orchestra, knocking the audience back into their seats. A heldentenor (literally, "heroic tenor") can be found most often in operas by Wagner.

mezzo [MET-soh] *soprano*: *n* Literally, "half soprano." This is a woman whose voice—and pay—is significantly lower than a (high-voiced) soprano's.

prima donna [PREE-muh DON-na]: *n* A soprano, literally the "first lady." This is the woman who plays the heroine in an opera. Throughout history, this first lady has often been demanding to the point of ridiculousness. As a result, the expression "prima donna" is often used to refer to people who think the world revolves around them. Also known as "diva" (literally, "goddess").

---

sounded dissonant, as if all the notes were wrong. Much of the time this music was cold and unemotional, almost as if composed by a computer. Meanwhile, the composer Igor Stravinsky brought about other innovations: weird rhythms that change every second, keeping you off balance; strange combinations of instruments; and music that's in more than one key at a time (different instruments playing in different keys simultaneously). These challenging styles, believe it or not, persisted in classical music until the very late 20th century—and now the pendulum has begun to swing again. In the first decade of the 21st century, serious classical composers are once again writing beautiful, emotional melodies, constant rhythms, and harmonies that we can get our ears around. Contemporary music is now more audience-friendly than it has been in a long time.

3 Skirts Who Shook the Music World

Who says girls can't rock? The following women took sound to the extreme, blasting music past its traditional boundaries and breaking every convention along the way.

_01:: Grace Slick

With her powerful vocals, strong lyrics, and "up against the wall" political activism, Grace Slick was the voice of the 1960s San Francisco music scene. A former model, Slick joined Jefferson Airplane in 1965 as its lead singer and songwriter and quickly started using her songs and performances to ignite audiences to her causes—she was one of the first rock voices against the military-industrial complex and the war in Vietnam. Slick's "everything goes" peace-and-love lifestyle kept her in the eye of the public and the authorities; on at least one occasion she was arrested for public disorder when she incited the concert crowd to turn on the police in attendance. Rumor also has it that Slick the prankster tried to drop LSD into the punch bowl at her college reunion (also attended by one of President Nixon's daughters).

_02:: Joan Baez

Baez was one of the first artists in the 1960s to speak out against racism, social injustices, and the war in Vietnam. Not only did this revitalize folk music but it actually helped to create the protest music of the later 1960s and 1970s. During the 1960s, Baez helped start the career of Bob Dylan by recording his songs and sharing concert billings with him. As Baez's preoccupation with the war in Vietnam grew, so did her political activism: she founded the Institute for the Study of Non-violence and married David Harris, a student antiwar protestor jailed for draft evasion. Using her three-octave voice to spread her message, Baez has remained politically active, and her influence is still felt today in the music of the Indigo Girls and Mary Chapin Carpenter.

_03:: Chrissie Hynde

After moving from Ohio to London in the mid-1970s, Hynde co-founded the Pretenders and quickly became the prototype female punk rocker. During a time when British punk rock was male dominated, Hynde overcame the barriers and gave punk rock accept-

ability to a larger audience. Her punk-tough stage presence, appearance (bangs hanging over her eyes), and witty, biting lyrics quickly made Hynde one of the most assertive female singers in rock and roll and a model for many artists who followed. Not one to shy away from a cause she believes in, Hynde still maintains her strong, assertive nature both on and off stage and has inspired a new generation, including Sheryl Crow.

6 Political Moments in Rock and Roll

You've heard of the separation between church and state, but what about rock and state? Here are rockers who used their power to make heavy political statements.

_01:: Frank Zappa and the Mothers of Prevention

Ah, the birth of being carded to buy a CD! In 1985 a group of four Washington, D.C., mothers founded the Parents Music Resource Center (PMRC) in an attempt to curb sexually explicit lyrics in contemporary music. Tipper Gore, wife of then-senator Al Gore, and Susan Baker, wife of Secretary of the Treasury James Baker, were two of the four founders. The PMRC persuaded the Senate Committee on Commerce, Science, and Transportation (including senior member Al Gore) to convene a hearing on truth in packaging on record albums. While notable musicians like Frank Zappa and John Denver were summoned to the stand, Dee Snider of Twisted Sister was

singled out for questioning, especially by Senator Gore. The PMRC accused Twisted Sister of advocating sadomasochism, bondage, and rape in their song "Under the Blade." In turn, Snider accused the PMRC of reading into the lyrics of songs, insisting that the song "Under the Blade" was written for Twisted Sister's guitarist, who was going into surgery and was afraid of the operation.

_02:: Sinead O'Connor Takes On the Pope

The Irish singer started making waves back in 1990 when she refused to perform at a New Jersey concert after "The Star-Spangled Banner," but her best-known public stance took place on *Saturday Night Live* in 1992. After she performed the Bob Marley song "War" (a bit of a scandal in itself), she proclaimed, "Fight the real enemy!" and tore up a picture of Pope John Paul II in front of the national television audience. NBC received over 5,400 letters and calls; the National Ethnic Coalition of Organizations hired a steamroller and crushed her albums, tapes, and CDs on Sixth Avenue in New York City; and two weeks later she was booed throughout her performance at a Bob Dylan tribute concert at Madison Square Garden. When reruns of that *SNL* show air, a sans-Pope rehearsal tape is substituted.

_03:: John, Yoko, and Bed-In for Peace

John Lennon and Yoko Ono knew better than to expect a paparazzi-free wedding, so they used the press to advance their peace movement cause. On March 20, 1969, Lennon and Ono were married and the next week, in what was surely the strangest honeymoon of all time, held the first Bed-In for Peace in the presidential suite at the Amsterdam Hilton. In May they attempted to resume the bed-in in the United States, but the U.S. government refused them entry because of earlier drug charges. Instead, the bed-in took place in Montreal at the Queen Elizabeth Hotel. In front of a crowd of friends, supporters, and 50 reporters, John and Yoko stayed in bed for a week growing their hair for peace. During the week, they had recording equipment brought in and recorded the antiwar anthem "Give Peace a Chance."

_04:: Bob Dylan and the Hurricane

In 1967 Rubin "Hurricane" Carter, a successful professional boxer, received a life sentence for the murder of three people in a bar in Pat-

terson, New Jersey. Carter proclaimed his innocence and said he was the victim of a racist court and corrupt white policemen. Carter's memoirs, *The Sixteenth Round*, written during his imprisonment, caught Bob Dylan's attention, and Dylan wrote the song "Hurricane" about the case and staged two benefit concerts to raise money for Carter's defense. The first

---

Myths and Misconceptions
EVERY BREATH YOU TAKE

With the emergence of new wave rock in the early 1980s, British group The Police fused punk, reggae, and jazz into a musical style that set the direction for the next evolution of rock. In 1983 The Police released the ballad "Every Breath You Take," which became their biggest hit. While most people viewed it as a beautiful love song, that couldn't be further from the truth. The group's lead singer, Sting, has stated that the song is really about a guy stalking his ex-girlfriend. With lyrics like "every breath you take/every move you make/every bond you break/ every step you take/I'll be watching you," how could so many be so wrong? Over the years another story has surfaced about the meaning of the song. Since The Police were known for making political statements, people have come to wonder if the song wasn't subtle social commentary on what the group thought was ever-increasing interference by government into private lives. After all, it was 1983--1984, and as irony would have it, drummer Stewart Copeland's father was an ex-CIA agent. George Orwell would have been proud.

concert took place in Madison Square Garden on December 8, 1975, and the second at the Astrodome in Houston, Texas, on January 26, 1976. Two months after the Houston concert, the New Jersey Supreme Court ordered a retrial for Hurricane Carter, but Carter was once again convicted and returned to prison. Finally, in 1985, Carter was released after his lawyers proved that Carter had been denied his right to a fair trial in his earlier cases.

_05:: Madonna's Prayer

Madonna's lyrics, concerts, and video performances have fueled her career and, in many cases, her critics. The 1989 video to "Like a Prayer" is the perfect example. In the video Madonna witnesses the murder of a white woman and the arrest of an innocent black man in a church, replete with religious imagery including stigmata and burning crosses. A statue of a black saint (the black man accused of the murder) comes alive when she kisses his feet. As expected, Madonna's message was lost in the public outcry over the overt erotic and perceived sacrilegious overtones of the video. Hundreds of calls and letters were sent to the networks asking the video to be removed from airplay. The video

was censured by the Vatican, and Pepsi-Cola canceled a multimillion-dollar endorsement deal with Madonna (she'd already been paid, though).

_06:: Bob Marley Gets Up, Stands Up

Marley interlaced social commentary with reggae sounds and became a major force in Jamaica's turbulent and sometimes deadly politics. During the hotly contested 1975 national elections, Marley agreed to give a concert in support of Jamaica's prime minister, Michael Manley. On the night prior to the scheduled concert, Marley was wounded in a failed assassination attempt, but he went on to play the concert the next night with his arm in sling. In an attempt to bring about reconciliation between the warring political factions in a Jamaica, Marley held a concert in 1978 that brought together Prime Minister Manley and opposition leader Edward Seaga. During the concert, both men joined Marley on stage and shook hands, an incredible development in Jamaica at the time. For his efforts, Marley received the United Nations' Peace Medal the following year. Rock's most visible spokesperson for peace and brotherhood died of cancer in 1981 at age 36.

by
Valarie Samulski

Condensed
PERFORMING ARTS

Contains

Tony Tony Tony: 3 Plays That Smashed (Plus 3 That Crashed!) ✳ Men in Tights: 5 Guys Who Sent the Dance World Spinning ✳ Men in Skirts?: 3 Traditions of Theatrical Cross-Dressing ✳ 6 Broadway Originals Now Available at Blockbuster ✳ 5 Barefoot Beauties Who Gave Birth to Modern Dance ✳ All the World's a Stage: 5 Traditional Theater Forms ✳ Pirouette Quartet: 4 Prima Ballerinas You Need to Know ✳ Taking It to the Street: 5 Tricks of the Trade for Aspiring Sidewalk Stars ✳ 5 Dance Styles Meant to Bring You Closer to God ✳ 3 Performance Artists Who Scare Us ✳ 6 Sexy Dances That Will Leave You Drooling ✳

Tony Tony Tony:
3 Plays That Smashed (Plus 3 That Crashed!)

Sometimes there's a fine line between *Mame* and lame. A few of these shows hit the Great White Way running, while others stumbled right from the start.

The Hits
_01:: *Cats* (1982–2000)

Who would've guessed that a bunch of human-size felines singing could make Broadway magic? Based on a book of poems by T. S. Eliot called *Old Possum's Book of Practical Cats*, the show was also unusual because it didn't have any dialogue. Entirely dependent on the music of the ubiquitous Andrew Lloyd Weber and spectacular dancing, *Cats* ran on Broadway for 18 years at the Winter Garden Theatre and eventually became the show people loved to hate before closing in 2000. Theatergoers and critics could never agree on the merit of this mighty but mindless spectacle. Reviewer Clive Barnes probably captured the ambivalence best when he said that the play was "breathtakingly unoriginal yet superbly professional."

_02:: *Deathtrap* (1978–1982)

Deathtrap, the longest running mystery play on Broadway, is a perfect example of how to steal from Shakespeare—in this case, drafting a play within a play—for stage success. Written by Ira Levin (who also wrote *A Kiss before Dying*), *Deathtrap* tells the story of a celebrated writer of Broadway thrillers suffering a dry spell, who plots to murder his student and steal the student's script to sell as his own. In a combination of suspense and humor, Levin confuses the audience with plot twists and references to his own play as it's being performed before delivering a surprise ending. *Deathtrap*, despite belonging to a rather obscure Broadway genre (the mystery play), had a story line that earned four Tony Award nominations and a film venture in 1982, starring Christopher Reeve and Michael Caine.

_03:: *Metamorphoses* (2002–2003)

Say it with us now: "More is more." Especially on Broadway. Fabulous dance routines and interesting stories aren't always enough. So, what exactly could push Ovid's Greek myths over the top? Sometimes you just have to throw in a swimming pool. And that's exactly what *Metamorphoses* did: The stage was transformed into a 27-foot-wide pool of water. It wasn't the first time that a swimming pool had been created onstage (the 1952 musical *Wish You Were Here* also had aquatic scenic design), but it was the first time audiences experienced anything of that scale. Who knows? By the next half century we might see actual tidal waves on stage.

The Flops
_01:: *Breakfast at Tiffany's* (1966)

There has to be some substance behind the hype if a Broadway play is going to make it. The famous movie *Breakfast at Tiffany's* (1961) crashed and burned on Broadway, despite being the most anticipated musical of the season. Based on Truman Capote's novella, the play starred two glamorous television names: Mary Tyler Moore and Richard Chamberlain. However, during the first preview, the author himself was quoted as saying, "I don't like the score or the leading lady," and members of the audience actually talked back to the actors and walked out. When the show closed prematurely, the producer, David Merrick, joked that "Tiffany's the jeweler promised to pay off the loss. Their competitor, Cartier's, wanted me to keep it open to damage Tiffany's."

_02:: *Miss Moffat* (1974)

Even Bette Davis couldn't pull off this Broadway save. At 66, she quit the play *Miss Moffat* and explained, "I'm too big a star to be giving a poor performance, which I'm now doing." Though she starred in the film of the same name in 1945, by 1974 she was too old to play the part, appearing visibly uncomfortable onstage and interrupting herself midsong to ask where she was. While the producer, Joshua Logan, would have liked to have placed all the blame on Bette's shoulders (especially since she had previously bailed on two other plays), the play itself was past its prime, struggling with a less-than-stellar score and frequently awkward lyrics.

Just the Facts

TOP 10 LONGEST RUNNING BROADWAY SHOWS

1. *Cats*
2. *Les Misérables*
3. *Phantom of the Opera*
4. *A Chorus Line*
5. *Oh! Calcutta* (revival)
6. *Miss Saigon*
7. *Beauty and the Beast*
8. *42nd Street*
9. *Grease*
10. *Fiddler on the Roof*

_03:: *Superman* (1966)

Is there really a Superman curse? Closing after only four months in performance, it seemed as if "It's a bird . . . It's a plane . . . It's Superman" just wasn't meant to grace the stage. However, the writers, David Newman and Robert Benton, knew that the Superman comic book phenomenon should be milked somewhere, so they persevered and wrote a screenplay. *Superman*, the movie, became a series of films and a cross-marketer's dream, spawning clothing, dolls, and a television series. For the Hollywood bound, sometimes bombing on Broadway is just the beginning.

Men in Tights:
Guys Who Sent the Dance World Spinning

Not that there's anything wrong with that. The male contingent of dancers may be small, but a few fantastic guys have ignored the "twinkle toes" comments long enough to dazzle audiences.

_01:: Bill "Bojangles" Robinson
(1878–1949)

Mr. Bojangles, the father of tapology, began his dance career on street corners and in local taverns. By the age of 11, Bill Robinson was hired by a vaudeville headliner, and soon after, he was playing shows everywhere from Broadway to Hollywood to Harlem's Cotton Club. Best known for his delicate, crisp percussions executed in strict tempo and even shift, Robinson often talked to his audience and his feet, as if surprised by the rhythm chattering below. In fact, it was this squabbling characteristic that earned him the nickname Bojangles. Clearly jealous, Robinson's contemporaries complained that he could do the easiest routine in the world and get away with it simply because of his charm and charisma.

_02:: George Balanchine (1904–1983)

The most famous ballet master and choreographer of the 20th century, George Balanchine left a legacy of 425 works, 60 full-length ballets, and one of the foremost dance companies in the world (plus a few brokenhearted ballerinas). As a child, George Balanchine was offered admission to the Russian Imperial Ballet School on a fluke while accompanying his sister to an audition. He had his heart set on joining the Imperial Naval Academy, but alas, their rolls were full, so George accepted the ballet gig. At 16 he created his first piece, *La Nuit*, and continued choreographing at every opportunity. After forming his own troupe of young dancers, Balanchine decided to leave Russia, traveling through Europe and then arriving in the United States in 1933. Once there, he founded the New York City Ballet and cofounded the School of American Ballet, where the making and marrying of ballerinas became his specialty. (Balanchine was romantically involved with several of his ballerinas and married at least three, including Maria Tallchief.)

_03:: Ted Shawn (1891–1972)

The first men to appear on the modern dance scene arrived by hitching a ride on the skirts of women. Ted Shawn intended to be a minister; he took up ballet only to help the temporary paralysis in his legs from an earlier illness. But in 1911 he saw modern dance pioneer Ruth St. Denis perform, and it changed his world. Just three years later Ted auditioned for her, made his big debut as her partner, married her, and then helped her cofound the Denishawn School and Company. Ted did the majority of teaching and choreographing at Denishawn until he broke away in 1929 to form his own company, Ted Shawn and His Men Dancers group. The company helped encourage dancing for men in colleges throughout the United States, and Shawn's repertoire grew to include 185 dances and 9 major ballets.

_04:: Alvin Ailey (1931–1989)

Alvin Ailey felt his first artistic stirrings at the age of 14 when he saw Katherine Dunham perform. Soon after, Ailey began studying at the first racially integrated dance school in California and joined its affiliated company, the Lester Horton Dance Company, in 1950. He took classes in studios all over the city of New York, searching for other dancers like himself. Eventually he formed his own dance company, which performed pieces to blues and gospel music and celebrated the heritage of African Americans. Ailey's work introduced African Americans to modern dance and introduced other people to the art and culture of African Americans. Ailey died in 1989, but his company is still among the most successful in the world.

_05:: Fred Astaire (1899–1987)

The most famous of all dancing men was a spry Nebraskan named Fred Astaire. He began his career as a tagalong little brother to his sister, Adele. At the age of six, he started performing with her in vaudeville shows, and the duo was one of the highest paid performance groups of the time. During their 27 years of performing partnership, they appeared in 10 Broadway musicals and enjoyed huge success in London. By 1932 Adele was ready to retire and Fred was faced with refashioning his career. Turning to film, he became the biggest star of the Hollywood musical era, with credits including seven highly successful films featuring his famed partnership with Ginger Rogers. He is the best-preserved choreographer because of his work on film, which includes 212 musical numbers and 133 fully developed dance routines.

Men in Skirts?:
Traditions of Theatrical Cross-Dressing

Even before there was Boy George, cross-dressing had its place in performance, stretching back to when holy men dressed up as women to merge with an androgynous god. Springboarding from this spiritual precedent, dramatic gender-bending around the world has evolved, with interesting and often shocking variations.

_01:: Japanese Kabuki Theater

Early Kabuki theater was a forum for female eroticism and prostitution, which soon blurred the boundaries between women's on-stage and "backstage" talents. After authorities forbid women to perform the theater style, men took over in 1629, performing the male and female parts. Both the Chinese and the Japanese dramatic cross-dressing traditions have developed highly refined techniques and detailed codes of movement, dress, and makeup. The Peking Opera of China and the Kabuki theater are the most popular classical theater forms in their respective countries today, and both have earned a global reputation.

_02:: Shakespearean Drama

Can you imagine watching Romeo profess his love to a boy in a wig on a balcony? In Shakespeare's time, even the most famous European dramatic traditions were initially performed by all-male casts. Sixteenth-century English society believed that the stage was no place for a woman, so all of the female Shakespearean roles were played by boys or young men. It wasn't until 1660 that the first woman, Margaret Hughes, appeared on a London stage, playing the role of Desdemona in *Othello*.

_03:: Paris Opera Ballet

Leave it to the French to throw a feminine twist into onstage gender-bending. The 19th-century danseur was a ballerina who impersonated male roles from the corps all the way to romantic leads. It turns out that the Paris Opera Ballet was actually a front for glorified prostitution during the 1830s, and women playing masculine roles became an erotic enticement, especially since the pas de deux (romantic duet) occurred between two women. The danseur usually exposed the most flesh onstage, with legs and buttocks revealed in tights or breeches instead of hidden beneath skirts. A splendid figure was a prerequisite for the position.

Broadway Originals Now Available at Blockbuster

Give 'em their regards; these shows made the jump to the big screen, creating a unique genre of American theater known as the Hollywood musical.

_01:: *Broadway Melody* (1929)

The first Hollywood musical wasn't ever an actual play. Produced by MGM, which became the greatest studio for musical films, *Broadway Melody* was simply a movie about two Broadway chorus girls in love with the same Broadway star. For audiences, the fact that it had never been a live theater show was lost amid the excitement of witnessing the very first all-singing, all-talking, all-dancing entertainment extravaganza on film. Charting the way forward from the era of silent films, *Broadway Melody* was extraordinarily original in content and craft, providing invaluable advances in sound production techniques. It was no surprise that it won the Academy Award for Best Picture in 1929, becoming the first musical film to receive that honor.

_02:: *Anything Goes* (1934)

The first real Broadway musical to be made into a film was Cole Porter's *Anything Goes* (1934). The play was the quintessential 1930s Broadway show, complete with a Depression era escapist story line that sailed the characters from New York to England on an Atlantic ocean liner. When the story traveled to the cinema, it was actually filmed twice, 20 years apart, and starred Bing Crosby both times. Yet despite its double effort, *Anything Goes* enjoyed less success as a movie than it did as a play. It seemed that the show didn't transfer well to the screen, perhaps because only three of Cole Porter's original songs were retained in the film. However, this practice of cutting and changing the original scores from stage to screen became a precedent for the many movie musicals that would follow.

_03:: *West Side Story* (1957)

It wasn't until the late 1950s and '60s that popular Broadway plays actually began to experience equivalent success on the silver screen. *West Side Story*, a modern recapitulation of Shakespeare's *Romeo and Juliet* set in New York City, was highly successful on Broadway as the brainchild of the famed choreographer Jerome Robbins, lyricist Stephen Sondheim, and composer Leonard Bernstein. It was made into a United Artist movie in 1961, filmed on location in the streets of New York. While the exciting choreography and virile dance sequences remained consistent between the stage and screen, *West Side Story* started another trend in movie musical production that blurred the boundaries between theater and film stars. Three of the main roles in the movie were vocally dubbed, seeing as the film stars recruited for the roles couldn't quite match the singing talents of their Broadway counterparts. Despite the lip-synch factor, *West Side Story* won Best Picture in 1961.

_04:: *My Fair Lady* (1956)

My Fair Lady shared a similar backstory. The play was a revised version of George Bernard Shaw's *Pygmalion* (1913). Opening on Broadway in 1956, it also harkened to the familiar themes of a classic: a Cinderella story, in which a lower-class girl is transformed into a lady of society. While Julie Andrews played the stage role to much acclaim, MGM didn't choose her for the movie version they produced in 1964. The part went to Audrey Hepburn, whose voice was then dubbed by the same Marni Nixon who had sung for Natalie Wood in the movie version of *West Side Story*. Maybe it was Marni who deserves all the credit, since *My Fair Lady* also won Best Picture in 1964.

_05:: *The Sound of Music* (1959)

As for Julie Andrews, she rebounded quite nicely the following year with a role in one of the greatest movie musicals of all time. *The Sound of Music* was a Rodgers and Hammerstein creation that opened on Broadway in 1959. When 20th Century Fox made it into a movie in 1965, it not only won Best Picture but also dethroned *Gone with the Wind* at the box office. Even today, it's hard to imagine a child unfamiliar with the Von Trapp family version of "Do Re Mi." In this way, *The Sound of Music* showed that moving pictures expanded the art of theater beyond the elitism of the stage. Films provided a cheap and accessible way to experience dramatic art, especially for people who didn't live in urban centers.

_06:: *Grease* (1972)

A new measure of success for movie musicals was set forth in 1978 with Paramount's release of *Grease*. The Broadway play by Jim Jacobs and Warren Casey opened in New York in 1972, replete with the tragic humor of a group of 1950s teens singing and dancing to a rock-and-roll score. By the time it made it to the big screen, several songs had been changed and all of the original actors had been replaced with movie stars like John Travolta, Olivia Newton-John, and Stockard Channing. While *Grease* never won Best Picture, it became the highest-grossing movie musical of all time and was even released in Mexico as *Vaselina*. These crossovers into popular culture and high-revenue ventures mark the moment when Hollywood surpassed Broadway to become the main event in modern dramatic performing arts.

5 Barefoot Beauties Who Gave Birth to Modern Dance

Burn your bras . . . and your pointe shoes! Modern dance grew out of women's desires to reclaim their bodies at the turn of the 20th century. Rebelling against classical ballet's physical deformation of the body (pointe shoes *hurt*!) and images of women as fragile flowers, these geniuses set out to craft their own styles of movement.

_01:: Isadora Duncan (1877–1927)

Isadora Duncan's dramatic personality and proclaimed spirituality managed to draw critical attention to modern dance. Duncan set out to realign dance with nature by linking her movement to the spirit. To free up her body, she decided her corset had to go. Isadora is famed for skipping and leaping around in gauzy-thin tunics, and her dances tended to expose previously hidden areas of her form, such as the inner arm, thigh, and neck. She legitimated her aesthetic choices by saying that "Nudeness is truth, it is beauty, it is art . . . my body is the temple of my art. I expose it as a shrine for the worship of beauty." Her status as a single woman who'd had two children out of wedlock made her free-spirited sensibilities even more controversial.

_02:: Ruth St. Denis (1877–1968)

Isadora gets the credit for starting the modern-dance trend, but Ruth St. Denis made it popular. She worked her whole life in variety and vaudeville theater before she and her husband, Ted Shawn, founded the Denishawn School and Company in 1915. Not only did the school provide a seedbed for the next generation of choreographers, but its touring schedule brought dance to several American cities and small towns. While Isadora Duncan made her reputation mostly in Europe, Ruth St. Denis single-handedly brought modern dance into the American consciousness and demonstrated how dance could be an avenue to self-sufficiency for women.

_03:: Doris Humphrey (1895–1958)

Doris Humphrey began her serious dance training at the Denishawn School in 1917 and worked closely with Ruth St. Denis. In 1928 she set out to refine the sociological lens of dance when she formed her own school and company with Charles Weidman. Her explorations harnessed the power of breath and highlighted the fall and recovery of the body in relationship to gravity. As a result, she created a physical dialogue of conflict between stability and imbalance. Humphrey often described dancing as "the arc between two deaths" and maintained that "[t]here is only one thing to dance about: the meaning of one's personal experience." It's not surprising, then, that her dance themes were often concerned with examining and expressing the individual's voice in relation to the masses.

_04:: Martha Graham (1894–1991)

Martha Graham, another Denishawn student and contemporary of Humphrey, explored similar themes in her work. However, she focused more specifically on the emotional reasons for movement. For Graham, the contraction of the torso and spine was the purest form of expression, and her art was focused on creating an expressive physical language with an integrity all its own. Graham believed that "[m]ovement is the one speech which cannot lie." Both Doris and Martha were revolutionary in that they created large bodies of work cultivated from women's social and emotional perspectives, and developed original female voices that still echo through modern dance today.

_05:: Katherine Dunham (1910–)

Once the grounds of physical self-expression had been broken, modern dance exploded in new directions. Katherine Dunham used this liberation to focus specifically on the experience of African Americans, as she retraced Caribbean, West African, and South American lineages in her dance. She expanded the developing modern-dance techniques to reflect traditional movements and styles, and she's used her PhD in anthropology to research and incorporate the folklore of the African diaspora into the American consciousness. Using her art form purposefully as a means of social commentary and political activism, Dunham set a new bar for how modern dance would confront a changing world.

Timeline

FEMINISM AND MODERN DANCE

1890s Industrialization and urbanization brings women into the workplace.

1898 Charlotte Perkins Gilman publishes a significant feminist text, *Women and Economics*, calling for the economic independence of women.

1900 Isadora Duncan gives her first concert in London, initiating her career as a world-renowned performing artist (as well as unmarried mother) and placing herself shamelessly in the public sphere.

1915 Ruth St. Denis cofounds the Denishawn School and Company—the first American modern dance company and the first successful female business venture in performing arts in the United States.

1919 Women's suffrage groups finally secure the right to vote, giving women an official voice.

1926 Martha Graham debuts her first choreography in New York, bringing women's issues into the physical realm.

1928 Doris Humphrey forms her own company with Charles Weidman and begins an important career as a female choreographer making statements about individual voices in a collective society.

1932 Katherine Dunham begins to create a visual language through body motion to specifically communicate ideas about the African American subculture.

All the World's a Stage:
Traditional Theater Forms

The first actors were probably primitive holy men, performing ancient religious rituals. That theatrical storytelling tradition lives on, perpetuating legends, rituals, and mysteries across the globe.

_01:: The Peruvian Chilinchili Festival

For many Native American cultures, theater has a cosmic significance, and the belief in immortality and the worship of the dead have always been essential features of religious practices. Because ancestral connections are so important, many theatrical traditions focus on re-creating those myths and legends. The Peruvian Chilinchili Festival features actors who represent the souls of the dead, while the rest of the community reacts as if the actors are actually the dead ancestors they are impersonating.

_02:: Chantways of the Navajo Indians

Native American theater also serves as a forum for communal celebrations, especially since the audience members often tend to be participants instead of just spectators. The Navajo Indians perform chantways, which are 100-hour-long celebrations involving the entire community, where no costume, word, gesture, movement, or song is left to chance. Because of the social and cultural destruction that colonization caused, theater is an essential way of preserving the ancient traditions and tribal histories.

_03:: Dō Ceremony of the Bambara People

Traditional communities in Africa use morality plays to instruct young adults about appropriate social roles. In fact, some initiation ceremonies actually simulate the death and resurrection of the initiates. Young men bid their final farewells to loved ones before their isolation period and continue to act dead for a few days upon returning to the village. In Mali, the Dō Ceremony of the Bambara people occurs every seven years at the end of the initiation period. It takes over three months to perform and features masked men speaking a private language. For African cultures, traditional theater often provides a vehicle for border crossing between life stages and spiritual states.

_04:: Javanese Shadow Theater

Shadow theater originated in China between 140 and 86 BCE and exists in Japan, Cambodia, Turkey, Egypt, and India (to name a few), but Java is the home of its highest and finest form. Javanese shadow theater began as part of ancient Malayo-Polynesian religions and incorporates themes from Javanese cosmology into elaborate puppet shows that may last anywhere from an entire night to a whole week. The showman, or *dalang*, acts as the spiritual leader in the community who possesses the ability to remember the long legends that make up the text of the performances. The *dalang* is capable of improvising at whim but also maintains the traditional movements of the ornate buffalo-leather puppets.

_05:: Japan's Nō Theater

Japan's nō theater has received as much international acclaim as the Javanese shadow theater. Originating in the late 14th century, nō theater survives unaltered as a living testimony to the values of samurai culture. In a blend of shamanistic traditions and Buddhism, nō plays emphasize spiritual energy over actual dialogue or movement. Performing with utmost simplicity, nō actors are highly respected in Japanese society, and their art form is passed down from father to son in organized stages and hierarchical progression. This theater of the warrior class isn't only a Japanese status symbol; it's also come to be known throughout the world as one of the most highly refined theatrical arts.

Pirouette Quartet:
Prima Ballerinas You Need to Know

So, you think prima ballerinas are just girly-girls who twirl through the air to pretty music? Actually, being a prima ballerina requires training more grueling than that of your average linebacker. And the better the ballerina, the more effortless it looks.

_01:: Marie Taglioni (1804–1884)

Marie Taglioni was born into a family of Italian dancers, choreographers, and ballet masters. Under the watchful eye of her father, Marie perfected a new and graceful method of rising up onto the tips of her toes and balancing there while executing the steps of her dances. Then, in 1832, she changed dance when she starred in *La Sylphide*. The ballet has come to be acknowledged as the first exhibition of pointework, and it earned her much praise. Marie's perfection and fantastic performance of this new technique in combination with the overall lightness, ease, and grace of her dancing style earned her the title of the first great romantic ballerina. Her romantic nature, however, didn't quite carry beyond the stage. She petitioned for divorce in 1835 when her husband, Count Gilbert de Voisins, tried to end her dancing career.

_02:: Anna Pavlova (1881–1931)

While Marie Taglioni set the precedent for the ethereal otherworldliness that's become the ballerina's hallmark, her Russian successor catapulted ballet into the international spotlight. Enrolling in the Imperial Ballet School at the age of 10, Anna Pavlova began her professional career at 16, and dreamed of following in Marie's footsteps. Performing throughout Europe to popular acclaim, her travels eventually brought her to the United States, where each of her performances received a standing ovation. America, along with the rest of the world, was taken by Pavlova's virtuosic technique blended with her sensuous charm. She created a dance style so lyrical that it appeared to be a bodily song. Undoubtedly, Pavlova's most famous solo was *The Dying Swan*, choreographed for her to the music of Saint-Saëns, which showcased her highly emotional dancing. The performance secured her reputation as the greatest interpretive ballerina and remains unsurpassed even today.

_03:: Margot Fonteyn (1919–1991)

The national ballet tradition that nurtured Russian greats like Anna Pavlova didn't exist in other places. In fact, British ballet was rather unimportant on the international scene until Margot Fonteyn began to grace its stages. Born in 1919, Margot began to study dance at the age of 4 in local classes in Surrey, England. She eventually enrolled in the Sadler's Wells School in London and made her first solo debut with the Vic-Wells Ballet (which evolved into the Royal Ballet) while she was still a student. At 16 she became the company's first prima ballerina and began her long career of international acclaim. It wasn't until 1949, however, when she made her New York debut in *Sleeping Beauty*, that Margot's faultless line and lyric musicality brought legitimacy to the British ballet. Her status as Britain's greatest ballerina continues even today, especially since Fonteyn never formally

retired but chose instead to make a graceful exit from England's Royal Ballet instead.

_04:: Maria Tallchief (1925–)

America was a rather late bloomer in the production of homegrown dancing divas. Elizabeth Marie Tallchief was born on an Osage Indian reservation in Oklahoma in 1925. When her dance talent became apparent, her mother took her to California, where she encountered two of Europe's most famous ballet lineages. (One of her teachers had worked directly with Enrico Cechetti, the great Italian ballet master who codified an entire ballet technique, and the other, Bronislava Nijinska,

---

Inventions and Innovations

SHOES THAT GO
STRAIGHT TO THE POINTE

Before Marie Taglioni stunned her audiences with pointework in 1832, ballerinas actually gave their performances in high-heeled shoes. But as the art of rising up and balancing oneself on the tips of the toes became a staple of ballet, new shoes became a necessity. In their earliest form, they arrived as satin slippers reinforced with cotton wadding, glue, and starch. Today's pointe shoes, however, are made with many layers of cloth (linen, felt, canvas, etc.) held together by special glue, though they feel much like wooden boxes. Of course, ballerinas have all kinds of tricks for breaking them in, including slamming them in doors, banging them with hammers, and soaking them in water, all in the course of becoming a podiatrist's worst nightmare.

was a famous Russian ballerina and ballet choreographer in her own right.) At 17 Tallchief moved to New York City, where she was almost immediately apprenticed to the Ballet Russe de Monte Carlo and chose *Maria* as her new stage name. It was at the Russian Tea Room in New York that her life intersected with the great ballet choreographer George Balanchine, whom she eventually married.

Their artistic collaboration contributed to the formation of the New York City Ballet. In 1949 Maria Tallchief danced the lead role in *Firebird* with such blazing speed, energy, and brilliance that it became the pinnacle of her success. She was the first true star of the New York City Ballet and the first world-famous ballerina who did not train in Europe or make her reputation there.

Taking It to the Street:
5 Tricks of the Trade for Aspiring Sidewalk Stars

Entire subcultures of people make their living as performers but have never set foot on a stage. For these sidewalk stars, busy thoroughfares in tourist hot spots provide the best display for talent.

_01:: Sword Swallowing

Sword swallowing originated among the magicians and priests of India as a demonstration of their invulnerability and connection with the gods. The art form was eventually undertaken by people in Greece, China, Japan, and across Europe, and made its American debut in 1817. The dangerous challenge of pushing steel blades down the throat requires a developed control of the gag reflex and an esophageal muscular strength capable of holding the sword in place. Because the blades are dulled, it is actually the peril of pushing the sword too far into the body and rupturing internal organs rather than the slicing of flesh that causes most injuries. Despite sword swallowing's popularity in sideshows and circuses throughout the 1900s, today there are fewer than 50 remaining performers worldwide.

_02:: Contortion

Contortionists first appeared in the pictorial and sculptural work of ancient Egypt, Greece, and Rome. Contrary to popular belief, there's no such thing as being double-jointed. The term is more like a slang word used to describe the extreme flexibility exhibited by contortionists, which is actually the result of constant stretching. While certain people may be born with a higher proportion of muscle to tendon, which increases flexibility, contortionists have also developed the ability to relax the antagonistic muscle groups involved in an action. This loosens their joints and extends their range of motion. In India, Yogic philosophy developed an entire physical practice that promotes the kind of relaxation and balance necessary to assume seemingly impossible postures. Today you don't even have to be lucky enough to catch a street show where someone crams herself into a small box; just stop by any yoga studio and check out the aspiring contortionists trying to put their legs behind their heads.

_03:: Juggling

Many performers of seemingly impossible feats attribute their abilities to hours of practice and impenetrable mental focus. Juggling has even been credited with a Zen-like quality. The trick is discovering your own perfect inner rhythm, which depends on the length, weight, size, and shape of the different parts of your body and their proportional relationship to the whole. The greatest skill of the juggler, however, is cultivated ambidexterity, which promotes rhythmic coordination between the two sides of the body and brain. Most importantly though, juggling masters claim that you have to cultivate a state of mind and being that allows for fluidity of release, lets the balls drop, allows them to land in your hands, and demonstrates the patience of return.

_04:: Mime

If they aren't busy thrilling us or demonstrating a higher level of consciousness, street performers perpetually endeavor to make us laugh. Mime, the art of silent acting, existed as three recognizable traditions in the 1800s: the Oriental, Italian, and French schools. While Oriental mime stayed closely connected to the traditional theater in China and Japan, Italian mime eventually evolved into the circus clown acts of today. It was the French mime Marcel Marceau, however, who helped establish mime as an art form in and of itself. The French style requires extraordinary balance, control, flexibility, strength, and coordination

---

Strange but True

STREET-FAIR TRIVIA

Brad Byers holds the official world record for the most swords swallowed. On August 13, 1999, he swallowed and turned ten 28-inch swords. In 2002 the first Annual Sword Swallowing Convention was held, and 19 delegates swallowed a total of 50 swords simultaneously.

Female hormones actually increase physical flexibility while male hormones reduce it, which may explain why many of today's contortionists are women.

Due to their ambidexterity, Leonardo da Vinci, Michelangelo, Muhammad Ali, Willie Mays, and Michael Jordan all could have been master jugglers in addition to their other famed vocations.

Mime was one of the earliest mediums of self-expression, giving preverbal people a way to communicate.

Ventriloquism is thought to be the explanation behind the famous oracle at Delphi in Greek mythology.

to subtly mimic human motions and create a physical landscape of illusion.

_05:: Ventriloquism

Ventriloquists pushed illusion in the opposite direction by developing vocal techniques that allowed them to speak without moving their lips or jaw. In fact, they've actually traced their lineage from ancient Egyptian and Hebrew civilizations to the early Romans and Greeks. Capitalizing on the fact that hearing is the least reliable sense, ventriloquists use controlled breathing; refined speech mechanics; and the relaxation of the face, lips, and throat

to project their voice into their inanimate partners. Edgar Bergen was America's most famous ventriloquist, though not necessarily one of the greatest. While he couldn't prevent his lips from moving, audiences overlooked the fault because it seemed he really believed in his dummy partner, Charlie McCarthy. The friendship between Edgar and Charlie made them stars of radio, television, nightclubs, and movies. When Charlie was finally retired to the Smithsonian Institution in 1978, he left with the humor that had endeared him to audiences for years, claiming, "Well, at least I won't be the only dummy in Washington."

5 Dance Styles Meant to Bring You Closer to God

If you're looking to attract some heavenly bodies to the dance floor, maybe you just need to refine your moves. The following styles were designed to drive dancers toward religious ecstasy.

_01:: Sufis, or Whirling Dervishes

One of the most common ways to transcend to the spiritual realm using movement is to induce a trance. In the eighth century Islamic mysticism began developing in the Middle East in a sect known as the Sufi order. Following the practices of their founder, Mawlawiyah Rumi, the Sufis, or whirling dervishes, developed complex rituals designed to send them into religious ecstasy and mystical union with God. Dance was used as a means for uprooting man's foot from the terrestrial and transporting him toward the celestial. As Sufi dervishes spin

they must expand their awareness to include several dimensions at once: consciousness of their own physical axis, inward pronunciation of God, awareness of where they are in space, and constant connection to the religious lineage. As their minds open to accommodate this simultaneity and their bodies engage in continuous circles, they find new spiritual consciousness and express their infinite love of God.

_02:: Yoruba Sacred Dance

In west Africa, the Yoruba people believe that dance is a way to bring one "nearer the time of the gods on earth." Their dances consist of complex rhythmic structures emphasized by the relationship between dancers and drummers. And as the dancer begins to express a myriad of rhythmic patterns, she simultaneously opens herself to receive the presence of a deity. The possessed dancer is described as being mounted by the deity, and she becomes the vessel for expressing the essence of its power and delivering messages to the community. Yoruba spiritual practices use dance as a way to communicate with the different representations of God, where dancers are thought to capture and spread the energy of God that is present in all things.

_03:: Vodun

The mass relocation of African people during the era of slavery caused a deprivation of family, community, and homeland, and created the need for spiritual systems that linked people to their ancestors. As a result, several branches of spiritual practice evolved in the New World that were rooted in Yoruba tradition. The most well-known derivative of Yoruba spirituality is vodun, Haiti's system of concepts describing the relation of humankind to ancestors and the natural and supernatural forces in the world. The sacred dances of Haiti were designed to open the body and consciousness for possession by the deities. In fact, the intensity of these interactions with deities can be so great that it requires an intervention with the *maison*, a particular dance that shifts the energy from religious to sexual ecstasy, to break the possession and purge the deity.

_04:: Brazilian Candomblé

Brazil also has its own version of the Yoruba spiritual tradition. Candomblé is based on the worship of nature deities (similar to those of Yoruba and Vodun traditions) that are paired with Roman Catholic saints. On the day of the patron saint, there are public ceremonies where song, drumming, and dancing are employed as attractive forces to the spirits, and trances are induced so that dancers can reenact spiritual myths under the deities' direction. The African origins of dancing divination have evolved even further in Brazil with the umbanda tradition—one of the first conscious attempts to create a national popular religion by combining Yoruba sacred dance with Native American and spiritualist practices.

_05:: The Shakers

Believe it or not, Christianity had it own version of ecstatic dancing despite a reputation as one of the world's most physically repressive religions. The Shakers, a Christian sect that existed during the late 18th and early 19th centuries, developed a repertoire of dances designed for worship. Their founder, Ann Lee, proclaimed that "[d]ance is the greatest gift that ever was made for the purification of the soul." In fact, as a sect that practiced celibacy, the Shakers believed that skipping, shouting, falling, and turning were all effective methods for "shaking" out the evils of carnal desire. It was by dancing that the Shakers believed they made themselves worthy of God. Whatever the specific motivation or actual discipline, people have found dancing to be a transformative and transcendent experience for millennia.

Performance Artists Who Scare Us

Performance artists are supposed to push our limits, but some go past the unexpected and into the unbelievable. Not only would we never do these things, but we would never think of them in the first place.

_01:: Allan Kaprow

If you were an audience member at Allan Kaprow's performances, chances are, you were also a participant. In 1967 Kaprow created a piece called *Self-Service*, which featured (1) people in New York standing on empty bridges and watching cars pass until 200 red ones went by (fun), (2) people in Boston tar-papering several cars in a parking lot, and (3) people in Los Angeles driving into filling sta-tions in cars that erupted with white foam from the windows. He intended the random-ness of these activities to question the iden-tity and value of each action as art and focus close attention on their enactment and the idea of performing in general. Do you get it?

_02:: Carolee Schneemann

Carolee Schneemann, one of the most famous female performance artists, has focused her

---

Fake Your Way through a Conversation

(ABOUT PERFORMANCE ART!)

If you really want to impress when talking about performance art, you've just got to remember that the entire genre is built on the idea that there are a variety of realities and views in society. So, essentially, any argument you make with conviction should pass. However, should you need a little reassurance, you might want to keep these important ideas in your back pocket. First off, you should think about the degree of *minimalism* and *pluralism* exhibited in the work, fancy words for whether the content is simple or complex. You should also identify the *taboo* that's being ex-posed, and focus on the *provocative* details of the performance. Combining these clues with your own response and emotional opinion should help you make a seemingly profound statement (thankyouverymuch!) about the piece. In fact, just crib the following mad-lib to help you in sticky situations: I felt the piece truly deconstructed the process of (*some societal problem*), challenged the accepted value of (*some concept taken for granted*), and related bril-liantly to (*insert political, artistic, or social issue here*).

work on gender issues. Her piece *Interior Scroll* (1975) featured Schneemann standing naked on a table and ritualistically painting herself with mud until she began to extract a paper scroll from her vagina and read from it. For Schneemann, this action was the embodiment of the various potentials of the female reproductive organ. She thought of her vagina "physically, conceptually: as a sculptural form, an architectural referent, the sources of sacred knowledge, ecstasy, birth passage, transformation." Creating pieces laced with subversive feminism, Schneemann uses her body as a representation of the larger social world.

_03:: Chris Burden

Chris Burden is the best-known American body artist. His work explores different means of self-mutilation; in past pieces he's dragged himself bare-chested through broken glass or shot a bullet through his arm. His 1974 piece, *Trans-Fixed*, featured Burden being nailed to the back of a Volkswagen and displaying his pseudo-crucifixion on the street. When it comes to performance art, we may never completely understand it, but it's certain that we'll at least have a response.

6 Sexy Dances That Will Leave You Drooling

OK, so we said dancing was all about religious ecstasy and preserving history. Very fine goals. But, we admit, almost every dance has a little something to do with sex.

_01:: Belly Dancing

Belly dancing, one of the oldest dance forms, is an expression of the process of creating and transmitting life through the act of giving birth. In fact, it existed thousands of years before Christ in countries as far apart as India and Spain. Temple dancers in India and in the Middle East actually used sex as a worshiping tool, and their dancing provided a release of energy that enabled them to unite with the divine spirit. Migrating populations of Gypsies eventually became the most famous belly dancers, including the Ghawazee of Egypt and the Cengi of Turkey. Flourishing in the harems

of the Middle East, belly dancing was performed by women for their own sex as a celebration of procreative power. Today it's still a popular living art practiced by a wide variety of people across the world.

_02:: Samba

One of the reasons Brazil holds the unofficial title of sexiest nation is because of its national dance, the samba. It was derived from a Congolese-Angolan dance known as *umbigada*, where soloists would swing their hips and stamp their feet in the middle of a circle, calling the next soloist forward with the thrust of the belly button. The female *sambista* assumes her sexuality via a whirlwind of the hips and thrusting, circular movements emphasizing the pelvis and buttocks. And she (deservedly) attracts attention for her frenetic exuberance and elation in liberating her sexual impulses. Beginning as a traditional dance called *samba de roda*, the samba was eventually popularized into several hybrid versions that have become a hallmark of Brazil's Carnaval and an international symbol of sexiness.

_03:: Argentine Tango

Once dance becomes a couple's event, sexual passions are expressed with exciting tension. The Argentine tango was the first social dance with overt sexuality to make the worldwide sweep. Originally a dance of the brothels, it became popular and stylized between 1907 and 1913 due to Parisian enthusiasm. The tango is based on the interlacing of legs and balancing of bodies as they strike one another, where the movements are joined in a way that melds two bodies into one. Author Angela Rippon captured it best when she described the tango as "a sensual coupling, forged by raw emotion. The closest thing you'll find to a vertical expression of the horizontal desire."

_04:: Cancan

The French, it seems, had a weakness for salacious dances. In the 1840s an acrobatic form of the quadrille, called the cancan, was introduced. Originally danced by couples, the excessive display of ankles that occurred when women kicked up their petticoats was simply shocking. After waning in the 1880s as a popular social dance, it was adopted and adapted by professional dancers in dance halls and cabarets, including the Moulin Rouge. The cancan quickly became a burlesque profession characterized by black stockings, high heels, garters, lace panties, and kicks with wide-spreading legs.

_05:: American Burlesque

American burlesque began as a frivolous appeal to the animalistic side of man and a forum for displaying female beauty. It all happened quite by accident when a group of stranded ballet dancers were incorporated into a vaudevillian musical extravaganza called *The Black Crook*. It didn't take long for producers and performers to realize the potential of scantily clad dancers parading onstage. Burlesque evolved through the era of minstrel shows and entered a golden age in 1905. The standard format included variety acts and bits mingled with musical numbers, and performed with bawdy humor by beautiful women. Burlesque flourished with honky-tonk flare, making its home in half beer hall–half brothel establishments, where Mae West soon became its biggest star.

_06:: Striptease

By the 1920s Broadway had more nudity than burlesque theater, so the novelty of the striptease was introduced. The Minsky brothers were the first to glorify the tease at their National Winter Garden Theater on the Lower East Side of New York City, which was considered to be the high temple of American burlesque. By the 1960s there were more than 8,000 women in America making their living as go-go dancers, and by the 1970s male strippers had formed their own contingent. Eventually, however, the comedy, the tease, even the stripping began to disappear from this performance art form. Instead, blatant nudity and pornographic undertones replaced what was once a more subtle and silly form of sexual expression. While there are varying levels of comfort with sexual expression, dance can often provide a way to balance our desire and need for such expression against the perils of overexploiting our sexuality.

by
William Irwin

Condensed
PHILOSOPHY

Contains

11 Quotes You Probably Heard in Your Graduation Speech ✻ 4 Great Books That Won't Put You to Sleep ✻ Behind the Philosophy: 9 Bad Boys of Thought ✻ 3 Eastern Sages Who Leave the West Behind ✻ Philosophy Doesn't Grow on Trees, but It Does Have 6 Branches ✻ 3 Isms Finally Put in Their Place ✻ Thinking Positive!: 5 Feel-Good Philosophies ✻ 3 Bad Catchphrases (and the Philosophies behind Them) ✻ Name-Dropping 101: 3 Schools of Thought That Will Impress the Opposite Sex ✻

11

Quotes You Probably Heard in Your Graduation Speech

Oh, the advice you'll get. Between all the lectures, scolding, and parental nagging you've probably been subject to, chances are some of these quotes should sound familiar by now. But do you actually know what they mean?

_01:: "The unexamined life is not worth living."—Socrates (470–399 BCE)

Socrates' belief that we must reflect upon the life we live was partly inspired by the famous phrase inscribed at the shrine of the oracle at Delphi, "Know thyself." The key to finding value in the prophecies of the oracle was self-knowledge, not a decoder ring. Socrates felt so passionately about the value of self-examination that he closely examined not only his own beliefs and values but those of others as well. More precisely, through his relentless questioning, he forced people to examine their own beliefs. He saw the citizens of his beloved Athens sleepwalking through life, living only for money, power, and fame, so he became famous trying to help them.

_02:: "Entities should not be multiplied unnecessarily." —William of Ockham (1285–?1349)

Commonly known as Ockham's razor, the idea here is that in judging among competing philosophical or scientific theories, all other things being equal, we should prefer the simplest theory. Scientists currently speak of four forces in the universe: gravity, the elec-

tromagnetic force, the strong nuclear force, and the weak nuclear force. Ockham would certainly nod approvingly at the ongoing attempt to formulate a grand unified theory, a single force that encompasses all four. The ultimate irony of Ockham's razor may be that some have used it to prove God is unnecessary to the explanation of the universe, an idea Ockham the Franciscan priest would reject.

_03:: "The life of man [is] solitary, poor, nasty, brutish, and short." —Thomas Hobbes (1588–1679)

Referring to the original state of nature, a hypothetical past before civilization, Hobbes saw no reason to be nostalgic. Whereas Rousseau said, "Man is born free, and he is everywhere in chains," Hobbes believed we find ourselves living a savage, impossible life without education and the protection of the state. Human nature is bad: we'll prey on one another in the most vicious ways. No doubt the state imposes on our liberty in an overwhelming way. Yet Hobbes's claim was that these very chains were absolutely crucial in protecting us from one another.

_04:: "I think therefore I am." —René Descartes (1596–1650)

Descartes began his philosophy by doubting everything in order to figure out what he could know with absolute certainty. Although he could be wrong about *what* he was thinking, *that* he was thinking was undeniable. Upon the recognition that "I think," Descartes concluded that "I am." On the heels of believing in himself, Descartes asked, What am I? His answer: a thinking thing (*res cogitans*) as opposed to a physical thing extended in three-dimensional space (*res extensa*). So, based on this line, Descartes knew he existed, though he wasn't sure if he had a body. It's a philosophical cliff-hanger; you'll have to read *Meditations* to find out how it ends.

_05:: "To be is to be perceived (*Esse est percipi*)." Or, "If a tree falls in the forest and no one is there to hear it, does it make a sound?" —Bishop George Berkeley (1685–1753)

As an idealist, Berkeley believed that nothing is real but minds and their ideas. Ideas do not exist independently of minds. Through a complicated and flawed line of reasoning he concluded that "to be is to be perceived." Something exists only if someone has the idea of it. Though he never put the question in the exact words of the famous quotation, Berkeley would say that if a tree fell in the forest and there was no one (not even a squirrel) there to hear it, not only would it not make a sound, but there would be no tree. The good news is, according to Berkeley, that the mind of God always perceives everything. So the tree will always make a sound, and there's no need to worry about blipping out of existence if you fall asleep in a room by yourself.

_06:: "We live in the best of all possible worlds."—Gottfried Wilhelm Leibniz (1646–1716)

Voltaire's famous novel *Candide* satirizes this optimistic view. And looking around you right now you may wonder how anyone could actually believe it. But Leibniz believed that before creation God contemplated every possible way the universe could be and chose to create the one in which we live because it's the best. The principle of sufficient reason holds that for everything, there must be a sufficient reason why it exists. And according to Leibniz the only sufficient reason for the world we live in is that God created it as the best possible universe. God could have created a universe in which no one ever did wrong, in which there was no human evil, but that would require humans to be deprived of the gift of free will and thus would not be the best possible world.

_07:: "The owl of Minerva spreads its wings only with the falling of the dusk."—G. W. F. Hegel (1770–1831)

Similar to "vision is 20/20 in hindsight," Hegel's poetic insight says that philosophers are impotent. Only after the end of an age can philosophers realize what it was about. And by then it's too late to change things. It wasn't until the time of Immanuel Kant (1724–1804) that the true nature of the Enlightenment was understood, and Kant did nothing to change the Enlightenment; he just consciously perpetuated it. Marx (1818–1883) found Hegel's apt description to be indicative of the problem with philosophy and responded, "the philosophers have only *interpreted* the world differently, what matters is to *change* it."

_08:: "Who is also aware of the tremendous risk involved in faith—when he nevertheless makes the leap of faith—this [is] subjectivity . . . at its height." —Søren Kierkegaard (1813–1855)

In a memorable scene from *Indiana Jones and the Last Crusade*, Indy deduced that the final step across his treacherous path was a leap of faith. And so it is in Kierkegaard's theory of stages of life. The final stage, the religious stage, requires passionate, subjective belief rather than objective proof, in the paradoxical and the absurd. So, what's the absurd? That which Christianity asks us to accept as true, that God became man born of a virgin, suffered, died, and was resurrected. Abraham was the ultimate "knight of faith" according to Kierkegaard. Without doubt there is no faith, and so in a state of "fear and trembling" Abraham was willing to break the universal moral law against murder by agreeing to kill his own son, Isaac. God rewarded Abraham's faith by providing a ram in place of Isaac for the sacrifice. Faith has its rewards, but it isn't rational. It's beyond reason. As Blaise Pascal said, "The heart has its reason which reason does not know."

_09:: "God is dead." —Friedrich Nietzsche (1844–1900)

Well, you might not hear this one in a graduation speech, but you'll probably hear it in college. Actually, Nietzsche never issued this famous proclamation in his own voice but rather put the words in the mouth of a character he called the madman and later in the mouth of another character, Zarathustra. Nevertheless, Nietzsche endorsed the words. "God is dead" is often mistaken as a statement of atheism. It is not, though Nietzsche himself was an atheist. "Dead" is metaphorical in this context, meaning belief in the God of Christianity is worn out, past its prime, and on the decline. God is lost as the center of life and the source of values. Nietzsche's madman noted that he himself came too soon. No doubt Nietzsche, too, thought he was ahead of his time in heralding this news.

_10:: "There is but one truly serious philosophical problem, and that is suicide."—Albert Camus (1913–1960)

Camus's solution to *the* philosophical problem was to recognize and embrace life's absurdity. Suicide, though, remains an option if the absurdity becomes too much. Indeed Camus's own death in a car crash was ambiguous. Was it an accident or suicide? For Camus, the absurd hero is Sisyphus, a man from Greek mythology who is condemned by the gods for eternity to roll a stone up a hill only to have it fall back again as it reaches the top. For Camus, Sisyphus typified all human beings: we must find meaning in a world that is unresponsive or even hostile to us. Sisyphus, Camus believed, affirms life, choosing to go back down the hill and push the rock again each time. Camus wrote, "The struggle itself toward the heights is enough to fill a man's heart. One must imagine Sisyphus happy."

_11:: "One cannot step twice in the same river."—Heraclitus (ca. 540–ca. 480 BCE)

Heraclitus definitely isn't alone here. His message was that reality is constantly changing; it's an ongoing process rather than a fixed and stable product. Buddhism shares a similar metaphysical view with the idea of *annica*, the

Fake Your Way through a Conversation
(WITH CORRECT PRONUNCIATION!)

If you fumble with a philosopher's name, nothing you say afterward will sound credible. So, learn to pronounce these names correctly, then start worrying about their ideas.

(George) Berkeley is properly pronounced like Charles Barkley (bark-lee). This name is commonly mispronounced "burk-lee," like Berkeley, California, which, ironically, is named after George Berkeley.

(Friedrich) Nietzsche is commonly mispronounced as "nee-chee." The correct pronunciation is "nee-ch-ya" and rhymes with "pleased ta meetchya." "Pleased ta meetchya, Neechya." Say it!

Lao-tzu (born ca. 604 BCE) is spelled several different ways in English transliteration from the Chinese. But no matter how you spell it, the proper way to pronounce it is "lau" (sounds like "ouch")-"dsuh." The stress goes on the first syllable.

(Charles Sanders) Peirce (1839–1914) is commonly mispronounced as "peer-s." The correct pronunciation is "purse," which is somewhat funny because Peirce rarely had a penny in his purse. Oddly, Peirce took his middle name, Sanders, as an anglicized form of Santiago, or "St. James," in honor of a fellow pragmatist, William James (1842–1910), who helped him out financially.

(Ludwig) Wittgenstein (1889–1951) is a name that demands authentic German pronunciation, and there are plenty of ways to slaughter it. Here's one that embodies all of them, "wit-jen-steen." The correct pronunciation is "vit" (rhymes with bit)-"ghen" (rhymes with Ken)-"shtine." The first name is pronounced "lude-vig." If you think it's hard to pronounce his name, try reading his *Tractatus*.

claim that all of reality is fleeting and impermanent. In modern times Henri Bergson (1859–1941) described time as a process that is experienced. An hour waiting in line is different from an hour at play. Today contemporary physics lends credence to process philosophy with the realization that even apparently stable objects, like marble statues, are actually buzzing bunches of electrons and other subatomic particles deep down.

Great Books That Won't Put You to Sleep

Reading philosophy has been known to cure insomnia, but these books will actually keep you awake at night . . . thinking . . . we swear!

_01:: Plato's *Republic*

Plato's *Republic* raises the questions, What is justice? And what is the just society? If given the ring of Gyges, which makes a person invisible while wearing it, most people would do immoral things they could not get away with otherwise, but in the just society, a person would have no such use for the ring. Plato thus gives his design for a utopia in which all men and women are equal but in which they are assigned roles based on the part of their psyche that dominates them. Warriors are dominated by spirit, workers by appetite, and guardians (philosopher kings) by reason. Children are raised communally with no knowledge of who their biological parents are, which makes everyone the child of the previous generation and the sibling of the members of his or her generation. Plato goes on to suggest that the epics of Homer should be banned as they provide false and corrupting images of the gods, and that the rigorous education of the guardians should culminate in the study of philosophy. Only rulers who understand what justice truly is will be able to implement it in governing society.

_02:: Aristotle's *Nicomachean Ethics*

Aristotle's *Ethics* addresses the question, What is the good life? Aristotle (384–322 BCE) argues that human flourishing, or becoming our best, results from using reason to govern our actions and feelings. The flourishing person possesses the virtues and good character traits that allow him to act rightly in any situation. Each virtue is a mean, a perfect balance point between two extremes, an excess and a deficiency. For example, courage is the mean between the excess, rashness, and the deficiency, cowardice. Virtue is learned through repeated practice, experiencing situations that call for acting virtuously. Ideally, Aristotle argues, practice makes acting virtuously become automatic. And in the highest form of friendship, peers reinforce the virtues in one another, making one another better.

_03:: Descartes' *Meditations on First Philosophy*

Descartes begins philosophy anew, suspending belief in everything he had taken to be true, seeking one thing he could know with absolute certainty, and using it to serve as the foundation on which to build all philosophical knowledge. Suspending belief based on his five senses and even belief in simple mathematical truths (because he could be dreaming them), Descartes discovers he cannot possibly suspend belief in his certainty that he thinks. And because he thinks, he exists. After playing with this notion for a while, Descartes reasons that the body is a physical thing that works like a machine, subject to the laws of nature, and thus is not free. The part of him that thinks, however, the mind, is not physical and thus free. We are left, though, with a question that continues to perplex philosophers: How can a nonphysical mind interact with a physical body?

_04:: Nietzsche's *On the Genealogy of Morals*

Nietzsche attempts to unravel and expose traditional morality by investigating etymology, the origin of moral terms. *Good*, he finds in his study of various languages, originally meant "godlike," and actions were considered good when done by those who were powerful, godlike. The English words *noble* and *classy* remind us that originally those who were powerful were considered good. *Bad* originally meant "common" or "simple," and those who were not powerful and the actions they took were thus deemed bad. The English words *base*, *poor*, and *villain* ("from the village") remind us that originally the bad were the powerless. This original morality, in which the chief virtue was power, Nietzsche calls the master morality. With the rise of Christianity comes the rise of the slave morality, in which the chief virtues are love and compassion and the propaganda tells us that "the meek shall inherit the earth." This moral reversal was born from the resentment the low and the slavelike felt for the powerful. As a result, what was good came to be called evil and what was bad came to be called good. Nietzsche didn't wish for a re-

Strange but True

HOW WAKING UP EARLY KILLED DESCARTES

They say getting up early won't kill you, but that may not be true. René Descartes never had a real job. After college he traveled throughout Europe, much of the time as a gentleman volunteer in the army, a pretty cushy gig requiring no actual combat. In his thirties Descartes retired to the Netherlands, not for weed and hookers, but for peace and toleration. And he often spent his mornings in bed, philosophizing a little and sleeping a lot. Descartes enjoyed success as a philosopher, mathematician, and scientist, his works drawing the attention of the powerful and the intelligent. One of the powerful who admired Descartes' work was Queen Christina of Sweden, who repeatedly invited him to join her court and instruct her in philosophy. Descartes repeatedly declined the offer, calling Sweden "the land of ice and bears." In 1649, finding himself flat broke, he finally broke down and accepted the queen's offer. When he arrived, Descartes discovered to his horror that Queen Christina—who could stand barefoot in the snow—wanted philosophy lessons at 5 a.m. Rising at the ungodly hour and trudging through the elements killed Descartes. The formal cause of death was pneumonia, but we all know the early wake-up call was to blame.

turn to the master morality but looked for a new morality that went beyond good and evil.

Behind the Philosophy:
Bad Boys of Thought

You'd think that a philosopher could reason out the best way to behave, right? But you'd be wrong, very wrong.

_01:: Socrates, the Barefoot Bum

Notoriously ugly, clad in one coat long beyond its years, and always shoeless, yet possessed of charisma that made the youth swoon, Socrates was a fixture in the marketplace of Athens. There he would engage people with the Socratic method, beginning with a question that seemed straightforward and easy enough to answer, such as, What is virtue? Never content with the first answer, his irony and follow-up questions would inevitably lead to contradictions or admissions of ignorance on the part of his interlocutors. Socrates rubbed some people the wrong way, though, and was brought to trial on trumped-up charges of impiety and corrupting the youth. Defiant to the end, Socrates suggested that the proper sentence for his "crimes" would be free meals at the public expense, as he had done the city good. The jury gave him a hemlock cocktail instead.

_02:: Diogenes, a Cynic's Cynic

Always suspicious of society and philosophers, Diogenes (died ca. 320 BCE) would stop at nothing to make a point. He once ripped the feathers out of a live chicken to disprove Plato's account of human beings as the only featherless biped. Asked once what wine he liked best, his cynical response was "other peoples'." Alexander the Great, intrigued by stories about Diogenes, sought him out and announced, "I am Alexander the Great. What can I do for you?" "Stand back—you block my light" was Diogenes' response. While the ordinary person would have lost his head after such an insult, Diogenes was admired all the more, as the great conqueror said, "If I were not Alexander, I would be Diogenes."

_03:: Peter Abelard (1079–1144), the Castrated Cleric

Sex scandals are nothing new to the Catholic Church. Take the case of Abelard, the influential medieval philosopher who, ironically, did important work in ethics and logic. The young cleric fell in love with a beautiful young girl named Héloïse, whom he was supposed to be tutoring, and they married secretly, though they lived apart. Héloïse's uncle, however, mistakenly thought Abelard had discarded Héloïse by placing her in a convent, and he took revenge by having servants castrate Abelard in his sleep. Abelard woke up and things were never the same between him and Héloïse (needless to say, things were never the same between his legs either). The ill-fated pair were, however, reunited in death, buried together at Père Lachaise cemetery in Paris and immortalized in song by Cole Porter: "As Abelard said to Eloise, 'Don't forget to drop a line to me, please'" (from "Just One of Those Things").

_04:: Marx: Big Heart, Skinny Wallet

Unable to find work as a philosophy professor, Karl Marx (1818–1883) plotted a revolution. Working intermittently as a journalist and largely relying on the charity of friends, Marx lost many apartments and even some children for lack of financial resources. Declaring religion "the opiate of the masses," Marx found no solace in a better world to come, but instead sought to change the one he inhabited. "A specter is haunting Europe," he said, "the specter of communism. The workers of the world have nothing to lose but their chains." History reveals that Marx didn't adequately anticipate capitalism's ability to shift and change to avoid the revolution, as later workers' movements won concessions in the form of labor laws, the welfare state, and five-day work weeks. So, the next time you sleep late on a Saturday, make sure to give props to the man who made the dream of the weekend off a reality.

_05:: Arthur Schopenhauer, Poodle-Loving Pessimist

The ultimate pessimist, Schopenhauer (1788–1860) viewed reality as a malicious trap, believing we live in the worst of all possible worlds. A notorious misogynist, Schopenhauer once pushed a woman down a flight of stairs. Grudgingly, he paid her regular restitu-

---

Pure Genius

THALES OF MILETUS

Thales of Miletus (ca. 624–546 BCE), the first Western philosopher, set the standard for absentminded professors to come. Lost in thought, gazing at the sky, Thales fell into a well. Ridiculed as an impractical dreamer, Thales set out to show that philosophers could do anything they set their minds to, including amassing wealth. One winter, using his knowledge of meteorology and astronomy, Thales predicted a bumper olive crop for the coming season. He cornered the market on olive presses in Miletus and made a fortune when the olive harvest met his expectations. Remarkably, Thales predicted the solar eclipse of 585 BCE. He also measured the height of the Egyptian pyramids using their shadows. Thales is perhaps best known for arguing that water is the basic source element, that ultimately all things are made of water. He also argued that "all things are full of gods and have a share of soul," a poetic rendering of the insight confirmed by much later science that all matter is always in motion.

---

tion for her injuries until her death, when he recorded in his journal, "The old woman dies, the burden is lifted." Schopenhauer despised noise but inexplicably had a fondness for something more odious, poodles. A series of disposable poodles were his constant companions for most of his life. Not a pleasant academic colleague, Schopenhauer resented the success of Hegel, whose philosophy he thought was the worst kind of nonsense. Perhaps planning to undo Hegel, Schopenhauer scheduled his course lectures at the same time as Hegel's. The result, however, was an early retirement for Arthur.

_06:: Nietzsche: A Bad Boy Who Wasn't

One might think he railed against the corrupting influence of Christianity and declared "God is dead," because of his own misery (Nietzsche suffered from migraine headaches and poor digestion, topped off with bouts of insomnia). But the guy whose autobiographical *Ecce Homo* includes such chapters as "Why I Am So Wise," "Why I Am So Clever," and "Why I Write Such Good Books" was actually an unassuming, mild-mannered man. His belief in "the will to power" as the most basic human drive finds little reflection in his own life outside his fantasies. Though he fancied himself a warrior and a ladies' man, Nietzsche's military service was brief and unspectacular, and he never had a lover. As a bad boy in college, he may have visited a brothel or two, though. One theory suggests that the insanity that cut his career short and institutionalized him for the last 11 years of his life was the result of untreated syphilis.

_07:: Heidegger, Nazi Sympathizer

Though he originally planned to become a Catholic priest, this philosopher of being was far from holy. He carried on an extramarital affair with his gifted student Hannah Arendt, who later fled Germany to avoid persecution as a Jew. This might seem a peccadillo, except that Martin Heidegger was an anti-Semite who embraced the rise of Hitler's Third Reich. Notoriously, Heidegger had his dedication page in his *Being and Time* removed in subse-

quent printings of the book, as it paid homage to Edmund Husserl, his former teacher, a Jew. At a time when intellectuals should have risen up, Heidegger sank to the lowest common denominator. What's worse, he never recanted or apologized.

_08:: Bertrand Russell, Cambridge Casanova

An innovator in mathematics and logic, and one of the founders of analytic philosophy, at first blush Russell sounds like a dry guy. Yet his life was anything but dull. Plagued by bouts of terrible depression as a young man, Russell learned to cultivate a zest for life. This heavy-drinking, pipe-smoking professor was notorious for having affairs with his friends' wives. He rejected organized religion with his famous essay "Why I Am Not a Christian," but nonetheless had a passion for social justice, flirting with runs for political office and doing jail time for political protest, that last time at age 94. Notably, Russell was a leading intellectual voice against the war in Vietnam.

_09:: Michel Foucault, the Marilyn Manson of Philosophy

Always the outsider, Foucault (1926–1984) was the voice of the marginalized and oppressed, notably as a supporter of and inspiration for the Paris student uprisings of 1968. Making use of Nietzsche's insights on the nature of power and the method of historical investigation and exposure known as genealogy, Foucault challenged the legitimacy of dominant cultural structures. Suspicious of institutions, in works such as *Madness and Civilization,* *The Birth of the Clinic,* and *Discipline and Punish,* Foucault called for the abolition of prisons and asylums. Himself a homosexual, Foucault challenged our idea of what is normal in *The History of Sexuality*. As a visiting professor at Berkeley, Foucault frequented the San Francisco bathhouses and developed a passion for

S&M. Though he kept his disease a private matter, he was the first (and to date only) major philosopher to die of AIDS.

3 Eastern Sages Who Leave the West Behind

The line between philosophy and religion isn't clearly drawn in the East. As a result, these thinkers go straight to the heart of fundamental human concerns in a way not often matched in the West.

_01:: Confucius: If the Mat Was Not Straight the Master Would Not Sit

Believing that the way of earth was out of line with the way of heaven and that societal order was necessary for personal order, the Chinese sage Confucius (551–479 BCE) stresses the importance of harmony in five basic relationships: ruler and minister, father and son, elder brother and younger brother, husband and wife, and friend and friend. There are three primary elements in Confucian ethics: jen, li, and chih. Jen calls for compassion and reciprocity: "What you do not want done to yourself, do not do to others." Li, or rituals like ancestor veneration, cultivate individual moralities and indicate our place in the cosmos. And jen and li come together in chih, a kind of individual integrity in which one lives virtuously and authentically in thought and action.

_02:: Lao-tzu and the Tao of Who?

In the *Tao te Ching* Lao-tzu sets forth a profoundly optimistic philosophy, calling for har-

mony with what is good, i.e., nature and our own original nature. We become sages by following the Tao, or the way. As Lao-tzu states, the universe has a natural way running through it like the current in a river, which we must simply get in touch with and follow. His teaching, wu-wei, calls for action by nonaction (effortless action), as when an athlete "in the zone" moves with effortless grace, or as nonviolent protest defeats the most stubbornly active opposition. Lao-tzu goes on to say that attempting to understand how the Tao works is actually counterproductive and trying to define and name the Tao is futile: "The Tao called Tao is not Tao."

_03:: Nagarjuna (ca. 150–250 CE), the Happy Medium

Despite the Buddha's silence on metaphysical issues, later Buddhist philosophers, notably Nagarjuna, wondered about the reality of the world. Nagarjuna applied the doctrine of the Middle Way, not going to extremes, denying the extreme view that reality is solely material and denying the opposite extreme that there is no material reality. The interdependence of all things on all things implies that everything is sunya—empty—and thus the same. There are no opposites; such concepts mislead us. There is no birth or death, destruction or permanence, unity or multiplicity, coming in or going out. Because, like all things, nirvana is sunya and the cycle of suffering—samsara—is sunya, they are not in essence different. Nirvana involves liberation from concepts, thus seeing nirvana and samsara as the same.

• •

Philosophy Doesn't Grow on Trees, but It Does Have Branches

6

• •

Just as science divides its labor among branches such as biology, chemistry, and physics, philosophy too divides itself into specialized branches.

• •

_01:: Metaphysics: We're Not Talking Tarot Cards Here

Metaphysics isn't just for crystal-carrying Capricorns any more. The most basic question of metaphysics is, What is real? To answer the question, metaphysics also asks, How can we distinguish what is real from what is not real? And are there different degrees and types of reality? Metaphysics considers the reality of the mind, space, time, free will, and God. Some philosophers, such as Plato, have argued that the reality we take in through our senses is just a pale shadow of a higher, more perfect reality. By contrast, other philosophers, such as David Hume (1711–1776), have argued that the only reality is that which we take in through our senses; all else is sheer fantasy. The truth may lie somewhere between those answers, but you can decide for yourself.

_02:: Epistemology: When You've Gotta Have the Truth

You come to a fork in the road and on a hunch choose the path that leads you to your destination. Did you know it was the right path? You had a true belief about which was the right path, but you didn't *know* it was the right path. Why? Because you didn't have justification or evidence, just a hunch. Epistemology, the study of knowledge, traditionally defines its subject as true, justified belief. But what counts as justification? Does the justification have to arise from the proper causal relations outside of us? Or does it have to arise from proper reasoning within us? What yields knowledge? Reason alone? The testimony of our senses alone? Both acting together? And can we ever have enough justification to claim knowledge of anything?

_03:: Ethics: A System Not Employed by Enron and Not Available from Microsoft

In opposition to relativism, which tells us that ethical standards are individually or culturally determined, philosophers seek universal ethical standards. Virtue theorists, such as Aristotle, argue that cultivating character traits such as patience, temperance, and courage through repeated practice leads to the good life and to the good person who can be counted on to do the right thing no matter what situation arises. Natural law theorists, such as Thomas Aquinas (1225–1274), argue that there are objective moral laws just as surely as there are objective physical laws. Intentionally killing innocent people, for example, goes against the law of nature. Utilitarians,

---

that reason dictates that we should act only in a way, in which we would want everyone else to act.

_04:: Political Philosophy: Lots of Debate but No Parties

Despite the shameful actions of politicians past and present, Plato and Aristotle considered ethics and politics inseparable. The good person and the good society depend on one another. In his *Republic* Plato raises the question of the legitimate role of the government and calls for the abandonment of democracy in favor of a protosocialist state, an ideal developed much later by Karl Marx. Thomas Hobbes viewed the government as an overbearing presence, a Leviathan, but one to which we must submit for our own protection. According to John Locke (1632–1704), all men are born with the inalienable rights to life, liberty, and property, and through the social contract, we form governments to protect those rights. Libertarian philosophers of today see the protection of those rights as the only legitimate function of governments. By contrast, communitarian philosophers argue that governments must take care of their citizens in the spirit of community, thus justifying, among other things, the welfare state. Other topics of discussion in political philosophy include justice, fairness, punishment, globalization, the family, paternalism, and autonomy.

such as John Stuart Mill (1806–1873), argue that we should judge actions right or wrong on the basis of the greatest happiness principle: act so as to produce the greatest good (i.e., happiness) for the greatest number. The categorical imperative of Immanuel Kant tells us

_05:: Aesthetics: Hey There, Beautiful!

"Beauty is in the eye of the beholder," some say, but philosophers from Aristotle to Kant and beyond have searched for objective standards by which to judge the beauty of art and nature. "There's no accounting for taste," some say, but philosophers, such as Hume, attempt to do just that. Anyone who's ever sampled both Hershey and Godiva chocolate can tell you the Godiva chocolate tastes better. While some food, painting, and music may be acquired tastes, the beauty of nature is readily apparent to a child. Why? Why do we seek beauty and value art? How can we find truth and meaning in art? And do the intentions of artists govern how we should interpret their work? It's all there in aesthetic debate.

_06:: Logic: It's Elementary, My Dear Watson

Logic comes naturally for Vulcans like Mr. Spock, but humans need to specify and study the rules of proper reasoning that take us from the premise of an argument to its conclusion. There are two types of logical reasoning or argument: deductive and inductive. Despite what your seventh-grade science teacher said, the difference between the two does not depend on moving from general premises to a specific conclusion or vice versa. A deductive argument is one in which the premises are intended, if true, to guarantee the truth of the conclusion. A deductive argument in which the reasoning accomplishes this is called valid, and if its premises are indeed true as well, it's called sound. An inductive argument is one in which the premises are intended to provide support, but not

Strange but True

MOTION IS IMPOSSIBLE— ZENO'S PARADOXES

The Greek mathematician Zeno of Elea (ca. 495–ca. 430 BCE) attempted to show that space and motion were impossible. It would take too long to explain and examine all the paradoxes, but one will illustrate his basic argument. Zeno asks us to imagine a runner moving from point A to point B. If we assume that the line from point A to point B contains an infinite number of points, then the runner must reach the halfway mark before he reaches the end. But before he reaches the halfway mark, he must reach a point halfway to that, and so on. Between each of these halfway points, there are an infinite number of points. Here comes the paradox: How can the runner traverse an infinite series of points in a finite time interval? Using this same principle, Zeno showed that an arrow in flight does not move and that Achilles can never outrun a tortoise if the tortoise has even the slightest head start. In short, if we can divide something at all, we can divide it ad infinitum.

absolute proof, for the conclusion, and an argument that produces likely support is called strong.

Isms Finally Put in Their Place

Struggling to find the philosophy that's just right for you? Why not take a little inspiration from your surroundings.

_01:: Stoicism: When You're on the Porch

Stoicism takes its name from the Greek word *stoa*, meaning "porch," as the original stoics gathered on a *stoa* in Athens. This folksy source of the name speaks to the very practical concern of stoicism—how to live a tranquil life in the midst of a chaotic world. Stoicism, a philosophy embraced by both the former slave Epictetus (ca. 50–ca. 135) and the emperor of Rome Marcus Aurelius (121–180), counsels self-control, detachment, and acceptance of one's fate. Stoicism holds that the events of the world are out of our control and fated to be. Our minds, however, are free and so our reactions to and feelings about what happens to us and in the world around us are under our control. We can live with peace of mind under any and all circumstances so long as we adjust our minds to accept things as they are. This does not mean we should never take steps to change things, but we should realize that ultimately we have only influence, never control, over things outside our own minds.

_02:: Cynicism: When You're in the Doghouse

Cynicism takes its name from the Greek *kynikos*, related to our word *canine*. The most famous Cynic, Diogenes, chose to live outside of Athens in a tub and in the company of dogs, whom he found nobler than the residents of the city. The Cynics scorned and distrusted the values and ways of society, and Diogenes displayed this attitude with philoso-

---

Strange but True

TOMMY PUTS HIS QUILL DOWN

Thomas Aquinas was a well-greased philosophical machine, writing on nearly every conceivable topic of philosophical or theological interest. Indeed his collected works in Latin comprise 25 volumes. Strangely, though, Aquinas stopped writing altogether in December 1273, three months before his death. Ill health was not to blame. Rather, at prayer one evening Aquinas had a mystical experience, and afterward is said to have remarked, "All I have written seems like straw to me." This was not to say that his previous writing and commitment to faith seeking understanding was without value, just that by comparison with the awe-inspiring vision he had, his writing and projects seemed the stuff of animal beds.

phy in the form of performance art. He would walk through the marketplace of Athens carrying a lighted lantern in the middle of the day and, when asked what he was doing, would reply that he was looking for an honest man. None could be found by his lights.

_03:: Thomism: When You're in the Pulpit (This One Has Mass Appeal)

The philosophy of Thomas Aquinas (1225–1274) is the most significant contribution to Catholic philosophical thought. Following the guiding dictum of medieval philosophy, "faith seeking understanding," Aquinas believed that faith gives the answers to questions of theological and philosophical importance, and

philosophical reasoning makes sense of those answers where possible. His major work, the *Summa Theologica*, is *the* landmark work of medieval philosophy, and every major medieval philosopher after Aquinas studied, commented on, and felt the influence of his work. In 1879 Pope Leo XIII declared Aquinas to be *Aeterni Patris* ("of the Eternal Father"), and to this day his metaphysics and natural law ethics are an important source of Catholic theology. Thomism isn't merely a historical entry in the story of philosophy but a vibrant and continuing school of thought. Notable 20th-century Thomists include Etienne Gilson (1884–1978), Jacques Maritain (1882–1973), and Bernard Lonergan (1904–1984).

Thinking Positive!: Feel-Good Philosophies

5

If contemplating life has you down in the dumps, maybe it's time you justified your existence with some peppy reasoning. Chin up, kid. Here are a few feel-good philosophies to get you grinning again.

_01:: Eat, Drink, and Be Merry! with Epicureanism

Today an epicure is a gourmet, and as his detractors had it, Epicurus (341–270 BCE) indulged in extravagant pleasures of food, drink, and sex. Nothing could be further from the truth. Epicurus lived in a kind of hippie commune called the Garden and subsisted on a modest diet of water, cheese, vegetables, and the occasional glass of wine. With

no belief in an afterlife, Epicureanism holds that pleasure is the highest good in this life and there is no fear of punishment in an afterlife. Simple pleasures taken in moderation are best. In fact, some pleasures are unnatural and unnecessary, for they return more pain than pleasure in the long run. Just watch any VH1 *Behind the Music* episode to see why Epicurus is right about the pain of overindulgence.

_02:: Seize the Day! with Existentialism

Existentialism may conjure images of a French recluse smoking stinky cigarettes and despairing at the meaninglessness of it all, but this just ain't right! Existentialism generally prescribes a seize-the-day attitude and offers consolation in the face of the void. Some existentialists, such as Kierkegaard and Marcel (1889–1973), have actually been committed Christians, hopeful of salvation. Heidegger and Karl Jaspers (1883–1969) rejected the label of existentialism, but Sartre embraced it and defined it as the doctrine that "existence preceded essence," which means that we have no given nature but can create a nature for ourselves. The common bond of philosophies that fall under the heading of existentialism is a focus on lived individual existence rather than grand systematic theoretical speculation.

_03:: It's All Good! with Relativism

"Everything is relative," they say. Relativism is the belief that there are no universal standards for what is true, right, good, beautiful, etc. Standards are determined by the individual or the culture. Varieties of relativism include moral (right and wrong are relative), epistemological (truth is relative), aesthetic (beauty is relative), and metaphysical (reality is relative). Cultural relativism asserts that accepted standards differ among cultures and individuals. This claim is undoubtedly true. But whether differing cultural and individual standards can all be correct is another matter. A simple version of relativism runs into the problem of being self-contradictory. If, for example, I believe that it is wrong for anyone to fly kites on Sunday and you believe everyone has an absolute duty to fly kites on Sunday, relativism must hold that we're both right. But logically speaking, we can't both be right.

_04:: It's the Thought That Counts! with Rationalism

Rationalism is the belief that some, perhaps all, knowledge can be obtained through reason alone. Some rationalists take the senses to be less reliable than reason, while others distrust the senses completely. The most ancient rationalist, a Greek philosopher named Parmenides (born ca. 515 BCE), argued that according to reason and despite what our senses tell us, change and multiple beings are impossible. So, there is only one being and it never changes. Parmenides' student Zeno elaborated on this thesis by arguing through a series of paradoxes that motion, a kind of change, is impossible. Descartes is the most important modern rationalist. He begins his philosophical system by acknowledging that the senses sometimes deceive us and so should not be trusted. Happily, he goes on to discover that reason unaided by the senses yields certain knowledge that "I exist."

_05:: Share the Wealth! with Marxism

While many know that Groucho said he'd never want to belong to a club that would have him as a member, few know that Karl declared, "I am no Marxist." Even in Karl's lifetime Marxism was interpreted and applied in many ways beyond Marx's original vision. Karl Marx argued that the story of human civilization is best understood as a history of economic class conflict. Asserting that previous philosophers had merely interpreted the world, Marx's goal was to change it. The contemporary class conflict Marx pointed to was that between the workers and the capitalists: the owners of the means of production. In *The Communist Manifesto*, Marx and his co-author, Friedrich Engels (1820–1895), conclude with the cry "workers of the world unite." The pair called for a workers' revolution that would ultimately lead to a communist society guided by the principle "from each according to his ability, to each according to his need." Significantly, Marxism has been applied to literary theory as a way of reading literature in terms of class conflict. Notable Marxists who interpreted Marx in light of their own political concerns include György Lukács (1885–1971), Louis Althusser (1918–1990), the later Jean-Paul Sartre, and Herbert Marcuse (1898–1979).

Bad Catchphrases (and the Philosophies behind Them)

Sure, you've seen the bumper stickers, or overheard annoying conversations where someone would mutter an overused phrase, then wave a hand in the air, expecting a high-five. But who knew they were really spouting philosophy?

_01:: Show Me the Money! (Pragmatism)

Pragmatism focuses on questions that make a difference to the way we live and seeks answers that have a "cash value." This stands in direct contrast to abstract concerns that have no clear payoff. A distinctly American product, pragmatism's three chief figures are C. S. Peirce (1839–1914), William James (1842–1910), and John Dewey (1859–1952). Rejecting the correspondence theory, which holds that a belief is true if it corresponds to the way things actually are, and the coherence theory, which holds that a belief is true if it fits in with the rest of our beliefs, the pragmatic theory of truth holds that something is true if it works. For James, free will and God are true because they are ideas that work to make our lives better. Pragmatism's most enduring legacy, Dewey's theory of education, makes children active learners in a classroom that is a laboratory in which they can openly follow and explore their interests.

_02:: Not! (Nihilism)

Taking its name from the Latin *nihil,* meaning "nothing," nihilism is the general term applied to the belief that nothing is objectively meaningful. Existentialists are often mischaracterized as nihilists. Nietzsche, for example, predicted that with the "death" of God—the loss of belief in what is central—the 20th century would face an unprecedented threat of nihilism. Nietzsche did not advocate nihilism, but rather warned against it and urged the creation of new, more vibrant beliefs. The absurdity of actually adopting nihilism is played for laughs in the offbeat Hollywood comedy *The Big Lebowski*, in which the hero, "the dude," is hounded by nihilists.

_03:: There's More Than One Way to Skin a Cat (Pluralism)

Pluralism subscribes to the old, now politically incorrect, adage, "there's more than one way to skin a cat." Rejecting relativism as giving away too much, pluralism remains wary of absolute universal standards. Not just any view of right and wrong, truth, beauty, etc., can be right. But more than one view can be right. Obviously, there's more than one way to get from New York to Chicago. Similarly, religious pluralism holds that despite their differences, all true religions are in touch with the same ultimate reality. Other forms of plural-

---

Strange but True

AVOID THE BEANS (AND OTHER PYTHAGOREAN THEOREMS)

The name Pythagoras (ca. 580–ca. 500 BCE) probably resonates in your mind because of distant memories of geometry or music class. He is known primarily as the person who connected mathematics to music; in fact, for Phythagoras, all is number. His passion for mathematics was expressed in a mystical way. For example, he thought that the number 10 was sacred, and he often had his disciples spend days contemplating a number or a geometric figure. His mysticism, however, included some strange taboos. Here is a partial list of the rules of the Pythagorean school:

One must not eat beans
One must not pick up what has fallen
One must not touch a white rooster
One must not break bread
One must not step over a crossbar
One must not stir the fire with iron
One must not eat from a whole loaf
One must not pluck a garland
One must not sit on a quart of anything
One must not eat the heart of anything
One must not walk on highways
One must not allow swallows to nest on one's roof
One must not look in a mirror beside a light

Bertrand Russell called Pythagoras intellectually one of the most important men who ever lived and one of the most interesting and puzzling men in history.

ism suggest there's more than one way to do the good, know the truth, conceive the beautiful, or experience reality. Though it's motivated by practicality and tolerance, pluralism may itself give away too much. At least that's what absolutists, believers in single universal standards, would say.

Name-Dropping 101:
3 Schools of Thought That Will Impress the Opposite Sex

If you want to swing and cruise in the hippest intellectual atmospheres, your cocktail party cheat sheet better include some of these words.

_01:: Feminism: Something in the Way She Thinks

Feminism argues that from its beginning, Western philosophy has been a boys-only "reindeer game." The dominant views and approaches of philosophy have been distinctly male, marginalizing, at times outright excluding the female perspective. Metaphysics has sought a stable, phallic account of reality and has privileged mind and intellect (associated with the male) over body (associated with the female). Epistemology has sought to establish knowledge on the basis of rigid justification rather than explore the insight and intuition that make knowledge possible. Ethics has centered around male conceptions of objective duty rather than understanding ethical decisions as really being made in contextual relationships. The most activist issue of feminism is the political and civil rights of women, who were so long deprived of such rights as voting and owning property. Today political femi-nism addresses issues of sexual harassment, domestic violence, the continuing inequality of women's rights in the third world, and more subtle forms of gender inequality such as the corporate glass ceiling.

_02:: Deconstruction: Razing a Good Point

Deconstruction simply means that the meaning can never be clear. Jacques Derrida (1930–), the father of deconstruction, played on the French words for *differ* and *defer* to coin the term *différance*, implying that meaning is derived from difference. Further, in Derrida's logic, meaning is never fully present but is always deferred or postponed. There is always something to come next that can destabilize the meaning we thought was there. Derrida looks for metaphors, wordplay, footnotes, and other marginal comments that suggest a meaning other than that intended by the author. So, to deconstruct a novel, a film, or anything else is not just to analyze its parts but to show how it contains inconsistencies that actually subvert its intended meaning.

_03:: Postmodernism: Truthless People

Though the term *postmodernism* has almost as many meanings as users, in general, philosophers of postmodernism are concerned with the implications of a new era that began with the loss of Enlightenment ideals. Postmodernism holds that we have come to the end of "totalizing narratives" such as science, Christianity, and Marxism, none of which can be taken seriously as telling the whole story or truth. All our knowledge is piecemeal, fragmented, and perspectival—and no one can see or describe the big picture. With mass production and simulation, with the *Mona Lisa* available on everything from postcards to mouse pads, with artificial flavors and the growth of virtual-reality technology, the nature and value of what is "real" is always called into question.

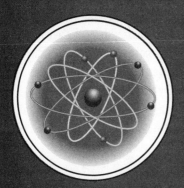

by
Richard A. Muller

Condensed
PHYSICS

Contains

4 Reasons to Have Your Physics Super-Sized ✳ 6 Swashbuckling Physicists (and Their Beautiful Minds)* ✳ Glowing Concerns: 5 Ways Radioactivity Lights Up Your Life ✳ Really Big Bangs!: Huge Explosions We're Actually Glad About ✳ 8 Scary Warnings That Could Have Been Placed on This Book ✳ 5 Miserable Screwups by a Famous Physicist ✳ 1 Nobel Prize That Should Never Have Been Awarded ✳ Say It Ain't So!: 4 Things Einstein Got Wrong ✳ 9 Laws of Physics That Don't Apply in Hollywood ✳ 2 Reasons Physics Doesn't Work in the Real World ✳

*Written by mental_floss

Reasons to Have Your Physics Super-Sized

Physicists love to use the term *super*. For some unexplained reason, they find the term superior to its synonyms, such as *big*, *great*, or *fantastic*. From superclusters to supernovas to supergravity to superheavy elements, physics is simply littered with the prefix. In fact, some day people may identify 20th-century physics ideas by the word's overuse, just as we can spot movies made in the 1940s by their frequent use of the word *swell*. The following are just a few of the ways the word *super* has attached itself to physics phenomena.

_01:: Superconductors

We like conductors: after all, they carry electricity into our homes so we can watch bad reality TV. In the name of cooler and better, in 1911 Heike Onnes discovered the property of superconductors—materials such as lead and mercury, which have no resistance to electricity when cooled near to absolute zero (−459.67°F). If an electric current starts flowing in a loop of superconductor, it will continue to flow forever. So, what's the catch? You have to keep it near −459.67°F—and that's extremely hard to do. Everyone got excited when high-temperature superconductors were discovered in the 1980s, but even those had to be kept at the temperature of liquid nitrogen. If and when we discover a superconductor that works at room temperature, our homes and countries will all be rewired with the superior wire.

_02:: Supersymmetry

Physicists classify all elementary particles into two groups, called fermions and bosons, based on their spin. Electrons, protons, and neutri-nos are considered fermions, while photons, gravitons, and gluons make up the boson camp. Prior to the theory of supersymmetry, these two classes of particles were considered to be quite different from each other. But the theory of supersymmetry romantically assumes that all particles come in pairs, with a boson for every fermion, and vice versa. In a sense, these pairs are actually two aspects of the same particle. If supersymmetry turns out to be true, then it could be the final unification of physics. Unfortunately, there are no known supersymmetric pairs, so the theory may be superfluous.

_03:: Superstring Theory

This is a theory that is even more far out than plain supersymmetry. In superstring theory, the ultimate fundamental particle from which all others are made is called a string (because of its geometry). And depending on how this string vibrates, it becomes an electron, a neutrino, a graviton, or a quark (the fundamental unit inside the proton and neutron). In ordinary string theory, the particles with different

THE MOST EXPENSIVE
MATERIAL IN THE WORLD

What's the most expensive material per pound in common use by physics? Diamonds? Nah. Gem-quality diamonds cost only about $15 million per pound. It's been estimated that Saddam Hussein was willing to spend $100 million per pound for weapons-grade uranium. But that isn't it. Moon dust? Nope. Russian-retrieved moon dust (they had a robot return some) has been sold on the black market for less than $5 million per pound. The most expensive substance per pound is actually an ultra-high vacuum. Although it's abundant in space, nobody has figured out a good way to bring it down to earth. The cost of making one is $4 followed by 21 zeros, so nothing else even comes close. And the price will only get more expensive per gram as the vacuums get better!

many extra spatial dimensions, typically 10 . . . not an easy thing to visualize. Super-string theory is considered superlative because it solves many of the mathematical problems that plagued particle theory—in particular, annoying infinities that wouldn't go away. But beware—there is no experimental evidence that string theory is true, i.e., that it represents physical reality rather than just superficial mathematics.

_04:: The Super

The Super is the name for the original version of the hydrogen bomb, and American nuclear physicist Edward Teller (1908–2003) worked for years trying to figure out how to make one work. The original model consisted of a stick of hydrogen ignited at one end by an ordinary atomic fission bomb, like the one dropped on Hiroshima. The hydrogen would ignite into fusion and burn down the stick. So, to make a bigger bomb, just make the stick longer, right? Nope. Calculations showed it wouldn't work, as it would cool down too much and put itself out. It was only when Teller discussed the problem with Stanislaw Ulam (1909–1984) that they came up with the solution: to compress the hydrogen using gamma radiation. That became the new design, and the Super was superseded.

spin rates are different strings; in superstring theory, they are the same. How can that be? The string has a more complicated geometry than the string you use to tie a package, with

6 Swashbuckling Physicists (and Their Beautiful Minds)

OK, so most physicists probably wouldn't be mistaken for Indiana Jones. But just because they don't tote snapping whips or fancy hats, it doesn't mean their stories don't get passed around. Here are the true tales of six colorful physicists you ought to know.

_01:: Albert Einstein (1879–1955)

Sure, you know all about Uncle Albert's famous equations, his knack for the violin, his love of sailing, or maybe even that he was offered the presidency of the newly created Israel in 1952. But did you know that he was a notoriously bad dresser? That's right, unkempt hair and all, Albert Einstein was a poster boy for unruly appearances. In fact, he was so underdressed on one occasion (a reception with the emperor of the Austro-Hungarian Empire no less) that he was mistaken for an electrician because of his work shirt. Not surprisingly, Albert also disliked extravagance, claiming that luxuries were wasted on him. Despite his intellectual celebrity status, the Nobel Prize winner refused to travel in anything but third class.

_02:: Nikola Tesla (1856–1943)

Tesla dreamed up AC current, won technical disputes with Edison, had ideas stolen from him by Marconi, and designed the tesla coil (that lovely spinning thing you find sparking light in every mad scientist's lab). But even more intriguing than all of this were his peculiarities. Nikola Tesla's personal life was one of crippling obsessions: washing his hands endlessly, counting every item on a dinner table before tucking in, and maintaining a hatred for earrings and other round objects. But perhaps most unusual was his fondness for pigeons. Tesla was so smitten by one bird in particular that when it passed away, he wrote, "Yes, I loved her as a man loves a woman, and she loved me. . . . When that pigeon died something went out of my life. . . . I knew my life's work was over."

_03:: Richard Feynman (1918–1988)

A real live wire of the science world, Richard Feynman was a giant in his field. One of the most famous physicists of the 20th century, Feynman contributed heavily to the Manhattan Project, won a Nobel Prize for his work in quantum electrodynamics, and contributed key insights as a member of the presidential team investigating the NASA *Challenger* disaster. He was also well known for banging away on his bongos whenever he got the chance and for trying to perfect the art of picking up women (from college parties to red-light districts). If you'd like some insight into his mischievous personality, though, consider how he let the great minds working on the Manhattan Project know that their classified documents weren't exactly safe. Feynman studied up a bit on safecracking, stole a few combinations, then picked the government locks with ease, taking nothing from the vaults. Instead he left amusing notes for the officials, letting them know just how good their security was.

_04:: Stephen Hawking (1942–)

Well known for authoring *A Brief History of Time*, the world-renowned theoretician has made his greatest contributions in the physics of black holes. He was also elected one of the Royal Society's youngest fellows and selected to Cambridge's Lucasian post, a professorship of mathematics once held by Isaac Newton. While all signs point to genius, that doesn't mean Hawking is always right. Back in 1975, he made a bet with Kip Thorne of Caltech that Cygnus X-1 did not contain a black hole. (The prize was a subscription to a racy magazine.) In 1990, when Hawking decided the evidence against him was overwhelming, he conceded in a waggish manner: he had a friend break into Thorne's office and steal the recorded terms of the bet. Hawking signed his defeat, then sneaked it back in for Thorne to find later. In the following months Thorne also received his promised issues of *Penthouse*.

_05:: Fay Ajzenberg-Selove (1926–)

As a little girl, renowned physicist Fay Ajzenberg-Selove had a knack for engineering. When she became bored with simple electronics, she turned to her true love—physics—but her path was far from easy. Her family fled Hitler's reign, and during the escape her father distributed small knives to each of his children, showing them how to slit their wrists in the event that they were caught. The experience was chilling, but surviving the Holocaust

---

Myths and Misconceptions

EVERYTHING YOU THOUGHT YOU KNEW ABOUT PHYSICS (BUT WERE AFRAID TO ASK)

Black holes don't suck things in, despite what you see on *Star Trek*. If we replaced the sun with a black hole of equal mass, the earth's orbit wouldn't change. It's only when you get very close to the surface of the black hole that the gravity becomes intense.

Einstein didn't make the atom bomb possible by showing that $E = mc^2$. The discovery of radioactivity had already shown that there was a million times more energy available than in ordinary chemical reactions, and the discovery of the chain reaction made fission power practicable. Einstein's equation just explains where the energy is coming from; it played no role in the development of atomic bombs or nuclear reactors.

Explosive detectors at airports don't detect hidden explosives. In fact, there's no reliable way to detect explosives remotely. The explosive detectors at work are just really fancy X-ray machines that look for suspicious shapes and wires. A chemical swipe can detect residual explosives on the outside of luggage but not the explosives within.

---

gave Ajzenberg-Selove tremendous courage for her later battles with sexism. In the 1950s Fay was invited by colleagues at Princeton to use some of the university's equipment for her experiments. The chairman of the physics department at Princeton, however, had a rigid rule: No women in the building. She ignored the warning, slinking through the halls late at night and conducting her experiments till the wee hours of the morn.

_06:: Archimedes (ca. 287–212 BCE)

Archimedes, of "give me a long enough lever and a place to stand, and I'll move the earth" fame, is also well known for popularizing the term *eureka*. The famous Greek mathematician, physicist, and inventor lived most of his life in Syracuse, where he was under the patronage of the royal family. The emperor asked him to de-termine whether a crown was pure gold, and the answer struck Archimedes while he was bathing. When the water started overflowing, he realized the crown's density was the key. He took the crown, placed it in water, and noted how much water was displaced. Then he took the crown's exact weight in pure gold and re-peated the process (surprise, surprise—the numbers were different). Supposedly, Archim-edes was so excited by his flash of bathtub in-spiration that he continued flashing: he jumped out of the tub and ran home nude, shrieking, *"Eureka!"* (or "I found it!") in delight.

Glowing Concerns:
5 Ways Radioactivity Lights Up Your Life

The word *radioactivity* always seems to bring up a number of glowing concerns. But maybe it's time you got over your fears and warmed up to the idea. Here are some reasons to grin about radioactivity.

_01:: If You Aren't Radioactive, You Just Ain't Livin'

The carbon dioxide in the air contains one part in a trillion of radiocarbon, which is ra-dioactive and produced by cosmic rays from space. Plants, of course, take in this carbon, so then they become radioactive. If you eat plants or animals that eat plants, then *you* be-come radioactive. So, why is this important? When you die, the radiocarbon will begin to decay. In 5,730 years half the radiocarbon will be gone. In another 5,730 years half of that will be gone. Because scientists can measure the age of ancient bones by measuring how much of the radiocarbon is gone, if a bone is not measurably radioactive, that means that its owner has been dead at least 50,000 years.

_02:: Radioactivity Helps You Get Your Drink On

It isn't that the Bureau of Alcohol, Firearms, and Tobacco tests alcoholic beverages for ra-dioactivity. What is surprising is that it rejects any alcohol that doesn't show radiation as "unfit." What's the reason? Any alcohol that has zero radioactivity must have come from very old carbon, and that usually means the alcohol has been manufactured from fossil fuels. After burial for 100 million years, the radiocarbon in the original organisms decays, and Congress has decreed that such alcohol may not be legally consumed. The argument that it's unfit probably has more to do with politics than with science, since there's no scientific reason why fossil fuel alcohol would be any worse than alcohol from grapes.

_03:: The Hills Wouldn't Be So Alive

Mountains come from the collision of large tectonic plates on the surface of the earth. Nobody knows what makes these plates move, but a reasonable guess is that the very slow flow of rocks (if they go slowly enough, they behave like fluids) is driven by the heat of radioactivity in the earth's depths. So, if it weren't for the fabulous effects of radioactivity, the plates wouldn't have moved, and those hills Julie Andrews and the Von Trapp family are so eager to sing about would never have existed.

_04:: You Might Be Speaking French

This is also related to the movement of the plates, discussed in the previous paragraph. About 100 million years ago, Europe and North America were one continent. And if you look on a modern map, you can still see how the continents once fit together. But the flow of rock, possibly driven by radioactivity, sent the continents apart. As a result, we have Europe and the United States. Why should we be thankful for radioactivity? Well, without it, the United States and France would probably be next-door neighbors!

Strange but True
FACTS AND PHYSICS

Chocolate chip cookies have 15 times as much energy as the same weight of TNT. (TNT is used as an explosive because it can release energy quickly, not because it has a lot.)

Compared to the rest of the atom, the nucleus is as small as a mosquito in a football stadium.

When you look at the sun, you aren't seeing it the way it is. You are seeing it the way it was eight minutes ago. If it blew up seven minutes ago, you wouldn't know immediately. (It takes light, and anything traveling at the speed of light, that long to travel the 93-million-mile distance.)

The speed of light is only 1 foot per computer cycle (assuming you have a 1 GHz computer). That's the same as 186,000 miles per second. That's why computers have to be small—so they can retrieve data as fast as they can think.

A meteor carries 100 times as much energy in its motion as does an equal weight of TNT in its explosion. (That's why an asteroid or comet hitting the earth had enough energy to kill the dinosaurs and most other life 65 million years ago.)

_05:: Ain't No Sunshine When There's No Radioactivity

The sun is driven by a process called fusion, which is actually a series of reactions that requires short-lived radioactive intermediaries to undergo a kind of radioactivity called beta decay. Simply stated, without radioactivity, the fusion on the sun could not proceed, and the sun would have cooled off billions of years ago. And guess what: without the sun, plants and animals wouldn't be here, and you wouldn't have that killer tan.

Really Big Bangs!:
Huge Explosions We're Actually Glad About

Baking soda and balloon explosions in the bathroom = bad; creation of the world = good.

_01:: Starting Off with a Bang

In 1948 physicist George Gamow said that the universe began as an explosion billions of years ago. The overwhelming majority of scientists today agree with him, but originally some thought the idea was a bit of a joke. A rival of Gamow's, the noted astronomer Fred Hoyle, ridiculed the theory and gave it the hokey name big bang theory—and of course the name stuck. The explosion produced all the hydrogen and most of the helium that fuels our stars and the sun. Some speculate that the big bang actually created space and maybe even time. And it's continuing to happen: all of the galaxies are flying away from one another in just the pattern predicted by the theory. But don't worry. There can never be an explosion to exceed the big bang; it involved all the energy of the universe.

_02:: From Stars to Supernovas

Sometime between 4 and 5 billion years ago, a giant star burned hydrogen and helium from the big bang and cooked them into carbon, oxygen, and nitrogen—the ashes of fusion. These remained buried in a star for millions of years until the star suddenly exploded, increasing its brightness by a billion for about a month and expelling all its ashes into space. We call those explosions supernovas, and they happen pretty frequently. One occurs in the Milky Way (our galaxy) about once every hundred years. Our own lucky star formed from the blobby ashes of a supernova, and presto! 4.6 billion years later it became the sun. A nearby little blob became the earth. So, you see, we really are all made of stars.

_03:: Lowest Comet Denominator

About 200 million years ago mammals evolved from reptiles. (And you were upset about the monkey rumors!) The mammals were small, had mediocre brains, and were always outfought and outthought by the bigger, smarter lizards. Finally, about 65 million years ago, a large comet or asteroid—the size of San Francisco—crashed into the earth. Its energy of motion was 100 times greater than we would have gotten from an equal mass of dynamite, and when it hit, that energy was turned into heat, causing the greatest explo-

sion that life has ever known. All the large animals were killed, including all the large lizards known as dinosaurs. A few of the smaller lizards, including some birds, survived, as did a few of the smaller mammals. Plants soon came back, and the mammals discovered that their terrible tormentors, the horrible dinosaurs, were all gone. Long live the mammals!

8 Scary Warnings That Could Have Been Placed on This Book

We dare you to keep reading!

_01:: This Book Is Radioactive

Paper contains carbon from trees, and such carbon contains the radioactive isotope carbon 14 at a concentration of about one part in a trillion. If that number seems small, then think about this one: there are about 100 trillion of those radioactive atoms. Every minute, about 100 of them decay (i.e., explode), releasing an energetic beta ray with an energy up to 156 thousand electron volts! And it's all true. It's just that it takes a lot more radioactivity than that to do harm. Of course, you're also partially made out of carbon, so you're radioactive too. In fact, the book and you also contain a whole host of other radioactive elements, including small amounts of potassium, uranium, and thorium.

_02:: Keep Out of Reach of Antimatter for Fear of Explosion

That's right! If this book were to come into contact with an equal amount of antimatter, it would likely explode, releasing an energy equivalent to 20 million tons of TNT. So would anything else. Contact with antimatter releases all the energy stored in the mass of the nucleus. That's why there appears to be no antimatter around. We think that all the original antimatter in the big bang was annihilated. Fortunately, there was a slight excess of matter, and that's why we're here. We can make antimatter, but it takes enormous power to do so. To make enough antimatter to annihilate this book would take the energy equivalent of 20 million tons of TNT.

_03:: Shocking: Parts of This Book Are Electrified at over 1 Million Volts

Should you be worried? For a heavy element, 1 million is a typical voltage near a nuclear surface. In fact, that's what keeps the electrons tightly bound to it. Voltage is dangerous only when there is no nearby electron to cancel it, because of the high energy that an electron can pick up from the attraction. But in this case the electron is already orbiting the nucleus, so there's no danger. The voltage would be 1 million volts only in a tiny region close to the nucleus.

_04:: Reading This Book Could Contribute to the Ultimate Heat Death of the Universe

Any work you do, be it manual or intellectual, requires the conversion of chemical energy into work and heat, and that increases the entropy (the disorder) of the universe. That's the third law of thermodynamics, but many people don't realize that the disorder you contribute consists of infrared radiation sent off to distant space. Locally, your entropy is actually decreased every time you learn something. There's a widespread belief that the gradual increase in entropy will eventually lead to complete disorder. This would be very cold, but for historic reasons it's still called a heat death. We don't know if this is in our future, but our own contributions will be negligible.

_05:: Parts of This Book Could Fly Off at Greater Than 60 Million MPH without Warning

The fastest electrons are those in the inner orbits of the heaviest elements, such as lead and uranium, which exist in microscopic amounts

Pure Genius
ENRICO FERMI

Though Fermi is virtually unknown to the public, he's considered by many in the field to be a contender for the greatest physicist of the 20th century, along with Albert Einstein. Unlike Einstein, though, Fermi made major experimental discoveries as well as theoretical ones. But while many might scoff at placing Fermi and Einstein on the same pedestal, we've got plenty of proof to back the claim up. Most common particles (the electron, the proton) are called fermions thanks to Fermi's theory. The Fermi level determines the behavior of transistors and computers. The Fermi pressure keeps stars from collapsing. His discovery of the surprising behavior of slow neutrons made nuclear reactors possible, and he built the first one, under Stagg Field in Chicago. The Fermi mechanism explains cosmic radiation. The Fermi theory explains how radioactive elements emit electrons. Fermi won a Nobel Prize, and so did four of his students. His reactor made the production of plutonium practical, and he's been called the father of the atom bomb. The highest award in the U.S. for a scientist is the Fermi Award. Fermilab was named after him. The 100th element is named fermium in his honor. And his photo has appeared on a U.S. stamp, strangely, with an incorrect equation on the blackboard behind him. Get the idea?

in all materials, including this book. Those electrons have a nominal velocity of about 10% of the speed of light. (The speed of light is usually given as 186,284 miles per second, or 671 million miles per hour.) If the nucleus were to suddenly vanish (e.g., by antimatter annihilation from a rare cosmic ray), then the electron would fly off with that velocity. But don't worry about it. In doing so, the electron wouldn't cause any more harm than the cosmic rays that are constantly penetrating your body anyway.

_06:: If This Book Is Moved Horizontally, the Type on This Book Will Become Narrower

This is a consequence of special relativity. According to the theory, any object in motion will become shorter by a factor of gamma (it's called the Lorentz contraction). We won't bore you with the equation; just know that the shortening, which is real (it's observed in laboratory experiments), is important only when the velocity is comparable to the speed of light. So just don't move the book around at the speed of light, and everything will be just fine.

_07:: The Weight of This Book Will Increase Significantly If It Is Moved Rapidly

Another consequence of special relativity, this increase in mass is noticeable only if you're moving the book rapidly. By rapidly, of course, we mean near the speed of light. However, if you choose to move the book around 67 miles per hour, then the mass will increase by only one part in 100 trillion. And while that may not sound like much, it's the same mass you would get by adding half a trillion carbon atoms to it. So, be careful not to throw your back out when hot-rodding with that bag full of books!

_08:: This Book Might Spontaneously Disappear and Reappear in the Middle of Your Stomach

One of the great, fun things about science is that everything has a probability. For example, the probability is greater than zero that you will pole-vault over the moon tomorrow. Tunneling is a theory in quantum mechanics that explains the passing of a particle through a seemingly impenetrable barrier without a cause that is explainable by classical physics. The probability of it happening to an entire book, over a distance of several centimeters, is so low that it will not happen, on average, in many trillions of years. But physics can't say that it won't happen, only that it's not very likely.

5 Miserable Screwups by a Famous Physicist

Oh, that Lord Kelvin (1824–1907). Sure, he made fundamental contributions to the theory of heat. And thermodynamics. And he had that temperature scale named after him. But really, when you make blunders this big, it's definite proof everyone's entitled to a few mistakes.

_01:: The Earth Is Young

When Darwin published his "Origin of Species," Kelvin came to the conclusion that it was a mistake. He convinced Darwin that the earth could not be more than 100 million years old (as Darwin had said in the book) because there was no process that could have kept the sun burning that long. In fact, we now know that the earth is 4.6 billion years old, 46 times Kelvin's limit. But Darwin was so awed by Kelvin's self-confidence that he removed his discovery from subsequent editions of his manuscript. In fact, Darwin's deduction for the age of the earth should have been taken as an indication that Kelvin's model of the sun was wrong. Now we know that the sun derives its heat from nuclear fusion, a process that hadn't yet been discovered.

_02:: The Earth Is Shrinking

So, how did mountains come about? Kelvin's belief was that mountains grow because of the reduced space on a shrinking earth. Unfortunately for his theory, the earth isn't shrinking, at least not a significant amount. Kelvin thought the earth must be shrinking because of all the heat coming from the interior, and he argued the point vigorously. Kelvin believed that the heat came from two sources: from primordial energy from meteor impact and from the continuing compression of rocks by the earth's gravity. What he didn't know was that the earth was so old that little primordial heat was left, and that present-day shrinkage from gravity is negligible. We now know that the heat comes from radioactivity in the rock, but again, radioactivity hadn't yet been discovered when Kelvin was making his explanations.

_03:: Airplanes Won't Work

Kelvin is often quoted as saying, circa 1899, that "heavier than air flying machines are impossible." But he knew that birds flew, so this is certainly a paraphrase at best. Perhaps more accurate is the version "the aeroplane is scientifically impossible." Giving him the benefit of the doubt, we can interpret his statement to mean "a commercially useful aeroplane is impossible." He might have said such a thing based on his mastery of thermodynamics; no motor that existed at that time could produce the required power with low weight. In fact, the engines built by the Wright brothers (four years later) were innovative, and the need for better airplane engines drove much of the subsequent engine development.

_04:: Radio Has No Future

Kelvin is reported to have said this in 1897. And while this sounds like typical arrogance today, he probably said it because he believed that radio would offer no realistic alternative to the proposed transatlantic cable, which he was backing. People undoubtedly were bugging him about Marconi's recent experiments showing that signals could travel through the air, thus making his transatlantic cable unnecessary. In fact, the cable proved enormously important, as radio waves travel poorly across the Atlantic. So, in a sense, he was right. What Kelvin didn't anticipate was the enormous growth of radio as a form of entertainment and as a way of conveying news to the populace.

_05:: Physics Is Dead

Near the turn of the 20th century, Kelvin asserted that virtually all the physics there was to know was known and that as an academic discipline, physics had almost completed its work. The outstanding problems of his lifetime had been the theory of heat, to which he had made many of the greatest contributions, and the theory of electromagnetism, which had been put in completed form by Maxwell. Kelvin admitted that there were a few loose ends, especially the blackbody radiation problem (the theory of heat radiation led to a prediction of infinite radiation—clearly not true) and the puzzling results of the 1887 Michelson-Morley experiment (where the duo tried to detect the motion of the earth by detecting differences in the speed of light in two directions). Kelvin was sort of right: the physics we now label classical physics was mostly complete, while the two puzzles he mentioned opened the door to modern physics. The blackbody radiation problem led Planck to hypothesize that radiation emission is quantized, and that led to quantum mechanics. The Michelson-Morley experiment, on the other hand, led to the theory of relativity.

1 Nobel Prize That Should Never Have Been Awarded

What's more depressing than spending your entire life in a lab and never winning a Nobel Prize? How about spending your entire life in a lab, winning the Prize, and then finding out your award-winning research was completely wrong!

_01:: Enrico's Error

Enrico Fermi received a Nobel Prize in physics "for his demonstrations of the existence of new radioactive elements produced by neutron irradiation." Of course, Fermi had done so much Nobel Prize–quality work that it's unfortunate that he won for one of his rare mistakes. We now know that the "new" radioactive elements discovered by Fermi were not new radioactive elements (presumably beyond uranium), as he had stated, but rather fission fragments, or pieces of the original nucleus. The same year Fermi was given the prize, two other physicists (Lise Meitner and Otto Frisch) performed the same experiment and correctly described the results as fragments from fission. Fermi's other great work is described in the sidebar on p. 248. Fermi's stature, however, goes so far beyond the Nobel Prize that very few physics professors are even aware of his gaffe.

Pure Genius

ALBERT EINSTEIN

Every year *Time* magazine makes headlines by picking the "person of the year." On January 3, 2000, they announced their person of the *century*: physicist Albert Einstein (1879–1955). His name is synonymous with genius. In 1905 Einstein solved the three outstanding physics problems of the time and, in the process, convinced other physicists that atoms exist (with his explanation of Brownian motion). He contributed to the invention of quantum mechanics (with his explanation of the photoelectric effect, for which he was awarded the Nobel Prize), and he created special relativity with the most famous physics equation of all time, $E = mc^2$. Eleven years later he invented general relativity, a theory of gravity that is still the foundation of our understanding of that force, as well as the basis for understanding all of cosmology (the big bang, the expansion of the universe, the size and future of space).

Say It Ain't So!: Things Einstein Got Wrong

4

Einstein's mistakes make a great point: in order to be right about anything important, you have to be willing to be dead wrong.

_01:: God Throws Dice

Einstein was one of the founders of quantum mechanics. His explanation of the photoelectric effect showed that light itself is quantized, and it was this work that won him his Nobel in 1921. (He didn't get it for relativity, which was more controversial.) Yet as quantum mechanics developed, he refused to believe what became a central tenet: that all events could be described only in terms of probability. Einstein summarized this by his famous statement, "God does not throw dice." According to quantum mechanics, two absolutely identical radioactive atoms will probably decay at different times. Einstein believed that there must be something hidden inside the nucleus, a hidden variable that was different for the two. Very sensitive statistical tests performed by experimentalists have shown that he was wrong. There aren't any hidden variables, at least not the simple kind.

_02:: Hubble Trouble

When Einstein developed his theory of gravitation, usually called general relativity, he found a problem. The universe, which he thought was static, could not be static according to his equations. Instead of predicting that the universe was changing, he modified his equations to introduce a cosmological constant that would support his theory. When physicist Edwin Hubble discovered that the universe was not static but was expanding, Einstein called his cosmological constant "the greatest mistake of my life."

_03:: Constant Hassles

Einstein effectively abandoned his cosmological constant when he learned of Hubble's discoveries. Ironically, calling this a mistake made for the second greatest mistake of his life! In the late 1990s Saul Perlmutter and his group at Berkeley discovered that the cosmological constant was not zero but was causing the universe to accelerate. Their result was soon confirmed by another group. So, had Einstein stuck to his guns, he could have been given credit for predicting one of the great scientific findings of the last 10 years—the accelerating universe.

_04:: A Field Day with Field Theory

Einstein spent the latter decades of his life trying to find a unified field theory that would illuminate a connection between gravity and electricity. In 1920, when he was in his forties, he decided to devote his career to unifying the theories of gravity and electromagnetism. He was so far ahead of his time that his major effort in this problem was doomed to failure. Although his work is full of mathematical insights, Einstein passed away before realizing his error. In the late 1960s and early 1970s, physicists Steven Weinberg, Abdus Salam, and Sheldon Glashow (and others) finally succeeded where Einstein couldn't—in unifying electromagnetism with the weak force—not the gravitational force that Einstein had worked on. The weak force is the force that makes for most radioactivity. It wasn't even known at the time Einstein began his work, so he couldn't have guessed that he was unifying the wrong forces.

9 Laws of Physics That Don't Apply in Hollywood

In general, Hollywood filmmakers follow the laws of physics because they have no other choice. It's just when they cheat with special effects that we seem to forget how the world really works.

_01:: Those Exploding Cars

When you're watching an action flick, all it takes is a crash, or maybe a stream of leaky gasoline that acts like a fuse, and suddenly, bang! You see a terrific explosion that's complete and violent. But gasoline doesn't explode unless mixed with about 93% air. Gas-induced car explosions were discovered on film relatively recently (you don't see them in the old black-and-white movies), and now audiences just take them for granted. In general, there's no need to rush out of a crashed car, risking injury, because you fear an imminent explosion—it's probably not gonna happen.

_02:: Sound That Moves at the Speed of Light

Hollywood always gets this one wrong. On film, thunder doesn't follow lighting (as in real life, because sound is slower); they occur simultaneously. Similarly, a distant volcano erupts, and the blast is heard immediately rather than five seconds later for each mile. Explosions on the battlefield go boom right away, no matter how far away spectators are. Even a small thing, like the crack of a baseball player's bat, is simultaneous with ball contact, unlike at a real game.

_03:: Everything Is Illuminated: The Myth of Radioactivity

Films would have you believe that radioactivity is contagious and makes you glow in the dark. Where did this idea come from? *The Simpsons*? Perhaps, but the truth is that the most common forms of radioactivity will make you radioactive only if the radioactive particles stick to you. Radioactivity is not contagious. If a person is exposed to the radioactive neutrons from a nuclear reactor, then he can become slightly radioactive, but he certainly won't glow. And because radioactive things emit light only when they run into phosphor—like the coating on the inner surface of a TV tube— you don't really need to worry.

_04:: Shotgun Blasts and Kung Fu Kicks Make Targets Fly across the Room

With the string of new kung fu films out (they run the gamut from *The Matrix* to *Charlie's Angels*), you just can't escape the small matter of bad physics. Yeah, the action scenes look great and all, but in reality momentum is conserved, such that every action has an equal and opposite reaction. So, when you see a gal kick someone across the room, technically the kicker (or holder of a gun) must fly across the room in the opposite direction—unless she has a back against the wall.

_05:: Legends of the Fall

We aren't surprised when the cartoon character Wile E. Coyote runs off a cliff and is suspended there momentarily before he falls. But in the movies, buses and cars shouldn't be able to jump across gaps in bridges, even if they go heavy on the accelerator. The fact is, a vehicle will fall even if it's moving at a high speed. During the 1989 San Francisco earthquake, a driver saw a gap in the bridge too late and, probably inspired by movies, accelerated to try to make it across. Unfortunately, the laws of physics were not suspended, and he fell into the hole and crashed on the other side. Movies with special effects should come with a warning: "Laws of physics are violated in this movie. Don't try these stunts at home."

_06:: The Sounds of Science

All across the silver screen, you'll catch people screaming as their car flies in slow motion across the gap in the bridge. The problem, though, is that their voices don't change. In reality, if you slow down motion by a factor of two, the frequency of all sounds should drop by an octave. Women will sound like men, and men will sound like Henry Kissinger. Sound is an oscillation of the air. Middle C, for example, is 256 vibrations per second. If time is slowed down, there are fewer cycles per second, and the resulting sound is lower in pitch.

_07:: Shell Shock! Exploding Artillery Shells That Blow Straight Up

In movies, shells tend to kill only the person standing directly over them. It seems like a waste of artillery, since—if you believe the movies—each shell can't kill more than a sin-all over. Movie directors like to have their actors running through a field of such shells, but they don't want their actors killed, so they arrange for underground explosions in holes that blow straight up, missing anyone who's more than 5 feet away.

_08:: The Sparking Bullet

Sparking bullets are a relatively recent invention in movie special effects. The gimmick provides a way of letting the audience know that the bullet just barely missed its target. In real life, sparks do occur when you scrape steel or other hard metals on hard surfaces (such as brick) because little pieces of the brittle material are heated to glow and fly off. The problem here is that bullets are generally made of lead because it's dense and soft, and you don't want the bullets scarring the steel of the gun barrel. Ever notice that no sparks fly from the front of the gun? That's because you're seeing lead bullets.

_09:: Sound Travels in Space

This is the granddaddy of all scientific complaints about space movies. For instance, in space the hero shouldn't be able to shout out instructions to the other astronauts from a spot several yards away. The movie *Aliens* corrected this misimpression with its tagline: "In space, nobody can hear you scream." And it's true. Sound is the vibration of air, and it's sensed when the air makes your eardrums vibrate. But try to forget this rule as soon as possible; it'll wreck a good many movies for you.

gle rifle bullet can. But in real life, artillery shells blow out in all directions, killing people

Reasons Physics Doesn't Work in the Real World

Admit it: you think physicists have it all figured out. But the fact is, some of the best theories just don't work anywhere but on the blackboard.

_01:: Science Friction: F = ma
(Force = Mass × Acceleration)

Sure, this fundamental equation of physics is simple to memorize, but it's virtually useless in real life. In fact, engineers almost never use it. The reason? Friction—that awful complication that keeps physics demonstrations from working. So, how do you calculate friction? If you ask an engineer, he'll give you an empirical coefficient that he measured from previous experiments. But the truth of it is that physics is useless for most everyday phenomena. That's why physicists like to confine their research to atoms, nuclei, and space. In these realms, friction is either absent or it behaves according to simple rules. Anything that doesn't obey simple rules in physics is labeled "engineering," "chemistry," or something else.

_02:: Light Concerns

The speed of light is about 186,284 miles per second. But when light goes through air or glass, it slows down. Einstein assumed when he made his theory of general relativity that everyone would know he was referring to the speed of light *in a vacuum*. Because light is thought to have no mass, it'll always move at this fundamental speed. The concern here, though, is that if we discover someday that light has a very small but non-zero rest mass, then even light would never travel at the speed of light. Who knows? If that happens, we might have to rename the fundamental speed the Einstein velocity.

by
Christopher
Smith

Condensed
POP CULTURE

Contains

6 Musicians Who May (or May Not) Have Choked on Vomit or a Ham Sandwich ✳ Comic Gold: 7 Comic Books Worth Stealing from Grandma's Attic ✳ 8 Films Worth Sneaking Past Customs ✳ 6 Album Cover Artists Who Wear Their Art on Their Sleeves ✳ Keeping It Reel: 6 Directors Whose Names Have Become Adjectives ✳ 5 Pop Culture Story Lines Plucked from the Classics ✳ 7 Classic TV Episodes That Should Be Sent into Space to Demonstrate to Aliens What We Earthlings Call "Funny" ✳ 6 Tricky Lyrics You'll Never Get Wrong Again ✳

Musicians Who May (or May Not) Have Choked on Vomit or a Ham Sandwich

What can we learn from the tragic deaths of all these talented people, taken from us far too soon? Stay the hell out of London.

_01:: Tommy Dorsey (1905–1956)

The first musician to die the archetypal rock-and-roll death was actually a trombonist. Tommy Dorsey and his clarinetist brother, Jimmy, were two of the biggest bandleaders of the swing era. The quarrelsome brothers split up in 1935 but reunited in 1953. The reunion would be short-lived, however. Tommy, a famed heavy eater, choked on vomit in his sleep at his country home in Greenwich, Connecticut, on November 26, 1956, thanks to a huge dinner with sleeping pills for dessert. It was just a week after the bone-slinging Lithuanian's 51st birthday.

_02:: Jimi Hendrix (1942–1970)

Much mystery surrounds the day guitar god Jimi Hendrix finally kissed the sky. But the facts are these: Jimi spent the night of September 17–18, 1970, in London, partying with a German girlfriend, Monika Danneman. At 3:00 a.m. she fixed Jimi a tuna fish sandwich, and they went to bed. She awoke around 10:20 the next morning to find Jimi with vomit around his mouth and nose, unable to wake up. He was rushed to St. Mary Abbott's Hospital, but en route he choked on his own vomit. He was pronounced DOA, the official cause listed as "inhalation of vomit due to barbiturate intoxication." The strange death also falls under the category of 3 Rock Gods Who Died at 27 (see page 185 for the rest of the list).

_03:: Eric "Stumpy Joe" Childs (1945–1974)

One of the many ill-fated drummers of the legendary (and completely fictional) British rock band Spinal Tap, John "Stumpy" Pepys—also known as the Peeper—died in a bizarre gardening accident that the police said was "best left unsolved." Two drummers, Mick Shrimpton and Peter "James" Bond, fell victim to spontaneous combustion. But the most bizarre death would have to be that of Childs, who, his bandmates sadly recall, choked on *someone else's* vomit. The originator of the vomit remains unknown because "you can't really dust for vomit."

_04:: Bon Scott (1946–1980)

When Ronald "Bon" Scott, hard-drinking Scottish front man of seminal rock group AC/DC, died, his band was on the verge of exploding internationally with the release of *Highway to Hell* (file under: Chillingly Prophetic Album Titles). But on February 19, 1980, after a night of heavy drinking, Scott passed out in the backseat of a friend's car in London. While speculative causes of his death have ranged from alcohol poisoning to hypothermia, the true cause was—you guessed it—asphyxiation by inhalation of vomit. The band replaced him with Brian Johnson and recorded *Back in Black*, one of the greatest rock albums of all time, as a tribute to their fallen comrade. (The album included, ironically, a toast to the high life, "Have a Drink on Me.")

_05:: John Bonham (1947–1980)

Many consider Led Zeppelin's John "Bonzo" Bonham the greatest rock drummer ever to pick up sticks. He was also, unquestionably, one of the greatest drinkers. The binge that finally sent him up the Stairway to Heaven occurred September 24, 1980, during which he reputedly downed 40 shots of vodka in four hours. Sometime during the night at Jimmy Page's home in Windsor, England, he vomited in his sleep and choked. Bassist John Paul Jones found him dead the next morning, and Led Zeppelin called it quits three months later. Some sources list alcohol poisoning as the cause of his death—a logical assumption, considering his blood alcohol content was a staggering 0.41. To put that in perspective, consider this: at 0.30, most people slip into a coma.

_06:: "Mama" Cass Elliot (1941–1974)

One of the most famous of all musicians to die by choking actually did not. Since her death in a London hotel room on July 29, 1974, the

What's the Difference?

RAP VS. HIP-HOP

There's no easy answer to this one. Some maintain that rap is a kind of music, whereas hip-hop is a lifestyle, one that includes rap, break dancing, DJing, and graffiti art. Rap pioneer and sage KRS-One says simply, "Rap is something you do, but hip-hop is something you live." Others insist that hip-hop is a musical style distinct from rap, for very specific reasons: hip-hop has a particular beat and uses scratching and "breaks" (samples). Just as heavy metal fans would never confuse a speed metal act with a hair band, true aficionados feel the same way about rap and hip-hop. They insist that rapping over a soul or heavy metal track could never be hip-hop. In other words, all hip-hop is rap, but not all rap is hip-hop.

legend has grown that Elliot, whose girth was as famous as her voice, died by choking on a ham sandwich. This, like all things pork, is not kosher. An autopsy determined that she died of heart failure due to fatty myocardial degeneration, a condition caused by her obesity. The ham sandwich legend grew from the fact that one was found on her bedside table. The sandwich was unresponsive to investigators' questions about its involvement in the singer's death.

Comic Gold:
Comic Books Worth Stealing from Grandma's Attic

Hey, Grandma never liked to read comics anyway, right?

_01::, _02:: Action Comics #1 (June 1938)

This is it, the comic book Holy Grail, the one that introduced the world to Superman. The cover bears the famous—if somewhat crude—drawing of Superman smashing a car against a rock. Written and drawn by Jerome Siegel and Joe Shuster, the comic introduced Superman as "Champion of the oppressed, the physical marvel who had sworn to devote his existence to helping those in need!" The last survivor of the doomed planet Krypton (duh), Superman could "leap ⅛th of a mile; hurdle a 20-story building . . . raise tremendous weights . . . run faster than an express train . . . and nothing less than a bursting shell could penetrate his skin!" Superman was so popular, he became the first character to get his very own comic book. Superman #1 hit newsstands in the summer of 1939. The Man of Steel has held up pretty well, you could say.

Action Comics #1

Cover price in 1938: 10¢
Estimated top value today: $350,000

Superman #1

Cover price in 1939: 10¢
Estimated top value today: $210,000

_03:: Detective Comics #27 (May 1939)

Less than a year later, an artist named Bob Kane decided to create a caped superhero of his own, one much darker, more mysterious, and more "human" than the squeaky-clean Superman. His creation: Batman. Unlike the campy '60s TV version of the character, the Batman in this first issue was a dark, vengeful crusader who stalked the night (he watches as a bad guy plunges into a vat of acid), presaging the hero's reemergence in the 1980s in *The Dark Knight Returns*. Perhaps this darkness was a reflection of the dread of war looming on the horizon in 1939? The cover proclaimed, "Starting this issue: The amazing and unique adventures of THE BATMAN!" and promised "64 pages of action!"

Cover price in 1939: 10¢
Estimated top value today: $300,000

_04:: Marvel Comics #1 (October 1939)

In 1939 a comic book house called Funnies Inc. approached pulp fiction publisher Martin Goodman with a proposal to provide him with ready-made comic book artwork. All he had to do was publish it. Seeing the kind of cash Action Comics and others were raking in, he agreed, and Marvel Comics was born. The first

Fake Your Way through a Conversation

THE LOWDOWN ON MARVEL AND DC

To the uninitiated, a comic book is a comic book. But to fans and collectors, the world of superheroes is divided into two camps: Marvel and DC. So, to avoid any embarrassing faux pas at your next comic book soiree, here's your handy guide to the two universes.

MARVEL COMICS

Founded: October 1939 (formerly Timely Comics)

Names to Drop: Stan Lee, Martin Goodman, Jack Kirby, Joe Simon, John Romita

Heroes: Captain America, Iron Man, Spider-Man, Thor, Namor the Sub-Mariner, Silver Surfer, Wolverine, Daredevil, the Punisher, Elektra

Villains: Dr. Octopus, the Red Skull, Kingpin, Dr. Doom, Magneto

Teams: The Avengers, X-Men, The Fantastic Four

Famous Green Guys: Green Goblin, the Lizard, the Incredible Hulk (who was originally gray)

Conversation starters: "I think I liked the Hulk better in his original gray." "Nobody could draw Iron Man like Jack Kirby!" "Mary Jane never looked hotter than when McFarlane was penciling *Spider-Man*. Meow!"

DC COMICS

Founded: 1934 (formerly New Fun Comics)

Names to Drop: Harry Donenfeld, Bob Kane, Frank Miller, Alan Moore, Jerome Siegel, Joe Shuster

Heroes: Superman, Batman and Robin, Wonder Woman, Hawkman, the Flash, Aquaman, Swamp Thing

Villains: Lex Luthor, the Joker, the Riddler, the Penguin, Darkseid, Catwoman

Teams: Legion of Super-Heroes, Justice League of America, Legion of Doom

Famous Green Guys: Green Lantern, Green Arrow

Conversation Starters: "I think Aquaman could totally perch-slap Sub-Mariner in an underwater fight, don't you?" "Which one had the scarier Joker—*Arkham Asylum* or *Batman: The Killing Joke*?" "Meanwhiiiiile, back at the Hall of Justice . . ."

issue introduced three legendary Marvel characters: the Sub-Mariner of Atlantis, prince of the Deep; the Human Torch (a different Human Torch than the one that would become part of the Fantastic Four 22 years later—let's not get them confused); and Ka-Zar the Great, a man who lived in the jungle among apes (strangely similar to another popular ape man whose name had a lot of the same letters).

Cover price in 1939: 10¢

Estimated top value today: $250,000

_05:: Batman #1 (Spring 1940)

After appearing in 13 issues of Detective Comics, Batman and his new sidekick—Robin the Boy Wonder (introduced in Detective Comics #38)—were so popular, they got their very own comic book. *Batman* began as a quarterly, but that wasn't enough for fans. Neither was a bimonthly. So, before long, readers could get a new Batman adventure every month. The first issue introduces two of Batman's most legendary nemeses: the Joker and Catwoman. More than 63 years and over 600 issues later, Batman is still fighting villains—as well as his own demons—on the streets of Gotham City.

Cover price in April 1940: 10¢
Estimated top value today: $100,000

_06:: All-American Comics #16 (July 1940)

How many times has this happened to you? Man finds alien metal lantern. Man makes ring out of lantern. Man presses ring to lantern. Man has incredible superpowers over everything. Except wood, obviously. That's the story in All-American Comics #16, a book published tangentially under the DC Comics umbrella. When regular guy Alan Scott made his ring, the superhero created was, of course, the Green Lantern. The idea of an everyday schmoe just lucking into superhero-ness proved incredibly popular. A similar idea struck gold in 1962 when a young nerd named Peter Parker got bitten by a radioactive spider (see below).

Cover price in 1940: 10¢
Estimated top value today: $115,000

_07:: Amazing Fantasy #15 (August 1962)

The word bubbles on the cover say it all: "Though the world may mock Peter Parker, the timid teen-ager . . . it will soon marvel at the awesome might of . . . SPIDER-MAN!" And writer Stan Lee (pseudonym of Stanley Martin Lieber) and artist Mike Ditko could not have been more right. Spider-Man was the first comic book hero to be a regular teenager, going through the same things his readers were dealing with: shyness, insecurity, a crush on a pretty girl, and trouble with the popular jock (Flash Thompson). No wonder people of all ages are still true believers.

Cover price in 1962: 12¢
Estimated top value today: $42,000

Films Worth Sneaking Past Customs (Note: *Crouching Tiger, Hidden Dragon* Not Included)

A trip across an ocean can add cachet and panache and a lot of other French words to just about anything. Even Jerry Lewis. And nothing makes you look classier than knowing a thing or two about foreign film. Here are some of the most *essentiel.*

_01:: *Un Chien Andalou* (France, 1928)

What do you get when you combine two of the greatest surrealist minds of the 20th century (Luis Buñuel and Salvador Dali) and throw in a heaping helping of existential ennui? You get *Un Chien Andalou*, one of the most bizarre, disturbing, and controversial films ever made. Thank God it's only 17 minutes long. A mishmash of unlinked dreamlike sequences, each prefaced with a meaningless time marker ("Eight years later . . . ," "Around 3 o'clock in the morning . . ."), the film challenges the very concept of film itself. Its most infamous image is its first, in which Buñuel himself sharpens a straight razor on a strop, then uses it to slash a woman's eyeball, an image paralleled by a sliver of cloud moving across a full moon. This leads to a string of unrelated images just as haunting: grand pianos full of rotting animal corpses that turn into dead priests, ants crawling out of a hole in a man's hand. You get the idea. The title (which means "An Andalusian Dog") has no reference in the film.

_02:: *M* (Germany, 1931)

Silence of the Lambs. Psycho. Seven. They all have their roots in *M*, Fritz Lang's expressionist masterpiece about a serial child killer. Lang anticipates Kubrick in his use of sound (and silence): the murderer whistles Grieg's cheery but ominous *Peer Gynt* before he kills. And, like Hitchcock, Lang terrifies you by what you *don't* see: a child's off-screen murder is symbolized by a balloon stuck in phone lines. Peter Lorre portrays killer Hans Beckert, who was based on a real child killer called the Monster of Düsseldorf. His scene before a mock court of his criminal captors, pitiful and pleading that he can't help himself, stands as one of the all-time great performances. And to think the Nazis almost suppressed *M* because they suspected its original title—*Murderers among Us*—referred to them.

_03:: *Seven Samurai* (Japan, 1954)

Like many Japanese products, this movie took an idea from America, improved on it, and was then remade in America. Akira Kurosawa's epic *Seven Samurai* drew inspiration from American Westerns by directors like John Ford. Ironically, it was eventually remade as a Western: *The Magnificent Seven.* Kurosawa's film is the magnificent story of seven out-of-work warriors coming together to help a village tormented by bandits in chaotic 16th-century Japan. The film combines epic sweep and personal detail to produce an incredibly rich story of real depth and power. And like all good heroic epics involving lots of guys (translation: *Spartacus*), it's vaguely homoerotic.

_04:: *The Seventh Seal* (Sweden, 1956)

Ah, Ingmar Bergman. No one else could make death, the black plague, rape, lost faith, metaphysical pondering, and chess all look so darn good. Max von Sydow plays a knight facing a crisis of faith. When Death (a white-faced figure in a hooded black cloak, lampooned in *Bill and Ted's Bogus Journey*, of all places) comes for him, the knight challenges him to a game of chess, during which he gives Death the third degree about the nature of God and all that. The film's last shot is its most famous: Death leads a line of people, silhouetted against a cloudy sky, in a final dance, uniting them all in the final equality of mortality. The shot was not planned: the dancing characters are actually grips and gaffers dressed up and ad-libbing.

_05:: *La Dolce Vita* (Italy, 1960)

Federico Fellini's *La Dolce Vita* is a symbol full of symbols. Marcello Mastroianni plays Rubini, a frustrated writer and wannabe playboy. Over a series of seven days and nights, Rubini prowls Rome's Via Veneto in search of "the sweet life." Each night is, both literally and figuratively, a descent into decadence, darkness, self-indulgence, and futility. Each dawn brings an ascension into light, selfdiscovery, shattered illusions, and regret. Packed with symbolism (a statue of Christ suspended from a helicopter; the seven hills of Rome = seven days and nights = the seven

---

Alphabet Soup
SOME LINGO FROM THE BACK LOT

Abby Singer [AB-ee SIN-gur]: *n* The second-to-last shot of a day of filming. The real Abby Singer, a production manager for numerous films and TV series, often called out, "Only one more shot," signaling to cast and crew that the workday was almost over. But the director frequently trumped him, asking for more takes or another shot. The Abby Singer is followed by . . .

martini [mar-TEE-nee]: *n* The very last shot of the day is called the martini because, the director hopes, the only shot left is a nice Bombay Sapphire.

Alan Smithee [AL-in SMIH-thee]: *n* A pseudonym used when a director wants nothing to do with the finished film, having lost creative control due to extensive reediting, studio meddling, or other interference. Directors can appeal to the Directors Guild of America (DGA, their union) to have their name taken off the film. If the appeal is successful, the name is replaced with Alan Smithee, the only pseudonym the DGA allows for directors, although writers, producers, and even actors have used it. John Frankenheimer, Dennis Hopper, Sam Raimi, and many others have all chosen to "Smithee" their films. So, get up and leave the theater if the opening credits say "An Alan Smithee Film." Or "Directed by Kevin Costner."

MOS [EM OH ES]: *adj* Describes a scene shot without live sound, such as panoramic landscapes or the like. Hollywood legend links the origin of MOS to Austrian actor and director Erich Von Stroheim, whose accent turned "without sound" into "mit-out sound."

deadly sins) and strange characters, *La Dolce Vita* depicts the sweet life as it is: a pretty, empty illusion.

_06:: *The Discreet Charm of the Bourgeoisie* (France, 1972)

This one is a doozy. Spanish filmmaker Luis Buñuel serves up this scathingly hilarious piece of social commentary with his trademark heapin' helpin' of surrealism. The plot—what there is of it—involves a group of hoity-toity types whose dinner plans keep getting interrupted by increasingly strange events. For example, the army marches through their party. The movie is a fable, a parable about the empty lives of the well-to-do and their detachment from real life. And it's actually funny.

_07:: *La Grande Illusion* (France, 1937)

Directed by Jean Renoir, this film portrays the relationship between French soldiers and their German captors in a World War I prisoner-of-war camp. Using innovative slow pans and long tracking shots, Renoir paints a picture of post-World War I Europe in microcosm: the aristocratic French and German officers commiserate about the looming death of Europe's rigid class system, while the enlisted men of both sides share their dreams about returning to live in a new, egalitarian, peaceful world. But the title reveals Renoir's attitude about the notion of war having the power to ultimately correct society's wrongs: it's simply an illusion.

_08:: *Trainspotting* (UK, 1996)

OK, so it's not *technically* in a foreign language. *Boot et mate as bloody wail beh!* The Scottish accents in director Danny Boyle's heroin-addled morality tale-slash-comedy-slash-antidrug manifesto are as thick as Edinburgh fog. One disco scene is actually subtitled. But the images in the film—the baby crawling on the ceiling, the harrowingly realistic heroin binges, the kitten sitting by the body of a toxoplasmosis victim—are unforgettable. Love it or hate it, *Trainspotting* can't be ignored. Extra trivia tidbit: the title refers to a curious British hobby. Trainspotters spend hours on train platforms meticulously recording the type and numbers of passing trains. Sound like a pointless waste of life? So's heroin.

Album Cover Artists Who Wear Their Art on Their Sleeves

Every art form has its giants, and album covers are no different. Some of the designers were so prolific, so recognizable, that their work became as famous as the bands themselves.

_01:: Hipgnosis

It sounds like "hypnosis" but, like, it's more about "gnosis," knowing spiritual truth, y'know? Only, like, more "hip." The name helps explain the distinctive style of Hipgnosis, a British design trio led by the prolific Storm Thorgerson. Hipgnosis covers combine enigmatic, symbolic images with a disturbing sense of timeless isolation. Consider the naked children on Led Zeppelin's *Houses of the Holy* or the empty black shape on *Presence*, the black eye bars on AC/DC's *Dirty Deeds (Done Dirt Cheap)*. And most of Pink Floyd's unforgettable covers, like the fiery handshake on *Wish You Were Here* or *Dark Side of the Moon*'s iconic prism. All classics. All instantly recognizable. And all Hipgnosis. Far out.

_02:: Neon Park

The pseudonym of quirky painter Martin Muller, Neon Park produced offbeat paintings for bands of all stripes, most notably Little Feat (some of his covers featured cakes on swings or ducks dressed up like Hollywood pinups). His bizarro style became popular after the equally unique Frank Zappa and his band, the Mothers of Invention, chose Neon Park's work for the cover of *Weasels Ripped My Flesh* (1970). The cheery cartoonlike draw-

ing of a white-bread father figure tearing his smiling face to bloody ribbons is the most famous example of the strange work of Neon Park.

_03:: Andy Warhol

Album covers were just one more medium for which pop art legend Andy Warhol changed the rules. He brought an interactive sense of fun to his covers. The Rolling Stones' 1971 classic *Sticky Fingers* featured a well-endowed man in tight jeans that had a real working zipper (contrary to legend, the dong behind the denim is *not* Mick Jagger's). The zipper left its mark on the album cover genre. Unfortunately, it also left its mark on the record itself (right in the middle of "Sister Morphine"). Warhol was also responsible for the peel-away banana on 1976's *The Velvet Underground & Nico*. The man just had a way with phallic symbols.

_04:: Pen & Pixel Graphics

Yo, for all the straight up hip-hop impresarios who want CD covers drippin' wit Benjamins, Bentleys, and plenty of bling bling, Pen & Pixel graphics is da shizznit. The Houston design firm all but defined the look of rap albums of the late '90s and beyond. Pen & Pixel's diamond-studded type treatments, metallic inks, and exaggerated photographs of fur-clad, jewel-encrusted rap artists have graced tons of rap albums, including *Da Game Is To Be Sold,* *Not To Be Told* by Snoop Dogg and Master P's *Da Last Don.* And like so many distinctive styles, theirs have also inspired a lot of blatant imitation. Or is it just "sampling"?

_05:: Reid Miles

Many cover artists have defined the look of a band, sometimes even a decade. The work of Reid Miles defines a legendary record label and an entire genre of music. From 1956 to 1967, Reid Miles produced hundreds of striking graphic covers for jazz artists on the Blue Note label including Freddie Hubbard, Jimmy Smith, and Art Blakey. Miles brought the graphic sensibilities of his commercial-art background to bear on his covers, using bright colors, clean type, and cropped black-and-white or duo-tone photos to evoke the moods of the music. His style, still imitated to this day, defined what cool looked like.

_06:: Honorable Mentions: Illustrators and the Bands Who Love Them

For some bands, their name on the front means one particular artist's name in the liner notes. For example, if you see YES over an otherworldly dreamscape, dollars to doughnuts the art is by Roger Dean. Prog-rock supergroup Asia liked him too. How about the Coca-Cola-esque Chicago logo? Of its more than 20 iterations, the original and 13 others were by John Berg. All those gruesome portraits of theatrical metal masters Iron Maiden's horrific mascot, Eddie, are the work of Derek Riggs. Journey's winged scarab beetle? Veteran designer Jim Welch.

Keeping It Reel:
Directors Whose Names Have Become Adjectives

When it comes to film, it's not enough to be good. You've gotta have style, meaning that film school schlubs everywhere will do their best to mimic your work.

_01:: Stanley Kubrick (1928–1999)

It's impossible to label Kubrick with a single genre, ranging as he did from historical epic to horror to sci-fi to war to black comedy about war. His films were always masterful and thought provoking. But the keys to being Kubrickian are deliberate pacing, a sense of contradictory emotion (claustrophobia caused by open spaces, complete silence shattered by loud noises, horrific images shot beautifully), and storytelling without words. Also, a director can be called Kubrickian when he is being his most difficult; Stanley Kubrick was legendary for his perfectionism, his need for control ("It is essential for one man to make a film"), and his exhaustive shooting, sometimes demanding 50 or 100 takes to get a scene just right.

Kubrick at his most Kubrickian: *Dr. Strangelove* (1964), *2001: A Space Odyssey* (1968), *A Clockwork Orange* (1971), *The Shining* (1980), *Eyes Wide Shut* (1999).

Spielberg at his most Kubrickian, at least until the last 10 minutes: *A.I.: Artificial Intelligence* (2001), a project conceived by Kubrick but shot (and killed) by Spielberg.

_02:: Ingmar Bergman (1918–)

For serious film buffs, Swedish director and writer Ingmar Bergman is God. His films are slow burns of pain and raw emotion, wrenching in their realism and jarring in their stark beauty. Bergmanesque films smolder with emotional tension, intellectual gravitas, symbolism, and religious imagery. If you're planning to see a film described as Bergmanesque, bring your tissues and prepare to think about things like love, death, your relationship with your father, and the nature of God. The 2001 drama *In the Bedroom* (directed by Tom Field) was considered very Bergmanesque. For younger or less sophisticated viewers who prefer explosions and poop jokes to naked emotional drama, *Bergmanesque* can be mistakenly used interchangeably with *boring*.

Bergman at his most Bergmanesque: *The Seventh Seal* (1957), *Cries and Whispers* (1972), *Scenes from a Marriage* (1973), *Fanny and Alexander* (1982).

_03:: Robert Altman (1925–)

While not all of his films necessarily fall into the category, Altman's films are often multi-character studies that portray the many layers of human social interaction with equal parts humor and venom (2001's *Gosford Park*, for example, had 30 speaking roles). Altman is renowned for his technique of giving all the actors in a scene their own microphones and encouraging them to ad-lib, mixing the results into a symphony of half-heard conversa-tional snippets, muttered insults, and naked confessions. But below it all, Altmanesque films demonstrate an understanding of the human condition and a contempt for pomposity and social castes. No wonder he is such an outspoken critic of the Hollywood system and considered a maverick.

Altman at his most Altmanesque: *M*A*S*H* (1970), *Nashville* (1975), *The Player* (1992), *Gosford Park* (2001).

Altman at his least Altmanesque: *Popeye* (1980).

_04:: Federico Fellini (1920–1993)

Like Bergman's, Fellini's films are full of symbolism and personal reflection. His Oscar-winning masterpiece *8½* is a painfully honest autobiographical study of a film director suffocated by success. But what has come to be most Felliniesque about Fellini's films are his characters. Through his lens, life was a carnival, a circus parade of bizarre characters whose very surrealism makes them all the more real—midgets, clowns, whores, circus folk, or even circus-clown-midget-whores. Think of the cover of the Doors' album *Strange Days*. That is, visually speaking, the essence of Felliniesque.

Fellini at his most Felliniesque: *La Strada* (1954), *Nights of Cabiria* (1957), *La Dolce Vita* (1960), *8½* (1963), *Juliet of the Spirits* (1965).

_05:: David Lynch (1946–)

There is a temptation to describe anything unexplained or bizarre as Lynchian. But the term implies something much more. To be truly Lynchian, a film or event must juxtapose something incredibly bizarre and unexplainable with something else completely mundane—

Pure Genius

ALFRED HITCHCOCK

The son of a greengrocer from Leytonstone, London, Alfred Hitchcock (1899–1980) directed his first film, *Number 13*, at the age of 23. After several hits in England (including *The Man Who Knew Too Much*), he moved to Hollywood. He had trouble finding a studio to hire him until David O. Selznick chose him to direct *Rebecca* (1940). It won Best Picture. Despite never winning an Oscar for any of his next 37 films, Hitch did receive the Irving Thalberg Memorial Award for lifetime achievement in 1967. His acceptance speech? "Thank you."

Hitchcock's films show his particular penchant for blondes. But his most famous technique was the use of a MacGuffin, an object that propels the action but has no real bearing on the story's outcome. Classic Hitchcock MacGuffins are the true identity of the spy in *North by Northwest* or the stolen $40,000 in *Psycho*. Other directors have used MacGuffins, like the contents of the briefcase in *Pulp Fiction*. Quentin Tarantino borrowed another page from Hitch's book: the cameo appearance in his own films. Hitchcock showed up in every film he made from *The Lodger* in 1926 until his last, *Family Plot*, in 1976.

like finding a severed ear in a perfectly mani-cured suburban lawn, as in *Blue Velvet*. Lynch likes to set his absurd happenings in the most white-bread small towns (he hails from Missoula, Montana), thereby increasing their strangeness and their universality at the same time. Lynch's weirdness is very self-conscious, very calculated, which is what makes it so creepy. Through people and places that (we hope) are nothing like us and our world, he shows us the worst parts of ourselves.

Lynch at his most Lynchian: *Eraserhead* (1977), *Blue Velvet* (1986), *Twin Peaks* (TV, 1990), *Lost Highway* (1997), *Mulholland Drive* (2001).

_06:: Alfred Hitchcock (1899–1980)

You may think that defining the characteristics of a director dubbed "the master of sus-pense" would be a no-brainer. But Hitch-cock's mastery goes deep. In almost 70 films, Hitchcock drew suspense from ordinary objects (who knew birds or shower curtains could be so terrifying?), from strained roman-tic relationships, and, most of all, from viewing the characters' reactions to violence rather than the violent acts themselves. No one could draw more terror from a single gaze than Hitchcock. As the master himself once said, "Film your murders like love scenes, and film your love scenes like murders." Many films are Hitchcockian—*Body Double, Dead Again, What Lies Beneath, Frantic*—but none of them are Hitchcock.

Hitchcock at his most Hitchcockian: *Rope* (1948), *Dial M for Murder* (1954), *Rear Window* (1954), *Vertigo* (1958), *North by Northwest* (1959), *Psycho* (1960), *The Birds* (1963).

5 Pop Culture Story Lines Plucked from the Classics

Why come up with a new plot line when you can recycle? Better yet, steal from a source with a built-in fan base.

_01:: *West Side Story* (1961) = William Shakespeare's *Romeo and Juliet*

This one's pretty common knowledge, and the parallels aren't hard to see. Instead of Romeo and Juliet, the star-crossed lovers are Tony and Maria. Instead of fair Verona you've got not-so-fair Spanish Harlem. Similarly, Shake-speare wasn't allowed to have a woman play the part of Juliet, and for some reason studios couldn't find a Hispanic actress to play the part of Maria. Instead of two warring families (Capulets and Montagues), you've got two warring gangs. And instead of wordy solilo-quies and gut-wrenching violence, you've got finger-snapping tunes and dynamite dance choreography. And instead of them both dy-ing, only Tony gets it. After all, how can you kill Natalie Wood?

Fake Your Way through a Conversation
(WITH A STAR TREK FAN!)

Say a Trekker (the polite term) approaches you with amorous intentions: "You're the most beautiful carbon-based life-form in the Alpha Quadrant. Would you care to join me for a Romulan ale? May I store your number in my tricorder?" Here's a quick primer for your convenience. If you're in a pinch, though, you can always say your Prime Directive prevents you from dating dweebs.

Aliens, Not-So-Friendly—the Borg, Jem'Hadar, Cardassians, Klingons (sometimes), Q Continuum: In the original series, the warlike Klingons were *the* bad guys. But sometime between then and *The Next Generation*, an uneasy truce came into effect. One of them, Worf, even joined the crew of the *Enterprise*. The Ferengi (big-eared merchant aliens that bear a strange resemblance to NBA star Reggie Miller) were too comical to be the new bad guys. Enter the ultimate menace, the robotic Borg, stalking the galaxy in giant cubes assimilating entire planets into their Collective: "You will be assimilated. Resistance is futile." The super-hottie on *Star Trek: Voyager*? That's ex-Borg babe Seven-of-Nine.

Kirk and Picard: The two big-name captains of the starship *Enterprise*. James Tiberius Kirk (William Shatner) commanded *Enterprise NCC-1701* in the original series and the first seven films. Jean-Luc Picard (Patrick Stewart) commanded several *Enterprise*s in *The Next Generation* and the later films.

"Live long and prosper": A Vulcan blessing/salute, accompanied by a hand sign: fingers spread in a V formation, thumb out, both ad-libbed by Leonard Nimoy. He derived it from a common blessing from rabbis to their congregation. The gesture symbolizes the letter *shin*, the first letter of the word *Shadai*, a secret Hebrew name for God.

Prime Directive: The guiding principle of all Starfleet interactions with alien species. The main clause: "No Starfleet personnel may interfere with the healthy development of alien life and culture."

Stardate: The way of marking time that replaced AD as the standard. There's a complicated method for determining stardate (SD), but here's a good one to know: SD 40759.5 = October 4, 2363 = commissioning date of the starship *Enterprise*.

Starfleet: The military arm of the United Federation of Planets, an alliance including Earth and over 150 other planets.

Tachyon pulse: An emission of a special kind of energy that seems to solve all kinds of problems, from temporal anomalies to subspace rifts. If that doesn't work, usually an *inverse* tachyon pulse does the trick. It is a common deus ex machina solution in the Trek series.

Warp speed: As Mach 1 is the speed of sound, Warp 1 is the speed of light.

_02:: *O Brother, Where Art Thou?* (2000) = Homer's *Odyssey*

So, you say you can't see the parallels between the George Clooney vehicle and Homer's epic poem of Odysseus' 10-year voyage home from the Trojan War? Look closer: three escaped convicts undergo a long journey from prison to get home, having lots of obstacles thrown in their way. The Sirens (three singing, bathing beauties on rocks) lure the men into trouble; they run afoul of a giant Cyclops (John Goodman as eye-patched Big Dan Teague). Rather than hiding under sheep, as in the *Odyssey*, they hide under Ku Klux Klan robes. And when the main character, Ulysses (Odysseus' name in the Roman version of the tale), returns home, he finds his wife being courted by another. One character, a gubernatorial candidate, is named Homer Stokes. And, well, both titles start with the letter *O*. However, scholars haven't been able to find a mention of Dapper Dan Hair Pomade in the original text.

_03:: *Rent* (1996) = Puccini's *La Boheme*

These two line up almost scene for scene. The original followed a group of starving artists in 1830s Paris. The musical is about a group of starving artists in 1990s Greenwich Village with Americanized versions of the original's names (Rodolfo the poet = Roger the musician; Marcello the painter = Mark the filmmaker; Mimi the seamstress = Mimi the exotic dancer; Benoit the landlord = Benny the landlord). Instead of tuberculosis, *Rent*'s characters are dealing with another plague: AIDS. And a whole lot of them are gay. Late composer Jonathan Larson even uses pieces of dialogue and music from the opera and doesn't hide it. Roger repeatedly plays a snippet on his guitar

that Mark dismisses for sounding too much like "Musetta's Waltz" from the opera.

_04:: *Star Trek II: The Wrath of Khan* (1982) = Herman Melville's *Moby Dick*

No, seriously. It does. Well, kind of. In *Moby Dick* a man's relentless pursuit of (and hatred for) his nemesis, a plump white whale, drives him to the edge. Ditto for the movie, only in this case the nemesis is a plump white William Shatner. References to *Moby Dick* occur throughout the movie (the book itself is on the shelf in Khan's ship *Botany Bay*). Khan's dialogue mirrors much of Captain Ahab's: "Thar she blows!" becomes "There she is!" Both men chase their prey because "he tasks me." Both vow to chase their quarry "around Perdition's flames." And Khan's last words are lifted directly from Captain Ahab: "From Hell's heart I stab at thee! For hate's sake I spit my last breath at thee!"

_05:: *Clueless* (1995) = Jane Austen's *Emma*

Never has such a seemingly brainless movie linked itself so closely to such a thoughtful book. But *Clueless* is actually a rigidly faithful retelling of Austen's romantic coming-of-age tale. Emma becomes Cher, the pampered, ditzy teenager with a heart of gold. The parallels are many, including her friendship with a social outcast, her matchmaking (a teacher and a guidance counselor instead of Mr. Weston and Miss Taylor), and imagined overtures from an unavailable male (in Emma it's for social reasons; in *Clueless* it's because he's gay). An adventure in a carriage becomes a failed driving test, and Gypsies that threaten Emma are replaced by a couple of reckless guys at the mall. One main difference: Alicia Silverstone is much, much hotter than any Austen character. Ever.

Note: Similar parallels occur between the 1999 film *10 Things I Hate about You* and Shakespeare's *The Taming of the Shrew*. The titles even rhyme.

7 Classic TV Episodes That Should Be Sent into Space to Demonstrate to Aliens What We Earthlings Call "Funny"

Some moments on TV are universally funny no matter whom you ask. But just what makes a show funny—is it the writing, the delivery? We're not sure, but we know it when we see it.

_01:: *Seinfeld*—"The Contest" (1992)

Of all *Seinfeld*'s memorable moments—Poppy peeing on Jerry's couch, George's "shrinkage," the Soup Nazi—"The Contest" stands out as an instant classic. The titular contest is a bet between Jerry, George, Kramer, and Elaine about who could go the longest without masturbating (or, in one of the series' many classic catchphrases, being "master of your domain"). All are tempted: George watches a silhouetted nurse give a woman a sponge bath, Jerry is dating a virgin, and Elaine does aerobics behind John-John Kennedy. But the first to succumb is Kramer, who, after watching a nudist in her apartment, slams his money down with an emphatic, "I'm out!"

_02:: *The Mary Tyler Moore Show*—"Chuckles Bites the Dust" (1975)

It's a premise straight out of Greek drama or Shakespeare: a parading elephant tramples to death a circus clown in a giant peanut suit. At first horrified by others' reactions to Chuckles's tragic death, Mary can't keep from giggling all through his funeral. Ted's solemn eulogy featuring a timeless quote from Chuckles—"A little song, a little dance, a little seltzer down your pants"—sends her over the edge. The scene turns bittersweet when a mourner reminds Mary that Chuckles would've wanted her to laugh. With that, her giggling turns to heartfelt tears.

_03:: *The Dick Van Dyke Show*—"That's My Boy???" (1963)

The brainchild of comic legend Carl Reiner, *The Dick Van Dyke Show* was known for its spot-on timing and sharp writing. The "That's My Boy???" episode builds around a flashback: Rob (Dick Van Dyke) is absolutely certain that he and Laura (Mary Tyler Moore) brought the wrong baby home from the hospital. To settle the matter once and for all, Rob invites the other couple to their home for dinner. When he

Timeline

MONEY FOR NOTHING AND CHICKS FOR FREE!

MTV began as a part of youth culture. Today it defines it. Here are some of the big dates in its influential history, going all the way back to the days when they played videos. (The "M" was for "Music," remember?)

August 1, 1981, 12:01 a.m.   MTV goes on the air. The first video: The Buggles, "Video Killed the Radio Star." Duh. Easy one. The next four? Pat Benatar, "You Better Run"; Rod Stewart, "She Won't Dance with Me"; The Who, "You Better You Bet"; PhD, "Little Suzie's on the Up." A real classic, that one.

March 1, 1982   Still not offered by many cable systems, MTV encourages potential viewers to shout, "I Want My MTV!"

March 2, 1983   MTV airs its first video by black artist Michael Jackson, "Billie Jean." Until then MTV videos were as white as a box of rice. Oh, how things change.

July 17, 1985   Where were you when MTV aired the Live Aid concerts for 17 straight hours?

1987   The switch from 24-hour music to a more traditional show-based format begins as MTV premieres dance show *Club MTV*, bizarre game show *Remote Control* (featuring such budding talents as Adam Sandler, Kari Wuhrer, and Colin Quinn), and, as late-night filler, episodes of *Monty Python's Flying Circus*.

August 6, 1988   Fab Five Freddie hosts the first episode of *Yo! MTV Raps*. Hip-hop fans find it def.

January 21, 1990   The acoustic revolution begins with the first airing of *MTV Unplugged*. First performers: Squeeze, Syd Straw, and the Cars' Elliot Easton.

June 2, 1991   Animation comes to the fore with *Liquid Television*, launching such characters as Aeon Flux and Beavis & Butt-head.

1992   MTV's still-running reality show, *The Real World*, debuts, a real-life look at the trials and travails of immature twentysomethings enduring the hardships of living in a huge, fabulously furnished, rent-free apartment together. Not having to work, they have plenty of time to party, argue, and/or screw.

May 15, 1994   Kurt Cobain commits suicide, world ends, MTV gives entire generation a shoulder to cry on.

September 14, 1998   Screaming teenage girls finally get their own forum when *Total Request Live* debuts.

February 26, 2000   MTV ends its one millionth video celebration with Peter Gabriel's "Sledgehammer." Appropriate, considering most viewers felt like they'd seen that video at least a million times.

opens the door to greet them, he (and we) learn for the first time that they are black. Van Dyke's priceless expression of shock, embarrassment, and relief caused one of the longest laughs by a studio audience in TV history.

_04:: Ed Ames's "Frontier Bris" on *The Tonight Show with Johnny Carson* (1965)

When singer-actor Ed Ames appeared on *The Tonight Show* on April 29, 1965, he and Johnny Carson thought it might be fun to show off his tomahawk-throwing skills, which he'd learned for his part on TV's *Daniel Boone*. Proudly declaring, "This is how you take care of an enemy," Ames hurled a tomahawk across the studio and embedded it, handle up, directly in the crotch of a man-shaped outline. The audience's and host's roars of laughter—which lasted several minutes—are television legend, as is Carson's perfect ad-lib: "Gee, Ed, I didn't even know you were Jewish!"

_05:: *I Love Lucy*—"Lucy Does a TV Commercial" (1952)

I Love Lucy erased any doubt that the sitcom would dominate prime time. Retail stores even changed their open-late night to Thursday from the traditional Monday, because everyone stayed home Monday to watch *Lucy*. Lucy and Ethel's adventure in a candy factory, the birth of Little Ricky, and Lucy's trouble in a grape-stomping vat are all classics. But when Lucy tries to shill a highly alcoholic "health tonic" called Vitameatavegamin, it's an absolute scream. Drunk after four takes, she slurs through the product's name, misses the spoon, then chugs right from the bottle. It's a brilliant showcase of Lucille Ball's impeccable

timing and fluid physicality. Besides, showing someone getting drunk on a network sitcom in 1952 was pretty ballsy.

_06:: *Sanford and Son*—"Fred Sanford, Legal Eagle" (1974)

Frequently when a sitcom tries to take on serious social issues, the result comes off ham-fisted and sappy. But Norman Lear's shows—*All in the Family, The Jeffersons, Sanford and Son,* and others—did it masterfully. One of the most daring examples is this episode of *Sanford and Son*, which first aired on January 11, 1974, during the show's third season. When Lamont receives an unfair traffic ticket from a white policeman, Fred decides to serve as his lawyer. Fred, famous for his great lines (to Aunt Esther: "I'm calling you ugly; I could push your face in some dough and make gorilla cookies!"), cracks off a doozy here. He accuses the cop of ticketing only black people. When the judge responds that justice is blind to color, Fred snaps back: "Look around here; there's enough niggers in here to make a Tarzan movie!" The studio audience howled. And white America squirmed.

_07:: *The Simpsons*—Pick 'Em

The Simpsons is like sex or pizza. When it's good, it's great. And when it's bad, it's still pretty good. Dozens of the show's more than 300 episodes are worthy of consideration. But which one to pick? Homer's stint as Mr. Plow or Bart's as Mr. Burns' heir? Marge's gambling problem or one of Sideshow Bob's murderous plots? Perhaps the episode that best encapsulates the show's brilliance, its crackling writing, its incredible cast of characters, and its references to—and skewering of—all pop culture is in fact *two* episodes: "Who Shot Mr. Burns?"* Airing in May and September of 1995, the shows parodied the "Who Shot JR?" phenomenon of *Dallas* 15 years earlier to hilarious effect. Even Tito Puente is a suspect.

*It was Maggie, by the way, although the show produced several alternates to confuse snoops.

6 Tricky Lyrics You'll Never Get Wrong Again

Here are some of the trickiest lyrics in pop music, spelled out and explained for all you driver's seat soloists.

_01:: That "Leonard Bernstein" section of "It's the End of the World as We Know It (and I Feel Fine)" by R.E.M., 1987

"The other night I dreamt of knives, continental drift divide. Mountains sit in a line. Leonard Bernstein. Leonid Brezhnev, Lenny Bruce and Lester Bangs."

Great. So, what's it mean?

Very little. But here's who all those guys whose names start with *L* are:

Leonard Bernstein: American composer and conductor whose most famous musicals include *On the Town* (1944) and *West Side Story* (1957).

Leonid Brezhnev: President of the Soviet Union from 1977 to 1982. As a member of the Presidium (or Politburo), he pronounced the Brezhnev Doctrine, which gave the USSR the authority to roll tanks into any Warsaw Pact country where "communism was threatened." Hence, the Prague Spring of 1968.

Lenny Bruce: Groundbreaking American comedian whose outspoken, obscene political humor got him in trouble with the government.

Lester Bangs: Outspoken rock critic for *Creem* magazine, who railed against the pretensions of hippie musicians and extolled the virtues of raw, iconoclastic rock and roll.

_02:: That Weird Last Line of "One Week" by Barenaked Ladies, 1998

"Birchmount Stadium, home of the Robbie."

Great. So, what's it mean?

Birchmount Stadium is a sports venue affiliated with Birchmount Park Collegiate school in Toronto, Canada. The Robbie is a soccer tournament held at the stadium. The song line is taken directly from a sign outside the stadium.

_03:: Some of the Garbled Lines in "Rock the Casbah" by the Clash, 1982

"The muezzin was a-standin' on the radiator grille."

"But the Bedouin they brought out the electric camel drum."

"Sharif don't like it, Rockin' the Casbah, Rock the Casbah."

Great. So, what's it mean?

muezzin: A Muslim crier who calls the faithful to prayer five times a day. He calls from towers attached to the mosque, called minarets.

Bedouin: A member of one of the nomadic desert tribes of North Africa, Syria, and Arabia.

sharif: Can be used to describe a descendant of the prophet Mohammad through his daughter Fatima, or the chief magistrate of the holy city of Mecca. In this context, a Moroccan ruler or prince.

casbah: The citadel and palace of a North African sovereign.

_04:: Some Lines from That Middle Part of "Bohemian Rhapsody" by Queen, 1975

"Scaramouche, Scaramouche, will you do the Fandango."

"Bismillah! No we will not let you go."

"Beelzebub has a devil put aside for me, for me, for me."

Great. So, what's it mean?

Bohemian: Originally referred to someone from the Czech region of Bohemia, or Gypsies. Today it can be either a wandering vagabond or, more commonly, an artistic or literary person who disregards conventional lifestyles.

rhapsody: A rambling, disconnected series of sentences or statements composed under excitement, with no natural connection.

Scaramouche: A cowardly braggart and boastful buffoon, used as a stock character in Italian commedia dell'arte.

fandango: A provocative Spanish courtship dance in 3/8 or 6/8 time; performed by a man and a woman playing castanets.

bismillah: Arabic for "In the name of Allah." In daily speech it is a way of expressing truth or sincerity, similar to "With God as my witness" or the like.

Beelzebub: Today, another name for Satan. In Milton's *Paradise Lost*, he was one of the fallen angels, second to Lucifer in power. The name comes from Baalzebub, a Philistine god of Ekron. Also called Baal in the Old Testament. *Baal-zebub* means literally "lord of the flies" or, some say, "dung-god."

_05:: What about That "Hippopotamus of Love" or Whatever in "The Joker" by the Steve Miller Band, 1973?

"Some people call me Maurice, 'cuz I speak of the pompatus of love."

Great. So, what's it mean?

No matter how you spell it—*pompatus, pompetous,* or *pompitude*—you won't find it in a dictionary, because it's not a word. It's actually a corrupted form of yet *another* made-up word. It comes from an obscure 1954 R&B tune by the Medallions called "The Letter" in which singer/songwriter Vernon Green croons about the "puppetutes of love." Turns out "puppetute" was Green's made-up word to refer to "a secret paper-doll fantasy figure who would be my everything and bear my children." So from "puppet" we get "puppetutes." And Steve Miller, a huge old-school R&B fan, borrowed the line for his song 19 years later. But, since he didn't know the right word, approximated it as close as he could. Thus, "pompatus."

_06:: The Granddaddy of Them All: What the Hell Is That "Douche" Line in "Blinded by the Light" by Manfred Mann's Earth Band, 1976?

"Blinded by the light, revved up like a deuce, another runner in the night."

Great. So, what's it mean?

deuce: '60s slang for a 1932 Ford, or "deuce coupe." Note: Don't blame Manfred for the bizarre lyrics. They were written by Bruce Springsteen.

by
Shane Pitts &
Royce Simpson

Condensed
PSYCHOLOGY

Contains

5 Common Myths about Human Behavior

Maybe Malcolm X said it best: "You've been hoodwinked. You've been had. You've been took. You've been led astray, led amok. You've been bamboozled." Face it, kid. Someone lied to you, and it's time you got the truth.

_01:: You Use Only 10% of Your Brain

Undoubtedly, you've heard this one, but it's just not true—we use it all. While the origin of the myth isn't known, there are several lines of evidence that expose it as false. Maybe what people mean is that only 10% of our neurons are essential or are used at a given time? That's not true either. Brain imaging techniques such as fMRI (functional magnetic resonance imaging) clearly show that the brain doesn't just sit there while we engage in many activities. Think about it from an evolutionary perspective: the brain comprises only about 5% of total body mass but consumes 20% of the body's oxygen and glucose. It makes little survival sense for a species to develop a large, energy-hungry organ to use only 10% of its capacity.

_02:: Listening to Mozart Will Make Your Child Smarter

The so-called Mozart effect is a good example of a scientific finding being distorted by the media through hype not warranted by the research. It all started when researchers reported that after exposure to a selection of Mozart's music, college students showed an increase in spatial reasoning for about 10 minutes on tasks like putting together pieces of a jigsaw puzzle. Note first that the research was done on college students, not infants, and that the effect was very brief. In addition, no one's been able to replicate the research. The increase in spatial reasoning, it turns out, can be generated by any auditory stimulation (e.g., listening to a short story or other types of music) that keeps people alert while being tested. However, none of this has stopped eager parents—spurred on by fantastic claims from unscrupulous companies—from purchasing Mozart CDs for their babies.

_03:: Subliminal Advertising Will Make You Buy Stuff

Maybe you've heard of the "Drink Coke and eat popcorn" study. Supposedly, these words were flashed outside of patrons' awareness on a movie screen, and this induced them to buy more Coke and popcorn. Not only was that "study" never published, but it was later exposed as a hoax—a publicity stunt by an advertising executive. In over 200 published studies, there is no clear evidence of subliminal messages persuading anyone to buy or do anything. In one study, participants listened to tapes with classical music embedded with subliminal messages designed to increase either their self-esteem or their memory. At the end of five weeks, participants completed self-esteem scales and memory tests. Did the

Just the Facts

THE AMAZING NERVOUS SYSTEM

Average number of neurons in the brain: 100 billion

Number of synapses (neural connections): 60 trillion, give or take a few billion

Average loss of neurons: 85,000 per day (≈31 million per year)

Brain weights (in grams): human: 1,300–1,400; sperm whale: 7,800; hippopotamus: 582; chimpanzee: 420; cat: 30; hamster: 1.4

According to the *Guinness Book of World Records* the world's heaviest human brain weighed 5 lb. 1 oz. The lightest healthy brain weighed 1 lb. 8 oz.

Rate of neuron growth (early pregnancy): 250,000 neurons per minute

Neurons can transmit information at over 200 miles per hour.

During the first three years of life, 75% of brain growth is completed.

tapes work? No. They had no real effect on memory or self-esteem. But those who thought they were exposed to memory tapes, for example, believed they had improved regardless of the actual content of the tape.

_04:: That Whole "Hot-Hand" Thing in Basketball

Sports fans, players, and coaches attest to the fact that players perform in streaks. They predict that it's more likely for a player to make his next shot if he has made his previous two or three shots rather than missing them. But as it turns out, streak shooting is an illusion. Statistically, NBA players are no more likely to make shots after hitting previous shots. The shooting percentages after one, two, or three misses and after one, two, or three hits are virtually identical. The same is true for free throws. Likewise, players' own perceptions of being "hot" or "cold" are not predictive of their shooting performance. Lots of factors go into hitting a shot, including player skill, the defense, and so on, but the "hot hand" is just an illusion.

_05:: The Right Brain and Left Brain Function Separately

The idea is that the right and left hemispheres of the brain are highly specialized and that each one has a separate mode of thinking and stream of consciousness. The two hemispheres are somewhat specialized for various tasks, but it's a drastic oversimplification to assume that various mental functions are completely handled by one hemisphere or the other. The superiority of one hemisphere over another on most mental tasks is very modest. In normal individuals, the two hemispheres work in concert on all tasks. Likewise, even patients who've had their brain hemispheres disconnected generally experience a unity of conscious experience. Despite popular opinion, there's no research that links being left- or right-brained to musical ability, occupational choice, or other personal preferences. And, no, you can't educate the two sides separately.

3 Famous Studies That Would Be Illegal Today

What happened to the good old days, when a scientist could just rustle together some test subjects and let loose in the lab? You know, without having to worry about petty humane things . . . like ethics!

_01:: Stanley Milgram's Obedience Studies

In this Yale University study, participants were told they were part of an experiment on the effects of punishment on learning. They were instructed to teach another participant (the "learner") a list of words and, whenever the learner made a mistake, deliver an electric shock via a generator with levers labeled in 15-volt increments (up to 450 volts—where the label read "Danger: Severe Shock" and "XXX"). The learner (who, unknown to the participant, was not actually receiving shocks) became increasingly vocal, at one point even screaming, "I can't stand the pain! Get me out of here!" Because the experimenter urged the participants to continue, nearly 65% of them continued to obey the experimenter to deliver the maximum 450 volts. The participants weren't sadistic, Milgram argued, just socialized to obey authority figures.

_02:: Stanford Prison Experiments

In the summer of 1971 Philip Zimbardo put Stanford University students in jail. Students, who volunteered and were paid, were randomly assigned to be either a guard or a prisoner. The prisoners were surprised at their homes, handcuffed, and taken by police cruiser to a makeshift jail in the basement of the psychology department. There they were stripped of their personal belongings and given smocks, nylon caps, and identification numbers. The uniformed guards were simply told to enforce the rules. In just a few short days, the guards began to devise sadistic and degrading rituals for the prisoners, many of whom became depressed, anxious, or apathetic. Although they knew that this was just an experiment, all of the guards and prisoners adopted their roles, completely overriding their own individuality. The outcome was so dramatic, the experiment was stopped after only six days.

_03:: Little Albert

John Watson and Rosalie Rayner conducted one of the most famous and controversial studies in psychology using an 11-month-old boy who came to be known as Little Albert. With Little Albert, Watson demonstrated that many fears are conditioned through an association with other fearful situations. Before the experiment, Little Albert was a normal baby who was afraid of loud noises but not much else. Little Albert loved playing with small animals until Watson taught him to become afraid of a white rat by repeatedly banging a steel rod with a hammer whenever

Albert was given a white rat to play with. Little Albert's fear generalized to other similar objects, such as Watson's white hair and a Santa Claus mask. Watson clearly demonstrated that fears could be conditioned, but his methods have been roundly criticized, especially since the conditioning was never reversed.

Funny Psychology Experiments (Both Ha-Ha *and* Peculiar!)

Forget the comedy clubs and must-see sitcoms. If you're looking for a really good time, you can always get your giggles at the campus psych department.

_01:: How Long Is That Line? Asch's Studies on Conformity

You're sitting at a table with six strangers (who are all privy to the study) and are shown two cards, one with a single line and another with three. You are to say aloud which of the three lines on the second card is the same length as the line on the first. The three lines are not close in length, so the judgment is straightforward. The first two rounds are uneventful, with everyone agreeing on the match, but on subsequent rounds, one by one, the others clearly say the wrong answer. What would you do? If you were like most of Solomon Asch's subjects in his 1951 and 1956 studies, at least part of the time you too would say the wrong answer. Why? In many cases we conform to group norms out of a need to be accepted or a fear of rejection.

_02:: Pavlov: That Name Should Ring a Bell

Ivan Pavlov, a Nobel Prize–winning physiologist, conducted experiments that formed the basis of what is now known as classical conditioning. While studying the digestion of dogs in the early 1900s, Pavlov noticed that they would begin to salivate *before* they were presented with food to eat. Through numerous experiments, Pavlov discovered that almost any stimulus (for example, a metronome or a buzzer) could come to elicit the salivary response if the stimulus had been reliably paired with food in the past. In a typical experiment, Pavlov would present meat powder to a dog while a metronome was ticking so that eventually just hearing the metronome would cause the dog to salivate. Pavlov's work was influential because it detailed the process by which learned associations are made.

_03:: Help! The Smash-Hit Psychology Study by Latané and Rodin

Under what circumstances will people in an emergency situation receive help? In a 1969 study by Bibb Latané and Judith Rodin, a female researcher greets a male participant and asks him to complete a questionnaire. The researcher then leaves to go to an adjacent room. After a few minutes there is a crash, and the female researcher screams, "Oh, my God, my foot . . . I . . . I . . . can't move it." Do you think the man helped? Would you? The determining factor seemed to be the presence of other people. About 70% of the men facing this situation alone helped the woman, but when a pair of strangers were confronted with the emergency, only 40% of the time did either person offer help. This counterintuitive finding illustrates the bystander effect: as the number of people witnessing an emergency increases, the likelihood that any given person will help decreases.

_04:: The Case of the Mathematical Horse: Clever Hans

In 1907 a horse named Clever Hans caused quite a stir in Germany when he and his owner toured the country, amazing crowds with the horse's mathematical prowess. Yes, Hans could add, divide, convert fractions to decimals, and even do simple algebra. Clever Hans would tap out with his hoof the correct answer in response to a question from his owner. Many scientists observed Hans and couldn't explain the ability. Enter psychologist Oskar Pfungst, who used controlled conditions to observe Hans. Pfungst discovered that Hans couldn't answer the questions if the questioner didn't know the answer. Likewise, Hans didn't answer questions correctly if he couldn't see the questioner. When people asked Hans a question, they made subtle, involuntary changes in posture such as leaning forward and then raising their head as Hans approached the correct answer. Hans started tapping when someone leaned forward and stopped when they changed pos-

---

Strange but True

A MAN WALKS INTO A BAR

On September 13, 1848, Phineas Gage's life changed forever. Gage, a railroad supervisor in Cavendish, Vermont, was blasting rock to make way for a new section of tracks when an accident sent tamping rod shooting through his skull. The rod was traveling so fast that it exploded through his left cheek and continued out the top of his head. Amazingly, Phineas survived the accident, but in many ways he was never the same. Before the accident Phineas was considered thoughtful by his friends and colleagues and was well-liked. But after the accident he became noticeably impulsive, foul-tempered, and rude. In fact, his friends commented that he was "no longer Gage." The Phineas Gage case continues to fascinate scientists today because it provides insight into the relationship between the workings of the brain and personality. Sadly, Gage never fully recovered from that fateful day and was reduced to working as a circus sideshow.

---

ture again. Hans was clever but not mathematical.

_05:: Child's Play: A "Touching" Experiment

Over 80,000 nurses practice therapeutic touch (TT), a technique designed to heal by influencing the patient's "human energy field." The healers claim to detect a human energy field when passing their hands over the afflicted regions of the patients and to transfer their energy to the patients. A nine-year-old girl, Emily

Rosa, decided to put these claims to the test. As described in her article, published in the *Journal of the American Medical Association* in 1998, Emily had 21 TT practitioners place their palms face up through slots in a screen, which prevented them from seeing their hands. On each of the trials, Emily randomly selected one of the practitioner's hands and hovered her hand palm down a few inches above the subject's palm. The subject had to detect Emily's energy field by identifying where her hand was placed. The practitioners were no better than chance at correctly locating Emily's hand, being correct only 44% of the time.

To Sleep, Perchance to Dream:
Insights on Snoozing

Hey, hey, hey! Before you go ahead and hit that snooze button for the 11th time, maybe it's time you think about what you're doing. Here are four things you should know about sleep.

_01:: Riding the Sleep Cycle

Think all sleep's the same? Actually, a 10-minute catnap is quite different from a 10-hour zonk. In stage 1 (about 10 minutes) you may imagine flashes of bright lights or have the distinct sensation of falling, which leads to a full body jerk (you've probably seen people doing it while napping on an airplane). During stage 2 you might talk incoherently, but don't worry—you're unlikely to divulge state secrets. While in the deeper sleep of stages 3 and 4, brain activity is at its lowest point, and you're most likely to sleepwalk during stage 4. At the end of stage 4 you cycle back up through the stages, except as you exit stage 2 you enter REM (rapid eye movement) sleep, when most dreams occur. As the night progresses you spend progressively less time in stages 3 and 4 and more time in REM sleep.

_02:: We All Dream a Little Dream

Many people simply don't remember their dreams, but when awakened during a REM period, those who claim not to dream typically report dreaming. People who consistently recall dreams tend to wake just as they exit the last REM period of the night, whereas others may wake up too long after their last REM period to recall much. Dreams do occur in all stages of sleep, but they're more prevalent and much more vivid during REM sleep. Dreams about falling, being chased, repeatedly failing to do something, flying, rejection, and being unprepared or late for an important event are common. Contrary to popular Freudian assumptions about the hidden sexual and aggressive content of dreams, most dreams are overtly and directly related to our everyday lives and concerns.

_03:: While You Were Sleeping: The Role of External Stimuli

Have you ever heard your alarm clock go off but continued sleeping and dreamed you were on a train or were hearing a car horn? Subjects who have water sprayed on their hands during REM sleep and are later awakened tend to report water-related dreams—waterfalls, leaky roofs, etc. Your brain doesn't "shut off" during sleep. It's simply in a different state from wakefulness. So, please don't put your roommate's hand in a glass of warm water during the night. Though we may incorporate some external stimuli into our dreams, we don't remember information conveyed to us during sleep. It's unfortunate but this means you won't be able to learn Spanish on tape while you snooze.

_04:: The Contagious Yawn

Everyone yawns, including in utero fetuses, some reptiles, birds, and most mammals. Fatigue and boredom certainly aren't the only reasons we yawn. One hypothesis is that yawning serves similar functions as stretching. Both activities increase blood pressure and flex muscles and joints. If you try to stifle a yawn, just as when restraining a stretch, the yawn is not very satisfying. A part of the brain, the hypothalamus, appears to be integral to yawning. It contains a number of chemicals that can induce yawns, some of which surge at night and when awakening. Yawns are catching, but there is little understanding of why they are contagious. One possibility is that at one time in our evolutionary history, yawns served to communicate changing environmental or internal bodily events to members of a social group.

6 Mind-Bending Ailments

Brains are pretty scary to begin with: they're pinkish gray, they're lumpy, and they blank out at the most inappropriate times. But what would happen if your brain really turned on you?

_01:: That's No Friend of Mine

Do your friends and family feel like strangers? You might be suffering from Capgras' syndrome, a rare condition in which family, close friends, or items of personal significance seem like imposters. What gives? When you see a familiar face, you don't just recognize the face; you also experience some sort of emotional reaction to it. Capgras' delusion arises when there's a disconnection between these two brain functions. You can identify your father's face and know it's familiar, but since there's damage to the pathways between face recognition and emotional reaction, you experience no jolt of emotion. Since it doesn't *feel* like your father, the man must be an imposter!

_02:: I Can't See, but I Can Slam-Dunk

Believe it or not, people with blindsight are blind due to cortical damage, but they can still unconsciously "see" some aspects of their environment. One famous patient, D.F., couldn't read the big E on the eye chart or identify how many fingers a doctor was holding up right in front of her, but she could put an envelope through a slit in the wall with a high degree of accuracy. How is that possible? There's more than one way to see. The "what" pathway is responsible for recognizing what an object is—for instance, is it a wolf or a banana? The "where or how" pathway determines where objects are and how to navigate and interact with them. Without visualizing the "what," people with blindsight are still able to figure out the "where."

_03:: Not for Weak Stomachs

Picture living your life under a strobe light. That's what it feels like to suffer from akinetopsia, or motion blindness. This very rare condition results from selective loss of motion perception because of damage to certain areas of the brain (the temporoparietal cortices). Patients with motion blindness can identify stationary objects and have no problems with other aspects of vision, but moving objects inexplicably seem to appear in one position and then another. For instance, when crossing the street, cars that at first seemed far away could suddenly be very near. And liquid pouring from a pitcher into a cup might look frozen until the cup finally overflowed, allowing the patient to infer that it was full.

_04:: Better Than Peyote

Can you imagine tasting music or smelling the color red? Most of us can't (or at least don't re-

Strange but True

THE HISTORY OF FRONTAL LOBOTOMIES

Many of us remember Nurse Ratched from the book and movie *One Flew over the Cuckoo's Nest*. This cold-blooded villain controlled the mental ward in part because it was understood that she had the therapies of shock treatments and frontal lobotomies at her disposal. Unfortunately, there was a time in our history when the use of frontal lobotomies to treat psychiatric disorders such as schizophrenia was as much fact as fiction. During a frontal lobotomy, a sharp object was inserted into the frontal lobes of the brain and moved back and forth to destroy tissue. The 1940s and 1950s represented the heyday of frontal lobotomies, with nearly 40,000 people receiving the treatment in the United States alone. One man in particular, Walter Freeman, worked tirelessly—traveling the country performing lobotomies and preaching about their effectiveness (while reportedly driving his "lobotomobile"). The advent of psychotropic drugs as well as a recognition that most patients did not improve after their surgery produced a sharp decline in the use of lobotomies during the 1960s. In very rare circumstances more precise psychosurgeries are performed today but generally only as a last resort.

member), but those with synesthesia can and do. Just as the word *anesthesia* means "no sensation," *synesthesia* means "joined sensation." For some reason, stimulating one sense triggers perceptions in another sense. For example, a bright light might seem loud, the sound of a bagpipe sour, the color after sex a static silver. No one's sure of the cause, but there are a few hypotheses. Some experts think that crossed wires in the brain cause the problem (the path to the taste buds gets hooked up to the sense of hearing path, for example), while others believe that it's a lack of inhibition (the natural pathways that squelch irrelevant sensory input just aren't working properly).

_05:: The Man without a Face

Prosopagnosics have no trouble recognizing noses, ears, eyes, chins, and so on, but they can't seem to fuse them together into a coherent, whole face. In extreme cases, they can't even recognize their own faces in the mirror. Prosopagnosia results from damage to structures just below the ears, stretching toward the back of the skull (otherwise known as the inferotemporal cortex). Dr. P, a famous case in the annals of neuropsychology, searched for his hat as he was departing his physician's of-

fice only to reach out and grab his wife's head and try to lift it off! Not being able to recognize faces clearly, he apparently mistook his wife's head for a hat.

_06:: Rent *Memento* and You'll Understand

If you haven't seen *Memento*, check it out. The main character suffers from damage to the hippocampus (one of the memory centers of the brain) and loses the ability to form new long-term memories (his pre-accident memories stay intact, though). Anterograde amnesiacs live life as though constantly waking from a dream. Leonard, the *Memento* character, takes to tattooing himself because he can't trust the people around him to tell the truth—even if they did, he'd just forget a few minutes later anyway. Strangely, sufferers of this condition can learn new tasks (for example, they improve while taking, say, tennis lessons), but they assume every lesson that it's just beginner's luck.

Crazy Kid Conundrums (That Are Somehow Still Cute)

Why do advertisers love to use kids in commercials? Kids can get away with things that would make an adult look stupid or smarmy—it's all about seeing things from a kid's perspective.

_01:: I'll Give You Five Shiny New Nickels for That Paper Dollar

If you've been around preschoolers and children up to the age of six or seven much, you may have heard something like, "Please cut

the pizza into lots of slices, I'm really hungry," or you may have seen an older child "exchange" five nickels for one paper dollar—much to the delight of the younger sibling. One reason for these cute behaviors is that preschoolers tend to lack what psychologists call conservation. They fail to understand that properties of an object, such as number or volume, don't change despite changes in the object's appearance. They tend to focus on only one dimension of an object at a time. With the pizza example, the child is focused on the number, but not the size, of the slices.

_02:: Enough about You; Let's Talk about Me

Preschoolers tend to be egocentric, meaning they assume that others share their point of view. Humorous examples are plentiful. Playing hide-and-seek with a three-year-old, you may find him standing in plain view with his eyes covered. If you ask one of your two preschool girls if she has a sister, she will say, "Yes." If you then ask her if her sister has a sister, she may look confused and say, "No!" because she can't see herself from her sister's perspective. Egocentrism also explains why

many young children stand in front of the TV. They can see, so everyone else must also be able to see. Egocentrism also helps explain "collective monologues," in which two preschoolers apparently are taking turns talking to each other, but it's clear that they're not talking about the same things.

_03:: I Saw Mommy Kissing Santa Claus

Preschoolers sometimes have difficulty distinguishing appearance from reality. When daddy puts on the Santa outfit, to a five-year-old, he *is* Santa. If a mother puts on a costume mask in front of her four-year-old, he may become confused and bawl, assuming that his mother is now a green, wart-faced monster. By around age four or five, children develop what psychologists call a "theory of mind," which is when the child begins to understand that others have mental states (beliefs/desires) of their own that influence how they behave.

6 Reasons You're an Unreasonable Reasoner

You're not crazy, really. Just highly unreasonable. But don't worry about it; we don't blame you at all. We blame your illogical brain.

_01:: I Must Be Psychic!

You're driving down the road, and a song comes on the radio that you were just humming in your head. The phone rings, and it's the long-lost friend you were just thinking of. These incidences seem strange, maybe even

mystical to most of us. But such incidences can be explained by the illusory correlation—the tendency to perceive a relationship between two events that are independent. When these surprising coincidences occur, we tend to remember them very well, but how often are we thinking about that song and it doesn't come on the radio, or how often does the song come on the radio when we're not thinking about it? The tendency to notice the hits and forget the misses can lead to some bizarre and erroneous beliefs, such as the full moon causing abnormal behavior.

_02:: My Point Exactly!

False beliefs are often maintained by a strong confirmation bias, or the tendency to seek information that confirms our preexisting beliefs rather than information that may disconfirm them. This bias becomes more than academic when social issues are considered. For instance, if someone believes that African Americans are hostile, that Republicans have the best agenda, or that a coworker is always wrong about everything, that person will seek information that confirms those beliefs and rarely examine, remember, or notice disconfirming evidence. The more this happens, the more firmly entrenched the false beliefs become.

_03:: It's All So Clear!

The availability bias occurs when our judgments are based on information that is vivid and memorable rather than reliable. Your opinion about an auto purchase may be more influenced by your salient knowledge of one friend who has a Honda that's frequently in the auto shop rather than on reliability information based on thousands of consumer experiences. Similarly, especially after televised airplane crashes, people overestimate the risk of flying by commercial airline compared with car travel. The gun lobby tries to focus consumers on vivid cases of home intruders, when the facts are that vastly more gun deaths in the home are due to accident and suicide

What's the Difference?

CLINICAL PSYCHOLOGIST, PSYCHOTHERAPIST, PSYCHOANALYST, AND PSYCHIATRIST

Sure, they sound interchangeable, but there are definite distinctions between clinical psychologists, psychotherapists, psychoanalysts, and psychiatrists. So, how do you tell them apart? A *clinical psychologist* has typically earned a PhD or PsyD in psychology and has completed an internship. The term *psychotherapist*, or therapist, is a generic term that may be applied to anyone who delivers therapy. Its use is unregulated in most states. The term *psychoanalyst* is associated with those who deliver psychoanalytic (Freudian-like) therapy. A *psychiatrist* is a medical doctor who has specialized in mental disorders after completion of basic training in medicine. Only psychiatrists can prescribe medications. Others who deliver therapy may include licensed social workers (LSWs), pastors, rehabilitation counselors, and anyone who has obtained a license to deliver therapy (an LPC—licensed professional counselor). People in these occupations typically have at least a master's degree in psychology or social work.

than to criminal intruders. The ease and vividness with which something comes to mind are no substitute for careful evaluation.

_04:: I'm Due for a Win!

Which of the following sequences of six coin tosses is most likely: (1) HHHTTT, (2)

HTTHTH, (3) HHHHHH? Most people pick the second sequence, though the three sequences are equally likely. People choose the second sequence because of a mistaken belief that if a process is truly random it should always look random—even in small runs. This belief can lead to the gambler's fallacy: people become more likely to bet on black numbers after a roulette wheel has come up red five times in a row. They believe that black must be "due." Of course, the five previous spins or coin tosses or lottery numbers have no bearing at all on the sixth.

_05:: Which Came First—the Chicken or the Pig?

It's almost irresistible to assume that since two variables are correlated, one must cause the other. One survey of elderly Americans noted a correlation between the amount of coffee the couples drank and the frequency of their sexual activity. The author suggested that the stimulants in the coffee might cause this increased sex drive. Before you run out and raid Starbucks, let's consider this further. There could be a third, unknown, factor. Or there could be a number of other variables related to both coffee drinking and sexual behavior—such as health, social activity, and so on. Even if we're sure that one caused the other, we can't be sure by using correlational research alone if A causes B or B causes A. Correlation is not causation.

_06:: The Glass Is Half Full!

Seemingly simple things have a way of subtly influencing our reasoning. Framing effects occur when the way an issue is worded influences a judgment or decision. For example, people think condoms are effective in controlling the spread of HIV or AIDS when condoms are said to have a 95% success rate but not when they have a 5% failure rate. People prefer meats that are 85% fat free compared to 15% fat. People sometimes make health choices based on wording. For example, people choose to use sunscreen if the message is framed in terms of a gain ("Using sunscreen increases your chances of maintaining healthy, young-looking skin") rather than in terms of a loss ("Not using sunscreen decreases your chances of maintaining healthy, young-looking skin").

Saying One Thing but Meaning Your Mother: Thoughts on Freud

9

Sigismund Schlomo Freud (aka Sigmund Freud) and his psychoanalytic theory have had an enormous impact on 20th-century culture, but his influence on psychological science is hotly contested. He's been described as a visionary, a genius, and an intellectual giant. On the other hand, some people just think he was a quack.

_01:: The "Talking Cure"

One of Freud's most significant contributions may very well be the emphasis he placed on talking about one's problems as a means of alleviating them. Talking with a therapist is still a widely used format of therapy today. (People generally do not lie down on couches, though.) The details of the therapeutic process are typically not Freudian unless you go to an analyst, but the general format is similar. The acts of creating a relaxing atmosphere and gaining acceptance are still integral parts of psychotherapy.

_02:: What Lies Beneath

Freud's most enduring idea is the role of the unconscious. Psychologist widely accept his general idea of the mind as an iceberg with the submerged unconscious playing a role in much of human behavior. Many empirical studies have demonstrated that we are often unaware of why we think or behave as we do and that we process extensive amounts of information outside conscious awareness. While some argue that unconscious processes account for most of our behavior, there's considerable dis-

agreement on the role the unconscious plays in human behavior.

_03:: Defense Mechanisms

A few of the ego defense mechanisms articulated by Freud and especially by his daughter Anna have received some empirical support over the years. Reaction formation, a defense mechanism in which one changes unacceptable impulses into their opposites, has garnered some support. Examples of reaction formation include a racist who behaves overly friendly toward someone of color or a young boy who derides a girl he really likes. However, defense mechanisms tied to Freud's ideas on "instinctual energy" such as displacement (shifting sexual or aggressive urges toward a less threatening target) have received very little support. Further, it seems that the basis of most defense mechanisms are not fuming, unacceptable impulses as Freud contended, but rather our motives to maintain our self-image.

_04:: The Role of the Unconscious

Whether Freud's ideas about the unconscious appear on a "contributions" or a "criticisms" list depends on whether we're speaking in generalities or specifics. Freud's ideas, in general, about behavior being influenced by the unconscious are well supported. The specifics of his views are another matter. Freud saw the unconscious as an analytically sophisticated, seething cauldron of repressed sexual and aggressive urges that controls nearly every thought and behavior. It was a place where boys harbored sexual feelings for their mothers and aggression toward their fathers, and little girls wrangled with feelings of inadequacy because they didn't have penises. Empirical research on the unconscious does not bear out this idea of the unconscious. Rather, research reveals a vast but simple, unanalytical information processor in which ordinary stimuli and tasks are handled.

_05:: After-the-Fact Explanations

One of the most damaging criticisms of Freud's psychoanalytic theory is that it provides explanations for behavior after the fact but predicts little about those behaviors in advance, which makes aspects of the theory unfalsifiable and therefore more akin to a pseudoscience than a science. If you are angry at your mother for remarrying, you illustrate the theory that "you have an unresolved Oedipal complex resulting in jealousy toward this new father figure." If you are not upset but rather quite happy about the marriage, you again exemplify his theory because you're "demonstrating a reaction formation" (see p. 294). A scientific theory must specify in advance observations that would contradict the theory if they were to occur. It's convenient that no behavior can ever contradict Freudian theory.

Strange but True
FREUD FUN FACTS!

Sigmund Freud's father, Jakob, was 20 years older than his young mother, Amalia. Freud had half-brothers very close to Amalia's age and a nephew older than he was. In fact, there may have been intriguing dynamics between his young attractive mother and his older half-brothers, of which Sigmund was likely aware.

Freud was a gifted student who was barely 10 years old when he entered high school. He began his studies in law before becoming more interested in medicine, and enrolled in medical school at 17. He received his medical degree at 25, specializing in clinical neurology.

Patients who visited Freud reclined on a small couch during therapy. He sat behind them because he couldn't bear to be stared at by his patients.

Freud never won a Nobel Prize in medicine or anything else for that matter. His only major award was the Goethe Prize for literature.

Freud was an unabashed cocaine advocate who regularly ingested the drug and gave it to his sisters, friends, and patients. He even published six articles describing its benefits. Freud avoided cocaine addiction but was clearly addicted to nicotine. He chain-smoked cigars, averaging 20 a day. He developed cancer of the palate and jaw at age 67 and underwent a series of 33 operations. He continued to smoke cigars until his death in 1939.

_06:: Ambiguous, Nebulous Concepts

Psychoanalytic theory falls short partly because many of the core concepts are too ambiguous and nebulous to be measured. For instance, how do you compute an id, castration anxiety, or penis envy? How do you know whether the latent, hidden content of interpreted dreams is valid and reliable? Science uses operational definitions, which means that variables and concepts are defined in terms of the operations or procedures used to measure them. Many central Freudian concepts, such as repression, are not measurable and are therefore untestable.

_07:: Overemphasis on Sex

Freud's ideas were a product of his time, so it's no surprise that his theory has been heavily criticized for its overemphasis on sexuality. Freud saw the expression or repression of sexual motivations as major, even primary, determinates of human behavior. Freud's dogged attachment to this idea was relayed in a letter to follower Carl Jung: "My dear Jung, promise me never to abandon the sexual theory. That is the most essential thing of all. You see, we must make a dogma of it, an unshakable bulwark." Some of Freud's original followers, such as Carl Jung and Alfred Adler, parted company with him in part because they viewed his ideas on sexual motivations as extreme and unnecessary to explain human behavior.

_08:: Biased Observations

Critics of Freud say that his theory was built on biased, nonobjective, and even fabricated observations of only a handful of patients. There is ample evidence that Freud pressured patients into accepting, for example, his suggestions that they had been abused. He subjected his patients to leading questions and may have planted ideas in their memory. Likewise, historical analyses show that Freud distorted many of his case studies to fit with his theory irrespective of the facts of the cases and regardless of what patients did or didn't say. A related criticism is that Freud's ideas were developed based largely on a very small, self-selected sample of wealthy, upper-class, 18- to 20-year-old, mentally unstable, single women from Victorian Vienna.

_09:: Bad Test Results

Of those specific psychoanalytic concepts that have been tested empirically, few have fared well. The structural theory—id, ego, and superego—has not received empirical support. The idea of progression of development through oral, anal, phallic, and genital psychosexual stages and the linking of adult personality characteristics to psychosexual stages of child development have no empirical underpinnings. The Oedipal complex, where a boy has sexual impulses toward his mother and comes to view his father as an unwanted rival, has likewise received no empirical support. Many psychologists suggest that Freud is of historical interest only and that a science of mind and behavior must move on without him.

Rational Explanations for Disorderly Conduct

While most people have a general understanding of what OCD (obsessive-compulsive disorder), depression, and schizophrenia are, the following disorders may be new to most.

_01:: Dissociative Fugue: Home Sweet Home, I Think?

Like Betty Sizemore, the title character in the film *Nurse Betty*, people with this disorder have complete amnesia and suddenly leave their home and work and may start a new life. They may also assume a new identity. The disturbance may last for hours, days, or even months. Neither the victim nor those around him or her are typically aware of the disorder. Fugues typically occur after extreme stress, such as severe marital quarrels, loss of a cherished job, combat, or natural disasters. The sufferers typically recover, are disoriented, and are eager to return home. They usually don't have much recollection of their altered lives. The disorder is very rare, with less than 0.2% of the American population experiencing it, and not much is known about the cause.

Stump the Expert

THE SCIENTIFIC PURSUIT OF CONSCIOUSNESS

Consciousness is one of the most profound puzzles of existence, and it's a cutting-edge topic of investigation among psychologists, biologists, neuroscientists, and others. How is it that lower-level physical processes in the brain give rise to the subjective, conscious experience of the color green or of the agony of an intense headache or of the resonating sound of a cello? Why should they give rise to experience at all? Some experts argue that explanations of consciousness are beyond the realm of science; others disagree. One of the more promising hypotheses for how consciousness arises comes from John Searle, who maintains that consciousness is a biological phenomenon caused by lower-level processes in the brain. He claims that as an emergent property, the processes and elements within the brain cause consciousness, but it's not a property of any individual elements and cannot be explained simply as a summation of the activity of those elements. For example, consider a cup of coffee. The liquidity of the coffee is explained by the behavior of the molecules that compose it, but none of the individual molecules are liquid. Consciousness, like the liquidity of brewed coffee, is a property that emerges from the behavior of many individual elements that cannot be reduced to or explained by any single element in the system.

_02:: Frottage (Unwanted Touching)

Frotteurism, from the French *frotter*, "to rub," involves the rubbing of one's genitals against a nonconsenting, unsuspecting person. A frotteur may rub his penis against the buttocks or thighs of women in a crowded public place such as a bus or subway. The frotteur tends to choose places that afford easy escape, such as crowded sidewalks or buses that make frequent stops. He may board a bus several times a day during rush hour in search of multiple victims. Frotteurs are typically men, between 15 and 25 years of age, and the behavior generally begins in adolescence. The impersonal nature of the sexual contact seems to be important to the frotteur. The number of the attacks may be considerable. In a large-scale study, researchers found that frotteurs in their sample averaged 901 victims during the course of their disorder.

_03:: Delusional Disorder: Brad Pitt Is So in Love with Me

Individuals with erotomanic delusional disorder, also known as de Clerambault's syndrome, are under the delusion that another person is in love with them. The person they have the delusion about is typically of higher social status and unattainable due to marriage or celebrity. The person with the disorder is often convinced that the sought-after individual is the one who initiated the relationship despite little or no contact between the two. Sometimes the disorder spirals into stalking, harassment, assault, and/or kidnapping. The most notorious case of this disorder involved John Hinckley Jr., who attempted to assassinate former President Reagan to capture the attention of actress Jodie Foster.

Fascinating Fetal Feats

It's amazing to realize how young you were when you first came to your senses—your five senses, that is. Sure, it might take us a little longer than most species to walk around or even lift our own heads, but that doesn't mean we're late bloomers in every department.

_01:: Taste and Smell

At 13 to 15 weeks, fetuses have taste buds that look like a mature adult's. Whether fetuses can taste the liter a day of amniotic fluid they ingest is not known, but we do know that premature infants and newborns prefer sweet tastes to sour tastes. Some researchers think that amniotic fluid serves as a flavor appetizer or precursor to breast milk. Newborns show a distinct preference for the smell of their mother over that of a stranger. A one-week-old will orient significantly more toward a gauze pad from its mother's bra than a pad from another nursing mother.

_02:: Hearing

Despite their insulated environment in the womb, fetuses can hear. They will jump at the sound of a slammed door or other loud noises. Newborns will fling their arms in the air and open their eyes wide when startled by a loud noise. As with smell, a newborn will display a preference for the sound of his or her own mother's voice. The newborn will suck more vigorously on a pacifier to turn on a recording of the mother's voice compared to that of a strange woman's similar voice. A 20-week-old will orient toward the sound of his or her own name more than that of similar-sounding other names. Newborns are particularly sensitive to high-pitched and melodic sounds and human voices. It's little wonder that people in all cultures speak to infants in the slow-paced, high-pitched, melodic, simple "motherese," or baby talk, that attracts the infant's attention.

_03:: Learning, Memory, and Language

In addition to displaying memory for their mother's voice, newborns show memory for other stimuli as well. In one study, mothers read passages from one of three different stories to their babies during the last six weeks of pregnancy. Shortly after birth, newborns donning headphones sucked faster or slower on an electronic pacifier to activate recordings of the story they had heard in the womb rather than a new story. Displaying a sensitivity to language, newborns not only prefer the sound of their own mother's voice but tend to prefer that voice when she speaks in her native language rather than a foreign language. By six months of age, infants from different-speaking countries show different auditory brain mappings, which helps explain why related languages (Spanish and French, for example) are easier to learn than dissimilar ones.

_04:: Vision

Despite popular myths, newborns can see, though they are very nearsighted. They can focus best on objects that are seven or eight inches away. A few hours after birth, newborns can tell the difference between light and dark shades and can track slow-moving objects. Newborns show a marked preference for complex patterns with lots of contrast—especially human faces. They stare much longer at complete, correctly featured faces compared to other complex stimuli, including face patterns with features rearranged. It seems as though newborns are especially attuned via evolutionary forces to attend to significant social stimuli in their environment.

Shrink Rap:

4

Giants of Psychology Discussed in Plain English

Who said psychologists don't have superpowers? Between these four brainiacs, your head could be shrunk down to nuthin' in no time flat.

_01:: Carl Gustav Jung (1875–1961)

A one-time close companion and disciple of Freud, Jung was Freud's heir apparent until their split over theoretical differences in 1914. Jung's version of psychoanalysis was built around the collective unconscious—ancestral experiences common to all humans. The contents of this unconscious, or archetypes, are innate psychological predispositions that converge ancestral experiences around common themes such as the anima (the representation of woman in man) and animus (man in woman). Jung focused heavily on the dreams and on the development of the self, which he viewed as the unifying core of the psyche. For inspiration, Jung delved into history, religion, mythology, mysticism, and archaeology. His most enduring contribution has been that of a typology of personality most popularly captured in the Myers-Briggs Type Indicator, which classifies people as introverts or extroverts, for example.

_02:: Jean Piaget (1896–1980)

The influence of Piaget's theory and work on child cognitive development has been compared to Shakespeare's influence on English literature. Born in Switzerland, Piaget was a precocious child, publishing a small article by age 10. He published 20 papers before receiving his doctorate in 1918 at age 21 and eventually published over 40 books and 100 articles on child psychology alone. Piaget is most famous for his stage theory of intellectual development, in which children sequence through four distinct stages of cognitive development: sensorimotor, preoperational, concrete operational, and formal operational. Piaget likened children to little scientists constantly conducting experiments on their environment as they actively seek information to better understand the world.

_03:: B. F. Skinner (1904–1990)

Burrhus Frederic Skinner was one of the most influential psychologists of his generation and is almost as well known to the public as to the scientific community. Skinner is best known for his research demonstrating the effects of reinforcers and punishers on behavior. It was his belief that virtually all behaviors are the result of environmental consequences; stated simply, behavior that is reinforced (or rewarded) will be more likely to be repeated, while punished behavior will be less likely to be repeated. So, according to Skinner, we may watch movies, eat chocolate cake, and even love our parents because these things supply us with ample reinforcement. While much of Skinner's research used pigeons and rats, often in controlled experimental chambers called Skinner boxes, his principles are regularly applied to humans using a technique called behavior modification.

_04:: Carl Rogers (1902–1987)

Carl Rogers was one of the pioneers of the humanistic approach in psychology. The humanistic perspective differs from Freud's psychoanalysis and Skinner's behaviorism in that individuals are assumed to be responsible for their actions rather than at the mercy of unconscious motives or environmental forces. The role of the therapist is to provide a supportive, nonjudgmental atmosphere while helping clients take responsibility for their betterment. Rogers's method of therapy reflected his belief that all individuals have an innate self-actualizing tendency, or a desire to understand their true selves and be the best they can be. Rogers believed that a complete understanding of the self can be obtained only when individuals are loved and respected unconditionally. The humanistic approach in psychology reached its heyday during the 1960s and '70s, but many of Rogers's views on human nature, and especially his client-centered therapeutic techniques, continue to be influential in psychology.

by
Greg Salyer

Condensed
RELIGION

Contains

5 Unusual Creation Stories ✳ 5 Religious Rituals That Hurt Like Hell ✳ Mmm-Mmm God: 4 Ways to Be Religious While Having Sex ✳ 8 Steps to Founding a World Religion ✳ 6 Versions of Heaven ✳ Abandon All Hope, Ye Who Enter Here: 7 Versions of Hell ✳ 6 Women Who Shaped World Religions ✳ 3 (or 3 Million) Famous Gods ✳ Straight from the Cutting Room Floor: 6 Texts That Didn't Make It into the Bible ✳

5 Unusual Creation Stories

If tales of Adam and Eve or earth being a seven-day job leave you yawning, here are a couple of alternative creation myths that have human beings arriving with flair.

_01:: If at First You Don't Succeed . . .

Like many gods, the Mayan deities created life on earth to be worshiped by it, and like many gods, they began with animals. As we know, with the exception of parrots, animals can't talk. The gods were displeased because they couldn't understand the animals' praise (or growls, as it were). Of course, when the gods are displeased, bad things happen, as in you might become food for a greater creation. Initially, that creation was a man of mud. He had mud for brains and eventually melted in the rain. Man, version 2.0, involved a being constructed of wood, but he had wooden expressions, so the gods felt unloved. Finally, the gods created human beings that were just like gods, knowing and seeing everything the gods did. Guess how long that lasted?

_02:: Bumba and His Digestive Problems

An unusual creation story from the Boshongo people of sub-Saharan Africa includes a high god who created the world by vomiting. As is often the case, the world begins in watery darkness, and Bumba, the only being in existence, is alone. He "wretches and strains" until he vomits up the sun. The sun dries up some of the water, and the earth begins to emerge. Next, Bumba vomits the moon and stars so that the night has lights as well. Finally, in one last regurgitative effort, Bumba

vomits animals and men. One of the men "was white like Bumba." This line indicates that the story was written down after contact with Europeans (and therefore contact with writing).

_03:: New and Interesting Uses for Masturbation

In the Egyptian Book of the Dead (1550 BCE), two major gods (Shu, the god who separated the earth and sky, and Tefnut) are born in a most unusual fashion: "When I rubbed with my fist, my heart came into my mouth in that I spat forth Shu and expectorated Tefnut." It would seem that these two divinities were created by one god's act of masturbation. Although it's not surprising to find sexual imagery in sacred texts, you just don't see many references to masturbation. In regard to the creation of humankind, the text reads, "I wept tears, the form of my Eye, and that is how mankind came into existence." Hey, we'll take the poetic with the raunchy.

_04:: I Don't Know, Do You?

This marvelous story comes from the oldest Hindu sacred text, the Rig Veda, and offers an interesting counterpoint to Western worry about the "true" story of creation. In this hymn, the author asks the same questions that others ask about creation but doesn't worry too much about the answers. He begins: "The

Timeline

'CAUSE YOU GOTTA HAVE
FAITH, FAITH, FAITH!

Here's a quick primer to when religious movements first got their big breaks.

125,000–30,000 BCE   The Neanderthals kick things off with possible burial rituals.

30,000 BCE   Cro-Magnon moves things forward with cave paintings and figurines.

7,000–3,000 BCE   The Neolithic age brings with it agricultural revolutions, fertility religions, and megaliths (e.g., Stonehenge).

3000–1500 BCE   Hinduism's Vedas appear in their oral form, Judaism's Abraham (1900–1700 BCE) makes his presence felt, and early elements of Shinto arrive on the scene.

1500–1000 BCE   Good age for religious texts. As the Egyptian kingdoms flourish, the Egyptian Book of the Dead hits shelves, while Hinduism's Vedas also make their way into print (1500 BCE). Judaism's superstar Moses (ca. 1300 BCE) also hits the scene.

1000–500 BCE   Definitely big years for religious movers and shakers. Zoroastrianism's Zoroaster (ca. 1100–550 BCE), Judaism's King David (1010–970 BCE), Taoism's Lao-tzu (ca. 600–500 BCE), Confucianism's Confucius (ca. 551–479 BCE), Buddhism's Siddhartha Gautama Buddha (563–483 BCE), and Jainism's Mahavira (599–527 BCE) all make their mark.

500 BCE–1 BCE   Christianity's Jesus Christ (ca. 4 BCE–30 CE) makes a memorable entrance.

1 CE–500 CE   As the Mayans make their presence felt (300), this era turns out to be huge for Christianity. Paul's ministry (ca. 50–60) explodes on the scene, the Gospels are revealed (ca. 70–95), and the religion gets a huge endorsement as it becomes the state religion of Rome (313). Looking eastward, Mahayana Buddhism emerges, and the religion known as Shinto formally picks up its name.

500–1000 CE   Islam's Muhammad (ca. 570–632); Buddhism: national religion of Tibet (700s); Christianity: pope rules Church and state (800–1100); Islam: dominates much of the world (750–1258).

1000–1500 CE   The Aztec and Inca empires flourish in the Western hemisphere (1325–1470), as Islam manages to expel Christian crusaders (1300) in the Middle East. Zen Buddhism hits the scene in Japan (13th century), and the Spanish Inquisition begins (1478). Sikhism also finds a founder in Guru Nanak (1469–1504).

1500–2000 CE   Big years for Christianity as the Protestant Reformation takes place (1521). The Baha'i religion is established in 1863. Jews are severely persecuted during the Holocaust, and Israel becomes a state in 1948.

nonexistent was not; the existent was not at that time. The atmosphere was not nor the heavens which are beyond. What was concealed? Where? In whose protection? Was it water? An unfathomable abyss?" The only thing for certain in this story seems to be that there was darkness in the beginning, or rather "darkness within darkness." But a spark of desire born on the sea of darkness sets things in motion and creation begins. Or does it?

_05:: The Woman Who Fell from the Sky

According to the Iroquoian legend "The Woman Who Fell from the Sky," a young woman journeys to another village, and there she meets a magician, the most prominent man in the village, and asks to be his wife. After she passes a series of strenuous and painful tests, he agrees. She soon realizes that a beautiful tree has drawn her there to be impregnated, and one day she spreads her legs to receive a blossom that falls lightly onto her vagina. Meanwhile, the magician is in dire straits because the village is suffering a drought, and some of the elders suggest that his new bride might be to blame. They plot to bury her under the tree, but when they lift it up, there's no hole in the earth, only an expanse of blue. The curious woman agrees to jump, and at that moment she becomes the woman who fell from the sky. Her offspring now populate the earth.

5 Religious Rituals That Hurt Like Hell

Religious rituals aren't just day-to-day affairs, like brushing your teeth. They're highly organized and symbolic efforts to place the body in touch with the sacred. In fact, a good number of religious groups agree that pain can help achieve this goal. Here are a few of the most painful exercises undertaken to achieve contact with the sacred.

_01:: Circumcision

Circumcision is practiced by a number of cultures all over the globe and has been throughout history. But why? The Ndembu of Zambia explain the ritual by way of a story of a boy who was accidentally circumcised while playing among sharp grasses. The name of their ritual is *Mukanda*, which means "to heal and make strong." Some sociologists and anthropologists have come up with a variety of explanations for circumcision: (1) to mark captives, (2) to attract the opposite sex, (3) to indicate tribal affiliation, (4) to maintain hygiene, (5) to increase sexual pleasure, (6) to cut the ties to the mother (the rite is usually performed by older men), (7) to test bravery, (8) to sacrifice, (9) to symbolically castrate, and (10) to simulate menstruation. No one really knows (or agrees on) the answer, but that doesn't keep people from snipping away.

_02:: The Sun Dance

The Sun Dance is a sacred ritual performed by a number of Plains Indians as a reflection of the cosmos and an offering of thanks for the life and aid given by the spirits. The ritual is situated around a pole ceremonially placed in the center of a specially built lodge. The dancers enter the lodge and begin moving up and down on the balls of their feet while blowing eagle whistles and looking beyond the top of the center pole and into the sun. They fast and dance for four days, and some of them drink only what is provided from the sky. As if that doesn't sound painful enough, the young men attach themselves to the pole by piercing their skin with bones wrapped with leather. The leather is tied to the center pole, and the men lean back and stretch their skin in hope of earning special blessings from Wakan Tanka, or the Great Mysterious. Ultimately, the men stretch their skin until it breaks.

_03:: Bloodletting

Bloodletting has been called the mortar of life for Mayan culture, a powerful and sophisticated civilization that existed in what is now Guatemala for about 1200 years, beginning in 300 BCE. Gods, kings, and priests all practiced it, and it became a prominent rite of passage in Mayan culture. So what was it? Let's say a king was ascending to the throne. He would take the spine of a stingray or a blade made of obsidian and perforate his penis. Then he would draw a rope through the wound so that the blood would run down the rope to bits of bark that were lying on the ground. Once the blood had saturated the bark, the king would burn it, and a sacred serpent would appear in the smoke to provide instructions for the king.

_04:: Human Sacrifice

While it's not as widespread as some cartoons and films might suggest, human sacrifice does

---

Fake Your Way through a Conversation

THE BUDDHIST ESSENTIALS

While Buddhism is relatively popular in the West, many people don't understand its full scope. Buddhism refers to the founder, Siddhartha Gautama, who was given the title of Buddha, or Enlightened One, after he received his enlightenment under a bo tree. The Buddha taught the "Middle Way," that is, a path that is neither hedonistic nor ascetic. The Middle Way is essentially the eightfold path of right view, intention, speech, action, livelihood, effort, mindfulness, and concentration. The basic teaching of the Buddha is called the Four Noble Truths: (1) Life is suffering, (2) Suffering is caused by desire, (3) Desire can be broken, (4) Desire can be broken by following the eightfold path. There are several sects of Buddhism, but two divisions predominate: Theravada and Mahayana. Theravada claims to follow the essential teachings of the Buddha and emphasizes life in the *sangha*, or monastic community. Mahayana Buddhism is the more expansive tradition that spread into China and Japan. It includes belief in bodhisattvas, or divine helpers, who have delayed their achievement of Nirvana so that they can help all living beings.

---

exist in the world's religions. The Aztecs, in particular, gave this exchange some horrific twists. Victims were kept in cages by the community temple and fed and taunted by the locals. At the time of the killing ceremony, victims were dressed in elaborate regalia, paraded through the streets, and forced to perform established routines before they ascended the pyramid to die. At the top, priests would place a victim over the altar so that the victim's chest would protrude for the ritual. Another priest would then drive a knife into the chest and drag out a beating heart, which was then raised to the sun before the gathered people. The body would fall off the altar, then roll down the steps of the pyramid, where it would be carried away for dismemberment.

_05:: Seppuku

The term for ritual suicide is *hara-kiri* (often mispronounced in America thanks to a number of World War II films), or *seppuku*, which involves ritual disembowelment. Because hara-kiri is a ritual suicide, there is a clear set of rules to follow that align with the Bushido code, such as refraining from any emotional expression. While seppuku was restricted to men, women performed *jigai* when they were dishonored, a slicing of the jugular vein. The seppuku ritual was often arranged by the victim himself and watched by family and officials. He would first recite his shame and ask the audience for the honor of witnessing his seppuku and then stab himself deeply below the waist and turn the knife upward (showing no emotion). After drawing out the knife, he would offer his neck to the presiding executioner (an honored position).

Mmm-Mmm God:
Ways to Be Religious While Having Sex

Thanks in part to theologians from St. Paul to the Puritans, westerners have a difficult time connecting sex and religion, except in terms of sin. But sex may be the oldest religious expression, and many religious traditions recognize sexuality as central to their understanding of the sacred. Here are four ways to get some God in your groove.

_01:: Tantrism

If you've seen the term *tantric* before, you were probably looking at a sex manual or reading about Sting, but the word is actually a religious one found in Hinduism and other Eastern religions. Tantrism includes a variety of rituals that focus on transcending dualities in hopes of achieving a holy union with the primal nature of this universe. Deep, eh? In the most advanced form of Tantrism, ritu-

alistic sex was used as a vehicle for this transformation, along with other practices that were considered forbidden. Unlike our current sex manuals, however, Tantrism indicated that there were severe karmic consequences for practicing tantric sex just for pleasure. The idea was to transcend such mundane concerns as sleeping or eating and use them as symbols of a greater union. The vehicle for this transformation, however, was the thing that was to be transcended—in this case, sex.

_02:: Mysticism

You wouldn't expect medieval monks and nuns to have a sex life, but many of their writings suggest that their desire for union with God takes on erotic qualities. The type of mysticism, espoused by Bernard of Clairvaux, William of St.-Thierry, and others, emphasizes the divine union of God and humans, or spiritual marriage. As such, there is a kind of intercourse associated with this union that is, well, mystical, and much was made of the notion of believers as the bride of Christ. Women mystics were especially interested in love-mysticism, and writers like Teresa of Avila, Catherine of Siena, Theresa of Liseaux, and Julian of Norwich wrote about God in a way that had more prudish readers squirming in their chairs.

_03:: The Song of Solomon

One of the most curious texts in the Bible is called the Song of Solomon, or the Song of Songs. It's nothing less than an erotic love poem and contains some of the most explicit sexual imagery in the Bible. For example, verses 7:7–8 read, ". . . your stature is like a palm tree, your breast like its fruit. I will climb up into the palm tree. I will take hold of its fruit." Scholars have struggled to make sense of this bit of biblical erotica by calling it an allegory of God's love or a statement on marriage, but the word God is never mentioned in this text, and it certainly isn't about marriage—it's about sex.

_04:: Shinto

The most ancient writings of Japan, the Kojiki (712 CE), explain the origins of the Japanese islands and reflect a much older oral tradition that has to do with the rhythms of nature, especially fertility and rebirth. In fact, the two main gods in the story, Izanagi and Izanami, have so much sex in the beginning that their offspring populate heaven and earth. The Shinto world, then, is dependent upon sexuality, and as such, sexuality is considered natural and good, and to have sex is to reflect the work of the gods.

Steps to Founding a World Religion (✳ = required, others optional)

Does your mom think you're special? Was your childhood boring and uneventful? Have you ever gone to extremes, been rejected by your friends, or been misunderstood? You could start your own religion! Be sure to read the fine print, though.

_01:: Have a Miraculous Birth

An eventful entrance is a surefire sign that you're going to have an eventful life, and Siddhartha Gautama, or the Buddha, shows just how it's done. There were signs in the heavens and on his body at the boy's birth, and a wise man (they're everywhere) predicted that the infant would become either a great ruler or a great enlightened one. The name Siddhartha means "one who attains the goal." In fact, as we know from Christianity, a miraculous conception doesn't hurt either. In the Buddha's case, he came to his mother in the form of a dream that a white elephant impregnated her by entering her right side.

_02:: Have an Uneventful Childhood*

With some exceptions, it seems that founders of the world's religions have a relatively normal childhood. This fact works well in terms of the "plot" of the leader's life because it allows potential followers to see them much like themselves, as well as covering up those embarrassing childhood incidents that don't really go with leading a world religion. Can you imagine pictures of Buddha, Jesus, or Muhammad in the bathtub, or getting scraped up on the playground? An uneventful childhood sets the stage for an eventful adulthood.

_03:: Go to Extremes*

Again, the Buddha is a perfect example. Kept from the suffering of life by his father, who wanted him to be a ruler instead of a religious figure, Siddhartha went from being a pampered pet to the greatest ascetic who ever lived. Asceticism, the belief that the body must be punished or denied for spiritual liberation, was the prevailing religious practice in India at the time, and the Buddha took this already extreme practice to new heights. It was said that at one point he could touch his backbone through his stomach, and he learned to live on one grain of rice per day. Of course, he eventually realized that such extremes—hedonism and asceticism—were just that, and he preached the Middle Way.

_04:: Be Rejected by Your Peers*

It seems that founders of the world's religions generally have to be rejected in one form or another. This can occur because they're weird, offensive, belligerent, or some combination of the above. In the case of Muhammad, his new religion was bad for business. His anti-idolatrous stance made it hard to sell idols along the Arabian trade routes, and the businessmen were not amused (are they ever?). Similarly, the Buddha's ascetic friends rejected him when they saw that he had abandoned their way, and of course Jesus was called a blasphemer by the religious leaders of the day and punished as a criminal. So cheer up! If people just don't seem to like you or think you're weird, there may be eternal glory in your future as a founder of a world religion!

_05:: Disappear for a While

A pretty good strategy in a number of areas (such as when you don't pay your taxes), the founders of world religion usually find that having lost years or days adds to their mystery and suggests that they have had experiences that are unique. Not a bad line on the résumé for the job. Consider Jesus, who spent 40 days and nights in the desert being tempted and came out of the experience ready to begin his work. St. Paul spent 14 years in the Arabian Desert before he became the apostle to the Gentiles and converted the world to Christianity. Moses too ended up tending sheep in the desert before he had that conversation with the burning bush and demanded that Pharaoh let his people go.

_06:: Die—the More Strangely the Better*

The Buddha died from eating bad mushrooms, Muhammad expired from eating poisoned lamb, and Jesus was hung on a cross. If your birth was special, then your death had better be spectacular. Of course all the founders have to die, and some, like Abraham, live long and full lives before they meet their maker. A

Strange but True

FOUNDERS FROM NONTRADITIONAL FAMILIES

Confucius, Moses, and Muhammad—three significant men in three significant religions. Sure, they lived in vastly different times and places, but they do share one trait: they each are products of single- or no-parent childhoods. Confucius lost his father shortly after he was born, and he claimed that the difficulties he and his mother faced enabled him to do the kind of work a noble would never have to consider. He did note, however, "It is not hard to chafe at poverty." The story of Moses is one of the most dramatic in the Hebrew Bible, or Old Testament, and the drama begins at birth and lasts to his death. Moses was born at a time when Pharaoh had declared that all male children born to the Hebrews were to be killed, so Moses' mother hid him for three months but eventually had to do something more drastic. The solution? She put him in a basket along the Nile River, and Pharaoh's daughter found him and raised him as her own son. As for Muhammad, he was born in 570 CE, but his father was already dead when he emerged from the womb. Even more tragic, his mother died when Muhammad was six years old. From then on, Muhammad stayed first with his paternal grandfather, then with his uncle Abu Talib, and like many other founders, he grew up in poverty.

bizarre death, however, puts a fine point on the unique life of a founder and makes for a dramatic ending to the story (plus guaranteed TV-movie success).

_07:: Live Again*

As we know, sequels can be good or bad, but they're never quite the same as the original. If you want to found your own religion, it really helps to be resurrected or live again in some fashion. The Buddha did it by passing into Nirvana, a state free from desire and suffering. Jesus had a more active post-death existence, proving himself to the doubtful Thomas and eventually judging the living and the dead. More important, perhaps, the second life of the founder promises a second life for the followers. Best to keep the details of this second life as murky as possible lest it appear to resemble this life too much, but promises of a new body and a cool place to live work well.

_08:: Watch Your Followers Misconstrue Your Teachings, Sometimes to the Point of Bloodshed*

There is always a crucial moment in the life of a religion when the founder dies (or just goes away). What to do then? When the founder is alive, there is opportunity for him to correct misinterpretations, adjust expectations, and comment on current events, but when he's gone, these functions are usually replaced by ethical systems that purport to get at the founder's teachings. Legend has it that a split occurred in the followers of the Buddha only one day after his death. Before a year was up, they had to call a council to sort things out, which didn't work. Soon there were 4 sects of Buddhism, and within 10 years of the Buddha's death, there were 16. The problem is that the death of the founder leaves a power vacuum, and history has proven that we are all too willing to fill that vacuum with our own ideas about what the founder meant, and all too often we are willing to prove our point with the point of a gun.

6 Versions of Heaven

Ah, heaven. Marx called it a carrot used by the wealthy to keep us working hard for little money. After all, the real rewards are supposed to come much later. But despite what Marx had to say, the notion of a happy afterlife won't quite go away. Here are six pleasant resorts the righteous can look forward to in the afterlife.

_01:: Heaven: Judaism

As one of the oldest and most influential religions in existence, Judaism might be expected to be the source of our most profound notions of heaven, but it isn't. In fact, there is no clear indication of a heaven or afterlife in the Jewish scriptures at all, which leads to a lot of debate on the subject. Two typical positions are those of the Pharisees, who believed that there was an implied notion of an afterlife, and the Sad-

THE PROBLEM OF EVIL

One of the most vexing problems in religion is the existence of evil, and the problem can be summarized in a series of propositions:

1. God is omnipotent, or all-powerful.
2. God is omniscient, or all-knowing.
3. God is omnipresent, or everywhere.
4. God is benevolent, or all-good.
5. Evil exists.

Logically, one of these statements must be false. Why? Because a god who has all the characteristics of propositions 1–4 cannot allow evil to exist. That does not mean of course that believers in God cannot hold all these beliefs; they often do. What it means is that they cannot hold them philosophically; they must resort to some kind of mysticism or lack of faith in the mind's ability to understand the world in order to hold them. Both of these options are unavailable to philosophers. Other believers, wanting to maintain their philosophical integrity, have rejected one of the four propositions (usually the first). But the revered St. Augustine tried a different approach: he rejected the fifth proposition. Augustine knew that if evil exists, and if God is the creator, then God had to create evil, so he argues that evil is "the absence of the good" and has no independent existence. It can, however, help us to appreciate the good by showing us what the absence of the good entails. Though he was trying to provide a solution to the problem of evil for Christians, some of them felt that Augustine's measures sacrificed too much of the Christian worldview since the fight against evil is central to their beliefs.

ducees, who pointed out that there was no biblical evidence of such. Over the millennia, Jews have come to believe in various versions of heaven, some of which occur after the Messiah comes and involve the righteous dead coming back to life. Still, overall, Judaism is more concerned with life in the here and now.

_02:: Paradise: Zoroastrianism

It was the ancient Persians who gave us the word *paradise*, which means a walled garden or park, and Zoroastrianism in particular gave

us notions of the afterlife that were adopted and/or adapted by Jews, Christians, and Muslims. Zoroastrianism is also interesting because, unlike other religions, it claims that everyone will eventually get to heaven, though it might take awhile. The paradise of Zoroastrianism is attained the fourth day after death by crossing the Bridge of the Separator, which widens when the righteous approach it. (See the next section for what happens to the wicked.) The righteous soul crosses the bridge and is met by a beautiful maiden who is the physical and feminine embodiment of all his good works on earth. He is then escorted into the House of Song to await the Last Day. On this day, everyone will be purified and live in a new world absent of evil and full of youthful rejoicing.

_03:: Heaven: Christianity

The Christian notion of heaven is one of singing and rejoicing before God in a "new heaven and a new earth." It also reflects Christianity's roots in Judaism because this new heaven contains a city called New Jerusalem. There are elaborate descriptions of the city in the book of Revelation. New Jerusalem has a wall and 12 gates, and on each gate is the name of one of the tribes of Israel along with an angel. There are also 12 foundations, 1 each for the 12 apostles. In fact, we even know the size of the New Jerusalem: 1400 miles square with a 200-foot wall. The structure itself is made of all kinds of precious stones, some of which have not yet been identified on this earth. There is a river of "the water of life," which flows from God's throne, and trees of life line the banks of the river and produce fruit every month. Believers will have God's name written on their foreheads, and all pain, tears, and death will disappear forever.

_04:: Paradise: Islam

The Islamic version of heaven is a paradise for those whose good works have outweighed the bad as determined by the straight path laid out in the Quran. Heaven is a garden where the faithful lie upon couches in a climate-controlled environment surrounded by "bashful, dark-eyed virgins, chaste as the sheltered eggs of ostriches." They will drink from crystal goblets and silver vessels as "immortal youths" hover about them looking like "scattered pearls." The believers will be clothed in green silk and brocade and will wear silver bracelets, and they will "drink a pure draught" drawn from Allah's own source as a reward for their striving and patience.

_05:: Moksha: Hinduism

Eastern religions don't really have notions of heaven like those in the West. Instead, they usually offer some kind of release from illusion and suffering in the present world. The Hindu Upanishads are philosophical portions of the Vedas, Hinduism's oldest sacred text, and in them the notions of the self and afterlife are developed. According to the Upanishads, our actions connect us to this world of appearances, which is in fact illusory. What is real is Brahman, the ultimate reality that transcends our sensory experiences. Unfortunately, we live in ignorance of Brahman and act according to our illusions. This action (karma) causes us to participate in the cycle of death and rebirth (samsara—see next section) from which it's difficult to escape. Thus, if you can escape your ignorance and realize that ultimately you are not you but Brahman itself, then you can achieve release from the cycle of death and rebirth. This release is called moksha.

_06:: Nirvana: Buddhism

One of the four noble truths of the Buddha is that suffering is caused by desire, the desire to have but also the desire to be. Desire is *tanha*, or a burning that keeps us caught in the web of illusion that is our ego. The Buddha taught that desire is a flame that burns us, causes suffering, and keeps us tied to the cycle of death and rebirth because the flame continues burning into the next life. What we hope for is Nirvana, or the extinguishing of that flame, which is also the end of suffering.

Abandon All Hope, Ye Who Enter Here: Versions of Hell

Walt Whitman wrote that "the fear of hell is little or nothing to me," but he was Walt Whitman. For most religious people, the fear of hell is a powerful motivation to believe in a faith, avoid sin, and generally behave. Here are seven pretty effective motivational scenarios.

_01:: Hell: Judaism

As with their view of heaven, Jews have an ambiguous version of hell. The Hebrew Bible makes little mention of it except as a place where the spirits of the dead reside (Sheol). There is, however, the term *Gehinnom*, which refers to a valley in which children were reportedly sacrificed to the god Molech. Eventually, this valley became a refuse dump that was constantly burning, which provided a powerful metaphor for a place to send sinners. In later Judaism, hell is the place of punishment for unbelievers, but according to the rabbinical texts, they will probably stay there for no more than a year.

_02:: The Chinvat Bridge: Zoroastrianism

The Bridge of Separation, as it's also known, is the one that all people must walk after they die. For the righteous it broadens and leads to a beautiful maiden, but for the less than righteous, it turns on its side and becomes like a razor. The ancient god Mithra is there with a scale to balance the good and evil deeds done during one's lifetime, and if evil deeds prevail, then the soul is tormented by an old hag before it falls off the bridge into hell. The torments of the evil go well beyond Dante's imagination and focus on punishments directly related to their evil deeds. Zoroastrian hell may be the most horrific of all, and a text called the Vision of Arda Viraf describes it in all its gory glory. Fortunately, everyone eventually leaves Zoroastrian hell. They are purified and join the righteous in the reign of the god Ahura Mazda.

_03:: Hades: Greek

Hades is actually the name of the lord of the dead and ruler of the netherworld, but the name became so associated with the place that the two merged, so Hades is also the place the dead go. Hades rules this world with Persephone—whom he abducted from the earth-goddess Demeter—and a number of other figures such as Thanatos, Hypnos, Charon, and Cerberus. Hades represents the place of eternal punishment for evildoers, where the sinners are put on horrifying display. Such examples include Tityos bound while a vulture eats his liver, Tantalus thirsty and hungry but unable to eat the fruit just above his head or drink the water at his feet, and Sisyphus forced to push a rock up a hill only to have it roll back again for eternity.

_04:: Hell: Christianity

Christian hell seems at one level to be a combination of the Jewish idea of Gehinnom, where there is eternal burning, and Hades, where there is eternal punishment. In fact, the Greek word for *hell* in the New Testament is often *hades*, and Jesus uses the word *Gehenna* (a version of *Gehinnom*) to indicate the place for sinners where the fire is not quenched and the worm does not die. The book of Revelation indicates that those whose names are not found written in the Book of Life are thrown into the lake of fire. In fact, Death and Hades themselves are thrown into the lake of fire in the end. In addition to these texts, Dante did much to embellish the Christian notion of hell in his *Inferno*.

_05:: Hell: Islam

The Quran, the sacred text of Islam, usually speaks of heaven and hell in the same passage, perhaps in order to provide a dramatic contrast. Hell is often described as "an evil resting place" and the "Fire." But fire is just the beginning of the torment in hell because the fire is like a wall enclosing the wicked, and when they cry out, they are showered with water as "hot as molten brass," which scalds their faces. It gets worse. The unbelievers wear garments of fire and are lashed with rods of iron, and if they try to escape, they are dragged back and told to "taste the torment of the Conflagration."

_06:: Samsara: Hinduism

Again, the Eastern religions have a very different notion of the afterlife, although in some sects of Hinduism, Buddhism, and Taoism, there are heavens and hells that are similar to Western ideas of the same. Hindu hell, however, is traditionally a continuation of life on earth called samsara. Samsara is the endless cycle of death and rebirth that is the result of our ignorance of the ultimate reality of the universe. The word means "to wander across," as in lifetimes, and samsara is the result of karma or actions taken in this life that will determine the nature of one's rebirth and the caste one is born into.

_07:: The Bardo: Tibetan Buddhism

One of the most detailed and elaborate depictions of the afterlife is from the Tibetan Buddhist text Bardo Thodol, or the Tibetan Book of the Dead. As the title suggests, the book deals with dying or, more accurately, with the state of Between, and there are many "betweens": birth and death, sleeping and waking, waking and trance, and three others within the death-rebirth between. The Bardo Thodol teaches that after death, the soul exists in the Bardo for 49 days in a between that can lead to Nirvana or back into rebirth. One of the factors that influences the soul's ultimate location is the dying itself. A good death tends to push the soul toward enlightenment, while a bad death can move it toward rebirth in the world. Tibetan Buddhists thus spend a lot of time and energy in helping the dying.

• •

Women Who Shaped World Religions

• •

If you haven't noticed it already, women don't play a prominent role in the world's religions. There are plenty of reasons for this, including patriarchy, sexism, and fear on the part of men. But there are significant moments when women appear in religion, and when they do, the effect is usually powerful. Here are some famous and not-so-famous women who shaped world religions.

• •

_01:: Buffalo Woman: Lakota

The story of Buffalo Woman is that of a Lakota sacred figure who comes to the people in a time of starvation and shows them how to use the sacred pipe. In the end she walks away and becomes in turn a black, a brown, a red, and a white buffalo calf. Just after she disappears, buffalo come in great numbers and give themselves willingly to the people, thus setting the stage for a long and harmonious relationship between the buffalo and the Lakota in which the former provide everything the latter need. The appropriate response of the Lakota is to perform the sacred pipe ceremony, which reminds them of all their relations and of Wakan Tanka, or the Great Mysterious.

_02:: Isis: Egyptian

Isis and her famous brother-husband, Osiris, were two of the most powerful gods in the ancient world, and Isis in particular was worshiped in Egypt and throughout the Mediterranean for centuries. She was also a favorite goddess of the Romans. Isis worship withstood the growth of Christianity and remained viable until the sixth century CE. Her qualities and attributes are those of the Great Mother, especially in her fertility symbolism. The daughter of the sky goddess Nut and the earth god Neb, Isis was often represented by a cow, and her power was considered great, especially for warding off evil.

_03:: Lilith: Judaism

The story of Lilith is one that has animated contemporary religious feminism because Lilith was a rebel, a woman who wanted to define her own sexuality and was punished for it. According to rabbinic legend, Lilith was Adam's first wife, and she refused to lie beneath him during intercourse because she too was made of dust and should not have to be in an inferior position. When Adam tried to take her by force, she uttered the secret name of God and fled to the desert. Later Jewish tradition (and superstition) has Lilith as a demoness who lives in the desert and gives birth to 100 demons a day. She also visits and strangles infants and sexually assaults men who sleep alone. Lilith's punishment and characterization are seen by some contemporary feminists as the result of male reaction to female independence.

What's the Difference?

SEPARATING THE SUNNIS FROM THE SHIITES

Like every religion, Islam has its different expressions, and these days it's become increasingly important to understand the differences between them. Most Muslims are Sunni (about 85%). They consider themselves to be in line with the most ancient understanding of Islam and focus their attention on the Quran and community and family life. The Shiites were formed as a result of a schism in Islam, one that initially concerned leadership succession but grew into a full-fledged theology of its own. Shiites believe that revelation can continue through the imams, religious leaders who speak for God, and these imams never die but wait in hiding to return to earth. There are either 7 or 12 imams, depending on the tradition. Shiites also have a messiah figure, called a Mahdi, who will bring justice to the earth. Because their first leader, Ali, was murdered, Shiites tend to understand martyrdom as a high expression of faith. Interestingly, Shiites tend to mistrust the Quran since it does not mention their leader.

_04:: Khadija: Islam

Khadija was unusual in the world of ancient Arabia. She was a 40-year-old woman who owned her own caravan. She was also a widow when she met a deeply religious and influential man named Muhammad, who was 15 years her junior. Soon Khadija became his only wife in a culture that permitted polygamy, and they were married for 25 years. Khadija's influence on Muhammad was enormous: She provided money and wisdom to a tortured orphan who was struggling with painful and strange visions. Her wealth alone enabled Muhammad to pursue his religious vocation, and Khadija was one of the first converts to the new religion of Islam.

_05:: Amaterasu: Shinto

Amaterasu is the sun goddess of Japan. This is unusual in itself since solar deities are usually male (Egypt is another exception). But in spite of that, the goddess has been extraordinarily influential. Amaterasu is so highly integrated into Japanese society that her emblem, a rising sun, adorns Japan's national flag. There is also a national Japanese holiday devoted to her; the Great Festival of the Sun Goddess is celebrated on July 17 with all-day street processions and parties. Amaterasu is also known as the ancestor of Japan's imperial family; consequently, all royal families in Japan trace their lineage back to her. Even today, an important part of the Japanese coronation ceremony takes place at the temple at Ise where Amaterasu is believed to reside.

_06:: Mary: Christianity

As the mother of Jesus, Mary is the most important saint in Catholicism, and reverence for her began early in the history of Christianity. She became the emblem of the pain of love in having to see her son crucified for the world, and her title as "bearer of God" elevated her to a status where she is seen as reigning with her son in heaven. Considered immaculately conceived—or born without sin—Mary was said to be taken directly to heaven upon her death. The Catholic use of the rosary is an expression of Mary's importance to the faith since it entails meditation on various aspects of the life of Jesus and Mary and includes the Ave Maria, or Hail Mary.

3 (or 3 Million) Famous Gods

While not all religions have deities (e.g., Confucianism, Taoism, Buddhism), gods do play an important role in the world's religions. Their personalities are varied, but they usually represent human ideals in some form and thus are recognizable to us. At the same time, they're certainly more than human and thus are objects of fear, reverence, and worship. Here are three gods everyone should know.

_01:: Yahweh

Yahweh is an approximation of the secret name that God gave to Moses as he spoke from the burning bush. Yahweh is also called Jehovah, and when the name is used in most bibles, it appears as small capitals to distinguish it from the other names of God, such as Elohim or Adonai. The reason Yahweh or Jehovah is an approximation is that the ancient Hebrews refused to pronounce the name for fear of taking it in vain, which is one of the Ten Commandments. Apparently, the name

FIVE MYTHS ABOUT THE BIBLE

1. There is a Bible.

There is no Bible; there are only copies of copies of copies. The original text(s), however, does not exist.

2. There is one Bible.

The Bible came into being over a long period and went through many revisions before its present form. Not surprisingly, not everyone agreed with the edits, so there are a number of Bibles in existence. For example, there are additional books in Catholic Bibles, a different order and structure in Jewish Bibles, and a whole series of other gospels and texts that did not make it into the New Testament. As late as the 1500s, Martin Luther was still arguing that the New Testament book of James should be expunged.

3. The Bible was written down from the beginning.

Both the Old and New Testaments begin in oral cultures—that is, cultures that depended on word of mouth and storytelling to convey information. This means that the stories we read in the Bible were circulated orally, sometimes centuries before they were written down.

4. The writers of the Bible knew the Bible.

If you think about it a moment, you'll realize that the biblical authors didn't have the Bible in front of them because it was still being developed. Often biblical writers show absolutely no awareness of other biblical texts. One exception of course is that the authors of the New Testament knew the Old. But Paul, for example, cannot refer to the Gospels because they weren't written down when he was writing. In fact, the Gospels weren't written until 40 to 70 years after Jesus died and was resurrected and some 20 years after Paul's first letters.

5. The author is the author.

Ever wonder how Moses wrote about his own death? Well, he probably didn't. Ever wonder how Paul got so many bylines in the New Testament? He probably shouldn't have. Our notions of authorship are relatively new, and during the time when the Bible was being composed, it was common for people to write using more famous or authoritative people's names.

was pronounced once a year by the high priest on the Day of Atonement, or Yom Kippur, but since that ceremony hasn't taken place for 2,000 years, the correct pronunciation's been lost. Add to this the fact that written Hebrew from this period didn't have vowels, and there's even more confusion. The name of this god, then, appears as YHWH or JHVH in English. Whatever the pronunciation, Yahweh is a unique god who acts in history on behalf of the Jewish people, such as when he led them out of slavery in Egypt.

_02:: The Hindu Pantheon

Hinduism, in addition to being the oldest of the recorded religions, has also given us a pantheon that is enormous and diverse. There is a god or goddess to help with anything in life, but Hindus are typically devoted to one god in particular. This god or goddess might be Parvati, a princess who nurtures her subjects, or Ganesha, the elephant-headed god who helps solve everyday problems, or a whole host of others. Three gods in particular, however, have received the most attention in Hinduism, and they are sometimes called the Trimurti, or "three forms." Brahma is considered the creator god, Vishnu is the preserver, and Shiva is the destroyer. Hindus do not, however, separate these functions as easily as one might think since each of the gods serves some of these functions.

_03:: Mithra

Mithra is an ancient god who appears in Persia and reached the zenith of his popularity in Rome. Older than Jesus by several centuries, the legend of Mithra has him being born of a virgin on December 25 and visited by shepherds and magi. He had 12 disciples, healed the sick, and cast out devils, and was often depicted as a lion or lamb. Mithra rose again around the vernal equinox (March 21) and later ascended into heaven. Obviously, there is some speculation that Christianity was a new kind of Mithraism. Mithra is associated with the bull because of a legend where he captured and then sacrificed a sacred bull, and from this sacrifice came everything that was good in the world. Mithra also appears in Zoroastrianism as the god who weighs a person's deeds on a scale.

Straight from the Cutting Room Floor: Texts That Didn't Make It into the Bible

6

That's right! If you've been looking for the director's cut of the Bible, with all the extra features, you've come to the right place. The reasons why these texts were cut vary, but they generally have to do with the prevailing theological and cultural concerns at the time the Bible was being assembled. Regardless, here are some texts that some people never wanted you to know about.

_01:: Susanna and the Elders (Daniel and Susanna)

Though it sounds like a '50s girl group, it's actually a wonderful little story that includes a beautiful woman unjustly charged and a young Daniel (of lion's den fame) who defends her with great cunning. Susanna was the wife of Joachim, a rich and honored man who was often consulted by the elders for his wisdom. Two of these elders began to lust after Susanna, and one day, while she was bathing in the garden, the two lecherous elders, who had

said, and as Susanna was being led away to be killed, a young man named Daniel called out that she was innocent. He proved it by questioning the men separately and asking under which tree in the garden Susanna had consorted with this man. When the men gave two different answers, they were killed and Susanna spared.

_02:: Judith

In another story about a powerful woman, Judith is a beautiful widow who is also a powerful warrior. Judith lives in Bethulia, which is being attacked by the hated Assyrians. Led by the Assyrian king's best general, Holofernes, the army captures the water supply, and the elders of Bethulia decide that they have five days before they must surrender. Judith, however, is having none of it. Until this point, she'd been in mourning for her dead husband, but now she removes her mourning clothes and dresses herself to be alluring. She then leaves the city and hands herself over to the Assyrians surrounding it. Holofernes is impressed with her and asks her to dine with him hoping to seduce her, but he gets drunk and passes out. Judith takes his sword and cuts his head off. Then she returns to the Hebrew camp and orders that the head be placed on the wall. When the Assyrians see it, they are routed by the Hebrews, and everyone praises God and Judith. While the story isn't included in Bibles, it has been the subject of several works of art.

_03:: Tobit

Tobit is another story of Jews in exile. In this case the main character, Tobit, is a man who has fallen on hard times in addition to being in exile. Part of his difficulty comes from trying

hidden themselves there, asked her to have sex with them or they'd tell everyone that they'd seen her with another man. Susanna bravely refused to sin with the men and chose to face execution instead. The men did as they

to be righteous under the reign of Sennacherib and other kings. In particular, Tobit buries the dead left behind by the evil king in direct opposition to him. He is blind and poor, but his fortunes change when his son Tobias and the archangel Raphael begin to work on his behalf. In the process, Tobias, gets a wife, the widow (seven times) Sarah. On their wedding night, Tobias and Sarah are attacked by a demon, but Tobit's pennance has paid off. The archangel Raphael has already forewarned the family, clueing Tobias in to a unique way of repelling the demon using fish guts and a scent that would repel any hound of hell.

_04:: The Infancy Gospel of Thomas

This gospel, which is very different from the Gospel of Thomas, is a narrative containing a number of stories about the childhood of Jesus. The Bible is silent on Jesus' childhood except for a brief mention of a visit to the Temple, but the Infancy Gospel of Thomas tells us that Jesus could be quite an unruly child with a temper and the power to act on it. For example, in one story Jesus is making clay figurines of birds by a creek on the Sabbath. When he is reproached by an elder, Jesus claps his hands and tells the birds to fly away—and they do. When Jesus is run over by a boy in the street, he tells the unfortunate boy that he will continue no longer. The boy falls down dead. Of course, Jesus does do some good things in this gospel. When his father, Joseph, a carpenter by trade, cuts a board too short, Jesus is able to stretch it for him.

_05:: The Gospel of Mary

This isn't Mary the mother of Jesus but Mary Magadalene, the woman from whom seven devils were cast. She is generally represented as a sinner whom Jesus saved. In this gospel, however, the disciples are anxious and fearful about going out to preach the gospel because if the ruling powers killed Jesus, surely they'll kill them too. Mary Magdalene stands up in their midst and tells them to be of good cheer and to remember the words of Jesus. Peter encourages her to continue because "we know that the Savior loved you more than other women." Mary goes on to describe her mystical vision of Jesus and their secret conversation, but Andrew and Peter turn on her and argue that Jesus would never have revealed such secrets to a woman. Levi (Matthew), however, comes to Mary's aid and reminds them once again that Jesus loved her more than them. They then go out and preach.

_06:: Acts of Paul and Thecla

The Apostle Paul was a traveler, and as travelers can, he got into some interesting situations. This text describes Paul preaching in a church (a house, really) of one of his friends. He is described as "a man small in size, bald-headed, bandy-legged, well-built, with eyebrows meeting, rather long-nosed, full of grace." Thecla, a virgin betrothed to a man named Thamyris, sits by her window, listening to Paul preach, and she finds that she cannot tear herself away. For three days and nights, she sits there without eating until her fiancé is called to deal with her. Thamyris makes inquiries as to this man Paul because Thecla "thus loves the stranger." His friends suggest having Paul brought up on charges of teaching heresy, and so it is done. Thecla, however, follows Paul and wallows on the ground where he is imprisoned. Paul is scourged, and Thecla is ordered to be burned, but when the fires reach her, she is not consumed.

Contributors

Will Pearson and **Mangesh Hattikudur** met as freshmen at Duke University. Cleverly ignoring the lures of law school and investment banking, the pair cofounded *mental_floss* magazine and have been grinning ever since. This is their first book.

When she's not flossing, **Elizabeth Hunt** works in the publishing department of the International Reading Association. Previously she worked as the project coordinator of the book *Watch It Made in the USA, 3rd Edition*. This is Liz's second project with Mangesh—they met while working on their high school newspaper, *Tiger Pause*.

Founded in 2001, ***mental_floss* magazine**, currently available at newsstands everywhere, has received rave reviews in a variety of publications including the *Washington Post*, the *Chicago Tribune*, *Entertainment Weekly,* and *Newsweek*. The publication is regularly featured on *CNN Headline News*, and was named one of the top ten new magazines of 2001 by *Library Journal*.

Alexei Bayer, a coauthor of *mental_floss*'s economics column "Know Your Dough," is a New York-based economist and writer contributing to a number of national publications and *The Globalist* Web site. He writes a column for *Vedomosti*, Russia's leading business daily.

Karen Bernd, Ph.D., is a professor of biology at Davidson College in Davidson, NC. A molecular biologist by training, Bernd has authored pedagogical material to help others integrate animations and current research in their biology courses, and her research has been published in leading scientific journals.

Robert Cumming is an art critic and writer. Initially a curator in the Tate Gallery Education Department, he went on to become the founder and chairman of the renowned Christies Education programs in London, New York, and Paris. He writes extensively for the British and American press, including *mental_floss*, and his bestselling art books have been translated into thirty different languages worldwide. He lives in Buckinghamshire, UK, with his wife and two daughters.

Curry Guinn is a researcher in artificial intelligence at RTI International in Research Triangle Park, NC, and an adjunct assistant professor at Duke University. His current research focuses on developing synthetic humans that converse, display emotion, and react to the world according to their personality.

Former newspaperman and sometime college journalism instructor **Peter Haugen** is the author of *World History for Dummies*. A contributor to *mental_floss*, he writes regularly for *History* magazine and is working on a history of biology in the 20th century. He lives in Madison, WI, with his wife and two sons.

Bill Hauser, Ph.D., is currently an assistant professor of marketing and an adjunct professor of sociology at the University of Akron in Akron, OH. After two decades of directing market research for Fortune 500 companies, Bill is currently fulfilling his lifelong dream of teaching, research, and writing.

William Irwin is associate professor of philosophy at King's College in Wilkes-Barre, PA. He is the editor of *The Matrix and Philosophy*, *The Simpsons and Philosophy*, *Seinfeld and Philosophy*, and *The Death and Resurrection of the Author*? He is the author of *Intentionalist Interpretation* and the coauthor of *Critical Thinking*.

Martin W. Lewis is a lecturer in international relations at Stanford University. He was educated at the University of California at Santa Cruz (B.A. in environmental studies) and the University of California at Berkeley (Ph.D. in geography). He is the author (or coauthor) of several books, including *The Myth of Conti-*

nents: A Critique of Metageography and *Diversity Amid Globalization: World Regions, Environment, Development*.

Richard A. Muller is a professor of physics at the University of California at Berkeley. His research includes astrophysics, geophysics, elementary particles, and climate. He has received a MacArthur Prize and the NSF Alan T. Waterman Award. He currently teaches a course called "Physics for Future Presidents."

Shane Pitts is a cognitive psychologist at Birmingham-Southern College in Birmingham, AL. His primary research interests are memory distortions, social cognition, and stereotyping. He enjoys art, basketball, spending time with his girlfriend, and diet Mountain Dew (not necessarily in that order). He isn't as good a swimmer, but is younger and taller than exactly one other author of the psychology chapter in this book.

Greg Salyer teaches English at Longwood University in Farmville, VA, and has taught courses in literature, philosophy, and religion for twelve years. He is the author of *Leslie Marmon Silko*, a critical introduction to the Native American writer's work, and the editor of *Literature and Theology at Century's End*. He has published numerous articles on Native American and contemporary literature, religion, and film, and is currently working on a book on Native American writer Louise Erdrich.

Valarie Samulski is a choreographer, dancer, and writer exploring the intersection of social, cultural, and political vertices in the arts. A summa cum laude graduate of Duke University, she is now teaching and performing throughout the United States, and makes her home in Fort Greene, Brooklyn.

Dr. Joe Schwarcz is a chemistry professor and director of the McGill University Office for Science and Society. He has received numerous awards for teaching as well as for interpreting science for the public. He writes a regular newspaper column entitled "The Right Chemistry" and is the author of four books.

Kenneth Silber is a writer based in New York City and coauthor of *mental_floss*'s economics column "Know Your Dough." Silber writes frequently for TechCentralStation.com. His articles have appeared in various publications, including *Book*, *Commentary*, *National Review*, the *New York Post*, *Reason*, and *Skeptical Inquirer*.

Royce Simpson received his Ph.D. in Experimental Psychology from the University of Alabama in 1992. He is currently an associate professor at Spring Hill College in Mobile, AL, where his teaching load includes courses in cognition, learning & behavior, and social psychology. His current research interests include an examination of gender differences in autobiographical memory.

Pop culture contributor **Christopher Smith** works as an advertising writer for The Richards Group in Dallas, TX. His own 30- and 60-second contributions to pop culture include award-winning spots for Motel 6 and many others. He is also a veteran performer with Dallas's Ad-Libs Improv Comedy Troupe. A native of upstate New York and graduate of Penn State, he lives in Dallas with his wife, Heather, and their baby daughter, Clara.

Scott Speck, conductor, regularly leads orchestras in the United States and around the world. He has conducted at the Kennedy Center, San Francisco's Opera House, the Paris Opera, and London's Royal Opera House at Covent Garden. Scott is the coauthor of three of the world's bestselling books on the arts: *Classical Music for Dummies*, *Opera for Dummies*, and *Ballet for Dummies*.

John Timpane is the Commentary Page editor for the *Philadelphia Inquirer*. He is also a musician, a poet, and the author of *Writing Worth Reading* (with Nancy H. Packer), *It Could Be Verse*, and *Poetry for Dummies*.

FORBIDDEN
KNOWLEDGE

Also from **mental**_floss:

mental_floss *presents: Condensed Knowledge*

mental_floss *presents: Instant Knowledge*

mental_floss presents:

FORBIDDEN
KNOWLEDGE

edited by

Will Pearson,
Mangesh Hattikudur,
and Elizabeth Hunt

HARPER

NEW YORK • LONDON • TORONTO • SYDNEY

Acknowledgments

mental_floss would like to thank the Devil for making a book about sins possible. Also, Napoléon, Caligula, Nero, Boss Tweed (and the entire Tammany Hall gang), Genghis Khan, Atilla and all the Huns, Shanta Hattikudur, the victors who wrote history (you know who you are), and Voldemort. It's your inspiration that truly fills this book.

We'd also like to thank Winslow Taft, Lisako Koga, Sandy Wood, and Kara Kovalchik.

Finally, we thank Greg Chaput at Collins for his expert editorial guidance and support.

now with 20% more evil!

FORBIDDEN KNOWLEDGE

CAUTION!
Contains Seven Deadly Ingredients

Introduction

There's no dearth of great literature in the library here at *mental_floss*. Sure, you've got your heavyweights: Beckett, Proust, even a little section dedicated to obscure Chilean playwrights. But perhaps the most telling title on the rack is a dog-eared copy of the picture book *The Fire Cat*.

From the outset it looks like an ordinary kid's tale. Oversized pages, colorful drawings, easy-to-pronounce words. But if you turn a couple of pages in, you'll learn in giant I Can Read Book print that Pickles, who's under the care of Mrs. Goodkind, is neither a good cat nor a bad cat. He is a good *and* bad cat.

Profound. He also has big paws with which he plans to do big things, but that's neither here nor there.

What we mean to say is that we can relate. See, the cats at *mental_floss* often get pegged as a little too good. You know? All toothy grins and saccharine-sweet reputations. And yeah, we've got the good grades to back it up. Not to mention the clean-cut hairstyles, and the finely honed sense for when to insert a please

or thank-you without overdoing it. And then there's the press: endless coverage of us helping old women cross streets and plucking kittens out of trees. But don't let that fool you. Look a little deeper and you'll find there's more than a little yin that comes with all this yang.

The truth is, we're kind of bad seeds. Rebels, baby. Catch us when the media's not around and you might see us doing something c-r-a-z-y. Like standing on a moving bus—you know, just for the thrill of it. Or going into a library and using our *out*door voices. Sometimes we'll even bite into a piece of fruit without giving it a good rinse first. Does it taste a little sweeter? Oh, you know it does.

Okay. While we might not be as bad as we'd like to believe, there is some comfort in knowing that someone's made up of more than just medals and virtues. And history's exactly the same. It's not the hearts of gold and battles won that are interesting. It's the smirks and quirks. It's juicy anecdotes. It's history's greatest figures telling Jiminy Cricket to shove off, then getting caught on the wrong side of their conscience.

Take Ben Franklin, for instance. Doesn't his whole perfect patriot, Renaissance man act get a little more intriguing when you find out he was sort of a man slut? Or Adam Smith's Invisible Hand of Capitalism. Don't the yawns come a little slower when you watch it waving at developing nations with just one finger?

Forbidden Knowledge is exactly that. It's the worst history has to offer, all deliciously broken up into seven sin-tastic chapters. If our first book, *Condensed Knowledge,* was every-thing you feel you're supposed to know, this follow-up is the exact opposite: it's all the stuff you shouldn't. It's every bawdy story and dirty secret your history teacher wanted to tell you, but couldn't for fear of losing his or her job. So thumb through the pages. Find a name, person, or place you used to admire. And then read on. We're betting the naughty ending will make you smile.

Enjoy.
Will, Mangesh, and Liz

PRIDE

④ Utopian Communities (That Bombed Miserably)
④ Dictator Grooming Tips ⑦ Pampered Celebrities
④ Greatest Hoaxes of All Time ④ Mandatory Fashion Trends
⑤ Writers Who Fancied Themselves Peerless ⑤ Artists Who Were
Full of Themselves ⑥ Secret Societies That Ain't All That
Secret ⑥ Worst Miscalculations ⑦ Insane Soviet Projects
⑤ Bodies That've Never Been Found ④ Structures Built as Symbols of
National Pride ⑤ World Leaders Obsessed with Their Own Images
⑥ Recent Cases Where Diversity Would Have Helped
⑤ Individuals Who Taught Us How to Sing the Blues
The Secret Lives of ④ Civil Activists ⑨ Famous Bastards Who Made
Their Mark   The Dish on ⑤ National Anthems ⑥ Ignominious Things
Named for Napoléon Bonaparte ⑤ Mortals with Minor God Complexes

Talk of the Town:
Utopian Communities (That Bombed Miserably)

4

Every once in a while a proud little community will sprout up just to let the world know how Utopia should be run. With chins raised almost as high as ideals, the community marches forth to be an example of perfection. But in most cases, all that harmonious marching gets tripped up pretty quickly. Here are four "perfect" communities that whizzed and sputtered thanks to human nature.

_01:: Brook Farm, or Ripley's Follow Me or Not

Probably the best-known utopian community in America, Brook Farm was founded in 1841 in West Roxbury, Massachusetts, by George and Sophia Ripley. The commune was built on a 200-acre farm with four buildings and centered on the ideals of radical social reform and self-reliance. For free tuition in the community school and one year's worth of room and board, the residents were asked to complete 300 days of labor by either farming, working in the manufacturing shops, performing domestic chores or grounds maintenance, or planning the community's recreation projects. The community prospered in 1842–1843 and was visited by numerous dignitaries and utopian writers. However, Ripley joined the unpopular Fourierism movement, which meant that soon the young people (out of a "sense of honor") had to do all the dirty work like repairing roads, cleaning stables, and slaughtering the animals. This caused many residents, especially the younger ones, to leave. Things went downhill from there. The community

was hit by an outbreak of smallpox followed by fire and finally collapsed in 1847.

_02:: Fruitlands: A Utopian Community (for Six Months Anyway)

After visiting Brook Farm and finding it almost too worldly by their standards, Bronson Alcott (the father of Louisa May) and Charles Lane founded the Fruitlands Commune in June 1843, in Harvard, Massachusetts. Structured around the British reformist model, the commune's members were against the ownership of property, were political anarchists, believed in free love, and were vegetarians. The group of 11 adults and a small number of children were forbidden to eat meat or use any animal products such as honey, wool, beeswax, or manure. They were also not allowed to use animals for labor and only planted produce that grew up out of the soil so as not to disturb worms and other organisms living in the soil. Many in the group of residents saw manual labor as spiritually inhibiting and soon it became evident that the commune could not provide enough food to sustain its members. The strict diet of grains and fruits left many of the members malnourished and sick. Given this situation, many of the members left and the community collapsed in January 1844.

_03:: The Shakers

Officially known as the United Society of Believers in Christ's Second Appearing, the Shakers were founded in Manchester, England, in 1747. As a group of dissenting Quakers under the charismatic leadership of Mother Ann Lee, the Shakers came to America in 1774. Like most reformist movements of the time, the Shakers were agriculturally based, and believed in common ownership of all property and the confession of sins. Unlike most of the other groups, the Shakers practiced celibacy, or the lack of procreation. Membership came via converts or by adopting children. Shaker families consisted of "brothers" and "sisters" who lived in gender-segregated communal homes of up to 100 individuals. During the required Sunday community meetings it was not uncommon for members to break into a spontaneous dance, thus giving them the Shaker label. As pacifists they were exempted from military service and became the United States' first conscientious objectors during the Civil War. Currently, however, there isn't a whole lot of Shaking going on. As the younger members left the community, converts quit coming, and the older ones died off, many of the communities were forced to close. Of the original 19 communities, most had closed by the early 1900s, with only one in existence today.

_04:: Pullman's Capitalist Utopia

Located 15 miles south of Chicago, the town of Pullman was founded in the 1880s by George Pullman (of luxury railway car fame) as a utopian community based on the notion that capitalism was the best way to meet all material and spiritual needs. According to Pullman's creed, the community was built to provide Pullman's employees with a place where they could exercise proper moral values and where each resident had to adhere to the strict tenets of capitalism under the direction and leadership of Pullman. The community was run on a for-profit basis—the town had to return a profit of 7% annually. This was done by giving the employees two paychecks, one for rent, which was automatically turned back in to Pullman, and one for everything else. Interestingly, the utopian community had very rigid social class barriers, with the management and skilled workers living in stately homes and the unskilled laborers living in tenements. Within 20 years the experiment failed miserably. Pullman began demanding more and more rent to offset company losses, while union sentiment grew among the employee residents.

Touch of Evil

Not all cult villages lose touch with pop culture. Reports indicate that, strewn among the bodies of the 900-plus dead at the People's Temple in Jonestown, Guyana, were cassette tapes featuring the vocal stylings of none other than Barry White.

The Totalitarian Style Guide: Dictator Grooming Tips

So, you wanna be a dictator? Sure, you've got the well-equipped, fanatically loyal army, you've selected a country for conquering, and you're ready to murder anyone who stands in the way (what commitment!). But if you want to be taken seriously in the Dictator Game, you'll need to look the part. Lucky for you, we've assembled a handy guide to get you started.

_01:: The Mustache

From Hitler to Mussolini to Saddam Hussein, dictators have long relied on the mustache to give them the illusion of stiff upper lips. And they're touchy about 'em, to boot! In 1923, Hitler's friend Ernst Hanfstaengl encouraged the future Führer to grow his mustache across the entire length of his lip. Hitler, naturally, later tried to have Hanfstaengl killed. Critics of Stalin's 'stache fared even worse. In a poem intended only for a small circle of friends, Osip Mandelstam compared Stalin's mustache to a cockroach. Thereafter, Mandelstam was repeatedly arrested and sent to deadly Soviet work camps—he died, probably in 1939, in one of the gulags. So whether you go pencil-thin or Selleck-thick, remember the mustache—and to crush any who question it.

_02:: Let Yourself Go a Little

Nothing establishes power over the people quite like making it abundantly obvious to them that you have access to more food than they do. Just think of the adorably pudgy (and slightly paranoid) Kim Jong Il, or the rotund Idi Amin. But by far the fattest autocrat is Taufa'ahau Tupou IV, the longtime king of Tongo. But don't let the chub fool you: despite weighing in at a chunky 300-plus pounds, the Tongan king is 100% dictator. In fact, he's led one of the strangest imperialist campaigns of all time to prove it. After an eccentric Nevadan named Michael Oliver piled sand onto a reef in the Pacific and declared his newly built paradise "The Republic of Minerva" in 1972, Tupou and a force of 350 Tongans invaded the one-man nation and annexed it in history's most minor act of colonialism.

_03:: Care for Your Hair, Not Your People

Although it may seem a little too metrosexual for totalitarian rulers, hair care is as vital to a proper dictatorship as erecting statues of yourself and murdering innocents. Historically, dictators lucky enough to have a full head of hair (sorry, Mao) have gone to great lengths to protect it. When he was plucked from his miserable little spider hole outside Tikrit in 2003, it immediately became clear that the suddenly salt-and-pepper Saddam Hussein had previously been using Just For Men. And North

It's a Mad, Mad, Mad, Mad Emperor

NORTON I, EMPEROR OF THE UNITED STATES OF AMERICA

Joshua Abraham Norton (1819?–1880) was just about as crazy as they come. Norton declared himself Emperor of the United States of America (and Protector of Mexico) in 1859, and although he never really left San Francisco to survey his domains, he became such a local celebrity that his "proclamations" were carried in San Francisco's newspapers. Not just that, he ate for free in the best restaurants in town, and stores all over the city accepted the special "currency" he made for his empire of one. Even more impressive, when he passed away, 30,000 San Franciscans turned out for Norton's funeral, perhaps just to see his new clothes.

Korea's Kim Jong Il, whose bouffant may seem out of style to those of us who aren't 70-year-old women, purportedly spends hours on his perms—and spikes his hair into peaks to appear taller than his 5 feet 2 inches (he also wears shoes with lifts).

_04:: Uniforms = The New Black

Durable, washable, and flattering to any build, a military uniform is another essential for any dictator. Suits and ties are for democratically elected pansies—a uniform reminds your citizens who has the guns: You do! When selecting your totalitarian couture, we recommend choosing from one of two classic schools of uniform thought. The Castro—no fancy medals or ornate accessories here—is just your classic, tailored-to-fit green fatigues, with a cigar and a Britney Spears–esque page boy cap to complete the ensemble. Or you can opt for a little more military bling, and fashion yourself in the school of the Amin. Like Idi Amin's bloodthirsty, over-the-top reign, the Amin is ostentatious and intimidating, with dozens of medals, some the size of a hockey puck, adorning a blue double-breasted general's coat. Have your minions sew some gaudy gold epaulets onto your shoulders, and you'll be ready to terrorize the people in style!

Touch of Evil

Some sources claim that Adolf Hitler purposely styled his short mustache after film legend Charlie Chaplin's. The silent film star wasn't exactly impressed and responded by mocking Der Führer in The Great Dictator, *his first "talkie" film.*

Ridiculous Contract Riders of Pampered Celebrities

Everyone knows rock and roll is about thrills and excess—we just didn't realize that spirit was supposed to extend to the greenroom buffet. The following are seven very pampered acts that made sure their laundry list of demands got tacked onto their contracts.

_01:: Van Halen and the Whole M&M'S Thing

Van Halen first gained notoriety for their stipulation that, at every gig, their dressing room was to contain a large bowl of M&M'S, but with all the brown ones removed. And while this has often been cited as proof of the band members' towering egos, it was actually included by the tour promoters as an easy way of seeing if the concert venues had read the contract thoroughly (particularly the parts about technical requirements, etc.). But sneaky M&M'S tactics aside, Van Halen's riders are also notorious for the sheer volume of alcohol they stipulate. One rider specified that their dressing room was to contain a case of beer, a pint of Jack Daniel's, a pint of Absolut, a 750 ml bottle of Bacardi Añejo rum, three bottles of wine, small bottles of Cointreau and Grand Marnier, and a 750 ml bottle of one of five specific premium tequilas. Don't forget six limes, margarita salt, shot glasses, ingredients for Bloody Marys, and a blender. Sure, there are only four dudes in the band, but shouldn't you expect this sort of behavior from a group whose bassist plays a guitar shaped like a bottle of Jack?

_02:: JLo's Trailer from the Park

There are divas, there are superdivas, and then there's Jennifer Lopez. That's right, the same sultry soulstress who preaches the "keep it real" street mantra also happens to require a trailer *at least* 40 feet in length, in which *everything* is white. That means drapes, couches, candles, tablecloths, lilies, and roses (she also requires yellow roses with red trim thrown in as well). And if you're hoping to keep a prolonged smile on "Jenny from the Block's" pretty mug, you can't forget the selection of current CDs she requires, chosen from a list of 43 artists, or her three favorite scented candles from Diptyque—Tuberose, Figuier, and Heliotrope. And that's just from her contract for a *charity* song benefiting AIDS victims in Africa! Oh, and did we mention Jenny was only at the event for a total of 90 minutes? It's almost as if her ego's as big as her . . . nope, too easy.

_03:: Guns N' (Long-Stemmed) Roses

They were one of the biggest bands of the 1980s and '90s. Just ask them. And in a band of big egos, the very biggest was lead singer

Axl Rose. He had his own dressing room, stocked with plenty of the things a vocal professional needs: hot water and honey (Sue Bee brand only); a rib-eye steak dinner; a large pepperoni pizza; a deli tray with a heavy emphasis on lean roast beef, ham, and turkey; and a bottle of Dom Perignon. His bandmates had much simpler tastes. Their dressing room was to contain lots of chips, nuts, exotic fruits, and cheese. Of course, they went a little less simple on the drinks. Aside from a few cases of soda, the band also required four cases of beer, two fifths of Jack Daniel's, two fifths of Stolichnaya vodka, two bottles of Chardonnay, and a bottle of Jägermeister. Oh, and don't forget to throw in a couple bottles of . . . carrot juice? Clearly, it's the cornerstone behind every successful rock act. As are the four *cartons* of cigarettes and the assortment of adult magazines you'll need to provide.

_04:: Meat Loaf
(Just a Little Overdone)

Yes, *that* Meat Loaf. The man who brought us *Bat Out of Hell* obviously requires quite a bit in return. His rider states that the promoters are to recognize that they are dealing with an international "superstar" and therefore all provisions must be first class, as befits a "superstar." And that's two words: *Meat. Loaf.* Sheesh! His dressing room spread must include, among many other things, a loaf of 100% multigrain bread (preferably Vogel's Flaxseed & Soy), two bags of potato chips, a package of low-fat chicken or turkey wieners, four Gala apples (specifically, hard and crunchy ones), four low-fat fresh-baked muffins *from a bakery,* steamed broccoli and green beans amandine (not too soggy), a sliced roast pork tenderloin, a sliced roast beef tenderloin, and two baked potatoes. And this is supposed to feed two people. Maybe they're both Mr. Loaf?

_05:: Poison's Poison

Pretty standard for a rock band, really. Deli trays, condiments, lots of booze, etc. But what was Poison's poison? Apparently, pyrotechnics. Their contract also required that all the venue's smoke and fire detectors be switched off due to the band's flair for flares. So how do we think the concertgoers would feel knowing that little tidbit? Also very odd, Poison's rider stipulates that an American Sign Language interpreter must be made available on request for the band's deaf fans. And the band will need 24 hours' notice if the ASL interpreter needs the lyrics beforehand. Of course, some disdainful critics would claim that *all* the band's fans *must* be deaf.

Touch of Evil

So, what were the Beatles' demands after a grueling, fast-paced 1965 concert at New York's Shea Stadium? Just a black-and-white TV and some Coca-Cola.

_06:: The Village People's
Payment Plan

You might think that a bunch of guys as past their prime as The Village People would just be glad to get a gig. Nope. They still draw a crowd, so therefore they still have demands in their rider. The front page of their rider contains one stipulation: that all balances to The Village People be paid in "CASH" (yes, it's in all caps). It goes on to say that they can only be photographed in costume, that they won't fly in prop planes, and that they prefer certain seats in the plane (as specific as "aisle, rear right side of plane" for the Navy guy) and certain airports of origin. Disco may be dead, but ego certainly seems to be staying alive.

_07:: Various Spoiled Artists

Oh, there are just so many. Celine Dion requires a children's choir with 20 to 24 children of all races. Pavarotti demands that there be no noise backstage or distinct smells anywhere near him; but he does want a golf cart. Cher simply can't perform without a wig room, cable TV that gets Turner Classic Movies, and a room for her massage therapist. "Weird Al" Yankovic is a strict vegan and forbids Dasani water. Elton John demands that his dressing room be kept at 60° in summer and 70° in winter. And Busta Rhymes insists that there be no pork or beef anywhere near his dressing room; but he does want a 24-piece bucket of KFC and a box of Rough Riders condoms (ribbed).

Hoaxing Hoaxers and the Hoaxes They Play: Greatest Hoaxes of All Time

4

Fool me once, shame on me. Fool me twice, well, shame on me again. But fool me 245 times, come on now! So, why do hoaxes work so well, and why are people always willing to fall for them? Well, maybe it's because there's a sucker born every minute. Of course, if you believe P. T. Barnum really said that, there's a sidebar waiting for you on page 11.

_01:: The "Computer" That Outsmarted Napoléon

Centuries before Deep Blue started whuppin' on Russian grand masters, a chess-playing automaton nicknamed "the Turk" was thrashing all manner of chess players. Atop a wheeled wooden cabinet was a seated, life-sized mannequin made of wood and dressed in Turkish garb. The Turk held a chessboard in his wooden lap, and he beat 'most all comers—including Napoléon Bonaparte and Benjamin Franklin. Premiering in the 1770s, the creation of Wolfgang von Kempelen moved its wooden arms, seemingly without human assistance, around the board. The secret? The Turk's arms were operated by a diminutive chess expert crouched inside the cabinet, who operated gears and pulleys to move the Turk's arms. After traveling the world for almost a century, the Turk ended up mothballed in Philadelphia—where it was destroyed in a fire in 1854.

_02:: Microsoft Buys the Catholic Church!

While the pranksters are still unknown, few press releases have had the impact of the 1994 doozy sent out supposedly by Microsoft, announcing Bill Gates's purchase of the Catholic

Church. As reported, Microsoft not only would get sole electronic rights to the good book, but also would pitch in to the church's efforts, namely by engineering a means for delivering the sacraments online. Needless to say, the prank tricked a few folks. So many customers rang up Microsoft in protest that the distraught company finally felt obligated to clear up the mess via (you guessed it!) another press release. The statement full-out denied the allegations, and further said that it hoped to alleviate customer concerns by declaring that the company had no intentions of purchasing any religious institutions, Catholic or otherwise. Of course, it wasn't long before another "press release" surfaced, this one touting IBM's response to Microsoft: a merger with the Episcopal Church.

_03:: **This Is Your Brain on Bananas**

When the alternative newspaper the *Berkeley Barb* published a satirical article in 1967 claiming that smoking dried banana peels could lead to intoxication, they never expected to be taken seriously. But the oh-so-square national news media didn't get the joke, and publicized the report throughout the nation. Since then, countless wayward teens have been duped into smoking bananas (which can make you nauseated, but not pleasantly so). The hoax really took off, though, in 1970 with the publication of William Powell's *The Anarchist's Cookbook,* which covers all manner of craft pleasantries from building pipe bombs to manufacturing LSD. Not surprisingly, it also provides a recipe for turning your banana peels into "a fine, black powder" suitable for smoking. Even though no one's ever gotten high from bananas (although they are a great energy fruit, according to Dr. Atkins!), the *Barb's* hoax has had a stunning shelf life.

Touch of Evil

In 1994, computer users worldwide panicked over the "Good Times" virus, which was spread by an AOL user and was able to "erase your hard drive" if you even read the corresponding e-mail message. Luckily, it was just a big hoax.

_04:: **The *Social Text* Fiasco**

In 1996, the respected cultural studies journal *Social Text* published several complex and dense articles, mainly because that's what respected academic journals do. But one, "Transgressing the Boundaries: Toward a Transformative Hermeneutics of Quantum Physics," was a hoax by NYU physics professor Alan Sokal, who sought to prove that academic journals will publish any paper that uses big words. To the extent that Sokal's article is readable, it makes a grandly silly argument about the political implications of quantum gravity. Among other ludicrous assertions, the article claims that physical reality does not exist, that the laws of physics are social constructs, and that feminism has implications for mathematical set theory. It's hilarious, if you like that kind of thing, but it's also utter nonsense. After Sokal revealed his hoax in *Lingua Franca,* many academic journals beefed up their peer review process.

Mandatory Fashion Trends

If you've ever been in a marching band, the Rockettes, or even a parochial school, you know what it's like to be told how to dress. Of course, getting those orders from a band director or a nun is a little different from being told what to wear by a snazzy dictator and his fashion police. The following are four mandatory fashions, instructed to be worn with pride.

_01:: Queue It Up

The braided pigtail, or queue, which became a worldwide stereotype of Chinese commoners, wasn't so much a Chinese fashion statement as it was a Manchu style. So, why the braid? The initial hairstyle edict occurred during the reign of Emperor Shunzhi in 1654, but since Shunzhi was only eight years old, the law—requiring all Chinese men to wear their hair in a long braid—was actually the work of his uncle and regent, Dorgon. Shunzhi and Dorgon were members of the Qing dynasty, the last dynastic family to rule China (until 1912). But they weren't ethnically Chinese. Since they were from what became known as Manchuria (today a northeastern region of China), forcing people to wear the Manchu hairdo helped indicate who was subservient to the emperor.

_02:: Shaving Grace

Czar Peter I dragged reluctant Russians kicking and screaming into the 18th century after he became sole ruler in 1696. He did not, however, drag them by their beards. Peter's far-reaching reforms involved trade, agriculture, shipbuilding, and more, but Russians became most upset when their "forward thinking" emperor said men should look more like their smooth-faced European neighbors to the west. At the time, the traditional Russian style was a long beard, never trimmed (not even the mustache), worn with close-cropped hair. Beyond the politics of style, though, men were proud of their beards, and many believed that a man wouldn't be admitted to heaven without one. Peter finally decided that every gentleman (nobles, landowners) who kept a beard would have to pay for it: a tax of 100 rubles a year if he kept the bush. A commoner, on the other hand, had to pay a kopek. In other crimes of fashion (or misdemeanors in this case), Peter also taxed traditionally long Russian coats to encourage the adoption of a shorter, above-the-knee French style.

_03:: Suit Yourself

You know the Mao suit: four patch pockets on the jacket front, a turndown collar, five to seven front buttons. And while Westerners link it to China's smiling chairman, its originator was actually Sun Zhongshan (also spelled Sun Yixian or Sun Yat-sen). Dr. Sun, as he was known in the West, ordered the new fashion for the Republic of China (1911–1949) and required civil servants to wear the suit beginning in the 1920s. Among other things, Mao Zedong usurped the fashion statement, and the Communist leader continued wearing it after the 1949 revolution. Millions of Chinese followed suit (literally), as the unisex style became a proud symbol of proletarian humility and Chinese unity. Essentially it became a style mandate: unless you wanted to draw attention to yourself (not the best idea in a totalitarian state), you wore the suit. When Mao died in 1976, though, fashions began to diversify.

_04:: Ankle Management

Throughout history, many religious authorities have dictated proper ways to dress. It's not surprising, though, that when state and religious authorities are identical, as in turn-of-the-21st-century Afghanistan, such dictates become law. The short-lived Taliban government took Muslim social conservatism to such extremes that women and girls could not go outside the home without a head-to-toe burqa—a dark-colored garment with a three-inch rectangle of mesh over the eyes—the only opening. Also on the taboo list: bright colors, cosmetics, and high-heeled shoes. In fact, women couldn't wear any shoes that made noise when they walked. And if an inch of ankle showed under the burqa hem, a woman could be beaten on the street for the violation. Men, meanwhile, could be beaten, jailed, or worse for wearing a beard of insufficient length or otherwise offending the government.

Lies Your Mother Told You

NAPOLÉON WAS A SHRIMP

Momma done led you astray again: While Napoléon wasn't exactly a big man, he wasn't "tiny," either. So, how'd the myth start? Pretty simple, really. The French foot measured 1.067877 English feet, or roughly 13 inches. So, in the French system of measurement, Napoléon was 5 feet 2 inches, but in the British system (which Americans still use today), he stood roughly 5 feet 6 inches, or about 168 centimeters. At the time, that wasn't much shorter than the average man, who stood about 5 feet 8 inches. All the stuff about Napoléon being so "little" may also stem from the fact that his royal guard was made up of 6-footers, making him look small by comparison. Political critics in France liked to perpetuate the idea that he was little (he also had a slight build) while simultaneously making fun of his short, military-style haircut. They called him *le petit tondu* ("the little crop-head"). The exaggerated notion of his diminutive stature may also be rooted in the contempt in which he was held by his enemies. After all, victors do tend to write history.

I Must Be the Greatest—
Writers Who Fancied Themselves Peerless

Book writing requires a certain measure of confidence—even great authors get repeatedly rejected by publishers. Afraid he'd die in World War I, F. Scott Fitzgerald quickly wrote "The Romantic Egotist," which was praised but rejected. But Fitzgerald, something of a romantic egotist himself, persevered. As did these egotists.

_01:: James Joyce (1882–1941)

The only time W. B. Yeats and James Joyce, the titans of 20th-century Irish literature, met, a young, unpublished Joyce told the 30-something Yeats, "We have met too late. You are too old for me to have any effect on you." From the beginning, clearly, Joyce admired his own genius, and his self-admiration only grew with time, as we see in his semiautobiographical masterpiece *A Portrait of the Artist as a Young Man.* Preparing to leave Ireland at the end of the novel (as Joyce did in 1902, at the age of 20), *Portrait's* hero, Stephen Dedalus, announces that he is off "to forge in the smithy of my soul the uncreated conscience of my race." A heady task for a kid who ought to still be in college, but Joyce eventually managed it—*Ulysses* is, most would agree, the Great Irish Novel.

_02:: Dante (1265–1321)

Fortunately for Dante Alighieri, who wrote *The Divine Comedy,* the proud only go to Purgatory. The *Inferno* section of Dante's afterlife epic depicts the poet Virgil taking Dante on a rip-roaring road trip through the nine circles of hell. In Canto IV, they find themselves in the first circle in the company of the greatest poets of antiquity—Homer, Horace, Ovid, and Lucan. In Dante's none-too-humble imagining of the scene, the poets "invited me to join their ranks" (although Dante does save a bit of face by claiming his position as the least among the Greats). In reality, though, Dante could never have chatted with Homer, nor did he ever read Homer's work. At the time, neither the *Iliad* nor the *Odyssey* had been translated, and Mr. Fancypants Dante couldn't read or speak Greek.

_03:: Walt Whitman (1819–1892)

He celebrated himself; he sung himself; he quite clearly liked himself. Walt Whitman's Great American Poem "Song of Myself" features the word *I* a stunning 487 times, so it's perhaps odd that when he self-published the first edition of *Leaves of Grass,* it named neither a publisher nor an author. (In a sacrifice to his ego, however, Whitman placed a sizable portrait of himself on the front cover.) "Song of Myself" is not simply an egotistical poem, of course—it's a celebration of humanity itself—as represented by Walt Whitman. After all, Walt was seeking to both reveal his tender soul and be crowned the great poet of the young nation he so loved. And, indeed, if we are half as confident when we sing of ourselves as Whitman was, America is a proud country indeed.

_04:: William Faulkner (1897–1962)

William Faulkner was not the sort of humble southerner who downplays the difficulty of his work. In his Nobel Prize acceptance speech, Faulkner called his career "a life's work in the agony and sweat of the human spirit." Of course, Faulkner knew his hard work had paid off—whenever asked to name the greatest living writers, he always included himself without embarrassment. In fact, he passionately sought to accomplish the impossible goal of the perfect literary creation, and often attacked lesser writers (we're looking at you, Ernest Hemingway) for having a paucity of "moral courage" when it came to taking chances with narrative style. But while he believed his books were great, Faulkner maintained a strange kind of humility, arguing that the work mattered but the author didn't. "If I had not existed," he said, "someone else would have written me."

_05:: Ayn Rand (1905–1982)

The egoist's egoist, author Ayn Rand (born Alissa Zinovievna Rosenbaum) is the patron saint of Thinking You're Better than Everybody Else. Her most famous novels, *The Fountainhead* and *Atlas Shrugged*, are massive dramatizations of objectivism, an Oscar the Grouch philosophy that champions ego and accomplishment, shuns all religion as folly, and condemns any form of charity or altruism as counterproductive to society. Ever the optimist, Rand created protagonists, invariably men, who were shunned by others because of their genius but then persevered over the foolishness of morons to prove said genius and emerge triumphant. Not surprisingly, she saw humility as weakness and regarded laughing at yourself as "spitting in your own face." So, just how much did Rand believe in her own philosophy? Let's just say a lot. With typical Randian modesty, she ranked herself right up there as a philosophical equal of Aristotle and Thomas Aquinas.

Touch of Evil

The anonymously published novels Zabeebah and the King *and* The Impregnable Fortress *are thought to have been written by Saddam Hussein. Lackluster sales of the latter improved after Iraqi newspapers printed 200-plus glowing reviews that praised the book and its "prodigious author."*

Pre-Madonna Prima Donnas:
Artists Who Were Full of Themselves

They say a lot of artistic expression is motivated by self-loathing. Not for these folks. These puffed-up virtuosos didn't just think they could walk on water; they knew they could. Here are a few creative types who raised egotism to an art form all its own.

_01:: Frank Lloyd Wright (1867–1959)

Frank Lloyd Wright may be *the* genius of 20th-century architecture. And boy, did he know it. The designer of the Robie House (Chicago), Fallingwater (Bear Run, Pennsylvania), Taliesin West (Scottsdale, Arizona), the Guggenheim Museum (New York), and countless other buildings was notorious for his belief in his superiority to mere mortals. In fact, the architectural egomaniac frequently acted as if the rules did not apply to him, including the rules of geography and climate. But when you're Wright, you're Wright. After Wright was commissioned in 1935 to design a Dallas home for department store magnate Stanley Marcus, the project quickly went sour when he insisted that his client sleep outdoors year-round on "sleeping porches." He also decreed that the Marcuses' small bedroom "cubicles" would have almost no closet space.

_02:: Salvador Dalí (1904–1989)

"Every morning when I awake, the greatest of joy is mine: that of being Salvador Dalí." Yep, he really said it. Everything about the legendary surrealist (he of the melting clocks), from his whacked-out paintings to his curled-up mustache, was designed to shock, destroy convention, cause scandal, and stir up controversy. If he wasn't getting enough attention, he was known to walk the streets of New York City clanging a handbell. In fact, Dalí once said, "The thought of not being recognized [is] unbearable." Not surprising when you consider that the man criticized for choosing to live in Franco's fascist Spain defended his position by stating that he didn't care about others so long as he himself could be king. Not exactly a man of the people. Need another telling quote? "At the age of six years I wanted to be a chef. At the age of seven I wanted to be Napoléon. My ambitions have continued to grow at the same rate ever since." Apparently, so did his ego.

_03:: Alfred Hitchcock (1899–1980)

Hitchcock was, without question, one of the towering geniuses of cinema. But like many geniuses, he wasn't exactly the best collaborator. In fact, he was particularly trying for screenwriters, who never felt he properly credited them for their work, and notoriously hard on actors (he was very outspoken in his negative opinion of Kim Novak's performance in *Vertigo*). He was even quoted as saying, "Actors are cattle." The quip stirred up such a huge outcry (actors can be so touchy) that he issued this correction: "I have been misquoted. What I really said is: Actors should be *treated* as cattle." Although it began by accident (he was short an actor for the film *The Lodger*), he soon made it his trademark to appear in his own films, amassing a total of 37 such cameos over his career.

_04:: Orson Welles (1915–1985)

When you create *Citizen Kane*—still considered by many the greatest film ever made—at the ripe old age of 26, you're going to get a bit of a big head. But Welles was pretty much convinced of his own importance well before then. In fact, it's said that he created *Citizen Kane* as a withering exposé of newspaper mogul William Randolph Hearst because Hearst slighted Welles at a dinner party. Bruised ego indeed. And as his body grew, so did his arrogance. Do yourself a favor: track down a recording of Welles's outtakes for a TV commercial for frozen peas. You'll hear everything you need to know about his oversized ego. Here's one classic quote from the outtakes: "In the *depths* of your *ignorance,* what is it you want?"

_05:: Al Jolson (1886–1950)

Lots of performers have been labeled "the world's greatest entertainer." But Jolson really, *really* believed it. The greatest star of vaudeville, the singer, actor, dancer, and comedian was born Asa Yoelson in Seredzius, Lithuania (Srednike in Russian), a Jewish shtetl in what was then part of imperial Russia. He was known for hijacking the action in the middle of shows, ad-libbing, or just stopping to talk to the audience. During a 1911 performance of the critically hated *Paris Is a Paradise for Coons* (title not edited for political correctness), Jolson stopped and asked the audience if they'd rather hear him sing than see the rest of the play. They roared their approval, and Jolson ditched the whole program and took over. From that moment on, no one else could really share the stage with him. Unlike some on this list, however, Jolson can be forgiven somewhat for his huge ego; from most contemporary accounts, he really *was* the greatest in the world. Despite the enormity of his contributions to stage and screen, Jolson's image remains a political hot potato because of his use of stage blackface (considered repellent now, but pretty common for the times).

Secret Societies That Ain't All That Secret

Is it possible that so many societies can proudly claim so many powerful and influential people and still be called "secret"? Well, no. Here are six of the most famous of the world's supposedly secret societies. But if anyone asks, you didn't hear this from us.

_01:: The Freemasons

This is the granddaddy of all not-so-secret secret societies. Freemasonry, or "The Craft" as its members call it, most likely has its roots in 17th-century stoneworkers' guilds. Mason lore, however, extends its origins back to biblical times, linking the society to the building of the Temple of Solomon. Freemasonry is split into numerous subgroups and orders, all of which consider God the Grand Geometrician, or Grand Architect of the Universe. At their hearts, these groups are all means of exploring ethical and philosophical issues, and their rituals and symbols are famous (or infamous). Take, for instance, the square-and-compass logo often seen on the backs of Cadillacs. Or the use of secret handshakes, passwords, and greeting postures/gestures called "due guards," all collectively known as the Modes of Recognition. The list of famous Masons is massive, a virtual Who's Who of modern history, explaining the many conspiracy theories regarding the Masons' influence and intentions. Mozart, FDR, Harry S. Truman, George Washington, Mark Twain, Voltaire, Benjamin Franklin, John Wayne, W. C. Fields, and Douglas MacArthur were all Masons. But perhaps the Masons' greatest strides have been made in fast food: KFC's Colonel Sanders and Wendy's founder Dave Thomas knew how to secret-shake with the best of 'em.

_02:: The Illuminati

Over the centuries, lots of groups have called themselves the Illuminati ("Enlightened Ones"), but the one we're talking about here began as the Bavarian Illuminati. A radical product of the Enlightenment and offshoot of the religion-based Freemasons, the Illuminati espoused secular freethinking and intellectualism and proved a threat to Europe's old order. Although they were officially banned by the Bavarian government in 1784, some claim that they live on to this day in other guises (see "The Trilateral Commission" on page 18). So, what's the Illuminati's goal? To establish a new world order of capitalism and authoritarianism, of course! They've been accused of manipulating currencies, world stock markets, elections, assassinations, and even of being aliens. One common myth is that the eye-and-pyramid image on the dollar bill is a symbol of the Illuminati watching over us. Nope. It's a symbol of strength and durability (though unfinished, symbolizing growth and change), and the all-seeing eye represents the divine guidance of the American cause. Or so the government says.

_03:: Opus Dei

This organization has a $42 million, 17-story headquarters building on Lexington Avenue in New York City, claims 85,000 members in 60 countries, and was featured in Dan Brown's bestseller *The Da Vinci Code*. Now that its existence has been significantly unsecretized, this ultraorthodox Catholic sect has definitely raised its share of eyebrows. Founded in 1928 by Saint Josemaría Escrivá (a Spanish priest who bore an uncanny resemblance to Karl Malden), Opus Dei is the short name for the Prelature for the Holy Cross and the Work of God. The sect (some would say cult) stresses a return to traditional Catholic orthodoxy and behavior, especially celibacy, with members falling into one of three levels. Numeraries live in Opus Dei facilities, devote their time and money to the prelature, attend mass daily, and engage in mortification of the flesh (wearing a spiked chain around the thigh called a *cilice,* taking cold showers, or flagellating themselves with a knotted rope called "the discipline"). Next come Associates (kind of like Numeraries, but living "off campus"), then Supernumeraries (the rank-and-file members). The group did gain the praise of Pope John Paul II, and has engaged in a lot of charity work. Yet, critics accuse the group of being linked to fascist organizations like Franco's government in Spain, and of anti-Semitism and intolerance, even of other Catholics.

_04:: Skull and Bones

Top dog among all the collegiate secret societies, Yale's Skull and Bones dates to 1832 and goes by other spooky names like Chapter 322 and the Brotherhood of Death. With a large number of Bonesmen who have attained positions of power, including the president and the head of the CIA, it's no wonder that rumors abound that the society is hell-bent on obtaining power and influencing U.S. foreign policy. The fact that they meet in an imposing templelike building on the Yale campus called (what else?) the Tomb doesn't really help. Bonesmen are selected, or "tapped," during their junior year and can reveal their membership only after they've graduated. But they can never talk about it. The Bones have been accused of all sorts of crazy rituals and conspiracies, including drug smuggling and the assassination of JFK (a hated *Hahvahd* man, after all). It's even rumored that the skull of Geronimo resides in the Tomb, stolen from its resting place by Prescott Bush, Dubya's granddad. In one of the more commonly known rituals, the initiate spends all night naked in an open coffin, confessing all his sexual experiences to the group. So, who's lucky enough to have made such a confession? George H. W. Bush, George W. Bush, John Kerry, William Howard Taft, McGeorge Bundy, William F. Buckley, and Henry Luce are just a few.

_05:: The Bohemian Club

This is a weird one. In the majestic forests of Sonoma County north of San Francisco lies the Bohemian Grove, the 2,700-acre wooded retreat of the Bohemian Club, the nation's most exclusive men's club. Every July since 1879, the "Bohos" have gathered at the Grove for a two-week encampment, where they're divided into more than 100 residential camps with names like Owl's Nest, Cave Man, and Lost Angels. Membership has included, well, just about everybody important: Ronald Reagan, Dwight Eisenhower, Richard Nixon (who once called it "faggy"), Gerald Ford, Colin Powell, Dick Cheney, and many CEOs and wealthy business leaders like Malcolm Forbes. Each encampment opens with a robed-and-hooded ceremony called the Cremation of Care, in which an effigy called "Dull Care" (symbolizing worldly concerns) is burned before a 40-foot concrete statue of an owl, symbol of wisdom and the club's mascot. Throughout the week, plays are staged (called High Jinx and Low Jinx), there's lots of eating and drinking (and, reportedly, urinating on trees), and members are treated to speeches called Lakeside Talks. Some opponents go so far as to accuse the group of Satanism, witchcraft, homosexuality, and prostitution, while more reasonable observers object to the Lakeside Talks as national policy discussions to which the public is not privy. But above all, it's seen as a way that some of the elite meet others of the elite, thereby ensuring that they'll all stay elite. All this makes the club's seemingly anticonspiratorial slogan—"Weaving spiders, come not here"—that much more ironic.

_06:: The Trilateral Commission

While not, on its face, as juicily sinister as some of the other societies on this list, the Tri-

lateral Commission has been accused of all sorts of underhanded shenanigans by its critics. Formed in 1973 by David Rockefeller, the Commission includes over 300 prominent citizens from Europe, Asia, and North America in a forum for discussing the regions' common interests. But conspiracy theorists hold that the Trilateral Commission, along with the Council on Foreign Relations and others, is really just a front for a larger, more sinister order called the Round Table Groups, founded in London over 100 years ago and bent on the creation of a new world order, a global capitalist police state. Yikes! (For the record, some say the Round Table Groups are themselves just fronts for *another* society, the Illuminati, so who knows?) American members of the Trilateral Commission have included Bill Clinton, Henry Kissinger, Jimmy Carter, Dick Cheney, and Dianne Feinstein.

Worst Miscalculations of All Time

To err is human, but to really screw up you need to think you know exactly what you're doing first.

_01:: Columbus and the Indies

Pepper used to be one of the most valuable substances in Europe, mainly because it was

effective in masking the taste of spoiled foods. But since it came from the "East Indies," or the modern-day countries of Southeast Asia, it took forever to get there and back over land. Enter Christopher Columbus, who was sure that the earth was round and that he could therefore sail west across the Atlantic Ocean to the Indies. Only problem: he got the math very, very wrong. Aside from using the calculations of French cartographer Pierre d'Ailly, which vastly underestimated the distance around the globe from the European side to Asia, Columbus also misread maps, believing that "miles" referred to the 5,000-foot Roman mile rather than the 6,082-foot nautical mile. So Columbus believed the circumference of the planet at the equator was 19,000 miles rather than 24,600 miles. Hiding in the missing 5,600 miles, of course, were North and South America.

_02:: Chernobyl

Ironically, the catastrophic 1986 explosion at the Chernobyl nuclear plant began with an experiment to increase reactor safety. As part of the experiment, engineers had to slowly power the reactor down—kind of like "idling" a car engine. But they reduced energy production too quickly, and the reaction was "poisoned" by an increase in neutron absorption. Rather than wait 24 hours to restore energy production, as recommended, the head engineer decided to remove graphite control rods to get power back up because he was impatient, eventually leaving just six rather than the minimum of 30 decreed by operating manuals. Shortly after, when the engineers cut energy to the cooling system, coolant water heated up and quickly began to boil. The water had stabilized the reactor by absorbing neutrons, but when it turned to steam it was less effective. Further, because the rods had been withdrawn they no longer moderated the

power production. When the production suddenly spiked, engineers started an emergency process to push all the graphite control rods back into the reactor core and stop the reaction, but because of a small design flaw with the graphite caps on the ends of the rods the exact opposite happened. The reactor overheated almost instantaneously and exploded, and approximately 50 tons of nuclear fuel vaporized into the atmosphere.

Touch of Evil

In 1999, the $125 million Mars Climate Orbiter burned and disintegrated prior to landing. After NASA investigated, simple "bad data" was shown to have caused the mishap. The gaffe? Engineers accidentally mixed up metric units with English units in certain calculations.

_03:: Custer's Last Stand

In 1876, to destroy the Sioux resistance and force them onto a reservation, the U.S. government sent three commanders—Generals Crooks, Terry, and Gibbon—to converge on the Ogalala Sioux encampment at Little Bighorn in Montana. Lieutenant General George Armstrong Custer was serving under Terry's command, and unbeknownst to Custer, by the time he arrived, other Sioux tribes had more than doubled the size of the village, bringing it to 7,000 inhabitants. After an initial skirmish Custer was afraid that the Sioux would retreat before he could attack, so he split up his command of 657 men into three groups—a fatal mistake—and attempted to surround them. When he finally located the village, he led his troops in an all-out assault, saying "Don't worry, boys—there's enough of them for all of us!" Indeed there were. Things turned bad very quickly, as the Sioux spread the alarm. In the end, Custer made his famous "Last Stand" with about 100 men on a small hill near the village, facing 1,500 Sioux warriors. A total of 263 men died that day, the worst defeat ever inflicted by Native Americans on the U.S. military.

_04:: The Big Dig

Boston's "Big Dig" is the most ambitious urban infrastructure project ever undertaken in the United States—but it's become infamous for cost overruns and schedule delays that can be measured in geologic time. Aiming to take Boston's highways and relocate them to tunnels, the Big Dig hoped to spur new development and revitalization. In fact, early on, plans were also added to build a new tunnel under Boston Harbor to Boston's international airport in the east. The price of the project? $2.6 billion, with a project completion date predicted for 1997 or 1998. Because of geologic conditions, design mistakes, shoddy construction work, and frequent public opposition, however, the Big Dig is still going on, with a price tag of over $14.6 billion. What's more, tunnels have sprung hundreds of mysterious leaks, cutting off traffic, and construction has lowered the water table, potentially damaging buildings as they settle. How Boston digs itself out of this one is yet to be seen.

_05:: Draining of the Aral Sea

Shortly after the Russian Revolution in 1917, Soviet planners started diverting water from two large rivers in Central Asia—the Amu Darya and the Syr Darya—to turn Central Asian deserts into fertile cotton plantations. And the project was successful! Except...the

---

It's a Mad, Mad, Mad, Mad Artist

TALENTS WHO WERE TOO HARD ON THEMSELVES

It's hard to imagine a greater artistic success than Leonardo da Vinci, but the original Renaissance man was a notoriously harsh judge of himself—his last words are reported to have been "I have offended God and mankind because my work didn't reach the quality it should have." The famously depressed Sylvia Plath's will to perfection led to a Leonardian sense of disappointment in her own work. She frequently felt like a failure, and one of her first suicide attempts (at which she also failed) occurred after she was rejected from a fiction-writing class at Harvard. And John Kennedy Toole, author of the brilliant comic romp *A Confederacy of Dunces*, fared no better. Toole wasn't entirely humble (he felt that the book was a masterpiece), but after it was rejected by a publisher, Toole believed he would never be anything but a failed writer, so he committed suicide in 1969. After Toole's death, his mother took the book to the novelist Walker Percy, who reluctantly read it and was surprised to enjoy it. *Dunces* was finally published in 1980 and went on to win the Pulitzer Prize for fiction.

only problem was that the rivers were the sole source of water for the Aral Sea, the second-largest lake in the world. Other rivers were supposed to be diverted to compensate but as the Soviet economy declined, those projects never got under way. By 1960, between 20 and 50 cubic *kilometers* of water were being diverted from the sea every year; during the 1960s, the sea level dropped by an average of 20 centimeters a year, during the 1970s 50–60 centimeters a year, and during the 1980s 80–90 centimeters a year. Currently the sea has lost about 80% of its volume, and 60% of its surface area, and is expected to disappear entirely in the near future.

_06:: Vietnam and Casualty Burdens

One persistent question remains about Vietnam: How could the U.S. government and military make such a bad blunder? Much of the responsibility lies with the top brass at the Pentagon, including Secretary of Defense Robert McNamara, appointed by President John F. Kennedy in 1960, who believed that if American forces killed a certain number of the enemy, their economy would break down and resistance would collapse. However, these calculations proved disastrously wrong. Because they believed they were fighting for their independence, the North Vietnamese absorbed at least one million casualties. After the war, American officials still didn't get it. General William Westmoreland, the highest-ranking American commander during the war, said, "An American commander who took the same losses . . . would have been sacked overnight." Later McNamara himself said, "What I thought was that a very high rate of casualties would soften them up for negotiations. They paid no attention whatsoever to casualties. It had no impact at all militarily, and it had no impact on negotiations."

Bigger Is Better:
Insane Soviet Projects

The Soviet Union decided the best way to show up the West was through building the biggest version of any given object. The following are just seven of the largest examples.

_01:: Magnitogorsk

Whether it was for guns, tanks, ships, railroads, or bridges, Stalin, whose name means "Man of Steel," knew he needed one thing above all else for his 1920s Soviet Union: steel. He also knew that to the east, in the southern Ural Mountains, there was a unique geologic oddity named Magnitka—an entire mountain of pure iron ore, the key ingredient for steel. In 1929, Stalin decreed that a city, "Magnitogorsk" (see what he did there?), be built from scratch around said mountain to mine the ore and turn it into steel. So began one of the largest construction projects ever undertaken. With expertise provided by Communist sympathizers from the West, a ready-made city for 450,000 inhabitants was constructed in about five years. Of course, Stalin saved on labor costs by having the heavy lifting done by political prisoners. In fact, 30,000 people died in the effort. Steel production began in 1934, but shortly after World War II the iron ore ran out and the city's economy collapsed.

_02:: The Baltic–White Sea Canal

Ever the optimist, this time Stalin wanted to connect the Baltic Sea, with its key port of Leningrad, to the White Sea's port of Archangelsk. The idea was that he could move the Soviet navy fleets back and forth. So Stalin had more political prisoners sent to work on the canal—there was a seemingly endless supply from the gulags—and after a few brutal years it was completed in 1933. Disease, poor nutrition, and brutal conditions took a huge toll, though, with as many as 250,000 of the slave laborers dead by the end of it. The icing on the cake? The canal was completely useless when finished. For most of its length it was too shallow to admit anything larger than a small barge. Later a book of propaganda detailing the biographies of "heroic" workers and engineers, intended for distribution in capitalist countries, had to be recalled because in the downtime Stalin had ordered all the main characters shot.

_03:: The World's Largest Hydrofoil

The world's largest hydrofoil wasn't really a hydrofoil at all. In fact, it was one of a series of unique machines called "ground effect" vehicles built by the Soviet Union beginning in the 1960s. The Soviets had a monopoly on this fascinating technology, relying on a little-known principle of physics—the "ground effect"—in which a dense cushion of air hugging the ground can provide more lift to a vehicle than air at higher altitudes. Hovering about 3–12 feet above the ground, these vehicles resemble Luke Skywalker's levitating craft from *Star Wars,* and are far more fuel-efficient than airplanes, helicopters, hydrofoils, or cars. And at 58 feet, the largest of these, the "Caspian Sea Monster" was given its distinctive name after CIA analysts saw it at the Caspian port of Baku in photos taken by spy satellites. The craft traveled at speeds of up to 240 mph, had a swiveling nose cone for cargo loading, and could carry up to as many as 150 passengers.

_04:: Avant-garde Design for a Funkier Parliament

Designed by Vladimir Tatlin (1885–1953) in 1920, the *Monument to the Third International* was a gigantic spiraling iron structure intended to house the new Soviet government. Taller than the Eiffel Tower (and the yet-to-be constructed Empire State Building) at more than 1,300 feet, this curving, funnel-shaped structure was meant to encase three successively smaller assembly areas rotating on industrial bearings at different speeds, faster or slower according to their importance. Rotating once a year in the lowest level was a giant cube for delegates attending the Communist International from all over the world. A smaller pyramid, rotating once a month above it, would house the Communist Party's executives. The third level—a sphere rotating once daily—would house communications technology to spread propaganda, including a telegraph office, radio station, and movie screen.

Unfortunately the giant structure would have required more iron than the entire Soviet Union produced in a year, and was never built.

_05:: A Palace for the People

In 1931, Joseph Stalin ordered that the largest Orthodox Christian cathedral in the world—335 feet high, the product of 44 years of back-breaking labor by Russian peasants—be dynamited so he could build an enormous "Palace of the People," to celebrate the Communist Party. Stalin wished to replace the church with a new structure taller than the Empire State Building, and capped with a gilded statue of Lenin taller than the Statue of Liberty, but the "Man of Steel's" mad scheme never came to fruition. Although the first phase was completed (the dynamiting was the easy bit), the construction never took place as necessary resources were diverted to fighting World War II. After Stalin died, his successor—Nikita Khrushchev—ordered a large swimming pool built where the cathedral had stood. Old women who remembered the original cathedral could be seen standing at the edge of the swimming pool, praying to forgotten icons. Recently Yury Luzhkov, Moscow's autocratic mayor, tried to make up for Stalin's mess by ordering the construction of a tacky reproduction of the original cathedral using precast concrete.

_06:: The World's Largest Hydrogen Bomb

Truth is always stranger than fiction, so it's no wonder that Stanley Kubrick's absurd comedy *Dr. Strangelove* is actually premised on fact. The strange truth here was that Nikita Khrushchev and company had actually been plotting to build a "doomsday" device. The plan called for a large cargo ship anchored off the Soviet Union's east coast to be loaded with hundreds of hydrogen bombs. If at any point the radiation detectors aboard the ship measured a certain amount of atmospheric radiation, indicating that the Soviet Union had been attacked, the bombs would detonate. Soviet scientists persuaded Khrushchev to drop this mad scheme. He did, however, order the construction of the world's largest nuclear bomb in 1961, the so-called "Czar Bomba" ("King of Bombs"), which weighed in at about 100 megatons—equivalent to 100 million tons of TNT. The largest nuclear test involved a smaller version of "Czar Bomba" that measured somewhere between 50 and 57 megatons—the Soviets weren't sure themselves.

Touch of Evil

Sociologists, historians, and cultural theorists have all written about the Soviet obsession with making things as big as possible, whether they be factories, vehicles, cities, dams, bombs, farms, or anything else. The large size was intended to convey the might, authority, and technical expertise of the Soviet Union, especially in comparison with capitalist countries.

_07:: World's Largest Icebreaker, the *Yamal*

And it's the world's only nuclear-powered icebreaker at that! Confronted with the world's largest piece of ice—the Arctic Ocean—the Soviets had no intention of letting nature stand in their way. So, they came up with a simple solution: the world's largest icebreakers. The first included the Lenin and Arktika class of nuclear-powered icebreakers, introduced in 1959 and 1975, respectively. The Arktika ice-breakers had not one but *two* nuclear reactors, powering 75,000-horsepower engines. None compare with the newest vessel, however—the *Yamal*—launched in 1993. Also powered by two nuclear reactors, it measures in at 490 feet long, displacing 23,000 tons of water, with a crew of 150 and an armored steel hull 4.8 centimeters thick. Recently reoutfitted for tourist operations, it has 50 luxury cabins, a library, lounge, theater, bar, volleyball court, gymnasium, heated indoor swimming pool, and saunas. A helicopter is stationed on the ship to conduct reconnaissance of ice formations.

A Gentleman Never Tells: Bodies That've Never Been Found

It's tough to have a real first-class funeral, especially when the guest of honor doesn't seem to show up. And whether the following five individuals are smiling down from above or quietly smirking about their fake demises, none of their bodies made it to the lost-and-found box.

_01:: Ambrose Bierce (1842–1914?)

He was wounded during the Civil War, drank with fellow journalists Mark Twain and H. L. Mencken, and kept a human skull on his desk. Bierce was also a devilishly fine writer who lampooned and skewered just about everyone in the American public eye during the last half of the 19th century. One thing he wasn't, however, was found. In late 1913, Bierce went to Mexico to cover the country's revolution. What happened to him when he got there is a mystery. Theories include: he was killed at the Battle of Ojinaga; he was executed by the revolutionary leader Pancho Villa; he shot himself at the Grand Canyon. Any of those ends would have doubtless suited Bierce. Death by bullet, he wrote before leaving for Mexico, "beats old age, disease, or falling down the cellar stairs."

_02:: Joseph F. Crater (1889–????)

On the evening of August 6, 1930, a New York Supreme Court associate justice stepped into a New York City taxi—and became a synonym for "missing person." When Crater didn't show up for court on August 25, a massive search was launched. But no trace of the judge was ever found. There were reports he was killed by the jealous boyfriend of a chorus girl, or by crooked politicians who feared what Crater knew. Conversely, there were rumors that he fled the country to avoid a judicial corruption probe. After 10 years, Crater was declared dead. But by then he'd already become a staple of pop culture: Groucho Marx would sometimes end his nightclub act by saying he "was stepping out [to] look for Judge Crater."

_03:: Amelia Earhart (1897–1937?)

It was the second time around when Earhart and her navigator, Fred Noonan, took off in May 1937 to try to circle the world in a custom-built twin-engine plane. A first effort by the famed aviatrix ended in a crash in Hawaii. Undaunted, however, Earhart had completed all but the last three legs of her second journey when the world last heard from her on July 2, and investigations into her fate have been almost ceaseless since then. U.S. government officials say she crashed at sea. Others claim she died on a South Pacific island, was captured and executed by the Japanese military, or lived out her life as a housewife in New Jersey.

_04:: Glenn Miller (1904–1944?)

On December 15, 1944, it was so foggy that Miller reportedly joked, "Even the birds are grounded." Still, the famed bandleader, who had joined the U.S. Army in 1942, boarded a small plane in Bedford, England, bound for Paris to prepare for a troop concert. He never made it. Depending on your level of credulity: the plane crashed in the English Channel; it was knocked down by Allied planes jettisoning bombs before landing; he was killed by the Nazis while on a secret mission; or he died of a heart attack in a Paris brothel. The big money, though, is apparently on the bomb theory. A Royal Air Force logbook indicating "friendly fire" as the cause of Miller's demise sold for about $30,000 at a 1999 auction.

_05:: Harold Holt (1908–1967?)

On December 17, 1967, the ocean was all motion off Portsea, Victoria, but Australian politician Harold Holt, known as the "sportsman prime minister," plunged into the surf anyway. The man had been PM for only two years, but sadly, he never came out, and an intensive search failed to turn up a trace. The result? 38 years of rumors: had Holt committed suicide; been assassinated by the CIA; been eaten by a shark; or had he swum out to a waiting Chinese submarine and been spirited away? Without a body, no inquest was held at the time. But in 2004, a change in Australian law prompted a formal inquiry to formally close the case of the missing PM. The ruling? A lackluster verdict to say the least: death by drowning.

Touch of Evil

In a 2003 episode of TV's Mythbusters, New York Giants coach Jim Fassel revealed that there was a "bump" at the 10-yard line near the south end zone of Giants Stadium, where many thought that missing labor leader Jimmy Hoffa's body had been buried. Radar indications showed nothing.

A Big Tower? What an Eiffel Idea!
Structures Built as Symbols of National Pride

Sure, any old nation can prove its global might by going out and subjugating the people of an inferior culture, but which of them can simply hint at their supremacy with a piece of art? A few, actually. The following structures weren't constructed just to insinuate their peoples' greatness to the rest of the world; they were meant to flat out proclaim it.

_01:: Colossus of Rhodes

In the third century BCE, the Macedonians had been laying siege to the Greek city-state of Rhodes for about a year when they finally decided that the war was too expensive and called it off. Failing to clean up after themselves, the Macedonians littered the landscape with various siege machines, which the enterprising Rhodesians made use of by selling off the equipment. Then they used their newfound cash to build a mammoth statue of the sun god Helios to commemorate their victory. The hollow bronze statue, which at 105 feet was not quite as high as the Statue of Liberty, took 12 years to complete. The Colossus stood tall for almost 60 years, until it was felled by an earthquake. Then it took to relaxing, lying around for about another 875 years, until the Arabs invaded Rhodes and sold off the statue's remains. Rhodes's scholars claim it took 900 camels to haul the Colossus away.

_02:: The Eiffel Tower

Vilified in the media as a monstrosity—one critic called it "a metal asparagus"—the Eiffel Tower wasn't supposed to stay up very long after it was built. In fact, it was offered for sale as scrap. It was spared only because the French army found its height made it an excellent communications tower. But Gustav Eiffel's 984-foot-high tribute to the 100th anniversary of the French Revolution welcomed its 200-millionth visitor in 2002, and has become one of the most recognizable man-made landmarks in the world. Constructed as the main attraction of the 1889 International Exposition, the tower was also the impetus behind the main draw at the 1893 World's Columbian Exposition in Chicago. Eager to one-up the French, the Americans unveiled a giant amusement ride named after its inventor—George Ferris.

_03:: Mount Rushmore

Meet America's greatest rock group: George, Tom, Abe, and Teddy. But how exactly did this presidential summit come about? And more important, why South Dakota? The fact is, a South Dakota state historian had a big idea in 1924: turn a cliff in the Black Hills into a tribute to heroes of the Old West. And sculptor John Gutzon de la Mothe Borglum liked the idea, but not the choice of subjects. So, the idea morphed a little, and a quartet of presidential busts was opened to the public in October 1941. Mount Rushmore, which cost about $1 million to build and is the largest American artwork ever created, attracts 27 million visitors a year—even though it was never finished. America got into World War II and funds ran dry. That's why Lincoln is missing an ear. Either that or that's van Gogh up there.

_04:: The Petronas Towers

Statues as national monuments are *so* passé, at least in Malaysia. The Petronas Towers, financed by the country's nationalized oil company and a private developer, are basically very tall office buildings, with a twist. They were built quite consciously as symbols of national pride. "We are showing the world we are a developing, industrialized country," the towers' chief operating officer told the Associated Press in 1995. To make sure the world was listening, though, the builders added spires to the towers to ensure they would be the world's tallest buildings. At 1,483 feet, they surpassed the Sears Tower in Chicago. Not to be outdone, however, in 2003, a spire was placed atop the Taipei 101 (Taipei Financial Center) building, in Taipei, Taiwan, just so it tiptoed above the Malaysian structures. And while Taiwan's building may have inched its way taller on a technicality, the view of Kuala Lumpur is still better at the Petronas.

I Want To See My Face in It:
World Leaders Obsessed with Their Own Images

There's no such thing as a face only a mother could love. After all, with the proper coercion (be it a gavel or a gun), a good tyrant can show you just how adjustable your aesthetic sense can be. Here are five world leaders who were obsessed with their own images, and made sure that their subjects were, too.

_01:: Mausolus (?–353 BCE)

For 24 years, Mausolus ruled over the city-state of Halicarnassus in what is now Turkey, and he spent a lot of time building up the city. So, maybe it was only fitting that in his final years Mausolus built a monument to himself. Mausolus's self-styled memorial wasn't finished until a few years after his death—with his wife, Artemisia I, carrying on the work. But when it was done, it was one of the fanciest tombs the world has ever seen: 140 feet high, 12,000 square feet, and tastefully adorned with tons of giant statues. The tomb stood for 16 centuries before it was toppled by earthquakes. But Mausolus's wish to be remembered did come true. His name is at the root of the word for "grand tomb": mausoleum.

_02:: Julius Caesar (100–44 BCE)

Things were looking pretty darn good for Jules in February 44 BCE. He'd stacked the Roman Senate with yes-men and he'd just changed his job title to "dictator for life." So he figured, what the heck, he'd ignore Roman tradition that prevented the images of living persons on coins of the realm. Caesar's portrait soon appeared on silver denari, along with the inscription "Divus Julius," or "Divine Julius." Alas, "divine" did not equate with "immortal." On March 15, Caesar was stabbed to death by a gang of senators. Pride had indeed gone before the fall. Not everyone was daunted by Caesar's recent stumblings, though. Brutus, the most famous of Caesar's killers, issued his own coins shortly after the assassination.

Touch of Evil

Many believe that stuffy old Richard Nixon won the 1968 presidential election largely due to four words he said on television. Those legendary words? "Sock it to me," uttered on America's counterculture comedy show Rowan & Martin's Laugh-In.

_03:: Nicolae Ceausescu (1918–1989)

Starting in 1965, Ceausescu was dictator of Romania, and boy did everyone know it. Portraits of the man hung everywhere, along with billboards extolling him as the "Genius of the Carpathians." Further still, images of him and his wife (the deputy prime minister) adorned postage stamps, and scores of books they allegedly wrote were crammed on bookstore shelves. But Ceausescu's biggest monument to himself was—insert ironic chuckle here—"the

People's Palace." The second-largest building in the world, after the Pentagon, in terms of area, the complex required the razing of a good part of downtown Bucharest in the late 1980s. Not surprisingly, the "people" weren't impressed. After a revolution and a one-day trial, the "people" took the First Couple out on Christmas Day, 1989, and shot them.

_04:: Saddam Hussein (1937–   )

For much of Saddam's 30-year-plus reign, it was probably easier to find something in Iraq that *wasn't* named after the dictator or *didn't* have his likeness on it. There was Saddam International Airport, Saddam Hospital, Saddam Stadium, dozens of palaces, and scores of statues. "Saddam has always been obsessed with building," observed *Time* magazine in 2000. So there was poetic justice on April 9, 2003, when Baghdad residents and U.S. marines pulled down a 40-foot statue of Saddam and triggered a symbolic, although as it turned out very premature, end of the Iraqi war. Still, there is something to be said for notoriety: Saddam portraits and bits of his statues are among the hottest souvenirs of the war.

_05:: Saparmurat Niyazov (1940–   )

What can you say about a guy who becomes his country's first president and promptly begins calling himself the "Turkmenbashi," or "father of all Turkmen"? That he has a golden statue of himself in the capital city that rotates so the face is always toward the sun? That his image appears on all the currency? That a book he wrote is the foundation of the educational system? That he renamed one of the months of the year after his mother? Well, yes, if the guy in question is Niyazov, who has been president of Turkmenistan since the Central Asian country broke free from the Soviet Union in 1991. Oh, did we mention the palace of ice he wanted to build in the middle of a desert? We're not kidding.

Pride and Prejudice: Recent Cases Where Diversity Would Have Helped

Discrimination in the workplace is a thing of the past, right? Well, not quite. These corporate giants had to find out the hard way that prejudice doesn't pay…though lawsuits certainly do!

_01:: Denny's

Usually associated with round-the-clock sausage links and "Moon Over My Hammy" specials, in the 1990s the name Denny's also became a byword for racism and discrimination lawsuits. Accused of making black patrons prepay for their meals, serving them slower than white patrons or not serving them at all, the national restaurant chain was thick in the midst of an investigation when things got even worse. Four black Secret Service agents who were assigned to protect the president reported not being served while their white colleagues were. In 1993, both the U.S. government and Kristina Ridgeway, a then-17-year-old who was asked to pay a cover charge before being served, brought class action suits against Denny's in California on behalf of all minority patrons nationwide. In 1994, the lawsuit was settled for an estimated $54 million and catapulted Denny's into a cultural transformation. Changes included diversity programs from the board membership on down. The results? Today, 50% of the 46,000 employees are minorities, 32% of supervisory positions are held by minorities, and contracts with minority-owned suppliers have increased from zero to $100 million a year.

_02:: Coca-Cola

In 2000, the Coca-Cola Company shelled out $192.5 million and agreed to establish new programs and reforms to settle a racial discrimination class action lawsuit brought by 2,000 black employees. The lawsuit claimed that Coca-Cola discriminated against black employees in pay, promotions, and performance evaluations. The amount (the largest award ever for a racial discrimination class action lawsuit) included $113 million in cash awards, $43.5 million to adjust salaries, and $36 million to establish oversight programs to monitor the company's employment practices. Talk about being the real thing! Coke also paid $20 million in attorney fees and took a fourth-quarter charge of $188 million against their profits to settle the lawsuit. As part of the agreed changes, a seven-member task force was assembled to examine the company to ensure fair hiring, pay, and other human resource practices until 2004. In late 2004, Coca-Cola requested that the task force supervision remain in effect until the end of 2006. Coca-Cola seems to have learned from its mistakes. Just like they did with New Coke.

Touch of Evil

Southwest Airlines broke their pattern as the "fun airline" when they began enforcing a regulation (from 1980) charging hefty passengers for two seats. Despite pending lawsuits, the rule has now been adopted by other airlines. Don't they know the human body swells at high altitudes?

_03:: Boeing

In 2004, Mary Beck and 11 other women filed a gender discrimination lawsuit against Boeing that triggered a class action lawsuit that included approximately 29,000 former and current employees of the company. Boeing agreed to pay $72.5 million to settle the gender discrimination lawsuit. The company was charged with paying female workers less and giving them fewer promotions than their male counterparts, and it actually took four full years to settle the lawsuit. The suit also contained allegations of sexual harassment, retaliation, and racial discrimination. For example, the plaintiffs claimed that they were consistently denied job training and promotions and reported that when they submitted complaints to the internal Equal Employment Opportunity office they were routinely punished with denial of overtime and other forms of retribution. Under the settlement, Boeing agreed to moni-

tor salaries and overtime assignments and to conduct annual performance reviews. Eligible nonexecutive and hourly female workers, from janitors to first-level managers, got $500 or more depending on when they worked and how much they earned. Mary Beck and the 11 other original plaintiffs were each awarded $100,000. The other women received settlements based on the amount of time they had worked and how much they had earned.

_04:: Morgan Stanley

Without admitting any culpability, in July 2004 Morgan Stanley agreed to pay $54 million, out of court, to settle claims that it didn't promote women and that it underpaid them. The financial powerhouse had been accused of passing over senior women employees in its institutional equity division for promotion and pay increases. Even worse, the Equal Employment Opportunity Commission lawyers alleged that women were groped and excluded from male-only outings with clients. Under the conditions of the agreement, a fund of $40 million was established to handle claims from more than 300 women who believed they were discriminated against. A separate payment of $12 million was awarded to the lead plaintiff whose original complaint in 1998 and subsequent firing in 2000 prompted the investigation, and the final $2 million was used to appoint an internal diversity ombudsman and outside monitor to conduct performance and compensation analyses, maintain a complaint database, and implement programs to address the promotion and retention of women.

_05:: Wal-Mart

As many as 1.6 million current and former female Wal-Mart employees alleged gender dis-

ALEXANDER HAMILTON'S HORRIBLE-TERRIBLE, NO-GOOD, VERY BAD DAY

July 11, 1804, Weehawken, New Jersey: Alexander Hamilton met his rival, Aaron Burr, for an "interview" (so called because dueling was illegal). Burr had challenged Hamilton to the duel as a result of years of squabbling and alleged libels that Hamilton could have defused many times but didn't because of his own pride and stubbornness. Both parties seem to have intended for it to be a relatively bloodless affair, simply going through the motions to "satisfy honor." But on July 11, everything seemed to be against Hamilton. First, he chose the north side of the ledge, which meant that the rising sun and glare off the water would be in his eyes. Second, he chose two ornate smoothbore pistols, fancy but highly inaccurate. Historians now believe that Hamilton purposely fired his shot high above Burr, intentionally missing him. Burr, not realizing this, fired back, but probably only to wound Hamilton in the leg. Hamilton's choice of weapon came back to haunt him, though: the inaccuracy of the pistol turned a flesh wound into a kill shot. The huge .54-caliber ball entered above his hip (leaving a two-inch hole), shattered a rib, ricocheted through his liver and diaphragm, and lodged in the second lumbar vertebra. He died at two the next afternoon. It was sort of a bad day for Burr, too. His "murder" of the popular Hamilton made him a villain in the eyes of the public and ruined his political career.

crimination, and a federal judge agreed in June 2004 that the case could proceed as a class action lawsuit. The suit claims that Wal-Mart consistently discriminated against female employees in its manager recruitment and promotion practices. Discrimination lawsuits are nothing new to everyone's favorite superstore, though. In 2001, Wal-Mart was cited and fined $6.8 million by the EEOC for a continued pattern of disability discrimination across 11 states. In fact, Wal-Mart's preemployment questionnaire violated the Americans with Disabilities Act (ADA) by seeking disability-related information from qualified applicants before formal job offers were made. As part of the settlement, Wal-Mart agreed to change its ADA policies and procedures, create an ADA coordinator, provide training in ADA compliance, and offer jobs to certain disabled applicants. Unfortunately, Wal-Mart didn't quite learn its lesson. The company has since paid an additional $720,000 for violating the terms of the agreement and was even ordered to produce a TV advertisement noting Wal-Mart's role in violating the Americans with Disabilities Act.

_06:: Costco

Not wanting to be left out, the Issaquah, Washington, retailer joined the ranks of known corporations embroiled in class action gender discrimination suits in August 2004. The lawsuit, which was brought by approximately 640 female employees, alleged that a "glass ceiling" had been imposed denying women promotions to assistant manager and general store manager positions. Worse still, the claims were well founded. According to company documents, approximately 50% of Costco's 78,000 employees are female, but less than 1 in 6 managers is a woman. Further, the complaints alleged that the company didn't announce openings for higher-paying managerial jobs. Instead, the selection process resembled a "boys' club"—with top-level male executives routinely selecting other men for the higher-level management positions.

Pride over Prejudice: Individuals Who Taught Us How to Sing the Blues

Despite all the terrible institutions that have been used to keep African Americans down, they still managed to turn their misery into the beautiful music of the blues.

_01:: W. C. Handy Discovers the Blues

William Christopher (W. C.) Handy was the prototypical bluesman of the early 1900s. Born in a log cabin in 1873, Handy learned to play music at a very young age. But it wasn't until he was 30 that he got his first taste of the blues. While sitting at a railroad station in Tutwiler, Mississippi, Handy heard a local musician playing blues on a guitar, strumming it with a knife and singing about a nearby location where two railroads crossed. At first, Handy thought the sounds emanating were a little too strange, but he soon became intrigued. Over the next few years, Handy collected and copyrighted the songs he'd learned from the rural Delta folk. Then, in 1909, Handy moved to Memphis and while playing at a political rally, he composed and sang a song about the politician Boss Crump. Three years later, Handy rewrote the lyrics and it became the widely known "Memphis Blues." It was just one of several hits he'd write. In 1914, Handy composed an instant classic, the "Saint Louis Blues," which went on to become the first nationally recognized song of the Delta blues movement and what many consider to be the first jazz recording.

_02:: Mamie Smith's "Crazy Blues" Sells a Million

By the second decade of the 20th century, the blues had gained a strong foothold in the South. Unknown to many, however, is the fact that female blues performers carried more than their share of the load during this time. And while the big names like Ma Rainey and Bessie Smith performed throughout the South, it was a vaudeville singer and dancer, Mamie Smith, who recorded the first blues songs in 1920. While her variety shows always included some blues and jazz numbers, her manager saw a new market for recordings in the large African American populations that had recently migrated to the North. Based on Smith's popularity in New York, her manager was able to persuade Okeh Records to record Smith's version of "Crazy Blues" and "It's Here for You." Not surprisingly, the recording was extremely successful, selling over 1 million copies in less than a year and eventually 2 million copies overall.

_03:: Charley Patton and the "Pony Blues"

Considered the founder of the Delta blues, Charley Patton was the model bluesman. The son of a sharecropper, young Patton moved with his family to the Dockery Plantation in the Delta region in Mississippi and soon began playing gigs around the area. Considered a "superstar" at a young age, Patton was always in demand to play at plantation dances and in juke joints. In fact, his slide guitar stylings became the standard imitated by other Delta musicians. In 1929 he recorded the "Pony Blues," which became a big hit for the Paramount Record Company. But it wasn't his music so much as his stage presence that made him a legend. Diminutive in size (5 feet 5 inches, 135 lbs), Patton became larger than life when he saw an audience. His raw, impassioned voice accompanied by his loud, fluid guitar playing to an unrelenting beat drove audiences into a

frenzy. Of course, Patton's persona carried over into his daily life as well. Loud, boisterous, drinking excessively, and with a woman on each arm, Patton defined the image of the early bluesman. Married eight times and imprisoned at least once, Patton was always on the move.

_04:: Leadbelly Meets John and Alan Lomax

Huddie Ledbetter, known to most of us as Leadbelly, was more than just a blues singer—he was one of America's greatest folk artists. Considered by some to be a murderer and by others a writer of children's songs, Leadbelly's life is legendary for its rumors and inconsistencies. In Texas in 1918, Leadbelly was accused of killing a man in a fight over a woman. And while many witnesses said it was in self-defense, Leadbelly pleaded guilty because he knew that as a black man he wouldn't get a fair trial. In 1930, he was involved in another murder (this time only attempted) and was imprisoned until 1934. Somehow, though, he still came to the attention of John and Alan Lomax, a father and son musicologist team who were commissioned by the Library of Congress to travel through the backwoods and rural areas of the South to record American folk music. The duo recognized Leadbelly's genius and promptly took him on tour with them in the northern United States, but audiences viewed him as more of a curiosity than a performer. Of course, the feelings were spurred by the press. A headline in the *New York Herald Tribune* (January 3, 1935), for instance, read, "Lomax Arrives with Leadbelly, Negro Minstrel/Sweet Singer of the Swamplands Here to Do a Few Tunes between Homicides." Like many a blues star, Leadbelly never achieved commercial success during his lifetime, but his songs "Goodnight Irene," "The Midnight Special," "Cotton Fields," and "Rock Island Line" are American classics today.

_05:: Muddy Waters and the Chicago Blues

In 1948, the blues got ratcheted up a notch when McKinley Morganfield and his Chicago sound hit the scene. Better known by his nickname, Muddy Waters, Morganfield helped create a new high-octane version of the music, which quickly became synonymous with contemporary urban blues. But just because he was pushing the sound forward didn't mean Waters had an easy time finding a label. After cutting some unissued recordings for Colum-bia, Waters finally persuaded the owners of Aristocrat (a small independent label that later became Chess Records) to put him in a studio. Luckily, one of the singles, "I Can't Be Satis-fied/I Feel Like Going Home," became a hit, and the modern Chicago blues was born. Waters's deep, majestic voice, coupled with an amplified guitar, introduced listeners to a sound that was exciting, powerful, and thoroughly compelling. In fact, the new music gave rise to a whole new generation of Chicago blues artists who played with Waters, including Willie Dixon, Otis Spann, Junior Wells, Buddy Guy, and Otis Rush. Later on, Waters was a significant influence on the careers of contemporary artists like Paul Butterfield, Michael Bloomfield, and Johnny Winters.

Disobedience School: The Secret Lives of Civil Activists

Sure, you know their names from textbooks. You've seen their statues and heard them praised as heroes for standing up (and sticking it) to the man. Heck, you might even get a day or two off in a year thanks to them. But just because history paints these proud figures heroes, it doesn't mean they didn't come with a couple of blemishes. The following are four civil activists—and a couple of their secrets that history likes to brush over.

_01:: Henry David Thoreau (1817–1862)

A civil activist and the author of *Walden* and "On Civil Disobedience," Thoreau was about as eccentric as they come. In 1837, Thoreau graduated from Harvard but saw little value in the courses he'd taken. After all, old Henry felt that true education came from communing with nature (sadly, the degree isn't widely accredited). Henry, not really fond of the idea of work, once lasted only two weeks at a teaching job because he couldn't keep his students quiet and refused to punish them. So, how'd he get by, exactly? The philosopher survived mainly on odd jobs, though not too many of them. Henry made it his policy to try not to work more than 15 to 20 hours per week. His laziness isn't all this "catch" had going against him; described as "ugly but in an agreeable fashion" by his friends, he once proposed marriage by letter to a young lady only to be rejected. He also took to calling himself Henry David (instead of his given name David Henry) and ticked off his neighbors, who thought this to be unnatural and unseemly. Preferring to live in a small cabin close to Walden Pond, Thoreau was known to spend inordinate amounts of time standing still watching nature. Of course, he did remain active in some aspects of his life. As an uncompromising abolitionist, Thoreau harbored runaway slaves and helped them reach Canada. As for his much-celebrated imprisonment for refusing to pay a poll tax, though, that only lasted one day.

_02:: Ralph Waldo Emerson (1803–1882)

To most of us, Ralph Waldo Emerson was the quirky sidekick and mentor to Henry David Thoreau. And while you might think of Ralph as the consummate Renaissance man, you probably don't consider inventing a religion to be one of his many talents. It's true, though. When Emerson started believing his Unitarian faith was a bit too limiting, he set out to create his own religion based on the relationship among nature, man, and the divine. Known as the Sage of Concord, Emerson was years ahead of others in understanding nature and its role. For example, his ideas on evolution preceded Darwin's, and his thoughts on matter and energy were 80 years ahead of Einstein. In fact, his discussions on the hierarchy of human needs even anticipated the work of Abraham Maslow in the 20th century. It's too bad most of this Renaissance thinking was lost during Emerson's time—and mainly because he took such a strong stance against slavery. His attacks on the morally bankrupt institution regularly got him in hot water, and calling John Brown a saint and a martyr didn't exactly help. In fact, it strongly curtailed his speaking engagements and left poor Emerson just that, poor.

Touch of Evil

While it's said that Dr. Martin Luther King Jr. had many secrets, things started with the name on his birth certificate. It wasn't Martin but Michael, which his father said was a mistake made by the attending physician.

_03:: Tom Hayden (1939–)

The poster boy for radical 1960s political movements, Tom Hayden was a chief ideologue of the student movement and the founder of Students for a Democratic Society. Gaining international attention as one of the Chicago Seven (who stood trial for disrupting the 1968 Democratic National Convention), Tom quickly became a celebrity, even marrying fellow political activist and movie actress Jane Fonda in 1973. Although he lost when he ran for the U.S. Senate in 1976, Hayden stayed involved in local California politics and ran unsuccessfully for mayor of Los Angeles in the late 1990s. Interestingly, this self-proclaimed defender of the poor and politically oppressed bought a 120-acre retreat with Fonda in 1977 to be used to train young political activists. The problem was, before they could move in Tom and Jane had to evict a number of low-income tenants.

_04:: Harriet Beecher Stowe (1811–1896)

Known as a moody, absentminded child, Harriet Beecher Stowe grew up to be one of the most influential social critics of the 19th century. Moving with her family from Hartford, Connecticut, to Cincinnati, Ohio, she soon came into contact with the mentality of the Mason-Dixon Line and with fugitive slaves. The effects were clearly profound. In 1851, Stowe became famous for her book *Uncle Tom's Cabin*, which depicted the evils of slavery. When the novel was attacked as being inaccurate fiction, she published "A Key to Uncle Tom's Cabin" in 1853 to refute the critics. Not only did the book make her an international celebrity, it actually made her quite wealthy during a time when writing wasn't viewed as a lucrative profession. Still, she managed to create arguably the most controversial piece of literature of the 19th century. In fact, when she met Abraham Lincoln in 1862, the president exclaimed, "So you are the little woman who wrote the book that started this great war!"

Who's Your Daddy?
Famous Bastards Who Made Their Mark

Accusing someone of illegitimate birth has long been one of the greatest insults possible, so it's not at all surprising that some of history's greatest shoulder-mounted chips have been securely fastened to people with murky parentage. In fact, by the look of the names on this list, it just might be a recipe for success.

_01:: Sargon the Great (ca. 2360–2279 BCE)

In his autobiography (recorded as *The Legend of Sargon*), Sargon admits, "My father I knew not." And while we don't know his genealogy, we do know the guy was "Great." Supposedly the son of royalty (at least that's what he told people), Sargon was actually abandoned in a basket on the Euphrates River and found by a gardener. Somehow, the clever kid worked his way up to cupbearer (sort of a prime minister) to the king of the Sumerian city of Kish, but his ambition didn't stop there. Eventually, Sargon founded his own kingdom among the Semitic peoples of Akkad. Of course, anyone who laughed at his supposed illegitimacy probably lived to regret it; in the span of a few decades Sargon conquered Sumeria and built one of the first true empires in world history, stretching from the mountains of southern Anatolia to the Syrian coast and the Persian Gulf. His Akkadian name, Sharru-kin, means "The King Is Legitimate." We think . . .

_02:: Confucius (ca. 551–479 BCE)

The early life of K'ung-Fu-tzu, better known in the West as Confucius, is largely a mystery. Born in the feudal kingdom of Lu, Confucius served as an adviser on political matters and court etiquette to several Chinese leaders during the mid- to late 500s BCE. The circumstances of Confucius's own birth, however, are hardly up to any Emily Post standards. According to the first complete biography of Confucius, the *Shiji*, his dad, a warlord named Shu Liang He, and his mom, a member of the Yan clan, "came roughly together," indicating either a rape, concubinage, or some other sort of extramarital shenanigan. His low birth, however, didn't stop him from attracting plenty of highborn followers, many of whom protected him when his outspoken manner offended his various employers.

_03:: William I of England (1028–1087)

Billy the Conqueror, as he liked to be called, was the son of Duke Robert of Normandy and a tanner's daughter named Arletta, who had a thing for guys in armor. By his early 20s, Billy had defeated his rivals for the throne, conquered the rich province of Maine, and become one of the most powerful men in France. But even after being crowned king of England, "William the Bastard" didn't stop his conquests—he died in Vexin during an attempt to seize control of the French province. Interestingly enough, though, little Billy wasn't the only great king of England to be a bastard; Athelstan (ruled 924–939), maybe the greatest of the Anglo-Saxon monarchs, was also the product of a somewhat less than legitimate union.

_04:: Juchi (ca. 1180–1227)

It almost sounds like a fairy tale: the bride of a young Mongol herdsman named Temudjin was kidnapped by an enemy tribe, but rather than abandon her to her fate (the custom at the time—Temudjin's own mother had been kidnapped by his father), Temudjin gathered an army and risked his life to get her back. When she came back, though, she was pregnant. Amazingly, Temudjin accepted the child as his own, but named him Juchi, "the Guest," just to make sure everyone knew that he didn't regard the kid's paternity as totally kosher. Temudjin soon became known to the world as Genghis Khan, and his son Juchi began the conquest of Russia, possibly to get away from his brothers, who, according to Mongol sources, taunted him and called him a bastard. The kingdom he carved out was ultimately known as the Golden Horde, the longest lived of the Mongol successor states.

Touch of Evil

It may not have been coincidence how Debbie Harry of the band Blondie resembled Marilyn Monroe. The adopted Harry used to dream that Monroe was her birth mother. Of unknown parentage herself, Marilyn would have been 19 when Debbie was born.

_05:: Leonardo da Vinci (1452–1519)

Everyone knows of Leonardo da Vinci, the *Homo universalis* who could be a painter, a naturalist, an engineer, a metallurgist, or a philosopher with equal ease. It's considerably less well known that this personification of the Renaissance was actually the son of a notary, Ser Piero, and a peasant girl of somewhat "easy virtue." In fact, the two simply took a tumble in the hay together before going their separate ways and providing Leonardo, from their mar-

Lies Your Mother Told You

THERE ARE PEOPLE BURIED IN THE HOOVER DAM

It's a good, spooky story. And with more than 100 fatalities occurring over the five years of its construction, there's a pretty good chance that at least one of them fell into the wet concrete and now rests there for all eternity, right? Nope. The construction of the Hoover Dam was notoriously devoid of safety considerations for the 16,000 workers who built the incredible structure. Men died from falls, rockslides, carbon monoxide poisoning (from the gasoline-powered dump trucks in the tunnels), and heat prostration (during the summer of 1931, the temperature routinely reached 140 degrees). But, oddly enough, the pouring of the 3,640,000 cubic meters of concrete went relatively smoothly. Nobody fell in. Well, nobody who didn't get out again, anyway. So the next time someone tells you there are people buried in the Hoover Dam, look them in the eye and tell 'em with confidence it's just a dam lie.

barrassment, and on his father's death in 1503 they conspired to deprive him of his share of the estate. Leonardo had the last laugh, however, when the death of an uncle led to a similar inheritance squabble, leaving him with sole custody of the uncle's lands and property.

_06:: Thomas Paine (1737–1809) and _07:: Alexander Hamilton (1755–1804)

Two of the best-known fathers of the American republic, Thomas Paine and Alexander Hamilton, were the results of extramarital bedroom high jinks. Paine, whose *Common Sense* helped bring widespread support to the American Revolution, and whose other writings, like the anti-Bible tract *The Age of Reason,* scandalized all and sundry, had to flee England a step ahead of treason charges. In the end, however, he died penniless in the United States. Hamilton, on the other hand, was the illegitimate son of West Indian colonials, and made a name for himself as a brilliant orator and writer. He eventually became one of the leaders of the American Federalist Party, but had the misfortune to be challenged to a duel by Aaron Burr. He also had the even greater misfortune of accepting, bringing his career to a dramatic close one fine New Jersey morning. (See "Alexander Hamilton's Horrible-Terrible, No-Good, Very Bad Day," page 31.)

_08:: Thomas Edward Lawrence (1888–1935)

The illegitimate son of a knight and his children's nanny, T. E. Lawrence became the model for generations of British diplomats blindly idolizing all things Arabian. One of the organizers of the much-touted (but in reality

riages to other people, with 17 half brothers and sisters. Needless to say, these assorted half siblings were none too fond of their renowned relation, whose birth was something of an em-

fought more on paper than on the battlefield) Arab revolt against the Turks during World War I, Lawrence later became embittered with Britain's imperial policy and spent the last few years of his life sulking and tinkering with motorcycles (he died in a motorcycle accident). Though he largely tried to keep a low profile, his much-exaggerated accomplishments led to him being dubbed "Lawrence of Arabia."

_09:: Eva Perón (1919–1952)

"Saint Evita" was the daughter of an adulterous relationship between two villagers in an impoverished part of Argentina. She made a name for herself as an actress before marrying Juan Perón in 1944, but, being illegitimate (and a peasant), she was never really accepted in the social circles in which he routinely traveled. As a rising military officer, Perón quickly found himself dictator of Argentina, and "Evita" was by his side. In fact, she was there to do more than just wave at crowds and manage the mansion. Evita actually ran several government ministries and almost became vice president in 1951 (the military bullied Perón into making her drop out of the campaign). And though she's best known to many from the musical and movie that bear her name, you really shouldn't feel obligated to cry for her. While the flick plays up the glamour and romance of her career, it largely ignores her corruption, oppression of political rivals, cozying up to Nazi war criminals, and other questionable doings.

Oh, Say Can You Sin: The Dish on National Anthems

A national anthem is supposed to symbolize everything that is good and true about a country. But these five patriotic songs have a slightly more disturbing past. Read on, and we guarantee you'll never watch Olympic medal ceremonies the same way again.

_01:: A Star-Spangled Drinking Song

What better place to start than with America's own national anthem? Every third grader knows the story of Francis Scott Key penning the great poem while watching the siege of Fort McHenry during the War of 1812. But that's just a poem. So where exactly did all this music hoo-ha come from? When Key wrote the anthem, he had a song in his head as a reference for the poem's meter (a song from *England,* ironically enough). The tune, notoriously difficult to sing, is from a drinking song written by John Stafford Smith originally titled "Anacreon in Heaven." It was the theme song of a club of rich London men who got together to eat, drink, and then—for good measure—drink some more. The Anacreontic Club took its name from Anacreon, a Greek poet who wrote about such things. Perhaps it's fitting, then, that the song is usually sung before sporting events, after fans have been tailgating (translation: drinking) for several hours.

_02:: The U.K.'s Illegitimate Anthem

Most Americans recognize the tune of the United Kingdom's national anthem as "My Country 'Tis of Thee," but the Brits clearly had it first. Like the U.S. anthem, "God Save the Queen" (originally "King," but they switch it depending on the gender of the current monarch) was first sung to commemorate a military victory: the capture of the South American port of Portobelo during the War of Jenkins' Ear (1739–1742). At least, that's what we think. Other traditions link it to the Jacobite rebellion, when George II's troops sang it to restore morale after losing to Bonnie Prince Charlie at Prestonpans (verse 5, now almost never sung, refers to crushing the rebellious Scots). Oddly enough, the well-known tune is the U.K.'s anthem only by default. It has no authorized version and has never been officially sanctioned by either royal decree or an act of Parliament. And get this—it's also the national anthem of Liechtenstein.

_03:: Australia's Beloved Sheep-Stealing Tune

Americans poke fun at themselves for not knowing all the words to the national anthem. But Australians share the same affliction. In fact, "Advance Australia Fair" has two official verses, but the second is usually a mumbled shadow of the first. And maybe it just comes down to the fact that Australians aren't really all that crazy for their national anthem. While most feel that it properly encapsulates good Australian values and whatnot, there are still mixed thoughts about it. So what song do Aussies really identify with? The correct answer is "Waltzing Matilda," a lovely and universally recognizable folk tune written by Banjo Paterson in 1895. There's a tiny problem with "Matilda's" lyrical content, though. It's about a *swagman* (itinerant worker or hobo) who steals a *jumbuck* (sheep), hides it in his *tucker bag* (food sack), and avoids arrest by drowning himself in a *billabong* (stagnant pool). Oh, and it's not about dancing with a gal named Matilda. In Australian slang, to "waltz Matilda" is to bum about from place to place looking for work, carrying your Matilda, or a blanket with all your possessions in it.

_04:: A Dutch Song of Defeat

The national anthem of the Netherlands, "Wilhelmus van Nassouwe," ranks as the world's oldest official anthem. Dating from around 1568, a turbulent time for the Dutch as they struggled with longtime enemy Spain, it's also one of the only anthems that's about a specific person, not a nation. But here's the really cool, borderline creepy part. If you take the first letter of each of the fifteen verses of the anthem, they spell WILLEM VAN NASSOV, the Dutch name of Prince William I of Orange-Nassau. And they did this on purpose. Amazing, huh? Well, maybe the content's a little less inspiring. The song recounts Prince William addressing the oppressed people of Holland after he tried—and failed—three times to free them from oppression under the Spaniards.

_05:: South Africa's Song: Something for Everybody!

Every time you struggle a bit with "The Star-Spangled Banner," just be glad that you're not from South Africa. Like the nation itself, the anthem is a combination of several different ethnic groups. During the apartheid era, the white government had its anthem, "Die Stem van Suid-Afrika" ("The Call of South Africa"). Nelson Mandela's African National Congress had its own separate but unofficial tune: "Nkosi sikelel' iAfrica" ("God Bless Africa"). Then, when apartheid finally ended, blacks and whites (and their anthems) were legally forced to coexist. That is, until 1995, when the pieces were melded to form the current national anthem in all its disjointed glory. Just how awkward is it? The anthem changes key in the middle and uses *five* different languages. Starting as "Nkosi," the tune goes on to sample the more prevalent of South Africa's many native languages. Verse 1 is in Xhosa. Verse 2, Zulu. Verse 3 is Sesotho. Then the key switches and "Die Stem" powers through. Verse 4 is in Afrikaans, and verse 5 is in English. Phew!

Ignominious Things Named for Napoléon Bonaparte

No matter what you think of him, Napoléon certainly did a number on this world. And whether it's as the savior of revolutionary France or the scourge of Western civilization, the little guy's name keeps on keeping on. Of course, not everything "Napoléon" adds luster to his legacy...here are a few examples to prove it.

_01:: His Son: Napoléon II

Sadly, Napoléon François Joseph Charles Bonaparte (aka Napoléon II, or, as we like to call him, "the Deuce"), never had a chance to fill his father's tiny shoes. Despite being the son of Emperor Napoléon I, and garnering the title King of Rome at birth in 1811, poor Napoléon II never ruled anything. By the time of his fourth birthday, the First French Empire had already collapsed. Then, after Napoléon I's brief return to power and his final military defeat at Waterloo in 1815, the emperor abdi-cated in favor of his son. This proved a futile gesture, however. The brilliantly resourceful statesman Charles-Maurice de Talleyrand, a high official in Napoléon's government, had arranged for Louis XVIII to take over a new royalist government. Napoléon's escape from exile on the island of Elba and his short-lived return as emperor didn't convince the French senate to anoint young Napoléon II instead of Louis XVIII. That wasn't the worst of it for junior, however. Under formal terms of the treaty ending the Napoleonic Wars, young Napoléon also was barred from ever ruling his mother's Italian lands. As duke of Reichstadt (a title based on his mother's Hapsburg lineage), Napoléon the younger spent his short life essentially under guard in Austria, where he died of tuberculosis in 1832. He wasn't confined to Austria forever, though. In 1940, a fellow with an even more nefarious name, Adolf Hitler, disinterred Napoléon's body and sent it packing to Paris, where it could be entombed beside his father's.

_02:: His Quirk:
The Napoleon Complex

A Napoleon complex is nothing more than an inferiority complex that vertically challenged individuals self-treat with an unhealthy dose of belligerence, a healthy pursuit of achievement, or both. Think of the tough little brawler, eager to take on all challengers, especially big ones. Think of singer-songwriter Paul Simon (5 foot 3) and actors Judy Garland (4 foot 11), Danny DeVito (5 feet), Michael J. Fox (5 foot 4), and David Spade (5 foot 7). Then there are basketball's Earl Boykins (5 foot 5) and football's Wayne Chrebet and Doug Flutie (both 5 foot 10). Overachievers all. Think of Britain's prime minister Winston Churchill, for that matter, or Soviet dictator Joseph Stalin. At 5 feet 6 inches each (the same, by modern measure, as Napoléon I—see "Lies Your Mother Told You: Napoléon Was a Shrimp," page 11), either of the World War II–era leaders could have had the complex named after him if Napoléon had not gotten there first. The idea of a psychological "complex," by the way, wasn't around in Napoléon's time. It arose in 1899, with the publication of Sigmund Freud's *Interpretation of Dreams*. In that groundbreaking book, Vienna's pioneer of psychoanalysis introduced the term "Oedipus complex," referring to a child's repressed sexual desire for the parent of the opposite gender. Freud can't claim "Napoléon complex," however. It seems to have arisen in the early 1900s as a casual term, more a backhanded insult than a psychological diagnosis.

_03:: A Pig Named Napoleon

George Orwell's 1945 novel *Animal Farm* tells of a revolt strikingly close to the one that transformed the Russian Empire into the Soviet Union. That is, except for one minor detail: Orwell's rebels and revolutionaries are a bunch of animals (in the farm sense of the word). Feeling a little oppressed, Mr. Jones's barnyard creatures turn against their owner, drive him off the land, and begin running things themselves under an "all animals are equal" banner. However, idealism crumbles pretty quickly as an unscrupulous pig named (you guessed it!) Napoleon wrests control, turns on his comrades, and becomes more tyrannical than old Jones ever was. In fact, the sacred "all animals are equal" mantra quickly finds itself warped into something significantly less utopian: "all animals are equal, but some animals are more equal than others." In an allegorical sense, Napoleon stands for the USSR's Stalin. But the evil porker's name, after the little corporal who hijacked the French Revolution, certainly fits.

_04:: Napoleon Solo
(1964–1968 Vintage)

The Man from U.N.C.L.E. premiered in 1964 as TV's answer to the James Bond movies, and each episode was packed with espionage, intrigue, sophistication, and action. With Robert Vaughn in the role of Napoleon Solo, a dashing secret agent and ladies' man, the

A Row Is a Row Is a Row

BEN YOSEF V. BEN ZAKKAI

In this corner: Sa'adya ben Yosef, one of the greatest minds of 10th-century Jewry—and he knew it. He authored dozens of philosophical, religious, and linguistic works (including the *Agron,* a Hebrew dictionary written when he was 20, an Arabic translation of the Bible, one of the first Hebrew prayer books, and the monumental *Book of Beliefs and Opinions*).

In the opposite corner: David ben Zakkai, the Exilarch (leader of Middle Eastern Jewry).

Round 1: David appoints Sa'adya as Gaon (rabbinic head) of the Talmudic academy of Sura (in modern Iraq) in 928.

Round 2: In 930, Sa'adya refuses to sign a court verdict that David issued, announcing repeatedly and loudly that he believes the decision unjust.

Round 3: David orders Sa'adya deposed from the academy.

Round 4: An outraged Sa'adya excommunicates David and announces that his brother Hasan is the new Exilarch (even though appointing Hasan wasn't really within his power).

Round 5: Sa'adya and David fight a decade-long war of foul words until they ultimately reconcile, but the experience makes Sa'adya a bitter man.

Round 6: In 933, Sa'adya pens the *Sefer ha-Galui,* a theological work in which he makes clear his belief that he is the most brilliant man who has ever lived.

show's popularity grew through the first two seasons. In season three, however, the producers fell under the spell of the competing TV series *Batman,* starring Adam West. Impressed by the ratings *Batman* was drawing with its tongue-in-cheek comedy approach to action-adventure, they began taking *The Man from U.N.C.L.E.* in distinctly comic book directions. The lowest comic denominator didn't work out for the show's ratings, though, and

Solo quickly degenerated from sophisticated to camp. In the worst episode, Vaughn danced with a man in a gorilla suit.

_05:: An Anthropologist Named Napoleon

Until 2000, Napoleon Chagnon was known as author of the best-selling anthropology text of all time: *Yanomamö: The Fierce People.* But since then, his research has been mired in controversy. The anthropologist, along with geneticist James Neel, inoculated many of the Venezuelan tribe's members. Unfortunately, it was right about this time that the Yanomami experienced their first-ever measles epidemic, leading to thousands of deaths in the region and reducing the tribe to half its original size. Coincidence? Perhaps. Allegations against Chagnon have divided the anthropological community. Many defend the expedition, claiming it would be impossible for a vaccine to spark such an outbreak. Critics, however, point to the expedition's financier, the Atomic Energy Commission, as proof that the accused were using the Yanomami as human test subjects. Either way, the scandal raised serious questions about the practices of studying indigenous peoples.

_06:: The Napoléon Complex Martini

What's terrible about one part Napoléon Mandarin Liqueur to three parts vodka with an orange peel twist? Nothing, we guess, unless you're a martini purist. No offense to Chez Napoléon on West 50th Street in Manhattan, where the Napoléon Complex is a bartender's specialty, but we'll take ours classic: fine, juniper-scented gin (not vodka); the merest suggestion of dry vermouth (wave the vermouth bottle in the general vicinity of the shaker); and a fat, green, pimento-stuffed olive on a toothpick.

Seriously Holier Than Thou: Mortals with Minor God Complexes

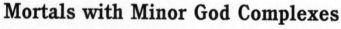

Sure, power corrupts, and absolute power corrupts absolutely, but what about Absolute power with a capital A? Here are four mortals who let their holier-than-thou attitudes go to other people's heads.

_01:: Narmer or Menes, or One of Those Really Old Egyptian Guys

Around 2925 BCE, Narmer united the upper and lower Nile Valley into Egypt. Pretty nice feat. Unfortunately, it was so long ago that historians don't know if Narmer is the same person as Menes, considered the founder of the First Dynasty, or if Menes was Narmer's son.

What they do know is that the ruler we're calling Narmer here definitely had a god complex—not that it wasn't merited! In unified Egypt, kings were considered gods. So, did that mean he was born divine? Early on, that seemed to be the idea. But during the First Dynasty, cunning priests did have a bit of veto power. If they deemed an ill king unfit, they were perfectly justified in killing him and making way for a more potent god (a practice done away with around 2659 BCE, presumably by a self-interested ruler). Slowly, though, Egyptian priests devised a better way to delay those holier-than-thou attitudes in their royalty. Instead of decreeing kings gods at birth, they created a ceremony in which a mortal royal heir was merged with his spiritual counterpart, or *ka,* to become a god only upon coronation.

_02:: Alexander the Really, Really Very Great (aka Almighty to You)

After his best friend (and presumed lover) Hephaestion died in 324 BCE, Alexander the Great demanded that his subjects (who by that point included the populations of Macedon, Greece, Persia, Egypt, and more) honor Hephaestion as a fallen hero. He also decided it was a good time to let people know that they could finally honor him as the god he was (or at least now claimed to be). Never a victim of modesty, Alex had been fond of comparing his accomplishments to those of the Greek gods for years. But, his newfound attitude adjustment indicated that he now believed he was equal to the immortals. Greek cities, which under his rule retained some semblance of self-government, complied with the order, but not necessarily with the spirit. The less-than-enthused Spartans, for instance, issued a decree that said, "Since Alexander wishes to be a god, let him be a god."

_03:: Augustus Caesar: Like Holy Father, Like Son...

On August 19 of the year 14 CE, Augustus Caesar died at age 77. Two days later, the Roman senate enrolled him among the gods of the Roman state. And while being deemed a god by committee isn't exactly the same as claiming godhood while alive, the emperor had the keen foresight to plan his ascension to divinity years before. How so? Just after his great-uncle and adopted father Julius Caesar's murder in 44 BCE, the young man interpreted a comet as evidence that Julius had entered the company of immortals. The strategic proclamation worked in his favor. Later, as a member of Rome's ruling triumvirate, he issued coins with his own image and the inscription "Son of a God." Then in 27 BCE, the "first citizen," as he'd dubbed himself, had a compliant senate name him Augustus, meaning "superior to humanity" or "godlike."

_04:: Caligula Declares Himself a God

Although he was emperor for just four years, Caligula (37–41 CE) was still able to take Rome on a wild ride, according to the ancient historians Suetonius and Flavius Josephus. The adopted son of the previous emperor, Tiberius, Caligula was initially very popular with Roman commoners. You can chalk it up to his spontaneous distributions of gold coins to them or his wacky, unpredictable sense of humor. Whatever the case, the public's opinion quickly turned when (according to Suetonius) Caligula began cross-dressing in public, impregnated his own sister, declared war on Poseidon (bringing back chests full of worthless seashells as "booty"), and topped it all off by declaring himself a god—the classical definition of "hubris." Poor Caligula. The seashell sovereign was assassinated by his own disgruntled bodyguards not long after.

_05:: Carl Jung, Full-time Psychologist, Part-time "Aryan Christ"

One approach to psychology is bringing your patients together to live with you, declaring yourself a god, and suggesting that they worship you. And as unconventional (read: cultish) as it may seem, that's the approach taken by famed Swiss psychologist Carl Jung (1875–1961). In fact, his mystical theory of a mass collective unconscious that unites the human race propounded that human psychological problems are caused by a separation from the divine. Further, he claimed the malady can only be treated through interpretation of visions, dreams, and the occult. Fleshing out some of his ideas when he temporarily lost his mind during World War I, Jung embraced the Hindu concepts of karma and reincarnation and began advocating polygamy. In the end, however, Jung claimed that the only way to reconnect with divine forces was to deify *yourself,* and he practiced what he preached, encouraging his followers to think of him as their connection with the sun god.

Ticket to Ride:
Things You Didn't Know about the Lottery

Call it the poor man's dream, a casino without walls, or a tax on the stupid, the lottery has deep and widespread roots. Here's a look at five stories about the numbers game.

_01:: Lotteries of Yore (It's Older Than You Think!)

Lotteries have been around as long as arithmetic. According to the Bible, God ordered Moses to use a lottery to divvy up land along the River Jordan (it's in the Book of Numbers, naturally). And that ain't all the "good book" has to say about it: lotteries are also mentioned in Joshua, Leviticus, and Proverbs. The lottery can also be traced back to China, where a warlord named Cheung Leung came up with a numbers game to persuade citizens to help pay for his army. Today, it's known as keno. Other famous lotteries? The Chinese used one to help finance the Great Wall; Augustus Caesar authorized one to raise money for public works projects in Rome. And in 1466, in what is now the Belgian town of Bruges, a lottery was created to help the poor—which lotteries supposedly have been doing ever since.

_02:: The Founding Fathers Took Their Chances

Displaying the astute politicians' aversion to direct taxation, early American leaders often turned to lotteries to raise a buck or two. John Hancock organized several lotteries, including one to rebuild Boston's Faneuil Hall. Ben Franklin used them during the Revolutionary War to purchase a cannon for the Continental Army. George Washington ran a lottery to pay for a road into the wilds of western Virginia. And Thomas Jefferson wrote of lotteries, "Far from being immoral, they are indispensable to the existence of Man." Of course, when he wrote it, he was trying to convince the Virginia legislature to let him hold a lottery to pay off his debts.

_03:: Louisiana: A Whole Lotto Love

By the end of the Civil War, lotteries in America had such bad reputations, they were banned in most states. But not in Louisiana, where a well-bribed legislature in 1869 gave an exclusive charter to a private firm called the Louisiana Lottery Company. The company sold tickets throughout the country, and for 25 years, it raked in millions of dollars while paying out relatively small prizes and contributing chump change to a few New Orleans charities. Finally, in 1890, Congress passed a law banning the sale of lottery tickets through the mail, and eventually all multistate lottery sales were banned. What's a corrupt U.S. company to do? Move offshore, of course! The Louisiana Lottery moved its operations to Honduras, and America was lottery free until

1963, when New Hampshire started the lottery cycle anew.

_04:: "Inaction" Jackson: Lottery's Biggest Loser

Clarence Jackson's luck began to run out on Friday, the 13th of October, 1995, when the Connecticut Lottery picked the numbers on Jackson's lotto ticket, making his family the winners of $5.8 million. Only he didn't know it—and he didn't find out until 15 minutes before the one-year deadline to claim the prize, despite a whole slew of lottery ads seeking the winner. Jackson, a 23-year-old who'd taken over the family's struggling office cleaning business from his ailing father, didn't make it in time, and lottery officials rejected the claim. In 1997, the Connecticut General Assembly voted to award Jackson the prize, but the state senate refused to go along. Up until 2004, Jackson was still trying each year to convince the legislature. And still losing.

_05:: And Some Other Jackson: Its Biggest "Winner"

Andrew Jackson "Jack" Whittaker was already wealthy when he won the multistate Powerball lottery in December 2002. A millionaire contractor from West Virginia, Whittaker became the biggest single lottery winner in history after snagging a $314.9 million jackpot. But the dough seemed to carry more curses than the Hope Diamond. And when Jack decided to take a $170.5 million lump sum instead of payments over 20 years, it wasn't the only lump coming his way. Whittaker was robbed three times, once of more than $500,000 at a strip club. He was also sued for assault, arrested for drunk driving, and even booked for getting into a bar fight. And in September 2004, three burglars broke into his house and found the body of a friend of Whittaker's granddaughter, whose death may have been drug related. The sad truth? Simply that money doesn't guarantee peace of mind.

You Can Take It with You: Kings Who Moved Their Entire Households into the Afterlife

We've all heard the old cliché "You can't take it with you." But that didn't stop a good number of royals from trying. Here are four examples of folks who didn't want just a thin slice of heaven—they wanted it served on the same silver plates they'd grown accustomed to.

_01:: Hauling Jeeves to the Afterlife

It might not have been the most profligate tomb in history, but considering that it was built only a few centuries after the idea of cities came into fruition, Pu-Abi of Ur didn't make out too badly. We know little about her except that she lived and died sometime in the 26th or 25th century BCE. The most ornate of Ur's royal tombs, Pu-Abi's *post vivos* abode was excavated in the 1920s and '30s by Leonard Woolley. Among the artifacts discovered there were a complex headdress of gold leaves, a solid gold comb, and a dress covered with gems and beads. Of course, Pu-Abi didn't go alone into the next world; a number of servants poisoned themselves after being sealed in (possibly willingly) with their late mistress. Still, we're guessing that whatever service the queen was getting in the afterlife, it probably wasn't coming with a smile.

_02:: Here Comes the Sun (King)

Since the Japanese traditionally revered their emperors as gods, it comes as no surprise that they spared no expense in preparing their rulers for the afterlife. Emperors of the Yamato era, particularly, were known for their enormous burial mounds. One grave in Sakai City, traditionally assigned to the late-fourth-century-CE emperor Nintoku, is especially impressive. If you think the Great Pyramid is the swankiest tomb around, well, you're gravely mistaken. Just the sheer scale of the mound dwarfs Khufu's resting place; the artificial hill marking the grave site is the length of five football fields and has an internal volume twice that of the Egyptian's pyramid. And as if that weren't enough, the keyhole-shaped tumulus is surrounded by a triple moat! Twenty years were spent building the massive structure and thousands of funerary offerings are enshrined inside.

_03:: Big Soldiers in Little China

In Chinese culture, death and dying are perceived as just another phase of life. So, it's no

---

Just the Facts

INCLUDED IN FORMER GE CEO JACK WELCH'S 2001 RETIREMENT PACKAGE

(Trimmed in 2003 in Response to Stockholder Outrage)

$9 million-plus: Annual pension

$86,535: Consulting fees for first 30 days of work each year

$17,307: For each additional day

$11 million: Resale of Trump Towers luxury apartment

$291,869: Unlimited use of corporate jet per month

$600: Leased luxury Mercedes-Benz per month

Priceless: Unlimited use of company limousine, security-trained chauffeur and bodyguards, country club memberships, full health and life insurance coverage, tickets (season courtside to New York Knicks at Madison Square Garden; season box seats at Yankee Stadium; season grand tier Metropolitan Opera; U.S. Open tennis; Wimbledon tennis; VIP seats at all Olympic events)

---

wonder that the emperor and other royalty have burial chambers that are designed to mirror their former opulence and prosperity. In fact, some tombs are so elaborate that construction begins *really* early. In Emperor Ch'in Shih Huang Ti's case, for instance, construction on his site started when he turned just 13 (the same age he was crowned king of Qin). Of course, the site was also filled with plenty of goodies the good king could appreciate in the afterlife: food supplies and utensils, carriages (just in case he got restless), pets, favorite objects, and more than a few subjects (aka dead servants) just in case something needed to be fetched. In fact, the emperor's large harem also accompanied him to his burial chamber while the majority of his servants and animals were spared and replaced with terra-cotta figures. The practice of human sacrifice eventually disappeared thanks to continued objections by notable philosophers like Confucius, Mozi, and Xunzi. Their arguments not only elaborated on the inhumanity of the sacrifices, but also pointed out that the preparations were extravagant, wasted time, and interfered with the daily labor needed to generate wealth. Pretty wise indeed.

_04:: Good Reason Not to Be a Mourning Person

On August 18, 1227, Genghis Khan, the most feared leader of the 13th century, was buried with a simple procession of 2,500 followers and a mounted bodyguard of 400 soldiers. Anyone unfortunate enough to happen upon the procession was immediately put to death by the soldiers. When the procession arrived at a remote mountain location in Mongolia, 40 virgins were killed to provide Khan with the needed pleasures in the afterlife. Then, at the end of the funeral ceremony, the soldiers killed all 2,500 members of the procession. When the 400 soldiers returned to Khan's capital city, they were immediately put to death by another group of soldiers so that no one could reveal where Khan's final resting place was. Since Khan was considered a god, it was important that no one know his whereabouts and plunder the site. In fact, only recently have archaeologists found a site that they think may be Khan's burial place. So did anyone survive the onslaught? Well, yes—a camel. The creature was spared since she could find her way back to the site if Khan's family needed to visit. Family members had to be led blindfolded—if they knew the whereabouts, they also would be put to death.

Take the Money (or the Gold Medal or the Notoriety or the Potato) and Run:
Great Sports Scams, Scandals, and Hoaxes

Some say the U.S. national pastime is baseball. Others say it's football. Or basketball. Or jai alai. But you can forget all those, because these seven examples prove that when it comes to sports, mankind's favorite pastime is lying, cheating, pulling pranks, and spreading hoaxes. Play ball!

_01:: A Black Pox on the Black Sox

This is pretty much the mac-daddy of all sports scandals. The 1919 Chicago White Sox was one of the greatest baseball teams ever to take the field, including superstar left fielder "Shoeless" Joe Jackson. But two gamblers, "Sleepy Bill" Burns and Billy Maharg, backed up by gangster Arnold Rothstein, changed that by bribing eight players with $100,000 to throw the World Series. The fix was a success, the Sox lost, and nobody really suspected a thing until late in the next season, when the eight players were indicted. Commissioner Kennesaw Mountain Landis suspended them all from baseball for life, and they all had it coming. Except one. "Shoeless" Joe did all he could to avoid being involved: he told Sox owner Charles Comiskey about the scam, but was ignored; he asked to be benched for the Series, but was refused; he even batted .375 for the Series and had 12 base hits (a Series record at the time) *and* the only home run. Due to the scandal, Jackson is still not in the Hall of Fame, though many players have supported his induction.

_02:: Stella "the Fella" Walsh

In 1980, a 69-year-old member of the National Track & Field Hall of Fame was shot and killed outside a Cleveland shopping mall. Police immediately ascertained that the victim was Stella Walsh, the greatest female track-and-field athlete of her day. Stella, born Stanislawa Walasiewiczowna in Poland, won a gold medal for Poland at the 1932 Olympics and a silver in 1936, and set 20 world records. But when the police took the body to be autopsied, they found something very unusual on the 69-year-old woman: male genitals?! Further studies showed that she ... er, *he* ... had both male and female chromosomes, a condition called mosaicism. When the shocking news got out, it took approximately 2.7 seconds for the great runner to get a new nickname: Stella the Fella.

_03:: Mighty *Sports Illustrated* Fans Strike Out

The greatest baseball pitcher of all time was actually a figment of George Plimpton's imagination. His article for the April 1, 1985, issue of *Sports Illustrated* was entitled "The Curious

Case of Sidd Finch." It told the story of an English orphan, raised by an archaeologist, educated at Harvard, and trained by a yogi in Tibet, who showed up at the Mets training camp in Florida. He could throw a fastball at 168 mph (the record at the time was a comparatively sluggish 103) and preferred to pitch with one foot bare and the other in a large hiking boot. As of the magazine's publishing date, Finch hadn't yet decided if he was going to play for the Mets. The response was massive. *Sports Illustrated* received over 2,000 letters immediately following the story, many expressing their hopes that Sidd would play. Two weeks later, the magazine fessed up to their hoax. Of course, the clever Plimpton had included a subtle clue in the article's subhead: "He's a pitcher, part yogi and part recluse. Impressively liberated from our opulent lifestyle, Sidd's deciding about yoga...." Confused? Just take the first letter of each word: "happyaprilfoolsday."

_04:: Rosie the (Underhanded) Runner

On April 21, 1980, a young woman crossed the finish line to win the 84th Boston Marathon in the record time of 02:31:56. For someone who had just run over 26 miles, Rosie Ruiz looked notably sweatless and un-rubbery in the legs. Race officials checked photos and video from various spots in the race, and Ruiz appeared in none of them. So how did she do it? Here's the prevailing theory: She started the race with the others, then left the course, *hopped a subway,* then reentered the course about a half mile from the finish line. She was disqualified and stripped of her title. So, how'd she fine-tune her con? By cheating in another mara-

thon, of course. Rosie had sneaked her way past New York Marathon officials, and her time qualified her for the Boston race.

_05:: Simonya Popova: aka How the Women's Tennis Association Got Served

With the advent of computer-generated imagery, the art of the hoax really came into its own. Take the case of Simonya Popova, a female teenage tennis sensation from Uzbekistan who made Anna Kournikova look like Billy Jean King. In the fall of 2002, a Jon Wertheim article in *Sports Illustrated* profiled Popova, proclaiming her the next great phenom on the tennis circuit. It covered five pages and even had a picture. But Popova was a complete fiction; her image was computer generated. Even the name Simonya was chosen as a reference to *SimOne,* a movie about a computer-generated actress who becomes a star. The story was done as a fictional what-if, intended to be a comment on tennis's need for a hot new superstar to give the sport some mojo. But the Women's Tennis Association wasn't exactly amused. A spokeswoman for the organization lambasted the magazine, claiming they should've used the five pages to cover *real* tennis players. And, for the record, they said, "We have tons of mojo."

_06:: The Great Potato Caper

The date: August 28, 1987. The scene: Bowman Field in Williamsport, Pennsylvania. The AA Reading Phillies were in town to play the hometown Williamsport Bills, when Bills catcher Dave Bresnahan decided to pull a stunt he'd been thinking about for weeks. With a runner on third, Bresnahan threw the ball over the head of the third baseman and into the outfield. The runner jogged home, thinking he had an easy run. But unbeknownst to him and the 3,500 fans at the game, Bresnahan still had the ball. The object he had thrown was a potato, meticulously peeled and shaped to look like a baseball. Everyone got a chuckle out of the hoax. Everyone, that is, except Williamsport manager Orlando Gomez, who promptly ejected Bresnahan and fined him a whopping $50. Bresnahan had the last laugh, though: Instead of the money, he gave Gomez 50 potatoes.

_07:: A Rose Bowl Is a Rose Bowl Is a Rose Bowl (Except When CalTech's Involved)

It seems fitting that what is widely regarded as the greatest college prank of all time was pulled off by the college where pranking is practically a major: CalTech. (Students once changed the well-known "Hollywood" sign to read "CalTech," despite the massive security around the joint.) Since the Rose Bowl game is played in CalTech's backyard of Pasadena, the students and their head pranksters, the Fiend-ish 14, were miffed at the lack of publicity the event generated for their school. So they finally decided to take it out on the game's participants in 1961 (neither of which happened to be CalTech—the game was between the University of Washington and the University of Minnesota). The students learned of an elaborate halftime spectacle planned by the Washington cheerleaders that involved 2,232 flip cards. One CalTech student, disguised as a high school newspaper reporter, interviewed Washington's head cheerleader to learn their plan. The CalTech students then stole one of the instruction sheets, made 2,232 copies of it, altered each one by hand, then swapped them with the real cards while the cheerleaders were visiting Disneyland. The next day, live on national television, thousands of Huskies fans held up cards to make a picture of a Husky. Instead, viewers saw a Beaver, CalTech's mascot. One of the next card formations read "Seik-suh" (read it backward and you'll get it). And finally, the *pièce de résistance:* The cards read, in giant letters, "CalTech."

Crime Does Pay:
Lifestyles of the Rich and Infamous

If you sell your soul to the devil, you might as well have something nice and shiny to show for it, right? If these dirty dealers didn't know how to live good, they sure knew how to live well.

_01:: John Palmer (ca. 1947–)

British bad boy John Palmer suckered over 16,000 people in a phony time-share scheme. Currently ranked Great Britain's wealthiest criminal, having amassed ill-gotten wealth of over £300 million, the notorious Mr. Palmer owns a fleet of cars and several houses all over England, including a huge estate at Landsdown in Bath. He even has a cool nickname: Goldfinger. Which doesn't mean he has a golden rep. Palmer defended himself in the fraud trial, lost, got eight years in the clink, and has so far been slapped with fines of £5 million. But this wasn't his first criminal activity. In 1983 he took part in the U.K.'s greatest-ever robbery, in which he and a partner stole £26 million in gold bullion from a cargo storage company at Heathrow Airport. He smelted the gold himself and was arrested when police found two gold bars, still warm, under his sofa.

_02:: Pablo Escobar (1949–1993)

Picture every stereotypical South American drug dealer you've ever seen in a movie. They're all based in part on Pablo Emilio Escobar Gaviria, head of the Colombian Medellin cartel. Escobar ran his empire from a lavish pad complete with Arabian horses, a miniature bullfighting ring, a private landing strip, a Huey 50 helicopter, and a private army of bodyguards. Clearly, money wasn't an object for the man. After all, he could afford to pay local authorities $250,000 each to turn a blind eye. Plus, he used his money to build schools and hospitals, and was even elected to the Colombian senate. But eventually the pressure from authorities, including the American DEA, got to be too much and he turned himself in. Of course, incarceration didn't stop him from living the lush life. Escobar used some of his loot to convert his prison into a personal fortress, even remodeling all the bathrooms and strengthening the walls. Once he left, he was a fugitive again, but he wasn't hard to track down. An obsessive misophobe, Escobar left a conspicuous trail of dilapidated hideouts with shiny, expensive new bathrooms. In the end, the cocaine kingpin was killed when the secret police tracked his cell phone to an apartment, stormed the building, and shot him. Many, many times.

_03:: Mother Mandelbaum (1818–1894)

One of New York City's earliest criminal godfathers was actually a godmother. Frederika "Mother" Mandelbaum, or "Marm" to her friends, was the top "fence" (buyer and seller of stolen goods) in post–Civil War New York. From 1862 to 1882, she's estimated to have processed almost $10 million in stolen stuff. In fact, Mandelbaum made enough money to purchase a three-story building at 79 Clinton Street. Running her business out of a bogus haberdashery on the bottom floor, and living with her family in opulence and comfort on the top two floors, "Mother" often threw lavish dinners and dances for the criminal elite, which included corrupt cops and paid-off politicos. Ma Mandelbaum could afford to eat well, too, and allegedly tipped the scales at over 250 pounds. But like any good criminal, she gave back. Well, kind of. Mandelbaum ran a school on Grand Street where orphans and waifs learned to be professional pickpockets and sneak thieves. She was finally arrested in 1884, but fled to Canada with over a million dollars in cash before the trial. She remained there in comfort and safety until her death in 1894.

Touch of Evil

Meyer Lansky was the syndicate crime boss who financed Bugsy Siegel's Flamingo Hotel in Las Vegas. While his cohorts died or went to prison, Lansky eventually retired in Florida with a cool $400 million.

_04:: L. Dennis Kozlowski (1946–)

OK, so he's not a criminal in the classic "bang bang, shoot 'em up" kind of way. But this scumbag still has it coming. The former CEO of Tyco International, along with CFO Mark Swarz, allegedly embezzled an estimated $600

million from his company, its employees, and its stockholders. He borrowed $19 million, interest free, to buy a house, a debt that the company then forgave as a "special bonus." He got an $18 million apartment in Manhattan and charged the company $11 million more for artwork and furnishings, including a $6,000 shower curtain and $2,200 garbage can. He even threw his wife a little 40th birthday soiree on the island of Sardinia that cost the company over two million clams. Special musical guest: Jimmy Buffett. And while a mistrial was initially declared in April of 2004, the best lawyers couldn't keep Kozlowski and his cohorts from changing residences from their very big houses to *the* Big House.

_05:: Leona Helmsley (1920–)

The famous New York real estate mogul and class-A witch lived the American Dream. Well, except for the whole prison thing. Leona was a divorced sewing factory worker with mouths to feed before she met and married real estate tycoon Harry Helmsley (the fact that he was already married mattered little). In 1980, Harry named Leona president of his opulent Helmsley Palace Hotel, which she ruled like a despot. Her tendency to explode at employees for the smallest infraction (like a crooked lampshade) earned her the title "Queen of Mean." The tyranny didn't exactly last. In 1988, Leona and Harry were indicted for a smorgasbord of crimes, including tax fraud, mail fraud, and extortion. And after numerous appeals, Leona served 18 months in prison and was forced to pay the government $7 million in back taxes. A healthy dose of irony for the woman who once said, "Only the little people pay taxes." Of course, that doesn't mean things turned out that badly for poor Leona. Said to

WILLIAM THE CONQUEROR'S HORRIBLE-TERRIBLE, NO-GOOD, VERY BAD DAY

Despite conquering England in 1066, William I spent more time back in Normandy, where greedy neighboring rulers tended to grab his lands if he left. In 1087, William, who had grown fat in his 50s, was on his way to take a "cure" (like going to a fat farm) when he made good on a threat to attack Mantes, taken from him by Philip I of France a decade earlier. The attack went well until the aftermath. As the village burned, a spark spooked Will's horse. It reared and the king lurched into the ornate saddle horn. Ugh! The painful result? It took William five agonizing weeks to die of internal injuries. Worse still, at his death, his attendants—including sons Henry and William Rufus—rode out quickly to defend their own properties as word got out. Meanwhile, servants robbed the unguarded body, stripped it naked, and dumped it on the floor.

be worth over 2.2 billion bucks, the dreaded Ms. H. still owns the lease to the Empire State Building and lives in luxury with her aptly named dog, Trouble.

_06:: Al Capone (1899–1947)

He killed people. He bought cops by the precinctful. He bootlegged liquor. He ran Chicago like his own personal kingdom. He was damn good at what he did, and he did it with style. Al Capone (aka Scarface) maintained a swank Chicago headquarters in the form of a luxurious five-room suite at the chic Metropole Hotel (rate: $1,500 a day). And when those Chicago winters proved a little too chilly for him, he bought a 14-room Spanish-style estate in Palm Island, Florida, which he spent millions turning into a well-decorated fortress. Capone's total wealth has been estimated at over $100 million (not a penny of which was kept in his vaults, as Geraldo Rivera learned on live TV). Not bad for a guy whose business card said he was a used furniture dealer. Of course, he didn't pay taxes on any of it, which is what eventually sent him up the river.

Friends of the Devil:
Figures Who Supposedly Sold Their Souls

3

If you really can't get a gig, and you're desperate to become a star, there's only one person who can help you out for sure. Of course, it's probably gonna cost you more than the standard 10%.

_01:: Robert Johnson at His Crossroads

Considered to be one of the most influential bluesmen of all time, Robert Johnson was also one of the most turbulent. And few musicians have achieved Johnson's mythical status, whether the devil had a hand in it or not. As the story goes, one night Johnson happened upon a large black man while walking near the crossroads of Highways 61 and 49 outside of Clarksdale, Mississippi. The man offered to tune Johnson's guitar, and as the story has it, claimed Johnson's soul in return. Within a year, Johnson was in demand throughout the region. Actually, the story may have started when Johnson sat in on a gig with Sun House and Willie Brown. House and Brown were so impressed with Johnson's playing they thought the only explanation was that he'd sold his soul. Of course, mythic lives require mythic endings. Known for his womanizing,

Johnson was fatally poisoned when he sipped some whiskey laced with strychnine—the act of a jealous husband. Johnson died in 1938 at the age of 27.

_02:: Led Zeppelin and Their Stairway to . . . ?

Did they or didn't they sell their souls to Satan for the rights to the classic "Stairway to Heaven" hit? While the debate has continued since the song came out in the early 1970s, it basically can be traced back to the allegation that, if played backward, the song makes numerous references to Satan. Even more damning, tons of people have interpreted the lyrics as being demonic. And Jimmy Page's and Robert Plant's interest in the occult didn't really help matters. In the 1970s, Page proclaimed himself a wizard and actually bought a house in Scotland known as "The Toolhouse," reputed to be a satanic temple. Then, when he played the chords of the rock anthem to Plant, Robert immediately sat down and wrote the lyrics right on the spot. Later, in interviews, Plant stated that he didn't seem to be writing and something else was moving his pencil across the page. Three decades later the debate continues, but the question remains as to who the piper ("the piper's calling you to join him")

Touch of Evil

Church of Satan founder Anton LaVey claims to have been born with a vestigial tail that was surgically removed when he was an adolescent.

is. Is it the devil, Jesus, or, maybe, just a plain old piper? Guess the rock world will never know.

_03:: The Darkness Crossover

It now appears that the fast rise of the British group The Darkness in the early 2000s may have had supernatural intervention. After struggling for many years playing in obscure pubs, the group's lead singer, Justin Hawkins, allegedly sold out to the devil. In 2002, Hawkins sought the assistance of Doktor Snake, a well-known British voodoo doctor. And in a scene reminiscent of Robert Johnson's rendezvous with the devil, Snake led Hawkins to a deserted country crossroads one evening at midnight and some unholy pact was consummated. Within the year, The Darkness was one of the hottest bands in the United Kingdom. Having been successful with The Darkness, Doktor Snake (who still hasn't figured out a cure for spelling his name incorrectly) now sells his dark side services over eBay.

I Want to Hold Your Handbag: Evangelists Who Received Until It Hurt

It's better to give than to receive, right? Well, that is unless you're one of the following fat wallet preachers. In a pay-to-pray world, this group of standouts would definitely make it into the evangelism hall of fame—one that no doubt has gilded walls and marble floors.

_01:: The Mail Order Order— The Reverend Ike

A forerunner to the televangelist frenzy of the 1980s, Frederick Eikerenkoetter, known as the Reverend Ike, unabashedly preached capitalism for years. In the 1970s, Ike broadcast weekly sermons on approximately 1,700 television and radio stations across the United States. Famous for saying that the lack of money was the root of all evil, Ike definitely practiced what he preached. In fact, it wasn't uncommon for Ike to tell his listeners that he didn't want to hear the sound of change hit- ting the collection plate, he wanted the folding stuff. Known for his expensive suits and a fleet of mink-trimmed Rolls-Royces, the Rev clearly didn't live the life of a monk. And while his television career appears to have diminished, old Ike continues his very lucrative mail-order business, which is more like a chain letter scam than anything else. Here's the setup: Normally a letter is sent containing a prayer hankie, a charm, or a curse. Then the recipient is told to send it back to Ike along with a $20 or $30 donation within a day and Ike will bless it or you. Of course, the failure to do so could bring about a whole host of unwanted problems, and no one wants that. Talk about the spirit of capitalism. We're not so sure John Calvin would be proud.

Touch of Evil

In 1987, Oral Roberts told viewers he needed $8 million or God would "call him home." He beat the deadline, thanks to a last-minute $1.3 million donation by dog track owner Jerry Collins, who admitted: "I think he [Roberts] needs psychiatric treatment."

_02:: The Miracle Worker— Benny Hinn

A throwback to the tent preachers of the early 1900s, Benny Hinn is a man of miracles, and estimates are that Hinn's organization receives over $100 million a year in donations (a miracle in itself!). Most of these donations, of course, are in response to Hinn's so-called faith healings, and his choreographed services are structured to elicit as much money as possible. In addition to the healings, he's happy to scare a little cash out of wallets as well, often telling his audience that worldwide disasters are going to occur, but only those giving to God's work will be spared. In 1999, Hinn announced that God had ordered him to build a $30 million World Healing Center. However, in 2003, Hinn stated that God still wanted the center built, but told him the time wasn't right. Like the loyal servant he is, Hinn told the Big Man (and all his followers) he'd hold the cash until then. In the meantime, Hinn lives in an $8 mil-

The Evil How-to

TAKING IT TO THE CLEANERS

Most people have a vague idea that money laundering is bad, but like the clueless protagonists of *Office Space*, have no idea what it is or how to do it. The most common method of laundering money is to give illegal income to a legitimate business already taking in large quantities of cash, so that it can be deposited without arousing suspicion. The term probably arose in the 1930s, when gambling rings opened up launderettes to disguise the influx of small change. Other methods in use are ingenious in their complex maneuvering around international financial reporting regulations. International terrorists, for instance, tend to use legitimate charities to funnel money into arms purchases and other nefarious doings. Of course, because of lax reporting laws and corrupt officials, some countries are better for cleaning one's cash than others. China, the Cayman Islands, the United Arab Emirates, Thailand, and Lebanon are generally among the favorites.

lion oceanfront home, travels by private jet, and stays in $3,000-a-night hotel suites. Apparently, for Hinn doing the Lord's work always feels good. Really, really good.

_03:: **You Gotta Pay to Pray— Robert Tilton**

In 1991, ABC-TV's *Prime Time Live* program investigated Robert Tilton's Word of Faith Outreach Center Church. At the time, Tilton's televangelist show appeared on 200 stations and he claimed his church had over 10,000 members. The truth was that his organization was also making $80 million a year through his direct marketing campaigns. The investigation found that prayer requests sent to Tilton were routinely discarded after the cash and checks had been removed—clearly not what Jesus would do. The exposé led to Til-

ton's downfall and in 1999 he sold the church and moved to Miami. However, in 1997 Tilton started buying time on independent stations, showing mostly reruns, in order to rebuild his mailing lists. Today, his mailings include financial prayer cloths, posters of Tilton, packets of oil, and other trinkets all for just the cost of a small donation. But sadly, old habits are hard to break: Reports state that employees are simply told to take out the dough and discard the prayer requests. But all in all, something seems to be working for him. Tilton owns a $450,000 yacht and property worth at least $1.5 million in Miami Beach.

Putting the Wind in Our Sales: Shameful Cases of False Advertising

No matter what the adage says, sometimes you just don't get what you paid for. And that's just about the time class action lawsuits somehow enter the picture. The following are three egregious cases where a little truth would have helped.

_01:: **BodyFlex**

In 2003, the FTC (Federal Trade Commission) sued BodyFlex, alleging that the company had deceptively advertised that the system caused users to lose 4–14 inches in the first seven days. The complaint charged that the loss of 4–14 inches was advertised as occurring without any reduction in calories, and that users burned enough body fat to achieve the claimed fat loss. In fact, the promotion also cited a clinical study that "proved" that the BodyFlex system caused significant fat and inch loss in the first seven days. No one knows how many

people actually bought into the hype, but according to the FTC, the BodyFlex commercial was one of the 10 most-aired infomercials in weekly U.S. rankings and aired more than 2,000 times from February through September 2003 on national cable channels. Of course, the company spent almost $20 million to promote the product. In September 2004, Body-Flex conceded, and agreed to set up a $2.6 million consumer refund program. They also agreed to stop making false weight-loss claims, effectively proving that not all liars are big, fat ones.

Touch of Evil

While they now do the healthy thing with Flintstone vitamins, when the Stone Age family originally appeared on television, old Fred and Barn were sponsored by (and appeared in commercials for) Winston cigarettes.

_02:: The Wedding

In September 1990, a group of drug crime suspects in Corunna, Michigan, received an invitation to a wedding from a well-known drug dealer in the area. Attendees were asked to check their guns at the entrance, apparently a common occurrence at these events. As part of a five-month undercover investigation, the police staged a wedding on a Friday night, figuring it was easier to make the drug suspects come to them than to round them up. The groom was an undercover investigator, the bride a Flint police officer, and the bride's father (and reputed crime boss) was the police chief. That evening, after the vows, the toasts, and the dancing, the band, called SPOC, or COPS spelled backward, played "Fought the Law," setting off the cue for the evening's real agenda. All the police officers were then asked to stand, and those who remained seated were arrested. A dozen suspects were booked and, by Saturday afternoon, 16 were in custody.

_03:: Sprint

In May 2004, the Florida attorney general charged Sprint with reaching out and scamming someone. Actually, it was charged with scamming many more than one, and to make amends the attorney general spearheaded an agreement with the phone company to pay Florida $2.4 million to settle charges that it switched consumers to their long distance services without permission, a practice known as "slamming." During 2002, consumers were unknowingly converted to Sprint long distance after purchasing unrelated items at electronics stores. The old switcheroo actually occurred when customers reached the checkout counter and were asked to sign what looked like a typical sales receipt but was in fact a letter of authorization. As a result, the customer would leave the store having unwittingly approved a change in his long-distance provider. Investigations that began in January 2002 also uncovered evidence that sales personnel forged consumer signatures on these letters to meet sales quotas and receive bonuses. Nearly 4,000 Florida consumers complained about the unsolicited switches and received restitution from Sprint in response to their complaints.

We Don't Need Another Nero: Leaders Who Spent Their Countries into the Ground for Fun

If you're looking for some bank-breaking works of less-than-staggering genius, look no further. Not only were these five leaders plagued by terrible ideas, they never bothered to get their money's worth.

_01:: Caligula's Bridge (Over Very Troubled Waters)

According to the classical chronicler Suetonius, as he was going mad the Roman emperor Caligula began spending money on increasingly bizarre and extravagant projects to satisfy his megalomaniacal whims. Among Caligula's best efforts: constructing a three-mile pontoon bridge across the Bay of Naples by confiscating merchant ships, having their bulwarks sawed off (making them useless afterward), spreading soil over the planks, and then planting trees, shrubs, and flowers to make the bridge more pleasant. When it was done, Caligula supposedly rode his horse across the bridge at the head of 20,000 troops to prove wrong an earlier prophecy that claimed he could no more become emperor than ride across the bay. After a night of partying, Caligula left and never came back. The bridge itself was destroyed by a storm a short while later. It was this kind of ridiculous spending that broke the Roman bank pretty quickly.

_02:: Nero's Extreme Home Makeover

As everyone's favorite gossip Suetonius tells it, the emperor Nero decided to go Caligula one better by building an extravagant mansion for himself in burned-down neighborhoods of Rome following the great fire of 64 CE. Called the Domus Aurea, or "Golden House," because its exterior was overlaid with gold leaf and mother-of-pearl embedded with gems and beautiful seashells, the building was far and away the largest private residence ever seen in Rome, covering a large part of three of Rome's seven hills. So, just how extravagant was Nero's crib? In the entrance hall stood a 120-foot statue (of Nero); a columned arcade ran for a mile; a pool the size of a small lake was surrounded by buildings shaped like cities and fake farms; exotic animals roamed everywhere; and the ceilings were carved ivory panels that could retract to allow a rain of perfume and flowers to fall on partiers. The Roman poet Martial said of it, "One house took up the whole city of Rome." When it was finished Nero famously said, "Good, now I can at last begin to live like a human being."

_03:: Prince of Thieves (Mainly the White-Collar Variety)

Prince Jefri Bolkiah, the brother of the sultan of Brunei, spent his small country into bankruptcy during the 1990s with a multibillion-dollar shopping spree that puts all the other royal contenders to shame. Clearly, Prince Jefri knew how to treat himself right, as the 300,000 citizens of Brunei found out when his purchases were put up for auction as part of bankruptcy proceedings. Included for sale were a golden toilet roll holder, rows of gold-plated Jacuzzis and showerheads, porcelain flamingos, gold-plated wastepaper baskets, a multi-million-dollar marquee complex, Comanche helicopter simulators, an Airbus jet, a Formula 1 racing car, and a bronze-plated eight-foot-high Trojan horse. Luxury hotels in Great Britain, France, and Singapore were also favorite purchases of Jefri. That's not to say he hasn't been caught with his fingers in more than a few (illegal) pies. Previously, a lawsuit had been brought against Jefri for the theft of approximately $16 billion from Brunei's state-run economic development agency. Needless to say, he didn't develop anything profitable with the funds.

_04:: Versailles and Everything After

Louis XIV was one of the most extravagant kings in French history. A lot of the stuff Louis spent money on was quite respectable—as a famous patron of arts he supported literary and cultural figures like Molière, Le Brun, and Lully, and he spent a great deal of money to improve the Louvre. Of course, Louis' most famous boondoggle was his palace at Versailles, a sprawling 700-room rococo residence on an 800-hectare estate with carefully tended gardens and woodlands about 15 miles to the southwest of Paris. In fact, Louis used so many luxurious materials—including gold leaf, crystal chandeliers and doorknobs, silk and satin window dressings, exotic hardwood furniture, ivory, mother-of-pearl, and precious stones—and his house contained so many famous works of art, that it's actually impossible to calculate a modern cost equivalent. If the spending wasn't bad enough, Louis also foolishly kicked out the Huguenots, or French Protestants, even though they provided many of the country's leading merchants and much of its tax income. Last but not least, Louis launched an endless series of unwinnable wars that were to put the last nail in the coffin of French finances. Who knew the nickname the Sun King referred to was one that was setting?

_05:: Empress Dowager's Ship That Never Sailed

In 1888, China had been on the ropes for a good three decades. Once an international powerhouse, the nation's world rep had suffered greatly since its humiliating loss to Great Britain in the Opium War. Foreign technical advisors told the mandarins who set policy that China needed a modern navy along Western lines if it was going to defend itself from further European and Japanese aggression, and the mandarins duly set aside 30 million taels of silver for new, modern ships. However, the dowager empress Cixi, who had the final say, decided that the money would be better spent on reconstructing the elaborate Summer Palace, which had served as a vacation spot for the Chinese imperial family for millennia.

When advisors complained that the only ship she had purchased was a marble pleasure yacht, she noted that while it was indeed immobile, "it's still a very nice place for a picnic."

Sticky Fingers: Celebrity Thieves

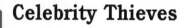

It's not surprising that celebrities steal—the sense of entitlement that accompanies wealth and adulation surely makes for a skewed sense of morality. It's *what* they steal that bothers us. Confederate battle plans? Cosmetics from a *drugstore?* And, most unfathomable, *figs?* Fame does funny things to people.

_01:: Hedy Lamarr (1913–2000)

Hedy Lamarr was a prototypical Hollywood sex symbol. Onscreen, the Austrian brunette sizzled as a femme fatale in movies like *White Cargo* and *Samson and Delilah*. And sure, her personal life was unstable: She married six times (twice more than Marilyn Monroe). But Lamarr was more than just a glamorous face. During World War II, she invented and patented an electronic device that made it more difficult to jam radio-guided torpedoes. Even though she understood the complexities of electrical engineering, Lamarr apparently couldn't outwit drugstore security guards. In the 1990s, she was caught shoplifting cosmetics on two occasions, but was never convicted. In the first case, she insisted on a jury trial and was acquitted by a 10–2 vote. After her second arrest, the charges were dropped.

_02:: Olga Korbut (1956–   )

Although the all-around gold medal for women's gymnastics in the 1972 Olympics went to Lyudmila Turischeva, the star that year was Turischeva's teammate, Olga Korbut. Diminutive and adorable, Korbut completed the first back flip on the uneven bars on her way to three gold medals in Munich. And then, a decade after moving to rural Georgia (the American one), cute little Olga Korbut was arrested outside a Publix supermarket. Her crime? Stealing chocolate syrup, figs, and cheese—begging the question: What in the name of God did she intend to cook? Korbut characterized the event as a misunderstanding, but apparently didn't feel strongly enough about it to make a case: She paid a fine of $300 to avoid trial.

Touch of Evil

In April 2005, the New York Post *reported that* Life & Style *star Kimora Lee Simmons not only pilfered props from the show's set, but also "made off with an entire rack of lamb from the lunch buffet table."*

_03:: Dean Martin (1917–1995)

Given the life story of Dean Martin, his klepto-mania shouldn't come as a terrible surprise. The former steelworker, prizefighter, and boot-legger never had much promise until he ran into Jerry Lewis at an Atlantic City night-club in 1946. Martin became the consummate straight man to Lewis's over-the-top clownish-ness, and it paid handsomely. But old Dean could never go *entirely* straight, even if he never wanted for money again. The Rat Packer once told the *Saturday Evening Post* that he couldn't go to a department store without steal-ing. His booty? "A necktie or a pair of gloves or a pair of socks. Everyone has a little bit of lar-ceny in them." Indeed. *When pocketing socks/ feels like adrenaline shots/that's amore*. Or klep-tomania, anyway.

_04:: Pauline Cushman (1833–1893)

And finally, a celebrity thief with real moxie and a heart of gold! Born in New Orleans, Pau-line Cushman became a successful, if minor, actress in New York in the 1850s. At the start of the Civil War, she offered her services as a spy to the Union. Cushman, who reportedly used her feminine wiles to gain favor with the Confederate troops (if you catch our drift), fol-lowed General (Braxton) Bragg's army around throughout much of 1863. She was eventually caught red-handed with secret papers and sentenced to death, but a hasty retreat by Bragg's men allowed Union soldiers to save her. Cushman stole for the right reasons, but she was no angel. She abandoned her children, married three times, exaggerated her military exploits, and eventually became addicted to opium. She committed suicide in 1893.

Rome Wasn't Burnt in a Day

SAN FRANCISCO'S BIG BLAST

By the time the Great Earthquake struck San Francisco at 5:13 a.m. on April 18, 1906, the city's fate had already been sealed by years of graft and greed. Corrupt mayor Eugene Schmitz and "Boss" Abraham Ruef had overseen years of shady deals that made the city a tinderbox. How so, you ask? Water mains were built *across* the San Andreas fault. Reservoirs under the city were filled with garbage from construction sites by cor-rupt contractors. And pillars in major build-ings were filled with newspaper, much cheaper than fireproof concrete. When the earthquake struck, fires began in the mostly wooden city and spread like, well, wildfire. What's a corrupt mayor to do? Schmitz turned over authority to General Frederick Funston, who had the (burning) bright idea of creating firebreaks by blowing up build-ings with dynamite. Without any water, the demolitions simply spread the fire further. By the time the fires were finally defeated four days later, 29,000 buildings were de-stroyed and over 3,000 people were dead, many of them shot as "looters" by the U.S. Army. Ironically, Schmitz and his cronies were set to be rounded up by authorities that very day, but the earthquake inter-rupted the operation.

Lowlife Perpetrates Art:
Greatest Art Heists and Scams of All Time

Everybody likes art in some form or another. In fact, some like it so much, they'll do anything they can to get their grubby hands on it. Here are six instances where the best of human artistry brought out the worst of human trickery.

_01:: When Greeks Lose Their Marbles

Since 1832, some of the greatest treasures of ancient Greek civilization have been residing in the British Museum. And the Greeks, who understandably consider themselves the rightful owners of things Greek, want their stuff back. The objects in question are the Elgin Marbles, so called because they were removed by Thomas Bruce, the seventh earl of Elgin, and British ambassador to Constantinople. Elgin claimed to have removed the friezes and sculptures because the Ottomans (who ruled Greece at the time) were neglecting them. Of course, critics are more than happy to tell you the good earl outright stole them. Whatever Elgin's motives, the workers who removed the sculptures did terrible, irreparable damage to the Parthenon. The marbles arrived in England between 1801 and 1805 to a mixture of awe and outrage. A profligate spender (earls just wanna have fun!), Elgin piled up huge debts and ended up selling the collection to Parliament in 1816. Since then, a cold war of sorts has simmered between the governments of England and Greece over the return of the sculptures. In fact, proponents of returning the marbles to Greece have removed Elgin's name and refer to them simply as the Parthenon Marbles.

_02:: "Just Judges" Just Disappeared

The Adoration of the Mystic Lamb, a 24-panel masterpiece by Flemish painter Jan van Eyck, is considered one of the most important Christian paintings in history. One panel, however, known as the "Just Judges," has been missing since it was stolen from a cathedral in the Belgian city of Ghent in 1934. Shortly after the theft, the archbishop received 13 ransom notes signed "D.U.A." demanding 1 million Belgian francs for the painting's safe return. D.U.A. turned out to be a transposition of the initials of Arseen Van Damme (with the "V" unlatinized into a "U"), alias of Arsène Goedertier, an eccentric who allegedly got the idea from a detective novel. Since then, numerous theories about the theft and the whereabouts of the painting have circulated: It was stolen by the Knights Templar; or the painting contains a map to the Holy Grail; or it's buried in the coffin of Belgium's King Albert I; or Goedertier was working for a Nazi spy, who was ordered by Hitler to obtain it as the centerpiece of his new "Aryan religion." The theories and clues have tantalized sleuths for three-quarters of a century, but the painting's location still remains a mystery.

Touch of Evil

In February 2005, two original Dogs Playing Poker *paintings by Cassius Marcellus Coolidge went up for auction in New York. Estimated to bring in $50,000, they instead commanded a bid just short of $600,000.*

_03:: The Case of the Missing Munch

The Scream, Edvard Munch's 1893 expressionist masterpiece depicting anxiety and despair, is one of the most famous paintings in the world. In fact, you'd be hard-pressed to find someone who couldn't recognize the ghostly figure on a bridge under a yellow-orange sky, with hands clasped over his (or her?) ears, mouth open in a shriek. And on Sunday, August 22, 2004, administrators at Oslo's Munch Museum were definitely given reason to let life imitate the art. In broad daylight, armed thieves barged into the museum, yanked *The Scream* and another famous Munch, *Madonna,* off the wall, then made a break for it. Police found only the getaway car and two empty frames. Understandably, Norwegians reacted with disbelief and outrage at the theft of two true national treasures. But, oddly enough, this wasn't the first time the painting had been purloined. There are actually *four* versions of *The Scream.* Another version was stolen in October 1994 from Oslo's National Gallery. That one turned up three months later, but the most recently ripped off version remains missing. Weird note: August 22 is a bad day for paint-ings. On that day in 1911, the *Mona Lisa* was stolen from the Louvre.

_04:: Pahk the Cah, Then Steal Some Aht

On March 18, 1990, in what still ranks as the biggest art theft in U.S. history, two thieves made off with masterpieces worth—get this—over $300 million. The robbery occurred at Boston's Isabella Stewart Gardner museum, where two men dressed as Boston cops pretended to respond to a disturbance. They cuffed the security guards, then helped themselves to 13 paintings, including works by Vermeer, Manet, and Rembrandt. While none of the paintings has yet been recovered, a theory has developed as to their whereabouts: the heist may have been masterminded by the Irish Republican Army, working in conjunction with Irish gangsters in Boston to ransom the paintings, then use the money to run guns to the IRA. Proponents of this theory say the paintings are hidden somewhere in Ireland, but IRA spokesmen vehemently deny this. Nevertheless, the FBI is said to be following this lead. Stay tuned.

_05:: The Disappearing Da Vinci

On Wednesday, August 27, 2003, two men posing as tourists walked into Drumlanrig Castle in Dumfries and Galloway, Scotland. During the tour, they made off with a painting, *Madonna with the Yarnwinder,* a masterpiece by Leonardo da Vinci valued at about £30 million. The thieves were seen on camera casually heading for their vehicle, a Volkswagen Golf GTI (whose slogan, "Getaway Drivers Wanted," seems appropriate), with the incredibly valuable painting tucked under one arm. Over 500 years old, the painting had been in the possession of the family of the castle's owner, the duke of Buccleuch, since the 18th century. In fact, the *Madonna* was the centerpiece of the duke's art collection valued at over £400 million and including works by Rembrandt and Holbein. Despite the theft, the castle reopened to visitors days later. As of this writing, the painting has not been recovered, but it's believed to be too famous to ever be sold by the thieves.

_06:: The Godfather of Fake

What made Elmyr de Hory infamous wasn't the sheer number of forgeries he sold. It was that they were damn *good* forgeries. For 30 years, de Hory sold forgeries of paintings by the world's greatest artists, including Picasso, Chagall, Matisse, Degas, and Toulouse-Lautrec. In fact, his forgeries were so good, so precise in every detail, that they fooled even the most experienced art buyers. So much so that the native Hungarian has even attracted his own cult following, who pay high prices for "authentic" de Hory fakes. Irony of ironies, the forger's forgeries are now being forged and sold by other forgers! Even more odd: today, legitimate museums host exhibitions of de Hory's works. De Hory told his story in *Fake!* a 1969 biography by Clifford Irving (who went on to, yes, forge a phony autobiography of Howard Hughes). But in the end the master forger wound up penniless (just like a real painter) and committed suicide in 1976, although rumors persist that he faked that, too.

Hey Judas:
Historical Tattletales and $nitches

Judas handed Jesus over to the Romans for 30 lousy pieces of silver (about $40 in today's money, by some estimates). And sure, some of the snitches in our roundup got a little more coin than that, but whatever their worth, today they're simply remembered as dirty rats.

_01:: Tonny Ahlers (1917–2000)

In August 1944, the Gestapo raided the warehouse annex in Amsterdam where Anne Frank and seven others had lived in hiding for more than two years. All eight ended up at Auschwitz—with only Anne's father, Otto, surviving. Clearly, someone ratted out the Franks, but only recently has attention started to focus on Anton "Tonny" Ahlers. Dishonest, violent, and virulently anti-Semitic, Ahlers was a business associate of Otto Frank, and knew the Frank family lived in hiding. But just how damning is the evidence? Well, let's put it this way: Ahlers's own son believes that his father betrayed the Franks. He also thinks Tonny might have blackmailed Otto after the war, noting that Tonny received a monthly check from mysterious sources until 1980—

the year Otto Frank died. That part of the story may be far-fetched, but even so, many historians seem to think that the mystery of Anne Frank's betrayal has been solved.

Touch of Evil

Police admitted they probably would not have solved the Manson murders without the help of Susan Atkins, a Manson Family member who spilled her guts to her cell mate.

_02:: Robert Hanssen (1944–   )

Widely believed to be the most damaging spy in the history of the FBI, Robert Hanssen snuck secrets to the Russians for millions of dollars in cash and diamonds between 1985 and 2001. His most damaging snitch? In October of 1985, Robbie informed the Soviet KGB that two KGB officers, Sergey Motorin and Valeriy Martynov, had been recruited to spy for the United States. Both men were promptly executed. Despite his handsome payoffs, though, Hanssen—known as Ramon Garcia to his Russian handlers—didn't exactly live like James Bond. The suburban snitch tooled around in a Ford Taurus and was happily married with six kids. And, like all the bad guys in *The Da Vinci Code*, Hanssen was also a member of Opus Dei, a secretive organization within the Catholic Church.

_03:: Richie Rich (1496–1567)

Believe it or not, the name Richie Rich had sinister implications even before Macaulay Culkin made it into a terrible film. After Henry VIII divorced Catherine of Aragon (without the pope's blessing), the devoutly Catholic Sir Thomas More, author of *Utopia,* refused to sign an oath swearing allegiance to the king

above the pope. On trial for treason, More's fate was sealed by the king's solicitor general, Richard Rich, who claimed More had told him that Parliament should have the right to depose the king. Rich, who never missed a chance to suck up to the powerful, was almost certainly lying, but More was convicted. A gentleman to the last, More comforted his executioners, saying, "Be not afraid to do thine office." He died on July 6, 1535—and was canonized by the Catholic Church in 1866.

_04:: Elia Kazan (1909–2003)

Although he directed such classic films as *East of Eden* and *A Streetcar Named Desire,* Elia Kazan is probably most famous for tattling on Hollywood communists to the House Un-American Activities Committee. In the 1930s, Kazan briefly joined the Communist Party but left, feeling betrayed (and rightly so, really) by Stalin's decidedly unegalitarian regime. When Kazan named names, helping to create the Hollywood blacklist, it provoked a firestorm of controversy within the artistic community—and when artists get mad, they do good work. Arthur Miller's play *The Crucible,* which portrays a Puritan who chooses to die rather than make a false accusation, is widely seen as an attack on Kazan. For his own part, Kazan made *On the Waterfront,* a movie about a heroic mob snitch, played by Marlon Brando.

_05:: Doña Marina (ca. 1501–1550)

Conquistador Hernán Cortés might never have conquered much without the able assistance of his slave, snitch, and mistress, Doña Marina. Originally named Malintzin, Marina abandoned her Aztec name after converting to Christianity. And because she understood

Aztec, Mayan, and Spanish (a triple threat!), Marina became a vital adviser and collaborator to Cortés... not to mention his lover. But besides blessing the conquistador with a son, she also aided his efforts in decimating the Aztec empire and people. Known in Mexico as *La Malinche,* Marina's betrayal has become part of the (Spanish, not Aztec) language—a *malinchista* is a person who abandons his or her language and heritage in pursuit of selfish goals.

Corruption, Corruption, What's Your Function? of the Worst Perpetrators

They say power corrupts and absolute power corrupts absolutely. Never was that more true than with these dirty (or should we say absolutely dirty?) rotten scoundrels.

_01:: Good Ol' Boss Tweed

The undisputed poster child for graft and greed in American politics, Boss William Tweed raised corruption to an art form. As a member of New York's Tammany Hall, Tweed and his cronies, including Mayor Fernando Wood, ran New York in the Civil War era as their own private money factory. Tweed once bought 300 benches for $5 each, then sold them to the city for $600 a pop. And that's just the tip of it. The building of City Hall was a clinic in graft: the city was charged $7,500 for every thermometer, $41,190 for each broom, and $5.7 million for furniture and carpets. One carpenter even received almost $361,000 for a single month's work. And although he was crooked as a dog's hind leg, Tweed does get a bit of credit from some historians for undertaking many important projects that improved life in New York (albeit at enormous financial gain to himself). Tweed's illicit profits were said to be in the range of $200 *million,* and that's in the 1860s! The law eventually caught up with the Boss, though, and he died in prison in 1878.

_02:: President Grant's Cronies

The 18th president of the United States was a great war general. But he was less skilled at avoiding scandal. To be fair, it wasn't so much Grant himself as the cast of characters around him that caused all the trouble. Grant's period in office (1869–1877) was marred by four major scandals: Crédit Mobilier, a railroad construction scandal during which the federal government and Union Pacific stockholders were bilked out of some $20 million; the Whiskey Ring, wherein over 100 Treasury Department officials were convicted of taking bribes and cutting deals for distillers; the Indian Ring, another scandal of bribes from companies licensed to trade on Indian reservations;

and Black Friday, a scheme involving Grant's brother-in-law that attempted to artificially inflate the price of gold. So, what's buried in Grant's Tomb? Let's just say a lot of dirty laundry.

_03:: The Entire Nation of Bangladesh?

Well, you have to be the best at something. The nongovernment watchdog group Transparency International repeatedly ranks Bangladesh and the regime of Prime Minister Khaleda Zia as the world's most corrupt (the runners-up for this dubious honor are Nigeria at number 2 and Haiti at number 3). You can barely walk a block in the capital of Dhakar without coming face-to-face with graft: you have to pay the postman to get your mail; bus drivers pay cops to let them drive their routes; victims of crime have to pay the cops to have someone arrested; doctors take bribes to dispense medicine; even meter readers get their palms greased for keeping energy bills low. It's estimated that 6% of the nation's GNP is spent on corruption. Not surprising in a place where the unemployment rate hovers around 70%.

_04:: The Less-Than-Honorable Judge Maloney

In the 1970s and '80s, the Cook County Circuit Court system based in Chicago was so corrupt and dirty that two federal investigations, Operations Greylord and Gambat, were undertaken to expose it. Lots of judges went to jail for their underhanded dealings, but the worst of the worst was the not-so-honorable Thomas J. Maloney. During the 13 years he spent on

the bench, from 1977 to 1990, Maloney "fixed" as many as six murder trials, taking bribes from $10,000 to $100,000 from gangs to convict members of other gangs of murder or manslaughter. Eventually, the justice got his own justice as he was indicted and sentenced to 15 years and 9 months in prison. The fact is he's the only judge in Illinois history to be convicted of fixing a trial. Of course, there would have been another in the same Greylord operation, Judge Frank J. Wilson, but he blew his own brains out just before the Feds came a-knocking.

_05:: Alexander the Waste

Sure, there have been some bad popes. With a list numbering 262 and counting, there's bound to be a few bad apples, right? But Alexander VI (reigned 1492–1503) was the baddest apple of 'em all. A member of the Spanish branch of the powerful and corrupt Borgia family, Alexander bought and bribed his way onto the papal throne, and used it to gather wealth and women for himself and influence for his children. By some accounts he had as many as seven illegitimate children and carried on with numerous mistresses while he was pope. Alexander also made a fortune selling indulgences, and married off his beautiful fair-haired daughter Lucrezia three times, each time to someone richer and more powerful. When the pope finally checked out, he was left to rot and turn purple in the Sistine Chapel, until his bloated corpse had to be stuffed and crammed into his coffin—a suitably rotten ending for a very rotten man.

Great Bank Robberies

When the famous bank robber Willie Sutton was asked why he robbed banks, he supposedly replied, "That's where the money is." Sutton claimed he never actually said it. Pity. Someone should have.

_01:: The Great Northfield, Minnesota, Raid

OK, in terms of actual success, this 1876 robbery was a bust. But it had a heck of a cast: legendary bandits Frank and Jesse James; Cole, Jim, and Bob Younger; and three lesser-known outlaws. Their target was Northfield's First National Bank, which the gang settled on after casing a half-dozen other towns. Clearly, not enough casing, as the robbery couldn't have gone worse. The bank's cashier refused to open the safe, an alert passerby sounded the alarm, and townspeople killed two of the robbers as the rest escaped. A week later, a posse killed or captured all of the other outlaws except the James brothers, who escaped home to Missouri. It was the beginning of the end for 19th-century America's most notorious bandits. Worse still? The take from the Northfield bank was a mere $26.70.

_02:: Hitler's Gold

As the German army rolled through Europe in World War II, it ransacked the banks of other countries, transferring the loot to the central Reichsbank in Berlin. But when the U.S. Third Army neared the German capital, the stolen booty was hidden in mines near the village of Merkers. Unfortunately for the Nazis, the Third Army captured Merkers before the treasure could be moved again. And it was truly a treasure: 55 boxes of crated gold, 8,198 bars of gold bullion, and a few tons of artwork. The total value of the precious metals and currency was put at $520 million, and it took 50 years to return the loot to the robbed countries. In 1997, several countries waived their remaining claims, and the funds were used to aid Holocaust survivors.

Touch of Evil

The 1951 robbery of Boston's Brink Express Company headquarters netted seven criminals more than $2.75 million. After the FBI spent nearly $30 million over six years to catch the crooks, less than 2% of the take was ever recovered.

_03:: Thinking Inside the Box(es)

In early 1976, the Lebanese capital of Beirut was in the throes of a civil war. Palestinian guerrilla groups had gained control of the city's aptly named Bank Street and set about knocking off a dozen banks. The biggest prize on the lot? The British Bank of the Middle East. To get to the loot, a PLO-affiliated group blasted through the wall of a Catholic church next door to the bank. Then imported Corsican safe-crackers were employed to open the vault to get to the safety-deposit boxes. Over a two-day period, the robbers loaded trucks with $20 million to $50 million in currency, gold, jewels, and stocks and bonds (not bad for a couple of days' work). The bad guys got away, though all was not lost. Eventually, some of the stocks and bonds were sold back to their owners.

_04:: More Francs Than a Wiener Schnitzel

How many Frenchmen does it take to rob a bank? Well, at least 10, if you're talking about the 1992 Bank of France robbery in Toulon. Using inside information from a bank employee, the gang kidnapped a guard's family and forced the guard to open the bank's doors. But just in case the "we've got your family and we'd be happy to off them" tactic wasn't convincing enough, the group decided to ensure the poor guy's cooperation by strapping explosives to him. Apparently, it was pretty effective. Once inside, the robbers removed the film from the surveillance cameras, emptied the vaults of 160 million francs (about $30 million), and took off in several vans—including one belonging to the bank. Within two months, most of the gang was caught, betrayed by the bank employee (not to be confused with the guard) who'd helped in the job. But several of the robbers still got away, and amazingly, less than 10% of the loot was ever recovered.

_05:: The Trench Coat Job

It was past quitting time when two men wearing buttoned-up trench coats let themselves into the Seafirst Bank in Lakewood, Washington, a suburb of Tacoma. Flashing a

Lies Your Mother Told You

IF THE SLOT MACHINE HASN'T PAID OFF ALL DAY, IT'S DUE

Sorry, Mom. You're a victim of what math professors call the "gambler's fallacy." And while it's possible that some olden-days mechanical slot machines may have responded to continuous play, today's computer chip–driven slots have no "memory" of previous plays. That means every pull is a brand-new game. Slot makers even claim their machines could pay off 19 times in a row, or not for years. A corollary to the gambler's fallacy is that things that happen in the long run should also happen in the short run. It ain't so. Oh, and for those of you still a little green to the machines, a "95% average payback" doesn't mean everyone who puts in $100 gets $95 back. Just think on it for a sec: a player who puts in $10 and wins $100 has a 900% payback. That means a lot of other players on the same machine are going to have a very small, or no, payback just to get the percentage back down to 95. There's a reason the house always wins.

gun, the pair stuffed 355 pounds of cash—$4.46 million—into sacks and made a clean getaway. Insane, right? The 1997 heist was actually the largest bank robbery in U.S. history, but this wasn't the work of amateurs. Nope.

Ray Bowman and William Kirkpatrick were real pros. In fact, between 1982 and 1998, Bowman and Kirkpatrick were believed to have robbed 28 banks around the country for a total of more than $7 million. Even more impressive: only once was there gunfire, and no one was hurt. A special FBI task force was formed, but it was stupidity that finally tripped them up. Kirkpatrick was stopped for speeding in late 1998 by a Nebraska state trooper. A search of the car turned up four handguns, fake badges, two ski masks—and $1.8 million in cash. Meanwhile, Bowman had failed to pay the rent on a storage locker in Kansas City, Missouri. When the owner opened it, and found a virtual armory of guns, he called the cops, and they collared Bowman at his suburban Kansas City home a few weeks after Kirkpatrick's arrest. The dapper duo was convicted in 1999, with Bowman getting slapped with 24 years, Kirkpatrick with 15.

Always Bet on the House:
Failed Attempts to Loot Las Vegas

Not all the bandits in Sin City are one-armed. Here are a few different ways people have tried to beat the odds.

_01:: A Little off the Top

Here's how it worked. In the 1970s, the Mob coerced the Teamsters Union into making loans to a San Diego businessman buying four casinos in Vegas. As hidden partners, Mob bosses then "skimmed" millions of dollars from the joints by rigging slots so they showed winners when there were none, or by fixing scales so they underweighed coins. One estimate had the wise guys swiping $7 million in quarters in just one 18-month period. In the end, though, federal wiretaps and informants broke the scam. The Feds even tapped conversations between mobsters in the visitors room at Leavenworth Penitentiary, and in 1986, a dozen bosses from gangs in Chicago, Kansas City, Milwaukee, and Cleveland were convicted in the biggest Mob-Vegas case ever.

_02:: Playing Your Cards Right

Blackjack is a beatable game—that is, if you can count cards well enough to know when the deck favors the player, not the house. And while solitary card counters are relatively easy to spot for most casino security outfits, it took them six years during the 1990s to tumble to the strategy used by a group of MIT students. Using card-counting *teams*, complete with diversionary players—the cavalier math-letes raked in millions. One player recounted walking from one casino to another carrying a paper hat stuffed with $180,000 in cash.

Amazingly, the MIT ring was never actually caught in the act. Some members retired. A few others were ratted out by a team traitor and banned from the casinos, which learned a lesson about the concept of team play.

_03:: The Genius

Like a football quarterback, Dennis Nikrasch needed his blockers. In Nikrasch's case, however, they were blocking surveillance cameras while he worked his sweet computer magic on slot machines. Once the machines were rigged, the clever hacker vacated the premises, leaving it to confederates to win the jackpots. Cops have reported that the Nikrasch gang raked in at least $16 million between 1976 and 1998, even with a 10-year time-out while Nikrasch spent time in federal prison and on parole. When he was caught again in 1998, Nikrasch indicated that he'd share his secrets in return for a lighter sentence. He got seven years—and apparently refused to talk. "I have no desire to explain anything to the public," he wrote to an Internet magazine in 1999 from jail. "Never smarten up a chump."

_04:: The Mechanic

Starting in 1980 in the back of his TV repair shop in Tulsa, Oklahoma, Tommy Glenn Carmichael invented, refined, then manufactured devices for cheating slot machines. Tommy's bag of tricks ranged from coins on strings to light wands that blinded machine sensors, fooling them into dropping their coins. For most of two decades, Carmichael and his partners raked in millions of dollars. But his luck finally ran out when federal agents tapped his phone and heard him discussing a new device that would rack up hundreds of credits per minute on slot machines. In 2001, Carmichael was sentenced to about a year in jail, and was ordered to stay out of casinos. In 2003, he told an Associated Press reporter he was developing a new gadget, called "the Protector." It was designed to stop slot cheaters.

_05:: And If All Else Fails...

Jose Vigoa was one cocky crook. After doing a five-year stint from 1991 to 1996 for drug dealing, Vigoa decided to change career paths in 1998. Well, only slightly. As the mastermind of a string of armed robberies over two years that rocked the Vegas Strip, Vigoa armed his outfit with high-tech weapons, body armor, and sophisticated planning. In fact, the Vigoa gang hit up the MGM Grand, the Desert Inn, the Mandalay Bay, and the Bellagio. Not looking to slack off, they even robbed an armored car in between gigs, and killed the two guards. Vigoa was tripped up, however, when video cameras at the Bellagio caught him without a mask during the robbery. He was sentenced in 2002 to life without parole, proving crime doesn't pay, even in Vegas.

My Kingdom for a Horse?
Really Bad Historical Trades

3

We've all made deals from time to time that we've instantly wished we could take back. But take heart, friends! Gather round and hear the tales of some of the worst barters in human history. With so much numbskullery to choose from, there's bound to be someone who made a worse bargain than you did.

_01:: Ephialtes Sells Out the Spartans

Nobody really remembers Ephialtes today, but for centuries after his treasonous deeds, Greeks would spit at the mere mention of his name. Here's how the story goes. In 480 BCE, about 7,000 Greek soldiers, led by King Leonidas of Sparta, were holding off King Xerxes' Persian army of over 200,000 men at the narrow pass of Thermopylae. Not exactly the greatest odds, but the troops were buying time for the allied Greek states to gather their armies and oppose the Persians. Enter Ephialtes, a local ne'er-do-well, and now renowned snitch. The Greek traitor decided to show the Persians a secret path around the pass, which would allow them to attack the Greeks from behind. A splendid little secret indeed. Facing attack from both sides, Leonidas sent most of his allies home, and he and his Spartans fought to the death. Of course, Ephialtes was supposed to have been rewarded handsomely for this tattling, no doubt with land, gold, and titles. But when an Athenian fleet destroyed the Persian navy at Thermopylae shortly thereafter, he had to flee the Persian camp without a penny to his name. After all, King Xerxes wasn't exactly in the rewarding mood at the time. On bad terms with the Persians, and wanted by the Greeks for his treason, the rascal fled to the wilds of Thessaly, where a few years later he was murdered.

_02:: The Dutch Buy Manhattan for a Pittance

In 1626, Peter Minuit, a representative of the Dutch government, bought Manhattan Island from an Algonquin tribe for 60 guilders. The old story about the Dutch buying the joint for 24 bucks' worth of beads is unlikely—there is no evidence that beads were part of the deal (iron tools were probably much more valuable to the natives). Nevertheless, considering the fact that a shoebox-sized apartment on the isle today sells for more than most people make in a lifetime, it seems that the Algonquins somewhat undervalued their own real estate. Only in America.

_03:: Cincinnati Gets Hosed: The Christy Mathewson–Amos Rusie Trade

Forget the Curse of the Bambino. Compared with this gaffe by the Cincinnati Reds, Boston's decision to trade Babe Ruth (and the subsequent 86-year curse) looks like a carefully orchestrated work of managerial genius. In 1900, the Reds traded relative newcomer and Renaissance man Christopher "Christy" Mathewson to the New York Giants for the ailing "Hoosier Thunderbolt," Amos Rusie. Following this brilliant move, Mathewson won 372 games for the Giants, including more than 20 games in 11 different seasons. He won wide renown as one of the greatest pitchers in baseball history. Rusie, on the other hand, pitched in three games following the trade, losing one and winning none—following which he promptly retired.

Touch of Evil

Manhattan for beads? No. The worst trade made between the Europeans and the Native Americans was much more gruesome: Europeans brought smallpox to America, which the Indians traded for syphilis!

An Offer I Can't Refuse: Generals Who Switched Sides in the Hopes of Reward

Military turncoats come in all shapes and sizes, motivated by all sorts of considerations: power, revenge, disillusionment, and, most often, the sound of a little extra coin. But not every turncoat seems to bear the tarnished rep old Benedict Arnold came away with. The following are some of history's lesser-known traitors, but ones who were pleased with the results.

_01:: Flavius Josephus (ca. 37–100)

Revolutionary governments, caught up in the heat of the moment, often make poor decisions. For example, the Jewish rebels fighting against Rome appointed Joseph ben Matthias to be military governor of Galilee. An inveterate coward, however, Joseph surrendered at the first opportunity and became the Roman general Flavius Vespasianus's adviser on Jewish affairs. A nice gig, for sure. And when Flavius became emperor in the year 69, Joseph (or Josephus, as his new pals called him) found himself vaulted to the top of Roman high society. After trying to encourage the surrender of Jerusalem by shouting propaganda at the walls, he retired to Rome and became a famous author. The guilt of his treason may have caught up with old Josephus in his old age; he penned numerous writings lauding Jewish civilization, possibly to try to clear his conscience.

_02:: Alaric (ca. 370–410)

A nobleman of the Visigoths, a Germanic tribe living in central Europe, Alaric fought for the Roman emperor Theodosius I against the rebel

Eugenius. The brilliant decision to hire Alaric, though, gave the cunning nobleman an insider's view of the empire's weaknesses, and he took careful note. When Theodosius died in 395, the empire was divided into eastern and western halves ruled by his quarreling sons—and Alaric decided opportunity wasn't just knocking, it was practically kicking down his door. Alaric marched on Constantinople and ravaged the Thracian countryside, capturing most of Greece before the Roman general Stilicho forced him to withdraw. Soon after, the eastern emperor Arcadius gave Alaric control of most of Illyria, all of which paved the way for his first invasion of Italy in 401. Alaric invaded the nation of his former employment several more times, and in 410 he became the first "barbarian" king to sack Rome in over 500 years. Though Alaric died in a plague in his 40s, his descendents carved out an empire of their own in what is now southern France, Spain, and Portugal.

_03:: Rodrigo Díaz de Vivar (El Cid, Campeador) (1043–1099)

His very title speaks of a checkered past: *El Cid* comes from the Arabic *al-Sayyid,* or "the lord," while *Campeador* is Spanish for "champion." Back when it all started, El Cid was a commander in the army of Castile. Of course, the cocky commander wasn't all roses to work with, and the Cid was forced to flee in 1080 after angering King Alfonso. What's an out-of-work commander to do, though? El Cid quickly decided to shack up with the enemy, joining forces with the Muslim emir (king) of Zaragosa. Despite the emir's cantankerous relationship with Castile, El Cid fought valiantly with his former foes for several years. That is, until Spain was invaded by Berber fanatics from

North Africa. Bathing in schadenfreude, El Cid was summoned back by Alfonso, profusely apologized to, and begged to defeat the seemingly invincible invaders. El Cid accepted, and in the course of the fighting, "the Champion" maneuvered himself into the top spot in Valencia, the gem of Spain's Mediterranean coast. He died in 1099 fighting off a new wave of North African attackers, but even after his death proved useful. The city's defenders strapped the Cid's rapidly-assuming-room-temperature form to the back of his horse and managed to trick the enemies into thinking El Cid, Campeador, was still in charge.

_04:: Francesco Sforza (1401–1466)

Warfare in 15th-century Italy was dominated by the *condottieri,* mercenary generals who commanded motley crews of hungry soldiers. Of course, the soldiers for hire weren't exactly loved by everyone, and were seen as particularly uncouth by those gallant few who fought for land instead of money. The son of one of the most successful of the condottieri, Francesco Sforza was known for his great strength: reportedly, he could bend iron bars with his bare hands. Of course, as a mercenary, his loyalties were just as easily bent. After signing on with various feudal lords in their endless wars, he settled down in Milan and joined forces with Filippo Visconti, the local duke. On Visconti's death in 1447, however, Francesco turned on the duke's family and exiled or killed many of them. He also broke up an attempt to establish a Milanese republic, and then made himself duke. It's not nearly as bad as it sounds, though. Francesco went on to usher in nearly two decades of the best rule Milan had ever seen.

Touch of Evil

The three Generals who have the most impact on the Department of Defense? General Dynamics, General Electric, and General Motors, all of which are among the companies with the most money tied up in military contracts.

_05:: Albrecht Wenzel Eusebius von Wallenstein (1583–1634)

A minor, though well-educated, Czech nobleman, Wallenstein became an officer in the armies of the Holy Roman Empire. He fought numerous battles against Venice and other powers and gained a reputation for military genius. But when his fellow Protestants rebelled against the empire in 1618, ushering in the Thirty Years' War, imperial generals worked themselves into a tizzy fearing that they would face Wallenstein on the field. They needn't have worried, though. A man whose eye was always on the bottom line, Wallenstein calculated that the rewards of serving the Catholic side of the war were greater. He helped crush Protestant armies in his native Bohemia as well as in western and northern Germany. Removed from command in 1630 on suspicion of preparing to switch sides, he was reinstated shortly thereafter on the rationale that a general thought to be disloyal was probably better than generals known to be incompetent. In retrospect, however, the reasoning was questionable, as Wallenstein was killed in 1634 while attempting to defect to the Swedes.

_06:: Shi Lang (1621–1696)

An admiral in the navy of China's Ming dynasty, Shi Lang came into conflict with Zheng Chenggong, a rival general. Deciding that the grass looked greener up north, he defected in 1646 to the Manchus, and left his family behind to be slaughtered as traitors. Was it worth the (very literal) sacrifice? Apparently so. Lacking experienced naval officers, the Manchu ruler Shunzhi welcomed Shi Lang with open arms, and the officer happily participated in the Manchu conquest of China. In fact, he became an official of the new Qing dynasty, made up of Shunzhi's descendents. Then, in 1681, he even got to lead the conquest of Taiwan, which culminated in the surrender of his old enemies, the Zheng family. In the end, Shi Lang made out pretty well, and was given the title "General Who Maintains Peace on the Seas" by a very grateful imperial government.

Double-crossing Agents (and the Countries That Paid Them)

In the trust-no-one world of espionage, an operative for one government may in fact be working for that government's enemy, and vice versa. Of course, the most successful double agents are the ones no one ever heard of. A few of the rest are listed below.

_01:: Numero Trece

An officer in the American Revolution, James Wilkinson moved after the war to Kentucky, where in 1787 he pledged loyalty to Spain. In return for a Spanish pension, Wilkinson (or "Numero 13" to his Spanish handlers) worked to make Kentucky part of Spanish Louisiana. Of course, Wilkinson had his fingers in a few pies at the time, and was simultaneously being promoted to lieutenant colonel in the U.S. Army. After the Louisiana Purchase of 1800, Wilkinson became a U.S. territorial governor, and began conspiring with U.S. vice president Aaron Burr to found an independent nation in Mexico. But like a good double-crosser, he's the one credited with exposing Burr's plot to President Thomas Jefferson, leading to Burr's trial for treason. Wilkinson emerged from the scandal with honor intact and commanded U.S. troops in the War of 1812. His incompetence, however, ended his U.S. service and he moved to Mexico, where he petitioned for and won a Texas land grant.

_02:: The Family That Spies Together...

In 1967, John Walker Jr., a petty burglar and U.S. Navy radioman, walked into the Soviet embassy in Washington, D.C., and offered to supply encryption keys—tools for decoding classified military messages—in exchange for a regular salary from the KGB. For the next 18 years, during and after his Navy career, Walker continued to work for the Soviets. When a transfer removed his access to classified codes and documents, he enlisted help from others, including his brother and his son. In fact, Walker talked his kid, Michael, into enlisting in the Navy just to pilfer shipboard documents. KGB officers later said that Walker had given them access to the most vital U.S. secrets. When the FBI finally caught up with him in 1984, Walker thought he could avoid prosecution by offering to turn the table on the Soviets. Under interrogation, however, he confessed, and is serving a life term in federal prison.

_03:: For a Fistful of Millions

Before his arrest in 1994, career CIA agent Aldrich "Rick" Ames exposed the identity of every U.S. agent working in the Soviet Union and its successor states. And the leak was used to full effect. Between 1985 and 1994, the Soviets executed at least 10 CIA operatives based solely on the info Aldrich and his Colombian-born wife were feeding them. A 31-year em-

Touch of Evil

Benedict Arnold probably wished he could've had a do-over. He never got even half the money the British promised him for switching sides.

ployee of the U.S. intelligence agency, Ames's job had been to discover Soviet spies within the agency. But like a fox guarding the hen-house, Aldrich betrayed his country and traded the lives of his comrades for a mere $2.5 million. Top government officials said the damage to U.S. security was potentially catastrophic. After pleading guilty to charges of conspiracy to commit espionage and tax fraud, Ames was sentenced to life imprisonment without chance of parole.

ALAN FREED'S HORRIBLE-TERRIBLE, NO-GOOD, VERY BAD DAY

On March 21, 1952, the Moondog Coronation Ball took place at the Cleveland Arena in Cleveland, Ohio, becoming the first rock-and-roll concert in history. The concert, which was promoted by Alan Freed (known for giving rock and roll its name), was also the event where the first rock-and-roll riot occurred. Why, exactly? Well, the concert hall only held around 10,000 people while over 20,000 tickets were sold. Also, even though most of the artists performing were African American, the fans able to get inside were white while those left outside were black. There was gate crashing and fights broke out between groups of fans and then quickly with the police. When the police finally closed down the concert, fans spilled out onto the streets of Cleveland, causing chaos and damage. As for Alan Freed, he was summarily arrested for inciting the riot. It seems that from day one, rock and roll and rioting were destined to happen together.

To the Victors Go the Soils: History's Most Blatant Land Grabs

5

God supposedly issued a commandment against it, and yet people have been stealing from each other since the world began. And sometimes on a ridiculously large scale. Here are just a few of the more outrageous instances.

_01:: Prussia, Austria, and Russia Partition Poland

Internal divisions accelerated by a ridiculous parliamentary system led to Poland's decline in the 18th century, and its neighbors—Prussia to the west, Austria to the south, and Russia to the east—were more than happy to bite off a large part of the struggling nation in the "First Partition" of 1772. All told, the nations usurped about half of its territory and a third of its population. In an attempt to save itself, the Polish government tried to institute internal reforms, but it was too little too late. In the "Second Partition," in 1793, Prussia and Russia took even more land, causing Polish rebellions that they quickly crushed. As if that weren't enough, the "Third Partition," in 1797, had Austria participating again, and it finished off Poland as a separate state. The nation wouldn't be independent again until 1918. And shortly thereafter, to add insult to injury, the Nazis and Soviets partitioned the country one last time, in 1939.

_02:: America Takes Most of the West from Mexico

In 1776, the 13 colonies covered about 900,000 square miles along the east coast of North America. Over the course of the next 75 years, the country would expand 300%, to about 2.9 million square miles, through five international treaties, two wars, and the Louisiana Purchase in 1803. Though the Purchase was a legitimate exchange of property—except for the claims of Native American inhabitants, of course, who were never really consulted—much of the later expansion was a blatant illegitimate land grab. The Mexican-American War of 1846, for example, began in part because slave owners in the American South wanted to add Texas as a new slave-owning territory. The war resulted in the transfer of all of California, Nevada, Arizona, Utah, and large parts of New Mexico, Colorado, and Wyoming to the U.S., all for a rather paltry payment of $15 million.

_03:: Japan Invades Manchuria and Then the Rest of Asia

In the decades before 1931, Japan needed iron ore and coal to outfit its rapidly expanding military and industrial base. On September 18, 1931, Japan invaded Manchuria, a large mineral-rich province in northern China. Of course, the invasion was justified. Sort of. Japanese officers fabricated an excuse for the war by blowing up a section of the Japanese-owned South Manchurian Railway and blaming Chinese saboteurs. The move was just the first in a long series of aggressive actions that would bring much of Asia under Japanese control, including unprovoked attacks on Shanghai, Hong Kong, and Nanking in south China, the occupation of many of China's coastal provinces, the sneak attack on the U.S. Navy at Pearl Harbor, and shortly thereafter the invasion and occupation of the Philippines, Vietnam, Laos, Cambodia, Thailand, Burma, Malaysia, Singapore, Indonesia, and New Guinea! Though estimates vary, it's certain that tens of millions of people died as a result of the Japanese aggression, which ended only with the country's defeat in the Second World War.

Touch of Evil

Colombia rejected a $10 million offer by the U.S. for the rights to build a canal across its land, so a "rebel force" was quickly organized, which broke free and became the country of Panama (with U.S. military support). The rebels got the bucks, and Teddy Roosevelt got his canal.

_04:: Cecil Rhodes, Zimbabwe, Botswana, and Zambia

Cecil Rhodes single-handedly added the modern countries of Zimbabwe, Botswana, and Zambia to British South Africa. Hardly content to stop there, Rhodes once famously declared, "I would annex the planets if I could." Rhodes moved to the British Cape Colony in South Africa in 1870 at the age of 17 and founded the British South Africa Company, which began at South Africa's diamond-rich Kimberly mine

and is now known as DeBeers. The company began expanding north into the tribal lands of present-day Zimbabwe in 1889, and subdued recalcitrant tribes there by force in 1893. The new territory was called Rhodesia in Rhodes's honor. Meanwhile, in 1890, company agents made treaties with local tribal leaders in present-day Zambia. Botswana was brought under British control after the controversial Boer War from 1899 to 1902. In the end, Cecil Rhodes had single-handedly taken control of an area more than three times the size of France.

_05:: Germany Invades Belgium in World War I

At the London Conference of 1838–1839, all the major European powers agreed to protect the neutrality of the small, newly created country of Belgium. However, as time went on Germany claimed that Belgium was not behaving as a neutral country because it had fortified its border with Germany but not with France. Although Belgium had a sovereign right to do this, a contingency plan for war with France was devised by General von Schlieffen in the 19th century, calling for a pincer offensive closing in on Paris, with one arm coming south across the Rhine—intended as a feint—and another arm launching a surprise attack from the north through Belgium. This plan was finally set in motion during the First World War, meeting with almost universal condemnation because it so blatantly disregarded treaty obligations and the rules of warfare, marking a new low in international relations and heralding the brutality to come.

I Got Mine, Now What?
Shady Business Moguls and
What They Did with Their Money

"A man who dies rich dies disgraced," said philanthropic industrialist Andrew Carnegie. And while not that many robber barons would agree, a few did try to give something back to society, no matter how unscrupulously their money was acquired.

_01:: An Erie Case of Corruption

Cattleman Daniel Drew turned to the passenger steamboat business in 1834 and prospered. Ten years later, he opened the Wall Street brokerage firm Drew, Robinson and Company. Then a decade after that, when a financial panic hit in 1857, Drew snapped up the undervalued Erie Railroad stock and became a company director. Not a bad few years. Although Drew routinely manipulated stocks, his old steamboat competitor Cornelius Vanderbilt outfoxed him in 1864 with company infighting and Drew lost heavily. Seeking revenge, he and two partners issued enormous amounts of Erie stock, driving down the value of Vanderbilt's investment. Both sides bribed judges in the "Erie War," which ruined thousands of investors, but never really hurt Vanderbilt. Then, in an unexpected twist, Drew's partners turned on him, leaving him ruined. Although dishonest in business, Drew did have a few good qualities. As a devout Methodist, he founded the Drew Theological Seminary (which later became Drew University) before he lost his money.

_02:: Whistle-stop Prosperity

After a few years of law practice in Wisconsin, Leland Stanford heard about all the money you could make selling equipment (at grossly inflated prices) to gold rush miners in California, so he promptly moved west. Once well established as a merchant, Stanford decided to seek public office and in 1860 he won California's governorship. Never bothered by conflicts of interest, Stanford used his position to secure public money and state land grants for himself and his three Sacramento partners—Mark Hopkins, Collis Huntington, and Charles Crocker—who built the western portion of the transcontinental railroad. After one two-year term, Stanford became president of the Central Pacific Railroad. A consummate (and ridiculously corrupt) businessman, Stanford's varied interests were greased with government influence, all of which brought him tremendous wealth. But he did give back a little. In 1885, after the death of his teenage son, Stanford founded and endowed Stanford University in the boy's memory.

DAVID HANNUM'S HORRIBLE-TERRIBLE, NO-GOOD, VERY BAD DAY

Turns out P. T. Barnum wasn't the man behind the memorable aphorism "There's a sucker born every minute." Though nearly always attributed to Barnum, the quote about suckers was actually from a first-rate sucker (and Barnum rival) named David Hannum. In 1869, Hannum and four business partners paid $37,500 for a 10-foot-tall stone giant man. The Cardiff Giant was in fact an elaborate hoax played by a tobacconist named John Hull, who had the stone man carved, then buried in Cardiff, New York, and then dug up again. Theories abounded about the giant (was he a petrified biblical figure? an ancient Native American statue?), and thousands of people paid good money to catch a glimpse. Of course, Hannum was looking to make back his investment easily. But then P. T. Barnum built a giant and claimed that *it* was the true Cardiff Giant. When people flocked to see Barnum's fake, Hannum—who didn't yet know he'd paid almost 40 grand for a fake giant of his own—mused incredulously, "There's a sucker born every minute." Sure is. And it takes one to know one, Mr. Hannum.

_03:: The Art of Making Money

The son of a financier, John Pierpont Morgan bought his way out of the Civil War draft for $300, giving himself plenty of free time to speculate in wartime gold. As Morgan quickly realized, the price of the metal rose against the dollar with each Union Army defeat. As a bank loan agent, J. P. Morgan earned a commission on a deal to buy defective rifles from a Union arsenal in New York for $3.50 apiece, then sell them to the Union Army in Virginia for $22 each. The underhanded deal (in, oh, so many ways) only helped him on his way to becoming a powerful banker, a railroad magnate, and one of the world's top financiers. Of course, he wasn't all bad. J. P.'s giant industrial consolidations reshaped American capitalism and his financial muscle held off national fiscal crises. Further, as a great art collector, Morgan gave many works to New York's Metropolitan Museum of Art. In fact, his book collection and the building that housed it have become a museum and public library in New York.

_04:: Oil Wells That End Well

John D. Rockefeller—originally a dealer in farm goods—got into the oil business in 1863 and founded Standard Oil in 1870. His ruthless competitive practices made Standard Oil a monopoly and made Rockefeller the world's first billionaire. To skirt antimonopoly laws, he reorganized the Standard Oil Trust and made the resulting companies appear in compliance. When the U.S. Supreme Court in 1911 declared Standard Oil to be in violation of federal law, it forced the company's breakup. But by then,

Rockefeller had found a new hobby: philanthropy. Before his death at age 97 in 1937, he had given away $500 million, including $80 million to the University of Chicago, which he had helped found in 1892. With son John D. Rockefeller Jr., the businessman also founded Rockefeller University, the General Education Board, and the Rockefeller Foundation.

_05:: Honeys, I'm Home!

Haroldson Lafayette Hunt speculated in cotton and Arkansas farmland before he became an oilman in the 1920s. As a real-estate operator, Hunt would find out a farmer's asking price, then find a buyer willing to pay a little more. In essence, the slick salesman would cut deals to sell the land before he actually acquired it. In 1930, though, Hunt took his eyes off land and set them on oil. He bought out East Texas oil wildcatter "Dad" Joiner and reaped hundreds of millions in profits. And while Hunt was pretty fond of money, he was also fond of pretty wives. A bigamist, Hunt was married to

first wife, Lyda, throughout his 17-year marriage to second wife, Frania. Then, after Lyda's death, he married secretary Ruth Ray, who had already borne him four children. But even with all the wives, and kids, and business dealings, Hunt made plenty of time to preach about the little things he really loved: like conservative values. The billionaire founded the nonprofit *Facts Forum* radio program, and also hosted the conservative radio show *Life Line*. Among his 14 children, daughters Margaret Hunt Hill, Helen LaKelly Hunt, and Swannee Hunt have been especially active in charitable work.

Touch of Evil

Tabloid and "yellow journalism" king William Randolph Hearst did more than buy flowers for his mistress, Marion Davies. He formed Cosmopolitan Pictures to make films starring only her, and put rave reviews in all his newspapers.

Pilfer While You Work:
Marauders to Know

3

Who invented the concept of "take the money and run"? Judging by the dates on these entries, we're guessing it wasn't Woody Allen.

_01:: Fur Pants, Iron Sword

The sketchy facts about Ragnar Lodbrok, prototypical Viking king, were spun into legend so long ago that the truth is elusive. Probably born in Norway, this Danish chieftain wore fur trousers that earned him the name Lodbrok ("Hairy Pants"). A proud pagan, Lodbrok enjoyed attacking the coasts of Europe on holy days, when townspeople were off guard. Legend says Ragnar fought Charlemagne (who died in 814 CE), but it's more likely that he led the 5,000 Norse warriors that besieged Paris in the 850s, until Charlemagne's grandson Charles II paid them off. (Ragnar often demanded and received huge bribes.) The Viking then hit up northern England on his European tour, but the strike proved unlucky. Hairy Pants was captured by the Saxon king Aella, who killed him by lowering him into a snake pit, Indiana Jones–style.

_02:: The Holy (City) Terror

At the culmination of the First Crusade in 1099, fair-haired Godfrey of Bouillon, a direct descendent of Charlemagne, led the first troops over the wall into Jerusalem. Bouillon and his fellow commanders from Western Europe, Raymond of Toulouse and Tancred Hauteville, were intent on taking the Holy City away from its Shiite Muslim rulers. Shortly after Godfrey's advance guard threw open the gates, the rest of the Christian troops stormed in. Immediately, the Muslim governor surrendered, but he was comforted when Tancred told him that those residents who took refuge in the Aqsa Mosque would be spared. Although Tancred may have been sincere, the rest of the Crusaders didn't show any mercy. They slaughtered everybody in the mosque in the name of Christ, and they killed virtually everyone else in Jerusalem as well—Muslim and Jew, grandmother and infant. When the raid was over, Godfrey declared himself ruler of Jerusalem under the title Defender of the Holy Sepulcher.

_03:: Black Beard, Black Heart

During the War of Spanish Succession (1701–1714), the Bristol-born Edward Teach sailed under a privateer's charter from Britain, attacking ships from hostile nations for profit. But in 1716 he began to freelance. Teach, better known as Blackbeard for his raven-colored chin whiskers, converted a captured French freighter into a 40-gun warship. As *Queen Anne's Revenge,* the vessel spread terror across the Caribbean and along the southern coast of colonial North America. Blackbeard raided ports and forced bribes from other sea captains in return for safe passage. He also cut deals with unscrupulous officials, including the colonial governor of North Carolina. The lieutenant governor of Virginia, however, called for a British naval force to put the pirate out of business. After a tough sea battle, the Brits killed Blackbeard, cut off his bearded head, and fastened it to the bowsprit of his ship.

Touch of Evil

Know which Marauder helped the Allies win World War II? The B-26 Marauder bomber. Thousands of them combined to drop 150,000 tons of explosives on Hitler and his cohorts.

LUST

The "Get Around, Get Around, I Get Around" Awards: Famous Scientists Who Shared More Than Equations

The nerdy scientist stereotype hardly presents the recipe for hot romance. After all, equations, beakers, and Bunsen burners rarely set the stage for love scenes except in the most absurd of parodies. And yet sometimes, while heating things up in the laboratory, scientists have been known to, well, heat things up in the laboratory.

_01:: Frederick's Hypothesis

To his friends, Frederick von Hohenstaufen was the *stupor mundi* ("wonder of the world"). To his enemies, he was the Antichrist. Of course, to the people of Sicily (1197–1250), Germany (1212–1250), and the Holy Roman Empire (1220–1250), he was simply the king. As a skilled warlord, Freddy kept power by overwhelming his enemies with his military expertise. As a clever linguist, he wrote scientific tracts in a dozen languages (including one of the first detailed manuals on the anatomy of birds). Not to mention that the guy was also an early advocate of the experimental method and performed some rather interesting (though highly unethical) experiments—such as raising children in silence to see if they would speak a "natural language." But Fred was best known for his decadent lifestyle—enamored of Islamic culture and philosophy, he kept a harem of nubile young ladies at his beck and call. And why shouldn't he? It's good to be the king.

_02:: Swingin' Ben Franklin

The kite-flying, bifocals-inventing, library- and post office–establishing Renaissance man of the American Revolution was a self-taught meteorologist, printer, inventor...and ladies' man? That's right, old Ben Franklin loved to get his groove on. And though he appears to have been faithful to his beloved wife Deborah during the years of their marriage (from 1730 until her death in 1774), historical records show big Ben was quite the man slut both before they married and after her death. In fact, Franklin fathered at least one illegitimate child, William, in 1728. While on diplomatic missions in Europe for the Continental Congress, Franklin developed a reputation that led more than one worried father to lock up his daughters when the American delegation was in town. And even in his old age, Franklin had so many affairs that we wonder if he might not be literally, as well as figuratively, the "Father of Philadelphia."

_03:: Einstein = Ladies' Man Squared

While he never had an actual harem like von Hohenstaufen or a gaggle of French mistresses like Franklin, old Al Einstein earns his place in the Horny Scientist Hall of Fame just the same for his work in seducing his colleague, Serbian scientist Mileva Maric. The lewd scientist snared more than just her heart when the two were graduate students working together in a lab. And Maric actually gave birth to an illegitimate daughter, whom the couple gave up for adoption, before marrying Einstein in 1903. Though the two went on to have more children (before divorcing in 1919), some have suggested that Maric made significant contributions to Einstein's theories. Albert didn't give up on love, though—he married his second wife, Elsa (not before contemplating marriage with her 20-year-old daughter, Ilse), shortly after his divorce, but maintained numerous affairs with other women throughout the 1920s and 1930s. Whether or not you consider it ethical, of course, remains a matter of relativity.

_04:: Alfred Kinsey Gets Kinky

An entomologist by training, Kinsey's tastes soon strayed far from insects. In 1947 he founded the Institute for Sex Research at Indiana University, single-handedly creating the academic field of sexology. In fact, his well-known Kinsey Reports were among the first scientific studies of human sexual behavior. It's little wonder that the guy was attacked by traditionalists, who accused him of promoting immoral behavior and sexual perversion. And though the first charge is a matter of opinion, they may have been more accurate on the second than they knew at the time. After Kinsey's death it became known that he was a masochist and a fan of group sex. Both Kinsey and his wife regularly engaged in sex with other men, but they stayed married for 35 years and remained devoted to each other until his death in 1956. Kinsey was also infamous for encouraging his assistants and grad students to engage in unusual sex acts with one another, which no doubt made for some rather interesting staff meetings.

Touch of Evil

After the death of her husband, Marie Curie began a scandalous affair with her married lab assistant. Despite her two Nobels and everything she did for science, the tryst ultimately cost her admission into the prestigious Académie des Sciences.

Biblical Girls Gone Wild:
Sinfully Amusing Snippets

6

It's part of the genius of the Bible that most of the great biblical figures aren't portrayed as supermen or saints. Abraham doesn't appear to have been in any danger of winning Father of the Year, Moses had serious anger management issues, and King Solomon's love of the finer things is criticized in the text, particularly his harem filled with 1,000 women. And because they're human, we can relate to them—well, most of the time. Here are a few biblical stories you probably didn't hear about in Sunday school.

_01:: Lot's Daughters Bark up the Family Tree (Genesis 19)

As they hid in a cave somewhere in the wilderness near the Dead Sea, Lot and his daughters were the only survivors of God's rampage through the streets of sinful, sinful Sodom (luckily, as the only righteous man in town, Lot was spared). Suspecting that they were the last people left on earth, and unwilling to die alone and childless, Lot's crafty lot got their father drunk and then had their way with him, making the previously righteous figure his own son-in-law and his two sons' father also grandfather and uncle at the same time. And while this probably made Lot family reunions a tad more interesting, sadly the details are lost in the mists of time. As for the kids, though, they did pretty all right for themselves. Lot's sons grew up to be the ancestors of the Moabites and Ammonites, two very powerful tribes of the highland region east of the Jordan River.

_02:: Jacob's Women (Genesis 29–30)

Need something even more Jerry Springer for your scandal-loving palate? Then get a load of the story of Jacob, grandson of Abraham. Things started off rocky for the kid as Jacob had to flee to his uncle's place after royally screwing his brother Esau in an inheritance swindle. Safe in the warmth of his uncle's home, he fell in love with his cousin Rachel, and married her, but not before his uncle Laban duped him into marrying Rachel's sister Leah as well. (For the privilege of all this cousin-marrying Jacob had to work 14 years, though some might say marriage is hard time enough!) More chaos ensued when Rachel, the beloved wife, was barren while her sister, Leah, (to whom Jacob was presumably relatively indifferent) produced kids with alarming regularity. Not to be outdone, Rachel gave her servant, Bilhah, to Jacob as a concubine, taking the kids produced as her own. Leah upped the ante by giving the probably exhausted Jacob her servant, Zilpah. All told, the competitive fivesome produced 13 children, 12 of which became the ancestors of Israelite tribes and the last of whom (see below) had the poor taste to be born a girl.

_03:: Dinah's Brothers Get Overprotective (Genesis 34)

Dinah was the only known daughter of the extraordinarily fertile Jacob. One day while her family was camped outside the town of Shechem, Dinah went to get some water and had a run-in with a local prince. Whether she ran off with him willingly (as feminist authors like to claim) or was raped by him (as the text seems to suggest) is unclear, but her 11 older brothers (the 12th, Joseph, was by this time in Egypt) had a rather dim view of such goings-on. After convincing the prince's buddies that circumcision was a great idea, Dinah's older brothers slaughtered the lot of them while they were recuperating from their ordeal. Dinah's ultimate fate has gone unrecorded, but folks who heard the tale were probably careful around girls with that many brothers for some time thereafter.

_04:: Tamar Tricks Judah (Genesis 38)

Another of Jacob's kids, Judah, married off his oldest son, Er, to a woman named Tamar. Er, who was "wicked in the eyes of the Lord," ended up dying young. The custom of the time (codified into law later in the Bible) was that his next oldest brother should "go in unto" his widow, and the child from that union would carry on the line of the dead man. Judah's second son, Onan, wasn't exactly up to the challenge, however. Unwilling to fulfill his obligation to his brother, Onan instead "spilled his seed on the ground" (hence "onanism," or masturbation). For the sin of refusing his brotherly obligation (not, as is often stated, for spanking his proverbial monkey), Onan too met an untimely end. So, what was a proud parent (albeit an embarrassed one at this point) to do? Unwilling to risk his youngest son's life, Judah sent Tamar home to her folks. But Tamar one-upped Jacob. Disguising herself as a prostitute, she tricked her father-in-law into performing the neglected duty himself. In fact, she bore him two sons, one of whom, Perez, was an ancestor of King David.

Touch of Evil

A 1631 printing of the King James version of the Bible was missing a rather important word. It became known as the **Wicked Bible** *for leaving "not" out of Exodus 20:14, which as a result read "Thou shalt commit adultery."*

_05:: Jael "Nails" Sisera (Judges 5)

Jael was the wife of Heber, the chieftain of a clan allied with the Israelites. After the Israelite chieftainess Deborah defeated Sisera, who was a general for the king of Hazor, Sisera made a hasty retreat that took him right by Jael's tent. The clever Jael, went on to play it just right. She invited him in, fed him, and, in a scene reminiscent of bad porn, may even have had sex with him. Once he was sound asleep, though, she took a hammer and drove a tent peg through his skull. Who knew the chieftain's wife would be so handy with a hammer? Or thoughtful? Jael went on to present Sisera's carcass as a gift to Deborah's army when they turned up shortly thereafter.

_06:: Bathsheba Nonchalantly Goes Skinny-dipping...in Plain Sight of the Royal Palace (2 Samuel 11)

One day King David glanced out his window and just happened to see a beautiful, completely naked woman taking a bath on a rooftop. She had no idea that David was going to be watching (and if you believe that, we have a river in Egypt to sell you), but he was immediately smitten. Just one problem: The woman, Bathsheba, was already married to a Hittite mercenary named Uriah. In one of David's less than stellar moments, he conspired to have Uriah moved too close to enemy lines and, with her husband out of the way, rushed to the altar with Bathsheba. Good thing, too, as it was just in time for her first son by him to be born. In an episode that is part tragic, part comic, and all shocking, the prophet Nathan exposed the adulterous union before the court. And though David and Bathsheba's first son died, their story takes an upswing as David and Bathsheba's second son eventually became King Solomon.

Weapons of Mass Seduction: Infamous Female Spies

Behind every good war are many good women. Using their feminine (and in at least one case masculine) wiles, the following five spies would make James Bond proud.

_01:: Mata Hari

While Margaretha Geertruida Zelle MacLeod (1876–1917) may not have caused World War I, she sure as heck kept it going. Having spent time in Java with her husband, Captain Campbell MacLeod, Margaretha returned to Holland and sued for divorce. To make ends meet she took up exotic dancing and the name Mata Hari (meaning "the light of day" in Malay). With her sensual performances becoming the attraction of the major European cities came the men and the gifts for her favors. Many of these favors came from royalty and high-ranking French and German military officers. As World War I progressed, both sides became suspicious that Mata was spying for the other side. The French eventually put her on trial and, although the charges were never proven, Mata Hari was convicted of espionage and was executed by a firing squad on October 15, 1917. Playing the seductress up until the end, Mata refused a blindfold, smiled, and blew a kiss to the firing squad as the fatal shots were fired.

_02:: Sarah Emma Edmonds (or Was It Frank Thompson?)

Born in 1841 in New Brunswick, Canada, Sarah ran away from home in her early teens. In order to survive she became an itinerant Bible salesman, by calling herself Frank Thompson and dressing like a man. In 1861, Frank (Sarah) enlisted in the Second Michigan Infantry and over the next two years not only fought in a number of Civil War battles, but also served as a spy for the Union Army. Solders in her unit called Frank "our woman" because of his feminine mannerisms and his extremely small boot size. However, none of her comrades ever figured out that Frank was really Sarah. This boded well for her spying, where she dressed as a young boy serving in Confederate camps, as an immigrant Irish peddler and, most interestingly, as a woman. In 1863, Sarah caught malaria and deserted the army out of fear that hospitalization would reveal her true identity. In 1884, though, Sarah applied for and was awarded a veteran's pension in which the secretary of war acknowledged that Sarah was a female soldier who had rendered faithful services to the ranks.

_03:: Noor Inayat Khan

Khan was born in the Kremlin in 1914 and at a young age moved with her family first to England and then to France. In 1940, Khan, along with her mother and sister, escaped back to England just before France surrendered to Germany. While in England she joined the Women's Auxiliary Air Force (WAAF), but her ability to speak fluent French soon caught the attention of the Special Operations group and Khan agreed to become a spy. Khan was flown to Le Mans, where she teamed up with other female spies and traveled to Paris. There they joined the French Resistance Prosper Network. Soon after their arrival, the network was infiltrated and many were arrested. Khan was ordered to return to England, but instead she stayed on and continued to pass information on to England. Eventually she was arrested again and interrogated by the Gestapo. When she refused to speak, she was sent to a prison in Germany and then to the Dachau concentration camp. On September 13, 1944, Khan and three other female British spies were executed by the Nazi SS. In 1949, Khan was posthumously awarded the George Cross.

_04:: Belle Boyd (aka "La Belle Rebelle")

Born Isabelle Boyd in Martinsburg, Virginia, in 1844, the beautiful Belle soon became the star attraction in Washington, D.C., social circles prior to the beginning of the Civil War. With the outbreak of the war, she returned to Martinsburg. When the Union soldiers occupied the city, Belle mixed with the officers and soon gathered information on troop movements, which she passed on to the Confederate forces. However, she is probably best known for warning Stonewall Jackson that the Union intended to blow up all the bridges around Martinsburg. With this information, Jackson, with a small number of troops, was able to surprise the Union troops and drive them from the area. In 1864, Confederate president Jefferson Davis asked Belle to carry letters for him to England. The Union Navy captured her ship, but the officer in charge fell in love with Belle and let her escape. The officer, Lieutenant Samuel Harding Jr., after being court-martialed and discharged from the Navy, traveled to England, where he married Belle. After the war, Boyd toured the United States as an actress under the stage name of La Belle Rebelle.

_05:: Elizabeth Van Lew

Crazy Bet, as she was known, was born in Richmond, Virginia, in 1818 but educated at a Quaker school in Philadelphia. After developing a hatred for slavery, Elizabeth returned to Richmond and freed all her family's slaves. She also went so far as finding where her freed slaves' relatives were and purchased and freed them also. After the Civil War started, Elizabeth asked to visit Union prisoners being held captive in Richmond. The Union prisoners gave her information, which she then passed on to the North. Among the slaves she freed was Mary Elizabeth Bowser, whom Van Lew got a job as a house servant in the home of Jefferson Davis. This allowed Bowser and Van Lew to collect and pass on information directly from the Confederate president's mansion. Elizabeth effectively used the Crazy Bet moniker to make the residents of Richmond think she was mentally ill. She would wear old clothes and bonnets and talk to herself. Because of this, most people thought that her Northern sympathies were just a part of her craziness. After the war, President Grant named Elizabeth the postmaster for Richmond. When the citizens of Richmond found out that Crazy Bet was an act, they shunned her. However, at her death, the state of Massachusetts placed a memorial marker on her grave.

Just the Facts

PORN BY THE NUMBERS

70: Percentage of visits to porn Web sites made between 9 a.m. and 5 p.m.

5.3 billion: Estimated number of dollars U.S. companies lost to recreational Web surfing during business hours in 2000

14 million: Number of porn pages on the Web in 1998

260 million: Number of porn pages on the Web in 2003

68 million: Daily number of pornographic search engine requests on the Web

25: Percentage of total daily Web search engine requests that are related to porn sites

12 billion: Number of dollars in revenues the U.S. porn industry gathered in 2003

33: Percentage of visitors to adult Web sites who are women

253: Number of arrests for pornography/ obscenity violations by the U.S. Postal Service in 2002

11: Average age at which men first see a copy of *Playboy* or *Penthouse* magazine

Harem Scarem:
Facts on Harems

You've heard about them. You've fantasized about them. You've dreamed about one day owning your own. But are you really mature enough to have your own harem yet? After all, who's going to cook for your harem? Who's going to feed 'em? And a harem doesn't just walk itself, you know. With great harems comes great responsibility. You might want to read the following five facts before you decide to invest in one.

_01:: The Primer: Just a Couple Harems to Know

Under Islamic law, a man can have as many wives as he can support, with the traditional number topping out at around four. However, concubines are unlimited and many harems grew into the thousands. Following are some of history's largest recorded harems. At the top of the list is the 6th century BCE's King Tamba of Banaras, whose harem numbered some 16,000 women. Not to be outdone, the 15th-century Sultan Ghiyas-ud-Din Kilji's harem numbered 15,000 and required him to build a separate walled city to house them. Next, during the 1800s, King Mongkut of Siam housed his 9,000 women in a totally contained city with its own government, recreational facilities, and a theater. Kublai Khan, the Mongol leader in the 13th century, had four empresses and around 7,000 concubines. Every two years he would get rid of a couple hundred concubines and replace them with a fresh supply. Finally, Emperor Jahangir of India maintained a harem of over 6,300 women during the early years of the 17th century. However, Jahangir also kept close to a thousand young men-in-waiting for those times when his appetite tended toward the other gender.

_02:: Getting Some Order in Your Harem

Contrary to the Hollywood view of scantily dressed beautiful women lounging around pools waiting for their romantic interlude with the sultan, harems were actually very elaborate and complex communities with rigid administrative and disciplinary systems. A harem was under the leadership of the Valide Sultan, or the sultan's mother. Directly responsible to the mother were the superintendent of the harem and a number of other female officials. Each of these officials had a number of younger harem members under them training for this and other future administrative assignments. Next in the pecking order after the sultan's mother was the mother of the sultan's heir apparent. After this came the mothers of the sultan's other children, who were ranked by the favor they held with the sultan. These female relatives and other officials were responsible for recruiting new harem members and annually presenting them to the sultan, usually on the 15th day of Ramadan.

Touch of Evil

Nizam Sir Osman Ali Khan Bahadur was perhaps the world's richest man in the early 20th century. He ruled Hyderabad both independently and as part of India, and his fat wallet helped him collect an enviable 42 concubines for his harem.

_03:: So You Want to Be a Eunuch?

Sounds like an exciting life being left to live among hundreds, if not thousands, of the most beautiful women in the empire. Let's look at some of the requirements. The first priority is castration. Most likely you'll want to have this procedure done during your childhood. Next, expect to be a part of a dowry offered by your master when his daughter is given in marriage. Okay, you've passed the entrance exam, now expect to spend years working your way up the ranks of eunuchs. Finally, you gain favor with the sultan and he makes you the chief eunuch. Your sole reason for being is meeting your master's needs. You need to know the master's mood and select his appropriate bedmate for the evening. You must also instruct the young lady on the master's whims and fantasies and have the appropriate aphrodisiacs ready. As the chief black eunuch you have become the sultan's most trusted servant and the third highest ranking official in his empire. You can enter the harem apartments, command the imperial army, and meet with the sultan. If you are the chief white eunuch, you get to run the bureaucracy and control all petitions, messages, and state documents sent to the sultan,

but you cannot enter the harem. Why? Because unlike the black eunuch, who lost everything (anatomically), you still have bits and pieces left and pose a threat.

_04:: How to Furnish Your Harem

The Arabic word *harem* means "the place of the women." The most important part of the harem was the zenana, or the inner sanctum where the sultan's fantasies were played out. The zenana was designed to replicate paradise. Each woman was given her own ornately decorated apartment with its own garden, waterfalls, and running streams. Because the ladies of the harem came from many different cultures, the apartments were furnished to make them feel comfortable and satisfied with their position in life. After all, one must be ready and willing for an unexpected visit from the master. Similarly, the attire was erotic and arousing. The goal was to remain naked while being dressed by wearing translucent muslin and silk garments. The material was so light that many outfits weighed about an ounce. In keeping with the opulence, the garments were adorned with diamonds, gold, rubies, and pearls. Shoes were also covered with precious stones. Finally, the outfit was topped off with an ostrich feather headdress with ruby-covered plumes. Many a sultan spent most of the empire's treasury keeping the ladies-in-waiting happy.

_05:: Keeping Your Harem Under Control

During the late 1500s, Mehmed III ascended to the throne of the Ottoman Empire. His mother, Safiye, as the Valide Sultan or leader of the harem, became one of his most important advisers. While not allowed to be directly involved in state politics, Safiye was able to influence the sultan's decisions, sometimes openly and directly. On one occasion, Safiye sat behind a curtain as Mehmed held a heated discussion with a leading mufti (religious cleric) and openly defended her son. As Safiye's influence increased so did the ire it raised among the vizier, the mufti, the chief black eunuch, and the sultan's favorite wives and concubines, who saw Safiye's excessive influence as overstepping her role of Valide Sultan. Mehmed found himself having to restrain his mother and, on at least one occasion, had her removed to another palace. Safiye's excessive greed, coupled with the ever increasing costs of the harem under her control, helped to bring about riots in Istanbul in 1600 over the devaluation of the empire's currency.

Original Cities of Sin (None of Which Had Elvis Impersonators)

Are you tired of Vegas and Havana? Is Bangkok just not providing the immoral rush you're looking for? Well, there's a quick fix for those of you with access to time machines. Just fasten up and warp your way back to some of these sin-sational locales. Judging by what we've heard (you know—what happened there but didn't stay there), it's a rollicking good time.

_01:: Sodom and Gomorrah

Who wouldn't want to check out the original cities of sin, Sodom and Gomorrah? Located in the beautiful arid wasteland around the Dead Sea (today in central Israel), the twin cities were near valuable mineral deposits, probably the sources of the cities' renowned wealth. Somehow, though, these locales became a byword for sin and corruption, in spite of the fact that the crime that supposedly led to the cities' destruction may not have been homosexuality at all, as some have suggested, but inhospitality—the worst of all sins in the ancient world. According to the Bible, God rained fire and brimstone on the region and destroyed the towns after promising Abraham that He would spare them if 10 righteous men could be found in their region. Apparently, only one could be found: Lot. Luckily for him, Lot offered hospitality to angelic visitors and was warned of the catastrophe. Oddly enough, the original sin cities sit on a seismically active gap between tectonic plates (where earthquakes and volcanic activity are possible), and the biblical account could be describing some sort of geological upheaval.

_02:: Pessinos

If you're looking for a wild night filled with religious ecstasy, you might want to set your time machine for the classical age, and check out Pessinos, in Asia Minor. As the center to a mother/goddess-oriented cult since the Stone Age, Pessinos was known for its worship of Cybyle, an Anatolian goddess dedicated to fertility. So, just how fertile was Cybyle? Well, to give you an idea, her statues are pretty easy to recognize since they feature an inordinately large number of breasts. And while the rites practiced by Cybyle's worshipers are poorly documented, the records tend to suggest that they included priests who castrated themselves while in a drug-induced trance, while presiding over midnight dances culminating in wild orgies.

Touch of Evil

The 12,000 citizens of Monaco are denied the right to enter Monte Carlo's casino rooms; that privilege is only allowed to visitors. Of course, the income helps keep the locals free from paying taxes, so the trade-off isn't that bad.

_03:: Münster

If you're looking for a polygamous good time, you might want to transport yourself back to 1530s Münster, a city in Westphalia, in what is today western Germany, which was a hotbed of Anabaptist agitation. A Christian sect that believed in rebaptizing people once they became adults (their theological descendents today include the Amish), the Anabaptists were persecuted mercilessly elsewhere in Europe both by Catholics and by more conservative Protestants. But in February 1534, the Anabaptists seized Münster in a relatively bloodless coup d'état, and had their way with the city. One of the Anabaptist leaders, Johann Matthys, declared himself a prophet. Unfortu-

nately, he seems to have believed in his own divinity: when the bishop of Münster arrived with an army, Matthys led 30 followers out to fight and, of course, was slaughtered with his men. Then his disciple, Jan Leiden, took over the town's defense, declared *himself* the Messiah, and introduced the townsfolk to polygamy (he took 16 wives). The party didn't last forever, though—after a solid 16 months of multiwife fun the city was taken by the bishop's army, which killed thousands, and tortured and executed the leaders of the revolt.

_04:: Port Royal

The original capital of British Jamaica, Port Royal, is certainly one town that's located on the wrong side of the tracks. The area was a hotbed for rascals, including plenty of pirates, and Limey officials who were happy to look the other way...for a piece of the action, of course. In fact, when pirate crews rolled in to town they could enjoy a wide array of vice to whittle down their profit margins, including prostitutes, gambling, liquor, and drugs smuggled from the Orient and the Middle East. If that doesn't sound like enough fun for you, the streets literally echoed with the sounds of sin: from raucous brawls to the incessant nursery rhyme "Sing a Song of Sixpence" (actually a recruiting jingle for the pirate Blackbeard). And just to prove how corrupt it was, Henry Morgan, an infamous pirate admiral, was actually made lieutenant governor of Jamaica in 1674. Of course, such dens of sin can't last forever, and Port Royal was destroyed in 1692 by an earthquake that dropped three-quarters of it into the sea. An initial attempt at rebuilding burned to the ground in 1704, hurricanes stopped several attempts at rebuilding in the early 1700s, and finally a 1907 earthquake caused the remaining parts of the city to sink. It seems someone upstairs had a grudge against this humble burg.

Self-proclaimed Casanovas

"How do I love thee?" Well, these guys were big fans of publicly counting the ways...just loud enough that *everyone* could hear it.

_01:: Clark "the Shark" Gable (1901–1960)

Despite sporting a pair of ears that were potential obstacles in revolving doors, silver screen legend Clark Gable was the leading male sex symbol of his generation. Known as "the King of Hollywood," Clark the Shark bragged that he had made love to women in a fire escape, a duck blind, a canoe, and a telephone booth. Apparently his choice of locations also said a lot about his technique. "God knows I love Clark," Gable's wife, Carole Lombard, once said, "but he's the worst lay in town. If he had one inch less, he'd be the Queen of Hollywood." As if Lombard's press release wasn't bad enough for his rep, Gable's *Gone With the Wind* costar, Vivian Leigh, complained that the "King of Hollywood's" breath had been atrocious on set. From his dentures, no less!

_02:: Frasier the Sensuous Lion (1951–1972)

This guy didn't actually do much bragging about his amorous exploits, but then again, he didn't have to—his proof was walking all around him! Frasier was about 20 years old, ancient for a lion, when he came to a wild animal park in southern California. The Mexican circus refugee was so doddering he could hardly walk, and his keepers figured his demise would occur any day. But that didn't stop the old lion from tomcatting about. Frasier hung on for 18 months and sired a stunning 35 cubs in his spare time. Amazingly, the press about the fertile feline was so widespread that Frasier fan clubs started sprouting up across the country. Wives even began writing in to find out what park rangers were feeding the beast. In fact, the lion's fame grew so much that a popular song was written about him, and a film was made. When the old cat's time finally came, it's said, Frasier the Sensuous Lion went with a smile on his face.

_03:: Good Wilt's Hunting (1936–1999)

When it came to basketball, very few people could take it to the hoop any better than Wilt the Stilt. But it's a wonder he had the stamina. In his 1991 autobiography, Chamberlain claimed to have slept with about 20,000 women

Lies Your Mother Told You

ALL AUTHORS ARE CADS

No matter what your momma (or your swooning lit teacher) told you, not all authors suffer from odd fetishes or omnivorous appetites. D. H. Lawrence, whose *Lady Chatterly's Lover* was so scandalous that it was banned in Britain until 1960, was happily and faithfully married (although his wife was, briefly, a bigamist, having failed to divorce her first husband before eloping with Lawrence). And some noted authors barely had sex at all. Most notable among them was the playwright George Bernard Shaw. Shaw didn't lose his virginity until his 29th birthday (July 26, 1885), when he slept with a 44-year-old widow. It may have been the only sexual encounter of his life. He married Charlotte Townshend in 1898, not because he loved her but because Shaw thought he was dying and wanted to offer his friend Charlotte the social and financial benefits of widowhood. As it turns out, the two were married—happily, but most likely celibately—for 45 years.

over a 38-year period. Of course, Chamberlain was roundly criticized for everything from propagating sexual stereotypes about African American men to having sex with women outside his race to just plain flaunting his conquests. But the lifelong bachelor said that, whatever else he might be doing, he wasn't bragging. "If you look at it," he said in a 1997 interview, "you can say that I had so many women because I was such a bad lover, they never came back a second time."

_04:: Hugh Hefner: Playboy Original (1926–   )

When Hugh Hefner was 75 years old, a reporter asked about his recent love life, and Hef replied it was "a natural one—except it involved five people." The founder of *Playboy* magazine and patriarch of the Sexual Revolution, Hefner virtually lives in his pajamas, and even a stroke in 1985 didn't slow him down. In 2001, Hefner told *Vanity Fair* magazine that thanks to Viagra, which came on the market two months after his second divorce, he was sleeping with seven women between the ages of 18 and 28, usually simultaneously. "And here's the surprise bit," Hefner said. "It's what *they* want." Hefner's mom lived to be 101, and he says his goal is to stay frisky at least that long.

They Did a Bad, Bad Thing:
So-called Virtuous Figures Who Got Caught with Their Flies Down (or Skirts Up)

This quintet of folks didn't exactly practice what they preached. Please bless them, Father, 'cause they've most certainly sinned.

_01:: Aimee Semple McPherson (1890–1944)

By the mid-1920s, evangelist McPherson was packing them in at her Angelus Temple in Los Angeles, preaching hope and warning against the sinful life. But in 1926, she disappeared while swimming at a local beach. She turned up a month later with a fantastic story about being kidnapped and taken to Mexico. Unfortunately, the evidence said otherwise: It appeared li'l Aimee had been shacked up with a married man. The evangelist was charged with perjury, but she stuck to her story and was eventually acquitted. Her popularity waned after the scandal, but you gotta hand it to her for chutzpah: instead of apologizing to her confused flock, McPherson bobbed her hair, bought some short skirts, and began dancing and drinking in public.

_02:: Jim Bakker (1941–   )

Simple people with a simple dream, Jim and Tammy Faye Bakker started out hosting a children's religious puppet show. By the mid-1970s, however, the fabulous Bakker duo had become the toast of televangelism. They pulled in millions of dollars in contributions to their PTL (Praise the Lord) ministry, and even built a sort of fundamentalist Disneyland called Heritage USA in South Carolina. But Jim had a couple of dirty little secrets. He had paid a former church secretary named Jessica Hahn to keep quiet about a sexual encounter they had in 1980. But when the scandal broke in 1987, questions began to be raised about Bakker's financial dealings. In 1989, he was sentenced to 45 years in prison for fleecing his flock of $158 million. In the end he only served five, and moved forward with his life, eventually opening a new ministry in a restaurant in Branson, Missouri.

_03:: Jimmy Swaggart (1935–   )

Swaggart was one of Jim Bakker's fiercest critics when the Bakker scandal broke, telling an interviewer he himself had never even kissed a woman other than his wife. Maybe not. But the bombastic and fantastically successful television preacher—and cousin to rock-and-roll legend Jerry Lee Lewis—was doing *something* with that prostitute in a cheap New Orleans hotel room in early 1988. Swaggart's tearful, televised confession kept his $12-million-a-year, 10,000-employee religious empire together—until he got caught with his pants down again. That's right, swingin'

Jimmy Swaggart was linked to (brace yourself!) another hooker in 1991. A couple of lost lawsuits, an IRS tax lien, and that was the end of the line for Jimmy Swaggart. Well, not exactly. As of mid-2004, he was still hurling rhetorical fire and brimstone on TV, albeit on a much smaller scale.

_04:: Amrit Desai (1932–   )

A onetime art student, Amrit Desai came to the United States from India in 1960. He began giving yoga lessons on the side and ended up training several thousand people, who in turn became yoga instructors around the country. With his followers calling him "guru dev," or "beloved teacher," one of the things Desai taught at the yoga center he founded in Massachusetts in 1972 was that celibacy was spiritually mandatory for unmarried people. Desai even took a vow of celibacy himself in 1974, despite being married with children. No wonder it was something of a shock (perhaps greatest to his wife) when in 1994, the beloved

teacher admitted to having affairs with three of his followers. The scandal forced Desai to resign his $150,000-a-year post. He eventually moved to Florida, but kept up the yoga.

_05:: Paul R. Shanley (1931–   )

In the 1970s, Shanley was known as "the hippie priest"; he was a Roman Catholic clergyman whose specialty was ministering to kids struggling with their sexual identity. By 2002, however, Shanley was a central figure in the greatest scandal ever to hit the Catholic Church in the United States. Shanley was accused of molesting more than two dozen boys over a 35-year span. Thrown out of the priesthood, Shanley was still awaiting trial at the end of 2004 on rape and indecent assault charges. Subsequent investigations into other allegations in the Boston archdiocese resulted in the Church paying $85 million in 2003 to 552 people who claimed to have been abused by priests. It also triggered similar probes, and similar results, in other areas of the country.

Presidential Affairs (Cigar Not Included)

Contrary to popular belief, Bill Clinton wasn't exactly the first president to get caught in the act. The following are some of the past presidents who helped unite the country in more ways than one.

_01:: The Many Loves of a Founding Father

Known for his extreme intellect and skills at diplomacy, Thomas Jefferson is truly one of America's founding fathers, but in more ways

than just patriotic. Considered a loving and faithful husband to Martha during their 10 years of marriage before her death, Tom Jefferson was actually a bit of a tomcat. In fact, the Virginia statesman had a notorious penchant for other men's wives. While on a trip to New York in 1768, John Walker asked Tom to look after his wife, and that he did, literally. Later, in 1786, as ambassador to France, Jefferson fell deeply in love with Maria Conway, the wife of portraitist Richard Conway. Legend has it that one day while walking through the countryside, Tom tried to show off for the blushing (Conway) bride and fell while jumping a fence only to break his wrist. But Tom's best-known relationship was with Sally Hemings, his slave and his late wife's half sister. Their relationship went on for 35 years and provided Jefferson a number of heirs.

_02:: Grover Cleveland, the Honorable Gentleman from New York?

In 1873, a young, politically aspiring bachelor named Grover Cleveland met Maria Halpin, a 35-year-old widow with two children. Maria's looks and personality made her the talk of Buffalo and Grover soon found himself among Halpin's many suitors. Well, more than just a suitor. In 1874, Halpin bore a son and insinuated that old Grover was the pop. Grover, not sure that he actually was the father, and not intending to marry Maria, decided to do the right thing and bear financial responsibility for the child. He also helped Maria get treatment for her alcoholism and actually set her up in her own business. During the 1884 presidential campaign, however, Cleveland's opposition dug up the old story and printed it in the press. Interestingly, a number of clergy members supporting Cleveland did a study of the case and found that after the "preliminary offense" Cleveland had done the responsible and honorable thing. More important in their minds, he'd shielded many married men in

Buffalo (and their families) from public scandal. Oddly enough, because of this, even many of Grover's opponents supported his run for the presidency.

Touch of Evil

FDR seemed like a ripe fit for The Jerry Springer Show. *Not only did he marry his cousin, but he was involved in multiple affairs, which his wife, Eleanor, countered by having a rumored 30-year lesbian affair with a reporter named Lorena Hickok.*

_03:: Warren G., Carrie P., and Nan B.

Far from the run-of the-mill tales you hear of political ambition, Warren G. Harding was a small-town Ohio newspaper editor who ran for senator because he liked the gentlemen's club atmosphere and the light workload of the U.S. Senate. However, his wife, Florence, had bigger plans, and Warren somehow found his way to the presidency in 1920. Not at all equipped to run a nation, Harding preferred to let Congress lead while he golfed and had sex with his mistress in closets throughout the White House. But Harding's philandering began well before his run for president. For 15 years, Warren maintained an active love interest with Carrie Phillips, the wife of his close friend. But when Harding ran for president, the Phillipses threatened to go public. So to secure their silence, the Republican National Party came to the rescue and sent Mr. and Mrs. Phillips on a world trip, plus they threw in $20,000 to boot. But it appears Warren didn't quite learn his lesson. Soon after winning the White House he began a secret relationship with Nan Britton, 30 years his junior. With the Secret Service ordered not to inform the First Lady, Nan was routinely ushered into the White House and many a West Wing closet became their intimate playground.

_04:: FDR and His Wife's Secretary

Best known as the president who brought the United States through the Great Depression, Franklin Delano Roosevelt is also known for his longtime affair with Lucy Mercer, his wife, Eleanor's social secretary. In 1918, upon FDR's return from a trip to Europe as assistant secretary of the Navy, Eleanor confronted Franklin with the love letters she'd found and offered him a divorce. Knowing that a divorce at the time would destroy his political ambitions, Franklin said he'd stop seeing Lucy if Eleanor would agree to remain married. Unfortunately, he didn't keep to his new deal. Lucy continued to visit the White House with regularity, especially when Eleanor was out of town. Years later, the widowed Lucy even became a frequent visitor to the South Carolina plantation where FDR was recuperating from his bad health. In fact, it was Lucy, not Eleanor, who was with FDR on April 12, 1945, when he was struck with the cerebral hemorrhage that killed him.

_05:: Ike and Kay— Did They or Didn't They?

Many a book, movie, and television show have portrayed the close relationship during World War II between Dwight Eisenhower and his Irish driver, Kay Summersby. As the Supreme Commander of the Allied forces, Ike found himself responsible for millions of lives, but not having anyone he could share his close thoughts and feelings with. With Ike's wife

Mamie over 3,000 miles away, the young, witty, and attractive Kay capably filled that role. But once the gossip columns got wind of this, talk of their so-called relationship spread on both sides of the Atlantic. With constant reassurances from Ike, Mamie believed that no sexual liaisons ever occurred between Ike and Kay and at the end of the war Ike returned to the States and Kay remained in England. Their lives moved forward, and Ike was elected president in 1952. As the decades proceeded, though, the private lives of the 1940s and '50s quickly became the public domain of the '60s, and the rumors of the affair again surfaced though no evidence of a sexual relationship was ever found. Years later, before her death, Summersby wrote that her relationship with Ike had been close, flirtatious, and intimate, but had never been consummated.

_06:: JFK and the Other Mistress

It's common knowledge that President Kennedy and Marilyn Monroe were an item. Less known, however, is the relationship that John F. had with Judith Campbell Exner, an affair that definitely falls under the category of dangerous liaisons. The extremely beautiful Exner was introduced to Kennedy by Frank Sinatra in 1960. However, Miss Exner was also romantically involved with Sam Giancana, one of the most powerful Mafia bosses of the time. And while their relationship remained secret from the public, it was well known around the White House and by Jackie Kennedy. FBI director J. Edgar Hoover, as he'd done with other presidents, had Exner tailed so that he had information to blackmail Kennedy with. In fact, Exner's affair with JFK remained a secret long after Kennedy's assassination, until in 1975 a number of Republican members of the Senate

Select Committee to Study Governmental Operations with Respect to Intelligence Activities (aka the Church Committee) leaked the information to the press. With the secret out of the bag, it quickly fueled the fires of conspiracy theorists wondering if the relationship in any way had played into JFK's assassination.

4 Crackers, Corn Flakes, and Chastity Belts, Oh My! Victorian Tricks for Restraining That Mojo

Ever play the game where someone tells you to picture anything in the world but an elephant? Anything but an elephant. And as you struggle to concentrate, all you can see are visions of Dumbo, Babar, and Snuffleupagus. Well, that's kind of what everyone in the Victorian age did with sex. It's a wonder they didn't produce more kids.

_01:: Fanning the Flames

In the Victorian age, an eligible Victor couldn't just cruise up to a Victoria and put the moves on her. No, in the extraordinarily prudish age proper etiquette had to be maintained at all times. A man, for instance, needed to be formally introduced to a woman before he could approach and talk to her. However, that didn't exactly mean that flirting was off-limits at social events. In fact, it was pretty en vogue. And one of the most subtle ways of demonstrating interest or disinterest was through the use of hand fans. In fact, a whole sign language was created around fan movements and placement. If a young lady let her fan rest on her right cheek, it meant she was interested; if she placed it on the left, however, it meant the guy was being passed over (subtle, but harsh!). Similarly, if she moved the fan slowly it was a signal that she was already engaged or married. If she held the fan in front of her face with her right hand, it was a signal for the young man to follow her. Finally, if she moved the fan across her forehead, it meant they were being watched. Whew! With all the mixed signals, restrictions, and rites of courtship, it's amazing anyone found time to procreate.

_02:: A Flaky Approach

If in the 19th century Victorians were very concerned about curtailing sexual urges, they were fanatic over masturbation. Dr. John Harvey Kellogg, a lecturer and so-called health "expert," proclaimed that masturbation caused a whole series of medical problems including enlarged prostate, kidney and bladder infections, piles, nocturnal emissions, and general exhaustion (guess blindness wasn't added until later). Kellogg actually came up with a list of 39 signs that could be used to spot masturbators running the gamut from sleeplessness to biting one's fingernails to using obscene lan-

Lies Your Mother Told You

CHASTITY BELTS

So, about those chastity belts...did they really exist or are they nothing more than a Victorian myth? Well, the fact is, the jury's still out. Thought to have been invented in Italy during the 14th century, the urban legend of the belts became popular in the rest of Europe. The antithesis of anything PC, the belts were basically used to maintain sexual control over women by covering the private area and keeping it under lock and key. And while many a suspicious husband may have lauded the invention, there's recent evidence that suggests the chastity belt may have been more of a Victorian myth than a reality. In 1996, two British historians reported that there was no medical evidence from the time of Chaucer through the Victorian period that chastity belts existed or were commonly used. Of course, they had the weight of the British Museum of London behind them. Agreeing with the two historians, the museum removed an alleged chastity belt that had been on exhibit since 1846.

originally called Granola. Unfortunately, another masturbation expert had already used that name so Kellogg changed the cereal's name to Corn Flakes. However, it should be mentioned that Kellogg never consummated his own marriage, preferring yogurt enemas instead.

_03:: Trojan Wars of the 19th Century

A number of mechanical methods of birth control were created and used in the 1800s, but they were only affordable for the wealthier Victorian women. Of course, they weren't exactly effective. The first generation of vaginal diaphragms and cervical caps were developed but the quality of the rubber was poor—that is, until the invention of latex in 1884. However, in keeping with the Victorian ethos, a law, known as the Comstock Law, defining condoms as obscene went quietly into effect in 1873. That didn't keep prophylactic science from making advances, though. Toward the end of the 19th century, the forerunners of IUDs (intrauterine devices), intracervical stems, or pessaries, became available. However, the devices were unpopular from the start, as they often led to infections. Oddly enough, the courts wised up to the fact that diaphragms and condoms were effective for disease prevention, and made them legal as medical treatment. However, they still weren't so fond of the idea of birth control, and the courts maintained that using the products as contraceptives should remain illegal.

_04:: Protection au Naturel

While not everyone could afford the premier forms of birth control, it didn't stop less affluent Victorians from jerry-rigging their own

guage. Like other thinkers of his time, Kellogg saw a connection between one's bowels and genitals with the proper diet being the answer. So he created a cold breakfast cereal, which he

homemade remedies. In fact, one of the most commonly used "natural methods" of birth control was the injection of fruit juices or naturally produced chemicals into the vagina, known today as "douches," shortly after intercourse. Of course, that wasn't the only recipe. A variety of mixtures were used, including baking soda, alum, vinegar, and quinine. Other birth-controlling techniques involved using small, natural sea sponges dipped in acidic or naturally spermicidal mixtures with a ribbon or string attached. And there were cheap solutions for the men, too! Condoms made of sheepskin, also known as "French letters," were particularly popular, and a notorious favorite with men who frequented brothels. After all, the rubbers didn't just aid in birth control, but also kept the syphilis at bay. In fact, it's this sordid use for birth control that gave condoms such a bad reputation and made them taboo in the eyes of the general public.

From Wags to Riches:
Royal Mistresses Who Made Good

4

It's no surprise that a lot of kings have kept a lot of ladies-in-waiting. Of course, not all of these gal pals were content just to wait. In fact, the following mistresses quickly found their way from the bedroom to the boardroom, making sure they were involved in more than just one of the king's affairs.

_01:: Diane de Poitiers (1490–1566)

Considered one of the most powerful women of the 16th century, Diane de Poitiers was the mistress to French king Henri II. And what a mistress! Although married to Queen Catherine, Henri basically let Diane run France by his side. In fact, she got all sorts of executive perks, from signing official documents to appointing ministers and handing out titles, to even dabbling in estates and pensions. And as a member of the Privy Council, Diane even routinely gathered money for the royal treasury. But for those skeptical few who want proof of her power in writing, just inspect any one of the numerous official documents the good king and his gal pal literally cosigned: they actually read "HenriDiane!" Of course, this dubious union did not exist without protest. When church officials questioned Diane's role, she simply had them sent to Rome. When Henri passed away, he was calling out Diane's name. However, Queen Catherine (pretty understandably) prevented Henri's mistress from attending the funeral and, in fact, demanded that she return any crown jewels. Strangely, though, Diane was not arrested for treason as expected—mainly because she was popular with the French people for helping Henri rule so well.

_02:: Nell Gwynne (1651–1687)

During the reign of Charles II of England, mistresses weren't exactly few and far between. In fact, less-than-chaste women were almost as plentiful around the palace as were catfights between them, and Charles was basically an equal opportunity cad. In fact, his favorite mistress was a prostitute from London's slum known as Kindhearted Nell. Renowned for using her influence with the king to help others, Nell also harbored a wicked sense of humor. For instance, when she heard that Charles planned to bed another mistress, Nell offered the gal a bunch of sweets. Little did the lady know Nell had laced the goodies with a laxative and an evening of bedding quickly turned into an evening of chamber-potting. But while Charles frolicked with Nell he let another mistress, Louise de Keroualle, run the country, and there was no love between the two. During a period of anti-Catholic sentiment, Nell's coach was surrounded by a mob thinking it contained the Catholic Louise. The quick-thinking Nell exclaimed, "Pray, good people, be civil, I am the Protestant whore." Amused, the crowd laughingly let her move on.

Touch of Evil

Camilla Parker-Bowles's family has been trying to get into the royal pants for decades. Her great-grandmother was reportedly the mistress to King Edward IV, Chuck's great-great-grandfather.

_03:: Madame de Pompadour (1721–1764)

Probably the most powerful of all royal mistresses, as King Louis XV's lady on the side,

Madame de Pompadour served as the unofficial French prime minister for 13 years. It worked out well for both parties. Louis, being a ridiculously lazy king, wasn't all that fond of making decisions, while Pompadour reveled in the power. All messages to the king and all requests for an audience had to go through her. Not just that, the Madame also controlled all titles, court positions, and honors and quickly began replacing high-level officials with her supporters. She even took over as France's minister of war during the Seven Years' War (1756–1763), and cleverly chose to appoint all the generals more on their social standing than their experience. Pompadour died of a lung disease in her early 40s, but for all her power-tripping she remained faithful to Louis till the end. In fact, court etiquette wouldn't allow Louis to attend Pompadour's funeral, but the casket was made to pass by his castle. Upon viewing the cortege, Louis reportedly cried, saying that tears were the only thing he could give her.

_04:: Mary, Countess von Waldersee (1866–1941)

Unlike most royal mistresses, Mary played the role of the matronly adviser. The daughter of a wealthy New York grocer, Mary was married to Colonel Alfred von Waldersee, the quartermaster general of the German army. As such, Mary opened a salon in Berlin and soon found herself entertaining German royalty, including young Prince William. Enamored of the old gal (she was, after all, two years senior to his mother), William decided to make her his private adviser. In 1888, William became Kaiser Wilhelm II, and he started referring all political matters to Mary before making decisions. However, the power went to Mary's head, and she attempted to get Wilhelm to replace Chancellor Bismarck with her husband. Wilhelm did remove Bismarck, but not for Alfred. Instead, Wilhelm began to view Mary as his biggest competition and to get rid of her he demoted her hubby and moved them both to Hamburg. Without mother Mary's sage advice, though, Wilhelm was lost, and his weak, egocentric decisions helped bring about World War I.

When Sex Doesn't Sell:
Risqué Ad Campaigns That Got Canned

There are two cardinal rules in advertising: "Sex sells" and "There's no such thing as bad publicity." Here are a few advertising missteps that proved one or both of them wrong.

_01:: **Abercrombie and Flesh**

It may sound odd for a clothing manufacturer to use nudity to sell clothes, but that's exactly the strategy campus mainstay Abercrombie & Fitch employed in their catalog/photo magazine *A&F Quarterly*. Over a series of years, the models somehow got younger and younger and began wearing fewer and fewer clothes. In fact, nudity wasn't uncommon, and consumers complained of suggestions of pedophilia, sexual irresponsibility, underage drinking, and homoeroticism. But the Winter 2003 edition was the one that went too far. The catalog featured over 100 pages of photos of young men and women frolicking naked in streams and waterfalls (in a *winter* catalog?), and one spread espoused the joys of group sex in both photos and text. The outcry from angry parents was so loud that sales for November 2003 dropped over 13%, and the company discontinued the *A&F Quarterly* altogether soon thereafter. Despite the hubbub, though, A&F has been a little slow to learn from their mistakes. Since then, they've been criticized for marketing T-shirts with ethnically insensitive slogans and for marketing thong underwear bearing phrases like "Kiss me" and "Eye candy" to teen girls.

_02:: **Calvin and Kiddies**

Designer Calvin Klein has always used sex to sell his clothes, and it's usually worked. After all, who can forget the slinky Brooke Shields proudly proclaiming "Nothing comes between me and my Calvins"? But in 1995, CK creeped out just about everyone with its ads for jeans and underwear. The commercials featured teenagers wearing almost nothing, standing in what appeared to be a poorly lit basement in front of cheap wood paneling. What's more disconcerting than cheap paneling? Well, maybe the fact that the models are being interviewed with eerie questions, like "That's a nice body. Do you work out?" Or "Why don't you open that vest up?" Although the resulting controversy did increase sales, it also prompted an investigation by the FBI to see if the ads qualified as child pornography. In fact, the campaign is still referred to in the industry as the "kiddie porn" campaign.

_03:: PETA's Sex Kittens (Literally)

It seems logical: What better use for sexual imagery than to promote...having your pets fixed? People for the Ethical Treatment of Animals, long known for their publicity stunts, tried it in 2001. The ad by industry giant Saatchi & Saatchi depicted animatronic cats "doing it" in all sorts of positions while their owner is away, while the copy reminded us that over 2.4 million unwanted kittens are born every year. It's actually very funny and effective, and PETA even tried to run it as a paid ad, not as a free public service ad. But MTV rejected it, saying they do not allow the depiction of "fornication" on their networks. Umm, excuse me? Apparently MTV's (s)executives have never actually *watched* MTV. And the aforementioned fornication wasn't even being done by real cats. They were *puppets*.

_04:: Candie's Bathroom Humor

Lots of companies use models to sell their shoes. But only Candie's used models *going to the bathroom*. A controversial series of ads from the late 1990s showed *Playboy* model Jenny McCarthy wearing a pair of Candie's shoes while sitting on a toilet, panties around her calves, reading a newspaper. So, just how racy was the spread? Both *Vogue* and *Cosmopolitan*

pulled the ads from their pages. Another series featured child-star-turned-sex-symbol Alyssa Milano in a bra and panties, rifling through a lover's medicine cabinet full of condoms. But she's stopped by an unexpected find: a bottle of Candie's perfume. Another has Alyssa about to be mounted by a naked man in the back of a limo. The ads weren't just suggestive, they were downright obvious. In fact, the ads were considered so risqué that they were banned in several countries, and the TV versions were even rejected by the WB, the network that carried Alyssa's hit show *Charmed*.

_05:: Miscellaneous: The DisGraceful Awards

At the height of the late 1990s dot-com boom, Silicon Valley professional Sylvia Paull founded GraceNet, a San Francisco–based networking group for the ever-growing number of women in high-tech fields. Every month GraceNet hands out the DisGraceful Awards for ads that crossed the line into sexism or offensiveness. And back during the boom, with all that ad money flying around, they had plenty to choose from. DisGraceful "winners" include an IBM Lotus ad showing a man using Lotus to learn "discounted cash flow techniques with 40 other analysts," while a woman uses it to finish her crossword by finding "a five-letter word for 'bellybutton'"; and an ad for Hong Kong–based games maker Lik-Sang International, featuring a young girl licking her lips over the line "We don't have young Japanese girls on sale right now, but we do ship more than 300 products directly from Hong Kong!"

Dear Dowry:
Crazy Historical Trades for Brides

Before the whole "old, new, borrowed, and blue" wedding tradition hoo-ha, there was another must-do part of any nuptials: the dowry. And through the years, lots of things have been given or received to sweeten the blessed deal. Here are a few things that have changed hands in exchange for (or in addition to) brides.

_01:: Foreskins: David and Michal

If you know where to look, you can find all kinds of crazy stuff in the good book. So grab your King James Version and flip to chapter 18 of the first book of Samuel for the story of David (yes, *that* David, with the stone and the sling and the Psalms) and Michal. After David smote the heck out of Philistine badass Goliath, he went to live with King Saul of Israel. Saul, afraid of David and troubled by evil spirits, began to plot his murder. When Saul's daughter Michal revealed her love for David, Saul made her a deal: Have David bring back 100 Philistine foreskins, and he can marry you. Now Saul had no particular affinity for foreskins; he just wanted David to get killed trying. But Dave and his posse, with God's help, brought back *200* for the good king. Saul couldn't help but bless his daughter's marriage to such a go-getter.

_02:: Heads: The Dayak
of Indonesia

Journey to the Indonesian island of Borneo and you'll find an indigenous tribe of people called the Dayak. But try not to overstay your welcome, as the Dayak were historically headhunters and cannibals. In fact, their economy seems to have been predominantly skull based. If, for example, someone wanted to marry a chief's daughter, the suitor would have to impress the chief by presenting him with three or four enemy skulls. This modern tribe had given up their headhunting ways—that is, until recently, when settlers from the overpopulated Indonesian island of Madura were caught encroaching on the Dayak's traditional land. The late-1990s ethnic struggle proved that old habits die hard. Thankfully, though, things seem to have simmered down since, as the Dayak have figured out better ways to get a head.

_03:: Political Prisoners:
Ramses and the Hittites

In the 13th century BCE, there were two superpowers in the Middle East: the Egyptians and the Hittites. And, as rival superpowers are wont to do, they hated each other. The main bone of their contention? The city of Kadesh, which served as a strategic linchpin located in modern-day Syria. After decades of fighting, King Hattusili III ascended to the Hittite throne, and he saw the wisdom of bargaining with the great Egyptian pharaoh Ramses II. So, he proposed a treaty. Ramses agreed to marry Maat-Hor-Neferu-Re (or Manefrure), Hattusili's eldest daughter, and in exchange he got an alliance with the Hittites, control of Kadesh, and the release of all political prisoners. Not a bad deal. But what did the blushing bride get out of it? Well, the lucky gal got only what every princess dreams of...to be the primary consort in a harem of more than 200 wives and concubines.

Touch of Evil

It was suggested that Henry VIII marry Anne of Cleves to help form a bond between England and Germany. After viewing a flattering portrait of Anne he agreed, but upon first meeting her he made it clear that he was disappointed by her looks, saying she resembled "a horse."

_04:: 100 Knights and a Table: Guinevere

The story of King Arthur has been told by many, and one of the best-known versions is Sir Thomas Malory's *Le Morte d'Arthur*. In his version, the famous Round Table was given by Uther Pendragon, its original owner, to a fella named Leodegrance, who happened to have a daughter by the name of Guinevere. When Guinevere was married off to a certain King Arthur, she brought to the marriage a most unusual dowry: the Round Table and, just for good measure, 100 knights to sit around it. But this was one serious table: it could seat 150. So magician Merlin threw in the rest of the knights to fill it. One hopes the happy couple registered for 150 place settings at Ye Olde Crate & Barrel.

_05:: England: "The Dowry of Mary"

Of all England's nicknames—Jolly Olde, Blighty, etc.—perhaps one of the most obscure is "the Dowry of Mary." At first blush, this may seem to refer to some medieval queen who married a king and got England as a wedding present. But it actually refers to the *Virgin Mary*. The story is linked to England's pious King Edward the Confessor, who, upon dedicating Westminster Abbey in 1055, allegedly offered England to the Virgin Mary as her "dowry" with the words *"Dos tua Virgo pia, haec est, quare rege, Maria"* (Thy Dowry this, O Virgin sweet, then rule it, Mary, as is meet). Legend has it that, a few years later, Mary responded to this piety by appearing to Lady Richeldis de Faverches in the tiny village of Walsingham, asking her to build a replica of the House of the Anunciation. This house became a major pilgrimage destination until it was destroyed unceremoniously during the Reformation.

_06:: India and Tea: Catherine of Braganza

In 1661, Catherine of Braganza, the daughter of Portugal's King John IV, was married off to King Charles II of England. The marriage was meant to cement an alliance between the two countries, and in exchange for taking Catherine's hand, Charles (and therefore England) received Tangier and Bombay. And while the natural deepwater harbor at Bombay became the headquarters of the British East India Company and a perfect foothold for England's growing colonial ambitions, the cities themselves might not have been Portugal's most treasured gifts in the exchange. Aside from the land (and a bride), Charles was also gifted a chest of tea from the far-flung Portuguese colonies. The present quickly turned him into an enthusiastic "tea" totaler, and drinking the steamy beverage soon became all the rage throughout England.

Eight Is Not Enough: Historical Dudes with Lots of Illegitimate Children

Some men produce many works of art. Or great symphonies. Or inventions that change the world. Other men just produce lots and lots of babies. Here are six examples of men whose sperm counts were obviously as healthy as their sexual appetites. Luckily for these prolific gents, Father's Day hadn't been invented yet.

_01:: Louis XV (1710–1774)

When you're made king of France at the age of five, you tend to grow accustomed to having your way. And Louis XV had his way whenever he could, eventually fathering dozens of illegitimate children. Two of his mistresses, Madame de Pompadour and ex-prostitute Madame du Barry, became famous in their own right as the Monica Lewinskis of their day. He also carried on with *five* sisters of a prominent family and kept several young concubines at a house used expressly for the purpose called the Deer Park. By the time of his death, he had a new nickname: Louis the Well Hated. Aside from all the bastard children, Louis' selfish lifestyle planted another seed: the French Revolution, which would commence just 15 years after his death.

_02:: Ramses II (ruled 1304–1237 BCE)

Of all the pharaohs of ancient Egypt, Ramses II is one of the biggies. When he wasn't commissioning statues of himself, or (as legend goes) forcing enslaved Israelites to build temples, or battling the hated Hittites, he was making babies. Estimates of his brood go as high as 96 sons and 60 daughters. Now, to be fair, many of these were born to the pharaoh's many wives, so they weren't all *technically* illegitimate. But, since he had a harem of around 200 wives and concubines, it's hard to keep track. So hard, in fact, that three of his wives—Bit Anoth, Maryamum, and Nebettawy—were *also* his daughters. And one was—wait for it—his *sister*. All together now: *Eeeeuuuw!*

_03:: Henry IV (1553–1610)

The French are world-renowned for romance, so it would make sense that they would revere a king whose many love affairs inspired the nickname *le Vert Galant* ("the Gay Old Spark"). Henry IV was one of France's greatest kings; he re-created Paris as a center of the arts, expanded France's presence in the New World, and soothed the bloody conflicts between France's Catholics and Huguenot Protestants. But he was quite the ladies' man as well. He fathered six children by his second wife, but only after he'd had three by a mistress named Gabrielle d'Estrée, the true love of his life. He also had five children by his three other principal mistresses. Henry is said to have had as many as 50 lovers over the course of his life, several of whom were his baby-mamas. Unlike many, though, he avoided the accompanying baby-mama drama by providing for his bastard offspring, making sure they were all given lands and titles and were well cared for.

_04:: King Augustus II (1670–1733)

How many Polish kings does it take to father an estimated 365 illegitimate children? Answer: one, and that one is Frederick Augustus of Saxony, better known as Augustus II ("the Strong"), king of Poland. Famous as a man of immense physical strength, unquenchable lust, and, apparently, considerable stamina, old Augustus wasn't called "the Strong" for nothin'. The first of his 300-plus love children was Hermann Maurice, comte de Saxe, a military genius who himself had several illegitimate children. The great female French novelist George Sand is descended from both these men. However, with that many children between them, we probably all are.

Scandalicious

POPE AND DAUGHTER CAUGHT GROPING AT SAME ORGY!

Not many women can claim the pope as her baby's daddy, but Vanozza dei Cattanei could. The mistress of Cardinal Rodrigo Borgia, she bore him four children before he became Pope Alexander VI in 1492. The most famous were Cesare and Lucrezia. Cesare was a ruthless general and politician, known for poisoning his enemies and conquering the cities of Romagna one by one in a three-year campaign (he also served as the model for Machiavelli's *The Prince*). His sister Lucrezia was married off to one noble after another as a pawn in her father's system of alliances. A little too fond of wealth, power, and luxurious decadence, Alexander VI was also accustomed to treating himself well by throwing notorious parties at the Vatican. The most infamous of his galas was the Ballet of the Chestnuts on October 30, 1501. Naked, painted men and women allegedly greeted guests as "living statues," and beautiful prostitutes danced nude, after which the party progressed into an orgy. Lucrezia's attendance reinforced rumors of incest. The pope supposedly lusted after his daughter as his sons Cesare and Juan fought over her as well. Some even claim Cesare murdered his brother Juan out of jealousy.

_05:: Genghis Khan
(ca. 1162–1227)

Nobody knows how many illegitimate children the great Mongol conqueror actually had. But modern genetic science has proven that he must have had an *awful* lot, a result of the Mongols' ample raping and harem collecting among their many conquered peoples. By tracing the lineage of modern populations of the former Mongol Empire (stretching from China to the Caucasus) through analysis of the Y chromosome, scientists have determined that roughly 16 *million* men, or about 0.05% of the earth's male population, are descended from Genghis Khan or his brothers. Genghis's eldest son, Tushi, alone had 40 sons. In fact, by the year 1260, less than 40 years after Genghis's death, a Persian historian estimated that he already had 20,000 descendants. Now that's what you call a *conquest!*

_06:: Alexandre Dumas
(1802–1870)

One of France's greatest literary figures, Alexandre Dumas brought the world adventures

Touch of Evil

England's king John battled his father, his brothers, and the pope, and was forced to sign the Magna Carta. He still had time, however, to connect with several mistresses and father illegitimate children, including Bartholomew, Eudes, Geoffrey, Joan, John, Maud, Oliver, Osbert, and Richard.

like *The Three Musketeers, The Count of Monte Cristo, The Man in the Iron Mask,* and many others. Turns out he was prolific at more than just writing. Dumas lived as colorful and adventurous a life as any of his characters, taking numerous mistresses and frittering away great gobs of money. He was purported to have fathered dozens of illegitimate children, but he acknowledged only three (by different women). Oddly enough, the one he named after himself went on to renown of his own. So to distinguish him from his son, Alexandre senior is known to the French as *Dumas père* (Dumas the Father). Well deserved, don't you think?

He Never Wants to Cuddle:
Famous People Who Died in the Act

It's not really surprising that people die from overexertion when they're having sex. What might shock you is *who.*

_01:: The Pope

Actually, that's "popes," plural. Apparently papal infallibility only gets you so far. First we

have Pope Leo VII (d. 939 CE), who died of a heart attack during the act. Then there's Pope John XII (d. 964 CE), who was reportedly bludgeoned to death, naked in bed, by the jealous husband of his sex partner. And who could forget Pope John XIII (d. 972 CE), who remarkably enough departed this earthly existence in exactly the same way as John XII. Then, of course, there's good ol' Pope Paul II (d. 1471 CE), who for variety's sake had a heart attack while being sodomized by a page boy.

_02:: The Duke of Orléans (1674–1723)

In 1723, after serving as prince regent and temporary ruler of France for eight years, Philippe II, the duke of Orléans and nephew of Louis XIV, "the Sun King," yielded the throne to Louis XV, who had finally come of age. And not a moment too soon—on December 23, 1723 (just two days before Christmas), Philippe had a stroke after a particularly strenuous night with his mistress, who was 30 years his junior. His only notable accomplishment had been allowing the mass-printing of paper money, which, by the way, bankrupted France.

Touch of Evil

According to a medical study published by the University Hospital of Johann Wolfgang Goethe University in Germany: "Over a period of 21 years (1972–1992), roughly 21,000 forensic autopsies revealed 39 cases (0.19%) of natural deaths occurring during sexual activity.... In most cases sudden death occurred during the sexual act with a prostitute."

_03:: Félix Faure (1841–1899)

Having served as president of France from 1895, Félix Faure seems to have experienced the "little death" and the "big death" simulta-

neously in 1899 while receiving oral sex from his mistress at the Elysee Palace. The woman's terrified screams alerted the president's aides, who broke down the door and found her still kneeling in front of the sofa where the president's corpse was seated, holding her head in his lap with the strength of a death grip. The aides freed the woman, made the president's corpse decent, and laid it out on a bed piously holding a crucifix. Typically, having caught wind of the truth, French newspapers were having none of this. They dutifully ran drawings of this Christian scene, but with the mocking caption "Death of Faure (Official Version)."

_04:: Lord Palmerston (1784–1865)

After a series of accomplishments that won the admiration of the whole world—including helping Belgium achieve independence, supporting the seizure of the French throne by Napoléon III, establishing friendly relations with France, winning the Crimean War, and criticizing the sale of opium in China—what would be the most dignified way for an English elder statesman to end his long life of public service? How about a heart attack as he diddles a parlor maid on a pool table in 1865? Nuff said.

_05:: Nelson Rockefeller (1908–1979)

Grandson of oil tycoon John D. Rockefeller, former governor of New York and vice president of the United States, Nelson Rockefeller left this world doing what he loved best—engaging in lively intercourse with America's free press. Seventy-one years of age, Rockefeller died while having sex with his mistress, a "thirty-one-year-old former news reporter who was working as his research assistant," according to the *New York Times*. The *Times* treated the sticky subject of just *how* Rocke-feller died rather delicately, saying only that he died as he lived, "with an enthusiasm for life in all its public and private passions." Ahem.

Can I Get Flies with That? World's Strangest Aphrodisiacs

If the one-two punch of Barry White and candlelight just ain't doin' the trick, maybe your lust needs some thrust from a less traditional source. Here are a couple of internationally acclaimed remedies from the days before Viagra.

_01:: Basil

If you're desperate for a quick trick to jump-start an ailing love life, just look to the sweetest herb on your spice rack for the remedy. That's right! According to practitioners of the voodoo belief system in Haiti, good ol' basil is the Spanish fly of your kitchen cabinet. Said to be sacred to the Haitian goddess of love, Erzulie, basil is added as an aphrodisiac to a special incense burned to invoke her spirit in voodoo love ceremonies—obviously, for romantic purposes. The Old World herb is also sprinkled liberally on food and eaten to stimulate that tingling feeling.

_02:: Antlers

Perhaps because they resemble erect phalluses, antlers have been considered aphrodisiacs in traditional Asian medical folklore for over 2,000 years. Practitioners of traditional medicine recommend grinding up the soft, velvety skin that covers deer antlers and sprinkling it on food or mixing it into a beverage. In fact, the bony outgrowths are so prized that one species, the Tibet red deer, has actually been hunted to near extinction. Luckily, scientists recently discovered a small herd of 200 of these animals near Lhasa, Tibet, we hope none of which will die in the name of love. Or lust.

_03:: Xanat

The flower of the vanilla orchid was reputed by the native cultures of Central America to be an aphrodisiac, and vanilla still carries this association in Mexico. In native folklore, Xanat, the youngest daughter of the fertility goddess, suffered from unrequited love for a young man of the Totonac tribe. In fact, she was forbidden to marry him because she was divine and he a mortal. Since she couldn't marry a human, however, the benevolent Xanat turned herself into a flower with aphrodisiacal qualities so she could help the human race do its thing.

_04:: Frog Legs

Sometimes you can have too much of a wood—er, good—thing. In the case of an unfortunate group of French Foreign Legion soldiers in North Africa, frog legs proved to be such an effective enhancer of "erectile function" that priapism—a prolonged, painful erection that will not go away—ensued. Subsequently, researchers from American universities found that the frog legs contained enormous amounts of cantharidin, better known as Spanish fly. It turned out the frogs had been eating meloid beetles, one of the main sources of the legendary aphrodisiac, eventually making things hard for the soldiers.

_05:: Nutmeg

Another salacious spice lurking in your pantry, nutmeg has long been thought of as an aphrodisiac by a variety of cultures. The ancient Greeks, Romans, and Hindus ate it for that purpose, and the tradition continued into both the Arab and Chinese civilizations. In fact, in contemporary India, couples eat a mix made of nutmeg, honey, and a half-boiled egg before sex to increase their endurance and make intercourse last longer. However, nutmeg may also have unpredictable hallucinogenic effects, and in large quantities can be fatal.

_06:: Sweet Potatoes

Shortly after Columbus made landfall in 1492, the natives of Hispaniola introduced him to the sweet potato, a member of the morning glory family. Spanish colonizers soon spread the sweet potato lovin' to Asia and Europe, the popularity to cultivate it driven in part by its reputation as an aphrodisiac. In *Health's Improvement*, a medical guide from 1595, Dr.

Thomas Muffet wrote that sweet potatoes increase not only libido, but apparently also the incidence of flatulence, claiming that they "nourish mightily . . . engendering much flesh, blood, and seed, but withal encreasing wind and lust."

_07:: Tiger

Today tigers are one of the most endangered species on earth, with the main population in Asia all but wiped out by poachers. Sadly, this is due in large part to a widespread belief in East Asian cultures that tiger flesh is medicinal for a variety of ailments and complaints. Tiger penis, bone, liver, fat, and whiskers are all reputed to stimulate sexual desire in men, driving the illicit trade and pushing the rare animals ever closer to extinction. Even worse? Despite the fact that its illegal, you can probably find a tiger parts dealer near you: tiger is commonly sold under the table in American cities that are home to large numbers of East Asian immigrants.

_08:: Unagi, Unagi

Served raw in sushi or cooked as part of an *udon* (noodle) dish, sea eel, or *unagi,* is reputed in Japan to be an aphrodisiac. The association likely springs from a rather obvious similarity between the shape of the eel and, as usual, an erect penis. Of course, there might be some science behind the belief as well. Unagi is high in vitamin A, which may help sexual function. Although *unagi* is an increasingly popular item on American sushi menus, most diners are unaware of its erotic associations in Japanese cuisine.

How Do You Solve a Problem Like Our Parents? Historical Eloping Tales

4

Love, they say, conquers all. But sometimes a little thing like parental permission can put up a tough fight. The following four couples didn't get their permission slips signed before taking field trips to the altar.

_01:: Peter Abelard and Héloïse Leonard de Selva

In 12th-century France, Fulbert, a priest of the Cathedral of Notre Dame in Paris, hired Abelard, a gifted but contrary theologian and Aristotelian philosopher, to tutor his brainy young niece, Héloïse. As you might have predicted, Abelard and Héloïse fell in love. What wasn't predicted, however, was that young Abelard would impregnate her. Understandably, Héloïse's uncle was enraged, shipping her off to Normandy for the duration of her pregnancy. After giving birth to a son, she returned to Paris, where, again defying uncle's wishes, Héloïse and Abelard slipped off for a secret wedding. What's an overprotective uncle to do? Fulbert organized his male relatives into a posse, ambushed Abelard, and castrated him, which effectively stopped history from repeating itself. Abelard became a monk and Héloïse reluctantly entered a convent. All wasn't lost, however, and their love affair continued in the form of letters, later collected in book form. In what can be considered a moderately happy ending (given the circumstances, not to mention the uncle), Héloïse ended her life as abbess of the Paraclete, an abbey that Abelard had founded, and was buried next to him.

_02:: John Scott and Bessy Surtees

John Scott was a graduate student at Oxford in 1722, but banker Aubone Surtees wanted more for his daughter Bessy than a merchant's son—especially one who'd been a notorious scamp as a boy. Yet, as songwriter Bob Dylan would put it more than 250 years later, "Love and only love, it can't be denied." Against the wishes of her father and his own (who thought John would imperil his academic career), Scott used a ladder to snatch young Bessy from an upstairs window, and they ran away to Scotland to marry. (It was easier for English couples to get hitched north of the border in those days.) Luckily for the couple, however, neither daddy knew best. John Scott bettered his father's and father-in-law's predictions by becoming the longtime lord chancellor of England. In fact, today, the once mischievous rascal is better remembered as the first earl of Eldon.

_03:: Henry Fitch and Josefa Carrillo

When sea captain Henry Delano Fitch—later a prominent California landowner—fell for 14-year-old Josefa Carillo in 1826, he fell hard. By the laws of Mexican California, however, the San Diego girl couldn't marry a Protestant foreigner, so the Nantucket-born Yankee converted to Catholicism and had himself rechristened Enrique Domingo Fitch. Josefa's father, after some persuading, agreed to the match. During the wedding, however, before the couple could say their vows, Josefa's uncle arrived with an order from the California governor to stop the ceremony. (She later claimed that the governor wanted her for himself.) At the bride-to-be's urging, Fitch took his gal aboard ship and they sailed off to Chile, where they wed. After they returned to California, Fitch was charged with kidnapping and jailed for three months until the governor could verify the legality of the nuptials.

Touch of Evil

Sixteen-year-old Konrad Falkowski eloped with Joan Kenlay in 1952. But to avoid being tracked down by their parents, the young man changed his name, and it's this moniker we still use to refer to the famous actor: Robert Conrad.

_04:: James Joyce and Nora Barnacle

Budding Irish writer James Joyce convinced his Dublin sweetheart, Nora Barnacle, to run away with him to Austria-Hungary in 1904. It wasn't exactly an elopement, though, because Joyce objected to the institution of marriage on philosophical grounds. So, they skipped the ceremony and dove straight into the happily-ever-after bit, living together and raising two children. Joyce, who had by now achieved fame and notoriety, especially for his complex masterpiece *Ulysses,* only agreed to marry his longtime love when the nagging got to be too much. We're not talking about Nora's whining here, but rather her daughter Lucia's. The young woman's incessant complaints about her parents' domestic arrangement drove them to the altar. In 1931, the couple finally legalized their union during a trip from their home in Paris to London. (So, in the end, they ran away to get married after all.)

Greatest Syphilitics of All Time

From Columbus to Gauguin to Al Capone, who knew that syphilis would be the great equalizer? The following are five notables who might have fared better if they'd kept their belts buckled and their legs crossed.

_01:: The Syphilitic Explorer

The long-held view was that Columbus's crew picked up syphilis in the Caribbean in 1492 and brought it back to Europe, where the "new" disease turned epidemic. But what about Columbus himself? He returned from his third voyage west in 1504 partially paralyzed, suffering edema, and mentally de-

The Evil How-to

HOW TO SPOT "THE SIGNS" (OTHER THAN JUST HAIRY PALMS)

Active physician, health innovator, and, yes, the founder of a cereal company, John Harvey Kellogg wrote a handbook for sexual behavior in 1877 (while on his honeymoon) called "Plain Facts for Old and Young, A Warning on the Evils of Sex." A key focus of this piece was a section containing 39 signs for parents to use to tell whether their children were masturbating or "performing the solitary vice," as it was called. The following are some of the signs that, according to Kellogg, all good parents should be on the lookout for: emaciation, paleness, colorless lips and gums, exhaustion, coughing, shortness of breath, chest pains, disobedience, irritability, a dislike for activity and play, sleeplessness, failure to get lessons done, forgetfulness, inattention, and liking to be alone. Kellogg went on to identify some other telltale signs, including bashfulness, boldness, mock piety, rounded shoulders, weak backs, pain in the limbs, lack of breast development in females, bad positions while sleeping, large appetites and the use of large amounts of spices, sunken and red eyes, and epileptic fits. Finally, especially be on the lookout for acne, bitten fingernails, moist, cold hands, bedwetting, the use of tobacco, and fondness for using bad language and listening to obscene stories. It's a good thing Kellogg was so specific; otherwise we might have started accusing everyone.

ranged. But can anybody be sure what caused those symptoms without examining Columbus's bones? Well, no. He could have had typhus or rheumatic fever, but syphilis can't be ruled out.

_02:: The Syphilitic King

A wound on Henry VIII's leg became a festering sore that wouldn't heal. Ulcers spread over his legs and feet. And as he grew hugely obese, the English king's toes turned gangrenous. Not exactly a thing of beauty, Old Hal had something going on. The latter-day diagnosis: advanced diabetes. So what's with the notion that Henry's late-life dementia came from syphilis? Some say first wife Catherine of Aragon's several miscarriages suggest a sexually transmitted disease. And then there's the sad case of Henry's son Edward VI, the boy king with the terrible skin rash whose hair and nails fell out. Tradition says Eddie died at age 15 of tuberculosis. Many, however, argue that he and his half sister Queen Mary I had congenital syphilis passed on from Henry. Of course, it's all unconfirmed. None of Henry's children, including Elizabeth I (another suspected but unconfirmed syphilitic), produced offspring.

_03:: The Syphilitic Philosopher

On a winter day when Friedrich Nietzsche was 54, the German-Swiss philosopher, clad in only his underwear, ran weeping into a street in Turin, Italy, where he tearfully embraced a horse. Stricken with diphtheria and bacterial dysentery during his service in the Franco-Prussian War (1870–1871), Nietzsche never fully recovered his health. His late-life dementia, however, more likely stemmed from tertiary syphilis. In other words, he had probably picked up the disease in his youth and it had run its course for decades. Nietzsche, a philosopher later admired (and grossly misunderstood) by Adolf Hitler, spent the last 11 years of his life totally mad.

Touch of Evil

One radical cure for syphilitic patients was to give them malaria. *The high fever worked to kill the syphilis, after which the malaria was easily cured with quinine.*

_04:: The Syphilitic Painter

Born in Paris, Paul Gauguin spent his early childhood in Peru before moving back to France. As a young man Gauguin signed on as a merchant sailor to see and sample the sensual riches of the world. Later, after he'd supposedly settled down, Gauguin and his wife moved from France to her native Denmark, where they raised their family and Gauguin had a career as a stockbroker. But then Gauguin chucked his family and his career to live a new life as a bohemian painter in Tahiti. So where did he pick up the syphilis that plagued him in his later years? It could have been in the South Seas, although it's more likely that a Parisian prostitute gave him the pox. Nearly blind, barely able to walk, and in terrible pain, this forefather of modern art died alone in his Maison du Jouir (House of Pleasure) in the village of Atuona in the Marquesas Islands.

_05:: The Syphilitic Gangster

When New York tough guy Alphonse "Scarface" Capone arrived in Chicago in 1919, one of his first jobs in the town where he would become America's most famous gangster was looking after mobster Big Jim Colosimo's string of brothels. So, did old Al sample the service? Well, a gentleman gangster never tells. What we will say, however, is that wherever he picked up the "goods," years later, he was discovered to be suffering from paresis—a psychosis that follows after the late-stage disease eats away a significant part of the brain. Released from Alcatraz Federal Prison in 1939, Capone entered a Baltimore hospital and spent his last years deep in syphilitic dementia.

The Cost of Free Love:
Not-So-Straitlaced Reformers of Victorian Times

A glimpse of stocking may have been shocking, but a vocal minority of 19th-century reformers fought for your right to hook up.

_01:: John Humphrey Noyes (1811–1886)

As a theology student at Yale, John Humphrey Noyes declared himself sin free and in a state of perfection. Not surprisingly, Johnny the Pure was denied a license to preach, so he organized fellow perfectionists into a "Bible Communist" community in Putney, Vermont. There Noyes taught a doctrine of free love. In 1846 the Putney group adopted what their leader called "complex marriage," such that all the women were "married" to all the men and vice versa. Arrested for adultery, Noyes jumped bail and fled to New York, where he founded a new community in Oneida. There, the Oneida Community practiced complex marriage up until 1879, when Noyes finally gave in to pressure from outside moralists and abandoned the practice. Oneida, once an agricultural-religious utopian community, reorganized as a joint-stock manufacturer of silver flatware. As for John Noyes? He fled again, this time for Canada.

_02:: Ezra H. Heywood (1829–1893)

Massachusetts liberal Ezra Heywood founded his publication *The Word* in 1872 as a voice for labor reform and other egalitarian causes. Heywood and his wife, Angela Tilton, also a writer for *The Word,* shared four daughters and a belief that traditional marriage amounted to slavery of women—both of the economic and sexual variety. So what did the couple do? They decided to pen their own emancipation proclamations, using *The Word* to advocate free love. "Sexuality is a divine ordinance elegantly natural from an eye-glance to the vital action of the penis and womb, in personal exhilaration or for reproductive uses," Tilton wrote. Of course, such salacious language was bound to offend a few Victorians, and Anthony Comstock, a smut-fighting special agent of the U.S. Post Office, was certainly one of them. Comstock took special offense to Heywood's pamphlet "Cupid's Yokes," which advocated birth control, and arrested Ezra in Boston in 1877. Many argued that Angela, known for her frank vocabulary (she used the "f" word in print) should have been jailed, too, but Ezra's the one who spent time in the slammer.

_03:: Moses Hull (1836–1907)

A gifted Seventh-day Adventist preacher, Moses Hull left the church and began lecturing

Touch of Evil

Despite having the Victorian era named after her, Queen Victoria didn't always act so Victorian. In fact, she was notorious for having a long-term out-of-wedlock relationship with her "personal attendant," John Brown—lavishing him with expensive gifts and constant affection—after her husband, Prince Albert, passed away.

instead on spiritualism in 1863. Well known for his eloquence, he was considered highly respectable. That is, until 1873, when old Moses printed a letter in *Woodhull & Claflin's Weekly* (copublished by Victoria Woodhull, see next item) unapologetically confessing that he'd strayed from his marriage. But he didn't stop there. Hull actually went on to praise sexual variety, claiming: "Many think they are improved . . . by a change of climate and scene, when their principal improvement is caused by a separation from their old sexual mate, and sometimes by the substitution of a new one." Hull and wife, Elvira, dissolved their marriage "by a law higher than man's" and Hull subsequently entered a "contract marriage" (no clergy, no license) with fellow spiritualist Mattie Sawyer. Luckily, the "contract" held until his death.

_04:: Victoria Woodhull (1838–1927)

Believe it or not, the first woman to run for U.S. president actually spent her childhood as a fortune-teller in her family's traveling medicine show. Luckily for Victoria Woodhull, she abandoned the psychic act for loftier goals, including stints as a stockbroker, magazine publisher, women's rights advocate, and, most notoriously, lecturer. Woodhull's talks on free love drew thousands—supporters and scandalized alike. Though few details about her own sex life are known (aside from the fact that she lived for a while with two husbands), Woodhull didn't argue in favor of promiscuity. In fact, she pushed sexual self-determination as essential to women's rights, condemning any copulation without love, inside or outside of marriage. In 1872, while seeking the White House on the Equal Rights ticket, Woodhull smeared clergyman Henry Ward Beecher, probably a former lover, who refused to publicly support her. Unfortunately, the first amendment didn't work in her favor in the Victorian climate. Woodhull's published account of Beecher's adultery with a married parishioner landed her in jail on obscenity charges.

Naked Lust:
Artists Who Did More Than Portray Their Models

Emotionally charged virtuosos plus beautiful nude models plus too many hours spent in the studio? These cases illustrate that high art and simple biology are anything but mutually exclusive.

_01:: Anselm Feuerbach and Nanna Risi

The 19th-century painter Anselm Feuerbach, nephew of philosopher Ludwig Feuerbach, admired and tried to emulate the art of the High Renaissance. That's a big part of the reason why he migrated from his native Germany to Italy. Yet Feuerbach also possessed a cool, northern European sensibility, which he brought with him to Rome when he moved there in 1856. In fact, his neoclassical scenes took on a bit of heat only after Italian model Nanna Risi (also seen in works by Frederick Leighton) began posing for him in 1860. It wasn't just his artwork that heated up, though. The chemistry between artist and model grew, and Risi eventually left her shoemaker husband and her child for Feuerbach. The affair didn't last, however, and she later abandoned the artist. Brokenhearted, Feuerbach tried to replace Risi with another model and lover, but he had little luck. After some time spent teaching art in Vienna, Feurbach moved to Venice, where he died poor and alone in 1880.

_02:: Suzanne Valadon and half of France...

Before 1892, when she became a painter, Suzanne Valadon was a teenage circus acrobat and then one of the most popular models in Paris—popular in more than one sense. Henri de Toulouse-Lautrec, Pierre Puvis de Chavannes, and Pierre-Auguste Renoir were among the many artists who depicted her. Toulouse-Lautrec's *The Hangover,* for example, is a portrait of Valadon. Usually, however, this model's relationships went well beyond the depicting stage. Valadon had numerous love affairs with Parisian artists, and perhaps the best documented is that with Renoir. Composer Eric Satie was also an intense lover of hers. More intriguing than a listing of the lovers she kept: Valadon never revealed which man fathered her son, painter Maurice Utrillo. Further, at age 44, Valadon was still on the prowl. She left a wealthy husband for the considerably younger artist André Utter, 23.

_03:: Pablo Picasso and Marie-Thérèse Walter

Picasso met Marie-Thérèse Walter either in 1925, when she was 15 and he was 43, or in

1927. In either case, they seemed to be lovers from early in their relationship, as Picasso's marriage to the former dancer Olga Koklova quickly deteriorated. Although Picasso first approached Walter to comment on her interesting face and his eagerness to paint her, Walter's likeness doesn't show up in Picasso's work until 1935, which is the same year she bore him a daughter. In any case, the reliably unreliable Picasso left Marie in 1936 for photographer Dora Maar, who turned the tables and used Picasso as a model. Sadly, Walter hanged herself in 1977. Even more unfortunate, she wasn't the only one of Picasso's former lovers to commit suicide.

_04:: Man Ray and Lee Miller

In 1929 Lee Miller, a 19-year-old art student from Poughkeepsie, New York, walked into innovative painter-collagist-photographer Man Ray's photo studio in Paris and introduced herself as his new assistant. Ray, who'd made his reputation as a surrealist and a pioneer of the Dada movement, said he didn't need an assistant but she persisted. Miller, already a top model who had adorned the cover of *Vogue* in 1927, was pretty persuasive (or persuasively

pretty). The affair lasted for a bit. Lee and Ray were together as lovers and collaborators for three years before she went on to a photo career ranging from studio fashion shoots for *Vogue* to feature spreads in *Life* to wrenching World War II battlefield coverage for the U.S. military.

_05:: Jeff Koons and Ilona Staller

In 1991, stockbroker-turned-controversial-artist Jeff Koons—earlier known for works depicting basketballs floating in aquariums and brand-new vacuum cleaners displayed under glass—took a turn toward the graphically sexual in 1991. The series of pieces included photographic tableaux and small glass sculptures depicting him engaged in sex acts with Italian porn star Ilona "Cicciolina" Staller. Oddly enough, there was nothing left to the imagination in these works—some of them barely distinguishable from the porn that was Cicciolina's career mainstay. Nonetheless, it was "art," just as a basketball in an aquarium was "art," because Koons pronounced it so. The pair married that year and produced a son (perhaps conceived on camera), but they separated in 1992.

Out of Order:
Divinity School Dropouts

Hell hath no fury like a former seminarian. From Hollywood superstars to adulterous dilettantes, several seminary dropouts have managed to find success in the secular world. But they've also strayed from the Christian path—whether it was for the teachings of L. Ron Hubbard or simply to reign terror over a Communist nation. Here's a sampling of the finest in almost-clergy.

_01:: Tom Cruise (1962–   )

In 1976, a deeply religious child named Thomas Cruise Mapother IV enrolled in a Franciscan seminary in New Jersey. Within five years, he'd ditched the church, dropped the Mapother, and landed a part in *Endless Love*. And in spite of his diminutive height (5 feet 7 inches) the man who might have been a priest became one of Hollywood's top leading men. Around 1986, though, he abandoned Catholicism altogether, embracing the Church of Scientology, which he once credited with helping him overcome dyslexia. Wildly popular with celebrities, Scientology is the path of choice to "clarity" for everyone from John Travolta to the guy who played Parker Lewis in *Parker Lewis Can't Lose*. Incidentally, Scientology does have ministers—but while Cruise remains an active member and apologist for the group, he has yet to seek ordination.

_02:: Casanova (1725–1798)

Everyone's favorite 18th-century libertine began his scandalous escapades at the seminary of St. Cyprion, from which he was expelled under cloudy circumstances (we're guessing he slept with someone). And as you well know, his postseminary life was as ungodly as it gets. By the age of 30 he was sentenced to prison for engaging in "magic," but he escaped after only a year to Paris. There, he made a fortune by introducing the lottery to France. But before settling down to write his ribald, self-aggrandizing autobiography, Casanova was expelled from more European countries than most of us ever visit. Along the way, he slept with tons of women, dueled with many of their husbands, and generally sinned his way to the top of European culture, befriending such figures as Madame du Pompadour and Jean-Jacques Rousseau along the way.

_03:: Joseph Stalin (1879–1953)

Lasting longer than the vast majority of divinity school dropouts, noted mass murderer Joseph Stalin studied at a Georgian Orthodox seminary in Tiflis (now Tbilisi) for five years, between 1894 and 1899. He left the seminary either because of poor health (his mom's story) or revolutionary activity (Stalin's story). Either way, Stalin clearly didn't take much of what he learned to heart (assuming he had one). After he became the Soviet leader in

1922, he was responsible for the deaths of thousands of religious leaders, and Stalin did more than any other premier to eliminate the role of Christianity in Soviet life. But his seminary wasn't exactly a study in Christian love, either. Prior to Stalin's arrival, a rector was murdered there—possibly by unruly seminarians.

Touch of Evil

When Charles Darwin hesitated to obtain a degree in medicine, his dad enrolled him in the University of Cambridge to study divinity. It wasn't long, though, before the "father of evolution" quit school (in 1831) to begin taking part in scientific expeditions around the world.

_04:: Michael Moore (1954–   )

Controversial documentary filmmaker Michael Moore began studying at a seminary in his hometown of Flint, Michigan, as an eighth grader in 1967. Brought up a devout Catholic, Moore aspired to a career as a priest, but he left the seminary the next year for thoroughly secular reasons. When the Detroit Tigers made it to the World Series in 1968, the seminary refused to let him watch the games—so he quit. Before his successful filmmaking career, in fact, Moore was something of a serial dropout. He dropped out of the University of Michigan because he arrived at school one morning and couldn't find a parking place, and he once got a job at an automobile factory in Flint—but called in sick on his first day and never returned.

_05:: Al Gore (1948–   )

Believe it or not, the winner of the popular vote in the U.S. presidential election of 2000 was actually a devoutly religious divinity school dropout. It's true! Al Gore graduated from Harvard cum laude in 1969 (although he earned several Cs and a D during his time in Cambridge), but he'd always been interested in theology, so he decided to continue his studies. It's no wonder, then, that he enrolled in Vanderbilt's prestigious divinity school, where, over the course of three semesters, he *failed* five of his eight classes! Gore's allies claim that the birth of his first child and his duties as a reporter at the *Tennessean* newspaper kept him from his studies. For the record, though, Gore also later dropped out of Vanderbilt's law school (in 1976), but this time for a truly higher purpose—to run for Congress.

Portraits of Artists as Young Perverts

In his memoir *A Moveable Feast*, Ernest Hemingway revealed that F. Scott Fitzgerald once confessed to being concerned about his diminutive penis size. Hemingway replied, "You're perfectly fine," but then of course went on to publish a book recounting the humiliating conversation. And if no less a writer than Ernest Hemingway can go around revealing authors' sexual quirks and insecurities, well, so can we.

_01:: Rousseau (1712–1778)

Jean-Jacques Rousseau, an 18th-century Swiss writer and philosopher, believed that humans were basically good but had been corrupted by the social order. And boy, did he know a thing or two about being corrupted. While you wouldn't know it from the dry prose of *Émile* or *The Social Contract,* Rousseau enjoyed the naughty—so long as he got spanked for his transgressions. "To lie at the feet of an imperious mistress," he once remarked, "was for me a sweet enjoyment." Yikes! In fact, he liked it so much that as a young man, Rousseau would drop trou and moon women in dark alleyways, hoping to get a spanking for his trouble. Surprisingly, the great philosopher's greatest impact might not have been made by his quill, but rather by his quirk. The phrase psychologists use to describe young men who get aroused when disciplined by older women: "the Rousseau effect."

_02:: Lewis Carroll (1832–1898)

The most famous sexual deviant in the annals of literature may, in fact, not have been: Lewis Carroll, children's book author and noted fan of taking little girls' pictures. Carroll, who spent most of his career teaching math, spoke with a terrible stammer around adults, but found it easy to talk to children (kind of like Michael Jackson). In fact, the sputtering author found it remarkably easy to engage his child friends in fantastic stories, which culminated with *Alice's Adventures in Wonderland.* Published in 1865, *Alice* is certainly a study in Freudian sublimation: there's a fair bit of squeezing through tiny holes, for instance. And then there are the pictures: Carroll photographed both adults and children, and also took several nude pictures of kids (he even sent a letter to a colleague at Oxford asking if he could photograph his girls nude without chaperones). Still, no evidence has ever surfaced that Carroll abused anyone—incapable of mature relationships, sure, but probably not an active pedophile.

_03:: René Descartes (1596–1650)

Perhaps the only example of a sexual eccentricity changing the history of Western thought can be found in the life story of the father of modern philosophy, René "I think therefore I am" Descartes. You see, Descartes had a fetish for cross-eyed women—due, he

Scandalicious

RUSSIAN CZARINA AND PEASANT SEEN SMOOCHING BY PALACE STEPS (PHOTOS INSIDE!)

How did an illiterate, raggedly dressed peasant with a well-known reputation for sexual debauchery become a trusted friend to Czar Nicholas II and Czarina Alexandra of Russia? Well, it may have been Rasputin's remarkable ability to heal their hemophiliac son, Aleksei. Or maybe, as many have thought, Alexandra was in love with him. When Czar Nicholas went to the front during World War I, Alexandra stayed behind to run the country, and the sex-crazed holy man Rasputin became her most trusted adviser. Meanwhile, she probably became the most prominent of his many mistresses. Though not the best-looking fellow you'd ever meet, Rasputin did have certain, uh, assets—his penis was supposedly more than a foot long. It's unlikely that Alexandra and Rasputin ever consummated their bizarre friendship, but by December 1916, the mere *rumor* of peasant-on-czarina loving was simply too much to bear for a group of Russian aristocrats, who finally decided to put Rasputin out of their misery. It wasn't easy. He survived poisoning and two gunshot wounds before finally being drowned in the icy Neva River.

believed, to his childhood fascination with a cross-eyed playmate. As he describes it in the *Principles of Philosophy,* Descartes was eventually able to condition his body to find straight-eyed women attractive (good for Descartes, maybe, but a disaster for the hard-up cross-eyed ladies of Europe). It was largely this experience that led Descartes to his belief in free will and to his assertion that the mind can control the impulses of the body.

_04:: James Joyce (1882–1941)

When an admirer once asked if he could "kiss the hand that wrote *Ulysses,*" James Joyce replied, "No. It has done a lot of other things, too." Indeed it had. *Ulysses,* the exemplar of 20th-century literature, was banned in much of the world for its purported obscenity. (For the greatest literary accomplishment of its time, *Ulysses* does feature a lot of smut.) In

Touch of Evil

Before Horatio Alger's rags-to-riches stories inspired a generation of youngsters, he was quietly dismissed as minister of the First Unitarian Church in Brewster, Massachusetts, for allegedly molesting two young boys who were members of the congregation.

America, Judge John M. Woolsey lifted the ban on *Ulysses* in December of 1933 (the same month Prohibition ended), and Joyce's sprawling, brilliant tale of one day in Dublin became an instant sensation. *Ulysses* may not be obscene, but Joyce himself was a bit of a perv. He admitted to finding women's unwashed underwear erotic—perhaps not coincidentally, panties and petticoats pop up in *Ulysses* rather frequently.

_05:: Edna St. Vincent Millay (1892–1950)

Many writers have been unfaithful to their spouses, but few can match Edna St. Vincent Millay. The first woman to win the Pulitzer Prize for poetry, Millay was married for 26 years to Eugene Boissevain. In a reversal of traditional gender roles, Boissevain did most of the housework and Millay most of the philandering. She took many lovers, both male and female, and one biographer described her as having a "megawatt libido." True enough, but so did a lot of male poets (like Lord Byron), and they didn't catch much flak for it. Millay was open, and funny, about her trysts. When she complained of headaches to a psychologist at a party, he wondered whether

Millay might have a subconscious attraction to women. "Oh, you mean I'm a homosexual!" Millay replied. "Of course I am, and a heterosexual, too. But what's that got to do with my headache?"

_06:: F. Scott Fitzgerald (1896–1940)

Another great modernist, F. Scott Fitzgerald, had his own quirks. Like many authors (Dostoyevsky and Thomas Hardy, among others), Fitzgerald may have had a foot fetish, at least according to biographer Jeffrey Meyers. In 1917, Fitzgerald became acquainted with the great love of his life, Zelda Sayre, outside of Montgomery, Alabama. They married in 1920, the same year his first novel, *This Side of Paradise,* was published. Then, five years later, his masterpiece, *The Great Gatsby,* hit the shelves. Shortly thereafter, Zelda lost her tenuous grip on sanity—she eventually landed in a sanitarium after she began practicing ballet day and night. All those hours en pointe couldn't have been good for her feet. But Fitzgerald might not have cared: most critics think he was only kidding when he made references to a "pedentia complex," which just goes to show you, be careful what you joke about.

A Pain in the Royal Horse: Sex Rumors About Royalty

Long before Prince Charles proved that love is blind by cheating on his beautiful wife with Camilla Parker-Bowles, bluebloods had already proudly renounced monogamy. Over the centuries, they've coveted their neighbors' wives countless times, sure, but what about their neighbors' livestock? It's time to separate the perverted facts from the perverted fiction about royal sex lives.

_01:: Catherine the Great (1729–1796)

The reign of Catherine II, the German-born czarina of Russia, began when she overthrew her alcoholic, incompetent, and purportedly impotent husband, Frederick (the not so Great), in 1762. If there was one thing Catherine the Great would not stand for, it was impotence. Although grossly overweight, Catherine loved men—a great many of them, in fact—over the course of her 34-year reign. And then, it was rumored, she died during a botched attempt to make love (if it can be called such a thing) to a horse. The rumor may have been spread by Catherine's Polish enemies, who resented her for annexing much of Poland. (On the list of European royalty's lei-sure activities, "overrunning Poland" has historically been a close second to "sex.") At any rate, Catherine never had sex with a horse, and one wonders why anyone felt compelled to make up such a story, since her actual death was plenty humiliating. While straining on the toilet, she had a stroke.

_02:: A Tale of Two Georges

In what seems to be an outlandish coincidence, England's king George II (1683–1760) also died of a stroke while on the commode. Some sources say that although he was quite happily married to his wife, Queen Caroline, George took mistresses so as to *maintain his reputation.* After all, a mistressless king could be seen as weak or, worse still, impotent. His son, George III, however, broke that streak of monarchial infidelity when he married the notoriously homely Princess Sophia Charlotte of Mecklenburg-Strelitz in 1761. Seeing her for the first time on their wedding day, George is said to have winced in disgust, but the two came to love one another immensely (and frequently—they had 15 kids), and George III was never unfaithful.

Touch of Evil

Supposedly, a priest attending Napoléon's autopsy ended up "saving" certain body parts, including the Bonaparte penis. Later bought by a collector and displayed in a New York museum, the organ was said to resemble "a shriveled sea horse."

_03:: Another Royal Horse

The Roman emperor Caligula (12–41 CE) redefined sexual debauchery during his reign. Aside from fancying himself a god and having an altogether creepy sexual fascination with his sister Drusilla, Caligula supposedly engaged in many orgies (which inspired a famous adult film). Plus, he had a suspiciously intimate relationship with his favorite horse, Incitatus. Some Roman historians claimed that Caligula intended to make his horse consul, but that appears to have been kind of a Roman urban legend. Roman historians despised Caligula so intensely that it's difficult to sort out the actual facts of his reign. And while Caligula did *like* his horse (he apparently built Incitatus a house), there's no reason to believe he "liked him" liked him.

_04:: Jahāngir (1569–1627)

Though there are plenty of excellent candidates for most sexually insatiable king ever, including Hal the Horny (the oft-married Henry VIII of England), our vote has to go to Jahāngir, the fourth Mughal emperor of India. Jahāngir had little to do with the day-to-day running of the empire—that work was accomplished by his favorite wife, Nūr Jahān. (The Taj Mahal was built for Jahān's niece, Mumtaz Mahal.) While Jahān became one of the most powerful women of the 17th century, Jahāngir busied himself with loving. He supposedly had 300 wives (296 more than allowed by the religion, Islam, he supposedly followed), 5,000 female concubines, and 1,000 male concubines. Jahāngir also kept a massive herd of 12,000 elephants, but we won't speculate.

_05:: And, of Course, Prince Charles! (1948–)

Of all the recent sex rumors about the British royal family, none has been kept quite so quiet as that of Prince Charles's supposed bisexual affair. For weeks in late 2003, the British press printed banner headlines about a royal sex scandal but, conscious of Britain's strict libel laws, never came out and openly revealed the accusations. Instead, they engaged in all manner of hints and innuendo. This led to the strange phenomenon of the royal family issuing a statement denying allegations that had never publicly been made. The rumor: Prince Charles had a love affair with his adviser Michael Fawcett. Scandalous, sure, but unlikely—it seems the prince only has eyes for Camilla. After decades of courtship, they finally wed in 2005.

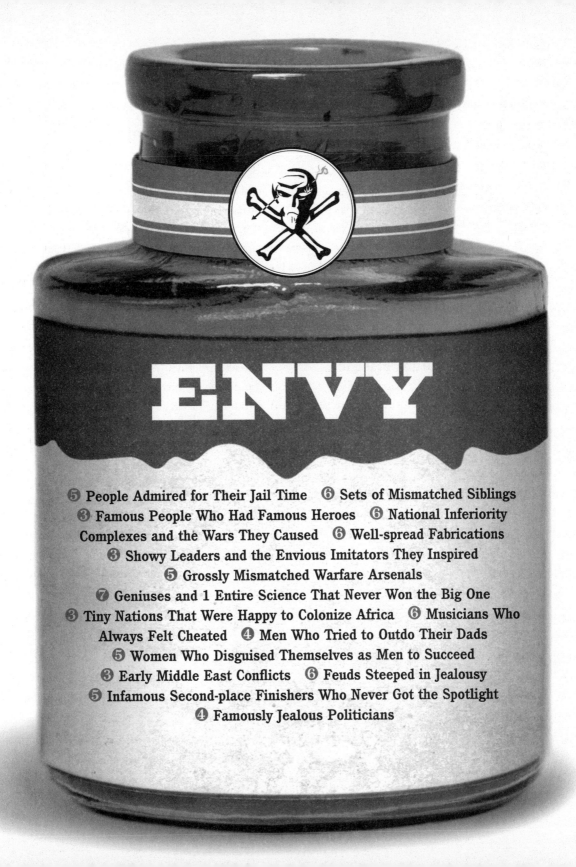

Does That Come in Stripes?
People Admired for Their Jail Time

Before she began serving her five-month sentence for illegal insider trading in 2004, Martha Stewart came perilously close to comparing herself to a somewhat more noble former inmate. "There's many other good people that have gone to prison. Look at Nelson Mandela." Oh, we'll look at him, Martha. But we're not so sure you'll stack up. While we wouldn't envy the following folks, they certainly earned respect by spending time in the clink.

_01:: Nelson Mandela:
The Political Prisoner

The son of a Tembu chief, Nelson Mandela worked as a lawyer (an honest lawyer!) until becoming a leader of the African National Congress in 1949. Today, Mandela has a reputation for nonviolence, but in reality he embraced armed struggle and sabotage after the appalling 1960 massacre of nonviolent protesters in Sharpeville. After admitting he helped found Spear of the Nation, the ANC's military wing, Mandela was sent to prison for life. During his 28 years in jail, the charismatic Mandela became even more popular among black South Africans, and his writings from prison, particularly *I Am Prepared to Die,* galvanized international opposition to apartheid. Released in 1990, Mandela made the most of his freedom. Within four years, he helped negotiate an end to apartheid, won the Nobel Peace Prize, and became South Africa's first black president.

_02:: 50 Cent:
The Platinum Prisoner

In the hip-hop world, nothing sells like street cred. Anybody can *rhyme* about prison and shootings and drug deals—but it's the precious rapper who can claim nine bullet wounds and several incarcerations that'll move those albums. For better or for worse, 50 Cent's payment of dues in jail certainly played a role in his seven-figure record contract. After all, the rap world was starving for authenticity, and 50 (aka Ben Jackson) was a true gangster in the Tupac mold. His résumé includes growing up selling crack and surviving being shot nine times in 2000 (he's also been stabbed!). Many critics, and some fellow rappers, have attributed his success more to his life's story than his mediocre rhyming. But it's probably not a trade worth making—most ex-con crack dealers who get repeatedly shot and occasionally stabbed tend not to end up with platinum albums.

_03:: Adolf Hitler:
The Palace-Bound Prisoner

These days, Adolf Hitler is perhaps history's least admired individual. But during his reign as Führer, Hitler's time in prison was seen as proof he sacrificed for National Socialism and Germany. In reality, though, his hard time wasn't particularly hard. Sentenced to five years in prison after failing spectacularly to take over the country in 1923, Hitler served only nine months. Also, he was "jailed" in a castle, and all his friends were either in jail with him or free to visit. What's a poor inmate to do? At the castle, Hitler decided to write (or dictate, actually) *Mein Kampf,* his self-aggrandizing autobiography/study in irrational hatred. Hitler originally gave the book the catchy title *Four and a Half Years of Struggle against Lies, Stupidity, and Cowardice,* which Nazi publishers smartly shortened to the catchier *My Struggle.* Soon enough, much of Germany admired Hitler's struggle—even if *he* was the real lying, stupid coward.

_04:: Leonard Peltier: The Pine Ridge Prisoner

While America was extricating itself from Vietnam in the early 1970s, a minor war was brewing on the home front. The American Indian Movement (AIM), advocating a return to Native traditions, was locked in a fierce battle with those Indians who supported, and were supported by, the federal Bureau of Indian Affairs. Some 60 Native Americans died, but the story didn't become big news until June 26, 1975, when two FBI agents were killed during a gunfight on the Pine Ridge Reservation in South Dakota. AIM activist Leonard Peltier was convicted of the murders. Although quite probably guilty, many (including Nelson Mandela, the Dalai Lama, and Amnesty International) have argued that Peltier is a political prisoner. President Clinton considered pardoning him in 2000 but didn't. Perhaps hoping to pardon himself, Peltier ran for president in 2004 as the candidate for the somewhat ironically named Peace and Freedom Party.

_05:: Dietrich Bonhoeffer: The Pacifist Prisoner

The most prominent theologian in Hitler's Germany, Dietrich Bonhoeffer openly and courageously opposed Nazism and condemned the church for "staying silent when it should have cried out." Although a pacifist, Bonhoeffer participated in a lengthy struggle to overthrow the Nazis that culminated in a failed assassination attempt on Hitler. Already imprisoned for helping Jews escape to Switzerland, Bonhoeffer's connection to the group resulted in his execution on April 9, 1945. His brilliant *Letters and Papers from Prison* remains in circulation, however, and is required reading for contemporary theologians. Among the first thinkers to consider the role of Christianity in an increasingly secular world, the suffering Bonhoeffer lived his theology. "God is weak and powerless in the world," he wrote, "and that is exactly the way, the only way, in which He is with us to help us."

Mom Always Liked *You* Best: Sets of Mismatched Siblings

Brothers wrestle; sisters scream. Siblings always compare themselves—how much they're loved, how much they inherit, how they look—and feelings always get hurt.

_01:: Jesus and Who?

The New Testament mentions brothers (*adelphoi* in Greek) of Jesus and even names them. Yet, many Christians teach that Jesus was an only child and that the *adelphoi* James, Simon, Judas (different from apostles James, Simon, and Judas), and Joseph were Jesus' cousins. In fact, according to Catholic theology, Jesus' mother, Mary, never had sexual intercourse and never bore a child other than the Messiah, so the *adelphoi* couldn't have been his brothers. Other lines of thought tell it a little differently, claiming that the Gospel writers used *adelphoi* literally and that Mary was a virgin only until after the birth of Jesus. We don't want to take sides, but if these four guys really were Jesus' brothers, they got the seriously short end of the sibling stick. Imagine—not only is your brother God Almighty, he's also the most famous man in history. Meanwhile, scholars are sitting around arguing about whether you ever even existed.

_02:: Charlotte Brontë and Her Five Siblings

Maria and Elizabeth Brontë couldn't help being eclipsed by younger sister Charlotte; after all, they died in girlhood in the 1820s. Sister Emily, second youngest, was the family's only poetic genius and wrote *Wuthering Heights* (1847). Seen in retrospect as one of the finest novels in English, it was panned in its own time and she produced no more. Youngest sister Anne's novels, *Agnes Grey* (1847) and especially *The Tenant of Wildfell Hall* (1848), were popular, if literarily undistinguished. Branwell, the one brother, drank too much, smoked too much opium, and died a failure in 1848. Emily and Anne died the next year. All of which leaves Charlotte the only Brontë to achieve popular, critical, and lasting success with her novels, especially *Jane Eyre* (1847). In the end, she was the longest-lived of the TB-plagued Brontë siblings, surviving until age 39. She was also the only one to marry (the show-off).

_03:: John and Tom Fogarty: Bad Blood Rising

In 1959, Tom Fogarty, two school chums, and Tom's little brother, John, formed a band. Playing in the Fogarty garage in El Cerrito, California, they called themselves Tommy Fogarty & the Blue Velvets. Then, in 1964, they landed a recording contract with Fantasy Records in nearby Berkeley. Renamed the Golli-

TOM WOLFE'S HORRIBLE-TERRIBLE, NO-GOOD, VERY BAD DAY

The 1998 publication of Tom Wolfe's novel *A Man in Full* brought healthy sales but brutal reviews from literary heavy hitters including novelists John Irving, John Updike, and Norman Mailer. Mailer, a longtime Wolfe nemesis, was particularly damning, comparing reading the book to having sex with a 300-pound woman. "Once she gets on top it's all over. Fall in love or be asphyxiated," Mailer wrote in *The New York Review of Books*. A decade earlier, the pugnacious Mailer had angered the Virginia-born Wolfe by making fun of his sartorial trademark, a natty white suit. At the time, Wolfe replied that "the lead dog is the one they always try to bite in the ass." After the attacks on *A Man in Full*, Wolfe dismissed critics Mailer and Updike as "old bags of bones" and said that all three of his novelist-rivals (whom he often refers to as "My Three Stooges") were panicked by his neorealist fiction. Either that, or his fancy-pants style.

wogs, the band floundered until John suddenly emerged as both a towering talent and a control freak. As lead singer, lead guitarist, lead composer, lead lyricist, lead arranger, and lead (if not sole) band manager, he could do everything but spell. John turned the group, now called Creedence Clearwater Revival, into an "overnight" sensation, cranking out top-10 singles ("Proud Mary," "Bad Moon Rising," "Down on the Corner") and No. 1 albums. Brother Tom? In 1971 he quit in disgust. Worse yet, he couldn't catch a break. He passed away in 1990 as a result of AIDS, a condition contracted from a blood transfusion.

_04:: Jimmy and Billy Carter: Not Like Two Peanuts in a Shell

Twelve years younger than brother Jimmy, Billy Carter found himself cast in the role of clown prince in the late 1970s. A beer-for-breakfast kind of guy who proudly wore a "Redneck Power" T-shirt, Billy sometimes embraced the role of buffoon and sometimes tried to shake the stigma. His bid to become mayor of Plains, Georgia, close on the heels of his brother's 1976 presidential victory, failed. He also failed as manager of the family peanut warehouse. His PR makeover wasn't helped by the fact that he regularly greeted reporters while perched on a stack of beer cases in his service station. It also wasn't helped by his business initiatives: Billy once tried to cash in on celebrity, promoting a brand of beer named for him. His biggest misadventure, however, came when he accepted money from the Libyan government in return for his supposed influence with his brother. Dubbed "Billygate," the episode prompted a congressional investigation and embarrassed Jimmy as his 1980 bid for reelection approached. Billy Carter died at age 51 in 1988.

_05:: Rajiv and Sanjay Gandhi: Who Gets Mom's Job?

Prime Minister Indira Gandhi had two sons: Rajiv and Sanjay. The elder, Rajiv, didn't want to follow in the political footsteps of his family (including grandfather Jawaharlal Nehru, founding prime minister of independent India). So, he became an airline pilot. Sanjay, on the other hand, was groomed by Mom to succeed her as leader of the Indian National Congress Party. Willful and aggressive, Sanjay pushed for his mother's 1975 declaration of a state of emergency—an unconstitutional abuse of power. After Sanjay's death in a 1980 plane crash, though, Rajiv agreed, reluctantly, to run for the Lok Sabha (lower house of the Indian parliament). After his mother's assassination in 1984, though, he was cast full force into the political sphere and elected prime minister. Unlike Sanjay, Rajiv was a reasonable leader, open to compromise. Yet financial scandals plagued his government and in 1989 he resigned as prime minister. He was seeking reelection to the Lok Sabha when a suicide bomber—linked to Tamil separatists in southern India—killed him. Today, his wife, Sonia, is active in Congress Party politics and continues the political legacy.

_06:: Bill and Roger Clinton: Little Rock

Like Jimmy Carter, Bill Clinton brought his own sibling of ill repute to the national spotlight. When Bill Clinton was Arkansas governor, Roger Clinton pleaded guilty to distributing cocaine and served 15 months in prison. When Bill was U.S. president, his half brother, 10 years younger, was supposedly a rock singer. After Bill left the White House, a congressional investigation in 2001 showed that much of Roger's considerable income during his brother's two terms had come from mysterious sources. His "musical gigs" overseas brought him big money from foreign governments, payments that suggest he was playing something other than rock and roll. (Clinton bashers say it was influence.) He also accepted money from organized crime figure Rosario Gambino, apparently in exchange for seeking leniency from a parole board. Hey, take "the work" when you can get it. Since Bill's White House departure, rockin' Roger's music career has fizzled.

If I Weren't Alexander (I'd Be Diogenes): Famous People Who Had Famous Heroes

Alexander the Great wanted to be Diogenes, Salvador Dalí wanted to be Napoléon, and J. Edgar Hoover wanted to be a lady. Hey, inspiration comes from strange places, so it's no wonder that even heroes have heroes. The following are three important figures and their unlikely influences.

_01:: Fathers of Their Countries

Growing up in China's Hunan province, young Mao Zedong loved to read. In fact, he liked it so much that his father, who wanted the boy to be a farmer, grew impatient. There was a less dreamy side behind the bookish Zedong, however. His heroes were military leaders, especially those who opposed established order. Though Mao concentrated on Chinese generals and great battles in Asia, he was also fascinated by ideas and stories from the Western world, including, believe it or not, the life of George Washington. In 1911, just before he turned 18, Mao joined a revolutionary army fighting Manchu authority in his province. And although he had yet to embrace the Marxist philosophy that would shape his life and China's history, the young man's stint as a soldier helped him begin to understand that he, like his hero, Washington, could use military force toward political ends.

_02:: A Mother of Innovation

Frank Zappa's early fans—most of them 13-year-old boys mesmerized by the vulgar weirdness of *Freak Out!*, his 1966 debut album—understood little about the artist. After all, Zappa came across like a zany cultural gadfly and wild-haired rock guitar hero—not the serious musician that he turned out to be. But an early clue to what was really going on lay in Zappa's frequent references to French-born composer Edgard (originally Edgar) Varèse. And while Zappa freaks didn't know that Varèse, a pioneer of electronic music, celebrated asymmetrical rhythms and dissonance, or that he died at age 81 in 1965, they did know that Zappa dug him, so he became cool by association. Over the course of Zappa's 30-year career, though—much of it as an ambitious, iconoclastic, and outright weird proponent of musical (and political) experimentation—his debt to Varèse became ever more apparent.

_03:: What'd I Say?

Born in 1944 in Sheffield, England, Joe Cocker went to work at age 16 installing gas pipes, but he was obsessed with rock and roll. And despite his appreciation for the vocal stylings of Chuck Berry, Little Richard, and Jerry Lee Lewis, young Joe fell in love with one voice that would shape his career as a music star of the 1970s and '80s—Ray Charles. Cocker said he got "hung up" on Charles, and French fans later referred to the gravel-voiced rocker as Le Petit Ray Charles. Although the blind genius's

Lies Your Mother Told You

MACBETH WAS A GOOD-FOR-NOTHIN' SOCIAL CLIMBER

Forget everything Shakespeare told you about Macbeth. The real Macbeth was a political genius who united the disparate Scottish lords and set Scotland on the path to nationhood. He was also beloved by the common people for his charity and piety and the fact that, unlike his predecessors, he preferred to rule in peace rather than involve them in disastrous wars abroad. In 1054, Malcolm, son of Duncan I (a hated egotist whom Macbeth had defeated fair and square in battle, not murdered in his sleep as Shakespeare would have it), invaded Scotland with an army of Anglo-Saxon mercenaries looking for land and power. Macbeth fought a three-year war against the invaders but was ultimately killed. As for Malcolm (III), he became one of Scotland's worst kings, and that's saying a lot; he fought numerous wars against England, losing every time, taxed the commoners to ruin, and put hated Sassenachs (Englishmen) in positions of power. Overall, one of the worst trades in the history of the British Isles.

influence can be heard in many corners of popular music, he had a particularly profound effect on boys growing up in the British Isles in the 1950s and '60s. You can note Charles's phrasing and intensity reflected in such Cocker hits as "A Little Help from My Friends" and "The Letter," but also in the vocal styles of Welsh pop star Tom Jones, Irish soul man Van Morrison, and English superstar Elton John, among others.

May I Have a Cup of Culture?
National Inferiority Complexes
and the Wars They Caused

If you think Polish jokes are bad, you should hear what they were saying about these other unsophisticated underdogs—that is, right up until they got bitten.

_01:: Macedonia v. Greece

In the fourth century BCE, the rest of Greece disdained the redneck Macedonians, and strangely enough, the Macedonians seemed to agree! Philip II, the king of Macedonia, and his son Alexander both learned the more sophisticated Ionian Greek dialect and aspired to educate themselves in the Greek style. In fact, Philip went so far as to hire the Greek philosopher Aristotle to tutor his young son (nothing's too great for my little Alexander!). The pair also wanted to reshape Macedonian culture and society along "sophisticated" Greek lines. Of course, the most logical way of making Macedonia more like Greece was to make Greece part of Macedonia, and so over the course of their reigns both Philip and Alexander brought the entire Greek peninsula under their control.

_02:: Rome v. Greece

Greek culture still carried its cachet a few hundred years later, when the rising power of Rome began to threaten the Macedonian kingdom from the west. The Romans venerated Greek culture even more than the Macedonians had, with educated upper-class Romans aspiring to read, write, and speak Greek as proof of good breeding. The Greek influence is even more evident, when you notice that Rome's public monuments are total imitations of Greek architecture. It's no wonder then that when Rome was expanding abroad, the Greeks, still resenting their Macedonian rulers, welcomed Roman intervention. At least they did at first. The Greeks figured that the Romans, respectful and assiduous students of their culture, would be honored to liberate Greece and set the Greeks free. Rather than letting the people go, however, the Romans simply took over the administration from Macedonia and incorporated Greece into their empire, marking the end of Greek independence for almost two millennia.

_03:: Arabs v. Persia

When the first Muslim Arabs came out of the Arabian Peninsula to conquer much of the known world in the seventh century CE, they were fairly simple bedouins with an oral tradition and little in the way of art or literature. Luckily, one of the first powers they encountered on leaving the deserts of the Arabian Peninsula, the Persian kingdom of the Sassanids, possessed the oldest and most refined culture in the Middle East. Hungry for Persia's wealth, great cities, material comforts, and beautiful art, the Arabs gobbled up the land beginning in 635. Within 20 years, these bedouin go-getters had incorporated the entire kingdom, including Afghanistan, and since they'd immediately adopted Persian art and literature as the gold standard of education and good breeding, its reach soon extended all the way from the Atlantic Ocean to the borders of India.

Touch of Evil

After General Leopoldo Galtieri seized control of Argentina in 1981, he ill-advisedly took the nearby Falkland Islands by force—a foolish move. Britain's Margaret Thatcher wasted no time regaining the land, and the general was quickly disposed of in a follow-up coup.

_04:: Mongols v. China

In the 13th century CE, the Mongol tribes of Central Asia had no written language, no cities, no knowledge of agriculture, and no real notion of the geography of the globe outside their own small corner of it. China of the Sung dynasty, by contrast, was the oldest continuously ruled empire in the world, with a highly refined culture and a complicated, evolved social structure that was the product of thousands of years of development. After all, Chinese agriculture produced enormous amounts of food—principally rice—supporting an extremely wealthy aristocracy and a Sung emperor who lived in opulent luxury. But all the money and refinement in the world couldn't protect the Sung dynasty from the maelstrom the Mongols unleashed on them. As masters of archery and cavalry combat, the Mongols, led

by Genghis Khan, swarmed over China in 1211 CE, killing millions of Chinese and establishing their bloody rule for decades to come.

_05:: England v. France

In the 15th century, France was the uncontested center of western European civilization. Paris had been the clearinghouse of medieval scholarship with its famous university at the Sorbonne, and France boasted the most productive agriculture; the largest population; the most creative painters, architects, and artists; and the most developed code of chivalry. As for England? During this time the nation was simply a small, poor, damp little backwater ruled by a French royal family descended from William the Conqueror. And believe it or not, the English aristocracy and royal family were all but French—they spoke French, drank French wine, ate French food, wore French clothes, read and talked about books by French scholars, and visited France frequently. So when a dispute over the succession to the French monarchy gave King Henry V an opening to conquer France, he naturally went for it—and won! Henry was crowned king of France shortly before his death in 1422.

_06:: Japan v. China

The Mongols weren't the only people attracted to China's refined, developed culture. In fact, the nation's sophisticated ways were alluring enough to draw the attention of another warlike neighbor, Japan, several times throughout history. And the effects are evident. The Chinese written language was adopted in its entirety by Japan; Buddhism, which dominated Japan for a long period, was a Chinese import, with Japanese Buddhist monks going to study in China; the Japanese borrowed Chinese architectural styles and governmental structures; and literate, well-educated Japanese studied Chinese literature. But as recently as the 1930s, even after Japan had modernized its economy and built a highly efficient armed forces, this Japanese obsession with China manifested itself in the desire to conquer and control the country. Sadly, the brutal attack resulted in the deaths of tens of millions of Chinese in the Second World War.

It's a Slanderful World: Well-spread Fabrications

The fifth-century-BCE dramatist Sophocles once said that "a lie never lives to be old." Clearly, Sophocles never heard the one about suicidal rodents, or about the world-famous animator frozen in suspended animation. Here's hoping that, at the very least, these lies don't live to be any older.

_01:: Elephants and Mice

In spite of what you may have seen at the circus, elephants aren't afraid of mice. Actually, they're not afraid of anything, which is why it's not all that hard for poachers to kill them for ivory. For decades, circuses have featured elephants rearing up and trumpeting with fear upon catching "sight" of a scurrying mouse. But in reality, the elephants probably can't even *see* the mouse in question—they have notoriously poor eyesight. Due to their excellent memories, however, elephants *can* learn a variety of tricks, including rearing up on their hind legs when ordered to do so by whip-brandishing circus trainers. And while we're dispelling elephant rumors: There's no such thing as an elephant graveyard. When elephants are ready to die, they just fall down and do it, like the rest of us.

_02:: Betsy Ross

In all likelihood, Betsy Ross did not design, or for that matter even sew, the first post–Union Jack American flag. Ross, a seamstress who took over her husband's upholstery business after he died fighting in the Revolutionary War, purportedly sewed the flag based on a pencil sketch from George Washington himself. But no evidence has ever been found to back up the Ross family story. In fact, most historians believe the flag was either based on the British East India Company's flag or designed by Francis Hopkinson, a signer of the Declaration of Independence and early member of Congress. Regardless of who designed it, the Continental Congress officially adopted the Stars and Stripes in 1777, on June 14, which, in an amazing coincidence, happens to be Flag Day.

_03:: Disney's Remains

Despite the ubiquitous rumor to the contrary, Walt Disney was not cryogenically frozen after his death. Disney, who won more Academy Awards (26) than any other person, expressed a desire to be cremated, and his wish was carried out two days after his death on December 15, 1966. There's scant evidence, in fact, that Disney even knew that cryogenic freezing existed. At any rate, it's highly unlikely that cryogenic freezing could have saved Walt. Putting aside the fact that most scientists think frozen bodies will never be resurrectable, Disney's lung cancer necessitated the removal of his left lung a month before his death. So even if future scientists could have brought Walt back from the dead, he would have been awfully short of breath.

Touch of Evil

It was a fascinating story how struggling musician Charles Manson auditioned for The Monkees back in 1965. Fascinating, and false! Manson was behind bars when the tryouts took place.

_04:: Lemmings

The poor, oft-maligned lemmings—you couldn't blame them for being suicidal, if they are, which they aren't. The notion of lemming suicide extends back at least to Freud, who in *Civilization and Its Discontents* (1929) explained the human death instinct in the context of lemmings. But the notion didn't really take hold until Walt Disney's 1958 so-called documentary *White Wilderness* hit the big screen. For his film, the lovable animator shipped dozens of lemmings to Alberta, Canada, herded them off a cliff, filmed them falling to their deaths, and passed it off as nonfiction. In reality, though, lemmings aren't suicidal. They're just dumb. Lemming populations explode in four-year cycles in Scandinavia, and when the tundra gets crowded, they seek out new land. Being stupid, they sometimes fall off cliffs, but not on purpose.

_05:: Rice at Weddings

These days, it's become common practice for eco-friendly couples not to feature rice throwing at their weddings. After all, the science-deficient theory claims, birds eat the rice, which expands in their stomachs and causes them to explode. Rice farmers from Thailand to Arkansas probably *wish* that rice-eating birds blew up, but quite simply, they don't. The fact is, nuptial rice poses no more danger to birds than combining pop rocks and soda does to kids. So, how'd the rumor come about? It all started in 1988, when old Ann Landers discouraged readers from the practice. Of course, the USA Rice Federation (motto: "Proving there is a federation for everything") immediately debunked Landers's story, but, surprisingly (and disappointingly), Ann Landers had a broader readership than the USA Rice Federation.

_06:: Van Gogh's Ear

In the fierce competition for the title of History's Most Tortured Artist, Vincent van Gogh certainly makes a compelling case. Impoverished, unloved, and underappreciated in his time, van Gogh led a miserable life, potently symbolized by his missing left ear. We've all heard the story: He chopped it off and Pony Express-ed it to a prostitute in a perverse act of love—here is an artist so tortured, even the prostitutes didn't love him! But wait! He didn't chop off his *entire* ear—just the lower half of it. And it wasn't about women at all. In a fit of rage after an argument with friend and fellow artist Paul Gauguin, van Gogh cut his ear to symbolize the end of their friendship, believ-

ing that Gauguin had grown "deaf" to his needs. Some claim van Gogh later visited a brothel to give the half-ear to a prostitute named Rachel (hey, we never said he wasn't crazy), but he certainly never *mailed* anything!

Playing the Palace:
Showy Leaders and the
Envious Imitators They Inspired

A smaller-than-average castle can give a guy a complex, so it's no wonder so many world leaders suffer from palace envy. The following are three characters who were pretty eager to overspend in an attempt to overcompensate.

_01:: Francis I and Henry VIII

In the first half of the 16th century, the kings of France and England were more than contemporaries, enemies, or allies. They were personal competitors. England's Henry VIII, especially, felt it important to keep up with French counterpart Francis I, and boy did it show. When the two were vigorous young men, handsome Hank fancied that his impressive physique outshone that of flashy Frank. But this was more than just a beauty competition. When Henry went on a state visit to France in 1520, he had an extravagant pavilion of gold cloth (like a luxury tent village) built to match that of Francis, nearby. The three-week diplomatic campout, known as the Field of Cloth of Gold, was a daily orgy of expensively competitive pageantry that nearly bankrupted both countries. The competition didn't end there. Later, Henry spent heavily on arts and

architecture, trying not to be outdistanced by the sophistication of Francis's capital.

_02:: Louis XIV and Leopold I and...

If a finance minister builds a house bigger than the king's, the king gets suspicious. That isn't exactly what happened to Nicolas Fouquet, who in 1661 threw a party for his boss, the "Sun King" of France, at Fouquet's magnificent new chateau, Vaux-le-Vicomte. Impressed, Louis XIV moved straight past the suspicion phase, and threw his host in jail. Then, he put Fouquet's former architects and builders to work on the royal estate outside Paris. Completed in 1682, the huge and incredibly ornate Palace of Versailles inspired envy in monarchs everywhere. In response, Leopold I of the Austro-Hungarian Empire commissioned a "hunting lodge" outside Vienna, the

1,440-room Schönbrunn Palace, completed in 1695. Other monarchs who retaliated with a Versailles of their own: "Mad" King Ludwig II of Bavaria (Castle Herrenchiemsee) and Empress Elizabeth of Russia (the Winter Palace).

Touch of Evil

As America's fifth president, James Monroe was so flattered by comments about his resemblance to George Washington that he dressed in the same style the Father of Our Country did. Sadly, that style was way out of date by then.

_03:: Richard Nixon and Queen Elizabeth II

U.S. president Richard Nixon liked a bit of pomp (with occasional circumstance). After all, Tricky Dick often saw other heads of state protected by guards in bright-colored uniforms with shiny trim or tall fur hats (as in Britain's famous Beefeaters outside Queen Elizabeth's official London residence). But what did the White House have? Guys in dark, plain security uniforms. Wanting a piece of the regal action, Nixon ordered a redesign of the outfits worn by White House guards (Secret Service Uniformed Division). Unveiled in 1970, the new duds featured gold-trimmed tunics and rigid, peaked hats reminiscent of 19th-century Prussia. The royalist look didn't go over so well with Americans. Critics howled. Comedians

Scandalicious

CAMBODIAN WIVES LASH OUT AGAINST ADULTERY (WITH BATTERY ACID)

Adultery is frowned upon in most societies, but in Cambodia it can mean taking your life into your hands. During the late 1990s, a rash of attacks by high-society ladies against their husbands' mistresses broke out. In the most famous case, Bun Ray, the wife of Prime Minister Hun Sen, hired hit men to murder Piseth Pilika, a Cambodian film star who was reputed to be assisting the prime minister with his homework after hours. Another infamous incident occured on December 5, 1999, when Tan Chhay Marina, a teenage actress and singer, was horribly disfigured when five liters of battery acid were dumped on her by the wife of Svay Sitha, an undersecretary of state.

snickered. And the White House immediately threw out the Prussian hats. Within a few years the fancy duds (along with their chief proponent) were retired entirely.

Who Throws a Shoe? Honestly!
Grossly Mismatched Warfare Arsenals

We know all's supposedly fair in love and war, but somehow these conditions still seem remarkably stilted.

_01:: Romans v. Celts

At the beginning of their long march to supremacy, the Romans had an early advantage because they knew how to make steel weapons that were much stronger than their opponents' iron weapons. Iron swords and spearheads were relatively simple to make, requiring that the blacksmith melt down iron ore in a furnace, hammer the metal into a blade, and then shape and sharpen it on a forge. To make steel, the Romans understood, the blade had to be put back in the furnace for a long period to allow carbon from the coals to infiltrate the metal, making it stronger. The results for their enemies were often disastrous: in a series of battles the Romans fought against the Celts, who were armed with iron weapons, the Celts' swords became so badly deformed that the Celtic warriors had to bend them back to their original shape over their knees in the middle of combat.

_02:: English v. French
at Agincourt

When the English, led by King Henry V, fought the French in the battle of Agincourt, they had a secret weapon: Welsh subjects trained in the use of the longbow. Amazingly, these weapons of war were simply five-foot-high yew arcs that could be used to shoot eight arrows a minute, each arrow about three feet long. And the rapid-fire assault was too much for the French. With a total force of about 5,000 archers, Henry slaughtered the pride of French chivalry before Genovese crossbowmen in French employ were even in range. In fact, it was said that the ground was covered with so many white feathers from the arrow fletching that it looked like snow.

_03:: Spanish v. Aztecs and Incas

When the Spanish invaded Mexico and Peru in the early 16th century, they wielded weaponry far superior to anything the Aztecs and Incas could have imagined. The 600 Spaniards who landed at the site of modern-day Vera Cruz in 1519, under the command of Hernando Cortés, carried firearms—muskets—and small cannons, and rode horses, all of which terrified the Aztec natives. And though the Aztecs fiercely fought back on foot with swords and spears made out of sharp pieces of obsidian, or black volcanic glass, set in pieces of wood, ultimately they were no match for the Spaniards. Despite Cortés's encountering a few setbacks, there was no contest, and he managed to subdue five million Aztecs with his tiny army. Similarly, beginning in 1530, the Spanish conquistador

Francisco Pizarro subdued the Inca empire with 180 soldiers, fighting a native army of about 40,000 men.

_04:: English v. Mahdi in Sudan

When the forces of British general Charles Gordon were surrounded and eventually destroyed by Islamic fundamentalist tribesmen at Khartoum, Sudan, in 1885, the blow to British prestige was tremendous. In fact, the imperialist nation was so embarrassed that it decided the event demanded a total and overwhelming response. To get revenge, the British shipped a well-trained army to fight the native Muslim rebels in central Sudan. But the army wasn't just well trained; they were well armed, and were even carrying Gatling guns—prototype machine guns that drew ammunition from a long straight clip filing through the firing chamber. The result at the battle of Omdurman in 1898 was decisive and horrendous, resulting in the slaughter of tens of thousands of native tribesmen with virtually no British casualties.

_05:: Germans v. Poles

One of the better-known instances of grossly mismatched weaponry in warfare occurred in 1939 when Nazi Germany under the dictatorship of Adolf Hitler invaded Poland. At the time Poland was an underdeveloped nation that had become independent only 20 years before. Itching to get his hands on more real estate, and determined to "restore" Germany's "original" borders, Hitler sent modern German tanks, at the head of regular and mechanized infantry, crashing into Poland. Simultaneously, the Führer sent the German air force to pound Polish cities from the sky. The Stuka dive-bombers railed on the virtually undefended towns, and killed tens of thousands of people in Warsaw alone. It wasn't exactly a fair fight. The impoverished Poles fielded horse-mounted cavalry and peasant brigades armed with old-fashioned muskets in an effort to resist the Germans. Their air effort was even more pathetic: the few antiquated World War I–era biplanes were no match for the Germans. In three weeks, Poland was finished.

They Put the "No" in Nobel: 7 Geniuses and 1 Entire Science That Never Won the Big One

Scientists are supposed to be above petty politics and popularity contests, right? Nope. Here are a few bright bulbs that never got the fancy Nobel gold medallion (or the 10 million Swedish krona that go with it). And you thought the Oscars were bad.

_01:: Joan Robinson, Economics

Great Britain's Joan Robinson may be one of the most exciting figures in the history of "the Dismal Science." An acolyte of the great John Maynard Keynes, her work covered a wide range of economic topics, from neoclassicism to Keynes's general theory to Marxian theory. Not to mention, her notion of imperfect competition still shows up in every Econ 101 class. Add to that the fact that Robinson's greatest work, *The Accumulation of Capital,* was published way back in 1956 but is still widely used as an economics textbook. So why no Nobel? The easy answer is that she's a female, and no female has ever won the Nobel in Economics. Others say that Robinson's work over her career was too eclectic, rather than hyper-focused like that of so many other laureates. Still others claim that she was undesirable as a laureate because of her vocal praise for the Chinese Cultural Revolution, a thoroughly anti-intellectual enterprise.

_02:: James Joyce and _03:: Marcel Proust, Literature

One wrote *Ulysses* and *Finnegan's Wake,* almost universally regarded as two of the most bril-liant works of the 20th century (in the case of *Ulysses, the* most brilliant). And the other is, well, Marcel Proust. Proust's towering work, *A La Recherche du Temps Perdu (In Search of Lost Time,* or, sometimes, *Remembrance of Things Past)* is considered one of the greatest literary achievements ever, combining seven novels and 2,000 characters for a celebration of life, consciousness, and sexuality spanning 3,200 pages. James Joyce's works and stream-of-consciousness style are the basis of countless college courses, doctoral theses, and poetic ru-minations. But the writings of Proust and Joyce were probably just too controversial and "out there" for the more conservative Nobel com-mittees of their day. And Nobel's stricture against posthumous awards hasn't exactly helped, especially since the influence of these two artists has continued to grow long after their deaths. Most ironic, Proust and Joyce have been major influences on many writers who went on to win Nobels themselves, like Saul Bellow, Samuel Beckett, Jean-Paul Sartre, Albert Camus, and Hermann Hesse. Other lit-erary giants who have gotten the Nobel shaft? Evelyn Waugh, Jorge Luis Borges, Bertold Brecht, Graham Greene, Henry James, Vladimir Nabokov, and Simone de Beauvoir, to name a few.

_04:: Dmitri Mendeleev, Chemistry

Why would this guy deserve a Nobel Prize for chemistry? After all, his only achievement was to devise the entire periodic table of elements, the miracle of organization and inference on which all of modern chemistry is based. Mendeleev's table was so good, it even predicted the existence of elements that hadn't yet been discovered. But here's where politics rears its ugly head. In 1906, Mendeleev was selected by the prize committee to win the honor, but the Royal Swedish Academy of Sciences stepped in and overturned the decision. Why? The intervention was spearheaded by Swedish chemist Svante Arrhenius, who had himself won the prize in 1903 for his theory of electrolytic dissociation. Mendeleev had been an outspoken critic of the theory, and Arrhenius seized the opportunity as the perfect chance to squeeze a few sour grapes.

_05:: Jules-Henri Poincaré, Physics

Although Poincaré was a mathematician, his genius was too universal to be confined to one category. Sure, he came up with all sorts of mathematical theories with crazy names: algebraic topology, abelian functions, and Diophantine equations. But he was into physics, too. Poincaré laid the foundation for modern chaos theory and even beat Einstein to the punch on certain facets of the theory of special relativity. And one of his math problems, the Poincaré conjecture, even remained unsolved for nearly 100 years! So why was Henri overlooked for the Big One? Due to Alfred Nobel's stipulation that his prizes go to those whose discoveries have been of practical ben-

efit to mankind, the Nobel committees have often been accused of rewarding experimental discoveries over purely theoretical advances. Poincaré's work in physics seems to be a victim of that prejudice.

_06:: Raymond Damadian, Medicine

Lots of deserving folks have been passed over for the Nobel, but few were as vocal about it as 2003 runner-up Raymond V. Damadian. He was the brain behind the science of magnetic resonance imaging (MRI), a technique that completely revolutionized the detection and treatment of cancer. But the 2003 Prize for Medicine went to Paul Lauterbur and Peter Mansfield, two scientists who expanded on Damadian's discovery. Enraged at the slight, Damadian ran full-page ads in the the *New York Times* and *Washington Post* featuring a photo of the Nobel Prize medal upside down and the headline "The Shameful Wrong That Must Be Righted." The ad featured quotes from other scientists backing up Damadian's claim, even a letter of protest to be cut out, signed, and mailed to the Nobel Committee. Some claim Damadian was slighted because his fundamentalist Christian belief in creationism made him anathema to the scientific community. Others say it was because his discovery wasn't really useful in medicine until Lauterbur and Mansfield improved upon it. Either way, 2003 left the poor scientist Nobel-less.

_07:: Mahatma Gandhi, Peace

The Susan Lucci of Nobel Peace Prize contenders, Mohandas "Mahatma" (Great-Souled) Gandhi was nominated like crazy: 1937, 1938, 1939, 1947, and 1948. He certainly deserved it, as his nonviolent methods helped kick the British out of India and became the model for future Peace Prize laureates like Martin Luther King Jr. Gandhi's final nomination came in 1948, and he was the odds-on favorite to win it that year. However, the "Mahatma" was assassinated just a few days before the deadline. Since the Nobel Prize is never awarded posthumously, the prize for peace went unawarded that year on the grounds that there was "no suitable living candidate." The decision was also motivated by the fact that Gandhi left no heirs or foundations to which his prize money could go.

_08:: Oh, and Anybody in Mathematics

When dynamite inventor (that's not a comment on his abilities; he really did invent dynamite) Alfred Nobel stipulated in his will that his fortune be used to establish a fund to award five annual prizes "to those who, during the preceding year, shall have conferred the greatest benefit on mankind," he mysteri-

ously left out mathematics. All kinds of theories have popped up to explain the omission, the most salacious of which claim that Nobel hated all mathematicians because his wife was schtupping one on the side. Nope. The most likely reasons for Nobel's ditching math are (1) He simply didn't like math all that much, and (2) Sweden already had a big, fancy prize for mathematics, bestowed by the journal *Acta Mathematica*. Although math is still a Nobel bridesmaid, a prize for economics was added in 1968, thereby giving the extremely boring sciences their due.

Touch of Evil

Before making a bang with dynamite and creating his famous prizes, Alfred Nobel lost his company to bankruptcy and *his brother to a nitroglycerine explosion.*

The Grass Is Definitely Greener: Tiny Nations That Were Happy to Colonize Africa

3

Historians call the gobbling up of territory at the end of the 19th century "the Scramble for Africa." And while the big European powerhouses—Germany, England, France—got much of the good stuff, there were plenty of scraps left for the little guys, too. Here are a few tiny nations that made out like bandits.

_01:: Portugal

While most people think of Portugal lurking in its big brother Spain's shadows, the tiny nation was quite the world power in the 15th and 16th centuries, and had early established outposts in West Africa. By the 1880s, however, Portugal's star had fallen, and it moved to being a second-tier global player. Still, it was pretty crafty in its imperial ways. While the big countries were occupied with bickering with one other, Portugal decided it was still occupied with, well, occupying. It took over most of both Angola and Mozambique, and by 1900 the nation controlled about 8% of the continent. Because it was a poor country, though, it could do little for its colonies except exploit them, which it did with gusto. In 1961, revolutions that had been brewing for years finally burst out. Five years of war were followed by seven years of unrest, and in 1974, Mozambique won its independence. In 1975, the Portuguese wisely left Angola and turned out the lights on their imperial ways.

_02:: Italy

Amazingly enough, Italy has the distinction of being the only European country to have had its butt kicked by an African nation, when it tried to conquer Ethiopia. How so? Italy had formed a colony in neighboring Eritrea. And while they were negotiating a friendship treaty with Ethiopia, the Italians cleverly decided that simultaneously invading the African nation would be a good way to seal their pact. Not so. In the Battle of Adova in 1896, Ethiopians under Emperor Menelik II soundly defeated the Italians. The loss didn't sit well, obviously, and in 1936, Italy attacked Ethiopia again. This time it was literally airplanes and tanks against spears, and the Italians held on for five years. With the outbreak of World War II, though, British troops and Ethiopian freedom fighters drove the Italians out, and expelled Italy from Eritrea and Italian Somaliland, too. So much for the Roman Empire's comeback.

_03:: Belgium

If there was a single infernal spark to the Scramble for Africa, it was King Leopold II of Belgium. After all, it was Leo who convened meetings of European nations to compromise on divvying up the continent. In fact, the Belgian king was so anxious to build an empire, he used his own money to buy a huge section of the Congo River Basin, 80 times the size of Belgium itself! As exploitation was the name of the colony-building game, Leopold followed the recipe to a T. The monarch literally bled his African kingdom, mutilating and torturing its residents when they failed to meet crop quotas or pay taxes. By 1908, however, the international outcry was so loud over Leopold's excesses that he was forced to transfer control of the Congo to the Belgian government. From then on, the Belgian government ruled the area, mostly badly, until 1960, when it was finally given its independence.

Touch of Evil

In 1821, the politically powerful American Colonization Society literally bought *what would become a country*. The land purchase in western Africa provided a home for freed slaves from America, and the citizens formed the independent republic of Liberia in 1847.

Musicians Who Always Felt Cheated

Sometimes it isn't just the guitar that's gently weeping. The following six musicians definitely felt they got the short end of the stick as far as their bands were concerned.

_01:: Syd "Wish You Were Here" Barrett (1946–)

During the early 1960s, a London art student named Syd Barrett teamed up with four kids from the Regent Street School of Architecture to form an R & B group. Barrett named the band the Pink Floyd Sound after a blues record by Pink Anderson and Floyd Council, and the group was off and running. Trading their sound in for a psychedelic one, the band became a huge hit around London. By 1968, however, Barrett's excessive drug use and mood swings made his onstage and offstage behavior a little too erratic and strange. The band brought in David Gilmour to cover the performances and Barrett was sacked within the year. Of course, Gilmour brought a heft of talent with him, and in 1973, Pink Floyd became an international success with the release of "Dark Side of the Moon." Some years later, they achieved superstardom with *The Wall* album and movie. At the same time, Barrett was working on solo projects but continued in a downward spiral of bad health. While not much of a consolation, Pink Floyd did dedicate their 1975 hit "Shine On, You Crazy Diamond" to Barrett, a cut off their album *Wish You Were Here*.

THOMAS CARLYLE'S HORRIBLE-TERRIBLE, NO-GOOD, VERY BAD DAY

Political scientist and historian John Stuart Mill showed up at his close friend Thomas Carlyle's house on March 6, 1835, with the only manuscript of Carlyle's *French Revolution*. It was a single burned scrap of paper. Why just one? Because Carlyle's manuscript had inadvertently been thrown into the fire—probably by Mill's maid. Mill apologized profusely, and Carlyle responded with remarkable kindness and empathy. After mourning the lost masterpiece, Carlyle restarted the project and eventually finished rewriting *French Revolution* in 1837. Published in three volumes, its first reviewer was Mill, who may or may not have noticed the abundance of "fire" imagery in the rewritten manuscript. Either way, Mill tried to make up for his maid's carelessness by hailing the book as a great work of genius. (Indeed, Dickens used Carlyle's book extensively when writing *A Tale of Two Cities*.) But their friendship never recovered from the burned manuscript—Mill went on to become a leading progressive member of Parliament, whose *On Liberty* is now required reading in political science courses, while Carlyle became something of an angry bigot.

_02:: Pete "I Want to Hold Your Hand" Best (1941–)

Having been the original drummer for an upstart Liverpool group called the Silver Beetles, Pete Best was sacked in favor of another, more experienced drummer named Richard Starkey, better known as Ringo Starr. As fate would have it, the Silver Beetles changed their name to the Beatles and became the best-known group in the history of rock and roll. Best's mom, who ran the Casbah Club in Liverpool, was their initial booking agent, landing them a two-month gig in Hamburg. But while in Germany the young group happened upon Ringo, and when they returned to London both Paul McCartney and George Harrison asked their new manager, Brian Epstein, to get rid of Best. On August 23, 1962, poor Pete found out that

he was no longer a Beatle, and although he later sued Ringo for libel, he received nothing for his early years with the band. Today he tours with his own group (he even put out an album under the tricky title *Best of the Beatles*) and freely discusses his sacking, although he doesn't accept the theories—Ringo's superior drumming, McCartney's jealousy, or his own unreliability. In the end, it was only John Lennon who ever sent Best a message about the way the Fab Three had treated him.

_03:: Keith "Can't Get No Satisfaction" Richards (1943–)

Although Keith Richards first met Mick Jagger in elementary school in 1950, it wasn't until 10 years later when they ran into each other that they found they shared a deep interest in American blues and R & B. Within the next two years they formed the Rolling Stones and began to proclaim themselves "the World's Greatest Rock-and-Roll Band." Of course, they backed up the claim with a long string of hits and concert performances. However, by the mid-1980s, Richards had grown resentful of Jagger's fame and the fact that Mick was receiving the majority of the credit for the Stones' success. Richards had always said that while the Stones existed he would never do a solo album and became angry that Jagger was performing outside the group. By 1986, the two were no longer speaking to each other and the group went into hiatus for the next three years. Richards and Jagger publicly went after each other in the press and with songs on their respective solo albums. In 1989, the two decided to end the feud and got together in Barbados to write a new album, which led to the Stones' first U.S. tour in over eight years, grossing over $144 million. Of course, the jealousy's probably still lurking. After all, Mick was recently knighted for his service to the British Empire, while Richards remains a rock star commoner. He just can't get no satisfaction.

_04:: Johnny "I'm a Lazy Sod" Rotten (1956–   )

In 1975, the 19-year-old John Lydon met a young entrepreneur, Malcolm McLaren, at McLaren's fashion boutique in London called Sex. McLaren, who was putting a rock group together, was on the hunt for a lead singer. Happy to oblige, Lydon accepted the position even though he'd never sung before...and somehow Britain's most notorious punk group, the Sex Pistols, came into existence. With his outrageously rude manner and his total lack of

personal hygiene, Lydon was soon dubbed Johnny Rotten. Because of their lyrics, the group was soon banned on British radio, but they still garnered a huge following. Of course, they garnered huge egos as well. Rotten soon became disenchanted with McLaren's management style and inability to move the group to a higher level of stardom. At the same time, he didn't feel that he was receiving his just due as a top performer, and after a concert in San Francisco in 1978, Rotten officially broke up the group, claiming that all of rock and roll and been played and now it was officially dead. The legal system, however, was not. Johnny Rotten eventually reverted to his given name and, teaming up with the other Sex Pistols, successfully sued McLaren for $1.44 million in back royalties.

Touch of Evil

As founder and original lead singer of The Supremes, Florence Ballard was more than a little peeved when Berry Gordy moved Diana Ross into the front spot. So, what good did her tantrums do? Ballard was ultimately fired and faded into obscurity, while lady Di became a Motown legend.

_05:: George "You Never Give Me Your Money" Harrison (1943–2001)

Known as "the quiet Beatle," George Harrison, who was the youngest of the lot, was also arguably the best musician among the Fab Four. Having attended school in Liverpool at one time or another with both Paul McCartney and John Lennon, Harrison started jamming with the two, forming a group called the Quarrymen, later to become the Silver Beetles, and eventually just the plain old Beatles. Harrison, who played lead guitar and occasionally sang lead ("Roll Over Beethoven"), was the first Beatle to get involved in Eastern religion. However, over the years, he found it more and more difficult for the group to take his compositions seriously and feature them on the albums. Interestingly, some of Harrison's works such as "I Need You," "While My Guitar Gently Weeps," "Here Comes the Sun," and especially "Something," are considered among the Beatles' greatest hits. By 1970, Harrison's resentment of his second-class status within the group had grown to the point that it became one of the factors that caused the Beatles to disband.

_06:: Big Mama Thornton (1926–1984)

In 1953, while playing at New York's Apollo Theater as part of the "Hot Harlem Revue,"

Thornton was asked by composers Jerry Lieber and Mike Stoller to record a song they had written for her. Thornton recorded "Hound Dog" and the single quickly sold nearly two million copies. As we all know, though, a young rockabilly recording artist with Sun Records named Elvis Presley also recorded said song and the rest is history. For her recording of "Hound Dog" and the two million copies sold, Thornton received one check for a whopping total of $500. Of course, that wasn't her only hit. Big Mama's song "Ball and Chain" became a huge hit for her in the 1950s. However, most of us remember that tune as the version recorded in the 1960s by another booming voice—Janis Joplin's. Like so many African American artists before her, Big Mama Thornton never received the financial and historical rewards she was due.

Oedipus Redux:
Men Who Tried to Outdo Their Dads

It's always tough to follow in your father's footsteps, particularly if Pops had big feet. Here are four guys who observed the massive footprints, and still decided to give it a shot.

_01:: Alexander the Great (356–323 BCE)

If Alexander was great, his old man was at least really pretty good. After all, Philip II did seize the throne of Macedon from his nephew,

reorganize the army, and conquer Greece at the age of 46. "My father will get ahead of me in everything, and will leave nothing great for me to do," Alexander reportedly whined. But Philip was killed during a wedding party brawl before he could put his plan to conquer the Persian Empire into operation. At age 20, Alexander took the throne, and he and his dad's well-trained armies not only conquered Persia, but also India and just about all of the known world. Not bad. And nice of Dad to leave the young Alexander something to do.

_02:: John Quincy Adams (1767–1848)

Unlike Alexander the Great, John Q. had a good relationship with his pa. Not only that, but they seemed to follow similar paths. John Adams had had a long diplomatic career and served as the country's first vice president and second president. Clearly, the apple didn't fall too far from the tree. Like his dad, John Q. was a veteran diplomat. And both fared similarly in their runs for the presidency, as in barely squeaking past their opponents on their way to the big house. But while Dad retired after being defeated for a second term, John Q. was elected to Congress. He served for 18 years, until he was fatally stricken while sitting at his House desk. Unfortunately for the Adams family, two Adamses were apparently plenty when it came to White House material. One of Q.'s three sons, Charles Francis, became a distinguished diplomat. As for the other two, one died of alcoholism and another became a heavy drinker who jumped or fell from a ship in New York Harbor.

_03:: Johann Strauss Jr. (1825–1899)

Junior was the oldest of five sons, and Johann Senior had no interest in his eldest being a musician. After all, he himself was a composer, orchestra leader, and leading Viennese waltz maestro, and he knew the musician's life to be a tough one. Be a banker, Pops said. But Junior wasn't having it. At the age of six Strauss the mouse tried to squeak out his first waltz, but by 19 he was conducting his own dance band in a Viennese restaurant. In 1845, Strauss the smaller became conductor of the city's second militia band, and a bit of father-son rivalry ensued. Pops was, after all, conductor of the first militia band, so for five years the two had a battle of the bands. All ended well enough, though. After Strauss Senior died, Junior was left sans competition at the top of the waltzing world.

_04:: Barry Bonds (1964–   )

Whatever else he was capable of accomplishing, Barry Bonds is baseball pedigree, and the kid was born to play America's game. Consider the facts: Not only did his dad, Bobby, play for 14 years in the major leagues, but his godfather was none other than the legendary Willie Mays. As a kid, Barry didn't much care for his father, who played for seven different teams and was often away from home. But whatever youthful ambivalence he had toward Dad was gone by the time Barry made the majors himself in 1986. And there's no question that both nature and nurture must have played a role in Bonds's development. In the 100-years-plus history of baseball, only four men have hit at least 300 home runs and stolen 300 bases in their careers. Three of them are Willie Mays, Bobby Bonds—and Barry Bonds.

Johnson Jealousy: Women Who Disguised Themselves as Men to Succeed

As sharp, determined women, these five gals didn't let the "It's a man's world" mantra dull their ambitions. Instead, they pulled their pants on one leg at a time, just like the guys, then set out to tackle their dreams.

_01:: Anne Bonney (1700–?)

The daughter of a big-shot South Carolina plantation owner, Anne fell in love with a sailor and went off to sea. But then her love life took an unusual turn—she fell in love with a pirate, Captain John "Calico Jack" Rackham. One of the most feared buccaneers of the day, Bonney dressed as a man, and shared Rackham's pirating adventures. But that's just the start of it. Rackham's Bonney, who seemed to be lying all over the ocean, found herself attracted to one of his lieutenants . . . only the officer turned out to be a disguised woman named Mary Read. In 1722, Rackham's ship was captured, and Bonney and Read were sentenced to hang. But—surprise—they were both found to be pregnant, and British law forbade executing pregnant women. Bonney escaped the gallows only to disappear into the mists of history.

_02:: Deborah Sampson (1760–1827)

Standing tall at 5 feet 8 inches and strong from years as an indentured servant, Deborah Sampson didn't have much trouble enlisting in the Continental Army in 1781. That is, until she got drunk and spilled her secret. Undaunted, she reenlisted under her dead brother's name and served with distinction for three years. Amazingly, even bullet wounds didn't prove to be Sampson's undoing. Once wounded in the thigh, she decided to remove the musket ball herself rather than jeopardize her secret. When she caught a fever, however, a doctor finally discovered the truth, and she was honorably discharged. In 1792, the state of Massachusetts paid her back wages for her service, and in 1804, with the help of an old friend, Paul Revere, she was awarded a veteran's pension by Congress.

_03:: Sarah R. Wakeman (1843–1864)

At least 400 women fought in the Civil War as men, but Wakeman got a head start on most of them. A farmer's daughter, she disguised herself as a man to get a job on a coal barge. Then, for a $152 bounty—or about a year's wages—she joined the Union Army in August 1862. Most of her stretch was spent in non-combat situations, but Sarah did fight in at least one battle. In 1864, our young patriot was stricken with dysentery and died in a New Orleans military hospital. But her secret wasn't revealed till years later. Her gravestone reads "Private Lyons Wakeman," and her identity surfaced only when her letters home were brought to light a century later. "I am as independent as a hog on ice," she wrote in one letter. Or as a woman in this man's army.

_04:: James Miranda Stuart Barry (1795?–1865)

Barry wanted to be a doctor in the worst way, which for a woman in the early 19th century meant pretending to be a man. Thus disguised, she enrolled at Edinburgh University, graduating at the tender age of 15. In 1813, Barry joined the British army, and by the time she retired in 1859, she had served all over the world and risen to the rank of senior inspector general. In fact, Barry is credited with performing the first successful caesarean section in the British Empire while in South Africa. Known as a skilled surgeon, and as a grump, she's recorded to have fought at least one duel and also publicly scolded Florence Nightingale. And while there was speculation about Barry's sexual preferences during her life, her gender itself stayed private until after her death.

_05:: Billy Tipton (1914–1989)

Dorothy Tipton wanted to swing, so at the age of 19, the Oklahoma City–born kitten reinvented herself as a jazz cat: the saxophone- and piano-playing Billy Tipton. A popular nightclub entertainer in the Pacific Northwest, Tipton played in big bands and fronted her own trio. More amazing, she had five common-law wives and three adopted sons. According to biographer Diane Wood Middlebrook, Tipton concealed her gender by using a prosthetic male organ, binding her breasts and having sex only in the dark. Even more amazingly, she explained it all away with vague references to "past accidents." Of course, the truth came out after Tipton's death when someone leaked the story to a Spokane newspaper and the dirt started a bitter fight among her survivors, thus ending a splendid deception on a somewhat sour note.

Touch of Evil

In 1950, 12-year-old Kathryn Johnston tucked her hair under a cap and tried out for the King's Dairy Little League team of Corning, New York, under the androgynous handle Tubby Johnston. She made the cut and clued her coach in to her secret two weeks into the season.

To the Victor Go the Oils:
Early Middle East Conflicts

Sometimes the oil looks greener on the other side. Long before huge reservoirs of oil were discovered in Persia in 1908, the Middle East was prize territory. Massive, waterless deserts, you say? One hundred twenty degrees in the shade in May? Well, sure. But like any good real estate professional will tell you: location, location, location. For millennia, the Middle East was a gateway from Europe to Africa, India, and East Asia. Combine that with the Middle East's cultural and religious diversity, and you've got a place worth fighting for.

_01:: The Battle for Mecca

Unlike Jesus or the Buddha, Muhammad founded a religion *and* a political entity. As the leader of the early Islamic community in Mecca, Muhammad found himself at odds with his clan's pagan leaders. Facing annihilation, Muhammad and his followers fled Mecca for Medina in 622 CE. Over the next eight years, the Muslims periodically engaged in bloody battles over Mecca (in one, the Prophet's uncle was partially eaten by the wife of a Meccan tribal leader). However grand a general he was, Muhammad was an even better negotiator: In 630, the Muslims finally overtook Mecca via a treaty with tribal leaders. After almost a decade of casualties, nary a drop of blood was shed in the final battle for Islam's holiest city.

_02:: The Battle of Karbala (Which Has *Nothing* to Do with Madonna)

Although the fighting lasted only a couple hours and the result was never really in question, the Battle of Karbala has come to symbol-ize the divide between Shia and Sunni Muslims—and, for many Muslims, represents the last stand of Islam's golden age. After the Prophet Muhammad's death, the Islamic community was led by a succession of four "Rightly Guided" caliphs. By 680 CE, however, a ruthless and distinctly Wrongly Guided caliph named Yazid held court, and the Prophet's grandson Husayn set out to defeat him. Husayn and just 72 followers (many of them young boys) met Yazid's massive army at Karbala, in present-day Iraq. And though Husayn and his supporters were slaughtered, the martyrdom is still remembered by Shia Muslims today with passion plays and public mourning.

_03:: The Crusades

Not content to let Muslims fight among themselves, Christian Europe decided to get into the act in 1095 CE. For the following two centuries, European Christians undertook eight major expeditions hoping to conquer Jerusalem and control Christ's tomb, the Holy Sepulcher (which seems like a lot of trouble—waging eight wars over a cave where Jesus spent three measly days). Armed with plenty of manpower, the Crusaders took Jerusalem in 1099, but Saladin then reconquered it in 1187. Long story made short, the back-and-forth kept on until everyone got tired and decided to postpone fighting over Jerusalem until the mid-20th century. Of course, the Crusades had a lasting effect on the therefore fairly peaceful relationship between the Islamic world and the Christian one, but they also deepened the divide between the Catholic and Eastern Orthodox churches, particularly when the Catholics decided to sack Constantinople during the fourth Crusade.

Touch of Evil

Italian porn star Ilona Staller tried to save everyone a peck of trouble back in 1990 when she told Newsweek *magazine that she'd sleep with Saddam Hussein "to achieve peace in the Middle East."*

When Opposites Attack:
Feuds Steeped in Jealousy

Jealousy has been likened to a green-eyed monster, much like Godzilla, a rampaging creature that leaves destruction in its wake. Unlike Godzilla, however, jealousy and the feuds it sparks are by no means limited to leveling Tokyo.

_01:: Feud like an Egyptian: The Petiese Saga

It was a time of renaissance in ancient Egypt, but for the town of Teudjoy the seventh and sixth centuries BCE were a little less enlightening. The tiny town became the venue for a multigenerational feud, leading to the demise of a noble family. Here's how the tragic happenings kicked off. In 660, the pharaoh Psammetichos I appointed a nobleman named Petiese to take charge of Teudjoy's Temple of Amun. If the local priests were nervous about this appointment, it was for good reason: Petiese punished corruption and incompetence with beatings and ended up taking personal charge of the temple's affairs. Even worse for the priests, within a few years the place was thriving. With less than holy spirit, the jealous priests took their revenge, murdering Petiese's grandsons in the temple itself. Of course, Petiese tried to get the pharaoh's support, but by then the king was too old and sick to do anything about it. Unfortunately, the vicious pattern of attack, reprisal, and appeal to authority continued for at least four generations, at the end of which the family of Petiese was reduced to utter poverty, still begging officials to take note and restore them to glory.

_02:: They're All Greeks to Me: The Peloponnesian War

In the early years of the fifth century BCE, the cities of Greece, led by Athens and Sparta in a Hellenic League, successfully fought off two separate Persian invasions. But the alliance developed cracks—instead of focusing on what they had in common (like wine, olive oil, and pedophilia), the Athenians and Spartans let their mutual jealousy and political and economic differences split the Hellenic League into two competing blocs, the Spartan-led "Peloponnesians" and the Athenian-dominated "Delians." Although it was difficult for the two sides to actually fight a battle (Athenian military might was mostly naval, while Sparta had few ships but large land armies), they finally worked out all the angles and settled in for nearly three decades of fighting in 431 BCE. Sparta won (sort of), but both sides were so exhausted from the fighting that in the end, both were left as prey for rival states, first Thebes and later the rising star of Macedon.

_03:: Viking Love Triangle: The Tragedy of Laxdaela

The Laxdaelas struggled to succeed in harsh 10th-century Iceland, and their tale (cleverly titled *The Laxdaela Saga*) reads like a veritable catalog full of soap opera–ish jealousy. It starts out with the family fleeing Norway because one of its ancestors, Ketill Flatnose, incurred the envy of King Harald for his able administration and great wealth. A good enough reason to leave, we suppose. But the drama just keeps coming: the tension between jealous half brothers Hoskuld and Hrut almost leads to combat; a chieftain named Olaf "the Peacock" incurs the jealousy of kinsmen and neighbors for, among other things, the ostentatious clothes that gave him his monicker; and a woman named Gudrun goads her husband, Bolli, into a feud against his cousin and foster brother, Kjartan (who had promised to marry Gudrun but later reneged). And if there weren't enough punches thrown in there for your taste, the emotional climax of the tale comes in 1003, when Bolli and some friends ambush Kjartan only to kill his foster brother in a duel. And while Bolli immediately regrets his actions, catching Kjartan as he falls, Gudrun probably does, too; just before her death in the mid-1000s Gudrun reportedly tells her son, "To him I was worst whom I loved best." Hey, sometimes love really hurts.

_04:: Sibling Rivalry among the Children of the Sun

When Inca Huayna Capac, the god-king of the Andes, died in 1525, he left his oldest son, Huascar, as the new king. But Huascar was dismayed to learn that his father had left the rich lands in and around the city of Quito to his younger son, Atahualpa. Apparently, the irritation was directed both ways. Atahualpa envied his older brother's rank and title, especially since Huascar was ugly, ill-tempered, and probably crazy. Fortunately, the two brothers decided to settle their differences like gentlemen. Unfortunately, they were Inca gentlemen, who also happened to have fully equipped armies at their disposal. The two brothers engaged in a brutal civil war in which tens of thousands died. In the end (1532) Atahualpa won, but the empire was so weakened that it was unable to offer serious resistance to the Spaniards, who conveniently showed up a few months later.

_05:: Blood Brothers: Jamuka and the Great Khan

Jamuka was chieftain of the Jadirat, a minor Mongol tribe, but through a combination of military skill and cunning diplomacy, he managed to acquire a large following in the closing years of the 1100s. Among his allies was a young chieftain named Temudjin; the two were so close that they became each other's *anda,* or blood brother. But things turned sour (much like fermented horse milk, the Mongol national drink) as Jamuka watched his little bro gain influence, followers, and herds of precious sheep and horses. The jealousy came to a head when Jamuka took the title of Gurkhan ("Warlord") in 1201 and declared war on his erstwhile buddy, which turned out to be a pretty unwise move. In 1205, after repeated defeats, Jamuka's own men murdered him and declared allegiance to Temudjin, who took the title "Genghis Khan" after rewarding the assassins by executing them.

_06:: Redneck Rampage: The Saga of Douglas County

Apparently, in the mid-1800s in Douglas County, Missouri, jealousy could be a deadly thing. It all started pretty innocently: two rival families, the Alsups and the Sheltons, gathered to engage in a little friendly horse racing. But during the race a Shelton hit an Alsup's horse with his whip. The Alsup then hit the Shelton back, with more fun ensuing. The games ended a few moments later when the Shelton killed the Alsup by shooting him in the heart. The Shelton was immediately blown away by an older Alsup, who in turn was made to resemble Swiss cheese by a hail of Shelton gunfire. The feud went back and forth until the Sheltons were forced to leave the county. Left without any family competition, the Alsups terrorized the region until the angry citizens banded together and killed enough of them to cow the rest into submission.

Born Losers:

Infamous Second-place Finishers Who Never Got the Spotlight

No one remembers who followed the Beatles on *The Ed Sullivan Show*. No one remembers the second dog to go into space, who Secretariat's closest competitor was, or who was the first man to break Roger Bannister's 4-minute mile. Nope, those names have been relegated to the same part of your brain reserved for high school chemistry and diagramming sentences. But we think it's about time you polished off your gray cells and gave some of these second-placers a second look.

_01:: Tenzing "I Could Have Climbed This Without You" Norgay

Tenzing Norgay was a Sherpa, one of the hardy mountain folk of Nepal. Like many Sherpa, he discovered that he could make a nice living guiding Europeans up the mountains of his homeland. In 1952, he led Sir John Hunt's expedition to the summit of Mount Everest, the highest point on earth. But few remember Norgay's name, because a New Zealander, Edmund Hillary, insisted on being the first person to stand on the summit. It took Hillary and company seven weeks to climb to the summit and three days to descend, though one suspects Norgay could have done better *without* the Europeans. In 2004, Pemba Dorji, another Sherpa, reached the peak in just 8 hours, 10 minutes.

_02:: Thorfinn "I Could Have Discovered This Without You" Karlsefni

Most Americans now know that Leif Eriksson was the first European to make a documented landfall in the New World. No one remembers the guy who got there second. In 1010, 10 years after Lucky Leif's expedition, an Icelander named Thorfinn Karlsefni led an expedition of two ships to North America, exploring regions he called Helluland, Markland, Furdustraands, and Straumford (probably the coast of Labrador and Quebec). Thorfinn's men even built a settlement called Hop, but they were forced to abandon it and head back to Greenland after coming under attack by the natives.

_03:: Gottfried "I Figured This Out Without You (and Didn't Even Get a Lousy T-shirt)" von Leibniz

Leibniz was a brilliant mathematician of the late 1600s as well as a philosopher, scientist, lawyer, librarian, and diplomat. Of course, today he is remembered (outside the wacky world of mathematicians) for none of these things. The reason? Independent of Leibniz, Sir Isaac Newton simultaneously developed many of the principles underlying the science

It's a Mad, Mad, Mad, Mad Scientist

MAYBE THAT APPLE *DID* FALL ON NEWTON'S HEAD

There's a fine line between genius and madness, and Isaac Newton skipped back and forth over it like a giddy schoolgirl. Often forgetting to eat, Newton would wake up in the morning and then sit on the edge of the bed for hours. Of course, all that time spent on his mattress didn't really help his attitude: Newton was notorious for being a champion grouch, even with his friends. And despite being one of the greatest scientists the world has ever known, Newton spent countless hours either practicing alchemy (trying to prove lead could be turned into gold) or trying to disprove the Christian religious tenet of the Trinity. That ain't all, though. While studying lights and colors, Newton once stuck a big needle in his eye socket to determine what was back in there, and stared at the sun so long that he had to spend days in a darkened room to recover his vision. It's been suggested he was mildly autistic. Or maybe just nuts.

of calculus. Newton turned out to be the better promoter. When schoolchildren today mutter about having to learn calculus, it's Sir Isaac's name they curse, and Sir Isaac alone they envision roasting in hell. As far as recog-

nition goes, Leibniz definitely got the short end of the stick.

_04:: Claudius

Most people with an interest in classics know that Julius Caesar was the first Roman general to lead an invasion of Britain. Few, however, remember that Caesar's expedition ended without a permanent occupation—he was forced to return to finish up a collection of outrageously one-sided battles in Gaul (which became known as the Gallic War). And it was four generations before a Roman commander again led troops to fair Britannia. In 43 CE the emperor Claudius, thought by many to be an imbecile, led a brilliant lightning conquest of the Britons, coordinating a number of legions and even bringing the first elephants ever seen so far north. In fact, "Claudius the Fool" was given the surname Britannicus in honor of his victories. Not bad for a moron.

_05:: Robert Falcon Scott

Captain Scott engaged in a famous and not-so-friendly contest with Norwegian Roald Amundsen to be the first human to reach the South Pole. Amundsen spent months preparing for his journey, learning cold-weather survival techniques from indigenous people of the Arctic. Scott, on the other hand, believed he needed no such instruction; ignoring sources on Inuit customs, refusing to use dogsleds, and otherwise, as the British say, "making a hash of things." On January 18, 1912, Scott and his party arrived after much hardship at the South Pole, only to discover that Amundsen's party had beaten them by over a month (Amundsen even left Scott a note advising him to help himself to whatever was left at the Norwegian camp). Amundsen returned home a hero; while Scott, well, didn't. Sadly, he and his entire party died on their re-

turn trek in weather that was harsh even by Antarctic standards.

It Ain't Easy Being Green: Famously Jealous Politicians

Sure, jealousy isn't exactly the best of traits, but occasionally it'll help a guy get a lot done. The following go-getters found plenty of things (and occasionally people) to cross off their to-do lists when plagued with a bit of the green.

_01:: Nero's Fiddling with Power

Poor old fiddling Nero was an unlikely candidate for emperor of Rome. But after his mother, Agrippinilla, conned her way into the bed of her uncle, Emperor Claudius, Nero was adopted by Claudius as coheir with Claudius's son, Britannicus. When Claudius died in 54, Nero became the emperor in name only. Of course, the real power was concentrated in the hands of his mother and her cronies, and Nero didn't like it. Jealous of his mom's power and her playing favorites with Britannicus, Nero most likely had the boy murdered in 55 and in 59 arranged for a series of mishaps for Agrippinilla (she had a strong survival instinct, so he eventually ordered her to be stabbed to death). Not exactly the best son, he wasn't exactly the best ruler, either. He went on to a reign of terror, killing anyone he perceived as a threat, including most of his surviving relatives. Of course, it all caught up with him in the end. Nero was eventually overthrown, declared a public enemy, and forced to kill himself while on the run.

_02:: Themistocles's Sleep Disorder

Themistocles was a brilliant orator and politician, but his jealousy knew no bounds. Furious after a rival named Miltiades won a victory over the Persians at Marathon (490 BCE), he famously declared "Miltiades' trophy does not let me sleep." And it didn't. Not only did Themistocles force his countrymen to build the largest navy in Greece, but as an expert on both battlefield tactics and psychological warfare, he was also largely responsible for the Greek victory over the Persian navy at Salamis (479 BCE). That was hardly the end of Themistocles' jealousy, however. The ugly green monster reared its head again not long after, and he became involved in a struggle against his rival, Aristides. Unfortunately for Themistocles, allegations of political corruption led to his exile in the late 470s BCE, and the architect of Greek victory over the Persians died in Asia Minor...living off a Persian government stipend. Strange bedfellows indeed!

_03:: The Bonaparte Black Sheep

It's not easy being the little brother, especially when your big sib is a self-made emperor. So it's no wonder relations between Lucien Bonaparte and brother Napoléon were often abrasive and strained. At first a supporter of Napoléon, Lucien became disillusioned by what he saw as the betrayal of the French Revolution. Unfortunately, he was sort of the Fredo Corleone of the family, being stupid enough to let a subversive pamphlet he had written fall into the hands of Napoléon's police. Obviously, it strained their relationship even further and made him one of the few Bonapartes who didn't end up king of something. In 1804, Lucien went into exile in Rome, and the pope named him prince of Canino, largely to annoy Napoléon. Not the brightest move. Napoléon imprisoned the pope in 1809. Lucien on the other hand was America-bound; captured by the British, he remained a prisoner for several years before returning to a comfortable, Napoléon-free retirement on the Continent.

_04:: Jealous Joe

Iosif Dzhugashvili, better known to the world as Joseph Stalin, was a man of complicated psyche, but jealousy was one of his most obvious traits. During the years leading up to and following the Russian Revolution, his idol, Lenin, scorned him in favor of intellectuals such as Leon Trotsky, Lev Kamenev, Grigory Zinoviev, and Nikolay Bukharin. But when Lenin died in 1924, Stalin was quite happy to take his revenge, spending several years playing his rivals off against each other before eliminating them all in the Great Purge of the 1930s. In deciding whom to eliminate, Stalin paid particularly close attention to those whose popularity rivaled his. Of course, his private life wasn't free of jealousy, either; his fights with his second wife, Nadezhda Alliluyeva, whom he sometimes suspected of infidelity, were legendary. After one such incident in 1932, Nadezhda died of a gunshot wound; the official line is that this was a suicide, though there's no dearth of historians who suspect Stalin of pulling the trigger himself. After all, he wasn't exactly of the "never harm a fly" mold.

Touch of Evil

Some believe that "sore loser" Richard Nixon might have been in on the plot to assassinate John F. Kennedy. The flimsy theory is based on the fact that Tricky Dick was actually in Dallas at *a Pepsi-Cola board meeting mere hours before the tragic event occurred.*

GLUTTONY

⑦ Unusual Food Competitions ③ Delicious Animals We Charbroiled into Extinction—and 1 That Tasted Nasty but We Killed It Anyway The ⑤ Most Excessive Weddings in History ④ Facts about Roman Excess ③ Diets to Avoid: Religious Councils through the Ages ⑥ Delicacies That Make You Gag ⑤ Facts on Cannibalism ④ Deaths of Famous People Caused by Overindulgence in Drugs, Drink, or Dessert ⑤ Monarchs Who Tipped the Scales ⑤ Fads from the Slimming Fashion Industry ⑤ Plants Known to Cause Hysteria World's ⑤ Oddest Cuisines ④ Dictators with Infamous Sweet Tooths ⑥ Servings of Swine: The Worst Pork Barrel Politics Revealed ⑧ Myths from Other Cultures about Gods' Strange Eating Habits ④ Pioneers of All-You-Can-Eat ③ Crazy Diets from Crazy Times ④ Presidents Who Overindulged ⑤ Deadly Digestive Problems ③ Philosophers Who Liked to Get Groovy Thoughts

I Eat Therefore I Am:
Unusual Food Competitions

The Nathan's Hot Dog–Eating Contest is only the most famous of all eating contests. And the ones on *Fear Factor* are only the most contrived. But if you're looking for a lesser-known chow challenge to show off your plate-cleaning prowess, these gastronomic free-for-alls might be just the place to start.

_01:: Matzo Balls

It ain't easy keeping kosher. Especially for contestants in the Ben's New York Kosher Deli Charity Matzo Ball–Eating Tournament. The contest is a charity fund-raiser for the Interfaith Nutrition Network sponsored by a New York–area deli chain. The record holder for 2004 is Eric "Badlands" Booker of Copaigue, Long Island, who ate 20 matzo balls in five minutes and 25 seconds. If that doesn't sound like a lot, you should know that these matzo balls were roughly the size of *tennis* balls. *Oy!* The winner gets a trophy and a $2,500 gift certificate to a stereo store, while runners-up get various prize packages, all of which involve tickets to a New York Islanders game. Umm...all that matzo for an Islanders ticket? We're thinking we'll pass.

_02:: Live Mice

The MTV show *Jackass* spawned a lot of copycat dumbasses. But two hungry fellas in Brisbane, Australia, win the prize. Participating in a contest at Brisbane's Exchange Hotel in which they were dared to eat a live mouse, the two men competed for a grand prize that was a vacation package worth a handsome $346. Both men chewed the tails off, and the "winner" actually chewed his mouse whole and spit it out. Needless to say, the RSPCA, Australia's version of our own SPCA, wasn't thrilled about the stunt and got the Queensland police on the participants'—um—tail. If caught, the winner will face fines of $75,000 and two years in the pokey. And just think how many big, fat, edible rodents must be in there!

_03:: Pickled Quail Eggs

Texas may have plenty of barbecue contests and chili cook-offs, but nothing holds a candle to the Pickled-Quail-Egg-Eating Contest held annually in Grand Prairie, a town between Dallas and Fort Worth. Begun as a publicity stunt by a flea market called Traders Village, the contest determines who can down the most pickled quail eggs in 60 seconds. Quail eggs are roughly the size of a large olive, and the rules stipulate that they must be eaten one at a time. In 2003, the contest was won for the seventh straight time by Grand Prairie resident Lester Tucker, who downed 42 in a minute. So, what's the secret to old Lester's success? He swallows them whole.

_04:: **Cessna 150**

Yes, that's an *airplane*. And the guy who ate it is a French gent named Michel Lotito, who goes by Monsieur Mangetout (French for "Mr. Eats Everything." See what he did there?). Lotito engaged in the stunt to earn a place in *Guinness World Records* (his actual record is for Most Unusual Diet: two pounds of metal per day), but his iron stomach's downed a lot more than just a plane. He's also the proud eater of 18 bicycles, a bunch of TVs, a wooden coffin, and several supermarket shopping carts. Not to mention all the light-bulbs, razor blades, and other knickknacks he's downed on variety shows. Looking for a reason why you shouldn't try this at home (or *with* your home)? Well, Lotito's got a natural advantage because his stomach lining is twice as thick as a normal person's. He's also aided by the fact that he's French, and the French will eat just about anything (*Escargot,* anyone?).

_05:: **Black Pudding**

It's hard enough to eat a little bit of some English food, much less a lot of it. And black pudding is not a dish you want to overindulge in. But don't let the name of this delicacy fool you. This treat from northern England and Scotland isn't pudding in the yummy, creamy, Bill Cosby sense of the word. It's more like a sausage, and it contains oatmeal, onions, spices, plenty of suet, and a whole lot of pig's blood. Hence the black. In 1998, the Robert Peel pub in the English town of Bury, near Manchester, decided to start a black pudding–eating contest. The first winner was Martin Brimelow, who ate nine black puddings. Though he was ahead, his victory was assured

when he ate a special black pudding injected with Tabasco sauce, which counted as two.

_06:: **Corned Beef and Cabbage**

Mo's Irish Pub in Milwaukee celebrates its very Irish heritage with dignity and class: an annual Corned Beef and Cabbage–Eating Contest. The winner in 2004 was Ed "Cookie" Jarvis, a veteran eating-contest competitor (he holds 29 titles) who weighed in at an intimidating 419 pounds. Jarvis packed away over five pounds of corned beef and cabbage in 10 minutes, beating the closest competitor by almost two pounds. Need an idea of just how fast that is? He packed away his first plate in a mere 80 seconds! As in many eating contests, there are only two ways to get disqualified: cheat or puke. It's a wonder this contest wasn't followed by an unofficial Gas-X Binge-Drinking Bout.

Touch of Evil

In 1990, Guinness World Records *stopped listing records for gluttony or eating contests. They later ended "heaviest pets" records, too, as demented folk were overstuffing Fido and Fluffy to try to gain entry into the book.*

_07:: **Vodka**

Sure, there are beer-drinking contests, so why not vodka-drinking contests? Well, here's why. In 2003 a bar in the southern Russian town of Volgodonsk decided to hold just such a competition. After all, Russians are famous for their ability to hold their vodka, and annual consumption is over 15 liters *per person*. The winner would get...well, more vodka.

Ten liters of it, to be exact. Sadly, the winner never got to claim his prize. After downing 1.5 *liters* of vodka in under 40 minutes (which is about 51 shots), the vodka champ passed away about 20 minutes later. What about the run-ners-up? The five other contestants got treated to full luxury stays in intensive care. Scary enough, many of the ones who weren't hospitalized actually showed up at the same bar the next night.

"Where the Buffalo Roast": Delicious Animals We Charbroiled into Extinction—and 1 That Tasted Nasty but We Killed It Anyway

"Good to the last drop" proved to be a great slogan for Maxwell House coffee. But the "Good to the last existing representation of the species" tagline hasn't worked so well for these delectable creatures. Here are four animals that prove that slow and tasty never wins the race.

_01:: The Dodo

Bigger than turkeys and more naive than happy taxpayers, the dodo didn't exactly have the best survival strategy on the block. Consider the evidence. Not only was the dodo a flightless bird, it also had tiny wings, a small tuft of curly feathers on its bum, and it laid only one egg a year. It's no wonder European sailors who landed on the shores of Mauritius in the early 16th century got a big laugh out of the clumsy bird, which, in addition to its previously lamented attributes, had absolutely no fear of man. The sailors also got quite a few meals out of the *aves,* even though they were said to be close to inedible (Dutch settlers called them *walgvogel,* or "disgusting bird"). No matter. Pigs, rats, and monkeys introduced to the island helped man kill off the bird by 1681. Which is why there aren't any Kentucky Fried Dodos today.

_02:: The Sea Cow

They were big, slow, tasty, and defenseless, all of which is a bad combination around a slew of hungry humans. A cold-water relative of the manatee and dugong, the sea cow was discovered by Europeans in 1741 when the explorer Vitus Bering and his crew were shipwrecked in the area between Siberia and Alaska. And since the adventurous lot couldn't really explore the land, they took to exploring their palate. Our shipwrecked gourmands quickly discovered that sea cow meat tasted like veal and remained fresh for a surprisingly long time. And there was a lot of meat, too, since the beasts reached as much as 26 feet in length and weighed up to 8 tons. They resembled a modern manatee, with looks like your mother-in-law—if your mother-in-law has big expressive brown eyes, a small head, external ears the size of peas, and bristling whiskers. Estimates are that only about 20% of the sea cows shot or harpooned were actually caught, but they all died. By 1768, the gentle, delicious beasts were naught but lip-smacking memories.

Touch of Evil

The Labrador duck went extinct not only because of its meat, but also because of its eggs. The bird could lay up to an egg per day, but that didn't stop humans and other predators from wiping them out by 1875.

_03:: The Great Auk

Rich in protein, chock-full of nutritious fats and oils, and great for baiting fishhooks, this flightless seabird was, well, great. Found on the rocky islands and coastal areas on both sides of the North Atlantic, great auks were like a somewhat smaller version of the dodo, and they had the brains to match. Starting in the early 16th century, sailors began marching the clueless creatures up the gangplank and pushing them into the ship's hold by the hundreds. Unlike the dodo, however, the auk was considered great grub, and the tasty bird was hunted for its feathers, skin, and eggs to boot. Unfortunately, you'll never get to feast on the great auk's tender meat, and you have your European brothers to thank for it. The last pair was killed on an island off the coast of Iceland back in 1844.

_04:: The Passenger Pigeon

The naturalist John James Audubon once reported seeing a flock of passenger pigeons so numerous, it took three days for them to fly over. And he wasn't exaggerating. In the early part of the 19th century, the birds, which were slightly larger than mourning doves, were estimated to make up as much as 40% of North America's entire avian population. But the abundance of the creatures made them easy marks. Effortlessly hunted, the birds were mowed down mostly for food but occasionally for sport, with some "sportsmen" bagging as many as 5,000 in a day. In fact, the birds filled entire train boxcars as they were shipped to markets in eastern cities. Unable to sustain themselves except in large flocks, the pigeons dwindled rapidly. In 1900, a 14-year-old boy shot the last wild passenger pigeon (boys *will* be boys). Fourteen years later, the last one in captivity died at the Cincinnati Zoo. Her name was Martha.

Nothing's Good in Moderation: The Most Excessive Weddings in History

Sure, there's lots to consider in planning a wedding: dresses, cakes, bands, halls…all of which can add up to a hefty bill for the parents of the bride (or, in some cultures, the groom). But perhaps those bellyaching about the substantial hit their bank account is about to take should pause for a moment to consider some of history's most ridiculously, outrageously off-the-wall weddings. Suddenly dropping a few grand on a one-wear gown doesn't seem so bad, does it?

_01:: Attila the Hun and Ildico (453 CE)

Attila the Hun, perennial barbarian bad boy, was apparently also a perennial playboy. Leader of the Huns, Attila somehow also found time to marry 12 women and father an unknown number of children. Never able to quite get enough, Attila still might have wanted to hold off on the last wife. On his last wedding night, in 453 CE, the royalty of every nation under Hun dominion, from the Rhine to the Volga, were in attendance, and thousands of gallons of booze and whole herds of sheep were brought in to slake their appetites. No ordinary nuptials, the drinking and feasting were to last for days, but on the morning after taking his 16-year-old bride to bed, the 50-something warlord was found dead. Whether his death was caused by poison, overdrinking, or just too much fun in the sack, the world will probably never know.

_02:: Margaret of York and Charles the Bold (1468)

Despite the protests of France's Louis XI, who was fearful of an alliance between the English and the Burgundians, Margaret of York was engaged to Charles the Bold, aka the duke of

Burgundy. And in spite of the king's objection, the crazy cats decided to go forth with said ceremony and party like it was 1469. Extravagant even by the standards of European royal weddings, the blessed event was accompanied by a tournament in which the most famous knights in Europe bludgeoned one another for days. And Margaret's crown, covered in pearls and diamonds, was so valuable that it's now on display in the treasury of Aachen Cathedral. Of course, the preceremony celebrations were equally grand. The nuptials themselves were preceded by parades through the streets of Bruges, a pageant reenacted every year during (coincidentally enough) the tourist season. Sadly, Margaret's subsequent life was a little less like a fairy tale: she lived to see the death of her husband in battle (1477) against the French and the overthrow of both Burgundy as an independent duchy (1482) and of her own family across the Channel (1485).

_03:: Prince Rainier of Monaco and Grace Kelly (1956)

Billed as "the wedding of the century," the union between the prince of Monaco (whose family is actually descended from Genoese pirates) and the Hollywood starlet was the talk of the civilized world for much of the mid-1950s. Rainier gave his bride a 10-carat diamond ring, and his subjects gave their new princess diamond earrings and a necklace to match and, for no particular reason, a Rolls-Royce. Of course, the gown was no joke, either, as Grace's dress was designed by an Oscar winner, Helen Rose. The couple had two wedding ceremonies, a private civil ceremony in the Riviera principality's throne room and a public religious ceremony in Monaco Cathedral. Over 600 of the world's rich and famous attended the reception, including Frank Sinatra, Cary Grant, and Ava Gardner. Tragically, Princess Grace was killed in 1982 in a car accident. Interestingly, commemorative U.S. postage stamps were issued in her honor, but they gave her name only as "Grace Kelly." Why? Because U.S. law bans the placement of foreign monarchs on its postage stamps.

Touch of Evil

Mariah Carey wore a $25,000 gown for her wedding to Sony Music Entertainment boss Tommy Mottola, an event that featured fifty flower girls and cost more than half a million bucks. If only the investment had paid off: the couple separated before celebrating their fourth anniversary.

_04:: Muhammad and Salama of Dubai (1981)

Things can be rough when you're constantly trying to "keep up with the Joneses," or the Hamids, as the case may be. Arab weddings are often such bank-breakers that Arab economists frequently bemoan the size and expense that have become culturally expected. But that didn't stop Rashid bin Sayid al-Maktoum, sheikh of Dubai, in planning his son Muhammad's 1981 wedding to Princess Salama. Lasting a mere seven days (seven!), the wedding was held in a stadium built expressly to host the festivities. Twenty thousand guests attended, and the bill came in at just over $44 million.

_05:: The Mittal Affair (2004)

In possibly the most luxurious wedding in history, Vanisha Mittal, daughter of Anglo-Indian steel tycoon Laxmi Mittal, married Amit Bhatia, an investment banker who literally cashed in. The wedding, held in June 2004 in a chateau in France, lasted six days and was reported to have cost over $90 million (yes, that's U.S. dollars). The guest roster included some of Bollywood's brightest stars and some of Europe's deepest pockets. Among the expenditures: $520,000 for a performance by pop diva Kylie Minogue, who performed for a half hour. That's almost $300 per second, a figure even more shocking when you factor in dollars per unit of talent.

Facts about Roman Excess

From insanely large feasts to the lewdest of lewd orgies, Romans certainly loved their excess and ohs. The following are just a few of the areas they really could have trimmed back on.

_01:: The Food

If you're throwing a vintage Roman orgy, you'll need to make sure your pantry's well stocked. For breakfast, the Romans served bread, grapes, olives, with cheese and eggs all at the fourth hour. Then followed a meal at the sixth hour and at the ninth hour, the *cena* (evening meal), when a three-part meal was served. The first part was the *gustus,* which was designed to whet the appetite with shellfish and spicy sauces. Second was the *fercula,* which consisted of many different courses of meats and vegetables, while the third, the *mensae secundae,* was a dessert composed of fruits and pastry. Of course, ancient orgygoers also chowed down on ram's head pies, stuffed fowl, and boiled calf and pastry stuffed with raisins and nuts. Don't forget that atmosphere counts for something, too! Dishes were often made of gold and silver and precious jewels, banquet rooms were strewn with lilies and roses, and the participants lived for the present. Of course, you'll want to make sure you've got an army of slaves wearing costly dresses, just to make sure your guests feel extra welcome. Also, any and all sorts of bodily functions were accepted and even encouraged during dinner: belching, farting, spitting, relieving oneself in slave-borne chamber pots in full view of other guests, and even vomiting to make room for more grub. Don't remember that scene in *Caligula.*

_02:: The Entertainment

Nothing *screams* entertainment, well, like the Roman entertainers of yore. And games, festivals, and gladiatorial shows were just another part of Roman society carried to excessive lengths. Generally speaking, spectators and participants were exposed to unnatural excitements, and somehow developed an entertaining perspective on acts of cruelty and suffering. In fact, historians estimate that over 500,000 people were regular attendees at these forms of entertainment, often staying for days at a time. To sweeten the deal, all concessions (food *and* drink!) were provided free of charge by a generous government. And boy could these people party! The amphitheater at Titus was built to hold 80,000 seated spectators arranged by rank. And from the emperor to the lowest of the population, all seated on marble benches, covered with cushions and protected from the elements by canopies. There, gladiators and political prisoners fought with people or animals to the death. And as the audiences got bored, organizers were forced to find new sources of entertainment. For instance, Pompey let loose 600 lions in the arena with the gladiators one day, while Probus, a wealthy Roman, at one of his festivals once reserved 600 gladiators for extinction and massacred another 200 lions, 20 leopards, and 300 bears (oh, my).

_03:: The Bath

Citizens of the Roman Empire regarded sexual relations and sexual freedom with passionate abandon. In fact, the indolent lifestyle of the rich focused more on pleasure than industry and the Roman baths were a focal point for daily relaxation, socializing, and idleness for both the rich and the poor. Originally designed for cleansing purposes, the baths quickly became hangouts for socializing, relaxing, and ultimately engaging in plenty of sex orgies. The baths were kept open all day and night and sometimes the wealthy classes, attended by armies of slaves, lived in them. Today, the

ruins of many of the baths indicate that the inside walls were extravagantly decorated with images made less to excite cleaning activities than the passions and senses.

Touch of Evil

Romans were too posh to commit bulimia themselves, so they actually employed slaves to tickle their throats. Once their systems were clear, they could go back for round two.

_04:: The Fashion

Amazingly, the Romans weren't always so fond of excess. Prior to the dawn of the empire, the Romans were a frugal people and actually dressed with great simplicity, but as the empire grew, so did the flamboyance of its citizens. Men started expecting their women, courtesans and wives, to wear extravagantly ornamented attire every day. And while pearls and rubies were treasured jewels and large amounts of money were spent to acquire them, women were also expected to don woven silk of various colors, with colorful, extravagant embroidery. Dyed hair and exotic cosmetics also came into fashion, as did gold thread, which was fashioned into hair jewelry. The Romans also got an eye for "bling" and more and more stoles were quickly fastened with diamond clips, with jewels being embroidered into clothing, and even footwear, whenever possible. However, there was a constant turnover of clothes and jewelry during banquets, where, depending on the generosity of the host, anything that wasn't bolted down was given to the guests as gifts. A pretty high price to pay for friendship, no doubt.

Diets to Avoid:
Religious Councils through the Ages

Religion means a lot of things to a lot of people. Some consider it to be the source of all compassion, others feel it's the opiate of the masses, and still others view it as a good reason to rent out a village and have a big, old get-together. We're just focusing on the latter.

_01:: Council at Clermont (1095)

By the 11th century, the Christian Church was split into eastern and western factions and the holy city of Jerusalem had been under control of the Muslims for a couple hundred years. Then, in 1095, Pope Urban II summoned the clergy and nobles to a council in the village of Clermont in central France. Urban's PR team had leaked a rumor that Urban was going to make a special announcement at the council, and the effort worked. On the first day the crowds were so large that the papal throne had to be set up in a field so that everyone could be accommodated. After listing a number of alleged atrocities on eastern Christians by the Muslims and arguing the need to recapture Jerusalem, the pope cajoled the crowd into taking up arms against the so-called heathens. And with a flair for the dramatic, the pope stated that "God wills it." He then summoned his followers to take up the cross and head east to fight for Christianity. Of course, Urban did come up with a clever scheme for paying the warriors. For going to the Holy Land and fighting the Muslims, crusaders were offered a heck of a deal: not only would their past sins be forgiven, but present and future ones as well! With free passes to heaven on the hori-

zon, armies of crusaders stormed toward the Holy Land, changing the climate of the region forever.

_02:: Diet of Worms (1521)

While the Diet of Worms doesn't sound particularly tasty, it was definitely historic. Having been excommunicated for his teachings, Martin Luther was invited by the German emperor to attend an imperial diet in the German village of Worms, where he could defend his teachings. And while the emperor expected Luther to recant his beliefs, German princes were actually hoping that the meeting would help loosen Rome's power over Germany. Because Martin hadn't officially been declared an outlaw just yet (as excommunicants normally were), he was allowed to travel freely to Worms and even spent two weeks preaching to large crowds along the way. There was less excitement upon his arrival, however, as Luther appeared twice before the emperor and was told both times to take back his teachings. Luther stated that he saw no reason to do so and simply said, "I am finished" (not the popularly believed "Here I stand. I cannot do other."). Clearly a little miffed, the emperor immediately declared Martin Luther an outlaw, and sentenced him to death. Like the religious fairy tale it was, though, Luther was saved from the sentence by kidnappers, who then hid him for his own safety. The Protestant Reformation was under way.

_03:: Council of Trent (1545–1563)

Arguably one of the most important councils in the history of the Roman Catholic Church, the Council of Trent not only served as the foundation for the Counter-Reformation, it also shaped the traditions and the doctrines of the church that remain to this day. In total, the council actually met three times over the 18-year period. The first two-year session ended abruptly when the city of Trent in northern Italy was attacked, not by the Protestants, but by the dreaded bubonic plague. Then, four years later, the council reconvened and then took the next 10 years off due to a war in Germany. When the third session finally ended, the council issued decrees on Holy Orders, the Mass, the sacraments of marriage, purgatory, and the doctrinal differences between the Roman Catholic Church and the Protestant faiths. And while the decrees from this council set the direction for the Roman Catholic Church for the next 500 years and helped create the chasms dividing the Christian faiths that remain until this day, ironically, the pope had little say or power at the council. Why not? Because the majority in attendance felt the big guy was too corrupt and incapable of fixing anything!

So Hungry I Could Eat a Horse: Delicacies That Make You Gag

Eager to figure out just how thick your stomach lining is? Well, the folks at *mental_floss* rounded up a couple Iron Chef recipes to put your iron stomachs to the test. Of course, you might need a bit of alcohol to work up the courage. The following are six courses to get you in the swig of things.

_01:: The Appetizer: Snails

From the ancient Romans to today's upper crust, snails, or as the French call them, *escargots,* have been a favorite starter of the rich and famous. As the Romans expanded their empire, the tasty little gastropods inched along with them and became a culinary prize, especially in France. In fact, Napoléon was even known to have issued snails as rations to his troops. But if you're about to get your grub on, you should know that a snail is not just a snail. While there are two basic snail groups, the achatine and the helix, you'll be dining on the latter. Helix snails are indigenous to Europe and are the snail gourmets' favorite. The young creatures feed on grapevines with the most famous coming from the Champagne and Burgundy regions. The *petit gris escargot* is considered the best, especially in November when they are the plumpest. And while rumor has it that the best snails are three to four years old, one question always remains for the uninitiated (mainly among the under-10 lot): If you salt the snail, will it disappear before you can eat it?

Touch of Evil

The Summer 1983 issue of Mothering *magazine featured recipes for the human placenta, including placenta stew, placenta cocktails, placenta lasagna, and placenta pizza. Some believe that ingesting the organ is natural and healthy.*

_02:: The Salad: Indonesian Sago Worm and Balinese Dragonflies

The Indonesian sago palm was once cultivated for its starchy substance used to thicken soup and make puddings. Today, however, the tree's extract has taken second place to its inhabitants. In fact, sago palm larvae, which seem to offer the same starchy taste, are a delicacy sold live in the marketplace. And harvesting the sago worm is actually an art form. It starts out by roaming the forest looking for fallen sago palms. If you happen to stumble across one, you knock on it checking for movement. If you hear a little rustling, you should feel free to hack open the tree and collect your jackpot. As for preparation, the worms can be eaten raw or toasted. And back to the salad, just combine the sago worms with deep-fried Balinese dragonflies, add a little coconut paste, fermented fish sauce, garlic, chiles, tamarind juice, basil leaves, ginger, and lime juice. Then, wrap the

whole thing in banana leaf and you have a salad that should tickle your taste buds (literally, if you decided to keep those larvae raw!).

_03:: The Soup: Bosintang (Dog Soup)

What's a full-course epicurean delight without the soup? For course number three, we've chosen Chinese Bosintang, or dog meat soup. Relatively easy to make, assuming Bowser is agreeable, the soup requires taking strips of dog meat and boiling them in a soy paste. Then vegetables like green onions, taro stalk, and perilla are added to the mixture, and the broth is brought to a boil. Finally, a sauce made from mashed garlic, red pepper, and ginger is mixed in. And before digging into your bowl of man's best friend, you should probably season the dish with pepper. Rumor has it that it goes very well with a glass of soju (liquor). Of course, the dish has a bit of versatility. Rice can be served with the soup or the combination can be mixed together to make sumptuous leftovers or a warm meal the kids can take in their lunch box . . . or a doggie bag.

_04:: The Entrée: Horse Meat Pie

Seabiscuit sautéed and simmered? No way! But outside the United States horse meat is accepted in such cultures as the French, Italian, Swiss, and Japanese. That's because horse meat is an excellent source of high-quality protein, vitamin B12, iron, and zinc. Plus, its lean red meat can easily be mistaken for premium beef. As for quality cuts, though, the mare is often considered the best source, followed by the gelding and then the stallion. There are actually numerous horse meat dishes, including horse meat stew, pony Stroganoff, horse parmesan, and chicken-fried horse meat. However,

Profiles in Carnage

IDI AMIN (1924/5?–2003)

Skeletons in the Pantry: Start with his fridge: Probably a big fan of plastic wrap and aluminum foil, Idi Amin kept the heads of some of his victims fresh by storing them in his fridge. Of course, he had plenty to choose from: Estimates are that Idi tortured and murdered up to 300,000 victims while he was president of Uganda.

Idi the Connoisseur: Of course, what good's a fridge if you can't make use of it? Amin once reportedly told his minister of health that he found human flesh "rather too salty." So, maybe Idi wasn't that into dark meat.

Idi the Sharp Dresser: If that isn't enough to make you retch, you should check out his style sense: The guy wore so many medals that his shirts sometimes tore.

Idi the Practical Joker: Amin often sent nonsensical telegrams to other countries' leaders, and he loved to romp about playing his accordion.

Idi "I Am the Most Modest Dictator in the World (and I Have a Medal to Prove It)" Amin: Apparently, he didn't suffer from low self-esteem. By the time Amin had fled into exile to Libya, and then Saudi Arabia, his official title was "His Excellency President for Life, Field Marshal Al Hadji Doctor Idi Amin, VC, DS, MC, Lord of All the Beasts of the Earth and Fishes of the Sea, and Conqueror of the British Empire in Africa in General and Uganda in Particular." Tough to get that on a business card.

---

today's entrée is Welsh horse pie. Just take strips of horse meat and sear them in a skillet. Next, arrange the strips in a stew pan with layers of potatoes, cheese, and tomatoes. Once tender, just remove the concoction to a baking dish lined with pie dough, cover the top with crust, and then bake until brown. You'll want to serve the dish with a heavy burgundy wine. Of course, caution while cooking is required. Underprepared horse meat can turn the epicurean into the Galloping Gourmet.

_05:: The Pièce de Résistance: Haggis

The crown prize of any culinary feast, haggis is typically served with great fanfare on January 25, or Burns Night, in celebration of the Scottish poet Robert Burns's birthday. In fact, the specially prepared feast is ceremoniously escorted into the room by a bagpiper, and Burns's poem "Address to a Haggis" is then read. So, what exactly is haggis, you ask? How about a sheep's stomach loaded with minced sheep liver and heart. Take one sheep pluck, or stomach bag, turn it inside out, scrape the surface with a knife, and then let it soak overnight in cold salt water. Boil the liver and heart and then parboil an onion. Simply mince this mixture, add toasted oatmeal and suet, and then fill the pluck, making sure to sew closed both ends. Now you just have to place the haggis in boiling water and slow boil for about four hours. For serving, you'll want to slice the haggis and garnish it with neeps (mashed turnips), tatties (mashed potatoes), and nips (sips of Scotch whisky). Actually, you may want to bring the whole bottle.

_06:: The After-Dinner Treat: Rocky Mountain Oysters

OK, so where does one find seafood in the Rocky Mountains? Well, you probably guessed it. Not really a seafood dish, Rocky Mountain oysters are actually bull testicles. And in fact, this famed western U.S. delicacy has its own testicle festival every September in Clinton, Montana. According to connoisseurs, the deep-fried gonads are best served with hot sauce and a beer. And for the strong of stomach the recipe's really quite simple. First, cut and pull away the skin around the testes, then place 'em in salted water for about an hour. Next, parboil the "oysters" in salt water, drain, and then let cool. Simply slice the delicacy into chip-size pieces and then roll them in a batter of flour, corn meal, and dried garlic. Finally, dip the oysters in red wine and fry 'em up. To serve, just place the oysters in a hot sauce, drain them, then pile on the potato chips and ply your guests with plenty of beer.

Fed Up with People: Facts on Cannibalism

You are what you eat, or is it who you eat? Following are five facts on the ritual value of cannibalism and some of its biggest gluttons.

_01:: Missionary Accomplished

Remember those cartoons showing natives placing captives in a big caldron of boiling water, tossing in the vegetables, and brewing up a large bowl of missionary stew? In most cultures, this couldn't be farther from the truth. While eating others' flesh may have been, at times, necessary for survival, in most cases it was out of ritualistic respect. In many locations cannibalism was the ultimate honor for the victim—when tribes ate their enemies, they did so to take on valued characteristics of that enemy. Blood was drunk in order to achieve some of the victim's bravery. Likewise, the brain was eaten for knowledge, the heart for courage, and the legs for swiftness. In some cases, a small portion of a recently deceased family member was also consumed out of respect as long as the departed one was not diseased or very elderly.

_02:: The Scottish Mr. Bean

During the time of Scotland's King James VI, later James I of England, there allegedly lived a highwayman named Alexander Bean, who along with his wife, eight sons, six daughters, 18 grandsons, and 14 granddaughters robbed any traveler unfortunate enough to cross their path. In order to hide the evidence and to feed an ever-growing family, each victim was killed and dismembered, with some body parts served immediately and the rest pickled for use later. Legend has it that close to 1,000 victims ended up the meal du jour for the Bean family. When finally captured, the adult male members of the Beans were executed by being dismembered and allowed to bleed to death. The women and children were then burned at the stake. However, there is no mention of what the Bean family had as its last meal.

_03:: Eddie Gein: Hollywood's Favorite Cannibal

On November 17, 1957, the Plainfield, Wisconsin, police began searching the farmhouse of Eddie Gein, a suspect in the robbery of a hardware store owned by Bernice Worden. As the police searched the dark, trash-covered house, they happened across a carcass hanging from the kitchen ceiling. At first they thought it was a deer, but upon closer inspection the officers discovered that it was the decapitated and gutted body of Bernice. But it didn't end there. More ghoulish items were soon found in the house. A bowl was made from the top of a human skull; lampshades, wastebaskets, armchairs, and an entire suit were made from human skin; and, most ghastly, a belt was made

from nipples, a human head, four noses, and a heart. The police could only speculate as to how many female victims were used to make Eddie's collection. Eddie soon became a Hollywood favorite. Norman Bates of *Psycho* fame is based on Eddie, bits and pieces of *The Texas Chainsaw Massacre* are taken from Eddie's story, and the character of Buffalo Bill in *The Silence of the Lambs* was inspired by Mr. Gein.

Touch of Evil

The word "cannibal" came from Christopher Columbus's journeys to the New World. He described the Caribs of Cuba and Haiti, whom he saw making meals of their own kind, as "Caníbalis."

_04:: Jeffrey Dahmer: Milwaukee's Notorious Cannibal

On July 22, 1991, Milwaukee police officers questioned an individual whom they had spotted wandering incoherently down a street with a handcuff on one hand. The individual told them that he had been drugged and handcuffed but was able to get away from his assailant. He then led them to the apartment of a 31-year-old chocolate factory worker named Jeffrey Dahmer. As they searched Dahmer's apartment, the police came across one of the most ghoulish scenes in American history. Upon opening the refrigerator, the officers found a recently severed head staring back at them. They also found three more heads and human meat stored in the freezer along with several hands and a penis in a stockpot. As the case unfolded, it became clear that Dahmer had killed, dismembered, and eaten as many as 17 victims, most of whom were poor transient blacks, Asians, or Hispanics. Dahmer would lure the victim to his apartment to watch TV and drink beer. Once there the victim was drugged and then stabbed or strangled. The body was then dismembered, with the head and genitalia saved as a trophy, the biceps and other muscles frozen to be eaten later, and the rest destroyed by acid and then disposed of. Dahmer was sentenced to 15 life sentences, or 957 years. He'd served only about two years when in 1994 he was murdered by another prison inmate.

_05:: Christian Cannibals and Communion

As with any upstart religion, the powers that be look at it with disdain and ridicule. This was the case with early Christianity. Late-first- and early-second-century Greek and Roman writers, such as Tacitus and Pliny the Younger, viewed the early Christian movement as a small group of superstitious fanatics who were a new sect among the hated Jews. Among both the upper class and common Romans gossip quickly spread about this group, including that as part of their religion they ate human bodies and drank human blood. Obviously a misrepresentation of the Christian ritual of communion, the rumored practice was viewed with disgust by the "civilized" Romans. Not only did this misinterpretation, coupled with other seemingly strange Christian practices, help to sway sentiment against the Christians, it made it easier for the Roman emperors to justify the persecution of the Christians. After all, there was no room in the Roman Empire for such barbarianism.

Too Much of a Bad Thing:
Deaths of Famous People Caused by Overindulgence in Drugs, Drink, or Dessert

Before you eat that last french fry, swallow that last dram of Drambuie, or sample a sedative or three, you should probably read on.

_01:: Henry I (1069–1135)

Henry I wasn't exactly given the throne. As the third son of William the Conqueror, Henry became king only after one of his older brothers died and he'd beaten the other out of the throne. He had quite a run of it, though, reigning for a good 35 years—that is, until he was toppled by one-too-many lampreys. If you're not familiar, a lamprey is a nasty-looking beast of a fish with a round mouth that can reach three feet in length. And it's as mean as it looks. Lampreys will attach themselves to other fish, rasp a hole in them, eat their flesh, then detach, leaving an often fatal wound. They are, however, reputed to be great eating (fit for a king, in fact), especially if you like meaty fish with a high fat content, which Henry clearly did. Sometime before Christmas, England's king sat down to a heaping platter of the fatty fish, ate a few too many, and breathed his last.

_02:: Honoré de Balzac (1799–1850)

"Coffee is a great power in my life," this French writer said in his essay "The Pleasures and Pains of Coffee." "I have observed its effects on an epic scale." The thing is, he wasn't kidding. Balzac consumed as many as 50 cups of strong Turkish coffee per day, and we're talking about the days before indoor plumbing! And he was no slouch at eating, either. At one meal old Balzac was reported to have eaten 100 oysters, 12 mutton cutlets, a duck, two partridges, and some fish, along with desserts, fruits, and wine. But coffee was clearly his passion, and he was faithful to the end. When Balzac couldn't get it strong enough, the addict was known to down pulverized coffee beans for the jolt he needed. This produced two results: Balzac was an incredibly energetic and prolific writer, writing more than 100 novels. He also died of caffeine poisoning at the age of 51.

_03:: Zachary Taylor (1784–1850)

Perhaps the most apolitical president in U.S. history, Zachary Taylor was an army veteran of four decades and a hero of the Mexican War, but he never voted or held office before being elected president in 1848. Even more amazingly, the cheapskate refused to accept mail with postage due, so he didn't even know he'd been nominated for the office until weeks after the fact! About 16 months after taking the oath of office, during which time he accomplished very little, old Zach attended a July Fourth cel-ebration at the Washington Monument on a sweltering day, and stood around in the heat for hours wearing dark heavy clothing. To cool off, he wolfed down a bowl full of iced cherries and polished 'em off with a pitcher of milk. Not the best idea. Turns out the milk and/or ice was tainted, and Taylor died five days later of typhoid fever or cholera.

Touch of Evil

Legend has it that the last words of heavy-drinking poet Dylan Thomas before his 1953 death were: "Eighteen straight whiskies... I do believe that's a record." Natural causes? Probably not.

_04:: Ira Hayes (1923–1955)

"It's funny what a picture can do," Hayes once said, but it had to have been said with bitter irony since it was a picture that ruined his life. Hayes was a Pima Indian from Arizona who, with four other U.S. Marines and a U.S. Navy pharmacist, raised a flag on the battle-ravaged island of Iwo Jima on February 23, 1945. The resulting photo made Hayes and the others heroes, but it embittered Hayes because he thought it denigrated the sacrifices of the thousands who'd died in the battle. The sad result? Hayes became an alcoholic who drifted from city to city and was arrested more than 50 times. In the end, the experience turned him into more of a hobo than a hero, and in the early morning hours of January 24, 1955, a drunken Hayes stumbled into a ditch that served as the water supply for his reservation. There the poor veteran froze to death.

It's Good to Be King, Especially If You Like Food: Monarchs Who Tipped the Scales

Throughout history, whether because of abundant food or lack of exercise or both, monarchs have been plagued with largeness of girth (what hardship!). Here are just a few of the fattest kings and queens on record.

_01:: Itey (ca. 1490 BCE)

Sort of an ancient Egyptian punch line, this corpulent queen ruled over the mysterious land of Punt, located somewhere in East Africa. So how exactly do we know of the great monarch's girth? Well, the Egyptian pharaoh Hatshepsut launched a trade delegation to Punt, and carvings on the walls of her temple complex at Deir el-Bahri record the expedition. Itey is depicted as grossly obese and is even pictured standing next to a diminutive husband and a tiny donkey. Under the donkey, in a delightful bit of Egyptian humor, is the inscription "This donkey had to carry the queen." A beast of burden indeed.

_02:: Eglon (ca. 1100 BCE)

According to the Bible, Eglon was the king of Moab (in modern Jordan) who united several tribes of highland and desert raiders to conquer the central Israelite tribes sometime in the 12th century BCE. An Israelite named Ehud gained the king's confidence, got him in a room alone, then killed him. Of course, the murder wasn't exactly a smooth operation. The Bible describes vividly that Eglon was so fat that Ehud couldn't retrieve his blade. Luckily, though, he managed to escape with little

trouble. As he fled, Ehud told Eglon's servants that the king was using the restroom. The stench coming from the room must have been fairly run-of-the-mill, because by the time they went in to check on their beloved king, Ehud had already rallied his followers and formed an army.

_03:: Charles the Fat (Ruled 881–888)

Not many kings actually have "the Fat" added to their names. A series of fortuitous deaths and abdications in the late 870s and early 880s left Charles the ruler of almost all of his great-grandfather Charlemagne's empire, encompassing most of modern-day France, Germany, and Italy. But Charles lacked the energy of his ancestor and namesake, possibly due in part to his obesity. During his reign Arab pirates raided Italy with impunity and Charles couldn't even be bothered to fight Viking marauders in northwestern France (he found it easier to pay them to go away instead). And while the dreaded moniker does have a certain ring to it, Charles wasn't the only French king of notable girth—Louis VI (ruled 1108–1137) also earned the appellation "the Fat."

_04:: George IV (Ruled 1820–1830)

George IV became king of England in 1820 after serving as prince regent while his father, George III, was alive but incompetent to rule. Apparently, though, the plush lifestyle being "Defender of the Faith" provided him seems only to have whetted his appetite. Known as a gambler, a drinker, and a laudanum addict, among other things, George IV enjoyed the dubious distinction of being far and away the fattest king in English history. His favorite breakfast was two roast pigeons, three beefsteaks, a bottle of white wine, a glass of champagne, two glasses of port, and one of brandy...after all, breakfast *is* the most important meal of the day.

_05:: Farouk (Ruled 1936–1952)

Farouk, the last king of Egypt with any real power, was crowned in 1936 and proceeded to live it up. He owned numerous palaces in Europe, hundreds of cars, and thousands of horses. But financing the royal lifestyle turned out to be a bit of a problem, so Farouk turned Egypt into even more of a kleptocracy than it had previously been. He was even renowned as a skilled pickpocket and was known to steal valuable items while on state visits to other countries (including a priceless pocket watch from Winston Churchill and a ceremonial sword from the shah of Iran!). In the end, Farouk was overthrown by a military coup in 1952 and briefly replaced with his newborn son, Fuad. But after a few months of infant rule, Egypt cleverly scrapped the monarchy thing altogether in favor of a very slightly less corrupt military dictatorship under Gamal Abdel Nasser (which degenerated into an arguably more corrupt system than Farouk ever could have dreamed possible). As for ex-king Farouk, he lived out the rest of his life in exile. Eating being one of his few pleasures, he died in 1965, at the age of 45, after gorging himself at the table. He weighed out at 300 pounds.

It's a Wrap:
Fads from the Slimming Fashion Industry

There's always the question of what to do with those extra pounds. Should you squeeze them back, tuck them in, wrap them up, camouflage them, or simply let hang? Well, whatever your preferred method for masking that extra chub, there's a manmade solution out there for you.

_01:: Kirtles, Corsets, and *Coches*

Women and men alike have used bindings either for religious or fashion reasons since time began. The origin of the use of corsets (derived from the French word *corps,* for "body") can be found in drawings discovered at a Neolithic archaeological site in Brandon, England. Not particularly confined to women's wear, the use of stays or corsets is documented back to 1700 BCE, when corsets were used to train small waists on young men and warriors as part of their culture. In the 13th and 14th centuries CE, dress construction incorporated a corseted effect known as "kirtles" into everyday wear. Iron was used in the 14th century to create the first known artificial support known as a *coche* in France and a busk in England. Used as a status symbol, Catherine de Medici, in the French court, ordered her ladies-in-waiting to cinch their waists to no bigger than 13 inches around, prompting the use of a steel framework to achieve this extreme state. In the late 20th century, the corset was resurrected as a piece of fashion outerwear made famous by Madonna in the late 1980s.

Touch of Evil

Some acupuncturists perform "ear stapling," in which a surgical staple is placed partially inside the ear. Why exactly? Because rubbing the device supposedly curbs hunger pangs.

_02:: Jeans and Slimming Cream

The quest to lift and shape our derrieres has become an economic boon for denim jean producers. A select line of jeans, trousers, and skirts produced by Miss Sixty carries an extra ingredient, Skintex, combining retinol, designed to stimulate collagen production, and chitosan, produced from shellfish skeleton bone. The serum embedded in the jeans material is designed to be released upon friction between the skin and fabric when worn. According to Cognis, the German manufacturers, 40% of the "medication" is absorbed after 48 hours and the clothing remains effective for another 30 washings. Hand washing is recommended. Doctors, however, are skeptical. One unforeseen problem is that the retinol reacts to sunlight so sunburn might be an interesting by-product of the slimming exercise. These clothes are not cheap; jeans retail at $139 a pair, pants range from $119 to $149, and skirts are $99 dollars. Already the company has said that it will not reissue this line of clothing next season.

_03:: These Shoes Were Made for Walking It Off

The latest cellulite-busting phenomenon, MBTs, gives a whole new meaning to the song "These Boots Were Made for Walking." Produced by Masai Barefoot Technology, the company's anticellulite sneakers are designed to help you mimic the gait of members of the Masai tribe in Africa. Why, exactly? Well, the lanky Masai are renowned for their perfect posture. Although definitely not a fashion winner, these bulky athletic shoes sit on a sole of rubber, curved thicker and higher in the middle, to force your legs to work harder with each step. Walking like a Masai ain't exactly cheap, though: it's about $255 for a pair of shoes. Despite the hefty tag, the sneakers move off shelves pretty quickly. And while there seems to be little scientific support for the shoes' anticellulite claims, they are credited with improving posture...a slightly pricey way to put some spring in your step!

_04:: Swimsuits

The art of wearing a swimsuit is an acquired technical skill, not necessarily apparent to the naked eye. Every year the agonizing ritual of searching for that ideal magic swimsuit begins. Reality strikes as women start the journey of accentuating the positive and camouflaging the negatives. This focus on body shaping and trend toward exposing more body parts increased in importance at the beginning of the 20th century, spurred in 1902 by the Australian swimmer Annette Kellerman, an "underwater ballerina" who dove into a glass tank clad in a swimsuit that showed arms, legs, and neck. Although she was arrested for indecent exposure, the damage had been done. Today, you can buy a swimsuit with panel-restricting tummy control, underwires to maintain bust shape, bust enhancers using a gel cup, bust reducers, bottom control and support, and even padded bottoms.

_05:: Wrapping It All Up

The fascination (and profit potential) associated with the magical effect of body wraps to reduce inches has survived for more than two centuries. Traced back to the time of the Romans, and used in Cleopatra's court, body wraps have worked by shrinking the size of fat cells to reduce, contour, and slenderize the body shape. Creams, lotions, and gels containing a mixture of either herbal extracts, chemicals, minerals, or vegetable products are applied to the skin before wrapping with terry cloth or cellophane. And while the older European full-body wraps sound closer to a variety of mummification, they promise up to six inches off original body measurements, which might last for a year. Using bandages soaked in sea-clay mud, the entire body is wrapped, starting with the feet and ankles, then going all the way to the jaws, with specialized wrapping procedures for the bustline. Recently,

Scandalicious

FEDS FIND COMMUNIST THREAT IN PUMPKIN!

In 1939, a down-and-out writer named Whittaker Chambers approached Assistant Secretary of State Adolf Berle, describing in detail an underground Communist network in the United States spying for the Soviet Union. Chambers, best known at the time for translating the book *Bambi* into English, was not regarded as a reliable expert on matters of espionage. Of course, it wasn't until 1948 that anyone decided to take Chambers at his word. Richard Nixon, then a congressman, perked up after Chambers provided a list of alleged Communist agents, a list that included Alger Hiss, a State Department lawyer. After first denying that he knew Chambers, Hiss launched a defamation suit. It proved to be a bad idea. Chambers led investigators to a farm where dozens of documents, some of them classified and some of them in Hiss's own handwriting, were hidden in a hollowed-out pumpkin. Hiss was eventually convicted of perjury (the statute of limitations barred trying him for espionage), though some people still dispute his guilt. One thing is sure, however: Alger Hiss lost his taste for pumpkin pie.

at-home body wrap kits sold directly to consumers at a lower price are competing against the high-priced wraps from the luxurious beauty salons.

Turning Over a New Leaf: Plants Known to Cause Hysteria

How about a nice cup of herbal tea? Better check which herbs you're talking about.

_01:: Blue Lily of the Nile

Remember your fourth grade history textbook, with all those pictures and drawings of life in ancient Egypt? If you can jog your memory enough, you might just recall a blue lotus or lily symbol that tended to be a fixture in those drawings. For centuries historians thought the blue lily to be a symbolic flower commonly placed in the sarcophagi of royalty such as King Tutankhamen. However, more recent findings suggest that the blue lily played a more hedonistic role in Egyptian society as a hallucinogen, creating states of ecstasy among the users. The flowers were prepared as a golden liquid tea with a sweet taste. After drinking, the individual entered into a euphoric state. The dried leaves were also smoked, but the favored way of ingesting the herb was mixed with wine. Maybe there is more to the Blue Nile than we thought.

_02:: A Button for Your Thoughts

If you're wondering where peyote comes from, look no further. Take one small Lophophora williamsii cactus and scrape off some of the buttons. Let the buttons dry until they are brown and ugly-looking. Serve in their natural form or grind them into a powder for tea or to mix with other drinks. For maximum effect, vomit early to get over the nausea. You are now ready for your peyote trip. Long a part of Native American culture, peyote was used by the Aztecs as a way to communicate with their gods. By the late 1800s, numerous North American tribes had integrated peyote into their religious ceremonies. In the early 1900s, a number of tribes formed the Native American Church, which still exists today. The basis of their communion is peyote.

_03:: Absinthe, or It's Not Easy Being Green

One of the most popular drinks of 19th-century Europe, especially in France, was absinthe, made from the herbs wormwood, green anise, fennel, and hyssop. The licorice-tasting drink contained more alcohol than wine and soon gained a reputation for causing addiction, excitability, hallucinations, and epileptic seizures. Questionable scientific research (usually funded by the French wine industry) found that the drink caused individuals to become criminally insane and that it brought on other illnesses, such as tuberculosis. In fact, one study found absinthe to be 246 times more likely to cause insanity than wine. By the 1890s, it became the leading target of temperance movements, a cause that reached its zenith in 1905, when Jean Lanfray, a Swiss peasant, murdered his pregnant wife and two daughters after having drunk two glasses of absinthe earlier in the day. What the press failed to mention was that in between the absinthe and the murders Lanfray had also had cognac, several glasses of wine at lunch, a glass of wine before leaving work, coffee with brandy, and a liter of wine after coming home. Absinthe was eventually banned in Switzerland (1910), the United States (1912), France (1915), and other countries.

_04:: Mold and Mass Hysteria: The Salem Witchcraft Trials

Was it sorcery or just a case of mold-induced food poisoning? In February 1692, young Betty Paris became ill and began manifesting hysterical behavior such as contorting in pain, appearing to be in a trance, complaining of fever, running around aimlessly, and diving under furniture. Things only got worse when Betty's playmates started showing similar symptoms. For the small Puritan village of Salem, Massachusetts, this was too strange and, therefore, must be the work of the devil. With this the witch-hunt began. By the time the mass hysteria had subsided over 100 individuals had been arrested and imprisoned on witchcraft charges. Nineteen were executed, four died while in jail, and one 80-year-old man was pressed to death under large rocks. But was it the devil? The winter of 1692 was extremely cold and wet. The main food source was the harvested rye wheat, which is now believed to have been infected with mold. Rye mold contains a chemical called ergot whose effects are similar to those of LSD, including hallucinations and seizures. It seems the devil was one "rye" character.

_05:: Designer Herbs: The Agony of the Ecstasy

The 1990s was a decade of designer drugs. What was a rave without ecstasy, or "X," as it is commonly called? But ecstasy is an illegal hallucinatory amphetamine. Leave it to American ingenuity to come up with a natural herbal alternative, called herbal ecstasy, and sell it as a "designer nutritional supplement." The main ingredients were a natural form of the stimulant ephedrine and the kola nut, a natural source of caffeine. What made the product appear to be more "in" was its slick packaging with pyramids, butterflies, mushrooms, and endorsements from (unknown) publications giving it a psychedelic mystique. Users said that it allowed them to party for hours with no side effects, while hard-core X users found it to be a weak version of the real thing. However, herbal ecstasy had a major problem. Many of its ingredients have been found to cause heart attacks, strokes, and seizures.

Are You Going to Finish That? World's Oddest Cuisines

There's no telling what someone's willing to put in their mouth if the right price is involved. Or the right condiments.

_01:: Eskimo Cuisine: Seal Oil

Forget ketchup and salsa, Inuits (often called "Eskimos") consider raw seal oil the king of all condiments. In fact, they're quite happy to slather the excellent sauce on baked salmon, sheefish, whitefish, caribou, moose, and anything else you can catch up north. Inuits also like their seal oil on "frozen-raw" moose or caribou and fish. So what's the secret to this not-so-secret sauce? The oil is produced by cutting up freshly slaughtered seal blubber into chunks and leaving them outside in a bucket for five days, stirring occasionally, until the blubber naturally renders and becomes oil. An adult seal produces about five gallons of usable seal oil. Once ready, just add A-1 or Tabasco to taste (really)!

_02:: Thai Cuisine: Insects I

Though most Americans and Europeans are familiar with Thai cuisine standards—the ubiquitous pad thai and thom yum goong soup—most are unaware of a small epicurean subgroup in Thai cuisine: connoisseurs who appreciate the variety of insect species native to Thailand's tropical jungles. It's true! This lot is quite happy to chow down on cicadas, locusts, mantises, deep-fried crickets, grasshoppers, and bamboo borers (grubs referred to on some menus as "fried little white babies"),

steamed giant water bug (which can also be eaten as a paste with chili and sticky rice), weaver ants and their eggs (eaten like the water bug as a paste), bamboo larvae, dung beetles, moth and butterfly pupae, wasp and bee larvae, grilled tarantula, and termite soup. A side of Raid will cost you extra.

_03:: Japanese Cuisine: Insects II

The Japanese also have a little-known gustatory affinity for insects. In fact, the practice of eating aquatic insects in particular probably originated in the Japanese Alps, where a hostile environment resulted in food scarcities. Now, however, insect larvae are considered a delicacy and are served throughout Japan, including the best restaurants in Tokyo. Well-known dishes include hachi no ko, or boiled wasp larvae; zazamushi or water insect larvae; inago, or field grasshoppers in fried rice; semi, or fried cicada; and sangi, or fried silk moth pupae.

_04:: Nigeria: Insects III

Asia isn't the only place you can get someone to rustle you up a couple of bugs. People from Kwara State in Nigeria also have a long-standing appreciation of insects as food. The particular technique used for catching termites is pretty interesting: termites are captured by putting a bowl of water under a bright light, attracting the termites, which then fall into the water and drown. A popular variation is winged termites—female queens and male drones that take flight to mate. Large, mature queens are considered a delicacy and are reserved for developed palates. Generally, the inhabitants of Kwara State roast termites over open coals or fry them in a pot before adding salt to taste. Nigerians also enjoy crickets disemboweled and roasted over open coals, except for the Yoruba because Ogun, their iron god, forbids eating animals that don't have blood. Grasshoppers, however, are the most popular because there's no religious taboo governing them, and field hands can eat them raw.

_05:: Guangxi, China: Live Monkey Brains

Disbelieving Westerners and Chinese have long asserted that the alleged practice of eating the brains of a live monkey directly from its skull in south China is a rumor, but in fact it isn't. Gourmets at Pingxiang, on the border with Vietnam, buy monkeys themselves at market and have them prepared by cooks at local inns. The cooks force the monkeys to drink large amounts of rice wine, and when they are passed out they bind their limbs, chop open their skull, and scoop out the brains into a bowl. Diners can tell the monkey has been prepared well when they can see the blood vessels still pulsing. The brains are eaten with condiments including pickled ginger, chili pepper, fried peanuts, and cilantro, and apparently taste like tofu. In less enlightened times monkeys were bound and gagged and then strapped under a special table with a hole in the center, and the tops of their skulls were sawed off while they were still sober. Thank God the TV show *Fear Factor* didn't exist back then.

They'd Steal Candy from a Baby:
Dictators with Infamous Sweet Tooths

4

After a busy day of oppressing your own people, murdering your enemies, and conquering foreign lands, sometimes a workaholic dictator just needs to treat himself to a little pick-me-up. These were four guys happy to do just that.

_01:: Napoléon: Keeping It Short and Sweet

Though he was originally from Corsica, Napoléon seemed to share the French obsession with pastries. In fact, his cook, Antonin Carême, who would eventually become a globe-trotting celebrity famous for his sugary confections, first made his reputation with an enormous wedding cake for Napoléon, celebrating his marriage to the empress Josephine. Of course, cakes were just the tip of the icing for the squirrelly French commander. Napoléon's favorite dessert was supposedly a pastry that resembled profiterole, made with chocolate and cream, and he was also said to favor a pastry called Turkish delight with pistachio filling. Later, when he was in exile on Elba, the sweet-toothed sovereign consoled himself with copious amounts of a sweet dessert wine from Klein Constantia in South Africa.

_02:: Hitler: Getting His Cake, and Definitely Eating It Too

Old Adolf probably had the most famous sweet tooth on record. And though he was a vegetarian who also abstained from hard alcohol, Hitler's weakness for candy and pastries was well known, and admirers always made sure to bring a box of chocolates or cake or pastries when they came to see the Führer. So, just how sweet were his teeth? Hitler was reputed to put seven teaspoons of sugar in each cup of tea, supposedly added sugar to wine because he found it too bitter otherwise, and plied all his guests with ice cream and candy. In fact, Hitler's favorite dessert chef, Gerhardt Shtammer, claims that Hitler asked him to make delectable desserts right up to the very end, when they were trapped in Hitler's bunker with hard-core Nazi holdouts. According to Shtammer, Hitler's favorite desserts were éclairs decorated with little swastikas and strudel.

_03:: Saddam Hussein and His Spider-Hole Snack Attacks

The bizarre contents of Saddam Hussein's residences—velvet paintings of Elvis and all—have provided endless fodder for cocktail conversations. Amid the revelations of Saddam's incredibly bad taste, it was also revealed that Saddam was a bit of a sugar fiend. In his last rather ignoble residence—the "spider hole" where he was finally apprehended in Ad Dawr in December 2003—American soldiers found a refrigerator filled with Mars and Bounty candy bars and 7-Up. Thank God! No

HIDEKI TOJO'S HORRIBLE-TERRIBLE, NO-GOOD, VERY BAD DAY (AND DENTURES)

General Hideki Tojo, who led Japan to disastrous defeat with his decision to attack Pearl Harbor, apparently enjoyed a lifetime of sweets. In fact, the condition of his teeth was even more abysmal than the condition of his army, because when he was captured he required a full set of dentures! Oddly enough, this led to one of the more bizarre stories of the Second World War: George Foster and Jack Mallory, Navy dentists on loan to the Army, were given responsibility for making Tojo's dentures and, realizing the identity of their famous patient, decided to play a youthful prank on him. Mallory made dentures that were an exact fit, causing no discomfort, but engraved a message— "Remember Pearl Harbor"—in Morse code on his false teeth.

longer relegated to the realm of middle school sleepovers, and Little League pizza parties, these snack foods have finally broken through to a new demographic: dictators evading prosecution for crimes against humanity.

Touch of Evil

In the Soviet Union, the role of Santa Claus was usurped by candy fan Joseph Stalin. Uncle Joe loved sweets so much that they were distributed to schoolchildren all across the country on his birthday (celebrated on December 21).

_04:: Fidel Castro: Near-Death by Chocolate

In a country known for its sugar production, the Cuban strongman's well-known fondness for a particular type of chocolate milkshake might very well have led to his demise had the CIA been a little more on top of its game. Among the approximately 600 assassination attempts the CIA is believed to have set in motion against Castro, one infamous failure called for covert agents to sneak poisoned aspirin into El Presidente's daily chocolate shake. And while they succeeded in getting the poison into the beverage, an overeager servant inadvertently foiled the plan by putting the shake in a freezer to keep it cold. Unfortunately, it froze and Cuba's temperamental dictator dictated a new one.

Servings of Swine:
The Worst Pork Barrel Politics Revealed

Sure, when it's served up as a McRib, or on a platter of chops at Grandma's, pork can be downright tasty. But as soon as a politician gets his grubby hands on the stuff, it becomes a little harder to stomach. The following are six of the worst cases of pork barrel politics, served high with a couple dollops of contempt!

_01:: The Pig Book and Oinker Awards

Every year, a pork barrel watchdog group called Citizens Against Government Waste produces the Pig Book, detailing the year's worst pork in Congress. CAGW picks the most outrageous examples from each year to bestow upon them the facetious Oinker Awards. The 2003 Sometimes You Feel Like a Nut Award went to the National Peanut Festival Fairgrounds in Dothan, Alabama, for the $202,500 allocated to them. The 2004 Soaking the Taxpayers Award was given to an Iowa senator for the $50 million he procured for an *indoor* rainforest in Coralville, Iowa. Montana's senator Conrad Burns took home the 2002 Shear Waste Award, as well as $400,000 for the Montana Sheep Institute. And 2001 had two notable winners: the Taxpayers Get Tanked Award, for $648,000 for ornamental fish research; and the Pillager from Pascagoula Award, bestowed upon Trent Lott for the $460 million he got for his state to develop an amphibious assault ship that the Department of Defense didn't ask for or want. Keep up the good work, CAGW.

_02:: Old Pork: Bonus Bill of 1817

The very first example of pork in American politics comes to us from the legendary and cantankerous South Carolina politician John C. Calhoun. In 1817, Johnny C. proposed the Bonus Bill in Congress, by means of which he planned on using the profits from the Second National Bank of the United States to finance the construction of roads and canals. While his stated objectives were to connect the country and aid all regions, critics said that Calhoun intended most of the money to go to the South, thereby strengthening its economic ties to the North and West and opening new markets for its goods (and considering his future cries for nullification of federal laws and secession from the Union, this argument had some pretty strong legs). After all, the North had already built its own good roads and canals, which was one of the main reasons why it was so far ahead of the South economically. But the whole thing is moot anyway: President James Madison vetoed it as unconstitutional.

_03:: Permanent Pork: The War Finance Corporation

In 1918, as the United States harnessed its economy for World War I, businesses in crucial war-related industries were having trouble borrowing money through bond sales. So Congress authorized the War Finance Corporation, setting aside $500 million to be made available for finance production. But when the war ended, the WFC didn't. Oddly enough, it lived on in various guises: first to finance the postwar European economy, then to help struggling farmers during the Depression. But money this big attracts plenty of opportunists, and through the 1930s and '40s chairman Jesse H. Jones from Texas doled out dough to his cronies in countless industries, including railroads, municipalities, insurance companies, and exporters. During World War II, the WFC payouts ballooned to over $50 billion. In some nifty political sleight-of-hand, the WFC was abolished in 1953 and replaced by the Small Business Administration, which is still with us and does basically the same thing. Same pork, different acronym.

_04:: Porkers-Come-Lately

Seems the two most recent additions to the U.S. community of states are making up for lost time at the pork trough. Alaska and Hawaii have traded the number one and two positions for several years in terms of pork spending per capita. In 2001, Alaska received 30 times the national average of pork spending per person; Hawaii got 15 times. And where did all this money go? It funded vital projects such as the pilot training simulator at the University of Alaska ($2,500,000); repairs on an Aleutian Pribilof church in Hawaii ($1,250,000); a parking lot and pedestrian safety access for the whopping 300 residents of Talkeetna, Alaska ($400,000); marijuana eradication in Hawaii ($2,500,000); and the Native Hawaiian culture and arts program ($742,000). Not bad for two states with combined populations of under two million people.

Touch of Evil

The Armour brand actually evolved from real pork barrel politics. Taking advantage of artificially high food prices, P. D. Armour sold futures to pork barrels he didn't own, gambling that the Civil War would end in a year, in which case prices would drop dramatically. The gamble paid off and he netted more than $2,000,000, leaving a bunch of disgruntled traders and government officials in the wake.

_05:: Out of This World Pork: NASA

With a humongous annual budget of around $14 billion, the National Aeronautics and Space Administration has turned into one fantastic place for pork. In 2000 alone, pork projects connected to NASA included $3 million for the Donald Danforth Plant Science Center's Modern Genetics Project "to permit studies that simulate specialized weather conditions, pathogen attacks, and development and characterization on genetically modified plants in controlled-environment chambers"; $15 million for upgrades to the Life Sciences Building at the University of Missouri–Columbia; and $3 million to enhance the University of South Mississippi's research of remotely sensed data for coastal zone management. The total amount of pork that went to NASA-related projects that year: $140.2 million. Three...two...one ...rip-off!

_06:: The Jumpstart Our Business Strength Act: Coming Soon to a Trough Near You

In a strange way, it's almost comforting to know that war, economic uncertainty, and massive budget deficits have not stopped our government from dysfunctioning normally. Almost. In 2004, a pork-packed piece of legislation called the Jumpstart Our Business Strength Act made its way up the Hill. According to CAGW, the bill was a mother lode of windfall tax breaks for all kinds of corporations: $519 million for makers of small aircraft, including Learjet; $310 million for makers of ships; $189 million for Oldsmobile dealerships (umm . . . *why?*); $92 million for NASCAR (the number-one spectator sport in the country gets a tax cut?); and, most vital of all in time of war, $8 million in tax breaks for makers of bows and arrows.

Let There Be Lunch:
Myths from Other Cultures about Gods' Strange Eating Habits

8

Eve gets a lot of bad press for the whole forbidden fruit incident. After all, who among us hasn't been tempted by a nice, shiny apple? But Eve's garden party foul doesn't even compare with these mythological munchers and their appetites for destruction.

_01:: Kronos and the Kids

If you thought your family was dysfunctional, you oughta meet the early Greek gods. Kronos, a Titan, overthrew his father, Uranus, and had him castrated. But Uranus warned Kronos that one of his children would kill him. So, among Uranus' first batch of offspring, he had the one-eyed Cyclopes and the hundred-handed Hecatonchires all imprisoned in the underworld. Fine. But then Kronos' sister and wife, Rhea, gave birth to a bunch of gods and goddesses. Panicky, Kronos ate them whole, one by one: Hestia, Hades, Poseidon, Demeter, and Hera. Chomp! But by the sixth, little Zeus, Rhea got wise. She hid the baby and presented Kronos with a stone wrapped in swaddling clothes. He ate the stone, and all was forgotten. That is, until years later when Zeus tricked Pops into upchucking the rest of the family (gods apparently don't digest so well). The new crew then joined forces with the other Olympians to overthrow Daddy and the Titans.

_02:: Zeus and Metis

Zeus had a lot—an awful lot—of sexual conquests. After all, it's good to be the king—especially of the gods. But his first was Metis, goddess of wisdom and knowledge (who says guys don't like girls with brains?). After much pursuit he finally consummated the relationship, resulting in her pregnancy. But leave it to an oracle to spoil the afterglow. A prophecy said that one of Metis's children would overthrow Zeus (surprising that this didn't sound familiar to big Z, isn't it?). So, naturally, he ate Metis. For a while it worked out: Metis gave Zeus wise advice from his belly. But pretty soon, he started to get wicked headaches. So bad, in fact, that he ordered Hephaestus to split his head open with a hammer and wedge (Excedrin wasn't around yet). Out of his split skull emerged Athena, fully grown and armed.

_03:: Demeter

The Greek goddess of grain and the harvest (the Romans called her Ceres, from whence we get "cereal") also bore quite a temper. When a mortal named Erysichthon foolishly tried to cut down her favorite oak tree, she appeared in the form of a priestess asking him to stop. What did our clever mortal do? Threaten her with his ax, of course. Oh, no you *didn't!* Demeter was, in a word, miffed. Because Erysichthon had wanted the wood to build himself a dining hall, Demeter cursed the man with an endless hunger (goddesses are nothing if not ironic). The more he ate, the hungrier he got. He ate his parents, their house, the dirt in the street, and, finally, himself. Yep. Ate himself, just like that.

_04:: Demeter, the Second Course

We've all heard the ironic punishment tale of Tantalus, the guy with the burning thirst and ravenous hunger who's stuck in a pool of cool water with grapes hanging just out of reach for all eternity. So how'd he get there? Turns out he was a son of Zeus, so he felt like he could have the gods over for dinner. To please

them, he chopped up his son Pelops, boiled him to a nice al dente, and served him to the gods. They were less than thrilled, and no one touched the Pelops platter except poor Demeter. Seems she was depressed and distracted because her daughter Persephone had just been whisked off to be the bride of Hades (and we all remember the pomegranate seeds and how *that* turned out). So, the distracted deity ate Pelops's shoulder. The gods, covering for her, restored the boy to life and gave him an ivory shoulder. Not so good for Dad, pretty good for the son. Apparently, Greek chicks dig ivory prostheses.

_05:: Finn and the Magic Salmon

The Greeks aren't the only ones who can come up with gustatory gems. Straight from the Celtic mythology of third-century Ireland comes the Fenian Cycle, tales of a brave group of warriors called the Fianna. The leader, Finn MacCunaill, was known for his wisdom and intelligence. So how'd he get so smart? Simple. He burned himself while cooking fish. OK, let's back up. Finn's mentor, a Druid, told him of the Salmon of Knowledge that swam in the River Boyne. Eat the salmon, know it all. So, the Druid caught the fish, and Finn dutifully set about cooking it. But salmon, as we all know, are fatty, and some of that fat sputtered from the fire and burned Finn's thumb. He licked the grease, and suddenly he was clairvoyant. The story goes that Finn used this knowledge to warn Ireland of the eventual coming of the Vikings. Lotta good it did 'em.

_06:: Set and the Semen

Every mythology needs a real bad guy, and the Egyptians had Set, the god of evil and darkness, nemesis and occasional homosexual lover of Horus, and slayer of Osiris, Horus's papa. Ever seen that Egyptian god with the head of a jackal? Yep, that's Set. To get revenge on Set, Horus and Isis, Horus's mother, hatched a strange plot: Isis made Horus ejaculate into a jar. She then spread the semen onto a piece of lettuce (a popular aphrodisiac for the ancient Egyptians). Set, suspecting nothing, ate the lettuce. In Egyptian belief, this meant that Set was symbolically "pregnant" by Horus, and thereby subservient to him. When the semen eventually "came forth" from Set, he was humiliated before all the gods. The obvious moral: When having lunch with an Egyptian god, skip the salad.

_07:: Karpakeli

This is an obscure one. Karpakeli is the ancestral god of the Pun Magar tribe of Nepal. One story tells of his nine wicked sons' plot to kill him. While gathering honey on a high cliff, Karpakeli was warned by a honey bird of his sons' scheme, so Karpakeli stored most of the honey in a cave, sending only empty combs down to his sons. They soon cut the rope, stranding him on the cliff, to kill him. But the clever Karpakeli was prepared, and he spent many months living off the honey he'd stored. Eventually, though, it ran out, so he started eating the only other food available: himself. Starting with his arms, then his thighs, then most of his own body. Luckily, the gods sent a series of animals to rescue him: a white monkey, a crow, even ants. Finally, the good god was rescued by a pair of vultures named Khakapati.

_08:: Amaterasu, Sword Swallower

As far as food goes, the Japanese mythmakers were pretty happy to get into the act as well. The chief deity in Japanese mythology was Amaterasu, the sun goddess from whom Japan's emperors were purportedly descended (Emperor Hirohito was forced to renounce this claim to divinity after World War II). She had a bit of trouble with her hot-tempered brother Susanowo, the *kami* (god or spirit) of the sea and storms. So, when she heard he was coming to visit her, she prepared for a battle (don't *any* gods get along with their families?). But they reached an understanding, and he offered her his sword. What's a gal to do? Well, Amaterasu promptly broke it into three pieces and ate them. When she exhaled (some sources say she spit them out), she created several more *kami* out of the pieces. After that, raw fish doesn't sound so bad.

Feeding Frenzies:
Pioneers of All-You-Can-Eat

4

Despite what you may have heard, the concept of all-you-can-eat wasn't invented by the owner of a Chinese restaurant (they just seem to have perfected it).

_01:: Death by . . . Hetvägg?

By the time Adolf Frederick came to occupy the throne of Sweden in 1751, a long period of monarchy-weakening reforms called the Age of Freedom left him with very little power. But his appetite didn't seem to suffer. In fact, the old Swede died in 1771 at the age of 61 from digestive problems caused by a giant meal (the dinner table being the only place left to him to indulge his power). His final feast? Smoked herring, lobster, caviar, sour cabbage soup, and a heapin' helpin' of a dessert called Hetvägg, a bun filled with marzipan served in a bowl of milk. It's no wonder the hapless monarch went down in history with an unfortunate (but accurate) epithet: "the King Who Ate Himself to Death." Maybe it's not *always* that good to be the king.

_02:: Mardi Gras' Great-Great-Great-Great-Great-Granddad

Just as the pagan Saturnalia was co-opted by Christmas and the Celtic Samhain got translated into All Hallow's Eve/Halloween, the pre-Lent binge of Mardi Gras has its origins in a pagan festival. On March 15, the ancient Romans celebrated the Lupercalia, a festival commemorating the founding of Rome and the suckling of the infants Romulus and Remus in a cave (the Lupercal) on the Palatine Hill.

While the festival had a solemn religious aspect to it—you know, the standard blood and animal sacrifice—the celebration was marked by much drinking, revelry, and general buffoonery. Boys clad in loincloths and smeared with blood would run through the city, as boys tend to do, lashing bystanders with strips of skin from sacrificed goats. After all, the lashings were said to promote fertility and easy childbirth, so young wives were particularly eager to meet the lash. When Rome became Christianized, the Lupercalia was replaced by Carnivale (literally "Good-bye to the Flesh"), the day before the beginning of the solemn season of Lent. In fact, the day before Ash Wednesday saw so much drinking and feasting that the medieval French dubbed it *Mardi gras,* or "Fat Tuesday."

_03:: The Sumo Diet

Like nearly every aspect of sumo life, the famed Japanese wrestlers' diet is based in centuries of tradition. So, what exactly makes up this traditional food? Sumo wrestlers put on their enormous weight—700 pounds and more—mostly by consuming a simple diet of *chankonabe,* a thick boiled stew containing tofu, carrots, cabbages, leeks, potatoes, lotus roots, daikon radishes, shiitake mushrooms, and giant burdock in chicken broth. Some rec-

Scandalicious

FATTY ARBUCKLE CRUSHES LOVER TO DEATH!

Media circuses around celebrity scandals long predate Michael Jackson and Robert Blake. One of the first involved Roscoe "Fatty" Arbuckle, a major star of silent films. Set around a three-day party hosted by Arbuckle at San Francisco's Saint Francis Hotel in 1921, the case involved a young woman named Virginia Rappe who died of peritonitis during the festivities. While Arbuckle claimed that her death was caused by too much alcohol (other sources say she'd recently had one of several abortions, which may have caused the illness), the papers went wild for the scandal. Based largely on the words of serial celebrity blackmailer "Bambina" Maude Delmont, the papers accused Arbuckle of raping Rappe, crushing her with his nearly 300 pounds, and violating her with various foreign objects. Arbuckle became the public's scapegoat for the amorality of Hollywood, and movie houses stopped showing his films. Even though he was eventually acquitted (he was already back in Los Angeles when Rappe died), Arbuckle was blacklisted by the Hays Office, a Hollywood monitoring organization established in the wake of the scandal. Fatty would eventually have to change his name to get work, directing several films under the pseudonym William B. Goodrich. He died of a heart attack in his sleep in 1933, at the age of 46. It was his one-year wedding anniversary.

ipes call for shrimp, noodles, raw eggs, or beer (interesting note: since falling to all fours in a match means a loss, many sumo wrestlers superstitiously avoid eating any four-legged animals. So there's no beef or pork in their chankonabe). Doesn't sound particularly fattening, does it? By itself, it isn't, even with the side of rice. In fact, chankonabe is actually quite healthy, high in both protein and vitamins. But three factors play into the whole weight-gaining aspect of it for sumo wrestlers: (1) They eat a lot of it—an *awful* lot of it; (2) they traditionally skip breakfast, consuming most of their calories at an enormous midday meal, after which (3) they immediately take a

three- or four-hour nap. As most nutritionists will tell you, skipping breakfast and then sleeping immediately after a meal is a guaranteed way to pack on the pounds.

_04:: The Babe's Bad Day at the Plate

Home wasn't the only plate at which George Herman "Babe" Ruth was a dominator. This guy had a big appetite for everything—food, drink, women, you name it. In fact, "the Sultan of Swat's" favorite breakfast was said to include a porterhouse steak, six fried eggs, and potatoes, all washed down with a quart mixture of bourbon whiskey and ginger ale. The

Babe also had a certain fondness for hot dogs, downing between 12 and 18 one day in April 1925. Shortly thereafter, he blacked out on a train and was hospitalized for an intestinal abscess (recent historians have attributed his hospital stay to gonorrhea, not a tummy ache). Disgustingly enough, one of the Babe's partially eaten hot dogs (now black and shriveled and nasty) is still on display at the Baseball Reliquary in Monrovia, California. And although Ruth became pretty hefty in the last few years of his career, the rumor that the Yankees adopted their famous pinstripes to make him look slimmer is false. The pinstripes first appeared in 1912, when the Yanks were still the New York Highlanders.

Touch of Evil

Realizing that all-you-can-eat buffets would attract customers (who would then pay to be entertained in other ways), the El Rancho casino in Las Vegas began to offer a smorgasbord with lobster, shrimp, roast beef, turkey, and more in 1946.

Crazy Diets from Crazy Times

Whether it's avoiding carbs, trans fats, or solid foods, diets generally ask a lot from you in the restraint department. Of course, when we heard about the following three diets, that meant restraining ourselves from laughing.

_01:: Gustave Jaeger: Don't Eat Animals, Wear Them

By 1885, the British critic and playwright George Bernard Shaw had already been practicing vegetarianism for a few years when he came under the influence of Dr. Gustave Jaeger's "sanatory [*sic*] system." The regimen was as much about what to wear as what to eat, and Jaeger rejected plant fibers such as "unhealthful" cotton and linen in favor of animal fibers such as wool. As a result, Shaw gave up using sheets in bed and took to wearing woolen clothing exclusively. In fact, his knitted "stockinette" suit became a personal trademark. Jaeger also allowed clothing made of hair and feathers—preferably unbleached, unprocessed, and free of dyes. Most of his followers came from Victorian reform movements such as the Fellowship of the New Life, which—like Shaw—preached a strict vegetarianism.

_02:: The Reverend Sylvester Graham: Stay Away from the Ketchup!

Graham crackers today are made from bleached white flour, which means, strictly speaking, that they are not graham crackers. Named for the Reverend Sylvester Graham (who coincidentally *was* a cracker), the sweet cupboard staple was part of a 19th-century diet meant to advocate temperance and vegetarianism in order to fend off excessive carnal desires and thus prevent disease. Graham preached that unsifted, coarsely ground wheat flour was healthier than the white stuff. He was right about that, but most people figured Graham for cuckoo. His regimen, aimed at reining in the sex drive, included sleeping on hard mattresses, taking cold showers, exercising, sleeping with the windows open (no matter the weather), and eating whole grains, fruits, and vegetables. Graham also warned that the use of ketchup and mustard led to insanity. Followers of his doctrine lived in special Grahamist boardinghouses and in an experimental commune near Boston.

_03:: Horace Fletcher: The Great Masticator

Also called "the Chew-Chew Man," Horace Fletcher was an American importer and art dealer who in 1890 donned a white jacket and began lecturing and writing about nutrition. His theme: chew. Fletcher advised that nothing should be swallowed unless it could be reduced to liquid first by chewing. Supported by studies that found chewing every morsel 32 times could be beneficial for weight loss (it slowed down the rate of eating, at the very least), Fletcher claimed such adherents as novelist Henry James and industrialist John D. Rockefeller. Health reformer Dr. John Harvey Kellogg was also a devotee of "Fletcherizing" for a while, and even made up a "chewing song" for patients. Many Fletcherizers spit out anything they could not chew to liquid, which eliminated a lot of dietary fiber and led to constipation.

Hail to the Chef: Presents Who Overindulged

4

Feeding an appetite for power rarely fills a guy's belly. These four pudgy heads of state were as happy raiding the pantry as they were creating policy.

_01:: Grover Cleveland: The Glass Is Always Half Empty

Large, jovial Grover Cleveland—also known as "Uncle Jumbo"—enjoyed his beer. In 1870 (15 years before he became president), Grover ran for district attorney of Erie County, New York, against Lyman K. Bass. It was a friendly contest. In fact, it was so friendly that Cleveland and his opponent drank and chatted together daily. In the interest of moderation, they agreed to have no more than four glasses of beer per day. But soon they exceeded that and started "borrowing" glasses from the next day and the next until they'd exhausted their ration for the whole campaign—with the election still weeks away. The solution: Each brought his own giant tankard to the tavern, called it a "glass," and went back to the four-a-day ration.

_02:: An Extra-Cuddly Teddy

The standard scoop on Teddy Roosevelt was that he was a scrawny, sickly weakling from New York City who built himself up into a rough, tough cowboy type through vigorous outdoor pursuits. What's seldom mentioned is that Roosevelt went from skinny boy to robust young man to plump (though vigorous) president to obese (though still active) ex-president. While running on the Bull Moose Party ticket in a 1912 attempt to regain the White House, Roosevelt was described as "an eager and valiant trencherman" (it meant he ate a lot). If the main course was roast chicken, TR would consume an entire bird himself, in addition to the rest of the meal. Not to mention the four glasses of whole milk the portly prez routinely threw back with dinner. Photos and films show an aging Roosevelt carrying a decidedly wide load.

_03:: W. H. Taft and His Presidential Privileges

William Howard Taft often dieted because his doctor and his wife told the 290-pound president that he must. But without supervision, Will "the Thrill" didn't just give in to temptation, he sought it. Once while traveling he asked a railroad conductor for a late-night snack. When the conductor said there was no dining car, Taft angrily called for his secretary, Charles D. Norton, who had probably—under instruction from Mrs. Taft—arranged for the diner to be unhooked. Norton reminded the president that his doctor discouraged between-meal eating. Taft would have none of it. He ordered a stocked dining car attached at the next stop and specified that it have filet mignon. "What's the use of being president," he said to Norton, "if you can't have a train with a diner on it?"

_04:: Bill Clinton: With an Assist from Helmut Kohl

President Bill Clinton, who famously frequented McDonald's, was known for eating whatever was put in front of him. He showed a more discriminating, if just as hungry, side in the company of Germany's chancellor Helmut Kohl, though. Kohl was called "Colossus," at least in part because he carried 350 pounds on his 6-foot-4 frame. But, in Kohl, Clinton found a gourmand soul mate. In 1994, Clinton hosted the chancellor at Filomena Ristorante of Georgetown for a lunch at which both consumed mass quantities of ravioli, calamari, and red wine, as well as plenty of antipasto, buttered breadsticks, Tuscan white bean soup, salad, and sweet zabaglione with berries. Each ended the meal by ordering a large piece of chocolate cake to go. Clinton once remarked that he and his German counterpart, though the largest of world leaders, were still too slim to be sumo wrestlers.

Deadly Digestive Problems

On the long list of unpleasant ways to die, it's hard to imagine anything topping "exploding colon." We'll take the stomach flu, heartburn, death by paper cuts even! Just please, please, spare us these fates.

_01:: Farting to Death

Sounds like a third-grade punch line, but maybe it's so funny because it's true. The average person expels about a half liter of gas per day. Put bluntly, that's somewhere between 13 and 17 daily farts. And although any 11-year-old with a matchbook and curiosity knows that gas passed is flammable (since it contains primarily hydrogen and methane), it's not dangerous for the excessively gassy to work around open flames. Once in a great while, though, someone will blow up from gas. The problem usually occurs during colonic surgery, when heat (or a spark) comes into contact with flammable intestinal gasses after inadequate "bowel evacuation." The resulting explosion is sometimes fatal. Anyone who's ever suffered through colon surgery can tell you exactly what "bowel evacuation" entails—you drink a laxative the day before surgery and find yourself in the bathroom with enough time to read *Anna Karenina*. Unpleasant, sure, but better than blowing up on the operating table.

_02:: Pica

Pica, an eating disorder in which sufferers feel compelled to eat nonfood items, is usually seen in children. At least 10% of kids enjoy eating dirt or paste or plaster, but adults suffering from pica often develop unusual tastes. Strangely, the same such cravings pop up so often they have their own names. Pagophagia is the compulsive eating of ice; coprophagia describes eating (often animal) feces; coniophagia involves—get this—the pathological consumption of dust from venetian blinds. And pica can be fatal. Too much plaster might lead to fatal lead poisoning, for instance, and consuming clay can lead to a potentially deadly intestinal blockage.

_03:: Roundworms

About 25% of the world's population is infected with roundworms (that's *Ascaris lumbricoides* to the Latin scholars), which is even more disconcerting when you consider that one generally contracts roundworms by swallowing egg-ridden human feces. Once infected, the eggs hatch in the stomach and intestines, then migrate throughout the body.

Touch of Evil

The most deadly digestive problem of all may prove to be bovine in nature. Cows emit so much methane in their flatulence that some experts claim it to be a contributing factor to the erosion of the ozone layer.

Although completely disgusting, roundworms are only occasionally deadly—they can cause edema in the lungs; and the female worms, which can grow 18 inches long, sometimes perforate the intestines, leading to peritonitis. But the most terrifying wormy complication involves anesthesia. Because worms find anesthesia irritating, they sometimes migrate up the trachea and nasal passages or down the intestines during surgery. It's been reported, for instance, that one pregnant woman had several of the nematodes worm out of her nose and mouth while she was giving birth.

_04:: Celiac Sprue

Dieters seeking a low-carb lifestyle might do well to seek out celiac sprue, an intestinal ailment that amounts to an allergy to the protein gluten—found in such foods as wheat, barley, and rye. When celiac sufferers ingest the dreaded stuff, the immune system responds by attacking the small intestine, which leads to a sort of intestinal baldness. Villi, hairlike protuberances that line the small intestine, absorb nutrients into the body, but when people with celiac eat gluten, the villi get flattened or otherwise damaged, making proper nourishment impossible. If left undiagnosed, celiac can lead to massive malnutrition, wasting, and even death. But people with celiac can lead perfectly healthy lives provided they forswear gluten. Which means no beer. Which is, frankly, unacceptable.

_05:: Megacolon

A blessedly uncommon but life-threatening disorder, megacolon is characterized by the one-two punch of a massively inflated colon (one), and the accompanying abdominal distension (two). Although generally a complication of bowel diseases like ulcerative colitis and Crohn's disease, megacolon occasionally develops from severe—and we mean *severe*—constipation. One such example is on display at Philadelphia's Mütter Museum, which collects all manner of medical oddities (from John Wilkes Booth's thorax to a tumor removed from President Grover Cleveland's jaw). The crown jewel of the Mütter Museum's collection is a five-foot-long megacolon. Bearing a distinct resemblance to Jabba the Hutt, the monstrosity was removed from a man who, unable to move his bowels, died with 40 pounds of excrement in his gut.

All You Need Is Drugs: Philosophers Who Liked to Get Groovy Thoughts

3

Philosophy requires precise reasoning and intense concentration on the most complex and intractable problems of human existence. But when your job involves developing elaborate proof about subjects like epistemology (the science of figuring out what we know, and how we can know it, and whether we can really know what we think we can know, and so on), perhaps you can be forgiven for winding down with a bit of illicit pleasure.

_01:: Aldous Huxley and His Rave New World

While no one confuses him with Aristotle, Aldous Huxley *is* considered something of a minor philosopher. Most famous for his tome *Brave New World* (1932), which featured the drug Soma, Huxley became fascinated with Hindu philosophy in the late 1930s, and eventually wrote a book *(The Perennial Philosophy)* and many essays on the subject. By the time 1953 rolled around, Huxley had tried the hallucinogen mescaline, and believed the visionary experiences he'd had reflected a truer world. In fact, Huxley was so enamored with hallucinogens that he dropped acid on his deathbed, passing away on November 22, 1963. For the record, C. S. Lewis, who abstained from drugs, and John F. Kennedy, who took copious amounts of tranquilizers, died on the same day.

_02:: Plotinus and the "Good" Life

Plotinus, the third-century Roman credited with founding Neoplatonism, traveled more extensively than most ancient philosophers. And in those days, the easiest way to see the world was by joining a war. So in 242, Plotinus accompanied Emperor Gordian III in his battles against Persia, where Plotinus likely encountered Persian and Indian philosophies. He also probably encountered opium. Upon his return to Rome, the older, wiser, and definitely groovier Plotinus founded a loosely affiliated school of philosophers who placed great emphasis on union with "the Good," or God. And while it's not clear whether or not he thought it helped him in his search for this union, Plotinus also became a regular opium

Touch of Evil

In 1963, Timothy Leary was fired from his job as a psychology professor at Harvard University due to continued experiments with psychedelic agents.

user. In fact, some scholars have even argued that his opium addiction shaped his high philosophical beliefs.

_03:: Foucault: The Thinking Man's Drinking Man

Being something of a postmodernist, the French philosopher and literary critic Michel Foucault (1926–1984) didn't believe drugs to be intrinsically good or bad, true or false. But he did use them. In addition to drinking heavily, Foucault dabbled in psychedelics and opium, and reportedly grew marijuana plants on the ledge of his Parisian apartment (he also enjoyed S and M, but that's neither here nor there). Luckily, the drugs didn't affect the quality of his intellect—books like *The Order of Things* and *The Archaeology of Knowledge* were the first major rebuttals to existentialism—and Sartre called the latter "the last rampart of the bourgeoisie." Foucault's books are also so exceedingly dense and his definition of "truth" and "knowledge" so nuanced that, frankly, it's difficult to imagine he ever wrote stoned.

Booze Is to Comedy as Pen Is to Literature: Funny Lushes

There's nothing funny about alcoholism. But for whatever reason, there's often something very funny about alcoholics. We can trace the phenomenon back at least 23 centuries, to the ancient Greek comic playwright Aristophanes, who is recorded as having said, "Quickly, bring me a beaker of wine so that I may wet my brain and say something clever." When full-blown alcoholism took hold of the comedians below, it was usually with tragic consequences—but until then, their wet brains made some great jokes.

_01:: W. C. Fields (1880–1946)

Of all the alcoholic comedians, the bulbous-nosed W. C. Fields (né William Claude Dukenfield) was by far the least embarrassed by his indulgence. Fields started his career as a juggler but found fame with his impeccable wit and comic timing, first on Broadway and then in the movies. Although also noted for his dislike of children ("Any man who hates children and dogs can't be all bad") and his ostentatious immorality (he claimed to religiously study the Bible—in search of loopholes), Fields is probably best known for his drinking. At his peak, Fields downed two *quarts* of gin daily. "I like to keep a bottle of stimulant handy in case I see a snake, which I also keep handy," he once remarked. Fields died on his least favorite of days—Christmas—in 1946.

_02:: Lenny Bruce (1925–1966)

Among his many contributions to American culture, we ought not forget that it was Lenny Bruce who coined the term "T and A." Who knows what other witty obscenities he might have added to the vernacular were it not for his prodigious drinking and drug abuse. Attacking everyone from JFK to Dear Abby, Bruce brought social commentary into stand-up (although it didn't always pay well...he once dressed up as a priest and "solicited money for lepers" to supplement his income). After repeated arrests for obscenity and worsening addiction, though, Bruce lost his sense of humor. He took to reading transcripts of his trials onstage, and on those rare occasions when he'd tell a joke, he'd often forget it midsentence. Sadly, Bruce passed away, bankrupt and alone, of a heroin overdose in 1966.

_03:: Bill Hicks (1961–1994)

Considered by many to be the Lenny Bruce of a new generation, Bill Hicks's innovative, ranting stand-up style inspired everyone from Sam Kinison (also an alcoholic, and also dead) to Denis Leary. Raised in Georgia, Hicks abandoned his conservative Baptist upbringing and quickly garnered critical acclaim on the comedy circuit. But his rages, both onstage and off, made him quite a misanthrope throughout much of the 1980s—heavily intoxicated, he once said Hitler "had the right idea, but was an underachiever." Unlike Lenny Bruce, though, Hicks managed to sober up. He never drank after 1988, making his 1994 death from pancreatic cancer all the more tragic.

_04:: Buster Keaton (1895–1966)

Buster Keaton, who was discovered by Fatty Arbuckle (and stood by him throughout his trials), also drank to excess. An innovative filmmaker, Keaton's masterpiece, *The General,* mixed his trademark slapstick comedy with his obsessive fascination with trains. But when Keaton's film company was bought in 1928, he soured on moviemaking, and his alcoholism worsened. In fact, by 1934 he was straitjacketed and placed in a sanitarium. Some claim that Keaton, whose godfather was none other than Harry Houdini, escaped the jacket using his godfather's tricks and then left the sanitarium to find some booze. Maybe so, but Buster eventually sobered up, and continued to be productive, if less famous. He starred, for instance, in playwright Samuel Beckett's only movie, cleverly titled *Film.* In the end, though, liquor didn't beat Buster Keaton; smoking did. He died of lung cancer in 1966.

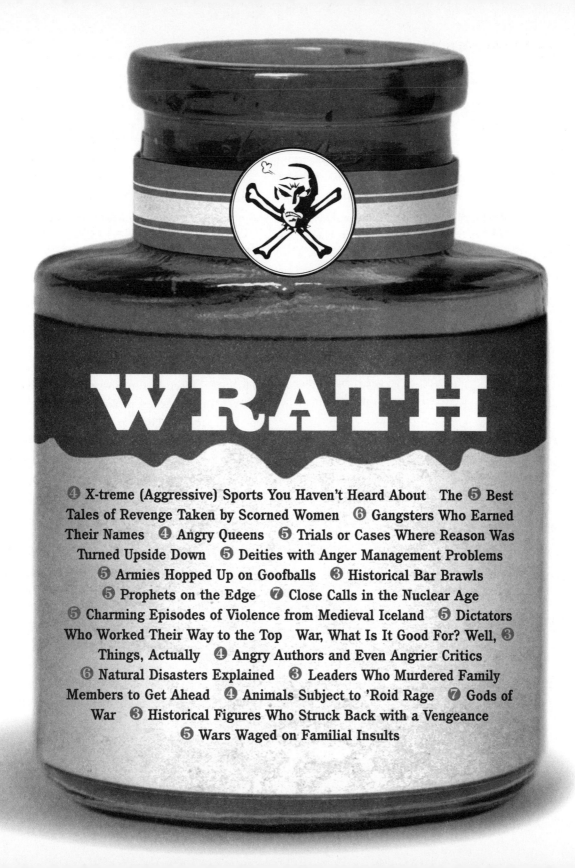

WRATH

Working It Out in Court: X-treme (Aggressive) Sports You Haven't Heard About

Ah, sportsmanship. It summons up images of competition, camaraderie, broken bones, disembowelment, and brutal, disfiguring death. No wonder players have always had fans to cheer them on.

_01:: Dead Goat Polo

The modern game of polo, favorite pastime of English aristocrats and snobbish upper-class wannabes, is usually played with a small ball about the size of a billiard ball, and almost never with a human head or a dead goat. But that's how the sport of kings began thousands of years ago under a different name—"bughazi." In fact, bughazi wasn't so much a leisure activity as military training for Persian cavalry, and it was possibly adopted from tribesmen in what is now modern-day Pakistan or Afghanistan. Aside from the dead goat factor, there were also other differences in play. Instead of four players on a side, for instance, the ancient version involved armies of men—literally—with hundreds or even thousands of players on each side. In fact, it's believed that the first tournament was won by Turkish tribesmen playing against the Persians in 600 BCE. And although the game was often played with animal heads, the Mongol conqueror Genghis Khan made a popular change, instituting the practice of decapitating military opponents and making a game ball of their noggins, still in their helmets.

_02:: Aztec Paddleball

"Ullamalitzli," a ceremonial ball game played by the Aztecs a few hundred years before the European discovery of America, called for players on two teams to don large stone belts or hip paddles. These paddles were used to bounce a small rubber ball back and forth down a narrow court with inclined stone walls. The players used each others' bodies and the walls as they attempted to maneuver the ball into a small stone ring high above mid-court. The game ended when either side scored a goal. Amazingly enough, the game actually enjoyed long popularity among the native peoples of Mexico and Central America before the Aztecs played it, including the Maya some thousands of years earlier. Of course, the stakes were a little greater when the Aztecs came to play. In their version of the sport, at the end of the game one of the captains was sacrificed to the gods, giving even more meaning to the phrase "sore loser."

_03:: X-treme Cricket

As with many aspects of their culture, it's unclear exactly what kinds of games the Vikings played, but one thing is certain—their games were incredibly brutal and violent, since they were considered training for personal combat. From vague descriptions in Icelandic "sagas"—histories of the Vikings that were passed down orally for hundreds of years before finally being transcribed in the 1200s—one ball game sounds a bit like an early and very violent version of cricket. The main difference being that most contemporary cricket players can expect to survive to the end of the game. Vikings, on the other hand, weren't always so lucky. "Egil and Thord played against Skallagrim, who grew tired and they came off better. But that evening after sunset, Egil and Thord began losing. Skallagrim was filled with such strength that he seized Thord and dashed him to the ground so fiercely that he was crushed by the blow and died on the spot."

_04:: Cheese Rolling

Though it's without a doubt one of the most absurd sports on record, the annual cheese-rolling contest at Cooper's Hill in Gloucestershire, England, is also incredibly dangerous. Which is not surprising when you consider how the sport is played: first, a master of ceremonies gives the countdown—"One to be ready, two to be steady, three to prepare, four to be off"—and then up to 20 contestants chase a seven-pound circular block of cheese down a steep, bumpy hillside, trying to catch it before it gets to the bottom 300 yards below. Four games are played over the course of one day, including one for women. Video footage of past events shows contestants breaking bones and splitting heads open, in addition to spectators suffering frequent injuries as contestants lose their footing and hurl themselves into the crowds. No one is quite sure how cheese-rolling started, though speculations include ancient pagan fertility rituals or harvest festivals.

Touch of Evil

Way back in 1984, a Japanese show called Za Gaman *("Endurance") broke open the whole* Fear Factor *TV genre by rewarding contestants who could withstand the most punishment. Physical and mental tortures included events with hot coals, snakes, cacti, and a wide range of scary implements.*

Served Cold: The Best Tales of Revenge Taken by Scorned Women

Who shot J. R.? A scorned woman. Who gave Mr. Bobbitt a belated bris? A scorned woman. Who bested Buttafuoco? You guessed it. Those guys could have picked up a thing or two from these poor saps, who quickly learned it's *never* a good idea to upset a lady.

_01:: "Mrs. Jack Johnson"

Black heavyweight boxing champion Jack Johnson was known for two things: (1) his conquests in the ring and (2) his conquests of the fairer sex. One of his favorites of the latter was Belle Schreiber, a prostitute at Chicago's glitzy Everleigh brothel. And though the Everleigh was for whites only, Johnson knew how to pull a few strings. In truth, Belle was only one of five white Everleigh girls Johnson saw, but when he married not one but *two* white women, Belle was crushed. Her high-class career ruined by her widely publicized affair with Johnson, Schreiber was broke and strung out on absinthe and drugs. Agreeing to testify for the government in their prosecution of Johnson for violating the 1910 Mann Act (which outlawed taking a woman across state lines for the "purpose of prostitution or debauchery") Belle's testimony got him a year in prison and seven years of exile in Canada. She also got her way: The stint put an end to Johnson, ruining his stellar boxing career.

_02:: Boudicca, One Badass British Babe

In the year 60 CE, the Romans were busy bringing Britain under their heel. Since anyone who resisted was crushed, it's no wonder that Boudicca, queen of the Iceni tribe in southeast Britain, decided to cooperate and offered to share her realm with Roman emperor Nero. Instead, Nero had a governor declare the region a slave province, and took Boudicca into custody (did Nero ever do *anything* right?). She was then flogged publicly while her two daughters were raped by Roman soldiers. Not a particularly clever move. In response, Boudicca raised an army, marched on the Roman city of Colchester, and burned it with thousands of Roman colonists trapped inside. Her army grew until it became unwieldy, and was eventually defeated by a disciplined Roman army. Defiant to the end, Boudicca killed herself on the battlefield rather than surrender.

Profiles in Carnage

VLAD THE IMPALER (1431-1476)

This guy was pretty much as bad as it gets. Most famous, of course, was his penchant for having people impaled—skewered alive through the anus or vagina on giant wooden spikes, to be slowly dragged down by their own weight. In fact, he liked the practice so much he once impaled 30,000 people *at one time,* for violations of some trade law or other (those of higher social standing got longer spikes). All told, good old Vlad is said to have impaled hundreds of *thousands* of people. And while his nickname Vlad the Impaler or, in Romanian, Vlad Tepes ("Vlad the Spike") only came about after death, his behavior certainly could have earned him lots of other colorful monikers.

Vlad the Daddy's Boy: As a boy, Vlad's father, Vlad Dracul ("Vlad the Dragon"), traded him to the Turks as a peace offering. That obviously tweaked the kid a bit. Upon his return, Vlad (called Dracula, or "the Little Dragon") invited his father's murderers, the boyars (Romanian nobility) to an Easter dinner. He arrested them all, sending the healthy ones into slavery to build him a palace (which many of them did naked). The rest he had impaled.

Vlad the Utopian: As ruler of Wallachia, Vlad wanted his realm to be a model of order and productivity and tried several innovative tactics to achieve this. He once had all the poor and sick invited to a great banquet. Like a good host, he fed 'em, got 'em drunk, then burned the hall with them all inside. The result: no more poor and sick people. To demonstrate his kingdom's absence of crime, he placed a golden chalice in the middle of a busy square in Tirgoviste and left it overnight. Not surprisingly, no one touched it, knowing what the penalty for thievery was under Vlad's rule (hint: it probably involved a tall spike).

Vlad the Literalist: When Turkish ambassadors said their custom prevented them from removing their hats in his presence, he had their hats *nailed to their heads.*

Vlad the Renaissance Man and Dietary Innovator: Impaling wasn't Vlad's only pastime. He also enjoyed having people physically disfigured, skinned, dismembered, boiled, eviscerated, or blinded while he watched, and frequently while he ate. His supposed habit of drinking his victims' blood and eating their flesh led to the Dracula vampire stories we all know so well. If you happened to be a guest at one of his impaling dinners and you got queasy or expressed disgust, guess what—you got impaled.

_03:: Perfect for the Part of Tyrant: Lady Mao

Before the Communists took power under Mao Zedong, China had a thriving film industry centered in Shanghai. There, as in Hollywood, thousands of young actresses flocked to the city hoping to become stars. One did become a star, but not in the way she'd originally intended. Her stage name was Lan Ping ("Blue Apple"), and as an actress she never got the big roles. Frustrated by her career and increasingly resentful of the system, Ms. Apple fell in love with and married a young revolutionary named Mao. Of course, her demeanor was to change quickly. As Lady Mao, she became the head of the notorious Gang of Four, who presided over their own purge of "unacceptable" elements. This reign of terror, ironically called the Cultural Revolution, is one of the most terrifying and chaotic periods in China's history, where freedom of thought and diverse opinions were effectively outlawed. As a former actress, Lady Mao put herself in charge of the film industry, and banned films that she felt did not exemplify good Communist values— and any film directed by someone who'd passed her over. Many were executed for their so-called crimes, and her ruthlessness earned her a nickname: "the White-Boned Demon."

_04:: Rhymes with "Odious"

Salome gets a lot of misdirected criticism for the death of John the Baptist, but the real villain of the story was her mother, Herodias. The Roman wife of Herod Philip, Herodias had come to Palestine with her beautiful daughter, Salome, and married her husband's brother, Herod Antipas. John the Baptist looked none too kindly on this royal scandal and made no secret of his disdain for the arrangement. In an effort to appease his new wife's anger, Herod reluctantly had John imprisoned. You probably know the rest: Herod threw himself a birthday bash, and Salome danced the oh-so-sexy Dance of the Seven Veils. Delighted, drunk, and probably more than a little lecherous, Herod granted her anything she desired. When she asked her mom what she should ask for, Herodias wasted no time in punishing her least favorite scandalmonger, the poor, locust-eating, camel-hair-wearing John the Baptist. She instructed Salome to ask for John's head on a platter, and Herod reluctantly complied. Even worse, in the historian St. Bede's version of the story, Herodias stabbed poor John's tongue repeatedly with a dagger.

_05:: Cochiti Caught Cheatin'

The Cochiti tribe are one of the native Pueblo peoples of New Mexico. Their colorful folklore and mythology includes the tale of a woman who suspected her husband of having an affair with her younger sister. One day, while the husband and younger sister were out on a rabbit hunt together, the wife looked into a bowl of clear water and saw an image of her husband and sister, umm, "hunting rabbits" under a cedar tree. Repeatedly. She began to cry, sat in the middle of a basket, and sang to the spirits to be turned into a snake. When the two lovers returned, she bit them both, killing them. She then appealed to the tribe's medicine men to be taken somewhere to live in peace. They took her to Gaskunkutcinako ("the Girl's Cave"). This is how the Cochiti explain the tearlike marks on a certain species of snake. And why rabbit hunting is not more popular.

Killing Is My Hobby:
Gangsters Who Earned Their Names

What's in a name? And would a thug by any other moniker still be as dangerous? We're guessing a definite "yes."

_01:: Vincent "Mad Dog" Coll (1908–1932)

His first nickname, "the Mick," was relatively harmless, since he hailed from Ireland and all. But his second one—it proved to be a keeper. The criminal with an ominous moniker, and a rep to boot, Mad Dog Coll was a top mob enforcer for New York bootlegger Dutch Schultz. And among his many talents, the versatile Coll also specialized in kidnapping and extortion. In fact, he had no qualms about torturing his victims. After falling out with Schultz, Coll touched off a gang war in which at least 20 people were killed. One was a five-year-old boy caught in a crossfire. Coll was charged with the shooting, and though he was acquitted, his days on the street were numbered. Mob bosses put a price on Coll's head, and on February 8, 1932, he was shot more than a dozen times while placing a call in a telephone booth. The Mad Dog had had his day.

_02:: Lester "Baby Face Nelson" Gillis (1908–1934)

He wanted to be called "Big George," but at 5 feet 4 inches and with the visage of a choir-boy, Lester Gillis was stuck with "Baby Face." No matter. Starting as a pickpocket, Lester put an even better face on things by graduating to enforcer (for Al Capone), bank robber, and psychopathic killer, sometimes shooting people for no reason midheist. By 1934, Baby Face was the FBI's Public Enemy No. 1. But on November 27 of that year, he went out with a bang. A lot of bangs, actually. In a gun battle with two FBI agents, Nelson killed both Feds, but not before they put 17 slugs in him. Amazingly, Nelson walked back to his getaway car and escaped. Of course, the 17 shots ended up doing the trick. Lester's body was found in a ditch the next day.

_03:: Frank "the Dasher" Abbandando (1910–1942)

Abbandando was one killer who was fast on his feet. A hit man for the New York mob's Murder, Inc., an organization of contract killers, Abbandando may have killed as many as 50 people. In one case, he walked up to a guy and pulled the trigger only to have the gun misfire. With his armed victim in pursuit, Frank "the Dasher" ran so fast around the block that he came up behind his quarry and coolly shot him in the back. Hence his nickname. But even Abbandando couldn't outrun a stool pigeon inside Murder, Inc. Convicted of a single murder, the speedy criminal was awarded a speedy trial, followed by a speedy execution via electric chair.

Touch of Evil

Al Capone was impressed with a story about his new trigger man, Tony Accardo, who took a liking to going to town on his rivals with a baseball bat. "That kid's a real Joe Batters," Capone said approvingly, and Accardo lived up to the moniker.

_04:: Albert "Lord High Executioner" Anastasia (1903–1957)

Also dubbed "the Mad Hatter" for his love of fancy fedoras, the dapper "Lord High Executioner," as his name suggests, was not a man to be messed with. In the early 1920s, Anastasia was sentenced to death for killing a fellow longshoreman. But he was granted a retrial and the conviction was reversed when four of the witnesses "disappeared." And that was just at the start of his career. After helping to kill crime boss Joe Masseria, Anastasia was made head of Murder, Inc. by new boss Lucky Luciano, and was dubbed the mob's "Lord High Executioner" by the press. And while the name stuck, his position didn't, as Anastasia eventually fell out with the other bosses. On October 25, 1957, Anastasia was shot six times while getting a haircut. As one New York paper put it the next day: "He Died in the Chair After All."

_05:: Tony "the Ant" Spilotro (1938–1986)

For the 15 years after he first hit Las Vegas in 1971 to the day he died, the mob's chief Vegas enforcer, Tony Spilotro, never spent a day in jail. Not bad for a guy who was implicated in at least 24 murders. In one case, he was even said to have squeezed a victim's head in a vise until his eyes popped out. Ugh. As for "the Ant" bit, though, li'l Tony hated the nickname, which was a reference to his diminutive stature (he was 5'5"). What he didn't hate, however, was the limelight, and it proved to be his undoing. Tony's bosses in Chicago figured he was getting a little too much press, so they came up with a quick remedy: Tony and his brother were beaten up, then buried alive in an Indiana cornfield. As for the slick lawyer who kept the Ant out of jail all that time? His name was Oscar Goodman, and he was elected Vegas's mayor in 1999, then reelected in 2003.

_06:: Aladena "Jimmy the Weasel" Fratianno (1914–1993)

"When the boss tells you to do something," Fratianno told a reporter in 1987, "you do it. You don't do it, they kill you." That's how he explained taking part in 11 murders. Of course, it didn't explain why he became a government witness in 1977 after 32 years in the mob. Fratianno, who got his nickname after speedily fleeing a crime scene as a kid, explained that he began ratting on his colleagues because they had a contract on his life. Fratianno spent 10 years in the Federal Witness Protection Program before being kicked out because he was costing taxpayers too much. Amazingly, he died peacefully in his sleep at the age of 89. Not bad for a weasel.

Hell Hath No Fury:
Angry Queens

Whether they were picking fights with the Arabs or torching all of the nation's heretics at the stake, these royal highnesses were definitely capable of a little rage, and more than a few people felt the burn.

_01:: Nitocris (2200 BCE)

OK, so Nitocris didn't exactly leave an archaeological record, but as far as the story goes, she was brave, beautiful, and married to her brother (which was common among Egyptian royalty). At some point, a mob killed her sib/hubby and put her on the throne, all of which made Nitocris the first woman known to rule Egypt. Her response wasn't exactly sweet, though. According to the Greek historian Herodotus, after a few years in charge, Nitocris built a big underground chamber, and then invited her brother-husband's slayers to a banquet. But just as they were settling in, Nitocris had the chamber flooded, to kill all of them. After the murders, she didn't exactly celebrate. Her life's work having been done, Nitocris then killed herself by jumping into a room full of hot ashes. At least her revenge was inspirational, though. In 1928, a 17-year-old kid had his first story published, in *Weird Tales* magazine. The story was called "The Vengeance of Nitocris." The kid was eventually called Tennessee Williams.

_02:: Dihya al-Kahina (ca. 694 CE)

The Berbers of North Africa were religiously a mixed lot in the last part of the seventh century: pagans, Christians, and Jews. But not Muslims. So when Arabs began pushing into the area with a convert-or-die message, the Berbers pushed back. Their leader was a tough, smart Jew said by some to be a prophetess. Keep the emphasis on tough. Al-Kahina took no mercy on the Arabs, and forced them to retreat almost out of Africa. Convinced they wouldn't come back if there were no riches to take, al-Kahina then mounted a scorched-earth campaign that decimated the region's settled areas. Irrespective of her efforts, the Arabs decided to return anyway, and al-Kahina's army was soundly defeated. It's unclear whether she died in battle or was captured and executed. Either way, legend claims she was 127 years of age when she died, which might be just a tad old to still be on the warpath.

_03:: Mary I (1516–1558)

Mary I had it pretty tough for much of her life, especially for a princess. Her dad, Henry VIII, had married her uncle's widow, which made her mom, Catherine of Aragon, her aunt, sort of. But never mind that. The important thing is that Hal divorced Catherine only to claim that it made Mary a bastard. Despite their religious differences (Henry being a Protestant and Mary an ardent Catholic), however, dad and daughter managed to reconcile. That is, until a crown was placed upon her head. When Mary became queen in 1553, she quickly decided there wasn't room for two religions in England. She was also quick to act on said belief. During her reign, about 300 people were burned at the stake for heresy, earning her a place in history as "Bloody Mary." Shortly after a disastrous war with France, she died alone, having been abandoned by her husband and being childless. Poor bastard.

Touch of Evil

Elizabeth I had known and loved Robert Devereux, the second Earl of Essex, since he was a child. And while she had no choice but to put him to death in 1601 after he had taken part in an uprising against her, the event triggered a bitter depression from which she never recovered.

_04:: Queen Isabella Offs Her Fella

Edward II was, surprise, the son of King Edward I of England. And, not to put too fine a point on it, the Deuce liked boys— particularly a French knight named Piers Gaveston. Although married to Isabella, daughter of the French king, Edward spent most of his time hunting and cavorting with Piers, showering him with gifts and, occasionally, playing some "hide the scepter." But Isabella didn't take kindly to being ignored. Taking a lover of her own, Roger de Mortimer, Izzy decided to oust Edward and proclaim her son the king. She and Mortimer imprisoned Edward II until, in 1327, they decided it would be better to just get rid of him. The method of execution was unbelievably gruesome. Edward was wedged between two tables. Then a hunting horn was inserted into his, ahem, royal exit door. *Then* a red-hot poker was shoved through the horn, cauterizing poor Ed's intestines and killing him. While this method was partly chosen as punishment for Edward's homosexuality, the more practical (and horrifically devious) reason was that it would leave no marks on Edward's body, so Isabella could claim he died of natural causes.

Good Witch Hunting:
Trials or Cases Where Reason
Was Turned Upside Down

Sometimes Lady Justice isn't blind, she's just massively embarrassed. The following are five cases where the light of truth could have used some more wattage.

_01:: Autun v. the Rats

When the French province of Autun's barley began disappearing in 1521, the local rats were charged with stealing. When they failed to answer a summons (yes, really!), their appointed lawyer, Bartholomew Chassenee, argued that a single summons was invalid because the rats lived in different villages. New summonses were issued. This time Chassenee argued some of his clients were aged and infirm and needed more time. After that, he argued the rats were afraid to come to court because of all the cats along the way. When villagers refused to obey a court order to lock up their cats, charges against the rodents were dismissed. Chassenee later became France's leading jurist. The dirty rats presumably returned to lives of crime.

_02:: Making a Monkey of the Prosecutor

It was a simple case. In 1925, a Dayton, Tennessee, teacher had taught Darwin's theory of evolution in defiance of a new state law. But the charges quickly became international news when Clarence Darrow, the era's most famous liberal lawyer, took up teacher John Scopes's defense. The case only got more intriguing when William Jennings Bryan, the three-time

Democratic presidential candidate, joined the prosecution. During the defense's case, Darrow stunned the courtroom and a national radio audience by calling Bryan to the stand. For two hours, the two dueled over Bryan's literal interpretation of the Bible. It was immensely entertaining, but had almost nothing to do with the case. Scopes was found guilty and fined $100. Bryan died a few days after the trial. And the state's ban on teaching evolution was reversed—in 1967.

Touch of Evil

In 1982, laid-off Detroit autoworker Ronald Ebens literally beat a Chinese-American man to death after mistaking him for Japanese and blaming him for the loss of jobs stateside. In the judicial farce that followed, Ebens pleaded guilty to manslaughter and received three years' probation.

_03:: The Scottsboro Boys

There were 11 of them: nine black male teenagers and two white women, all traveling in a freight car through Alabama in 1931. When they hit the town of Scottsboro, though, all 11

Scandalicious

IROQUOIS WARFARE SPURS LACROSSE GAME!

Think lacrosse is a game for high schoolers in pleated skirts? Despite the sport's growing popularity around the world, the history of lacrosse isn't generally known. Originally dubbed *Gatciihkwae*, or "Little Brother of War," lacrosse began as training for young men from tribes in the Iroquois federation of what is now upstate New York, preparing them for hunting and combat. The equipment resembled that used in the modern game—small baskets attached to the ends of sticks, which were used to catch and volley a small round stone. The game itself, however, has changed pretty drastically. "Little Brother of War" exhibitions lasted for two or even three days on a "field" that ranged from 500 yards to a few miles in length, and involved up to 1,000 players. Needless to say, the game was incredibly violent (no sideline medics or oxygen tanks), and extreme injury or even death was considered just a part of the play.

were arrested for vagrancy—and the two women quickly cried rape. Defense attorneys were given 25 minutes to prepare their case. In the kangaroo court proceedings that followed, all nine boys were quickly convicted by an all-white jury, and eight were sentenced to death. The U.S. Communist Party hired attorney Samuel Leibowitz for the boys, and he convinced the U.S. Supreme Court to overturn the convictions. The nine were retried—and reconvicted, despite the confession of one of the victims that the rapes never happened. Then, a third trial was ordered. This time, four were acquitted. Of the other five, one escaped and the other four were eventually paroled. The whole thing took almost 20 years.

_04:: The Twinkie Defense

There wasn't much question it was Dan White who climbed through a window at San Francisco City Hall in 1978 and methodically shot to death Mayor George Moscone and Supervisor Harvey Milk, one of the nation's most prominent gay politicians. So lawyers for White, who was an ex-cop and county supervisor, relied on a "diminished capacity" defense. They argued White was too depressed to commit premeditated murder. As proof, they briefly mentioned White's recent consumption of sugary snack foods. Oddly enough, the defense worked, and White was convicted of manslaughter instead of murder. The verdict, however, triggered a night of rioting in the city's gay community. White served five years in prison and then killed himself a few months after his release. In 1982, California voters abolished diminished capacity as a legal defense.

_05:: "Can't We All Just Get Along?"

On March 3, 1991, a 25-year-old black man named Rodney King was stopped by Los Angeles police for reckless driving. While a passerby videotaped the affair, several cops began viciously beating King, and four were charged with assault. In a controversial move, the trial was shifted from L.A. to the suburban community of Simi Valley, where a jury of 10 whites, an Asian American, and a Latino acquitted the police, despite the videotaped evidence. And while the ruling made no sense, what happened next was unimaginable. The verdict triggered one of the worst riots in U.S. history, with more than 50 people killed, 4,000 injured, and $1 billion in property damage done. The violence was so great that it spurred King to make his famous query: "Can't we all just get along?" The following year, two of the cops were convicted in federal court of violating King's civil rights. The other two were again acquitted.

My God's More Furious Than Yours: Deities with Anger Management Problems

5

There are more than a few deities from world mythology that had serious issues reining in their powerful emotions—and with omnipotence to match, the results were often devastating, as well as really entertaining.

_01:: Artemis: The Angry Bathing God

The ultimate definition of a woman scorned, Artemis, the Greek goddess of the hunt, of nature, and of chastity, had a temper notorious even by the standards of her fellow anger-prone Olympians. The fact that she killed her follower Maera and changed another friend, Callisto, into a bear was the least of it (in both cases, by the way, the hapless ladies had committed the "crime" of losing their virginity). Along with her brother Apollo, Artemis slaughtered the children of the Theban queen Niobe, for no more than insulting their mother. On two separate occasions young men had the misfortune to stumble upon Artemis while she bathed naked in the forest; one was turned into a stag and promptly killed by his own hounds, while the other got off easy (only being turned into a woman). Artemis even killed a girl named Chione for the sin of being too beautiful—which became more of a sin when the girl's beauty was said to rival the goddess's.

_02:: Kali: The Badly Dressed God

A Hindu fertility goddess, Kali is the female aspect of divine energy and the consort of Shiva, the Destroyer. As the slayer of evil spirits and the somewhat unpredictable mother of all life, she also moonlights as the goddess of death. Not a bad gig, except the uniform's a little scary. To show how many evil spirits she's slain, Kali's usually depicted wearing a necklace of human skulls and a girdle of severed arms, children's corpses as earrings, and cobras as bracelets. The outfit is pulled together, however, by her ferocious grimace and the blood smeared on her face. And in her eight arms she holds weapons or the severed head of a demon, representing both her creative and her destructive power. Some followers honored her with animal sacrifices, though a few even took things to the next level. One India-wide sect, the Thuggee, kidnapped and murdered humans as sacrifices to "the Dark Mother" until they were wiped out by British colonial authorities in the 1800s.

_03:: Huitzilopchtli: The Needy (in a Human Sacrificial Way) God

Huitzilopchtli, the Aztec god of the sun and war, was worshiped with rites so horrific that they probably couldn't be shown in the most demented of horror movies today. As far as the mythology goes, he's been causing a violent ruckus since birth. Right after he was born, Huitzilopchtli killed his own sister, Coyolxauhqui, and hung her head in the sky as the moon. He then killed thousands of his other siblings and placed them in the sky as the stars and planets. Not easily appeased, Huitzilopchtli, like virtually all Aztec deities, demanded constant human sacrifice as his price for not destroying the world. And boy did he get 'em! Every day, people were slaughtered in his temples and their hearts offered to the sun. Of course, during festivals, you could count on Huitzilopchtli's wrath to make sure that thousands of people were sacrificed at a time.

_04:: Thor: The God of Hammer Time

The Norse god of thunder and protector of the common man, Thor wielded a war hammer so heavy that only he could use it. In fact, the weapon was so unwieldy that he was known from time to time to fly off the handle (no pun intended). Of course, that wasn't his only unusual gimmick. Like any god who commands respect, Thor enjoyed rolling around town in a pimped-out chariot drawn by—what else?—magic goats. And as if that doesn't sound tough enough, his ride also was equipped to scorch the earth wherever it went. But back to his wrath; nothing could get on Thor's nerves like Loki, the divine trickster. And eventually, it was Thor's anger that became the driving force behind Loki's torturous imprisonment, strapped down to a rock under a mountain with venom dripping into his face. Not that the rascal didn't deserve it. You can't, after all, just go around stealing the hair off Thor's wife's head and expect not to have to pay. Aside from cruelty to Loki, though, Thor's anger also emerged when he treated a group of dwarves rather roughly for making advances on the goddess Freya. But then again, Thor was generally on the hunt for a good fight. What more can you expect from a god whose favorite pastime is killing giants and monsters?

_05:: Balor: The Never-Look-Him-in-the-Eye God

Balor of the Evil Eye, as he was called, was the Celtic god of the underworld and king of the Fomorians, a race of giants whom myth assigned to the Emerald Isle. As the story goes, Balor's mere gaze was enough to kill anyone it fell on (though, he normally kept his eye closed). That, of course, didn't keep him from doing plenty of wrong. Among his more nefarious doings was locking up his daughter Ethlinn in a vain attempt to keep her from having her child, a prophesied savior. (Her son, Lugh, eventually became god of the sun and killed Balor by throwing a spear into his eye.) Balor was also pretty fond of picking wars in order to use his evil eye. In fact, in one of them, Balor was thrilled to put an end to King Nuada, the Celtic sea god, using just his fearsome gaze.

Take Two of These and Maul Me in the Morning: Armies Hopped Up on Goofballs

The disinhibiting and pain-numbing effects of drugs make them perfect for turning people into killing machines. In fact, criminals on PCP have been reported to withstand multiple shocks with Taser guns, pepper spray, and Mace, and even direct gunshot wounds to the chest, without slowing down. It's no wonder that so many generals have relied on drugs to bring out the so-called best in unwitting soldiers.

_01:: Thai and Burmese Bandit Armies

"The Golden Triangle"—an area straddling Thailand, Laos, and Myanmar, where poppy plants grow particularly well—has long been a center of the international drug trade, and for centuries national armies, revolutionaries, and criminal gangs have waged war for control of the income it generates. Recently, however, bandits and rebels from all three countries have begun recruiting children, feeding them opium, hashish, amphetamines, and tranquilizers to give them courage, then sending them out on "human wave" attacks. The disturbing phenomenon leaves a huge proportion of the children dead. One adult soldier from Burma who had to fight these poor child soldiers recalled, "There were a lot of boys rushing into the field, screaming like banshees. It seemed like they were immortal, or impervious, or something, because we shot at them but they just kept coming."

_02:: U.S. Army "Go Pills"

Though amphetamines are essentially off-limits for the civilian population of the United States, American armed forces have long made use of them to enhance the fighting abilities of pilots, soldiers, and sailors, and to keep them awake for long periods of time. Interest peaked in World War II, when all the major combatants on both sides conducted extensive research and distributed large amounts of stimulants to their soldiers. Surprisingly enough, America's armed forces continue the practice to this very day. The amphetamine most often dispensed to American servicemen and-women is Dexedrine, short for dextroamphetamine sulfate, also referred to as "go pills." In one April 2002 incident in Afghanistan, pilots from the Illinois Air National Guard accidentally dropped bombs on a Canadian unit, killing four and wounding eight. In the inquiry that followed, the pilots claimed that they were disoriented because they had been forced to take Dexedrine "go pills" by their superiors and would have been declared unfit for combat if they had not.

_03:: Nazi Shock Troops

During World War II, Nazi Germany definitely led the pack in its use of amphetamines, cocaine, and other "performance-enhancing" drugs. In fact, amphetamine pills were included in every German soldier's first-aid kit, and Nazi researchers developed chewing gum that delivered a dose of cocaine with each piece. But that wasn't all! According to a book by German author and criminologist Wolf Kemper on the subject, *Nazis on Speed,* one of the substances tested by the Nazis in 1944, D-IX, was actually a cocaine-based compound that included both amphetamine and a morphine-related chemical to dull pain. The experimental drug was tested on prisoners of war, and Nazi doctors found the test subjects could march 55 miles without a rest before they collapsed. The Nazis hoped that the drug could put some fighting spirit into their armies, which were by that time being defeated on all fronts, but luckily the war ended before production could begin.

_04:: West African Child Soldiers

In the brutal civil wars that have bedeviled West Africa over the last two decades, much of the fighting is done by children who are teenagers or younger. Armed with automatic weapons, the children are rewarded with sex, candy, tobacco, or alcohol—anything that encourages them to fight. However, sometimes the temptation isn't great enough, so their adult commanders often find it helps to ply them with more powerful drugs that inhibit their judgment. In Sierra Leone, Western observers met children between the ages of 9 and 16 who had been given amphetamines, while children of similar age in the militias of Liberian president Charles Taylor were routinely given cocaine, opium, marijuana, and palm wine to encourage their killer instincts. Often dressed in outlandish costumes out of a belief that strange clothing would protect them in combat—a wedding dress with fright wig was a favorite—these children were described by the journalists who met them as borderline psychotic.

_05:: Medieval Iranian "Assassins"

In the 12th century CE, the invading Seljuk Turks encountered resistance from a small but fanatical group of Shiite Muslims in Persia. Unable to defend against the attacks, the resisters, known as the Ismailis (ancestors to today's second largest Shi'a community), retreated to the impenetrable mountain fortress of Alamut, where they continued their life as a separate society. To protect his people, the Ismaili prince Hasan-i Sabbah began recruiting young men and training them to be fanatical religious killers. The training wasn't exactly kosher, though. During one part, he supposedly gave his men huge amounts of hashish and other drugs and led them to a luxurious chamber. There they were plied with copious amounts of drugs and sex by beautiful women, who told them that they were getting a preview of the heaven that awaited if they died in battle. The fanatics were then sent out, still lost in a hashish haze, to kill the prince's opponents. Interestingly, the modern English word "assassin" comes from *hash-shashin,* the Persian word for "hemp eaters."

Black Eye for the Straight Guy: Historical Bar Brawls

3

What's a good bar without a good brawl? The following are a few famous fisticuff events and the watering holes where they were thrown.

_01:: Truckee, California

One of the best barroom brawl scenes isn't plucked from an old classic or Western, but rather from a real-life saloon in Truckee, California. In 1891, Jacob Teeter was the constable and James Reed the sometimes deputy of Truckee. But over the years, their friendly rivalry (they always ran against each other for constable) escalated, and the constable-deputy feud finally exploded on November 6. That's the day James Reed and a couple of his pals happened upon Teeter in the local bar. A fight ensued and Reed grabbed Teeter's gun. Embarrassed, Teeter left the bar only to return later on a mission. As Reed walked by, the constable shot point-blank at his deputy. The problem was, he missed. He did, however, succeed in shooting a hole through the hat of a man sitting at the next table. Anyway, the stir set patrons diving in all directions, and Reed pulled his gun (actually the one he'd taken from Teeter) and shot him four times. Teeter died and Reed turned himself in to the law. Instead of being arrested, though, Reed was released and at the coroner's inquest the next day was found innocent by reason of self-defense. However, it appears that Teeter got the best of old Reed in the end. His oversized gravestone lies prominently in the Truckee cemetery, while Reed lies quietly in the same cemetery, condemned to an unmarked grave.

Touch of Evil

Twins Reggie and Ronnie Kray, two of England's most infamous gangsters, loved a good punch-up at the local pub. Reggie spent hours perfecting his "sucker punch," whereby he'd offer a man a cigarette with one hand, and crack the guy's jaw with the other.

_02:: John Wayne v. Randolph Scott

Car chases and bar brawls are staples of certain genres and the viewing public plays an important role in what survives the director's cutting room. And while a real-life bar brawl might take just minutes to complete, picture-perfect re-creations take a little longer. The movie *The Spoilers,* for instance, was rereleased five times with different leading casts, the 1942 version starring John Wayne and Randolph Scott. In fact, the flick is well known for having the longest and most complex bar brawl in cinema history. The six-minute fight scene involved over *30* experienced stuntmen and acrobats, and the bar (understandably) was completely trashed by the end of it. And to get the scene just right, the actors went through their paces breaking everything in their paths: from fake breakaway furniture to mirrors to doors, and just for good measure (and cinematography) they slammed each other against walls, too. The scene actually took 10 days to wrap up, much to the satisfaction of John Wayne, who was quite happy to perform some of the stunts himself.

_03:: The Ugly American in Paris

Following World War I, French–American relations weren't exactly improved by the racist behavior of white American tourists. So in 1923, in a desperate effort to appease wealthy white American tourists, a number of French bars and dance hall owners defied national laws and refused admittance to blacks, including French blacks. Despite government warnings, a group of white Americans drinking one night in a bar in the Montmartre district demanded that two black men who had entered the bar be removed. When the men refused, the ignorant Americans responded by physically throwing them out. The next day the French press announced that Kojo Tovalou Houénou, a prominent leader of the Pan-African movement in Paris and a renowned philosopher, was one of the victims. Outraged and disgusted, President Raymond Poincaré denounced the scandal and ordered the bar closed—a warning that any French bar trying

---

Just the Facts

THE HUNGRY DUCK BAR BY NUMBERS

Since the Hungry Duck Bar opened in Moscow, Russia, in 1995, the civilized world hasn't been the same. The bar is notorious for its rowdiness and raunchiness, as the numbers show. In fact, the Hungry Duck is the only bar ever denounced by a national parliament, but the club continues to pay "favors" to stay open.

256: Cases the Moscow police have had involving the bar

8: Number of bullets that have been fired inside

2: Number of bomb threats

8-plus: Number of times the police have raided the establishment

5: Number of owners

4: Death threats each owner has received

1: Kidnapping attempts made

2: Number of full-time carpenters employed by the bar on account of all the regularly broken bar stools

40-plus: Number of customers that have had to receive medical treatment from falling off the bar while dancing

2: Types of draft beer available

0: Food items on the menu

---

to exclude blacks, French or otherwise, would be immediately shut down.

Prophets on the Edge

People are always a little skeptical of prophets. After all, when you're telling the world that God's decided to use you to pass on His message to the masses, or to lead people to some promised land, you're bound to get a few strange looks. Of course, your chances of being believed get even slimmer when you're preaching the gospel of semiautomatics and mass suicides like the following folks did.

_01:: David Koresh (1959–1993)

Best known as the leader of the ill-fated Branch Davidians, David Koresh led a short life as a prophet of doom. Born Vernon Wayne Howell (which didn't quite have that same son-of-God ring to it), Koresh joined the Branch Davidian sect in 1981. Founded in the 1930s by Ben and Lois Roden, the Davidians believed the return of the Messiah was imminent. Soon after joining, Koresh had an affair with Lois Roden, who by then was in her late 60s. While on a journey with Koresh to Mount Carmel in Israel, Roden died, and a power struggle for control of the group took place between her son, George, and Koresh. Shortly thereafter, David returned with seven followers, a great amount of conviction, and a couple of semiautomatic assault weapons (for good measure) to back up his claim. Choosing violence over, say, putting it to a vote, David Koresh attacked George Roden, wounding him in the chest and hands. At a subsequent trial, the seven were acquitted and Koresh's case was declared a mistrial. Believing that he was now the head of the biblical House of David, Koresh moved with his followers to Waco, Texas. Of course, living by the sword (or in this case, the rifle) also meant dying by

it. In 1993, Koresh and 74 of his followers perished in a fire during a shootout with federal agents.

_02:: Amos

Once upon a time, the Old Testament character Amos was satisfied to herd his sheep and tend to his sycamore trees. But the part-time prophet, as he saw himself, accepted "the call" and quickly became a thorn in the side of the religious establishment. At the time, part of Judea was true to Yahweh, while the religious establishment in Bethel worshiped Baal and the Golden Calf. Yahweh had decided to punish them and famous Amos got the job of providing the bad news. First, Amos accused the wealthy Judeans of being greedy, oppressive, and exploiting the poor. Then, he went after the rich who used their money to bribe judges and political officials. Finally, he accused them of perverting the true Israelite religion by moving the temple to Bethel and worshiping the Golden Calf instead of Yahweh. Not mincing any words, Amos told the leaders that Yahweh wasn't bluffing about the imminent punishment and that they'd better get their act together pretty soon. After that, Amos was no longer welcome at most banquets of the wealthy, with most townsfolk wishing that he'd just go back to his sheep and sycamores.

Touch of Evil

David "Moses" Berg, founder of the Children of God, developed "flirty fishing" to support his flock. Female acolytes had sex with wealthy men for money to earn funds for the church. Of course, any detractors who cried "Prostitution!" were labeled as not having enough faith.

_03:: Edgar Cayce (1877–1945)

Known as "the Sleeping Prophet," Edgar Cayce must have been a real bore at social gatherings. Considered to be one of America's greatest psychics, Cayce would close his eyes and appear to go into a trance before making his prophecies. A story has it that an angel appeared to Cayce at the age of 13 asking him what his greatest desire was, to which he allegedly replied that it was to help people. Another story has Cayce placing books under his pillow and absorbing the contents while he slept. Not bad for someone who was illiterate. However, Cayce was best known for his medical prognostications, performing thousands of medical readings for his legion of followers. While there was little or no scientific proof that anyone was actually cured by Cayce's clairvoyance, his followers were quick to spread the word. However, there was an interesting catch: Cayce's followers claimed that if one doubted the mystic his diagnosis wouldn't work. If only Miss Cleo had had such foresight.

_04:: Ezekiel

Talk about a genuine fire-and-brimstone preacher; today's ragamuffin evangelists would run a distant second to the Old Testament prophet Ezekiel. Consider how the guy gave solace to the exiled Israelites. When the bunch found themselves exiled in Babylon, far from their holy city of Jerusalem, Ezekiel didn't hold a pity party. Instead, the sweetheart prophet told the captives that they were directly responsible for their own exile and needed to change their ways if they ever hoped to return home. Probably not the comforting words the people wanted to hear. He also did something entirely revolutionary: he put God in a chariot throne, thus giving Him the mobility to get out of the temple and visit His people in Babylon. The idea of the chariot came to old Zeke in a vision that looks like something straight out of *Independence Day*. As described by the prophet, the glowing chariot emerged from a large storm cloud with fire flashing all around it, and couched in the middle of all the action was a fiery humanlike figure. To religious scholars this was obviously Yahweh coming in loud and clear on a mobile throne (can you see Him now?), though one still wonders if Ezekiel hadn't just had the fiery dream as the result of late-night indigestion.

_05:: The Reverend Jim Jones (1931–1978)

Hanging around with the Reverend Jim Jones was certainly detrimental to more than a few people's health. As an ordained minister in the Disciples of Christ denomination, Jones created a large congregation of followers among the poor in the San Francisco Bay area. Proclaiming himself a prophet and one who could raise the dead, Jones quickly became a local religious celebrity and his congregation numbered over 8,000. But by the early 1970s, a number of local newspapers published articles accusing Jones of using church money to buy political influence. Then, in 1976, another article was published accusing Jones of performing fake healings and coercing church members to sell their possessions and give the money to the church (clearly he was better at raising funds than the deceased). With the pressure on, Jones and a group of his followers moved to Guyana and set up a compound modestly named Jonestown. Things came to a nasty halt in November 1978 when, feeling trapped (especially after killing U.S. congressman Leo Ryan), Jones ordered his followers to down a grape drink laced with cyanide. Over 914 people died in the mass suicide, including Jones. Contrary to popular belief, though, the drink was not Kool-Aid, but one of its competitors.

You Say "Potato," I Say "Nuclear Annihilation": Close Calls in the Nuclear Age

There's a formula for fun: Arm two superpowers to the teeth with thousands of nuclear warheads. Make sure they are deeply hostile and suspicious of each other. Now, cut off diplomatic communication, stir in about 50 smaller countries with their own agendas on each side, and—voilà!—cold war in a jiffy!

_01:: Suez Crisis

On November 5, 1956, during the Suez crisis, the North American Aerospace Defense Command (NORAD) received warnings that seemed to indicate that a large-scale Soviet attack was under way: a Soviet fleet was moving from the Black Sea to a more aggressive posture in the Aegean, 100 Soviet MiGs were detected flying over Syria, a British bomber had just been shot down in Syria, and unidentified aircraft were in flight over Turkey, causing the Turkish air force to go on high alert. All signs pointed to the ominous, except that, not long after, each of the four warnings was found to have a completely innocent explanation. The Soviet fleet was conducting routine exercises, the MiGs were part of a normal escort—whose size had been exaggerated—for the president of Syria, the British bomber had made an emergency landing after mechanical problems, and, last but not least, the unidentified planes over Turkey? Well, they turned out to be a large flock of swans.

_02:: SAC-NORAD
Communication Failure

On November 24, 1961, all communication links between the U.S. Strategic Air Command (SAC) and NORAD suddenly went dead, cutting off the SAC from three early warning radar stations in England, Greenland, and Alaska. The communication breakdown made no sense, though. After all, a widespread, total failure of all communication circuits was considered impossible, because the network included so many redundant systems that it should have been failsafe. The only alternative explanation was that a full-scale Soviet nuclear first strike had occurred. As a result, all SAC bases were put on alert, and B-52 bomber crews warmed up their engines and moved their planes onto runways, awaiting orders to counterattack the Soviet Union with nuclear weapons. Luckily, those orders were never given. It was discovered that the circuits were not in fact redundant because they all ran through one relay station in Colorado, where a single motor had overheated and caused the entire system to fail.

_03:: U2 Spy Plane Accidentally Violates Soviet Airspace

U2 spy planes were high-altitude aircraft that took pictures of the Soviet Union with extremely powerful long-distance telephoto lenses. During the Cuban Missile Crisis of 1962, U2 pilots were ordered not to fly within 100 miles of the Soviet Union to avoid antagonizing the Soviets. However, on October 26, 1962, a U2 pilot flying over the North Pole made a series of navigational errors because the shifting lights of the aurora borealis prevented him from taking accurate readings with his sextant. As a result, he ended up flying over the Chukotski Peninsula in northern Siberia, causing the Soviets to order a number of MiG interceptors to shoot his plane down immediately. Instead of letting him be shot down, however, the United States responded quickly by sending out F-102A fighters armed

with nuclear missiles to escort the U2 back to American airspace and prevent the MiGs from following it. Unbelievably, the tactic worked. Even more amazing: the decision whether to use their nuclear missiles was left to the American pilots, and could have easily resulted in a nuclear conflict.

_04:: When Camping, Make Sure to Hide Your Food and Your Nuclear Weapons

On October 25, 1962, again during the Cuban Missile Crisis, a security guard at an air base in Duluth, Minnesota, saw a shadowy figure scaling one of the fences enclosing the base. He shot at the intruder and activated an intruder alarm, automatically setting off intruder alarms at neighboring bases. However, at the Volk Field air base in Wisconsin, the Klaxon loudspeaker had been wired incorrectly, and instead sounded an alarm ordering F-106A interceptors armed with nuclear missiles to take off. The pilots assumed that a full-scale nuclear conflict with the Soviet Union had begun, and the planes were about to take off when a car from the air traffic control tower raced down the tarmac and signaled the planes to stop. The intruder in Duluth had finally been identified: it was a bear.

_05:: A Terrifying Crash

On January 21, 1968, fire broke out on a B-52 carrying a nuclear payload near Greenland, forcing the crew to bail out. The unmanned plane then crashed about seven miles from the early warning radar station in Greenland. The damage done could have been remarkable. The plane exploded, as did the explosives surrounding the radioactive core of the nuclear weapons (which require conventional explosives to detonate). Given the state of nuclear weapons technology at the time, this type of unintentional detonation of conventional first-stage explosives could have theoretically triggered the second-stage fission reaction, resulting in a nuclear explosion. Luckily for the world, it didn't. The resulting explosion would have not only severed regular communications between the early warning station and NORAD, it would have also triggered an emergency alarm based on radiation readings taken by sensors near the station. The only conclusion at NORAD headquarters, in this grisly hypothetical but very plausible scenario, would have been that the Soviets were launching a preemptive nuclear strike, and the United States would have responded in kind.

Senator Charles Percy, who happened to be at NORAD headquarters during this event, said the reaction was one of overwhelming panic and terror. Justifiably so.

Touch of Evil

Western intelligence analysts believe that by the end of the Cold War, the Soviet Union—shortly before it went broke—was spending approximately $350 billion, or a third of its gross national product (GNP), on military spending. The United States, by comparison, was spending only 6 to 7% of its GNP at that time.

_06:: Comp Fear

On November 9, 1979, four command centers for the U.S. nuclear arsenal received data on their radar screens indicating that the Soviet Union had launched a full-scale nuclear first strike on the United States. Over the next six minutes, planes were launched and nuclear missiles initialized for an immediate retaliatory strike. The president's National Emergency Airborne Command Post—an armored jumbo jet with radiation shielding and advanced communications capabilities, meant to allow the president to remain in contact with the government and armed forces during a nuclear war—was also launched, though curiously without the president aboard. However, the alarm was canceled because no sensors or satellites detected an actual Soviet missile launch. The alarm had been caused by computer software used for training exercises depicting a nightmare scenario Soviet first strike.

_07:: Comp Fear, Part 2

Electronic displays at NORAD, the SAC, and the Pentagon included prominent, highly visible numeric counters showing the number of enemy nuclear missiles detected. They normally displayed four zeros—"0000"—indicating that no nuclear missiles had been launched. However, on June 3, 1980, at 2:25 in the morning, the counters started randomly substituting the number "2" for "0." As a result, crews manning bombers carrying nuclear weapons were ordered to begin to warm up their engines, Minuteman missiles were initialized for launch, and airborne command posts were also launched. It was determined that this first event was a false alarm, but three days later it happened a second time—causing the entire emergency response procedure to start rolling once again. The problem was eventually traced back to a single faulty computer chip combined with faulty wiring.

An Eye for an Eye: Charming Episodes of Violence from Medieval Iceland

The sagas of early medieval Iceland (written down between 1100 and 1300) are some of the great works of Western literature. Heck, they've got it all: lust, envy, large-scale violence, widespread failures. Plus, these charming tales are all set in a time when a man just had to do what a man (generally with anger-management issues and a club) had to do.

_01:: Hallgerd the Petty (Njal's Saga)

One of the bloodiest feuds in Icelandic history arose from the seating chart at a wedding, when Bergthora asked Hallgerd Hoskuldsdattir to move over at a banquet to a less prestigious seat. It only makes sense that the slighted Hallgerd took the instruction as a deadly insult. Unfortunately for Bergthora, though, Hallgerd knew how to hold a grudge. After all, this was the same woman whose husband, Gunnar, once slapped her for stealing from one of his enemies. Then, years later, when besieged in his home by his enemies, Gunnar begged Hallgerd to give him a lock of her hair to repair his bowstring, and she refused, reminding him of the slap he'd given her. Gunnar was killed, and Hallgerd was finally happy. Bergthora wasn't any luckier. Despite the attempts of Njal, Bergthora's husband, to make peace, things quickly got out of hand. Eventually, a gang attacked Njal's family on their farm and set fire to the farmhouse, killing everyone inside except for a brother-in-law, a Viking who didn't take kindly to his in-laws being barbecued. In response, he cobbled together a small army and successfully wiped out most of the conspirators before finally ending the bloody feud as all good feuds end...with a strategic marriage.

_02:: Hrafnkel's Comeback (Hrafnkel's Saga)

Hrafnkel was the perfect villain: a callous chieftain who murdered without paying compensation (this being rather bad manners at the time). Overthrown but spared by the kinsmen of a man he had killed, Hrafnkel was banished to the life of a penniless vagrant. But he managed to learn from past mistakes, gaining wisdom, kindness, and followers while his enemies grew weak and complacent. And while the wisdom and followers would definitely help him in his greater plan, we're not quite so sure we buy the kindness. Hrafnkel waited seven years for the opportunity to serve his revenge ice cold. And when it finally came, he killed the most dangerous of his enemies, then chased the rest out of his former holdings.

_03:: Thorstein Replaces the Men He Kills (The Tale of Thorstein the Staff-Struck)

What's a poor farmer to do when his honor is insulted by three servants of a wealthy landowner? If you're Thorstein Thorarinsson, you kill 'em, announcing your actions after the fact in accordance with Icelandic custom. Luckily for Thorstein, the three he killed were so worthless that their own boss didn't particularly want to avenge them. Thorstein and the chieftain, Bjarni, fought a rather halfhearted duel, punctuated by frequent water breaks, pauses to examine one another's weapons, and even stops to tie their shoes in midbattle. Finally, they reached a settlement: Thorstein, who was strong enough to do the work of three men, became the perfect replacement for the three he had killed. Downsizing, Icelandic style.

_04:: Egil Rewrites a Poem in His Head (Egil's Saga)

Egil was a raider, a pirate, a murderer, and, oh so predictably, an accomplished poet to boot. On his way to deliver a poem to King Athelstan of England, he fell into the clutches of Eirik, the Viking king of York. This was most unfortunate, as Egil had made a career of being quite a pain in Eirik's royal rear. Given one night's reprieve while the king decided the method of execution, Egil stunned everyone by delivering, in perfect meter, a poem in praise of Eirik. He was released well before anyone realized that he had just replaced "Athelstan" with "Eirik" (the Old Norse form), maintaining the rhythm of the poem and saving his own neck. Long after he died of old age, Egil's grave was excavated and his abnor-

Lies Your Mother Told You

REMEMBER THE *MAINE*

In full, the U.S. battle cry during the Spanish-American War of 1898 was "Remember the *Maine*, to hell with Spain!" It referred to the sinking of the U.S. battleship *Maine* in Havana Harbor in February of that year. But it's never been shown that Spain—then fending off a Cuban independence movement—attacked the ship. Sent to protect U.S. interests, the *Maine* was preparing to leave when it exploded. In reality, though, Spain had nothing to gain by provoking the United States, and much to lose. Many think the onboard explosion was accidental. Or maybe Havana rebels planted a bomb, hoping to bring America into their fight. If so, the tactic worked. U.S. newspapers—especially those owned by mogul William Randolph Hearst—took up the "Remember the *Maine!*" cry and agitated for war. It worked out well for the U.S. government, though...the United States came out of the fight with the Philippines, Puerto Rico, and Guam, while Cuba was happy to win its independence.

mally bulky skull was discovered, proving that you can have a thick head and still do some quick thinking.

_05:: Gudmund Negotiates a Deal (Gudmund the Worthy's Saga)

When a chump named Skaering had his hand cut off by Norwegian merchants, he turned to his kinsman Gudmund to get him justice. Ever helpful, Gudmund arranged a monetary settlement, but as soon as he left the scene the Norwegians refused to pay. Summoned back, a rather annoyed Gudmund made the following proposal: "I will pay Skaering the amount that you were judged to pay, but I shall choose one man from among you who seems to me of equivalent standing with Skaering and chop off his hand. You may then compensate that fellow's hand as cheaply as you wish." Not surprisingly, the Norwegians quickly coughed up the money, no doubt to the sound of Skaering's one hand clapping.

Quit Your Day Job:
Dictators Who Worked Their Way to the Top

In the dreary monotony of daily life, the best most of us can hope for is a promotion and 3% raise. But a small subset of the human population dreams big—of bloody coups and secret torture chambers, personality cults and absolute power. Frankly, it's enough to turn us off ambition entirely. Just imagine if Idi Amin had remained an assistant cook in the British colonial army. Or if these folks hadn't thought to quit their day jobs.

_01:: Pol Pot, the Frustrated Teacher

Before he became a world-famous war criminal, Pol Pot was named Saloth Sar. As a young man, Sar studied carpentry and radio engineering, but proved a poor student so he became—what else?—a teacher. (And you thought *your* classrooms were scary.) From 1954 to 1963, Sar taught at a private school in Phnom Penh before being forced out because of ties to communism. Ever fond of alliteration, Saloth Sar became Pol Pot and devoted himself full-time to Cambodia's Communist Party, eventually becoming the party's leader, and by 1975, his Khmer Rouge guerrilla army had overthrown the same government that once fired him. In his four years of rule, Pot killed more than a million Cambodians. When the Vietnamese came to the rescue and invaded Cambodia in 1979, Pot retreated to the jungle, though he continued to orchestrate guerrilla attacks until his arrest in 1997.

_02:: Hitler, the Frustrated Painter

As a child, Adolf Hitler attended a monastery school and harbored dreams of becoming a priest, but he dropped out after his father's death in 1903. By then, Hitler had a new career in mind: professional artist. And though the Führer's precise but emotionless landscapes showed moderate promise, he was rejected twice from Vienna's Academy of Fine Arts. Bitter, poor, and lonely, young Adolf moved between boardinghouses and hostels, earning a meager living painting postcards. Oddly enough, he might have been just another failed artist had it not been for World War I. Turning in his paintbrush for a pistol, Hitler volunteered as a runner for the German army. Turns out he enjoyed that world war so much that, a few decades later, he decided to start another one.

_03:: Mussolini, the Frustrated Author

Many dictators were also authors. Stalin wrote scintillating screeds like *Building Collective Farms;* Mao's *Little Red Book* is considered to be the second-best-selling book of all time; and Hitler's *Mein Kampf* made him a millionaire. Even Saddam Hussein found a little time to pen two horrible bodice-rippers while performing his duties as president of Iraq. But the most famous dictatorial romance is *The Cardinal's Mistress,* written by Benito Mussolini. Before becoming the world's first fascist dictator, Mussolini worked for a socialist paper, *Il Popolo d'Italia,* for which he wrote a serial later published as a novel. *The Cardinal's Mistress* tells the tragic story of, you guessed it, a 17th-century cardinal and his mistress. And boy is it bad. It's the sort of book where "terrible groan[s] burst forth from" characters' breasts, and characters ask one another to "cast a ray of your light into my darkened soul." No wonder Il Duce gave up his day job.

_04:: Papa Doc, the Frustrated Doctor

Unlike Doc Holliday (brilliant gunfighter and amateur dentist) and Elmer Fudd (inept gunfighter known to Bugs Bunny as Doc), François "Papa Doc" Duvalier was, in fact, a doctor—although we can only imagine his bedside manner. Favoring hypocrisy to the Hippocratic oath, the dangerous dictator was first a physician in Port-au-Prince for nearly a decade before immersing himself in politics full-time in 1943. Even more surprising, he actually rose to power in a legitimately democratic election. And though he was voted in as president in 1957, Duvalier promptly showed his gratitude to the Haitian nation by killing anyone who expressed the slightest opposition to his government. By the mid-1960s, Duvalier had established himself not only as President for Life but also as a quasi-divine manifestation of Haiti's greatness (he claimed to have supernatural powers; Papa Doc even said he placed a curse on John F. Kennedy that resulted in Kennedy's assassination). Incidentally, his son, "Baby Doc" Duvalier, who ruled from Papa Doc's death in 1971 until 1986, was not a doctor. Just a dictator.

_05:: Castro, the Angry Ballplayer?

Persistent rumors would have you believe that old Fidel was a talented baseball player who once tried out for a major-league team in America…which is completely untrue. The fact is, Castro did play a little ball back in school: he seems to have been the losing pitcher in a 1946 intramural game between the University of Havana's business and law schools. But the point here is that he was in law school not so much to win ball games as to study law. Castro graduated and practiced in

Havana between 1950 and 1952, when he failed miserably in his first attempted coup d'état. After a brief stint in prison and a few years exiled in Mexico and the United States, Castro and his army finally took control of Cuba in 1959. Just goes to show you, there's more to life than sports!

War, What Is It Good For? Well, Things, Actually

War gets a bad rap. Sure, it's often fatal and frequently unnecessary. But if war is so terrible, why do we keep on trying it? Hoping to shed some rosy light on the fog of war, we've collected a few possible, if minor, benefits to starting one.

_01:: Medicine

It seems like nothing brings about a good medical breakthrough like a solid war. Antibiotics, anesthesia, and countless advances in surgery were all discovered or perfected during wartime. In fact, one of the most interesting war-related medical breakthroughs came from Dr. Charles W. Drew, an African American doctor in World War II, who helped pioneer technology allowing the preservation and transfusion of blood plasma. Drew worked from 1940 through the end of the war, and his efforts saved the lives of thousands of soldiers who otherwise would have bled to death. Drew himself, however, was not so fortunate. After falling asleep at the wheel in North Carolina years after the war, Drew sustained massive trauma and bled to death. A persistent rumor claims that Drew was given poor treatment at the hospital because of his race, but friends with him that fateful night vehemently deny it.

_02:: Engineering

War can also bring technological advances. Believe it or not, the phrase "civil engineering" wasn't coined until the 19th century because before that "engineering" had been exclusively a military endeavor. It's common knowledge that math and science have both civilian and military implications, but one prominent example of the type is cybernetics, the mathematical field pioneered by the unfortunately named Norbert Wiener. Cybernetics is the study of control within complex systems, and our boy wonder (Wiener actually got a Ph.D. in math from Harvard when he was just 18) began by applying it as a World War II tool. Amazingly, he used the science to figure out how best to aim artillery fire at speeding airplanes. But he didn't stop there. Wiener went on to write about the nonmilitary political and social uses of cybernetics in his best-selling *The Human Use of Human*

Beings (1950). Today cybernetics helps ther-
mostats anticipate rising and falling temperatures. Do better artillery fire, finely tuned
air-conditioning, and one good book make a
war worthwhile? Well, that brings us to . . .

_03:: Literature

Peace just doesn't have the same ring as War
and Peace. And quite frankly, it couldn't get
All Quiet on the Western Front until after
things had gotten awfully loud. From The Iliad
to Tim O'Brien's The Things They Carried, good
yarns have often used war as their setting. It's
good for visual art, too. Picasso's Guernica and
Delacroix's Liberty Leading the People would
have been impossible without the Spanish
Civil War and the French Revolution, respectively. Sometimes, in fact, good art is all that
emerges from a battle. Kurt Vonnegut wrote
the best-selling Slaughterhouse-Five about the
firebombing of Dresden, an utterly superfluous attack that Vonnegut witnessed as a prisoner of war in 1945. Of the bombing, Vonnegut
once wrote: "Only one person on the entire
planet got any benefit from it. I am that person. One way or another, I got two or three
dollars for every person killed."

Angry Authors and Even Angrier Critics

Nothing sours a literary friendship quite like a bad review. The Irish playwright
Brendan Behan once said, "Critics are like eunuchs in a harem; they know how
it's done, they've seen it done every day, but they're unable to do it themselves."
Whether warring writers keep their feud on paper or let things escalate to physical
violence, a great literary feud is always entertaining.

_01:: Amis v. Amis

You'd think that the father-and-son dynamic
duo of contemporary Brit lit would stand by
one another, but Kingsley Amis (1922–1995)
was awfully hard on his son, Martin (1949–).
Kingsley, most famous for Lucky Jim, once told
The Guardian, "If I was reviewing Martin under a pseudonym, I would say he works too
hard and it shows." (Kingsley received his own
bad reviews—the novelist Robertson Davies
called his work "an awful bore.") But Kingsley's critique was nothing compared with attacks on Martin since. In one of the snarkiest
reviews of all time, author Tibor Fischer wrote
that reading Martin Amis's Yellow Dog (2003)
was akin to "your favourite uncle being caught
in the school playground, masturbating." Martin responded by calling Fischer "a wretch."
So much for British politeness.

_02:: Keats v. Quarterly Review

Before he became a central figure in British
Romantic poetry, John Keats apprenticed with
a surgeon. When he published the now-classic

Profiles in Carnage

PRINCESS OLGA OF KIEV

Olga the Widow: In 945, Prince Igor of Kiev took an army to the land of the Derevlian tribe. The Derevlians weren't exactly amused by Igor's demands for tribute so they defeated his forces and murdered him. In a great display of chutzpah, they then suggested that his widow, Olga, marry their ruler.

Olga the Agreeable: Surprisingly, Olga consented and invited the Derevlian leaders to Kiev to discuss the arrangements.

Olga the Hostess: Arranging a ceremonial steam bath for her guests, Olga had them burned alive inside. She then led an army against the Derevlian capital. When the Derevlians offered her tribute to leave, Olga showed her magnanimity by only asking for three doves per household.

Olga the PETA Nightmare: Their relief turned to horror when she had the birds set on fire (PETA not being around at the time); the doves returned home and set the town ablaze. The survivors were enslaved.

Olga the Saint: As for the Kievan princess, she had a fairly happy ending. She later converted to Christianity and is venerated today as Saint Olga.

Endymion at the age of 23, one critic wrote that Keats ought to go back to medicine, arguing that it's better to be "a starved apothecary than a starved poet." The widely respected *Quarterly Review* was even harsher, using adjectives like "absurd" and "unintelligible." Keats seemed largely unaffected by the criticism—the following year, he wrote his most famous poems, including "Ode on a Grecian Urn." But fellow Romantic Percy Bysshe Shelley later claimed that the bad reviews hadn't just angered Keats; they'd killed him. That led Lord Byron to write in *Don Juan* that Keats had been "snuffed out by an Article." Nice rhetoric, but in reality, Keats was snuffed out by tuberculosis. Immune to the critics, he remained a poet to the last. His entire last will and testament, in fact, was a single line of perfect iambic pentameter: "My chest of books divide amongst my friends."

_03:: Voltaire v. Fréron

In spite of his so-called passion for rationalism, Enlightenment stalwart Voltaire held ferociously unreasonable grudges. He once published a pamphlet claiming Rousseau had abandoned his children, and he even called Shakespeare "a drunken savage." But Voltaire's greatest literary feud was with Élie Fréron, founder of the literary journal *Année littéraire.* Fréron virulently attacked both the underlying philosophies of the Enlightenment and Voltaire's writing. Not one to take it lying down, Voltaire quickly fought back, penning the play *L'Écossaise* to ridicule Fréron. "A serpent bit Fréron," Voltaire said. "But it was the serpent that died." (Incidentally, the play is widely regarded to be one of Voltaire's very worst.) The rivalry didn't exactly die down. In fact, the bitterness seemed to last a lifetime: for example, Voltaire kept a painting in one of his dining rooms depicting a bunch of demons horsewhipping Élie Fréron. How's that for rationalism?

_04:: Gore Vidal v. Norman Mailer

While Norman Mailer and Gore Vidal were serving as commentators for ABC at the 1968 Democratic National Convention, their private feud became fairly public when Mailer called Vidal a "queer." Of course, he had his reasons—after all, the openly gay Vidal had just referred to him as a "crypto-Nazi." End of round one. Three years later, Vidal (most famous for his historical novels) compared Mailer's view of women to that of Charles Manson in the *New York Review of Books.* Mailer, whose gritty *The Naked and the Dead* established his reputation, *was* a misogynist—he once remarked, "I don't hate women, but I think they should be kept in cages." Even so, he didn't appreciate the Manson comparison. Just how much didn't he appreciate it? In the *Dick Cavett Show* greenroom a few months later, Mailer headbutted Vidal, who cleverly responded with a punch to Mailer's gut. The show itself was a disaster, with Mailer insulting both Vidal and Cavett while Vidal stared blankly like, well, like someone who'd just been headbutted.

Touch of Evil

After e. e. cummings' poetry collection was rejected 14 times, he borrowed $300 from his mom and printed it himself. Titled No Thanks, *the book's dedication listed all the publishers that had turned him down, arranged on the page in the shape of a funeral urn.*

When Nature Is a Real Mother: Natural Disasters Explained

There's nothing quite as frightening as when Mother throws one of her temper tantrums. Mother Nature, that is. And while there's some comfort in knowing that at least there's a little science in her madness, the explanations are enough to keep you up at night.

_01:: Krakatoa's Really, Really Big Bang

The terrible tsunami that devastated Indonesia in December 2004 wasn't the first time nature had vented its fury on the South Asian nation. At 10:02 a.m. on August 27, 1883, the volcano on the island of Krakatoa, in the Sunda Strait between Java and Sumatra, erupted. More accurately, it exploded. The detonation threw smoke and ash 17 miles in the air. In fact, the ferocity of the burst echoed so loudly that the sound of the explosion was heard on Rodriguez Island, nearly 3,000 miles away (imagine being in New York and hearing a boom from *San Francisco!*). The pressure wave caused barometers to twitch as far away as London seven times as the shock bounded and rebounded around the globe. But the eruption itself wasn't the worst of it. The explosion sent tsunami waves over 100 feet high toward Java and Sumatra. Ships were carried a mile and a half inland and dumped in the jungle. The disruption was so great, the tide actually rose several inches *in New York*. In all, more than 36,000 people were killed by the tsunami, and most of the nearby coasts of both islands were laid waste. As for Krakatoa, the island blew itself out of existence. It reemerged years later, the result of continued volcanic activity in this turbulent part of the Pacific "Ring of Fire."

_02:: "Bring Out Your Dead!" The Black Death

Between 1347 and 1351, a plague raged through Europe. Arriving in Messina, Sicily, on a Black Sea merchant ship, the disease was initially thought of as solely an animal sickness—like bird flu or mad cow disease. But somehow fleas managed to transmit the condition from rats to people. Called the Black Death because of the dark spots that appeared on victims' skin, the pandemic wasn't just the bubonic plague. In fact, the vicious strain was actually a lethal combination of four variations of plague: bubonic (causing buboes, or inflammations of the lymph nodes), enteric (intestinal), septicemic (an infection of the blood), and pneumonic (filling the lungs with fluid). Quadruple yuck. Even worse, the Black Death worked fast. People who were perfectly healthy at midday were dead by sunset. And the staggering death toll reflects it. An estimated 12 million people in Asia and 25 million in Europe (or one-third of Europe's population) were wiped out. An indiscriminate killer, the disease destroyed rich and poor alike, though only one reigning monarch is known to have died: King Alfonse XI of Castile, who refused to abandon his troops when plague struck his army.

_03:: Russia Dodges a Bullet from Space: The Tunguska Blast

At 7:17 a.m. on June 30, 1908, a 15-megaton explosion (more than 1,000 times that at Hiroshima) flattened a massive part of the Tunguska region of Siberia. The devastated area was 57 miles across, and the explosion shattered windows 400 miles away. A real investigation of the event wasn't undertaken until 1927. But that's not the weird part. The strangest fact about the incident is that there was no impact crater. An entire forest flattened, but there was no hole, meaning the object had exploded *in the air*. Scientists now believe that the object was an asteroid or extinct stony comet; the pressure of its descent simply blew it apart before it hit the ground. But the mysterious nature of the event has led to a whole literature of ludicrous theories, blaming the blast on everything from a black hole passing through the earth to a chunk of antimatter to an exploding UFO to—we love this one—an energy death ray built by Nikola Tesla and test-fired from the Wardenclyffe Tower on Long Island. Whatever they believe, scientists have shuddered and thanked their lucky stars, contemplating what might have happened had the object decided to explode over, say, Central Park. Due to the remoteness of Tunguska, not a single person was killed by the blast.

_04:: The Day the Little Conemaugh Got Much Bigger

Lake Conemaugh lies 14 miles up the Little Conemaugh River from the town of Johnstown, Pennsylvania. On May 31, 1889, the dam that held back the lake waters burst after two days of torrential rain. The results were devastating. A wall of water 60 feet high, moving at 40 mph, crashed down on the unsuspecting people of Johnstown, and the water and debris it carried all but flattened the entire town. In an utterly tragic twist, the town was downstream from a wire factory that was also flattened by the water. Many townspeople caught in the deluge got so entangled in barbed wire that they couldn't escape. In the end, 2,209 people were killed, including 99 entire families. But Mother Nature was not wholly to blame for the tragedy. The Lake Conemaugh Dam was the property of the South Fork Fishing and Forestry Club, which had turned the area into a mountain retreat for the wealthy. However, the club had neglected proper maintenance on the dam. Despite its culpability, though, it was never held legally responsible.

_05:: From the People Who Brought You World War I: The Flu

Just as the Great War was ending and the world looked like it might finally get back to normal, the influenza pandemic of 1918–1919 struck. The pandemic most likely originated in China, but its huge and devastating impact on Spain's population earned it the name "Spanish flu," while the French called it "La Grippe." Even such luminaries as President Woodrow Wilson caught the bug, in his case while attending the Versailles Peace Conference. In the end, one-fifth of the world's population would become infected, and more people would die—some estimates are as high as 40 million—than had during four years of fighting in the First World War. Ironically, the war can be held partly responsible not only for spreading the flu, but also for checking it. Populations were weakened, and thereby made more susceptible, by shortages and rationing and the fact that many of the strongest and healthiest members had been killed in some trench or no-man's-land. But the war had also advanced medical learning and germ theory, and steeled people to hardship. They were used to self-sacrifice and putting the nation before the individual. So they were more calm and cooperative with the measures taken by their public health departments, some of which were tremendously restrictive.

Touch of Evil

"Typhoid Mary" Mallon wasn't quite the walking natural disaster she was made out to be. Although she did spread typhoid to 33 known victims, only three of those died from the disease. The 1903 spread of typhoid through New York was caused by several different carriers.

_06:: Yellowstone National . . . Supervolcano?

So what exactly is a supervolcano? Just picture a volcano with 10,000 times the explosive force of Mount St. Helens. And unlike Mount Fuji, supervolcanoes aren't available in nice cone shapes. Rather, these extreme volcanoes form in depressions called calderas, where the magma gets so thick that gas can't escape. The pressure keeps building and building until all hell literally breaks loose. We have our very own supervolcano (U-S-A! U-S-A!) under Yellowstone National Park. The *entire* park. In fact, the caldera under Yellowstone is so big—

4,000 square kilometers—no one knew it was there until satellite images told us so. By all estimates, it erupts about every 600,000 years, and the last eruption was 640,000 years ago. We're due. So what happens if it blows? The last eruption of a supervolcano was at Lake Toba in Sumatra 75,000 years ago. So much ash was released into the atmosphere that the sun was blocked out, the global temperature dropped 21 degrees, and three-quarters of all plant life in the Northern Hemisphere died. Ice age, anyone? Hopeful geologists contend that we may be saved by the venting that occurs at Yellowstone through geysers like Old Faithful, relieving a bit of pressure from the caldera. Let's hope they're right.

_07:: Better Disasters through Science: The China Syndrome

OK, so it's not *technically* a purely natural disaster. But it involves a lot of physics and stuff, and it would certainly *cause* one heck of a natural disaster. The name (from the film *The China Syndrome* of 1979, the same year as the Three Mile Island snafu) comes from the theory that, in the event of a meltdown, molten nuclear material would be so hot that it would melt all the way through the earth and come out in China. Of course, we all know that's just plain silly. But experts do tell us that a melting reactor core would be able to sink about 15 meters into the earth's crust, at which point it would hit the water table. The resulting massive release of hot steam would then throw the material back out of the earth with tremendous force, causing the radioactive fallout to be spread across an even wider area. Feel any better about it? We certainly don't.

Leaders Who Murdered Family Members to Get Ahead

Sometimes passive aggression will only get you so far. But is straight aggression really the key? Hey, sometimes you've got to get a head to get ahead. The following are three achievers who'd kill for their relatives' jobs.

_01:: Attila the Hun Gives Brother Bleda the Ax

When Rua, king of the Huns, died in 434 he left an empire to be coruled by his nephews Bleda and Attila. At first the brothers made a good team, negotiating a new treaty in which they agreed not to attack the Eastern Roman Empire (the part that became the Byzantine Empire, based in Constantinople) in exchange for a fee: an annual 700 pounds of gold. Not a bad deal, since it was twice what the Eastern Romans had been paying Uncle Rua. But when Constantinople failed to fork over the protection money, Attila attacked. On his rampage, the Hun destroyed every town and city (including Belgrade) along his way in a succession of battles that devastated the Eastern Roman forces. Finally, Constantinople cried "uncle" and in 443 the city agreed to pay the Huns 6,000 pounds of gold in a lump sum and to triple the annual tribute. Perhaps all the success went to Attila's head because two years later he murdered brother Bleda and took over as sole ruler of the Huns. Why kill Bleda? Historians aren't sure, but it's likely that with all the loot coming his way, Attila wasn't big on sharing.

_02:: Enrique the Fratricide Takes It to Pedro the Cruel

Born in 1334, Enrique de Trastámara was the illegitimate son of Alfonso XI, king of Castile (before Castile became part of a unified Spain). Of course the illegitimate bit brought up a legit concern: the issue of the crown. When half brother Pedro succeeded Alfonso on the throne, it didn't sit so well with little Enrique. With reinforcements from France, he invaded Castile in 1366 and took over, getting himself crowned king. But Pedro, known as "the Cruel," wasn't easily shoved aside. Securing help from England and, with Edward the Black Prince in his corner, Pedro regained the upper hand in a bitter civil war. So, Enrique responded. Rounding up even more French, he captured his brother, then personally murdered him (no one's sure how, exactly) on March 23, 1369. As Enrique II, he became known as El de las Mercedes ("He of the Largess") for awarding a new class of noble titles (with estates included) to his loyal followers. Those still loyal to Pedro's line, however, called the new king Enrique el Fratricida ("Henry the Fratricide") or simply El Bastardo.

_03:: Richard III Snuffs His Nephew

When England's Edward IV died in the spring of 1483, his brother Richard, duke of Gloucester, was appointed protector of the realm. That's because old Eddie's son, the new king Edward V, was only 12. Not only did Richard chafe at the idea of doing Ed V's job, but he didn't get along with brother Ed Sr.'s widow, Elizabeth Woodville. In fact, he thought she and her family had become too powerful, so he arrested and executed a bunch of Woodvilles and locked up his two nephews, young Edward V and Eddie's nine-year-old brother. Then he got priests to annul his brother's marriage to Elizabeth, which unseated her son Eddie as king. Guess who took the throne in the boy's stead. In August of that same year, the two little princes disappeared. Nobody knows for sure what Richard III did with them, but in 1674 workmen repairing a stairway at the Tower of London discovered the bricked-in skeletons of two boys.

Animals Subject to 'Roid Rage

The hormone hydroxy steroid ketone—better known as testosterone—is considered the biological font of maleness. And though it's often linked to muscle-headed gym dwellers, the hormone/drug actually works in pretty mysterious ways when it comes to aggressive behavior. From elephants to monkeys to the tremendously masculine antbird, check out what too much "juice" does to creatures with slightly larger brains.

_01:: Musth You Be So Aggressive?

In 1995, rangers at South Africa's Pilanesberg National Park began finding dead rhinos, brutally battered and mutilated. An investigation was launched, and it led them to a surprising realization: that the raucous culprits behind the beatings were actually teenage bull elephants. Many of the thuggish elephants were turning increasingly violent, and had added rhino murder to their rap sheets. But why all the charges? Apparently, the young bulls were entering a period known as musth, or heightened aggression related to mating, at a younger age and for longer periods than normal for teens. Wildlife biologists realized that the youngsters in the park—populated by relocated animals—lacked the biological and social structure they needed. When a few older, and perhaps wiser, bulls were added to the park, it forced the young'uns to return to their place in the elephant hierarchy. But not only did the adult supervision give them a bit of social order; it actually repressed the teens' testosterone levels, delaying and shortening musth. The elephant-on-rhino crimes stopped soon after.

A Row Is a Row Is a Row

THE CAMPBELLS AND THE MACDONALDS

In the Ring: In one corner we have Clan MacDonald, descendents of half-Viking warrior Somerled and hereditary lords of the western Highlands and isles of Scotland. In the other there's Clan Campbell, lords of Argyll and pets of the Scottish kings, rightful or not.

Round 1: Early 1300s. Robert the Bruce makes his play for the Scottish throne, supported by the Campbells. The MacDonalds (mostly, except for one smart son) support the other claimant, John Comyn. Bruce wins. MacDonalds rebel and lose their lands, many of which are given to the Campbells.

Round 2: 1692, Glencoe. After adhering to the laws of hospitality and sheltering several Campbells through a winter storm, 38 men, women, and children of the MacDonald Clan are massacred by their guests. Three MacDonald chieftains escape to spread news of the massacre and carry on the hatred.

Round 3: The Jacobite Rising of 1745. The MacDonalds are Jacobites (supporters of Catholic claimant Charles Edward Stuart, or "Bonnie Prince Charlie"). The Campbells fight alongside the redcoats of the earl of Cumberland, son of King George II. The two forces meet outside Inverness on April 16, 1746, at the Battle of Culloden. The exhausted Jacobites are driven off and all the wounded are slaughtered, many by the Campbells, while the fugitive prince is secreted "over the sea to Skye" by the brave Flora MacDonald. Punitive laws soon put an end to the Highland way of life.

Last Laugh: To this day, some descendents of Clan MacDonald refuse to eat Campbell's soup.

_02:: Fight Winner Gets (Monkey) Girl and a Hormone High

Surprisingly enough, scientists have measured the testosterone in rhesus macaque monkeys before and after a fight, and found that testosterone levels don't necessarily trigger violence. What they did find, however, was that aggression and violence definitely affect testosterone levels. For instance, if a male macaque sees an attractive, approachable female, his testosterone spikes. Then, if another male challenges monkey number one for that female, both will experience a sudden surge of testosterone. After the juices have been flowing for a while, and the fight's gone a few rounds (by the way, macaques have long, sharp canine teeth, so things can get pretty ugly), the winner's testosterone level will remain high. In fact, it might even rise higher than during the fight and stay high for 24 hours. The testosterone level in the loser, on the other hand, plummets and stays low for a much longer period.

_03:: Homebody Birds Rise to Testosterone Challenge

In migrating birds, the testosterone level is rather low—at baseline—except in the spring when the birds settle into new territories and compete for, well, chicks. On the other hand, testosterone levels of birds that don't migrate rise less, spiking only during their short mating season. But in at least one case of nonmigrating *aves,* the spotted antbirds of the Panama rainforest, males can actually raise their testosterone levels in the off-season when they need to be aggressive against territorial invaders. In fact, the sight or sound of an intruder—or even a tape of an intruder's song, played by scientists—will cause the antbird's testosterone levels to spike, and for a short period he'll become aggressive. Even odder than that: Though his gonads manufacture the hormone, they won't "come to life" sexually until the correct season.

_04:: "Bad Dad" Hormone Gets Bad Rap

What makes male mice go so bad that they need to attack and kill their own young? Strangely, it's not excess testosterone, but another steroid hormone, progesterone. Although essential to the female reproductive system, and present in both males and females, progesterone hadn't been thought to play much of a role in male chemistry. That's because females produce it in much greater volume, as they do estrogen. In 2003, however, scientists in the United States and Canada used both genetic manipulation and drugs to block progesterone receptors in otherwise normal male mice. The results were shocking. Instead of being aggressive, the male mice no longer attacked their young but actually acted tenderly toward them. The results are even more amazing when you consider that three-quarters of a control group of daddy mice killed their own babies, making a strong argument that papas and progesterone just don't mix that well.

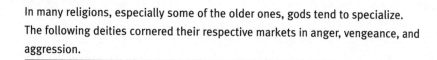

Anger from Above:
Gods of War

In many religions, especially some of the older ones, gods tend to specialize. The following deities cornered their respective markets in anger, vengeance, and aggression.

_01:: Huitzilopochtli: You Gotta Have Hearts

According to Aztec legend, Huitzilopochtli's 401 older siblings tried to kill him, but the clever god turned the tables on them and wiped 'em out with his weapon of choice, the *xiuhcóatl* (or for those of you who don't speak Aztec, a turquoise snake). Represented either as a hummingbird or as a warrior with armor and helmet made of hummingbird feathers (not exactly bulletproof), Huitzilopochtli was both god of the sun and the god of war. As such, Aztecs believed that he needed a steady diet of human hearts—preferably of the warrior variety—and human blood. In fact, the need to feed Huitzilopochtli fueled the Aztecs' ambition, and increased their urgency for fighting and conquering other peoples.

_02:: Ishtar: Not Just the Goddess of Box Office Death

Bizarrely enough, Babylon's goddess of sexual love, fertility, and plenty was also a principal goddess of war. Known by the Sumerians to the west as Inanna, Ishtar became one of the most complex and contradictory deities in the pantheon of the ancient Middle East—representing both rejoicing and grief, harvest and devastation. Ishtar also doubled as protector of prostitutes (who probably worked in her temples), and is identified with Astarte, the goddess of war and sexual love worshiped by the Egyptians, Canaanites, and Hittites (a long-ago civilization in what later became part of Turkey). Needless to say, the goddess had nothing to do with the 1987 movie flop that bears her name...unless perhaps she put a curse on it? How else can you explain the eerie flop of a big-budget buddy pic starring Warren Beatty and Dustin Hoffman?

_03:: Ares: No Dog's Best Friend

Although fiercely warlike, ancient Greeks rarely held Ares, god of war, in high regard. Sure, the guy represented brutality and slaughter—the spirit of war at its most savage. But as an Olympian—that is, among the inner circle of Hellenic deities—he was disliked by his divine peers and even his dad, the great Zeus. So, why the lack of love? Whenever Ares was wounded in battle, he'd come running to Daddy to fix things (mainly bones). And while his pops wasn't always supportive, Ares' sister Eris (Strife) and sons Phobos (Panic) and Deimos (Annihilation) stuck by him. All that isn't to say that Ares didn't have any earthly followers: he was most popular in Thrace, a region to the north of the Greek peninsula. The so-called worship, however, was an SPCA nightmare, as Spartans annually slaughtered dogs in sacrifice to him.

_04:: Mars: The God of Rome Improvement

Unlike Ares, Mars, god of war, carried more clout among Romans than his counterpart had in Greece. According to one story, Romulus, the founder of Rome, was a son of Mars. As such, the fierce battle god was seen as protector of Rome, and the month named for him, March, was festival time, as well as the time to prepare for battle. (Fighting tended to die down over the winter and resume again in spring.) The Mars fan club didn't end with the early Romans, though. In the time of Augustus (around 1 CE) Mars came to be considered avenger of the murdered dictator Julius Caesar (Augustus's great-uncle), and the war god's prominence continued to grow through the early Common Era.

_05:: Tÿr: The Sound of One Hand Pounding

The old Norse god Tÿr governed rules of battle, oaths, alliances, and even treaties. And he did it all with an iron fist... but just one of them. According to legend, Tÿr placed his hand in the mouth of Fenrir, a sort of monster-wolf, as a gesture of good faith. Then other gods tied down Fenrir so he could rampage no more. When the wolf realized he'd been duped into being docile for the purposes of being tied down, he retaliated by biting off Tÿr's hand. Of course, Tÿr's image changed from people to people. As envisioned by the Goths, barbarians who were originally from southern Scandinavia but later spread southward, Tÿr wasn't just one-handed but also one-armed. As such,

after a battle, the Goths would hack off the arms of enemy dead and suspend them from tree branches in tribute to their one-armed god. The practice was also pretty effective for terrifying the surviving enemy. While he isn't worshiped with the same vigor today, Tÿr does live on via the calendar, as Tuesdays (Tÿsdagr in Norse) are named for him.

_06:: Skanda: Six Heads Are Fiercer Than One

For early Hindus, the thunder god Indra and his brother, Agni, god of fire, were battle deities until Skanda (also called Karttikeya and Kumara) came on the scene. Devoted to nothing but war and violent adventure, this divine bachelor is depicted as a six-headed, armored archer who rides—what else?—a peacock. According to one myth, Skanda was born only because other gods, including Indra and Agni, needed a warrior to defeat the tyrannical demon Taraka. Since Taraka had been deemed invulnerable against all but a son of the god Siva—a childless, mourning widower—other deities conspired to arouse Siva's interest in the beautiful young goddess Parvatti. It took much meddling to awaken Siva from his mourning, but the matchmaking worked and eventually the six-headed Skanda was born. Enormously strong, Skanda could plunge his spear into the earth so firmly that no one but the god Vishnu could pull it out, shaking mountains and rivers in the effort.

_07:: The Eye Has It

Also called Wotan or Wodan, Odin was the Norse father god—a sort of Teutonic Zeus, but more often identified with the Roman Mercury. (The Latin *dies Mercurii* became Wotan's day, or Wednesday.) The warlike god of a warring culture, Odin presided over Valhalla, where slain fighters went to drink forever in bliss. Odin, often depicted as a tall, long-bearded old man observing the world from beneath the wide brim of his hat, rode an eight-legged flying horse, his cloak billowing behind him. He's also depicted with just one eye, not because he'd lost it riding with scissors, but rather because he'd traded the other in for eternal wisdom. Both wise, and bloodthirsty—definitely the makings of a god you can love.

Historical Figures Who Struck Back with a Vengeance

It's better to give than to receive. But then there's the whole issue of giving back, as in "some of their own medicine." The following are three cases where a little bit of vengeance went a long way.

_01:: The Charlemagne Attraction

On August 15, 778 CE, Charlemagne suffered the only major military defeat of his long reign. The king of the Franks and his army were passing through the Pyrenees when Basque fighters struck the column's rear guard. Why? The attack was simply revenge for the pillaging that Charlemagne had ordered on Basque villages. Among those killed in the skirmish, though, was a young paladin, nephew of the king, called Hrudoland. Today, historians know nothing about the real Hrudoland except for a legend of his heroism that was turned into the 12th-century epic poem *The Song of Roland*. In the poem, the attackers aren't Basque fighters but Muslims, carrying out a plot against Roland hatched by his scheming stepfather. The poet goes on to tell of Charlemagne's victory over the Muslims to avenge Roland's death, and of the evil stepfather being tried, convicted, then gruesomely executed. A bit of poetic license, to say the least: in history, Charlemagne did gain the upper hand against Muslim rulers of northern Spain, but it wasn't until a decade later. And it didn't have much to do with Roland.

_02:: Murder in the Cathedral

On a Sunday in 1478, a gang led by Francesco de' Pazzi attacked the Medici brothers, Lorenzo and Giuliano, during high mass in Florence's cathedral. The attack on the city's rulers seemed marginally successful at the time, as Pazzi and his pals stabbed Giuliano to death while his other conspirators tried to kill Lorenzo. Wounded, Lorenzo Medici managed to flee the scene. Amazingly, Pazzi's conspirators were wide-ranging, and included the archbishop of Pisa, the duke of Urbino, and Pope Sixtus IV (who wisely stayed in Rome). And while the gang had worked out most of the angles in their plot, they hadn't accounted for the Florentine people's reaction. Outraged Florentines mobbed the attackers, killed them, and dragged their bodies through the streets. When the archbishop tried to take over the government palace, Florentines slaughtered him and hung his corpse on a wall. Eventually, Lorenzo felt he'd gotten more revenge than he sought, and he tried to rein in the people's rage. As for the Pazzi family, business rivals of the Medicis, they lost everything, and many changed their names or dropped out of sight.

_03:: **Russian Reversal of Fortune**

Czar Alexander I hadn't wanted to declare war on Napoléon's France, but what's a czar to do? When France attacked Russia's European allies, he felt obligated to come to their aid. And Russia certainly paid a price. Suffering terrible defeats at Napoléon's hands in 1805 and 1807, Alexander was left with his army decimated, and thus signed a humiliating treaty with France. But Alex, it turned out, had no intention of honoring the bargain. When Napoléon's patience with his "ally" wore thin in 1812, the French corporal decided it would be a good idea to invade Russia. It wasn't. The Russian commander, Prince Kutuzov, devised a controlled retreat, allowing Napoléon to capture an evacuated Moscow—soon destroyed by fire. When Napoléon had to pull back, Kutuzov forced him to return west by the same now-ravaged route he had come, with the fierce winter closing in. The devastating retreat from Russia marked the beginning of Napoléon's end. In March of 1814, Alexander triumphantly entered Paris, vengeance achieved.

All in the Family:
Wars Waged on Familial Insults

Wars can start for all sorts of reasons: to secure trade routes, to capture resources, to eliminate a dangerous rival...but the most interesting wars flare up because of personal insults that lead to family feuds. After all, when a king's starting his speeches with a "your momma" joke, you know trouble's on its way.

_01:: **The Face That Launched a Thousand Ships**

Homer tells the story brilliantly: thousands killed, cities burned and pillaged, and giant equines built out of wood in a country that had barely any trees. And the root cause of the entire affair, as the ancients told it, was a woman: Helen, queen of Sparta. For reasons totally outside her comprehension, she was abducted by Paris, the wimpy prince of Troy. Once thought to be a myth, the story of the Trojan War is being reevaluated by scholars. In the centuries since, documents discovered in Hittite cities in Asia Minor make references to some of Homer's characters and the places he mentions. Did the war really start over the theft of Menelaus' wife? We will probably never know; though control over the lucrative trade routes to the Black Sea probably didn't hurt the cause.

_02:: Sister Pact

After the death of Gaius Julius Caesar, the most important men in Rome were two of his kinsmen, Gaius Octavianus (his great-nephew and adopted heir) and Marcus Antonius (aka Mark Antony). Realizing they could be even stronger with their powers combined, the two united with their good pal Lepidus, and formed a triumvirate that would determine the fate of all Roman territories. But the two needed something to seal the deal, and what better than a couple of marriage vows to do the trick? Octavianus wedded Antony's stepdaughter, and Antony took Octavianus's sister, Octavia, for better or for worse. Of course, for Octavia it was definitely for worse. Once old Mark caught sight of Cleopatra, he wanted a divorce. Meanwhile, this didn't really help matters between Octavianus and Antony, as the two men had remained rivals through their dealings. But news of the Antonys' divorce helped Octavianus decide he'd had enough. The civil war between the two lasted from 33 to 30 BCE. By the end of it, Octavianus was the undisputed ruler of the Roman world; he changed his name to Augustus and became the first Roman emperor. Antony, on the other hand, had committed suicide to avoid capture, having learned the hard way that you just don't mess with a man's sister.

_03:: How a Little Bullying Went a Long, Long Way

Tan Shi Huai was the illegitimate son of a Xianbei (Mongol) mercenary serving the Han dynasty of China. As a result of his low birth, he was considered little better than a slave by his fellow tribesmen. The insults served his way must have stuck in his young craw, particularly given his (as yet unrevealed) ambition, intelligence, and strategic skill. His injured pride may have spurred him on as he gathered a following of malcontents, somehow finagled his way into the supreme overlordship of all Xianbei tribes around 170 CE, and organized a powerful empire north of the Great Wall, even defeating the Huns who had previously ruled the region. Then, in 177, he defeated the Chinese army and threatened the imperial court, though an attack on the capital never materialized because of supply problems. Sadly, however, his empire, which had been held together largely through his own force of will, didn't survive his death. Still, the guy defeated both the mighty Hans and Huns. All because he was picked on as a kid? Makes you wonder how much more effective our politicians could be if we started insulting their families a little more.

_04:: The Great Islamic Schism

Politics in sixth- and early-seventh-century Mecca were dominated by a feud between two clans, the Hashemites and the Umayyads. And though the feud continued into the mid-600s, a generation after Muhammad's rise to power, things really came to a head in 656, when the caliph Uthman (an Umayyad) was murdered. The new caliph, Ali (a Hashemite cousin and a son-in-law of Muhammad), didn't really help smooth things over when he failed (or refused) to track down and punish the assassins. It's little wonder, then, that the Umayyads saw this as somewhat suspicious and, even worse, kind of insulting to their clan. A five-year war broke out, and eventually ended in a truce, but Ali's subsequent murder (not exactly truceful) and replacement by the Umayyad leader Muawiyya (whose kinsmen would rule the Islamic world for a century to come) exacerbated the conflict. Ali's followers, however, have remained faithful to the end. Driven underground, they called themselves Shiat Ali, or "the Party of Ali," and their spiritual descendents are known today as the Shiites. The rift caused by the fiasco survives to the modern day in Islam's two largest sects.

_05:: The Princess Bride (and a Decidedly Less Happy Ending)

In 758 CE, Caliph Abdullah al-Mansur, the titular ruler of all Islam, decided to order one of his nobles to take a royal Khazar bride and bring about some peace (the Khazars had fought two brutal wars to stop Islamic expansion into the Caucasus Mountains and Eastern Europe). To carry out this seemingly easy task, al-Mansur picked the military governor of Armenia, Yazid ibn Usayd al-Sulami, for the great marriage mission. Of course, Yazid was happy to comply, and took home a daughter of Khagan Baghatur, the Khazar leader. Things were going very well when the girl somehow died, possibly in childbirth, though the details are vague. Her attendants, however, didn't need details. They returned home convinced that some Arab faction had poisoned her (not unreasonable, all things considered). Needless to say, Pops got angry, and took his revenge on the Abbasid Caliphate. The Khazars quickly invaded what is now northwestern Iran, plundering and raiding as only nomads can.

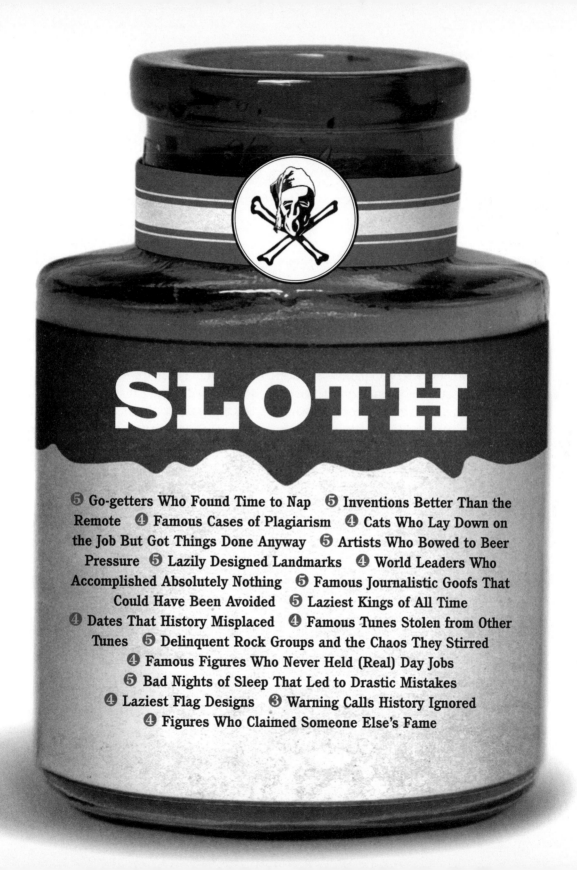

SLOTH

⑤ Go-getters Who Found Time to Nap ⑤ Inventions Better Than the Remote ④ Famous Cases of Plagiarism ④ Cats Who Lay Down on the Job But Got Things Done Anyway ⑤ Artists Who Bowed to Beer Pressure ⑤ Lazily Designed Landmarks ④ World Leaders Who Accomplished Absolutely Nothing ⑤ Famous Journalistic Goofs That Could Have Been Avoided ⑤ Laziest Kings of All Time ④ Dates That History Misplaced ④ Famous Tunes Stolen from Other Tunes ⑤ Delinquent Rock Groups and the Chaos They Stirred ④ Famous Figures Who Never Held (Real) Day Jobs ⑤ Bad Nights of Sleep That Led to Drastic Mistakes ④ Laziest Flag Designs ③ Warning Calls History Ignored ④ Figures Who Claimed Someone Else's Fame

Sleeping Giants:
Go-getters Who Found Time to Nap

Call it a power nap. Call it a break. Whatever you call it, don't assume that somebody who sneaks in a few winks in the middle of the day can't also take care of business.

_01:: Thomas Edison: Highly Inventive Napping

Prolific inventor Thomas Edison didn't like to go to bed at night. In fact, he didn't like to take his clothes off or change into pajamas because he thought it somehow interfered with his creativity. The solution? The "Wizard of Menlo Park" chose instead to sleep a few hours at night—often no more than three—then catch naps in the lab around the clock, whenever he felt tired. Colleagues referred to it as his "genius for sleep." After Edison built his laboratory and home together in Menlo Park, New Jersey, in 1876, he could indulge his odd sleep habits with little trouble—except with his wife, Mary, who found his eccentric hours bothersome. But he kept on doing it anyway. Edison loved to stretch out atop a lab table when catching a quickie, but he was known to make do on a stool if nothing more comfortable was handy.

_02:: Warren G. Harding: Late to Bed and Early to Rise

Although he seldom went to bed before midnight and frequently stayed up until 2 a.m., President Harding was not a very late riser. In fact, he always got up at 8. His White House schedule, however, left him increasingly fa-

tigued, perhaps signifying sleep deprivation, but also a sign of the advancing heart disease that would kill him in office in 1923. Friends told Harding that he would be more rested if he stayed in bed in the morning but the president refused, saying that to do so would be "too much like a woman." Irwin "Ike" Hood, chief usher of the White House, recalled that instead, the sleep-deprived president would steal the occasional presidential power nap in the Oval Office.

_03:: Salvador Dalí: Surreal Sleep

Salvador Dalí, the Spanish surrealist painter, arrived at the startling images of his most productive period—between 1929 and 1937—using what he called the "paranoiac-critical method." Apparently, this involved fishing "delirious associations and interpretations" out of his unconscious. It's less than clear how he accomplished this, but he used no intoxicants. "I don't do drugs," he once said. "I am drugs." Dalí wasn't above manipulating his consciousness in other ways, though. He reportedly took odd little catnaps that brought him right to the edge of deep sleep, but then jerked himself out of it. His method was simple: Seated in an armchair, Dalí held a metal spoon in one hand. Then, next to his chair,

It's a Mad, Mad, Mad, Mad Scientist

OLIVER HEAVISIDE REJECTS THE BATH

Maybe it was the scarlet fever he had as a boy that left him partially deaf. Or maybe it was the years he spent isolated in his parents' house studying electricity. Or maybe it was the lack of recognition he received from the scientific community. Whatever it was, something drove British mathematician and physicist Oliver Heaviside (1850–1925) certifiably loony. Heaviside made lots of important discoveries, like operational calculus, impedance, and a layer of the ionosphere now called the Kennelly–Heaviside layer (he's also got moon and Mars craters and a song in *Cats* named after him). But his twilight years were marked by all kinds of kooky behavior, brought on by bitterness and a persecution complex. Oliver refused to bathe, but kept his fingernails impeccably manicured and painted bright pink. He signed all his letters "W.O.R.M.," which stood for ... well, worm (how he saw himself or, perhaps, everyone else). And here's the best one: He replaced all the furniture in his house with giant blocks of granite. Yes, really.

he'd place a metal pan. He'd quickly nod off, and as soon as he was relaxed enough to let go of the spoon, it would fall against the pan. The sudden clang waking him up, Dalí was immediately reacquainted with his subconscious, and went back to work.

Touch of Evil

Calvin Coolidge took the oath of office at 2:00 in the morning following Warren Harding's death, but he was rarely up that late during any other night of his term. In fact, he was publicly reported to sleep an average of eleven hours every single day.

_04:: Samuel Goldwyn: Cinematic Snoozer

One of Hollywood's most prominent film producers for over 30 years, Sam Goldwyn believed in hard work. Indeed, he demanded it from his employees. He also believed in taking care of himself. Every day after lunch, Sam would take a siesta, disappearing into a room adjacent to his office, changing into pajamas, and sleeping for an hour. According to biographer Arthur Marx, Goldwyn—the man behind such classics as *Wuthering Heights* and *The Best Years of Our Lives*—believed a 60-minute afternoon nap was the secret to good health. One day he recommended the practice to two writers working on a script for a Danny Kaye picture. "You ought to try it, too," he said. Then, realizing that he didn't want the scribes sleeping on company time, he added, "In your cases, eat a half hour, sleep a half hour."

_05:: Ronald Reagan: To Nap or Not to Nap?

Ronald Reagan supposedly took a nap every day. In fact, it was frequently mentioned in newspaper columns and widely accepted as fact. But First Lady Nancy Reagan vehemently denied the accusations. What he did, Nancy said, was take a short break in the afternoon, away from staff, visitors, and the press. It was, after all, on doctor's orders after Reagan was wounded in a 1981 assassination attempt. Maureen Reagan, the president's daughter, also insisted that Reagan hated to take naps. So maybe the Gipper didn't nap in private, but as a president who was nearly 70 when he took office, he was definitely observed from time to time nodding off in public. Reagan even joked about falling asleep in cabinet meetings and once dropped off in the middle of a speech by Pope John Paul II.

Slacker's Paradise: Inventions Better Than the Remote

Oh, the horrors of the past. Although it's hard to fathom why people bothered to go on living, there was once a time when folks had no choice but to sit up straight in their chairs, fiddle with buttons and zippers, climb stairs, hike to the outhouse, and add numbers with pencil and paper. Below, a paean to the inventions that made it easier to enjoy the simple pleasures of sinful idleness.

_01:: Velcro

Isaac Newton beneath the apple tree. Archimedes shouting "Eureka!" in the bathtub. And Georges de Mestral going for a walk in the woods. The greatest discoveries often stem from mundane observations, and while gravity (Newton) and measurable density (Archimedes) are cool and everything, nothing beats the sweet music of parting Velcro. Mestral, a Swiss engineer, returned home after a walk in 1948 to find cockleburs stuck to his coat. After examining one under a microscope, he noted that cockleburs attach to clothes and fur via thin hooks. Eureka! It took Mestral eight years to develop his product. But in the end, the twin nylon strips worked precisely like a cocklebur on a coat—one strip features burr-like hooks and the other thousands of small loops to which they attach, forming an unusually strong bond.

_02:: Calculator

Ah, the calculator—a handy device that makes 55378008 look like a naughty word when you turn it upside down. Oh, and it also makes math class a whole lot easier. Oddly enough, it was a 19-year-old boy named Blaise Pascal (yes, that Pascal) who invented the first mechanical adding machine. But Pascal's device was cumbersome and couldn't record results, so the vast majority of people continued calculating by hand until 1892, when William Seward Burroughs patented the first commercially viable adding machine. Although Burroughs died before reaping much profit from his invention, his grandson (also William Seward Burroughs) was one sure beneficiary. The younger Burroughs became famous for writing *Naked Lunch,* a book that would likely have been impossible if Burroughs hadn't had all that inherited calculator money to waste on heroin.

_03:: Lay-Z-Boy

In 1928, when he was a mere lad of 21, Edwin Shoemaker forever blurred the distinction between sitting up and lying down by developing the world's first reclining chair. His initial model, a wood-slat chair intended for porches, was fashioned out of orange crates and designed to fit the contours of the back at any angle. It took an early customer, appreciative of the concept but rather unexcited about the prospect of lying down on bare slats of wood, to suggest *upholstering* the chair. Shoemaker and his partner (and cousin) Edward Knabusch then held a contest to name the invention. "La-Z-Boy" beat out suggestions like "Sit 'n Snooze" and "The Slack Back." The next time someone tells you an active lifestyle is the key to long life, reply with this tidbit: The man who invented the recliner lazed his way up to the ripe old age of 91.

_04:: The Toilet

Contrary to popular belief, we do not have Thomas Crapper to thank for the conveniences of the flushing toilet (more on him in a moment). Toilets with drainage systems date to 2500 BCE, but Sir John Harrington invented the first "water closet" around 1596 (it was also used by his godmother, Queen Elizabeth I). However, toilets never caught on until Alexander Cummings invented the "Strap," which featured a sliding valve between the bowl and the sewage trap. As for Mr. Crapper (1837–1910), he was a plumber who sold, but did not invent, a popular type of toilet, although he did hold several plumbing-related patents. Not surprisingly, Crapper has been unfairly linked to the less-than-pleasant word "crap." The two, however, are unrelated. In 1846, the first time "crap" is recorded as having been used in English, little Tommy-poo was just nine years of age.

_05:: The Escalator

In 1891, Jesse Reno patented the first moving staircase, paving the way for today's world, in which we choose not to use staircases, just StairMasters. Reno's invention was more of an inclined ramp than the escalator we know today; passengers hooked into cleats on the belt and scooted up the ramp at a 25-degree angle. Fairly soon after, he built a spiral escalator— the mere thought nauseates us—in London, but it was never used by the public. Reno's first escalator, however, *was* widely used, albeit not practically. In a testament to how utterly unamusing amusement parks were in the 1890s, 75,000 people rode Reno's "inclined elevator" during a two-week exhibition at Coney Island in 1896. Let's be clear: The escalator was not the means by which one traveled to a ride. It was *the ride itself.*

Say My Name, Say My Name:
Famous Cases of Plagiarism

No writer can be fully convicted of imitation except there is a concurrence of more resemblance than can be imagined to have happened by chance; as where not only the thought but the words are copied. And we ought to know a thing or two about plagiarism, since we stole that previous sentence from the great Samuel Johnson (1709–1784), who himself was accused of it. But even by Johnson's strict definition, these folks are all guilty as sin.

_01:: Martin Luther King Jr.: I Heard a Dream (Which Subsequently Became My Dream)

When writing about the Lord God Almighty, one is generally well advised not to break the seventh commandment, but Martin Luther King Jr. managed to turn out pretty well in spite of his tendency to borrow others' words without attribution. King received a doctorate in systematic theology from Boston University in 1955 on the strength of a dissertation comparing the theologians Paul Tillich and Henry Nelson Weiman. In a 1989–1990 review, though, the university discovered that King had plagiarized about a third of his thesis from a previous student's dissertation. And although it was closer to liberal adaptation than outright plagiarism, King's seminal "I Have a Dream" speech was, well, let's say "inspired by" a speech that an African American preacher named Archibald Carey Jr. gave to the Republican National Convention in 1952.

_02:: Stendhal: The Politician's Plagiarist

When asked by Oprah Winfrey about his favorite book during the 2000 presidential campaign, Al Gore cited Stendhal's *The Red and the Black*, a novel set in post-Napoleonic France. The book's protagonist, Julien Sorel, is an ambitious young womanizer who adopts the hypocrisy of his time in order to move up in the world. In his own time, Stendhal, whose real name was Henri Beyle, was most famous not for his novels, but for his books about art and travel. In one, *The Lives of Haydn, Mozart and Metastasio,* Stendhal plagiarized extensively from two previous biographies. Confronted with overwhelming evidence of theft, Stendhal added forgery to the list of his literary crimes, manufacturing correspondence in the hopes of exonerating himself.

_03:: Alex Haley and the Roots of *Roots*

Haley initially gained prominence for being the "as told to" author behind *The Autobiography of Malcolm X* and then went on to publish the epic *Roots: The Saga of an American*

Family in 1976, supposedly a true story that traced Haley's ancestry back to an African man, Kunta Kinte. Haley won a Pulitzer the next year, and the book was made into a wildly popular miniseries (which, curiously enough, featured the PBS show *Reading Rainbow*'s LeVar Burton as Kinte). After the book's publication, though, Haley admitted that he made up large swaths of the *Roots* story and, in a further embarrassment, was sued by author Harold Courlander for plagiarism. Haley acknowledged lifting (accidentally, he claimed) three paragraphs from Courlander's work and settled the suit out of court.

_04:: John Milton: In His Own Words

Was the half-blind creator of *Paradise Lost* a plagiarist? Well, no. But William Lauder, an 18th-century scholar, sure wanted you to think so. Bitter about his professional failures, Lauder published several essays in 1747 claiming to "prove" that Milton had stolen almost all of *Paradise Lost* from various 17th-century poets. One problem, though. Lauder had forged the poems, interpolating text from *Paradise Lost* into the original documents. For a while, many (including the great Samuel Johnson) supported Lauder, but it soon became clear by studying extant copies of the old poems that Lauder, not Milton, was the cheat. And cheating, at least in this case, didn't pay: Exiled to the West Indies, Lauder died an impoverished shopkeeper.

Supine Successes:
Cats Who Lay Down on the Job But Got Things Done Anyway

Parents and coaches have the annoying habit of urging people to get up and at 'em. Someone should remind them that the "up" part isn't always necessary.

_01:: Florence Nightingale: Don't Just Do Something, Lie There

As a hero of the Crimean War, nurse Florence Nightingale revolutionized the care of wounded and ill soldiers. And she's been remembered by British soldiers in the Crimea as the tireless "Lady with the Lamp," for patrolling field hospitals all through the night. It's no wonder, then, that Nightingale returned from the Crimea to London in 1856 with enough clout to lobby Queen Victoria for improvements in military living conditions. The next year, however, the 37-year-old healthcare advocate lay down and seldom again got up. Doctors who examined her found her perfectly healthy, with no apparent physical reason for her sudden unwillingness to rise. Living as an invalid for the last 53 years of her life, Nightingale remained inert yet rarely indulged in idleness. She supervised fundraising, advocated better training for nurses and midwives, received official visitors, took care of correspondence, and oversaw substantial projects—such as founding a London nursing school—all from the comfort of her couch.

_02:: Mark Twain: "A Pretty Good Gospel"

"Whenever I've got some work to do I go to bed," said the 69-year-old Mark Twain in 1905. In an interview with the *New York Times,* he explained: "I got into that habit some time ago when I had an attack of bronchitis. Suppose your bronchitis lasts six weeks. The first two you can't do much but attend to the barking and so on, but the last four I found I could work if I stayed in bed and when you can work you don't mind staying in bed." At his mansion in Hartford, Connecticut, the writer—whose real name was Samuel Clemens—ran a rubber hose from the gas chandelier in his bedroom to a gas lamp on his bedside table so that he would have enough light to write by. "Work in bed is a pretty good gospel," he told the *Times.* Of course, this is also coming from the man who said, "Whenever I feel the urge to exercise I lie down until the feeling passes away."

_03:: Winston Churchill: We Will Fight Them from the Bedroom

Britain's cigar-chomping prime minister during World War II conducted considerable state business from his bed. Tucked under the covers, the people's PM would dictate letters, tele-

---

It's a Mad, Mad, Mad, Mad Scientist

THOMAS MORGAN AND HIS FLY PLATE

Thomas Hunt Morgan, the Nobel Prize–winning geneticist whose research with fruit flies established the role of the chromosome in inheritance, was a meticulous thinker, but he was unspeakably sloppy about everything else. So, how sloppy was he? Morgan once wore a length of string as a belt and often sported shoes and shirts with holes in them. In his Columbia University laboratory, which smelled of fermented bananas (food for the insects), Morgan's staff threw discarded fruit flies into a jar of oil that they called "the morgue." Their boss, by contrast, simply smashed his flies against the white porcelain plate he used for counting them. He would leave the accumulating mess for days, even weeks, until someone—often the wife of one of his graduate students—felt compelled to wash the plate. Need more? His mail, which was usually unopened, lay in a massive pile that cluttered his lab table workstation until somebody else threw it away.

---

grams, and speeches—including his famous "Battle of Britain Speech" of 1940—to his secretaries until the early hours of the morning. He worked so late that secretaries were given sleeping quarters in the official residence, 10 Downing Street, so that one would always be on hand. In the morning, Churchill breakfasted and read the newspaper in bed, then would dictate again, to a secretary sitting on the end of his bed. If he had no meetings scheduled, he stayed in bed, working all the while, until noon. Then he would rise, bathe, and go to the House of Commons.

_04:: Hugh Hefner:
All Play Is All Work

Given the subject matter of *Playboy* magazine, publisher Hugh Hefner could have claimed the most enjoyable hours spent in the revolving circular bed of his mansion as work time. Nice work if you can get it. That's not what got him on this list, however. Especially in the swingin' 1960s, when his home and headquar-

ters was the 70-room Playboy Mansion on Chicago's Gold Coast, the workaholic's office wear was always silk pajamas, and it wasn't unusual for him to sprawl across that hedonistic bed along with stacks of photos to select from or copy to be reviewed for the next issue. In 1971, Hefner ditched midwestern winters in favor of southern California, where he brought his style of relaxed labor to a Playboy Mansion in Beverly Hills.

Touch of Evil

Xaviera Hollander, famous prostitute and author of The Happy Hooker, *still makes her living in the sack, kinda. She owns a bed-and-breakfast in Amsterdam.*

Hooked on Tonics:
Artists Who Bowed to Beer Pressure

Asked to give advice to aspiring writers, novelist William Styron once said, "You ought not to drink; you ought to write." The advice is a lot easier given than followed.

_01:: Patrick Branwell Brontë:
Black Sheep in a Snowy Flock

As a boy, Patrick Branwell Brontë (called Branwell) created an elaborate imaginary world with his big sister Charlotte. Including younger sisters Emily and Anne, the Brontë children of Haworth, Yorkshire, spun fantasies that fueled the girls' later careers as novelists.

Branwell wrote, too, but never published anything beyond a few poems in local newspapers. A gifted musician and artist, he opened a portrait studio, hoping to thrive as a painter. Lacking commissions, though, he spent more time in pubs than at the easel. Fired from the few jobs he tried—either for incompetence or (in the case of one tutoring position) questionable behavior toward his employer's wife—Branwell Brontë took to drinking more and to opium. By many accounts as promising a creative force as his sisters were, Branwell died a failure at 31.

_02:: F. Scott Fitzgerald: The Sodden Side of Paradise

Famed novelist (and the guy responsible for plenty of required high school reading) F. Scott Fitzgerald died of a heart attack in L.A. in 1940, believing himself a failure. Aside from his first book, 1920's *This Side of Paradise,* his works had not sold well. That included the critically well received *The Great Gatsby.* Fitzgerald did, however, earn good money writing stories for magazines, but had not saved any. His glamorous marriage had gone adrift upon a sea of alcohol and, in wife Zelda's case, insanity. Although an alcoholic, Fitzgerald typically wrote sober, before his first cocktail of the day. Free of alcoholism, however, he would likely have completed many more novels and may even have been able to hold his family together. When he died, Fitzgerald was writing a novel, *The Last Tycoon,* and it was going well—largely because he was staying away from the bottle. Too bad he never finished the book. After he died, scholars placed Fitzgerald among the best American novelists.

Touch of Evil

Original KISS drummer Peter Criss won an out-of-court settlement after the Star depicted him as a homeless drunk living under a Santa Monica bridge in 1991. The person photographed wasn't Criss but a look-alike alcoholic.

_03:: John Barrymore: Good Night, Sweet (Hiccup!) Prince

Decades before granddaughter Drew appeared on the scene, matinee idol John Barrymore was the most celebrated member of a show business dynasty, along with brother Lionel, a character actor, and sister Ethel, a leading lady of the stage. The three grew up as theater royalty, since parents Maurice Barrymore and Georgiana Drew were 19th-century stars. John took after his famous father, and the resemblance extended to their drinking—a trait that killed them both. When drunk, John made public scenes. He flew into screaming rages. He urinated in public. And the effects played into his career. In his final decade, John—once considered the greatest actor of his time for roles such as Hamlet—was reduced to taking degrading parts in trashy films. His mind was so riddled by booze that he couldn't remember his lines and he often had to read them from a blackboard off camera. A tragic ending for the brilliant talent, he died in 1942 at the age of 60.

_04:: Dylan Thomas: "Do Not Go Gentle…"

Precocious Welshman Dylan Thomas caught the attention of the London literary world when he was only 20 with the publication of his first book, *18 Poems,* in 1934. The Celtic rhythms of his English verse, and their themes—gnawing at elusive love and inevitable death—came across as startlingly full of feeling. Thomas, who had quit school at 16 to become a newspaper reporter, was a writer for the rest of his 39 years, producing poetry, prose, and drama, but he was also a heavy drinker. Constantly in debt to the Inland Revenue (Britain's counterpart to the IRS) and frequently broke, Thomas used alcohol for solace and inspiration. When away from wife Caitlin on a visit to London or on a speaking tour of U.S. universities, the poet was almost certain to get roaring drunk. It was on just such a trip that he died in New York, in 1953, of acute alcohol poisoning.

_05:: Charles Bukowski: When Life Inebriates Art

Some artists lose precious years of their productive life to the bottle. Bukowski, on the other hand, drank as he wrote and wrote as he drank. The prolific Los Angeles poet, who also wrote short stories (collected in the volume *Notes of a Dirty Old Man*) and novels (such as *Post Office*), wrote about drunks, prostitutes, and down-and-outers. His frequent main character, the hard-drinking and often pathetic Henry Chinaski, was a thinly veiled portrayal of Bukowski himself. The violence and graphic frankness in his work flowed from a dissolute life that Bukowski embraced, exposed, mocked, and—in an odd way—romanticized. His one screenplay, for the 1987 movie *Barfly,* was a love story featuring alcoholics on skid row.

If I Had a Hammock: Lazily Designed Landmarks

Attention do-it-yourselfers: You aren't the only ones to ever screw up a project. And you can take comfort in the fact that, most likely, your botched projects aren't on public display. Here are five high-profile screwups that don't have the luxury of anonymity.

_01:: Don't Lean on Me: Pisa's Towering Problems

The best known of the world's landmark blunders, the famed Leaning Tower is actually a *series* of blunders. Begun by Bonanno Pisano (whose name, ironically, means "A good year in Pisa") in 1174, the tower started leaning almost immediately, due to the incredibly poor soil conditions beneath it. Only three floors were completed before Pisa's frequent wars halted construction for 94 years. Then, by the time construction resumed in 1272, the lean was considerable. Of course, rather than demolishing it and starting over (preferably on more stable ground), the builders decided to *correct* for the lean by building the rest of the tower at a compensatory angle. Which is why, today, the tower doesn't just lean. It actually curves.

_02:: That Sinking Feeling: The Story of Folsom Library

The goof-ups in the construction of the Folsom Library at upstate New York's Rensselaer Polytechnic Institute are made even more ironic by the fact that they occurred at an engineering school. The library's floors were originally intended to bow upward slightly, so the weight of the books would level them. Unfortunately, the construction crews were a little foggy on this concept and built them nice and level. Like floors should be, damn it! Once the books were added, though, the floors developed a pronounced sag. RPI legend also has it that the contractor hired to design the foundation did so without knowing the building was a library, so he didn't account for the weight of the books. The resulting wimpiness of the foundation causes Folsom Library to sink about one inch every year. It's one of several buildings on campus that are sinking, sagging, or moving, phenomena the students refer to generally as "sliding down the hill into Troy."

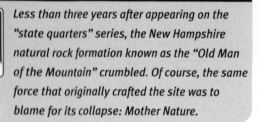

Touch of Evil

Less than three years after appearing on the "state quarters" series, the New Hampshire natural rock formation known as the "Old Man of the Mountain" crumbled. Of course, the same force that originally crafted the site was to blame for its collapse: Mother Nature.

_03:: Foul Ballpark: Houston's Disastrous Dome

OK, for its time it was pretty amazing. But the Houston Astrodome had some major problems when it first opened in 1965. Proclaimed a masterpiece of engineering and "the Eighth Wonder of the World," its original roof was made of clear Lucite panels. All of which sounds fine, but actually caused such a bad glare that outfielders routinely lost sight of the ball. So the roof panels were painted to block out the sun. Also not a bad idea, except that it caused the

Lies Your Mother Told You

DON'T THROW RICE (THROW BUTTERFLIES?)

Under the sway of the widespread but ridiculous myth that wedding rice poses a threat to birds, thousands of newlyweds have sought out rice alternatives, with questionable results. One of the more popular, ostensibly eco-friendly solutions is butterflies: They're pretty, they're totally natural, and they'll make you—a terrorist? So say the generally genial folks at the North American Butterfly Association, who argued in 1999 that releasing butterflies into the wild amounted to "environmental terrorism." Nonnative butterflies can cause a host of problems—introducing new parasites to native populations, interbreeding, and messing up migratory patterns. Some lepidopterologists (yes, there's a word for butterfly scientists) have even expressed concern that the growing popularity of butterfly releases has led to overharvesting of wild monarchs, the world's most popular butterfly species. Popular alternatives for true environmentalists include bubbles and rose petals. Or, you know, rice also works.

grass on the field to die almost immediately (its life may have been prolonged by the notoriously leaky roof, which let in so much rain during a game on July 30, 1972, that ushers handed out plastic rain shields). What to do? Officials replaced the grass with a new invention: a green carpet called AstroTurf, an abomination that can be blamed for enough wrenched ankles, torn anterior cruciate ligaments, and "turf toes" to fill a Hall of Fame. Texas tidbit: When the stadium was originally proposed, the team was called the Houston Colt .45s. The groundbreaking was performed by city commissioners firing real Colt .45 pistols at the ground (they used blanks).

_04:: Tacoma Narrows Bridge Is Falling Down

Motorists noticed movement of Washington's Tacoma Narrows Bridge on windy days almost immediately after it opened, quickly dubbing it "Galloping Gertie." But it would take a degree in structural engineering to understand precisely what went wrong on November 7, 1940. That's the day old Gertie shook herself to pieces and crashed into Puget Sound. But it can be summed up (kinda) by saying that strong winds induced vibrations in the bridge's rigid steel side girders that started out as vertical oscillations and then became torsional nodes. Got that? In short, it twisted itself to smithereens. At the worst extremity of the twisting motion, the sidewalk on one side of the bridge was 28 feet higher than on the other. Remarkably, there was only one casu-

alty in the collapse: a three-legged, paralyzed black spaniel named Tubby, who was stranded in a car when his owner, Leonard Coatsworth, fled the bridge. Tubby's death earned Coatsworth $364.40 in compensation from the Washington State Toll Bridge Authority. Not too shabby; he only got $450 for the car.

_05:: Putting Your Hancock Where You Shouldn't: Boston's Most Notorious Building

The tallest structure in New England, Boston's John Hancock Tower is a shimmering geometric tower of 10,000 squares of reflective glass. Designed by I. M. Pei, the world-famous architect who created the Rock and Roll Hall of Fame, the controversial addition to the Louvre, and many other structures, this Beantown creation was unfortunately snakebit from the start. After completion in 1976, the building became a menace as pressure differentials and poor securing techniques caused its huge glass panels to routinely pop out and plummet the 62 stories to Clarendon Street below. The high Boston winds caused an inordinate amount of swaying. And the tower's weight caused nearby buildings, including a historic hotel and church, to sink and suffer structural damage. Eventually, all 10,000 glass panels had to be replaced to correct the sway. During the process, it earned the nickname "Plywood Place."

"Fortunate Son": World Leaders Who Accomplished Absolutely Nothing

Inept people in positions of power? So many to choose from, so little space. Ah, well. Here are four to get you started.

_01:: Commodus (161–192 CE)

Commodus has the dubious distinction of being one of the worst Roman emperors—and that's saying something. He was cruel, sadistic, vicious, and crazier than an outhouse rat (perhaps that's all par for the course). He also renamed Rome, as well as days of the week, after himself, thought of himself as the reincarnation of the demigod Hercules, dressed in lion skins, and killed hundreds of animals and people in the gladiator arena in rigged fights. Need more? Commodus was so swept up in the Hercules/gladiator thing that he let others run the empire, until they showed too much competence. Then he'd have 'em killed. As for his own life, Commodus was strangled by a wrestler while taking a bath. In his wake came a long line of really lame emperors, and one not-so-lame movie, as 2000's *Gladiator* was very loosely based on the Commodus administration.

_02:: Pope John XII (937–964)

There were a lot of bad popes in the Middle Ages, but this guy, whose birth name was Octavian, was a pip. As Daddy's little boy (and son of the secular ruler of Rome), John XII was given the keys to the pope-dom at just 18. But things didn't exactly start off on the right foot. After a disastrous military expedition against a rebellious lord in the Papal States, John XII settled for less ambitious pursuits. In the eight years to follow, John XII was guilty of rape, fornication, looting the church treasury, and gambling. After being briefly (and rightly) deposed, John struck back at his deposers with even more unholy behavior . . . by killing some and mutilating others. Good Catholics can be comforted in knowing that he died with almost as little grace as he lived: John's less-than-saintly life was ended in 964 by an enraged husband, who caught his wife being given more than just the sacrament. John's reign accomplished only one thing: it ensured the pope's office would become politically trivial during the rest of the Middle Ages.

_03:: Edward II (1284–1327)

Lazy and incompetent, Eddie II got to be king of England only because his three older brothers all died. Quite an honor indeed! Taking the throne in 1307, Edward abandoned his father's efforts to work through the nobility to get things done. Instead, he chose to irritate them by conferring power to a guy from France who was his best friend and possibly his lover (not the best decision). Edward also had his royal rump handed to him by the Scots, who were fighting under Robert the Bruce at the time. But that isn't the worst of it. Edward finally agreed to a set of limits on his authority imposed by English nobles, but reneged. His disaffected wife, a French princess, then invaded England with her new boyfriend. Ever incompetent, Edward was deposed, imprisoned, and eventually murdered. A tough end, even for a nincompoop.

_04:: James Buchanan (1791–1868)

Whenever there is talk of America's worst presidents, Buchanan's name is almost sure to come up. Which is too bad, even if warranted, because old James had one of the best political pedigrees. When elected in 1856, Buchanan had been a legislator, congressman, U.S. senator, minister to Russia and Great Britain, and secretary of state. Unfortunately, he was also a Northerner with Southern sympathies at a time when America was rife with sectional

Touch of Evil

Before his death, George V predicted that once his son took the throne, he would "ruin himself in 12 months." He was wrong, however, as Edward VIII abdicated the throne to marry divorcée Wallis Simpson two months before the full year was up.

tensions, thus pleasing no one. Thoroughly incompetent in the post, President Buchanan cleverly confronted the tensions over slavery by doing nothing. Of course, the economic depression triggered by a bank panic didn't really help matters. It's no wonder Buchanan didn't run for reelection on the Democratic ticket. One good thing did result from his incompetence, though. Buchanan's paralysis caused a split in his party, which helped ensure the election of a Republican candidate in 1860: a fellow by the name of Lincoln.

The Inconvenience of Fact-checking: Famous Journalistic Goofs That Could Have Been Avoided

There's an old adage in journalism: "If your mother says she loves you, check it out." Here are five instances in which journalists forgot to call someone other than Mom.

_01:: The Amazing Tasaday

They lived in caves, wore leaves, used stone tools, and had no word in their language for "enemy." At least that's what Manuel Elizalde Jr., the Philippine government minister who "discovered" them in 1971, said. The "Stone Age" tribe of about 25 was called "the anthropological find of the century," featured on the cover of *National Geographic* and idealized by media around the world. They were also declared off-limits by Philippine dictator Ferdinand Marcos. That is, until Marcos was deposed in 1986, and journalists and anthropologists got to revisiting the Tasaday. This time, tribe members had a slightly different story: that they'd been coerced by Elizalde into posing as primitives. While some scientists still insist the Tasaday are unique in some ways, no one claims they're the 21st-century version of the Flintstones, as they were originally hailed.

_02:: A Cooked-Up Tale

In journalistic terms, it was a world-class "weeper"—the story of an eight-year-old heroin addict named Jimmy. In fact, the September 28, 1980, story in the *Washington Post* was so good, magazines and other newspapers reprinted part or all of it. And the mayor of Washington, D.C., even ordered city police to find the poor kid. It's no wonder, then, that the reporter, Janet Cooke, won a 1981 Pulitzer Prize. Of course, her spoils proved to be her undoing as well. The publicity quickly raised questions about her background, and it soon became clear she'd fudged the story from her imagination. An embarrassed *Post* fired Cooke and gave the Pulitzer back. Where to go from here? Cooke took a job as a $6-an-hour department store clerk. But in 1996, she did sell the movie rights to her tale. Presumably it's based on a true story.

_03:: Hitler's Diaries

"I've got to have a really serious talk with Eva," read one entry. "She thinks that a man who leads Germany can take as much time as he wants for private matters." According to the German magazine *Der Stern*, that quote was from Adolf Hitler's secret diaries, and the magazine was willing to fork over 5 million big ones to a guy named Konrad Kujau, for the pages. Supposedly discovered in East Germany, the diaries were authenticated by the eminent

Just the Facts

SLUMBER BY THE NUMBERS

60 million: Number of American adults who suffer from inadequate sleep

77: Percentage of American adults who drink coffee on a daily basis

100 billion: Estimated annual loss in dollars because of sleep-deprivation-related problems in the United States

100,000: Number of fatigue-related traffic accidents per year in the United States

65: Percentage of Americans who lose sleep due to stress

32: Percentage who lose sleep due to stress on a weekly basis

18 million: Number of Americans who suffer from sleep apnea

8.6: Average number of hours of sleep Americans got daily in 2000

1: Ranking of Honolulu, Hawaii, in 2003 survey as best U.S. city in which to get a good night's sleep

2: Ranking of Fresno, California, in same survey

British historian Hugh Trevor-Roper, and the London *Sunday Times* even agreed to buy the reprint rights. But much to everyone's chagrin, the German government revealed the diaries were a rather amateurish fraud. Kujau and the *Der Stern* reporter who arranged the seven-figure deal went to jail. And in 2004, one of the fake volumes sold for $7,741 at a Berlin auction. Go figure.

_04:: The Scoop

The *New York Post* will never be confused with the *New York Times,* at least not by anyone who can read. But the *Post* had a big scoop on July 6, 2004: Democratic presidential candidate John Kerry had picked Congressman Richard Gephardt as his running mate. Of course it was wrong—Kerry had picked Senator John Edwards. Trying to manage the damage done, the *Post* apologized the next day for their error, while the *Times* gleefully reported that the source of the scoop was none other than *Post* publisher Rupert Murdoch. Of course, Murdoch hotly denied it. Whoever was to blame, the *Post*'s July 6 edition quickly took its place in history alongside the *Chicago Tribune*'s 1948 "Dewey Beats Truman" headline and was selling for $10 and up on the Internet within days, all of which says something about accuracy being its own reward.

_05:: A Rather Bush Story

Well, they looked authentic, unless you looked pretty closely, and CBS didn't. Instead network news anchor Dan Rather reported on September 8, 2004, that CBS had obtained documents showing President George W. Bush had received special treatment while in the Texas Air National Guard. And for nearly two weeks, CBS and Rather steadfastly defended the story, despite almost immediate doubts raised about the documents and their source. Finally, on September 20, the network cried "uncle" and Rather apologized for airing the story, confessing his staff had failed "to properly scrutinize the documents" or properly check out the sources behind them. Subscribers to the "liberal media conspiracy" theory had a field day, and the incident gave the network a black eye. It also left an indelible mark on Rather's long and storied career.

Royal Bums:
Laziest Kings of All Time

When you're born with a silver spoon in your mouth, it's no wonder you grow up expecting someone to pull said spoon out, pile it high with delicious food, then put it back where they found it. The following are just a few of the spoiled royals who managed to get away with doing nothing, both for themselves and their doting subjects.

_01:: Louis XIV and His Shirt-Sighted Attendants

Louis XIV may have gotten a lot done in his life, but he seems to have been profoundly lazy when it came to personal care. According to contemporary accounts, to get up in the morning Louis XIV required the assistance of literally hundreds of servants and favored courtiers, who helped him bathe, dress, and shave. It was a great honor to hand the king his shirt, and courtiers and sycophants vied with each other for the singular prestige associated with forking over the emperor's new clothes.

_02:: Charles II: A Royal Drain on England

Charles II is on record as one of the laziest kings to rule Britain. And sure, he played an important role just by showing up, since his restoration to the throne signaled a return to peace and tranquility after a bitter civil war.

But once he got there, Charles didn't do much of anything. A contemporary English chronicler, Samuel Pepys, described Charles as "a lazy Prince, no Council, no money, no reputation at home or abroad." Not the best PR. Even worse, a common saying at the time had it that Charles "never said a foolish thing, and never did a wise one." Ironically, the high point of Charles's popularity came when he survived an assassination attempt during the "Rye House Plot," named after the place where the would-be assassins allegedly wanted to kill him...after a lifetime spent not doing things, not getting killed was Charles's biggest accomplishment.

_03:: Ethelred the Unready

With a nickname like "the Unready," old Ethelred's place in history is pretty obvious. The poor royal seemed unable to make any decisions by himself, and generally found it easier to put them off. And sure, this governing-by-procrastination strategy worked just fine when England was at peace, but not so well when it was attacked from abroad, which is exactly what happened in 1009, when Sweyn Fork-beard and his Danish Vikings invaded England. The Danes had given plenty of warning, threatening England for several years, but rather than organize an army to fight them, Ethelred thought it would be less work to just buy them off. Unfortunately, the easy loot only encouraged the Danes, and they demanded successively larger sums. When finally pushed to make a decision, the one Ethelred made proved to be the wrong one. By ordering the slaughter of Danish settlers in 1002, he simply provoked the Danes even further. Truly unready in the end, it's no wonder he was deposed by Sweyn Forkbeard in 1012.

_04:: Sultan Selim II: Lazy Like a Fox

Sultan Selim II, "the Drunk," is generally considered one of the most disgracefully lazy rulers of the Ottoman Empire, which is no small accomplishment. But perhaps his indolence was even more noticeable because of the contrast with his father. Selim's pop, Süleyman the Magnificent, ruled from 1520 to 1566 and in that time conquered much of the Middle East and North Africa. His progeny, on the other hand, preferred to spend almost all his time in the harem, never once led his army in a campaign, became an alcoholic, as his nickname suggests, and generally withdrew from all administrative duties. Historians of the Ottoman Empire often mark the beginning of its decline from his completely useless reign.

Touch of Evil

Were King Kong of normal size, perhaps he wouldn't have been so hyper. Gorillas sleep about 13 hours a night, and sometimes nap during the day as well.

_05:: Nicholas II and His Royal Ramblings

Nicholas II, the last czar of Russia, was a bit slow and didn't care for the tasks of government at all. He did keep a diary through most of his reign, though, and it's remarkable to read how little time he seemed to spend on affairs of state compared with, say, the latest news about his dogs. The journal is filled with entries like "At about 6 my dog Shilka whelped 2 puppies whose father was Iman. It caused a lot of fuss in the house." Looking for something deeper? Try this: "I've been hanging pictures upstairs in the new bedroom with green furniture." Or this: "The 3 of us had dinner together at 8:30. We were awfully hungry after our trip and . . . I stuffed myself in an indecent way." Even more remarkable than his complete lack of competency, after the Russian Revolution of 1917 he spent most of his remaining time happily working in his small garden. That is, until he was shot.

Next Time, Mark It Down:
Dates That History Misplaced

4

From Momma's birthday to the Wilkersons' anniversary to, you know, the time Eadweard Muybridge figured out that horses have all four of their hooves in the air while running, there are just some dates that you know are important...but somehow end up being a little harder to remember.

_01:: October 24, 1942: Smithsonian Admits Its Plane Wrong

For decades children have been taught that Wilbur and Orville Wright were the first to fly a machine-powered airplane. However, for more than a couple of years the Smithsonian Institution thought differently. The fact is, an inventor named Samuel Langley unsuccessfully attempted to fly over the Potomac River in an airplane he'd designed nine days before the Wright bothers made their famous Kitty Hawk flight. A few years later, though, after Langley had passed away, a number of his colleagues repaired the crashed plane and displayed it in the Smithsonian as the first manned flying machine. For two decades, a bitter debate ensued with the Wright broth-

ers, who by then had loaned their original aircraft to the Science Museum in London. Finally, on October 24, 1942, the Smithsonian apologized to Orville Wright (Wilbur had died years before) and declared that he and his brother were in fact the first to fly a machine-powered aircraft. With history corrected, Orville donated his airplane to the Smithsonian.

_02:: October 13, 1307: A Terrifying Friday for the Templars

While there are tons of stories about how the dreaded Friday the 13th date came about, the one with the most historical significance happened on October 13, 1307. During the previous century, a religious order of warrior monks had sprung up in France to fight in the Crusades. Known for their religious piety and courage in battle, the Knights Templar soon became wealthy and actually served as Europe's first banking system. Meanwhile, the French king Philip IV, needing money to run his kingdom, turned on the Templars after coercing the pope to drop their protected status. Then he craftily sent out secret orders to every bailiff in his kingdom. Under penalty of death, the documents were to be opened on October

Touch of Evil

"I am apt to believe it will be celebrated, by succeeding Generations, as the great anniversary Festival." John Adams wasn't talking about July 4, though, but July 2, when the Continental Congress first actually declared American independence.

Lies Your Mother Told You

NEW YEAR'S DAY WAS ALWAYS JANUARY 1

The new year begins on January 1, right? It's always been that way. Wrong. In fact, the selection of the date has been a little more like getting everyone to convert to the metric system—some people love it, but there's plenty of resistance. The Romans traditionally celebrated the beginning of their year on January 1, but the early Christian Church actually thought otherwise. So, in the seventh century, the church decided that one of its major religious festivals should signify the start of the new year, and Christmas was selected. This lasted only until the 12th century in most of Europe. In the ninth century, however, parts of southern Europe had already splintered and began celebrating the new year on March 25, the Feast of the Annunciation. Then, starting in Italy in 1522, the date for New Year's Day reverted back to the Roman date of January 1, but it took almost another 225 years for the majority of European countries to adopt this day. England and its American colonies didn't switch over until 1752. Just think what a computerization mess Y1K would have been.

12 and executed the next day, Friday, October 13. The orders demanded the arrest of any and all Templars and the forfeiture of all their possessions to the king. As a result, over 2,000 Templars were arrested and tortured into making confessions. Interestingly, a couple years later, Jacques de Molay, the Templars' grand master, while being burned at the stake, cursed Philip and the pope, saying that they would both join him in death within the year. They both did!

_03:: June 15, 1878: Muybridge (and a Horse) Invent Motion Pictures

The photographer was Eadweard Muybridge and the horse was Abe Edgington. Commissioned by Leland Stanford (the railroad tycoon and the cofounder of the university bearing his name), Muybridge was attempting to photograph the horse running in full stride to see whether all four of the horse's hooves left the ground at the same time. Twelve box cameras, fitted with special trip wires, were placed 21 inches apart along the track; the cameras essentially recorded what was too fast for the eye to see. Not only did this prove that horses become airborne while running, but the camera technique became the foundation for motion pictures. Despite a quick run-in with the law (Muybridge was also known for tracking down a journalist and shooting him for allegedly having an affair with his wife and fathering his son—later ruled a justifiable homicide), Muybridge continued to experiment with motion photography, and even earned the title "Father of Motion Pictures."

_04:: March 3, 1879:
The Supreme Court Finally Listens to a Woman

On March 3, 1879, Belva Ann Lockwood won the right to plead a case before the U.S. Supreme Court, thereby becoming the first woman admitted in the court. The case involved the right of Samuel Lowery, an African American attorney, to practice law. However, this wasn't the first "first" for Ms. Lockwood. After moving to Washington, D.C., at the end of the Civil War, Lockwood applied to law school only to be told that, as a woman, her attendance would be an "injurious diversion" to the other students. Eventually she did receive a law degree from National University Law School, but the school refused to award her a diploma. She then wrote to President Grant, the titular head of the school, telling him to either award her the diploma or take his name off the letterhead. Two weeks later she got her diploma. In 1884, as the candidate for the Equal Rights Party, she became the first female to run for president, receiving 4,000 popular votes (women weren't allowed to vote) and two electoral college votes. Lockwood also may have been the first to foresee the Beltway gridlock as she was frequently seen riding a tricycle through the streets of Washington, D.C.

Songs in the Key of Trite:
Famous Tunes Stolen from Other Tunes

Ever had a catchy song you just couldn't get out of your head? Well, have you ever taken said song, thrown in a couple of new lyrics, and told everyone it was your own? That's just what these cats did, and it landed them in a boatload of trouble. The following are four cases where imitation was a pretty expensive form of flattery.

_01:: "My Sweet Lord"/
"He's So Fine"

After a pretty successful run with the Beatles, George Harrison recorded his solo album *All Things Must Pass* in 1970 and released "My Sweet Lord" as its first single. The song quickly became a big hit. The problem was that back in 1962 a group called the Chiffons had recorded a hit song by Ronald Mack in the United States called "He's So Fine." Actually, the problem wasn't just that the Chiffons had released a song, but that the songs sounded pretty much the same. In early 1971, Mack and the Bright Tunes Music Corporation filed suit against Harrison and his American and British music companies. In order to settle the lawsuit, Harrison initially offered to purchase the entire Bright Tunes catalog, but it wasn't agreeable to Bright Tunes. The company countered the suit with a proposal whereby Harrison would surrender the copyright to "My Sweet Lord" and they'd share 50% of the royalties on the song with Harrison. Neither side gave in and the suit went on for years. Finally, the suit was settled with Harrison admitting that he "unknowingly" plagiarized the melody.

_02:: "Ice Ice Baby"/"Under Pressure"

On his 1990 album *To the Extreme,* Vanilla Ice sampled some very identifiable riffs in his hit "Ice Ice Baby" from the Queen/David Bowie song "Under Pressure." While it's a pretty common technique to hook audiences and generate sales, the problem was that Ice didn't bother to license the song or give Queen or David Bowie any credit. The album's liner notes credit Vanilla Ice and two others as the composers, and while it goes on to thank other artists, there's no mention of either Bowie or Queen. Although the case never went to court, Vanilla Ice was threatened with a lawsuit, which he settled for an undisclosed amount. Interestingly enough, Queen rereleased "Under Pressure" as part of its 1992 *Classic Queen* album. The liner notes stated that not only was the song a hit in the U.K., but that in 1990, the bass and piano were featured again in Vanilla Ice's number one single "Ice Ice Baby."

_03:: "Avalon"/*La Tosca*

Using someone else's musical composition isn't just an epidemic of the rock era. In 1920, the song "Avalon" was introduced to the American public by Al Jolson. Considered a classic American love song, it was later recorded in 1937 by the Benny Goodman Quartet and featured in at least five movies. Of course, the music and lyrics are attributed to Vincent Rose

and Al Jolson (aka "the Jazz Singer"). And while it wasn't common for Jolson to take credit for many of his hit songs, in this case he probably wished he hadn't. Soon after the song was published, the Italian composer Puccini and his publisher filed suit against Jolson, claiming that the melody was plagiarized from the aria "E Lucevan le Stelle" from his opera *La Tosca.* Puccini won the case and all future royalties. He also received settlement of $25,000, not a small sum for that time.

Touch of Evil

While the Beach Boys' "Surfin' USA" seemed like an obvious update of Chuck Berry's "Sweet Little Sixteen," Berry was only credited on the label after initiating a lawsuit.

_04:: *Ghostbusters/* "I Want a New Drug"

Is the Stay Puft Marshmallow Man the new drug that Huey Lewis & The News were looking for? Say it ain't so! When the movie *Ghostbusters* came out in 1984, the theme song ("Who You Going to Call?") sounded very much like Lewis's "I Want a New Drug," and Lewis quickly decided he was going to call his lawyer. Understandably, the suit was settled out of court in 1995, and while Ray Parker never admitted that he copied Lewis, he did agree to pay Huey an undisclosed amount. However, the story doesn't end there. In 2001, as part of a *VH1: Behind the Music* segment, Huey Lewis, in discussing the battle over the *Ghostbusters* tune said, "They bought it," referring to Parker and the settlement. Of course the segment gave Parker some ammunition of his own, and Parker filed suit against Lewis for violating their agreement, whereby the fact that money had changed hands was never to be made public.

Riot Back At'cha: Delinquent Rock Groups and the Chaos They Stirred

Just because you're a big-shot, world-famous rock-and-roll band doesn't mean you have the right to play with people's emotions. At least, that's probably what these rock bands' moms told them after they came home stoned (we're talking bruised from having rocks pelted at them, not high on drugs!).

_01:: Guns N' Roses— December 6, 2002

The rock group Guns N' Roses had a history of canceling concerts, or just plain deciding not to show up for 'em. On December 6, 2002, however, South Philadelphia fans struck back. When the group didn't arrive as scheduled, the warm-up act continued to play for close to two hours. Understandably, the crowd grew increasingly irritated, and unlike the GNR anthem, they didn't "have a little patience." Tempers quickly moved toward the boiling point when the crowd saw the warm-up group removing their equipment from the stage and nothing was being set up in its place. Unknown to the crowd of 20,000, Guns N' Roses had canceled right before the show because their lead singer, Axl Rose, was "too sick" to perform. No one told the audience, though, and after standing around for even more time, they quickly realized their own "Appetites for Destruction." Chairs, drinks, and even ceiling tiles were tossed as the crowd went berserk. In

fact, it took over 100 police officers to restore order, and while no one was arrested, a number of individuals did require hospital treatment. Interestingly, concert officials denied that there was any trouble and claimed the fans left in an orderly fashion.

_02:: Creed—December 29, 2002

Some musicians show up at a concert but aren't really there. And while Bob Dylan's been accused of it for years, it was definitely the case with Scott Stapp, the lead singer for Creed, in Rosemont, Illinois. Once onstage, Stapp was so under the influence of alcohol and drugs that he was unable to sing the lyrics to any of the group's songs. On a number of occasions he actually left the stage and didn't return for several minutes. When he did choose to return, he fell to the floor and rolled around in pain; then it appeared like he'd passed out. Many angry fans left the arena, but four of them decided to take things into their own hands. By filing a class action suit against Creed and their promoters, the fans sought over $2 million in refunds for the 15,000 concertgoers attending that night. The group later apologized for what they called their "most unique" experience and reminded the fans that it's only rock and roll, even if you don't like it.

_03:: Punked in Montreal— October 2003

Fans weren't exactly happy when organizers canceled a midweek punk rock show in Montreal in mid-October 2003. After all, the concert attendees had already gathered to hear their bands, Total Chaos and The Exploited, play when they received the bad news. Of course, a different sort of total chaos did eventually show up: police reports indicate that at roughly 8 p.m., when they were informed of the cancellation, hundreds of punk rock concert fans immediately expressed their anger by rioting, smashing windows, overturning cars, and setting things on fire. In fact, the Canadian press reported that one city block had 24 cars and at least six stores with smashed windows. When things finally calmed down, an unknown number of people had been arrested and two police officers had sustained injuries. The French-language TV channel LCN said that the band had to cancel after Canadian customs officials had barred some members of The Exploited band from entering the country.

_04:: Jefferson Starship— June 17, 1978

The Jefferson Starship was known for inciting their fans to riot when they did perform at concerts. Unfortunately, things didn't change much when they didn't. In Germany, as part of a European tour, the Starship was scheduled to play at the Lorelei Amphitheater outside Wiesbaden when Grace Slick (the group's lead singer) allegedly became ill and stated that she wasn't going to perform. Without Slick, the group couldn't go on, and decided to cancel the concert. Of course, the crowd of over 10,000 didn't quite understand. They had, after all, waited for a couple hours, and when the announcement came they erupted. Angry fans started throwing bottles and rocks at the stage, injuring one of the crew. When the crew finally gave up trying to save the band's stuff, the crowd attacked the stage and destroyed over a million dollars' worth of equipment. And whatever wasn't torched was thrown over a cliff into the Rhine! Apparently, the fire could be seen from miles away, and when the fire brigade showed up they were pelted with bricks and forced to flee the scene. As for the police, they never did show up.

_05:: Hot Fun in the Summer Sun— July 21, 1973

The city of Milwaukee runs an annual 11-day festival called Summerfest. And in the summer of 1971, Sly and the Family Stone caused a riot among the 100,000 fans in attendance when they failed to show up on time (something they were known for doing). Essentially, the old pattern of a crowd getting rowdy and police making numerous arrests occurred. Unfortunately for the Summerfest, though, lightning did strike twice. On July 21, 1973, the group Humble Pie failed to show up on time and the large crowd went even crazier, this time throwing bottles and cans, torching food tents, and stealing barrels of beer. The crowd then set bonfires using chairs and fences as the fuel. And then they took their show on the road, going over to a nearby circus, beating up two workers, and swinging on the trapezes. In the end, police managed to clear the area using nightsticks and tear gas, though seven officers were injured in the event, and damages totaled in the thousands.

Born Retired:
Famous Figures Who Never Held (Real) Day Jobs

What do these dictators, witty writers, spiritual leaders, terrorists, and philosophers all have in common? Well, there's one thing they didn't have: a job.

_01:: Oscar Wilde (1854–1900)

"Cultivated leisure is the aim of man," Oscar Wilde once famously said, and he certainly lived his life by that dictum. Wilde was brilliant, winning a gold medal in Classics at Trinity College in Dublin in 1874 before earning a scholarship to Oxford. When his father died, however, Wilde left the family's finances to his older brother Henry, and worked only once in his life, a brief two-year stint as the editor of a women's magazine called *The Woman's World*, from 1887 to 1889. Wilde spent the rest of his time writing, giving lectures on aesthetics, coining pithy epigrams, and generally being a wit. Sadly, Wilde was forced to do hard labor near the end of his life after he was found guilty of immoral conduct for homosexual activities. A broken man, he died shortly thereafter, in 1900.

_02:: Socrates (468–399 BCE)

Aside from a possible brief stint as a sculptor, Socrates seems to have spent most of his hours ambling around the *agora*—the gymnasia where Athenians exercised, which was also Athens's central public meeting place and marketplace. When he wasn't milling about the town, the old philosopher could be spotted going to parties and loitering in taverns where citizens and foreign guests gathered. All this isn't to say the poor guy enjoyed the lush life. Socrates lived and dressed simply, wore neither shoes nor shirt, and owned only one coat. He also ate poorly, lived hand to mouth, relied heavily on the charity of his friends, and refused gifts when they were offered. Like, for instance, the time his friend Charmides offered to give him slaves who could have made money to support him. He also refused to accept presents from powerful leaders of Greek cities, not wanting to ever compromise his integrity. When the great philosopher was put on trial for allegedly teaching sacrilege, Socrates tweaked the Athenian assembly by suggesting that far from being a criminal, he deserved free room and board at their expense. Unamused, they condemned him to death.

_03:: Buddha (ca. 563–483 BCE)

Buddha, like Socrates, was a full-time thinker whose schedule of meditation, contemplation, and conversation didn't leave any time for work. Born around 563 BCE, Siddhartha, as he was called when young, was the son of a king who ruled a small kingdom in the northern floodplains of the Ganges River in India. The young prince led a life of leisure in his early years before growing disgusted with the materialism of the royal palace. Instead of sticking around, Siddhartha wandered off into nature at the age of 28, and after seven years of travel, meditation, and conversation with Hindu mystics, he attained enlightenment under a *Bodhi* tree. Receiving visitors and teaching students from under the tree, he spread the message of moderation and separation from material want that became Buddhism—and never did get a job.

_04:: Osama bin Laden (1957–)

Before he started fighting for his own violent version of Islam, terrorist Osama bin Laden led the life of a playboy. Born around 1957 to a wealthy Yemeni father and Syrian mother, bin Laden was heir to part of the massive fortune his billionaire father had accumulated in the Saudi construction business. As such, he squandered his days, acquiring a reputation for drinking too much and womanizing in his teens and early 20s in Beirut, which was then a cosmopolitan tourist hot spot. In fact, he didn't become a firmly committed, full-time Islamic radical until he went to fight the Soviet invasion of Afghanistan in 1979. That's where Osama began his improbable transformation from a rakish ladies' man to a mass-murdering zealot, never having worked a day before then.

Less-Than-Golden Slumbers: Bad Nights of Sleep That Led to Drastic Mistakes

"To sleep, perchance to screw up." OK, we'll admit that's not exactly what the good bard said, but it does fit these five slices of somnambulistic history.

_01:: A Christmas Wake-up Call

Colonel Johann Rall was a proven fighter, having already led his Hessian, or German mercenary, troops in successful battle against the American rebels. But he was contemptuous of his foe, and boy did he like to drink. In the end, the happy juice proved to be his undoing.

On December 25, 1776, Rall ignored warnings that rebels under General George Washington were on the march toward Trenton, New Jersey. Instead, he got drunk and went to sleep, as did many of his 1,400 soldiers. Washington, meanwhile, made a daring predawn crossing of the ice-choked Delaware River. At daylight on December 26, the rebels attacked and routed the Hessians. Rall, who was under the covers when the battle began, got dressed just in time to be killed . . . proving that some days it really doesn't pay to get out of bed.

Touch of Evil

Cyril Evans, the wireless operator aboard the Californian, forgot to set the automatic signal detector in his haste to catch some shut-eye. As a result, the ship didn't receive any warnings from the nearby Titanic, *and (despite being the closest to the wreck) failed to lend a hand until far too late.*

_02:: "Get the Phone, Eva, I'm Schnoozing"

The weather seemed too rough over the English Channel the evening of June 5, 1944, to launch the greatest military invasion in history. So Adolf Hitler figured, "What the hell, I'm going to bed." Der Führer took a sleeping pill and left orders not to be disturbed. Big mistake on old Adolf's part: D-Day was several hours into effect before aides got the courage to wake Hitler up to get his permission to mobilize needed troops and equipment. Even then, the dictator dallied. He had tea, took a nap, and met with the premier of Hungary. Finally, about 5 p.m. on June 6, he issued orders, mostly bad ones that kept German generals from being able to move reinforcements to the invasion area. Good thing for the Allies that he woke up.

_03:: Asleep at the Switch?

During a clear, sunny morning, February 8, 1986, the 114-car Canadian National Railway

It's a Mad, Mad, Mad, Mad Author

ONE WORD, TWO WORDS

The charming children's books (and wartime propaganda) of Theodor Seuss Geisel (Dr. Seuss) have entertained young and old alike for generations. One commentator described his work, which included *If I Ran the Zoo, Horton Hears a Who!, How the Grinch Stole Christmas,* and *The Cat in the Hat,* as wonderful stories of "ludicrous situations pursued with relentless logic." Starting in 1957, Seuss's work becomes noticeably laconic: the number of different words drops considerably. With *Green Eggs and Ham,* Seuss won a bet with his editor, who wagered that he couldn't write a book using fewer than 50 different words. Brilliance or laziness? You decide.

freight train rolled west near the small town of Hinton in the province of Alberta. Rolling east was a passenger train. But because the freight train's three-man crew missed a stop signal, the two trains were on the same track. The result was a horrific collision, killing 23 people, including the freight train's engineer and brakeman. Just why the crew missed the signal has never been resolved. What was reported, however, was that the engineer had worked 26 of the 30 days before the wreck, and the crew had had little sleep. In the wake of the tragedy, the rail company introduced sweeping measures to combat crew fatigue.

_04:: Oil on the Waters

The reef was well marked on the charts, the weather was OK, and the 984-foot-long *Exxon Valdez* had all the latest navigational equipment. But the oil-laden ship still went aground on Prince William Sound just after midnight on March 24, 1989. The result—only the worst oil spill in American history, which led everyone to ask the same question: What happened? Despite the popular notion that it was caused by a drunken captain, the U.S. National Transportation Safety Board attributed the spill to other causes. Among them was that the third mate, who was at the helm at the time of the accident, was "impaired by fatigue," as was the rest of the crew. Exxon, it turned out, had a policy of increasing crews' workload to save money. The spill cost the company $2.2 billion, which translated into a lot of overtime.

_05:: "I Object: My Attorney's Asleep"

Calvin Burdine was scheduled to die on April 11, 1995, 12 years after being convicted of killing his boyfriend in Houston. But a federal judge stopped the execution a few hours before it was scheduled. What prompted the justice's change of heart? Well, among other things, he was troubled that Burdine's lawyer had slept through portions of the trial. Amazingly, a three-member federal appeals court panel overruled the judge, reasoning that a defendant had no constitutional right to a conscious attorney. Fortunately for Burdine, a full appeals court ordered a new trial, and the U.S. Supreme Court concurred. As of 2004, Burdine was doing life in a Texas prison after a plea bargain. And lawyers all over the country were trying to stay awake.

What's That You're Flying? Laziest Flag Designs

Flags are an important reminder of who we are and what we stand for, so it's surprising how often a flag design is chosen in a seemingly careless manner, with little attempt at originality of appearance. What follows is a list of just four of the many, many lazily designed flags that have still waved proudly from masts across the globe.

_01:: Libya: It's Ridiculously Easy Being Green

In 1977, Libya left a federation of Arab states (the other members were Syria and Egypt) that had all used a pan-Arab banner with horizontal stripes of red over white over black. As part of an effort to forge a new, uniquely Libyan identity, the ever-wacky Muammar al-

Gadhafi unveiled a new flag design for the "Socialist People's Libyan Arab Jamahiriya." The flag, representing Islam and fertility, was completely green.

Touch of Evil

The flags of Denmark, Finland, Iceland, Norway, and Sweden are all nearly identical in design; each depicts a cross with its intersection in the first third of the field.

_02:: Haiti: Get the White Out

The modern Haitian flag features two horizontal stripes, blue over red. But the original version, adopted upon independence in 1804, featured two stripes arranged vertically like those on the French flag. The flag originated when Jean-Jacques Dessalines, a leader of the Haitian revolt against France, tore the white stripe out of a French flag and told his goddaughter to sew the two remaining stripes together. Ironically, while Dessalines meant this as a gesture of contempt for his country's former white masters (many of whom were massacred by their former slaves during the fight for Haitian independence), the color white in flags traditionally stands for peace, something Haiti unfortunately has known little of in its 200 years as an independent country.

_03:: Alaska: The Best Darn Artist in the Whole Eighth Grade

Alaska had been a U.S. possession since 1867 and a territory since 1912, but apparently no-body ever bothered to make a flag for the place until 1927, when the territorial government of Alaska farmed out the responsibility of flag design to the Alaska Department of the American Legion. The Legion, in turn, decided flag design was too important to leave to anyone but teenage children, and so sponsored a contest. The winner, John Bell Benson, was a 13-year-old boy. He actually did a fair job, all things considered—the flag is dark blue, with eight five-pointed gold stars in the shape of the Big Dipper and a larger gold star representing the North Star, Polaris. The lazy, lazy inhabitants of Alaska even let Benson pick the state flower—he chose the forget-me-not.

_04:: China: Getting By with a Little Help from Communist Friends

The Chinese Communists developed their own flag during the terrible decades-long civil war with the Nationalists and various warlords. The clever design featured a red background with a golden hammer and sickle. The only problem: This flag was identical to that of the Soviet Union, minus a star. Not to be outdone, the later Communist parties in Vietnam and Laos adopted their own flags. For some reason, however, these were simply copies of the Chinese version. This intrepid spirit of innovation would serve the Communists well in defeating Western democracy and capitalism in the cold war. Oh, wait . . .

The Sound of Sirens:
Warning Calls History Ignored

3

Tsk-tsk! If you hear the warning bells a-ringing (or see that a certain group has been looting and plundering your neighbors and is now making a beeline for your home), maybe it's time to put down the remote and start planning your defense. Of course, if you're too lazy to make a move you could always cross your fingers and take your chances. Unfortunately, that genius tactic didn't work out so well for the following folks.

_01:: Beware Macedonians Bringing Gifts

Demosthenes (384–322 BCE) was a brilliant Athenian orator, though apparently he was pretty good as an oracle as well. Throughout the 340s BCE, he begged, harangued, and pleaded with the feuding Greek city-states to unite against what he saw as the growing threat of Macedon, under its brutal, one-eyed King Philip. But Philip wasn't without his charms, either: the wily warlord threatened, flattered, and bribed the city-states until they were either too scared, too vain, or too rich to risk fighting the Macedonians. When they finally realized the danger, it was a little too late. With the evidence all pointing to Philip's plot for total domination, Demosthenes did finally succeed in scrounging up a coalition against him, but they lacked the time and resources to prepare. At Chaeronea in 338 BCE, Philip and his son Alexander (a few years shy of being "the Great") destroyed the united Greek armies. Demosthenes lived on until 322, giving him plenty of time to tell his fellow Hellenes, "I told ye so."

_02:: Norse by Norse-West: The Vikings Arrive on the Scene

In 789, Viking marauders made their first appearance in the British Isles. Then, four years later, a major force of Norsemen sacked the famous monastery at Lindisfarne. Doing pretty darn well for themselves, the Vikings' raids became a regular part of life in England, Scotland, Wales, and Ireland over the next few decades. Across the Channel, the nobles of what is now Germany and France heard of the attacks and tried to build up their defenses, but the Carolingian rulers opposed such efforts, fearing (not entirely without reason) that nobles could use these bases to rebel. By the

Touch of Evil

No one blinked when Swedish scientist Svante Arrhenius predicted a global warming scenario that would cause problems around the world. Maybe it's because his alert came about a hundred years too early, in 1896.

Lies Your Mother Told You

THE "SURPRISE" PROTESTANT REFORMATION

Teachers often describe the Protestant Reformation as if it came out of nowhere, but Martin Luther and Ulrich Zwingli were hardly the first to take stabs at reforming the increasingly corrupt Catholic Church. From about 1300 until the rise of the Protestant movement, would-be reformers popped up everywhere—John Wyclif in England, the fire-and-brimstone Savanarola in Florence, and Jan Huss in Bohemia. Though they tried to effect change from within the Church, most of these folks ended up burning at the stake or meeting some other sticky end. Simony (buying a position in the Church), nepotism (riding on your relatives' coattails), and indulgences (buying forgiveness for your sins) all continued unabated, eventually sparking the Reformation and the splintering of Western Christianity.

mid-800s, entire provinces were in the hands of Scandinavian marauders; and Carolingian monarchs, too, had to pay vast bribes to keep them happy. One group of these pirates was even granted land in northwestern France; the province of Normandy is named after these "Northmen."

_03:: Winnie Prophesies Doom

Winston Churchill, dismayed by the rise of Hitler, was reported to have said that "the hottest part of hell is reserved for those who, at a time of grave moral crisis, steadfastly maintain their neutrality." During the 1930s, Churchill did his best to alert his fellow Britons to the danger on the horizon, but no one was particularly interested, since everyone was focused on the Depression. When Prime Minister Neville Chamberlain signed a peace deal with Hitler, Churchill told the House of Commons, "You were given the choice between war and dishonor. You chose dishonor and you will have war." The irrepressible Churchill was right, of course—within months Germany had unleashed war, and Britain and France were caught with their proverbial pants down.

Resting on Someone Else's Laurels: Figures Who Claimed Someone Else's Fame

When "'Tis a far, far better thing he does than you'll ever be able to do" happens to be the case, maybe you should take a page out of these guys' playbook. After all, it's a great thing to be able to produce something that will be remembered for all time. It's even better to let some other chump do the work while you just steal the credit.

_01:: Darius "I'm the Greatest" the Great

In 522 BCE, the Persian king Cambyses died while at war, and the relatively young Persian Empire erupted into rebellion. The Persian prince Darius became the new king after leading six other conspirators to kill off the most prominent challenger. And while Darius did succeed in arranging the end of the various rebellions (largely through the efforts of said six coconspirators), the age of Persian expansion was largely over. Sure, old Darius defended the empire well, but his best-known foreign campaign, the invasion of Greece in 490 BCE, ended in defeat. But that didn't stop the Persian from stealing a bit of glory for himself. On a monument erected in his honor in Behistun (in modern Iran), Darius claimed the kingship of 23 nations, virtually all conquered by his predecessors.

_02:: Pope Gregory's Calendar

In 1582, Pope Gregory XIII ordered the Catholic world to adopt an adjustment to the old Roman "Julian" calendar then in use. And while many people can tell you the new "Gregorian" calendar corrected some of the misplaced leap years of the old system, which had resulted in the year being slightly too long, few people knew the identity of the real inventor. The calendar was actually designed by Aloysius Lilius, a Neapolitan doctor. And Lilius himself had relied upon the calculations of Roger Bacon, a 13th-century English philosopher who had once been incarcerated by the Church for heresy. Not surprisingly, Pope Gregory got all the credit because the system change was mandated in the papal bull *Inter Gravissimas*, but we're pretty sure he didn't mind too much.

_03:: The Many Inventors of the Telescope

Most people credit Galileo Galilei (1564–1642) with the invention of the telescope. But then most people are wrong! Until recently it was believed that Galileo was the first to use the telescope for observation of the heavenly bodies, and that Hans Lippershey (1570–1619) was the first to build a workable telescope. This conventional view, however, may be mistaken as well—various cryptic remarks in Leonardo da Vinci's (1452–1519) notebooks, which discuss the science of optics, actually seem to refer to the use of telescopic devices to study the moon. And in 1938, Domenico Argentieri discovered a previously ignored diagram in a Leonardo manuscript that appears to depict the plans for a primitive telescope. Chalk another great invention up to old Leonardo.

Touch of Evil

After Hank Ballard failed to show up on American Bandstand to promote "The Twist," host Dick Clark asked his protégé, Chubby Checker, to record the tune for the program. He did, and it became the biggest dance record of its era.

_04:: Morseward Bound

Forget what you learned in grade school: Samuel Morse was at the least a second placer when it came to the telegraph. Instead, set your sights on the true champ, Sir Charles Wheatstone (1802–1875). It's true! The British inventor built the first practical electric telegraph in 1837 or 1838, at the very least four years before Morse received his U.S. patent (and around the time he was conducting his early experiments with electric telegraphy). Even in America, though, Morse's "invention" of the telegraph is fraught with controversy: a friend, Dr. Charles Jackson, accused the inventor of stealing his idea (which could move Morse from second into third place). Also in dispute is the extent to which Morse's assistant, Alfred Vail, contributed to both the design of his telegraph machine and the development of the "Morse code," which was originally called the "Morse-Vail." (Does that even leave Sammy in the running anymore?) Well, whatever the case, you can always trust that the telegraph system will forever bear the good old Morse name.

About the Editors

For the first 22 years of their lives, **Will Pearson** and **Mangesh Hattikudur** were really well rounded, in the "wow, nice résumé" kind of way. Joining and starting any clubs they could, doing anthropological research in Tibet, trying to save whales, wetlands, and any other bumper-sticker cause they saw. So, what happened to those days? Now they're only well rounded in the "you should really slow down on the chips and queso" kind of way. Ever since the duo started *mental_floss* as Duke University students, all they want to do is talk trivia. In fact, it's kind of a problem. If anyone knows of a good trivia-addicts support group, please contact the *mental_floss* staff immediately.

mental_floss presents: Forbidden Knowledge is their fourth book together. The pair also worked on *mental_floss presents: Condensed Knowledge, mental_floss presents: Instant Knowledge,* and *Lolita,* published under the pen name Vladimir Nabokov.

Elizabeth Hunt was not a trivia buff—for years she felt compelled to share her SAT scores to look smart at social gatherings. Then Mangesh introduced her to *mental_floss,* and she discovered that trivia knowledge is even more impressive than high school achievements. Now she often opens bar conversations with the classic line "So...did you know that beer is made by bacteria feeding on yeast cells, then defecating?" *mental_floss presents: Forbidden Knowledge* is her second *mental_floss* book. When she's not flossing, she works as a book editor at the International Reading Association.

***mental_floss* magazine,** currently available at newsstands everywhere, was founded in 2001 with the mission of blurring the lines between education and entertainment. The magazine has received rave reviews in a variety of publications, including *Newsweek,* the *Washington Post,* the *Chicago Tribune,* and *Entertainment Weekly.* The *mental_floss* staff has contributed to more than 80 segments on CNN *Headline News* and recently released its first board game, *mental_floss: The Trivia Game.* Daily trivia and the *mental_floss* store are easy to find online at www.mentalfloss.com.

About the Contributors

Erik Sass is a freelance journalist in Brooklyn, New York, covering American foreign policy, New York's immigrant communities, and anything else that strikes his fancy. His interests include geography, espionage, guerrilla warfare, and microbrewed beers from around the world. He's good at the history questions in Trivial Pursuit but is completely clueless about sports, science, and entertainment, so don't choose him as your partner.

John Green writes for *Booklist* magazine, where his reviewing niches include books about Islam, Christianity, boxing, and conjoined twins. John's background in religious studies prepared him for a lifelong study of sin, which culminated in his work for this book. Besides writing for *mental_floss* and regularly contributing to NPR's *All Things Considered*, John is also the author of the novel *Looking for Alaska*.

Christopher Smith is a regular contributor to *mental_floss* magazine and also contributed to its first book, *mental_floss presents: Condensed Knowledge*. As a writer and creative director in the advertising field, he has written for some of the industry's best-known brands, including Motel 6, Home Depot, 7-Eleven, Red Lobster, Chick-fil-A, Red Roof Inn, and Bennigan's. Since 1997 he has performed with Ad-Libs, one of America's most successful comedy troupes. A native of upstate New York and graduate of Penn State, he lives in Dallas with his wife, Heather, and their toddler, Clara, who, at the time of this writing, is looking forward to the expected addition of twin baby brothers.

Steve Wiegand is a senior writer for the *Sacramento Bee*, where he specializes in covering vice—sex, drugs, and gambling. Wiegand's 30-year newspaper career has also included stints at the *San Francisco Chronicle* and the *San Diego Tribune*. He's the author of two books, *Sacramento Tapestry* and *U.S. History for Dummies*. In his spare time he's a woodworker, and plays blues harp and sings with the nearly legendary Sacramento band Deadline.

Brian Gottesman is (he assumes) the only contributor to *mental_floss presents: Forbidden Knowledge* to be put in apprehension of imminent attack by a feral reindeer while hiking in Iceland. He is a Phi Beta Kappa graduate of the University of Rochester, where he earned a B.A. in history, and of Harvard Law School. An aficionado of the obscure (he enjoys reading Icelandic sagas, and his college thesis was on Eurasian nomad tribes so obscure that they are widely thought to be mythological), Brian is making his first contribution to a *mental_floss* project. He is the author of *The King of Zion: A Tale from the Age of Faith,* as yet unpublished, and *Lords of the Steppe,* a work in progress. Brian practices law in Wilmington, Delaware.

Peter Haugen (rhymes with "now then"), author of *World History for Dummies* and a contributor to *mental_floss presents: Condensed Knowledge,* has been theater critic of the *Sacramento Bee,* a regional news editor of the *St. Petersburg Times,* and a contributor to *mental_floss, History Magazine,* and *Psychology Today,* among many other publications. A Phi Beta Kappa graduate of the University of California, Berkeley, he once held a job stacking wet turkey feathers with a pitchfork (really). Trained in journalism at the Defense Information School, he was awarded the Keith L. Ware Award and a Meritorious Service Medal during his hitch as a U.S. Army journalist. He has taught journalism at the University of Wisconsin and at California State University, Fresno. He lives in Madison, Wisconsin, with his wife, two sons, and assorted pets of various species.

Bill Hauser, Ph.D., contributed to *mental_floss presents: Condensed Knowledge,* and is currently an assistant professor of marketing and an adjunct professor of sociology at the University of Akron in Akron, Ohio. After two decades of directing market research for Fortune 500 companies, Bill is currently fulfilling his lifelong dream of teaching, research, and writing.

Index